# ACCA

## PAPER F7

### FINANCIAL REPORTING (INTERNATIONAL AND UNITED KINGDOM)

BPP Learning Media is the **sole ACCA Platinum Approved Learning Partner – content** for the ACCA qualification. In this, **the only Paper F7 study text to be reviewed by the examiner**:

- We **discuss** the **best strategies** for studying for ACCA exams
- We **highlight** the **most important elements** in the syllabus and the **key skills** you will need
- We **signpost** how each chapter links to the syllabus and the study guide
- We **provide** lots of **exam focus points** demonstrating what the examiner will want you to do
- We **emphasise key points** in regular **fast forward summaries**
- We **test your knowledge** of what you've studied in **quick quizzes**
- We **examine your understanding** in our **exam question bank**
- We **reference all the important topics** in our **full index**

BPP's **i-Pass** product also supports this paper.

FOR EXAMS IN 2012

**BPP LEARNING MEDIA**

First edition 2007
Fifth edition October 2011

ISBN 9781 4453 7763 6
(Previous ISBN 9780 7517 8923 2)

e-ISBN 9781 4453 7586 1

British Library Cataloguing-in-Publication Data
A catalogue record for this book
is available from the British Library

Published by

BPP Learning Media Ltd
BPP House, Aldine Place
London W12 8AA

www.bpp.com/learningmedia

Printed in the United Kingdom

We are grateful to the Association of Chartered Certified
Accountants for permission to reproduce past
examination questions. The suggested solutions in the
exam answer bank have been prepared by BPP Learning
Media Ltd, unless otherwise stated.

# Contents

# A note about copyright

Dear Customer

What does the little © mean and why does it matter?

Your market-leading BPP books, course materials and e-learning materials do not write and update themselves. People write them: on their own behalf or as employees of an organisation that invests in this activity. Copyright law protects their livelihoods. It does so by creating rights over the use of the content.

Breach of copyright is a form of theft – as well as being a criminal offence in some jurisdictions, it is potentially a serious breach of professional ethics.

With current technology, things might seem a bit hazy but, basically, without the express permission of BPP Learning Media:

- Photocopying our materials is a breach of copyright

- Scanning, ripcasting or conversion of our digital materials into different file formats, uploading them to facebook or emailing them to your friends is a breach of copyright

You can, of course, sell your books, in the form in which you have bought them – once you have finished with them. (Is this fair to your fellow students? We update for a reason.) But the e-products are sold on a single user licence basis: we do not supply 'unlock' codes to people who have bought them second-hand.

And what about outside the UK? BPP Learning Media strives to make our materials available at prices students can afford by local printing arrangements, pricing policies and partnerships which are clearly listed on our website. A tiny minority ignore this and indulge in criminal activity by illegally photocopying our material or supporting organisations that do. If they act illegally and unethically in one area, can you really trust them?

# Helping you to pass – the ONLY F7 Study Text reviewed by the examiner!

As ACCA's **sole Platinum Approved Learning Partner – content**, BPP Learning Media gives you the **unique opportunity** to use **examiner-reviewed** study materials for the 2012 exams. By incorporating the examiner's comments and suggestions regarding the depth and breadth of syllabus coverage, the BPP Learning Media Study Text provides excellent, **ACCA-approved** support for your studies.

## The PER alert

Before you can qualify as an ACCA member, you do not only have to pass all your exams but also fulfil a three year **practical experience requirement** (PER). To help you to recognise areas of the syllabus that you might be able to apply in the workplace to achieve different performance objectives, we have introduced the '**PER alert**' feature. You will find this feature throughout the Study Text to remind you that what you are **learning to pass** your ACCA exams is **equally useful to the fulfilment of the PER requirement**.

## Tackling studying

Studying can be a daunting prospect, particularly when you have lots of other commitments. The **different features** of the text, the **purposes** of which are explained fully on the **Chapter features** page, will help you whilst studying and improve your chances of **exam success**.

## Developing exam awareness

Our Texts are completely **focused** on helping you pass your exam.

Our advice on **Studying F7** outlines the **content** of the paper, the **necessary skills** the examiner expects you to demonstrate and any **brought forward knowledge** you are expected to have.

**Exam focus points** are included within the chapters to highlight when and how specific topics were examined, or how they might be examined in the future.

## Using the Syllabus and Study Guide

You can find the syllabus and Study Guide for both the International and UK papers on page IX of this Study Text

## Testing what you can do

Testing yourself helps you develop the skills you need to pass the exam and also confirms that you can recall what you have learnt.

We include **Questions** – lots of them - both within chapters and in the **Exam Question Bank**, as well as **Quick Quizzes** at the end of each chapter to test your knowledge of the chapter content.

# Chapter features

Each chapter contains a number of helpful features to guide you through each topic.

**Topic list**

| Topic list | Syllabus reference |
|---|---|
|  |  |
|  |  |
|  |  |

Tells you what you will be studying in this chapter and the relevant section numbers, together the ACCA syllabus references.

## Introduction

Puts the chapter content in the context of the syllabus as a whole.

## Study Guide

Links the chapter content with ACCA guidance.

## Exam Guide

Highlights how examinable the chapter content is likely to be and the ways in which it could be examined.

**Knowledge brought forward from earlier studies**

What you are assumed to know from previous studies/exams.

**FAST FORWARD**

Summarises the content of main chapter headings, allowing you to preview and review each section easily.

## Examples

Demonstrate how to apply key knowledge and techniques.

**Key terms**

Definitions of important concepts that can often earn you easy marks in exams.

**Exam focus points**

Tell you when and how specific topics were examined, or how they may be examined in the future.

**Formula to learn**

Formulae that are not given in the exam but which have to be learnt.

This is a new feature that gives you a useful indication of syllabus areas that closely relate to performance objectives in your Practical Experience Requirement (PER).

 Question

Give you essential practice of techniques covered in the chapter.

 Case Study

Provide real world examples of theories and techniques.

## Chapter Roundup

A full list of the Fast Forwards included in the chapter, providing an easy source of review.

## Quick Quiz

A quick test of your knowledge of the main topics in the chapter.

## Exam Question Bank

Found at the back of the Study Text with more comprehensive chapter questions. Cross referenced for easy navigation.

# Studying F7

F7 is a demanding paper covering all the fundamentals of financial reporting. It has five main sections:

1. The conceptual framework of accounting
2. The regulatory framework
3. Preparation of financial statements which conform with IFRS
4. Preparation of consolidated financial statements
5. Analysis and interpretation of financial statements

All of these areas will be tested to some degree at each sitting. Sections 3 and 4 are the main areas of application and you must expect to have to produce consolidated and single company financial statements in your exam.

Some of this material you will have covered at lower level papers. You should already be familiar with accounting for inventories and non-current assets and preparing simple income statements, statements of financial position and statements of cash flows. You should know the basic ratios.

F7 takes your financial reporting knowledge and skills up to the next level. New topics are consolidated financial statements, construction contracts, financial instruments and leases. There is also coverage of the substance of transactions and the limitations of financial statements and ratios. The examiner wants you to think about these issues.

If you had exemptions from lower level papers or feel that your knowledge of lower level financial reporting is not good enough, you may want to get a copy of the study text for F3 Financial Accounting and read through it, or at least have it to refer to. You have a lot of new material to learn for F7 and basic financial accounting will be assumed knowledge.

The way to pass F7 is by practising lots of exam-level questions, which you will do when you get onto revision. Only by practising questions do you get a feel for what you will have to do in the exam. Also, topics which you find hard to understand in the text will be much easier to grasp when you have encountered them in a few questions. So don't get bogged down in any area of the text. Just keep going and a lot of things you find difficult will make more sense when you see how they appear in an exam question.

## Important note

If you are sitting the F7 UK paper you will be studying under International standards and approximately 10 marks will be for comparisons between International and UK standards. See the 2012 F7 UK syllabus on page xix and the article entitled 'Reporting Changes' dated 8 September 2010 by Steve Scott and Graham Holt on the ACCA website.

This text covers all the topics you need to know under International standards and we have produced a supplement and practice questions covering the additional UK issues. This is available at: www.bpp.com. Follow links to Learning Media/Supplements.

# The exam paper

The exam is a three hour paper with five compulsory questions.

## Format of the paper

|  | Marks |
|---|---|
| Question 1 | 25 |
| Question 2 | 25 |
| Question 3 | 25 |
| Question 4 | 15 |
| Question 5 | 10 |
|  | 100 |

Question 1 will be on consolidated financial statements.

Question 2 will be on single company financial statements.

Question 3 is likely to be on cash flow statements or interpretation of accounts

Questions 4 and 5 will be on other areas of the syllabus

The examiner has in the past used questions 4 and 5 to test construction contracts, deferred tax, provisions and issues relating to non-current assets.

### Syllabus and Study Guide

The F7 Int and F7 UK syllabi and study guides can be found below.

## Syllabus

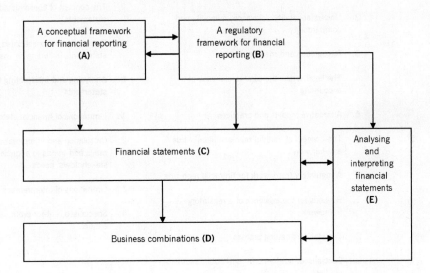

**AIM**

To develop knowledge and skills in understanding and applying accounting standards and the theoretical framework in the preparation of financial statements of entities, including groups and how to analyse and interpret those financial statements.

**MAIN CAPABILITIES**

On successful completion of this paper candidates should be able to:

**A**   Discuss and apply a conceptual framework for financial reporting

**B**   Discuss a regulatory framework for financial reporting

**C**   Prepare and present financial statements which conform with International accounting standards

**D**   Account for business combinations in accordance with International accounting standards

**E**   Analyse and interpret financial statements.

**RELATIONAL DIAGRAM OF MAIN CAPABILITIES**

**RATIONALE**

The financial reporting syllabus assumes knowledge acquired in Paper F3, *Financial Accounting*, and develops and applies this further and in greater depth.

The syllabus begins with the conceptual framework of accounting with reference to the qualitative characteristics of useful information and the fundamental bases of accounting introduced in the Paper F3 syllabus within the Knowledge module. It then moves into a detailed examination of the regulatory framework of accounting and how this informs the standard setting process.

The main areas of the syllabus cover the reporting of financial information for single companies and for groups in accordance with generally accepted accounting principles and relevant accounting standards.

Finally, the syllabus covers the analysis and interpretation of information from financial reports.

**DETAILED SYLLABUS**

**A    A conceptual framework for financial reporting**

1.    The need for a conceptual framework

2.    Understandability, relevance, reliability and comparability

3.    Recognition and measurement

4.    The legal versus the commercial view of accounting

5.    Alternative models and practices

6.    The concept of 'faithful representation' ('true and fair view')

**B    A regulatory framework for financial reporting**

1.    Reasons for the existence of a regulatory framework

2.    The standard setting process

3.    Specialised, not-for-profit, and public sector entities

**C    Financial statements**

1.    Statements of cash flows

2.    Tangible non-current assets

3.    Intangible assets

4.    Inventory

5.    Financial assets and financial liabilities

6.    Leases

7.    Provisions, contingent liabilities, and contingent assets

8.    Impairment of assets

9.    Taxation

10.  Regulatory requirements relating to the preparation of financial statements

11.  Reporting financial performance

**D    Business combinations**

1.    The concept and principles of a group

2.    The concept of consolidated financial statements

3.    Preparation of consolidated financial statements including an associate

**E    Analysing and interpreting financial statements**

1.    Limitations of financial statements

2.    Calculation and interpretation of accounting ratios and trends to address users' and stakeholders' needs

3.    Limitations of interpretation techniques

4.    Specialised, not-for-profit, and public sector entities

## APPROACH TO EXAMINING THE SYLLABUS

The syllabus is assessed by a three-hour paper-based examination.

All questions are compulsory. It will contain both computational and discursive elements.
Some questions will adopt a scenario/case study approach.

Question 1 will be a 25 mark question on the preparation of group financial statements and/or extracts thereof, and may include a small discussion element. Computations will be designed to test an understanding of principles.

Question 2, for 25 marks, will test the reporting of non-group financial statements. This may be from information in a trial balance or by restating draft financial statements.

Question 3, for 25 marks, is likely to be an appraisal of an entity's performance and may involve statements of cash flows.

Questions 4 and 5 will cover the remainder of the syllabus and will be worth 15 and 10 marks respectively.

An individual question may often involve elements that relate to different subject areas of the syllabus. For example the preparation of an entity's financial statements could include matters relating to several accounting standards.

Questions may ask candidates to comment on the appropriateness or acceptability of management's opinion or chosen accounting treatment. An understanding of accounting principles and concepts and how these are applied to practical examples will be tested.

Questions on topic areas that are also included in Paper F3 will be examined at an appropriately greater depth in this paper.

Candidates will be expected to have an appreciation of the need for specified accounting standards and why they have been issued. For detailed or complex standards, candidates need to be aware of their principles and key elements.

# Study Guide

## A   A CONCEPTUAL FRAMEWORK FOR FINANCIAL REPORTING

### 1.   The need for a conceptual framework

a)   Describe what is meant by a conceptual framework of accounting.[2]

b)   Discuss whether a conceptual framework is necessary and what an alternative system might be.[2]

### 2.   Understandability, relevance, reliability and comparability

a)   Discuss what is meant by understandability in relation to the provision of financial information.[2]

b)   Discuss what is meant by relevance and reliability and describe the qualities that enhance these characteristics.[2]

c)   Discuss the importance of comparability to users of financial statements.[2]

d)   Distinguish between changes in accounting policies and changes in accounting estimates and describe how accounting standards apply the principle of comparability where an entity changes its accounting policies.[2]

e)   Recognise and account for changes in accounting policies and the correction of prior period errors.[2]

### 3.   Recognition and measurement

a)   Define what is meant by 'recognition' in financial statements and discuss the recognition criteria.[2]

b)   Apply the recognition criteria to: [2]
   i)   assets and liabilities.
   ii)  income and expenses

c)   Discuss revenue recognition issues; indicate when income and expense recognition should occur.[2]

d)   Demonstrate the role of the principle of substance over form in relation to recognising sales revenue.[2]

e)   Explain the following measures and compute amounts using: [2]
   i)   historical cost
   ii)  fair value/current cost
   iii) net realisable value
   iv)  present value of future cash flows.

### 4.   The legal versus the commercial view of accounting

a)   Explain the importance of recording the commercial substance rather than the legal form of transactions – give examples where recording the legal form of transactions may be misleading.[2]

b)   Describe the features which may indicate that the substance of transactions differs from their legal form.[2]

c)   Apply the principle of substance over form to the recognition and derecognition of assets and liabilities.[2]

d)   Recognise the substance of transactions in general, and specifically account for the following types of transaction: [2]
   i)   goods sold on sale or return/consignment inventory
   ii)  sale and repurchase/leaseback agreements
   iii) factoring of receivables.

### 5.   Alternative models and practices

a)   Describe the advantages and disadvantages of the use of historical cost accounting.[2]

b)   Discuss whether the use of current value accounting overcomes the problems of historical cost accounting.[2]

c)   Describe the concept of financial and physical capital maintenance and how this affects the determination of profits.[1]

4

**6. The concept of 'faithful representation' ('true and fair view')**

a) Describe what is meant by financial statements achieving a faithful representation.[2]

b) Discuss whether faithful representation constitutes more than compliance with accounting standards.[1]

c) Indicate the circumstances and required disclosures where a 'true and fair' override may apply.[1]

**B  A REGULATORY FRAMEWORK FOR FINANCIAL REPORTING**

**1. Reasons for the existence of a regulatory framework**

a) Explain why a regulatory framework is needed also including the advantages and disadvantages of IFRS over a national regulatory framework.[2]

b) Explain why accounting standards on their own are not a complete regulatory framework.[2]

c) Distinguish between a principles based and a rules based framework and discuss whether they can be complementary.[1]

**2. The standard setting process**

a) Describe the structure and objectives of the IFRS Foundation, the International Accounting Standards Board (IASB), the IFRS Advisory Council (IFRS AC) and the IFRS Interpretations Committee (IFRS IC).[2]

b) Describe the IASB's Standard setting process including revisions to and interpretations of Standards.[2]

c) Explain the relationship of national standard setters to the IASB in respect of the standard setting process.[2]

**3. Specialised, not-for-profit and public sector entities**

a) Distinguish between the primary aims of not-for profit and public sector entities and those of profit oriented entities.[1]

b) Discuss the extent to which International Financial Reporting Standards (IFRSs) are relevant to specialised, not-for-profit and public sector entities.[1]

**C  FINANCIAL STATEMENTS**

**1. Statements of Cash flows**

a) Prepare a statement of cash flows for a single entity (not a group) in accordance with relevant accounting standards using the direct and the indirect method.[2]

b) Compare the usefulness of cash flow information with that of an income statement or statement of comprehensive income.[2]

c) Interpret a statement of cash flows (together with other financial information) to assess the performance and financial position of an entity.[2]

**2. Tangible non-current assets**

a) Define and compute the initial measurement of a non-current (including a self-constructed and borrowing costs) asset.[2]

b) Identify subsequent expenditure that may be capitalised, distinguishing between capital and revenue items.[2]

c) Discuss the requirements of relevant accounting standards in relation to the revaluation of non-current assets.[2]

d) Account for revaluation and disposal gains and losses for non-current assets.[2]

e) Compute depreciation based on the cost and revaluation models and on assets that have two or more significant parts (complex assets).[2]

f) Apply the provisions of relevant accounting standards in relation to accounting for government grants.[2]

g) Discuss why the treatment of investment properties should differ from other properties.[2]

h) Apply the requirements of relevant accounting standards for investment property.[2]

### 3. Intangible assets

a) Discuss the nature and accounting treatment of internally generated and purchased intangibles.[2]

b) Distinguish between goodwill and other intangible assets.[2]

c) Describe the criteria for the initial recognition and measurement of intangible assets.[2]

d) Describe the subsequent accounting treatment, including the principle of impairment tests in relation to goodwill.[2]

e) Indicate why the value of purchase consideration for an investment may be less than the value of the acquired identifiable net assets and how the difference should be accounted for.[2]

f) Describe and apply the requirements of relevant accounting standards to research and development expenditure.[2]

### 4. Inventory

a) Describe and apply the principles of inventory valuation.[2]

b) Define a construction contract and discuss the role of accounting concepts in the recognition of profit.[2]

c) Describe the acceptable methods of determining the stage (percentage) of completion of a contract.[2]

d) Prepare financial statement extracts for construction contracts.[2]

### 5 Financial assets and financial liabilities

a) Explain the need for an accounting standard on financial instruments.[1]

b) Define financial instruments in terms of financial assets and financial liabilities.[1]

c) Indicate for the following categories of financial instruments how they should be measured and how any gains and losses from subsequent measurement should be treated in the financial statements: [1]
 i) amortised cost
 ii) fair value ( including option to classify equity instruments through other comprehensive income)

d) Distinguish between debt and equity capital.[2]

e) Apply the requirements of relevant accounting standards to the issue and finance costs of: [2]
 i) equity
 ii) redeemable preference shares and debt instruments with no conversion rights (principle of amortised cost)
 iii) convertible debt

### 6. Leases

a) Explain why recording the legal form of a finance lease can be misleading to users (referring to the commercial substance of such leases).[2]

b) Describe and apply the method of determining a lease type (i.e. an operating or finance lease).[2]

c) Discuss the effect on the financial statements of a finance lease being incorrectly treated as an operating lease.[2]

d) Account for assets financed by finance leases in the records of the lessee.[2]

e) Account for operating leases in the records of the lessee.[2]

6

7. **Provisions, contingent liabilities and contingent assets**

a) Explain why an accounting standard on provisions is necessary.[2]

b) Distinguish between legal and constructive obligations.[2]

c) State when provisions may and may not be made and demonstrate how they should be accounted for.[2]

d) Explain how provisions should be measured.[1]

e) Define contingent assets and liabilities and describe their accounting treatment.[2]

f) Identify and account for: [2]
   i) warranties/guarantees
   ii) onerous contracts
   iii) environmental and similar provisions
   iv) provisions for future repairs or refurbishments.

8. **Impairment of assets**

a) Define an impairment loss.[2]

b) Identify the circumstances that may indicate impairments to assets.[2]

c) Describe what is meant by a cash generating unit.[2]

d) State the basis on which impairment losses should be allocated, and allocate an impairment loss to the assets of a cash generating unit.[2]

9. **Taxation**

a) Account for current taxation in accordance with relevant accounting standards.[2]

b) Record entries relating to income tax in the accounting records.[2]

c) Explain the effect of taxable temporary differences on accounting and taxable profits.[2]

d) Compute and record deferred tax amounts in the financial statements.[2]

10. **Regulatory requirements relating to the preparation of financial statements**

a) Describe the structure (format) and content of financial statements presented under IFRS.[2]

b) Prepare an entity's financial statements in accordance with the prescribed structure and content.[2]

11. **Reporting financial performance**

a) Discuss the importance of identifying and reporting the results of discontinued operations.[2]

b) Define and account for non-current assets held for sale and discontinued operations.[2]

c) Indicate the circumstances where separate disclosure of material items of income and expense is required.[2]

d) Prepare and explain the contents and purpose of the statement of changes in equity.[2]

e) Describe and prepare a statement of changes in equity.[2]

f) Earnings per share (eps)
   i) calculate the eps in accordance with relevant accounting standards (dealing with bonus issues, full market value issues and rights issues) [2]
   ii) explain the relevance of the diluted eps and calculate the diluted eps involving convertible debt and share options (warrants) [2]
   iii) explain why the trend of eps may be a more accurate indicator of performance than a company's profit trend and the importance of eps as a stock market indicator [2]
   iv) discuss the limitations of using eps as a performance measure.[3]

g) Events after the reporting date
   i) distinguish between and account for adjusting and non-adjusting events after the reporting date [2]

   ii) Identify items requiring separate disclosure, including their accounting treatment and required disclosures[2]

7

**Introduction** XV

**D   BUSINESS COMBINATIONS**

**1.   The concept and principles of a group**

a)   Describe the concept of a group as a single economic unit.[2]

b)   Explain and apply the definition of a subsidiary within relevant accounting standards.[2]

c)   Identify and outline using accounting standards and other applicable regulation the circumstances in which a group is required to prepare consolidated financial statements.[2]

d)   Describe the circumstances when a group may claim exemption from the preparation of consolidated financial statements. .[2]

e)   Explain why directors may not wish to consolidate a subsidiary and outline using accounting standards and other applicable regulation the circumstances where this is permitted.[2]

f)   Explain the need for using coterminous year ends and uniform accounting polices when preparing consolidated financial statements.[2]

g)   Explain why it is necessary to eliminate intra-group transactions.[2]

**2.   The concept of consolidated financial statements**

a)   Explain the objective of consolidated financial statements.[2]

b)   Indicate the effect that the related party relationship between a parent and subsidiary may have on the subsidiary's entity statements and the consolidated financial statements.[2]

c)   Explain why it is necessary to use fair values for the consideration for an investment in a subsidiary together with the fair values of a subsidiary's identifiable assets and liabilities when preparing consolidated financial statements.[2]

d)   Describe and apply the required accounting treatment of consolidated goodwill.[2]

**3.   Preparation of consolidated financial statements including an associate**

a)   Prepare a consolidated statement of financial position for a simple group (parent and one subsidiary) dealing with pre and post acquisition profits, minority interests and consolidated goodwill.[2]

b)   Prepare a consolidated income statement and consolidated statement of comprehensive income for a simple group dealing with an acquisition in the period and minority interest.[2]

c)   Explain and account for other reserves (e.g. share premium and revaluation reserves).[1]

d)   Account for the effects in the financial statements of intra-group trading.[2]

e)   Account for the effects of fair value adjustments (including their effect on consolidated goodwill) to: [2]
   i)   depreciating and non-depreciating non-current assets
   ii)  inventory
   iii) monetary liabilities
   iv)  assets and liabilities not included in the subsidiary's own statement of financial position, including contingent assets and liabilities

f)   Account for goodwill impairment.[2]

g)   Define an associate and explain the principles and reasoning for the use of equity accounting.[2]

h)   Prepare consolidated financial statements to include a single subsidiary and an associate.[2]

**E   ANALYSING AND INTERPRETING FINANCIAL STATEMENTS**

**1.   Limitations of financial statements**

a)   Indicate the problems of using historic information to predict future performance and trends.[2]

8

b) Discuss how financial statements may be manipulated to produce a desired effect (creative accounting, window dressing).[2]

c) Recognise how related party relationships have the potential to mislead users.[2]

d) Explain why figures in a statement of financial position may not be representative of average values throughout the period for example, due to: [2]
   i) seasonal trading
   ii) major asset acquisitions near the end of the accounting period.

2 Calculation and interpretation of accounting ratios and trends to address users' and stakeholders' needs

a) Define and compute relevant financial ratios.[2]

b) Explain what aspects of performance specific ratios are intended to assess.[2]

c) Analyse and interpret ratios to give an assessment of an entity's performance and financial position in comparison with: [2]
   i) an entity's previous period's financial statements
   ii) another similar entity for the same reporting period
   iii) industry average ratios.

d) Interpret an entity's financial statements to give advice from the perspectives of different stakeholders.[2]

e) Discuss how the interpretation of current value based financial statements would differ from those using historical cost based accounts.[1]

3. Limitations of interpretation techniques

a) Discuss the limitations in the use of ratio analysis for assessing corporate performance.[2]

b) Discuss the effect that changes in accounting policies or the use of different accounting polices between entities can have on the ability to interpret performance.[2]

c) Indicate other information, including non-financial information, that may be of relevance to the assessment of an entity's performance.[1]

4. Specialised, not-for-profit and public sector entities

a) Discuss the different approaches that may be required when assessing the performance of specialised, not-for-profit and public sector organisations.[1]

9

## SUMMARY OF CHANGES TO F7 (INT)

### RATIONALE FOR CHANGES

ACCA periodically reviews its qualification syllabuses so that they fully meet the needs of stakeholders such as employers, students, regulatory and advisory bodies and learning providers.

**Note of significant changes to study guide Paper F7 INT**

The main areas to be added or deleted from the syllabus from that date are shown in Table 1 and 2 below:

### Table 1 – Additions to F7 INT

There have not been any additions to the 2011 study guide. However there have been minor amendments to the wording of some of the study guide outcomes corresponding to changes within examinable documents and to ensure greater clarity.

### Table 2 – Deletions to F7 INT

There have not been any additions to the 2011 study guide. However there have been minor amendments to the wording of some of the study guide outcomes corresponding to changes within examinable documents and to ensure greater clarity.

# Syllabus

## AIM

To develop knowledge and skills in understanding and applying accounting standards and the theoretical framework in the preparation of financial statements of entities, including groups and how to analyse and interpret those financial statements.

## MAIN CAPABILITIES

On successful completion of this paper, candidates should be able to:

A   Discuss and apply a conceptual framework for financial reporting

B   Discuss a regulatory framework for financial reporting

C   Prepare and present financial statements which conform with International accounting standards

D   Account for business combinations in accordance with International accounting standards

E   Analyse and interpret financial statements.

## RELATIONAL DIAGRAM OF MAIN CAPABILITIES

**RATIONALE**

The financial reporting syllabus assumes knowledge acquired in Paper F3, *Financial Accounting*, and develops and applies this further and in greater depth.

The UK syllabus is primarily based on International accounting standards together with elements of UK legislation governing the preparation of financial statements both for individual and group entities. Selected differences between UK and International accounting standards will also be tested.

The syllabus begins with the conceptual framework of accounting with reference to the qualitative characteristics of useful information and the fundamental bases of accounting introduced in the Paper F3 syllabus within the Knowledge module. It then moves into a detailed examination of the regulatory framework of accounting and how this informs the standard setting process.

The main areas of the syllabus cover the reporting of financial information for single companies and for groups in accordance with generally accepted accounting principles and relevant accounting standards.

Finally, the syllabus covers the analysis and interpretation of information from financial reports.

**DETAILED SYLLABUS**

**A    A conceptual framework for financial reporting**

1.    The need for a conceptual framework

2.    Understandability, relevance, reliability and comparability

3.    Recognition and measurement

4.    The legal versus the commercial view of accounting

5.    Alternative models and practices

6.    The concept of 'faithful representation' ('true and fair view')

**B    A legal and regulatory framework for financial reporting**

1.    Reasons for the existence of a regulatory framework

2.    The standard setting process

3.    Specialised, not-for-profit, and public sector entities

4.    Legal requirements relating to the preparation of single entity financial statements

**C    Financial statements**

1.    Statements of cash flows

2.    Tangible non-current assets

3.    Intangible assets

4.    Inventory

5.    Financial assets and financial liabilities

6.    Leases

7.    Provisions, contingent liabilities, and contingent assets

8.    Impairment of assets

9.    Taxation

10.   Regulatory requirements relating to the preparation of financial statements

11.   Reporting financial performance

**D    Business combinations**

1.    The concept and principles of a group

2.    The concept of consolidated financial statements

3.    Preparation of consolidated financial statements including an associate

**E Analysing and interpreting financial statements**

1. Limitations of financial statements

2. Calculation and interpretation of accounting ratios and trends to address users' and stakeholders' needs

3. Limitations of interpretation techniques

4. Specialised, not-for-profit, and public sector entities

## APPROACH TO EXAMINING THE SYLLABUS

The syllabus is assessed by a three-hour paper-based examination.

All questions are compulsory. It will contain both computational and discursive elements.
Some questions will adopt a scenario/case study approach.

Question 1 will be a 25 mark question on the preparation of group financial statements and/or extracts thereof, and may include a small discussion element. Computations will be designed to test an understanding of principles.

Question 2, for 25 marks, will test the reporting of non-group financial statements. This may be from information in a trial balance or by restating draft financial statements.

Question 3, for 25 marks, is likely to be an appraisal of an entity's performance and may involve statements of cash flows.

Questions 4 and 5 will cover the remainder of the syllabus and will be worth 15 and 10 marks respectively.
An individual question may often involve elements that relate to different subject areas of the syllabus. For example the preparation of an entity's financial statements could include matters relating to several accounting standards.

Questions may ask candidates to comment on the appropriateness or acceptability of management's opinion or chosen accounting treatment. An understanding of accounting principles and concepts and how these are applied to practical examples will be tested.

Questions on topic areas that are also included in Paper F3 will be examined at an appropriately greater depth in this paper.

Candidates will be expected to have an appreciation of the need for specified accounting standards and why they have been issued. For detailed or complex standards, candidates need to be aware of their principles and key elements.

4

# Study Guide

## A  A CONCEPTUAL FRAMEWORK FOR FINANCIAL REPORTING

### 1.  The need for a conceptual framework

a)  Describe what is meant by a conceptual framework of accounting.[2]

b)  Discuss whether a conceptual framework is necessary and what an alternative system might be.[2]

### 2.  Understandability, relevance, reliability and comparability

a)  Discuss what is meant by understandability in relation to the provision of financial information.[2]

b)  Discuss what is meant by relevance and reliability and describe the qualities that enhance these characteristics.[2]

c)  Discuss the importance of comparability to users of financial statements.[2]

d)  Distinguish between changes in accounting policies and changes in accounting estimates and describe how accounting standards apply the principle of comparability where an entity changes its accounting policies.[2]

e)  Recognise and account for changes in accounting policies and the correction of prior period errors.[2]

### 3.  Recognition and measurement

a)  Define what is meant by 'recognition' in financial statements and discuss the recognition criteria.[2]

b)  Apply the recognition criteria to:[2]
   i)   assets and liabilities.
   ii)  income and expenses

c)  Discuss revenue recognition issues; indicate when income and expense recognition should occur.[2]

d)  Demonstrate the role of the principle of substance over form in relation to recognising sales revenue.[2]

e)  Explain the following measures and compute amounts using:[2]
   i)   historical cost
   ii)  fair value/current cost
   iii) net realisable value
   iv)  present value of future cash flows.

### 4.  The legal versus the commercial view of accounting

a)  Explain the importance of recording the commercial substance rather than the legal form of transactions – give examples where recording the legal form of transactions may be misleading.[2]

b)  Describe the features which may indicate that the substance of transactions differs from their legal form.[2]

c)  Apply the principle of substance over form to the recognition and derecognition of assets and liabilities.[2]

d)  Recognise the substance of transactions in general, and specifically account for the following types of transaction:[2]
   i)   goods sold on sale or return/consignment inventory
   ii)  sale and repurchase/leaseback agreements
   iii) factoring of receivables.

### 5.  Alternative models and practices

a)  Describe the advantages and disadvantages of the use of historical cost accounting.[2]

b)  Discuss whether the use of current value accounting overcomes the problems of historical cost accounting.[2]

c)  Describe the concept of financial and physical capital maintenance and how this affects the determination of profits.[1]

6. The concept of 'faithful representation' ('true and fair view')

a) Describe what is meant by financial statements achieving a faithful representation.[2]

b) Discuss whether faithful representation constitutes more than compliance with accounting standards.[1]

c) Indicate the circumstances and required disclosures where a 'true and fair' override may apply.[1]

**B   A REGULATORY FRAMEWORK FOR FINANCIAL REPORTING**

**1.   Reasons for the existence of a regulatory framework**

a) Explain why a regulatory framework is needed also including the advantages and disadvantages of IFRS over a national regulatory framework[2]

b) Explain why accounting standards on their own are not a complete regulatory framework.[2]

c) Distinguish between a principles based and a rules based framework and discuss whether they can be complementary.[1]

**2.   The standard setting process**

a) Describe the structure and objectives of the IFRS Foundation, the International Accounting Standards Board (IASB), the IFRS Advisory Council (IFRS AC) and the IFRS Interpretations Committee (IFRS IC).[2]

b) Describe the IASB's Standard setting process including revisions to and interpretations of Standards.[2]

c) Explain the relationship of national standard setters to the IASB in respect of the standard setting process.[2]

3. Specialised, not-for-profit and public sector entities

a) Distinguish between the primary aims of not-for profit and public sector entities and those of profit oriented entities.[1]

b) Discuss the extent to which International Financial Reporting Standards (IFRSs) are relevant to specialised, not-for-profit and public sector entities.[1]

4. Legal requirements relating to the preparation of single entity financial statements

a) Identify and outline the circumstances in which a single entity is required to prepare and present statutory financial statements.[2]

b) Recognise and apply the laws, regulations, accounting standards and other requirements to the preparation of statutory financial statements of an entity[2]

**C   FINANCIAL STATEMENTS**

**1.   Statements of Cash flows**

a) Prepare a statement of cash flows for a single entity (not a group) in accordance with relevant accounting standards using the direct and the indirect method . Describe the differences in format under a UK presentation of a cash flow statement. [2]

b) Compare the usefulness of cash flow information with that of an income statement or statement of comprehensive income.[2]

c) Interpret a statement of cash flows (together with other financial information) to assess the performance and financial position of an entity.[2]

**2.   Tangible non-current assets**

a) Define and compute the initial measurement of a non-current (including a self-constructed and borrowing costs under International and UK rules) asset.[2]

b) Identify subsequent expenditure that may be capitalised, distinguishing between capital and revenue items.[2]

6

c)  Discuss the requirements of relevant accounting standards in relation to the revaluation of non-current assets. Outline how revaluation guidance differs under UK rules including frequency of valuation, methods of valuation given different property types. .[2]

d)  Account for revaluation and disposal gains and losses for non-current assets. Outline how accounting for revaluation gains and losses differs under UK rules (including non specialised property and situations where an asset is subject to revaluation and is now subject to clear consumption of economic benefit)[2]

e)  Compute depreciation based on the cost and revaluation models and on assets that have two or more significant parts (complex assets).[2]

f)  Apply the provisions of relevant accounting standards in relation to accounting for government grants.[2]

g)  Discuss why the treatment of investment properties should differ from other properties.[2]

h)  Apply the requirements of relevant accounting standards for investment property.[2]

3.  Intangible assets

a)  Discuss the nature and accounting treatment of internally generated and purchased intangibles.[2]

b)  Distinguish between goodwill and other intangible assets.[2]

c)  Describe the criteria for the initial recognition and measurement of intangible assets. Outline how under UK rules the recognition criteria for intangibles. [2]

d)  Describe the subsequent accounting treatment, including the principle of impairment tests in relation to goodwill.[2]

e)  Indicate why the value of purchase consideration for an investment may be less than the value of the acquired identifiable net assets and how the difference should be accounted for.[2]

f)  Describe and apply the requirements of relevant accounting standards to research and development expenditure including the choice for deferment under UK rules. [2]

4.  Inventory

a)  Describe and apply the principles of inventory valuation.[2]

b)  Define a construction contract and discuss the role of accounting concepts in the recognition of profit.[2]

c)  Describe the acceptable methods of determining the stage (percentage) of completion of a contract.[2]

d)  Prepare financial statement extracts for construction contracts and outline how construction contracts should be accounted and presented under UK rules.[2]

5   Financial assets and financial liabilities

a)  Explain the need for an accounting standard on financial instruments.[1]

b)  Define financial instruments in terms of financial assets and financial liabilities.[1]

c)  Indicate for the following categories of financial instruments how they should be measured and how any gains and losses from subsequent measurement should be treated in the financial statements: [1]
    i)   amortised cost
    ii)  fair value ( including option to classify equity instruments through other comprehensive income)

d)  Distinguish between debt and equity capital.[2]

e)  Apply the requirements of relevant accounting standards to the issue and finance costs of: [2]
    i)   equity
    ii)  redeemable preference shares and debt instruments with no conversion rights (principle of amortised cost)
    iii) convertible debt

6. **Leases**

a) Explain why recording the legal form of a finance lease can be misleading to users (referring to the commercial substance of such leases).[2]

b) Describe and apply the method of determining a lease type (i.e. an operating or finance lease). Outline how under UK rules a lease is classified. [2]

c) Discuss the effect on the financial statements of a finance lease being incorrectly treated as an operating lease.[2]

d) Account for assets financed by finance leases in the records of the lessee.[2]

e) Account for operating leases in the records of the lessee.[2]

7. **Provisions, contingent liabilities and contingent assets**

a) Explain why an accounting standard on provisions is necessary.[2]

b) Distinguish between legal and constructive obligations.[2]

c) State when provisions may and may not be made and demonstrate how they should be accounted for.[2]

d) Explain how provisions should be measured.[1]

e) Define contingent assets and liabilities and describe their accounting treatment.[2]

f) Identify and account for: [2]
   i)   warranties/guarantees
   ii)  onerous contracts
   iii) environmental and similar provisions
   iv)  provisions for future repairs or refurbishments.

8. **Impairment of assets**

a) Define an impairment loss.[2]

b) Identify the circumstances that may indicate impairments to assets.[2]

c) Describe what is meant by a cash generating unit.[2]

d) State the basis on which impairment losses should be allocated, and allocate an impairment loss to the assets of a cash generating unit.[2]

9. **Taxation**

a) Account for current taxation in accordance with relevant accounting standards.[2]

b) Record entries relating to income tax in the accounting records.[2]

c) Explain the effect of taxable temporary differences on accounting and taxable profits.[2]

d) Compute and record deferred tax amounts in the financial statements and distinguish between International and UK treatment for revaluation of non-current assets and in the discounting of the deferred tax liability.[2]

10. **Regulatory requirements relating to the preparation of financial statements**

a) Describe the structure (format) and content of financial statements presented under IFRS.[2]

b) Prepare an entity's financial statements in accordance with the prescribed structure and content.[2]

11. **Reporting financial performance**

a) Discuss the importance of identifying and reporting the results of discontinued operations.[2]

b) Define and account for non-current assets held for sale and discontinued operations.[2]

c) Outline the different definitions and treatment of discontinued operations and assets held for sale under UK standards. [1]

d) Indicate the circumstances where separate disclosure of material items of income and expense is required.[2]

e) Prepare and explain the contents and purpose of the statement of changes in equity.[2]

f) Describe and prepare a statement of changes in equity.[2]

g) Earnings per share (eps)
   i) calculate the eps in accordance with relevant accounting standards (dealing with bonus issues, full market value issues and rights issues)[2]
   ii) explain the relevance of the diluted eps and calculate the diluted eps involving convertible debt and share options (warrants)[2]
   iii) explain why the trend of eps may be a more accurate indicator of performance than a company's profit trend and the importance of eps as a stock market indicator[2]
   iv) discuss the limitations of using eps as a performance measure.[3]

h) Events after the reporting date
   i) distinguish between and account for adjusting and non-adjusting events after the reporting date[2]

   ii) Identify items requiring separate disclosure, including their accounting treatment and required disclosures[2]

## D   BUSINESS COMBINATIONS

### 1.   The concept and principles of a group

a) Describe the concept of a group as a single economic unit.[2]

b) Explain and apply the definition of a subsidiary within relevant accounting standards.[2]

c) Identify and outline using accounting standards ,other applicable regulation and UK legislation the circumstances in which a group is required to prepare consolidated financial statements.[2]

d) Describe the circumstances when a group may claim exemption from the preparation of consolidated financial statements under accounting standards, other applicable regulation and UK legislation .[2]

e) Explain why directors may not wish to consolidate a subsidiary and outline using accounting standards and other applicable regulation the circumstances where this is permitted.[2]

f) Explain the need for using coterminous year ends and uniform accounting polices when preparing consolidated financial statements.[2]

g) Explain why it is necessary to eliminate intra-group transactions.[2]

### 2.   The concept of consolidated financial statements

a) Explain the objective of consolidated financial statements.[2]

b) Indicate the effect that the related party relationship between a parent and subsidiary may have on the subsidiary's entity statements and the consolidated financial statements.[2]

c) Explain why it is necessary to use fair values for the consideration for an investment in a subsidiary together with the fair values of a subsidiary's identifiable assets and liabilities when preparing consolidated financial statements.[2]

d) Describe and apply the required accounting treatment of consolidated goodwill.[2]

### 3.   Preparation of consolidated financial statements including an associate

a) Prepare a consolidated statement of financial position for a simple group (parent and one subsidiary) dealing with pre and post acquisition profits, non-controlling interest (at fair value or proportionate share of subsidiary's net assets) and consolidated goodwill.[2]

b) Prepare a consolidated income statement and consolidated statement of comprehensive income for a simple group dealing with an acquisition in the period and non-controlling interest..[2]

c) Explain and account for other reserves (e.g. share premium and revaluation reserves).[1]

d) Account for the effects in the financial statements of intra-group trading.[2]

e) Account for the effects of fair value adjustments (including their effect on consolidated goodwill) to:[2]
   i) depreciating and non-depreciating non-current assets
   ii) inventory
   iii) monetary liabilities
   iv) assets and liabilities not included in the subsidiary's own statement of financial position, including contingent assets and liabilities

f) Account for goodwill impairment.[2]

g) Outline differences under UK rules of accounting for goodwill (initial measurement and subsequent treatment), minority interest, contingent consideration and acquisition expenses.

h) Define an associate and explain the principles and reasoning for the use of equity accounting.[2]

i) Prepare consolidated financial statements to include a single subsidiary and an associate.[2]

**E    ANALYSING AND INTERPRETING FINANCIAL STATEMENTS**

**1.    Limitations of financial statements**

a) Indicate the problems of using historic information to predict future performance and trends.[2]

b) Discuss how financial statements may be manipulated to produce a desired effect (creative accounting, window dressing).[2]

c) Recognise how related party relationships have the potential to mislead users.[2]

d) Explain why figures in a statement of financial position may not be representative of average values throughout the period for example, due to:[2]
   i) seasonal trading
   ii) major asset acquisitions near the end of the accounting period.

**2    Calculation and interpretation of accounting ratios and trends to address users' and stakeholders' needs**

a) Define and compute relevant financial ratios.[2]

b) Explain what aspects of performance specific ratios are intended to assess.[2]

c) Analyse and interpret ratios to give an assessment of an entity's performance and financial position in comparison with:[2]
   i) an entity's previous period's financial statements
   ii) another similar entity for the same reporting period
   iii) industry average ratios.

d) Interpret an entity's financial statements to give advice from the perspectives of different stakeholders.[2]

e) Discuss how the interpretation of current value based financial statements would differ from those using historical cost based accounts.[1]

**3.    Limitations of interpretation techniques**

a) Discuss the limitations in the use of ratio analysis for assessing corporate performance.[2]

b) Discuss the effect that changes in accounting policies or the use of different accounting polices between entities can have on the ability to interpret performance.[2]

c) Indicate the effect that the application of the different UK rules contained in this syllabus guide may have on an assessment of an entities performance.[1]

d) Indicate other information, including non-financial information, that may be of relevance to the assessment of an entity's performance.[1]

**4.    Specialised, not-for-profit and public sector entities**

a) Discuss the different approaches that may be required when assessing the performance of specialised, not-for-profit and public sector organisations.[1]

**SUMMARY OF CHANGES TO F7 (UK)**

**RATIONALE FOR CHANGES**

ACCA periodically reviews its qualification syllabuses so that they fully meet the needs of stakeholders such as employers, students, regulatory and advisory bodies and learning providers.

These changes are summarised in Table 1 and 2 below:

**Table 1 – Additions to F7 UK**

There have not been any additions to the 2011 study guide. However there have been minor amendments to the wording of some of the study guide outcomes corresponding to changes within examinable documents and to ensure greater clarity.

**Table 2 – Deletions to F7 UK**

There have not been any deletions to the 2011 study guide. However there have been minor amendments to the wording of some of the study guide outcomes corresponding to changes within examinable documents and to ensure greater clarity.

11

# Analysis of past papers

The table below provides details of when each element of the syllabus has been examined and the question number and section in which each element appeared. Further details can be found in the Exam Focus Points in the relevant chapters.

| | | Dec 2008 | June 2009 | Dec 2009 | June 2010 | Dec 2010 | June 2011 |
|---|---|---|---|---|---|---|---|
| **A** | **A CONCEPTUAL FRAMEWORK FOR FINANCIAL REPORTING** | | | | | | |
| **A1** | The need for a conceptual framework | | | | | | |
| **A2** | – Framework qualitative characteristics<br>– Accounting policies, changes in accounting estimates and errors | Q4(a) | | | | Q4 | Q4(a) |
| **A3** | Recognition and measurement | Q4(a) | | | | | |
| **A4** | The legal versus the commercial view of accounting | | Q2 | Q2 | Q2, Q4 | | Q2 |
| **A5** | Alternative models and practices (accounting for inflation) | | | | | | |
| **A6** | The concept of 'faithful representation' ('true and fair view') | | | | | | |
| **B** | **A REGULATORY FRAMEWORK FOR FINANCIAL REPORTING** | | | | | | |
| **B1** | Reasons for the existence of a regulatory framework | | | | | | |
| **B2** | The standard setting process | | | | | | |
| **B3** | Specialised, not-for-profit and public sector entities | | | | | | |
| **C** | **FINANCIAL STATEMENTS** | | | | | | |
| **C1** | Statements of cash flows | | Q3 | Q3(a) | Q3(a) | | Q3(a) |
| **C2** | Tangible non-current assets<br>– Property, plant and equipment<br>– Investment properties<br>– Government grants<br>– Borrowing costs | Q2, Q5 | Q2, Q5 | Q2, Q3 | Q2, Q3<br><br><br>Q5 | Q2, Q4 | Q2 |
| **C3** | Intangible assets | Q2 | | Q3, Q4 | | | |
| **C4** | Inventories and construction contracts | | Q2, Q4(b) | Q2 | Q2 | Q4(b) | Q2, Q5 |
| **C5** | Financial assets and financial liabilities<br>– Fair value through profit or loss/OCI<br>– Amortised cost<br>– Convertible debt | Q2 | Q2 | Q2<br><br>Q2, Q3 | Q2<br>Q2 | Q2<br>Q2 | Q2 |
| **C6** | Leases | | Q2 | | Q3(a) | | |

| | Dec 2008 | June 2009 | Dec 2009 | June 2010 | Dec 2010 | June 2011 |
|---|---|---|---|---|---|---|
| **C** **FINANCIAL STATEMENTS (CONT'D)** | | | | | | |
| **C7** Provisions, contingent liabilities and contingent assets | Q2, Q4 | | | | Q2, Q5 | |
| **C8** Impairment of assets | | | | | | |
| – Group accounting | | | Q1(a) | Q1(a) | | |
| – Other | | | Q2, Q4 | | | |
| **C9** Taxation | | | | | | |
| – Current tax | Q2 | Q2 | Q2 | Q2 | Q2 | Q2 |
| – Deferred tax | Q2 | Q2, Q4(b) | Q2 | Q2 | Q2 | Q2 |
| **C10** Regulatory requirements relating to the preparation of financial statements | | | | | | |
| – Income statement | | | | Q2(a) | | |
| – Statement of comprehensive income | Q2(a) | Q2(a) | Q2(a) | | Q2(a) | Q2 |
| – Statement of financial position | Q2(c) | Q2(b) | Q2(b) | Q2(b) | Q2(c) | Q2 |
| – Statement of changes in equity | Q2(b) | | | | Q2(b) | Q2 |
| **C11** Reporting financial performance | | | | | | |
| – Discontinued operations | | | | | Q5 | Q4(b) |
| – Non-current assets held for sale | | | | Q2 | Q5 | |
| – Earnings per share | | | Q5 | | | Q4(b) |
| **D** **BUSINESS COMBINATIONS** | | | | | | |
| **D1** The concept and principles of a group | | | | | | |
| **D2** The concept of consolidated financial statements | | | | Q1(b) | | Q1(b) |
| **D3** Preparation of consolidated financial statements: | | | | | | |
| – Consolidated income statement | Q1(a) | | Q1(b) | | | |
| – Consolidated statement of comprehensive income | Q1(b) | Q1 | | | Q1(a) | Q1(a) |
| – Consolidated statement of financial position | | Q1 | Q1(a) | Q1(a) | | |
| – Associates | | Q1 | Q1(b) | Q1(a) | Q1(b) | Q1(a) |
| **E** **ANALYSING AND INTERPRETING FINANCIAL STATEMENTS** | | | | | | |
| **E1** Limitations of financial statements | | | | | | |
| **E2** Calculation and interpretation of accounting ratios and trends to address users' and stakeholders' needs | Q3(a)(b) | Q3(b) | Q3(b) | Q3(a)(b), Q4(c) | Q3 | Q3(b) |
| **E3** Limitations of interpretation techniques | Q3(c) | Q4 | Q5 | | | |
| **E4** Specialised, not-for-profit and public sector entities | | | | Q3(b) | | |

# The conceptual framework

| Topic list | Syllabus reference |
|---|:---:|
| 1 Conceptual framework and GAAP | A1 |
| 2 The IASB's *Conceptual Framework* | A1 |
| 3 The objective of financial statements | A2 |
| 4 Underlying assumptions | A2 |
| 5 Qualitative characteristics of financial statements | A2 |
| 6 The elements of financial statements | A3 |
| 7 Recognition of the elements of financial statements | A3 |
| 8 Measurement of the elements of financial statements | A3 |
| 9 Fair presentation and compliance with IFRS | A6 |

## Introduction

The IASB's *Framework for the preparation and presentation of financial statements* has now been replaced by the *Conceptual Framework for Financial Reporting*

A conceptual framework for financial reporting can be defined as an attempt to codify existing **generally accepted accounting practice (GAAP)** in order to reappraise current accounting standards and to produce new standards.

# Study guide

| | | Intellectual level |
|---|---|---|
| **A** | **A CONCEPTUAL FRAMEWORK FOR FINANCIAL REPORTING** | |
| **1** | **The need for a conceptual framework** | |
| (a) | describe what is meant by a conceptual framework of accounting | 2 |
| (b) | discuss whether a conceptual framework is necessary and what an alternative system might be | 2 |
| **2** | **Understandability, relevance, reliability and comparability** | |
| (a) | discuss what is meant by understandability in relation to the provision of financial information | 2 |
| (b) | discuss what is meant by relevance and reliability and describe the qualities that enhance these characteristics | 2 |
| (c) | discuss the importance of comparability to users of financial statements | 2 |
| **3** | **Recognition and measurement** | |
| (a) | define what is meant by 'recognition' in financial statements and discuss the recognition criteria | 2 |
| (b) | apply the recognition criteria to: | 2 |
| | (i)   assets and liabilities | |
| | (ii)   income and expenses | |
| (c) | discuss revenue recognition issues and indicate when income and expense recognition should occur. | 2 |
| (d) | demonstrate the role of the principle of substance over form in relation to recognising sales revenue. | 2 |
| (e) | explain the following measures and compute amounts using: | 2 |
| | (i)   historical cost | |
| | (ii)   fair value/current cost | |
| | (iii)   net realisable value | |
| | (iv)   present value of future cash flows. | |
| **6** | **The concept of 'faithful representation' ('true and fair view')** | |
| (a) | describe what is meant by financial statements achieving a faithful representation. | 2 |
| (b) | discuss whether faithful representation constitutes more than compliance with accounting standards. | 1 |
| (c) | indicate the circumstances and required disclosures where a 'true and fair' override may apply. | 1 |

# 1 Conceptual framework and GAAP

 There are advantages and disadvantages to having a conceptual framework.

## 1.1 The search for a conceptual framework

A **conceptual framework**, in the field we are concerned with, is a statement of generally accepted theoretical principles which form the frame of reference for financial reporting.

These theoretical principles provide the basis for the development of new accounting standards and the evaluation of those already in existence. The financial reporting process is concerned with providing information that is useful in the business and economic decision-making process. Therefore a conceptual framework will form the **theoretical basis** for determining which events should be accounted for, how they should be measured and how they should be communicated to the user. Although it is theoretical in nature, a conceptual framework for financial reporting has highly practical final aims.

The **danger of not having a conceptual framework** is demonstrated in the way some countries' standards have developed over recent years; standards tend to be produced in a haphazard and fire-fighting approach. Where an agreed framework exists, the standard-setting body act as an architect or designer, rather than a fire-fighter, building accounting rules on the foundation of sound, agreed basic principles.

The lack of a conceptual framework also means that fundamental principles are tackled more than once in different standards, thereby producing **contradictions and inconsistencies** in basic concepts, such as those of prudence and matching. This leads to ambiguity and it affects the true and fair concept of financial reporting.

Another problem with the lack of a conceptual framework has become apparent in the USA. The large number of **highly detailed standards** produced by the Financial Accounting Standards Board (FASB) has created a financial reporting environment governed by specific rules rather than general principles. This would be avoided if a cohesive set of principles were in place.

A conceptual framework can also bolster standard setters **against political pressure** from various 'lobby groups' and interested parties. Such pressure would only prevail if it was acceptable under the conceptual framework.

## 1.2 Advantages and disadvantages of a conceptual framework

**Advantages**

(a) The situation is avoided whereby standards are developed on a patchwork basis, where a particular accounting problem is recognised as having emerged, and resources were then channelled into **standardising accounting practice** in that area, without regard to whether that particular issue was necessarily the most important issue remaining at that time without standardisation.

(b) As stated above, the development of certain standards (particularly national standards) have been subject to considerable **political interference** from interested parties. Where there is a conflict of interest between user groups on which policies to choose, policies deriving from a conceptual framework will be **less open to criticism** that the standard-setter buckled to external pressure.

(c) Some standards may concentrate on **profit or loss** whereas some may concentrate on the **valuation of net assets** (statement of financial position).

**Disadvantages**

(a) Financial statements are intended for a **variety of users**, and it is not certain that a single conceptual framework can be devised which will suit all users.

(b) Given the diversity of user requirements, there may be a need for a variety of accounting standards, each produced for a **different purpose** (and with different concepts as a basis).

(c) It is not clear that a conceptual framework makes the task of **preparing and then implementing** standards any easier than without a framework.

Before we look at the IASB's attempt to produce a conceptual framework, we need to consider another term of importance to this debate: generally accepted accounting practice; or GAAP.

## 1.3 Generally Accepted Accounting Practice (GAAP)

**GAAP** signifies all the rules, from whatever source, which govern accounting.

In individual countries this is seen primarily as a **combination** of:

- National company law
- National accounting standards
- Local stock exchange requirements

Although those sources are the basis for the GAAP of individual countries, the concept also includes the effects of **non-mandatory sources** such as:

- International accounting standards
- Statutory requirements in other countries

In many countries, like the UK, GAAP does not have any statutory or regulatory authority or definition, unlike other countries, such as the USA. The term is mentioned rarely in legislation, and only then in fairly limited terms.

There are different views of GAAP in different countries. The UK position can be explained in the following extracts from *UK GAAP* (Davies, Paterson & Wilson, Ernst & Young, 5th edition).

'Our view is that GAAP is a dynamic concept which requires constant review, adaptation and reaction to changing circumstances. We believe that use of the term 'principle' gives GAAP an unjustified and inappropriate degree of permanence. GAAP changes in response to changing business and economic needs and developments. As circumstances alter, accounting practices are modified or developed accordingly..... We believe that GAAP goes far beyond mere rules and principles, and encompasses contemporary permissible accounting **practice**.

It is often argued that the term 'generally accepted' implies that there must exist a high degree of practical application of a particular accounting practice. However, this interpretation raises certain practical difficulties. For example, what about new areas of accounting which have not, as yet, been generally applied? What about different accounting treatments for similar items – are they all generally accepted?

'It is our view that 'generally accepted' does **not** mean 'generally adopted or used'. We believe that, in the UK context, GAAP refers to accounting practices which are regarded as permissible by the accounting profession. The extent to which a particular practice has been adopted is, in our opinion, not the overriding consideration. Any accounting practice which is legitimate in the circumstances under which it has been applied should be regarded as GAAP. The decision as to whether or not a particular practice is permissible or legitimate would depend on one or more of the following factors:

- Is the practice addressed either in the accounting standards, statute or other official pronouncements?
- If the practice is not addressed in UK accounting standards, is it dealt with in International Accounting Standards, or the standards of other countries such as the US?
- Is the practice consistent with the needs of users and the objectives of financial reporting?
- Does the practice have authoritative support in the accounting literature?
- Is the practice being applied by other companies in similar situations?
- Is the practice consistent with the fundamental concept of 'true and fair'?'

**This view is not held in all countries**, however. In the USA particularly, the equivalent of a 'true and fair view' is 'fair presentation in accordance with GAAP'. Generally accepted accounting principles are defined as those principles which have 'substantial authoritative support'. Therefore accounts prepared in accordance with accounting principles for which there is not substantial authoritative support are presumed to be misleading or inaccurate.

The effect here is that 'new' or 'different' accounting principles are not acceptable unless they have been adopted by the mainstream accounting profession, usually the standard-setting bodies and/or professional accountancy bodies. This is much more rigid than the UK view expressed above.

A **conceptual framework** for financial reporting can be defined as an attempt to codify existing GAAP in order to reappraise current accounting standards and to produce new standards.

# 2 The IASB's Conceptual Framework

FAST FORWARD

The 1989 *Framework for the Preparation and Presentation of Financial Statements* was replaced in 2010 by the *Conceptual Framework for Financial Reporting.* This is the result of a joint project with the FASB.

The IASB *Framework for the Preparation and Presentation of Financial Statements* was produced in 1989 and is gradually being replaced by the new *Conceptual Framework for Financial Reporting.* This is the result of an IASB/FASB joint project and is being carried out in phases. The first phase, comprising Chapters 1 and 3, was published in September 2010. Chapter 2 entitled 'The reporting entity' has not yet been published. The current version of the *Conceptual Framework* includes the remaining chapters of the 1989 Framework as Chapter 4.

The *Conceptual Framework for Financial Reporting* is currently as follows:

Chapter 1: The objective of general purpose financial reporting

Chapter 2: The reporting entity (to be issued)

Chapter 3: Qualitative characteristics of useful financial information

Chapter 4: Remaining text of the 1989 Framework:
- Underlying assumption
- The elements of financial statements
- Recognition of the elements of financial statements
- Measurement of the elements of financial statements
- Concepts of capital and capital maintenance

We will look briefly at the introduction to the *Conceptual Framework* as this will place the document in context with the rest of what you have studied for this paper and in particular the context of the *Conceptual Framework* in the IASB's approach to developing IFRSs.

As you read through this chapter think about the impact it has had on standards, particularly the definitions.

## 2.1 Introduction

The Introduction to the *Conceptual Framework* points out the fundamental reason why financial statements are produced worldwide, ie to **satisfy the requirements of external users**, but that practice varies due to the individual pressures in each country. These pressures may be social, political, economic or legal, but they result in variations in practice from country to country, including the form of statements, the definition of their component parts (assets, liabilities etc), the criteria for recognition of items and both the scope and disclosure of financial statements.

It is these differences which the IASB wishes to narrow by **harmonising** all aspects of financial statements, including the regulations governing their accounting standards and their preparation and presentation.

The preface emphasises the way **financial statements are used to make economic decisions** and thus financial statements should be prepared to this end. The types of economic decisions for which financial statements are likely to be used include the following.

- Decisions to buy, hold or sell equity investments
- Assessment of management stewardship and accountability
- Assessment of the entity's ability to pay employees
- Assessment of the security of amounts lent to the entity

- Determination of taxation policies
- Determination of distributable profits and dividends
- Inclusion in national income statistics
- Regulations of the activities of entities

Any additional requirements imposed by **national governments** for their own purposes should not affect financial statements produced for the benefit of other users.

The *Conceptual Framework* recognises that financial statements can be prepared using a **variety of models**. Although the most common is based on historical cost and a nominal unit of currency (ie pound sterling, US dollar etc), the *Conceptual Framework* can be applied to financial statements prepared under a range of models.

## 2.2 Purpose and status

The introduction gives a list of the purposes of the *Conceptual Framework*.

(a) to assist the Board in the **development of future IFRSs** and in its review of existing IFRSs.

(b) to assist the Board in **promoting harmonisation** of regulations, accounting standards and procedures relating to the presentation of financial statements by providing a basis for reducing the number of alternative accounting treatments permitted by IFRSs.

(c) to assist **national standard-setting bodies** in developing national standards.

(d) to assist **preparers of financial statements** in applying IFRSs and in dealing with topics that have yet to form the subject of an IFRS.

(e) to assist **auditors** in forming an opinion as to whether financial statements comply with IFRSs.

(f) to assist **users of financial statements** in interpreting the information contained in financial statements prepared in compliance with IFRSs.

(g) to provide those who are interested in the work of the IASB with **information** about its approach to the formulation of IFRSs.

The *Conceptual Framework* is not an IFRS and so does not overrule any individual IFRS. In the (rare) case of conflict between an IFRS and the *Conceptual Framework*, the **IFRS will prevail**.

### 2.2.1 Scope

The *Conceptual Framework* deals with:

(a) The **objective** of financial statements

(b) The **qualitative characteristics** that determine the usefulness of information in financial statements

(c) The **definition, recognition and measurement** of the elements from which financial statements are constructed

(d) Concepts of **capital and capital maintenance**

### 2.2.2 Users and their information needs

Users of accounting information consist of investors, employees, lenders, suppliers and other trade creditors, customers, government and their agencies and the public. You should be able to remember enough to do the following exercise.

Question

**Users of financial information**

Consider the information needs of the users of financial information listed above.

Answer

(a) **Investors** are the providers of risk capital

(i) Information is required to help make a decision about buying or selling shares, taking up a rights issue and voting.

(ii) Investors must have information about the level of dividend, past, present and future and any changes in share price.

(iii) Investors will also need to know whether the management has been running the company efficiently.

(iv) As well as the position indicated by the statement of profit or loss and other comprehensive income, statement of financial position and earnings per share (EPS), investors will want to know about the liquidity position of the company, the company's future prospects, and how the company's shares compare with those of its competitors.

(b) **Employees** need information about the security of employment and future prospects for jobs in the company, and to help with collective pay bargaining.

(c) **Lenders** need information to help them decide whether to lend to a company. They will also need to check that the value of any security remains adequate, that the interest repayments are secure, that the cash is available for redemption at the appropriate time and that any financial restrictions (such as maximum debt/equity ratios) have not been breached.

(d) **Suppliers** need to know whether the company will be a good customer and pay its debts.

(e) **Customers** need to know whether the company will be able to continue producing and supplying goods.

(f) **Government's** interest in a company may be one of creditor or customer, as well as being specifically concerned with compliance with tax and company law, ability to pay tax and the general contribution of the company to the economy.

(g) The **public** at large would wish to have information for all the reasons mentioned above, but it could be suggested that it would be impossible to provide general purpose accounting information which was specifically designed for the needs of the public.

# 3 The objective of general purpose financial reporting

FAST FORWARD

The *Conceptual Framework* states that:

'The objective of general purpose financial reporting is to provide information about the reporting entity that is useful to existing and potential investors, lenders and other creditors in making decisions about providing resources to the entity.'

These users need information about:
- the **economic resources of the entity**;
- the **claims against the entity**; and
- changes in the entity's **economic resources and claims**

Information about the entity's **economic resources and the claims against it** helps users to assess the entity's liquidity and solvency and its likely needs for additional financing.

Information about a reporting entity's financial performance (the **changes in its economic resources and claims**) helps users to understand the return that the entity has produced on its economic resources. This is an indicator of how efficiently and effectively management has used the resources of the entity and is helpful in predicting future returns.

The *Conceptual Framework* makes it clear that this information should be prepared on an **accruals basis**.

Key term

**Accruals basis.** The effects of transactions and other events are recognised when they occur (and not as cash or its equivalent is received or paid) and they are recorded in the accounting records and reported in the financial statements of the periods to which they relate.

Financial statements prepared under the accruals basis show users past transactions involving cash and also obligations to pay cash in the future and resources which represent cash to be received in the future.

Information about a reporting entity's cash flows during a period also helps users assess the entity's **ability to generate future net cash inflows** and gives users a better understanding of its operations .

# 4 Underlying assumption

FAST FORWARD

**Going concern** is the underlying assumption in preparing financial statements.

## 4.1 Going concern

**Key term**

**Going concern.** The entity is normally viewed as a going concern, that is, as continuing in operation for the foreseeable future. It is assumed that the entity has neither the intention nor the necessity of liquidation or of curtailing materially the scale of its operations. *(Conceptual Framework)*

It is assumed that the entity has no intention to liquidate or curtail major operations. If it did, then the financial statements would be prepared on a **different (disclosed) basis.**

# 5 Qualitative characteristics of useful financial information

FAST FORWARD

The *Conceptual Framework* states that qualitative characteristics are the attributes that make financial information useful to users.

Chapter 3 of the *Conceptual Framework* distinguishes between **fundamental** and **enhancing** qualitative characteristics, for analysis purposes. Fundamental qualitative characteristics distinguish useful financial reporting information from information that is not useful or misleading. Enhancing qualitative characteristics distinguish more useful information from less useful information.

**The two fundamental qualitative** characteristics are **relevance** and **faithful representation**.

## 5.1 Relevance

**Key term**

**Relevance.** Relevant information is capable of making a difference in the decisions made by users.  It is capable of making a difference in decisions in decisions if it has **predictive value**, **confirmatory value** or both. *(Conceptual Framework)*

The relevance of  information is affected by its **nature** and its **materiality**.

**Key term**

**Materiality.** Information is material if omitting it or misstating it could influence decisions that users make on the basis of financial information about a specific reporting  entity. *(Conceptual Framework)*

## 5.2 Faithful representation

**Key term**

**Faithful representation.** Financial reports represent **economic phenomena** in words and numbers.  To be useful, financial information must not only represent relevant phenomena but must **faithfully represent** the phenomena that it purports to represent. *(Conceptual Framework)*

To be a faithful representation information must be **complete, neutral** and **free from error.**

A **complete** depiction includes all information necessary for a user to understand the phenomenon being depicted, including all necessary descriptions and explanations.

A **neutral** depiction is without bias in the selection or presentation of financial information. This means that information must not be manipulated in any way in order to influence the decisions of users.

**Free from error** means there are no errors or omissions in the description of the phenomenon and no errors made in the process by which the financial information was produced. It does not mean that no inaccuracies can arise, particularly where estimates have to be made.

### 5.2.1 Substance over form

This is **not a separate qualitative characteristic** under the *Conceptual Framework*. The IASB says that to do so would be redundant because it is **implied in faithful representation**. Faithful representation of a transaction is only possible if it is accounted for according to its **substance and economic reality**.

## 5.3 Enhancing qualitative characteristics

### 5.3.1 Comparability

**Key term**

> **Comparability**. Comparability is the qualitative characteristic that enables users to identify and understand similarities in, and differences among, items. Information about a reporting entity is more useful if it can be compared with similar information about other entities and with similar information about the same entity for another period or date. *(Conceptual Framework)*

**Consistency**, although related to comparability, **is not the same**. It refers to the use of the same methods for the same items (i.e. consistency of treatment) either from period to period within a reporting entity or in a single period across entities.

The **disclosure of accounting policies** is particularly important here. Users must be able to distinguish between different accounting policies in order to be able to make a valid comparison of similar items in the accounts of different entities.

Comparability is **not the same as uniformity**. Entities should change accounting policies if those policies become inappropriate.

**Corresponding information** for preceding periods should be shown to enable comparison over time.

### 5.3.2 Verifiability

**Key term**

> **Verifiability**. Verifiability helps assure users that information faithfully represents the economic phenomena it purports to represent. It means that different knowledgeable and independent observers could reach consensus that a particular depiction is a faithful representation. *(Conceptual Framework)*

### 5.3.3 Timeliness

**Key term**

> **Timeliness**. Timeliness means having information available to decision-makers in time to be capable of influencing their decisions. Generally, the older information is the less useful it is. *(Conceptual Framework)*

Information may become less useful if there is a delay in reporting it. There is a **balance between timeliness and the provision of reliable information**.

If information is reported on a timely basis when not all aspects of the transaction are known, it may not be complete or free from error.

Conversely, if every detail of a transaction is known, it may be too late to publish the information because it has become irrelevant. The overriding consideration is how best to satisfy the economic decision-making needs of the users.

### 5.3.4 Understandability

Key term

> **Understandability**. Classifying, characterising and presenting information clearly and concisely makes it understandable.
>
> *(Conceptual Framework)*

Financial reports are prepared for users who have a **reasonable knowledge of business and economic activities** and who review and analyse the information diligently. Some phenomena are inherently complex and cannot be made easy to understand. Excluding information on those phenomena might make the information easier to understand, but without it those reports would be incomplete and therefore misleading. Therefore matters should not be left out of financial statements simply due to their difficulty as even well-informed and diligent users may sometimes need the aid of an advisor to understand information about complex economic phenomena.

#### The cost constraint on useful financial reporting

This is a pervasive constraint, not a qualitative characteristic. When information is provided, its benefits must exceed the costs of obtaining and presenting it. This is a **subjective area** and there are other difficulties: others, not the intended users, may gain a benefit; also the cost may be paid by someone other than the users. It is therefore difficult to apply a cost-benefit analysis, but preparers and users should be aware of the constraint.

# 6 The elements of financial statements

> Transactions and other events are grouped together in broad **classes** and in this way their financial effects are shown in the financial statements. These broad classes are the **elements** of financial statements.

The *Conceptual Framework* lays out these elements as follows.

A process of **sub-classification** then takes place for presentation in the financial statements, eg assets are classified by their nature or function in the business to show information in the best way for users to take economic decisions.

## 6.1 Financial position

We need to define the three terms listed under this heading above.

Key terms

> - **Asset**. A resource controlled by an entity as a result of past events and from which future economic benefits are expected to flow to the entity.
>
> - **Liability**. A present obligation of the entity arising from past events, the settlement of which is expected to result in an outflow from the entity of resources embodying economic benefits.

**10**    **1: The conceptual framework** | F7 Financial reporting

- **Equity**. The residual interest in the assets of the entity after deducting all its liabilities.

*(Conceptual Framework)*

These definitions are important, but they do not cover the **criteria for recognition** of any of these items, which are discussed in the next section of this chapter. This means that the definitions may include items which would not actually be recognised in the statement of financial position because they fail to satisfy recognition criteria particularly the **probable flow of any economic benefit** to or from the business.

Whether an item satisfies any of the definitions above will depend on the **substance and economic reality** of the transaction, not merely its legal form. For example, consider finance leases (see Chapter 16).

## 6.2 Assets

We can look in more detail at the components of the definitions given above.

**Key term**

> **Future economic benefit**. The potential to contribute, directly or indirectly, to the flow of cash and cash equivalents to the entity. The potential may be a productive one that is part of the operating activities of the entity. It may also take the form of convertibility into cash or cash equivalents or a capability to reduce cash outflows, such as when an alternative manufacturing process lowers the cost of production.
>
> *(Conceptual Framework)*

Assets are usually employed to produce goods or services for customers; customers will then pay for these. **Cash itself** renders a service to the entity due to its command over other resources.

The existence of an asset, particularly in terms of **control**, is not reliant on:

(a) **physical form** (hence patents and copyrights); *nor*
(b) **legal rights** (hence leases).

Transactions or events **in the past** give rise to assets; those expected to occur in the future do not in themselves give rise to assets. For example, an intention to purchase a non-current asset does not, in itself, meet the definition of an asset.

## 6.3 Liabilities

Again we can look more closely at some aspects of the definition. An essential characteristic of a liability is that the entity has a **present obligation**.

**Key term**

> **Obligation**. A duty or responsibility to act or perform in a certain way. Obligations may be legally enforceable as a consequence of a binding contract or statutory requirement. Obligations also arise, however, from normal business practice, custom and a desire to maintain good business relations or act in an equitable manner.
>
> *(Conceptual Framework)*

It is important to distinguish between a present obligation and a **future commitment**. A management decision to purchase assets in the future does not, in itself, give rise to a present obligation.

**Settlement** of a present obligation will involve the entity giving up resources embodying economic benefits in order to satisfy the claim of the other party. This may be done in various ways, not just by payment of cash.

Liabilities must arise from **past transactions or events**. In the case of, say, recognition of future rebates to customers based on annual purchases, the sale of goods in the past is the transaction that gives rise to the liability.

### 6.3.1 Provisions

Is a provision a liability?

**Key term**

> **Provision**. A present obligation which satisfies the rest of the definition of a liability, even if the amount of the obligation has to be estimated.
> *(Conceptual Framework)*

## Question

Consider the following situations. In each case, do we have an asset or liability within the definitions given by the *Conceptual Framework?* Give reasons for your answer.

(a)    Pat Co has purchased a patent for $20,000. The patent gives the company sole use of a particular manufacturing process which will save $3,000 a year for the next five years.

(b)    Baldwin Co paid Don Brennan $10,000 to set up a car repair shop, on condition that priority treatment is given to cars from the company's fleet.

(c)    Deals on Wheels Co provides a warranty with every car sold.

## Answer

(a)    This is an asset, albeit an intangible one. There is a past event, control and future economic benefit (through cost savings).

(b)    This cannot be classified as an asset. Baldwin Co has no control over the car repair shop and it is difficult to argue that there are 'future economic benefits'.

(c)    The warranty claims in total constitute a liability; the business has taken on an obligation. It would be recognised when the warranty is issued rather than when a claim is made.

## 6.4 Equity

Equity is defined above as a **residual**, but it may be sub-classified in the statement of financial position. This will indicate legal or other restrictions on the ability of the entity to distribute or otherwise apply its equity. Some reserves are required by statute or other law, eg for the future protection of creditors. The amount shown for equity depends on the **measurement of assets and liabilities.** It has nothing to do with the market value of the entity's shares.

## 6.5 Performance

Profit is used as a **measure of performance**, or as a basis for other measures (eg Earnings per share). It depends directly on the measurement of income and expenses, which in turn depend (in part) on the concepts of capital and capital maintenance adopted.

The elements of income and expense are therefore defined.

**Key term**

> - **Income**. Increases in economic benefits during the accounting period in the form of inflows or enhancements of assets or decreases of liabilities that result in increases in equity, other than those relating to contributions from equity participants.
> - **Expenses**. Decreases in economic benefits during the accounting period in the form of outflows or depletions of assets or incurrences of liabilities that result in decreases in equity, other than those relating to distributions to equity participants.
> *(Conceptual Framework)*

Income and expenses can be **presented in different ways** in the statement of profit or loss and other comprehensive income, to provide information relevant for economic decision-making. For example, income and expenses which relate to continuing operations are distinguished from the results of discontinued operations.

## 6.6 Income

Both **revenue** and **gains** are included in the definition of income. **Revenue** arises in the course of ordinary activities of an entity.

> **Gains**. Increases in economic benefits. As such they are no different in nature from revenue.
>
> *(Conceptual Framework)*

Gains include those arising on the disposal of non-current assets. The definition of income also includes **unrealised gains**, eg on revaluation of marketable securities.

## 6.7 Expenses

As with income, the definition of expenses includes losses as well as those expenses that arise in the course of ordinary activities of an entity.

> **Losses**. Decreases in economic benefits. As such they are no different in nature from other expenses.
>
> *(Conceptual Framework)*

Losses will include those arising on the disposal of non-current assets. The definition of expenses will also include **unrealised losses**, eg the fall in value of an investment.

## 6.8 Section summary

Make sure you learn the important definitions.

- Financial position:
    - Assets
    - Liabilities
    - Equity
- Financial performance:
    - Income
    - Expenses

# 7 Recognition of the elements of financial statements

> Items which meet the definition of assets or liabilities may still not be recognised in financial statements because they must also meet certain **recognition criteria**.

> **Recognition**. The process of incorporating in the statement of financial position or statement of profit or loss and other comprehensive income an item that meets the definition of an element and satisfies the following criteria for recognition:
>
> (a)  it is probable that any future economic benefit associated with the item will flow to or from the entity; and
>
> (b)  the item has a cost or value that can be measured with reliability.
>
> *(Conceptual Framework)*

Regard must be given to **materiality** (see Section 5 above).

## 7.1 Probability of future economic benefits

Probability here means the **degree of uncertainty** that the future economic benefits associated with an item will flow to or from the entity. This must be judged on the basis of the **characteristics of the entity's environment** and the **evidence available** when the financial statements are prepared.

## 7.2 Reliability of measurement

The cost or value of an item, in many cases, **must be estimated**. The *Conceptual Framework* states, however, that the use of reasonable estimates is an essential part of the preparation of financial statements and does not undermine their reliability. Where no reasonable estimate can be made, the item should not be recognised, although its existence should be disclosed in the notes, or other explanatory material.

Items may still qualify for recognition **at a later date** due to changes in circumstances or subsequent events.

## 7.3 Assets which cannot be recognised

The recognition criteria do not cover items which many businesses may regard as assets. A skilled workforce is an undoubted asset but workers can leave at any time so there can be no certainty about the probability of future economic benefits. A company may have come up with a new name for its product which is greatly increasing sales but, as it did not buy the name, the name does not have a cost or value that can be reliably measured, so it is not recognised.

## 7.4 Recognition of items

We can summarise the recognition criteria for assets, liabilities, income and expenses, based on the definition of recognition given above.

| Item | Recognised in | When |
|------|---------------|------|
| Asset | The statement of financial position | It is probable that the future economic benefits will flow to the entity and the asset has a cost or value that can be measured reliably. |
| Liability | The statement of financial position | It is probable that an outflow of resources embodying economic benefits will result from the settlement of a present obligation and the amount at which the settlement will take place can be measured reliably. |
| Income | The statement of profit or loss and other comprehensive income | An increase in future economic benefits related to an increase in an asset or a decrease of a liability has arisen that can be measured reliably. |
| Expenses | The statement of profit or loss and other comprehensive income | A decrease in future economic benefits related to a decrease in an asset or an increase of a liability has arisen that can be measured reliably. |

# 8 Measurement of the elements of financial statements

**FAST FORWARD**

A number of different measurement bases are used in financial statements. They include

– Historical cost
– Current cost
– Realisable (settlement) value
– Present value of future cash flows

Measurement is defined as follows.

**Key term**

**Measurement**. The process of determining the monetary amounts at which the elements of the financial statements are to be recognised and carried in the statement of financial position and statement of profit or loss and other comprehensive income.

*(Conceptual Framework)*

This involves the selection of a particular **basis of measurement**. A number of these are used to different degrees and in varying combinations in financial statements. They include the following.

**Historical cost**. Assets are recorded at the amount of cash or cash equivalents paid or the fair value of the consideration given to acquire them at the time of their acquisition. Liabilities are recorded at the amount of proceeds received in exchange for the obligation, or in some circumstances (for example, income taxes), at the amounts of cash or cash equivalents expected to be paid to satisfy the liability in the normal course of business.

**Current cost**. Assets are carried at the amount of cash or cash equivalents that would have to be paid if the same or an equivalent asset was acquired currently.

Liabilities are carried at the undiscounted amount of cash or cash equivalents that would be required to settle the obligation currently.

**Realisable (settlement) value**.

- **Realisable value**. The amount of cash or cash equivalents that could currently be obtained by selling an asset in an orderly disposal.

- **Settlement value**. The undiscounted amounts of cash or cash equivalents expected to be paid to satisfy the liabilities in the normal course of business.

**Present value**. A current estimate of the present discounted value of the future net cash flows in the normal course of business.

*(Conceptual Framework)*

**Historical cost** is the most commonly adopted measurement basis, but this is usually combined with other bases, eg inventory is carried at the lower of cost and net realisable value.

Recent standards use the concept of **fair value**, which is defined by IFRS 13 as 'the price that would be received to sell an asset or paid to transfer a liability in an orderly transaction between market participants at the measurement date'.

### Example

A machine was purchased on 1 January 20X8 for $3m. That was its original cost. It has a useful like of 10 years and under the **historical cost convention** it will be carried at **original cost less accumulated depreciation**. So in the financial statements at 31 December 20X9 it will be carried at:

$3m – (0.3 x 2) = $2.4m

The current cost of the machine, which will probably also be its fair value, will be fairly easy to ascertain if it is not too specialised. For instance, two year old machines like this one may currently be changing hands for $2.5m, so that will be an appropriate fair value.

The **net realisable value** of the machine will be the amount that could be obtained from selling it, less any costs involved in making the sale. If the machine had to be dismantled and transported to the buyer's premises at a cost of $200,000, the NRV would be $2.3m.

The **replacement cost** of the machine will be the cost of a new model less two year's depreciation. The cost of a new machine may now be $3.5m. Assuming a 10-year life, the replacement cost will therefore be $2.8m.

The **present value** of the machine will be the discounted value of the future cash flows that it is expected to generate. If the machine is expected to generate $500,000 per annum for the remaining 8 years of its life and if the company's cost of capital is 10%, present value will be calculated as:

$500,000 x 5.335* = $2667,500

* Cumulative present of $1 per annum for 8 years discounted at 10%

## 9 Fair presentation and compliance with IFRS

Most importantly, financial statements should **present fairly** the financial position, financial performance and cash flows of an entity. **Compliance with IFRS** is presumed to result in financial statements that achieve a fair presentation.

The following points made by IAS 1 expand on this principle.

(a) **Compliance with IFRS** should be disclosed

(b) **All relevant IFRS** must be followed if compliance with IFRS is disclosed

(c) Use of an **inappropriate accounting treatment** cannot be rectified either by disclosure of accounting policies or notes/explanatory material

There may be (very rare) circumstances when management decides that compliance with a requirement of an IFRS would be misleading. **Departure from the IFRS** is therefore required to achieve a fair presentation. The following should be disclosed in such an event.

(a) Management confirmation that the financial statements fairly present the entity's financial position, performance and cash flows

(b) Statement that all IFRS have been complied with *except* departure from one IFRS to achieve a fair presentation

(c) Details of the nature of the departure, why the IFRS treatment would be misleading, and the treatment adopted

(d) Financial impact of the departure

This is usually referred to as the 'true and fair override'.

## 9.1 Extreme case disclosures

In very rare circumstances, management may conclude that compliance with a requirement in a Standard or interpretation may be so **misleading** that it would **conflict with the objective** of financial statements set out in the *Conceptual Framework*, but the relevant regulatory framework prohibits departure from the requirements. In such cases the entity needs to reduce the perceived misleading aspects of compliance by **disclosing**:

(a) The title of the Standard, the nature of the requirement and the reason why management has reached its conclusion.

(b) For each period, the adjustment to each item in the financial statements that would be necessary to achieve fair presentation.

IAS 1 states what is required for a fair presentation.

(a) Selection and application of **accounting policies**

(b) **Presentation of information** in a manner which provides relevant, reliable, comparable and understandable information

(c) **Additional disclosures** where required

# Chapter roundup

- There are advantages and disadvantages to having a conceptual framework.

- The 1989 *Framework for the Preparation and Presentation of Financial Statements* was replaced in 2010 by the *Conceptual Framework for Financial Reporting*. This is the result of a joint project with the FASB.

- The objective of financial statements is to provide information about the reporting entity that is useful to existing and potential investors, lenders and other creditors in making decisions about providing resources to the entity.

- **Going concern** is the underlying assumption in preparing financial statements.

- The *Conceptual Framework* states that qualitative characteristics are the attributes that make financial information useful to users.

- Transactions and other events are grouped together in broad **classes** and in this way their financial effects are shown in the financial statements. These broad classes are the **elements** of financial statements.

- Items which meet the definition of assets or liabilities may still not be recognised in financial statements because they must also meet certain **recognition criteria**.

- A number of different measurement bases are used in financial statements. They include:
    - Historical cost
    - Current cost
    - Realisable (settlement) value
    - Present value of future cash flows

# Quick quiz

1 Define a 'conceptual framework'.
2 What are the advantages and disadvantages of developing a conceptual framework?
3 The needs of which category of user are paramount when preparing financial statements?
4 Define 'relevance'.
5 In which two ways should users be able to compare an entity's financial statements?
6 A provision can be a liability. True or false?
7 Define 'recognition'.
8 The cost or value of items in the financial statements is never estimated. True or false?
9 What is the most common basis of measurement used in financial statements?

# Answers to quick quiz

1  This is a statement of generally accepted theoretical principles, which form the frame of reference for financial reporting.

2  *Advantages*
   - Standardised accounting practice
   - Less open to criticism
   - Concentrate on statement of profit or loss and other comprehensive income or statement of financial position, as appropriate

   *Disadvantages*
   - Variety of users, so not all will be satisfied
   - Variety of standards for different purposes
   - Preparing and implementing standards not necessarily any easier

3  Needs of investors

4  Information has relevance when it influences the economic decisions of users by helping them evaluate past, present or future events or confirming (or correcting) their past evaluations.

5  - Through time to identify trends
   - With other entities' statements

6  True. It satisfies the definition of a liability but the amount may need to be estimated.

7  See Key Term Section 7.

8  False. Monetary values are often estimated.

9  Historical cost.

Now try the questions below from the Exam Question Bank

| Number | Level | Marks | Time |
| --- | --- | --- | --- |
| 1 | Examination | 10 | 18 mins |

# The regulatory framework

| Topic list | Syllabus reference |
|---|---|
| 1 The need for a regulatory framework | B1 |
| 2 The International Accounting Standards Board (IASB) | B2 |
| 3 Setting of International Financial Reporting Standards | B2 |

## Introduction

We have already discussed the IASB and IFRSs to some extent. Here we are concerned with the IASB's relationship with other bodies, and with the way the IASB operates and how IFRSs are produced.

Later in this text we look at some of the theory behind what appears in the accounts. The most important document in this area is the IASB's *Conceptual Framework for Financial Reporting*.

# Study guide

| | | Intellectual level |
|---|---|---|
| **B** | **A REGULATORY FRAMEWORK FOR FINANCIAL REPORTING** | |
| **1** | **Reasons for the existence of a regulatory framework** | |
| (a) | explain why a regulatory framework is needed, also including the advantages and disadvantages of IFRS over a national regulatory framework. | 2 |
| (b) | explain why accounting standards on their own are not a complete regulatory framework. | 2 |
| (c) | distinguish between a principles based and a rules based framework and discuss whether they can be complementary. | 1 |
| **2** | **The standard setting process** | |
| (a) | describe the structure and objectives of the IFRS Foundation, the International Accounting Standards Board (IASB), the IFRS Advisory Council (IFRS AC) and the IFRS Interpretations Committee (IFRS IC). | 2 |
| (b) | describe the IASB's Standard setting process including revisions to and interpretations of Standards. | 2 |
| (c) | explain the relationship of national standard setters to the IASB in respect of the standard setting process. | 2 |

# Exam guide

You may be asked about these topics as part of a longer question.

# 1 The need for a regulatory framework

## 1.1 Introduction

The regulatory framework is the most important element in ensuring relevant and faithfully presented financial information and thus meeting the needs of shareholders and other users.

Without a single body overall responsible for producing financial reporting standards (the IASB) and a framework of general principles within which they can be produced (the *Conceptual Framework*), there would be no means of enforcing compliance with GAAP. Also, GAAP would be unable to evolve in any structured way in response to changes in economic conditions.

## 1.2 Principles-based versus rules-based systems

**FAST FORWARD**

> A principles-based system works within a set of laid down principles. A rules-based system regulates for issues as they arise. Both of these have advantages and disadvantages.

The *Conceptual Framework* provides the background of principles within which standards can be developed. This system is intended to ensure that standards are not produced which are in conflict with each other and also that any departure from a standard can be judged on the basis of whether or not it is in keeping with the principles set out in the *Conceptual Framework*. This is a **principles-based** system.

In the absence of a reporting framework, a more **rules-based** approach has to be adopted. This leads to a large mass of regulation designed to cover every eventuality, as in the US. As we have seen over the past few years, a large volume of regulatory measures does not always detect or prevent financial irregularity. One presumed advantage of rules-based systems is that the exercise of judgement is minimised. Auditors who fear litigation tend to prefer rules-based systems. It could be that a rules-based approach is appropriate for controversial areas in accounting.

# 2 The International Accounting Standards Board (IASB)

The organisational structure consists of:

- The IFRS Foundation
- The IASB
- The IFRS Advisory Council
- The IFRS Interpretations Committee

## 2.1 Introduction

The International Accounting Standards Board is an independent, privately-funded accounting standard setter based in London.

In March 2001 the IASC Foundation was formed as a not-for-profit corporation incorporated in the USA. The IASC Foundation is the parent entity of the IASB. In July 2010 it changed its name to the IFRS Foundation.

From April 2001 the IASB assumed accounting standard setting responsibilities from its predecessor body, the International Accounting Standards Committee (IASC). This restructuring was based upon the recommendations made in the *Recommendations on Shaping IASC for the Future*.

## 2.2 How the IASB is made up

The 15 members of the IASB come from nine countries and have a variety of backgrounds with a mix of auditors, preparers of financial statements, users of financial statements and an academic. The Board consists of 12 full-time members and two part-time members.

## 2.3 Objectives of the IASB

The formal objectives of the IASB, formulated in its mission statement are:

(a) To develop, in the public interest, a single set of high quality, understandable and enforceable global accounting standards that require high quality, transparent and comparable information in general purpose financial statements

(b) To promote the use and vigorous application of those standards

(c) To work actively with national accounting standard setters to bring about convergence of national accounting standards and IFRS to high quality solutions.

## 2.4 Structure of the IASB

The structure of the IASB has the following main features.

(a) The IFRS Foundation is an independent corporation having two main bodies – the Trustees and the IASB. The IFRS Foundation holds the copyright of IFRSs and all other IASB publications.

(b) The IFRS Foundation trustees appoint the IASB members, exercise oversight and raise the funds needed.

(c) The IASB has sole responsibility for setting accounting standards.

(d) There are also two further bodies, the IFRS Advisory Council and the IFRS Interpretations Committee (see below).

The structure can be illustrated as follows.

**Trustees**. The Trustees comprise a group of twenty two individuals, with diverse geographic and functional backgrounds. The Trustees appoint the Members of the Board, the IFRS Interpretations Committee and the IFRS Advisory Council. In addition to monitoring the Foundation's effectiveness and raising its funds, the Trustees will approve the budget and have responsibility for constitutional changes. Trustees were appointed so that initially there were six from North America, six from Europe, four from Asia Pacific, and three others from any area, as long as geographic balance is maintained. Trustees were selected as follows:

(a) The International Federation of Accountants (IFAC) suggested candidates to fill five of the nineteen Trustee seats and international organisations of preparers, users and academics each suggested one candidate.

(b) The remaining Trustees are 'at-large' in that they were not selected through the constituency nomination process.

**IFRS Advisory Council**. The IFRS Advisory Council provides a formal vehicle for further groups and individuals with diverse geographic and functional backgrounds to give advice to the Board and, at times, to advise the Trustees. It comprises about fifty members and meets at least three times a year. It is consulted by the IASB on all major projects and its meetings are open to the public. It advises the IASB on prioritisation of its work and on the implications of proposed standards for users and preparers of financial statements.

**IFRS Interpretations Committee**. The Interpretation Committee provides timely guidance on the application and interpretation of International Financial Reporting Standards. It deals with newly identified financial reporting issues not specifically addressed in IFRSs, or issues where unsatisfactory or conflicting interpretations have developed, or seem likely to develop.

## 2.5 Other international influences

There are a few **other international bodies** worth mentioning. You are not required to follow their workings in detail, but knowledge of them will aid your studies and should help your general reading around the subject area.

### 2.5.1 IASB and the EC/intergovernmental bodies

The European Commission has acknowledged the role of the IASB in harmonising world-wide accounting rules and EC representatives attend IASB Board meetings and have joined Steering Committees involved in setting IFRSs. This should bring to an end the idea of a separate layer of European reporting rules.

The EC has also set up a committee to investigate where there are conflicts between EU norms and international standards so that compatibility can be achieved. In turn, the IASB has used EC directives in its work.

**All listed entities in member states have been required to use IFRSs in their consolidated financial statements since 2005.**

The IASB also works closely with the United Nations Working Groups of Experts on International Standards of Accounting and Reporting (UN IASR group), and with the Working Group in Accounting Standards of the Organisation for Economic Co-operation and Development (OECD Working group). These bodies support harmonisation and improvement of financial reporting, but they are not standard-setting bodies and much of their output draws on the work of the IASB (eg using the IASB's *Framework* document).

### 2.5.2 United Nations (UN)

The UN has a Commission and Centre on Transnational Reporting Corporations through which it gathers information concerning the activities and reporting of multinational companies. The UN processes are highly **political** and probably reflect the attitudes of the governments of developing countries to multinationals. For example, there is an inter-governmental working group of 'experts' on international standards of accounting and reporting which is dominated by the developing countries.

### 2.5.3 International Federation of Accountants (IFAC)

The IFAC is a private sector body established in 1977 and which now consists of over 100 professional accounting bodies from around 80 different countries. The IFAC's main objective is to co-ordinate the accounting profession on a global scale by issuing and establishing international standards on auditing, management accounting, ethics, education and training. You are already familiar with the **International Standards on Auditing** produced by the IAASB, an IFAC body. The IFAC has separate committees working on these topics and also organises the World Congress of Accountants, which is held every five years. The IASB is affiliated with IFAC.

### 2.5.4 Organisation for Economic Co-operation and Development (OECD)

The OECD was established in 1960 by the governments of 21 countries to 'achieve the highest sustainable economic growth and employment and a rising standard of living in member countries while maintaining financial stability and, thus, to contribute to the world economy'. The OECD supports the work of the IASB but also undertakes its **own research** into accounting standards via *ad hoc* working groups. For example, in 1976 the OECD issued guidelines for multinational companies on financial reporting and non-financial disclosures. The OECD appears to work on behalf of developed countries to protect them from the extreme proposals of the UN.

### 2.5.5 International Organisation of Securities Commissions (IOSCO)

IOSCO represents the world's securities markets regulators and has worked closely with the IASB on the development of standards. In 2000 it recommended to all its members that they allow multinational users to submit financial statements based on IFRS.

## 2.6 Generally Accepted Accounting Practice (GAAP)

We also need to consider some important terms which you will meet in your financial accounting studies. GAAP, as a term, has sprung up in recent years and signifies **all the rules, from whatever source, which govern accounting**. The rules may derive from:

(a)     Local (national) company legislation
(b)     National and international accounting standards

(c)     Statutory requirements in other countries (particularly the US)

(d)     Stock exchange requirements

A complete regulatory framework encompasses all of these, where they exist.

## 2.7 True and fair view (or presented fairly)

It is a requirement of national legislation (in some countries) that the financial statements should give a true and fair view of (or 'present fairly, in all material respects') the financial position of the entity as at the end of the financial year.

The terms 'true and fair view' and 'present fairly, in all material respects' are not defined in accounting or auditing standards. Despite this, a company's managers may depart from any of the provisions of accounting standards if these are inconsistent with the requirement to give a true and fair view. This is commonly referred to as the 'true and fair override'. It has been treated as an important **loophole** in the law in different countries and has been the cause of much argument and dissatisfaction within the accounting profession.

## 2.8 IFRS-advantages and disadvantages

The advantages and disadvantages of adopting IFRS have to be considered by each adopting country and are being widely debated in the US at the moment.

The main advantages are seen to be:

- A business can present its financial statements on the same basis as its foreign competitors, making comparison easier.

- Cross-border listing will be facilitated, making it easier to raise capital abroad.

- Companies with foreign subsidiaries will have a common, company-wide accounting language.

- Foreign companies which are targets for takeovers or mergers can be more easily appraised.

The disadvantages are perceived to be:

- The cost of implementing IFRS

- The lower level of detail in IFRS.

Countries which have national standards which are very prescriptive are worried about the principles-based standards in IFRS which require the application of judgement. This is particularly so in the US. US accountants are subject to a high degree of litigation and their defence in court is usually that they complied with the relevant sub-section of one of the hundreds of detailed standards which make up US GAAP. They fear that adoption of IFRS will remove this defence.

Question                                                                                          Harmonisation

In accounting terms what do you think are:

(a)     The advantages to international harmonisation?

(b)     The barriers to international harmonisation?

Answer

(a)     Advantages of global harmonisation

The advantages of harmonisation will be based on the benefits to users and preparers of accounts, as follows.

(i)     Investors, both individual and corporate, would like to be able to compare the financial results of different companies internationally as well as nationally in making investment decisions.

(ii) Multinational companies would benefit from harmonisation for many reasons including the following.

(1) Better access would be gained to foreign investor funds.

(2) Management control would be improved, because harmonisation would aid internal communication of financial information.

(3) Appraisal of foreign entities for take-overs and mergers would be more straightforward.

(4) It would be easier to comply with the reporting requirements of overseas stock exchanges.

(5) Preparation of group accounts would be easier.

(6) A reduction in audit costs might be achieved.

(7) Transfer of accounting staff across national borders would be easier.

(iii) Governments of developing countries would save time and money if they could adopt international standards and, if these were used internally, governments of developing countries could attempt to control the activities of foreign multinational companies in their own country. These companies could not 'hide' behind foreign accounting practices which are difficult to understand.

(iv) Tax authorities. It will be easier to calculate the tax liability of investors, including multinationals who receive income from overseas sources.

(v) Regional economic groups usually promote trade within a specific geographical region. This would be aided by common accounting practices within the region.

(vi) Large international accounting firms would benefit as accounting and auditing would be much easier if similar accounting practices existed throughout the world.

(b) Barriers to harmonisation

(i) Different purposes of financial reporting. In some countries the purpose is solely for tax assessment, while in others it is for investor decision-making.

(ii) Different legal systems. These prevent the development of certain accounting practices and restrict the options available.

(iii) Different user groups. Countries have different ideas about who the relevant user groups are and their respective importance. In the USA investor and creditor groups are given prominence, while in Europe employees enjoy a higher profile.

(iv) Needs of developing countries. Developing countries are obviously behind in the standard setting process and they need to develop the basic standards and principles already in place in most developed countries.

(v) Nationalism is demonstrated in an unwillingness to accept another country's standard.

(vi) Cultural differences result in objectives for accounting systems differing from country to country.

(vii) Unique circumstances. Some countries may be experiencing unusual circumstances which affect all aspects of everyday life and impinge on the ability of companies to produce proper reports, for example hyperinflation, civil war, currency restriction and so on.

(viii) The lack of strong accountancy bodies. Many countries do not have strong independent accountancy or business bodies which would press for better standards and greater harmonisation.

## 2.9 The IASB and current accounting standards

The IASB's predecessor body, the IASC, had issued 41 International Accounting Standards (IASs) and on 1 April 2001 the IASB adopted all of these standards and now issues its own International Financial Reporting Standards (IFRSs). So far thirteen new IFRSs have been issued.

## 2.10 The IASB and FASB

The IASB is currently involved in a joint project with the FASB (Financial Accounting Standards Board) to develop a common conceptual framework. This would provide a sound foundation for developing future accounting standards. The aim is that future standards should be principles-based and internationally-converged. This represents a movement away from the rules-based approach which has characterised US accounting standards.

The new framework will build upon the existing IASB and FASB frameworks and take into account subsequent developments.

## 2.11 European Commission and IFRSs

**All listed entities in member states have been required to use IFRSs in their consolidated financial statements since 2005.**

To this end the IASB undertook **improvements projects**, dealing with **revisions to IFRS**, for example in the area of materiality, presentation, leases, related parties and earnings per share. This has been matched in, for example, the UK, by a **convergence project**, bringing UK GAAP into line with IFRSs where these are better.

# 3 Setting of International Financial Reporting Standards

**FAST FORWARD** »

IFRSs are developed through a formal system of due process and broad international consultation involving accountants, financial analysts and other users and regulatory bodies from around the world.

## 3.1 Due process

The overall agenda of the IASB will initially be set by discussion with the IFRS Advisory Council. The process for developing an individual standard would involve the following steps.

**Step 1** During the early stages of a project, the IASB may establish an **Advisory Committee** to give advice on issues arising in the project. Consultation with the Advisory Committee and the IFRS Advisory Council occurs throughout the project.

**Step 2** IASB may develop and publish **Discussion Papers** for public comment.

**Step 3** Following the receipt and review of comments, the IASB would develop and publish an **Exposure Draft** for public comment.

**Step 4** Following the receipt and review of comments, the IASB would issue a final **International Financial Reporting Standard**.

The period of exposure for public comment is normally 90 days. However, in exceptional circumstances, proposals may be issued with a comment period of 60 days. Draft IFRS Interpretations are exposed for a 60 day comment period.

## 3.2 Co-ordination with national standard setters

Close co-ordination between IASB due process and due process of national standard setters is important to the success of the IASB's mandate.

The IASB is exploring ways in which to integrate its due process more closely with national due process. Such integration may grow as the relationship between the IASB and national standard setters evolves. In particular, the IASB is exploring the following procedure for projects that have international implications.

(a) IASB and national standard setters would co-ordinate their work plans so that when the IASB starts a project, national standard setters would also add it to their own work plans so that they can play a full part in developing international consensus. Similarly, where national standard setters start projects, the IASB would consider whether it needs to develop a new Standard or review its existing Standards. Over a reasonable period, the IASB and national standard setters should aim to review all standards where significant differences currently exist, giving priority to the areas where the differences are greatest.

(b)     National standards setters would not be required to vote for the IASB's preferred solution in their national standards, since each country remains free to adopt IASB standards with amendments or to adopt other standards. However, the existence of an international consensus is clearly one factor that members of national standard setters would consider when they decide how to vote on national standards.

(c)     The IASB would continue to publish its own Exposure Drafts and other documents for public comment.

(d)     National standard setters would publish their own exposure document at approximately the same time as IASB Exposure Drafts and would seek specific comments on any significant divergences between the two exposure documents. In some instances, national standard setters may include in their exposure documents specific comments on issues of particular relevance to their country or include more detailed guidance than is included in the corresponding IASB document.

(e)     National standard setters would follow their own full due process, which they would ideally choose to integrate with the IASB's due process. This integration would avoid unnecessary delays in completing standards and would also minimise the likelihood of unnecessary differences between the standards that result.

## 3.3 IASB liaison members

Seven of the full-time members of the IASB have formal liaison responsibilities with national standard setters in order to promote the convergence of national accounting standards and International Financial Reporting Standards. The IASB envisages a partnership between the IASB and these national standard setters as they work together to achieve convergence of accounting standards world-wide.

In addition all IASB members have contact responsibility with national standards setters not having liaison members and many countries are also represented on the IFRS Advisory Council.

**Exam focus point**

> This topic is likely to be examined as a short discussion question.

## 3.4 Current IASs/IFRSs

The current list is as follows.

| International Accounting Standards | | Date of issue |
|---|---|---|
| IAS 1 (revised) | Presentation of financial statements | Sep 2007 |
| IAS 2 | Inventories | Dec 2003 |
| IAS 7 | Statements of cash flows | Dec 1992 |
| IAS 8 | Accounting policies, changes in accounting estimates and errors | Dec 2003 |
| IAS 10 | Events after the reporting period | Dec 2003 |
| IAS 11 | Construction contracts | Dec 1993 |
| IAS 12 | Income taxes | Nov 2000 |
| IAS 16 | Property, plant and equipment | Dec 2003 |
| IAS 17 | Leases | Dec 2003 |
| IAS 18 | Revenue | Dec 1993 |
| IAS 19 * | Employee benefits | Dec 2004 |
| IAS 20 | Accounting for government grants and disclosure of government assistance | Jan 1995 |
| IAS 21 | The effects of changes in foreign exchange rates | Dec 2003 |
| IAS 23 (revised) | Borrowing costs | Jan 2008 |
| IAS 24 | Related party disclosures | Dec 2003 |

| International Accounting Standards | | Date of issue |
|---|---|---|
| IAS 26 * | Accounting and reporting by retirement benefit plans | Jan 1995 |
| IAS 27 (revised) | Consolidated and separate financial statements | Jan 2008 |
| IAS 28 | Investments in associates | Dec 2003 |
| IAS 29 * | Financial reporting in hyperinflationary economies | Jan 1995 |
| IAS 30 * | Disclosure in the financial statements of banks and similar financial institutions (not examinable) | Jan 1995 |
| IAS 31 * | Interests in joint ventures | Dec 2003 |
| IAS 32 | Financial instruments: presentation | Dec 2003 |
| IAS 33 | Earnings per share | Dec 2003 |
| IAS 34 | Interim financial reporting | Feb 1998 |
| IAS 36 | Impairment of assets | Mar 2004 |
| IAS 37 | Provisions, contingent liabilities and contingent assets | Sept 1998 |
| IAS 38 | Intangible assets | Mar 2004 |
| IAS 39 | Financial instruments: recognition and measurement | Dec 2004 |
| IAS 40 | Investment property | Dec 2003 |
| IAS 41 * | Agriculture | Feb 2001 |
| IFRS 1 | First time adoption of International Financial Reporting Standards | June 2003 |
| IFRS 2 * | Share-based payment | Feb 2004 |
| IFRS 3 (revised) | Business combinations | Jan 2008 |
| IFRS 4 * | Insurance contracts | Mar 2004 |
| IFRS 5 | Non-current assets held for sale and discontinued operations | Mar 2004 |
| IFRS 6 * | Exploration for and evaluation of mineral resources | Dec 2004 |
| IFRS 7 | Financial instruments: disclosures | Aug 2005 |
| IFRS 8 * | Operating segments | Nov 2006 |
| IFRS 9 | Financial Instruments | Nov 2009 |
| IFRS 10 | Consolidated financial statements | May 2011 |
| IFRS 11* | Joint arrangements | May 2011 |
| IFRS 12* | Disclosures of interests in other entities | May 2011 |
| IFRS 13 | Fair value measurement | May 2011 |

* These standards are not examinable at F7.

## 3.5 Alternative treatments

Many of the old IASs permitted two accounting treatments for like transactions or events. One treatment was designated as the **benchmark treatment** (effectively the **preferred treatment**) and the other was known as the **alternative treatment**. This is no longer the case. The last standard to have a benchmark alternative was IAS 23 which was revised to remove the benchmark treatment. Under the revised standard allowable borrowing costs **must** be capitalised. However, some standards do still allow more than one policy – for instance IAS 16 allows property, plant and equipment to be carried at cost or revalued amount.

## 3.6 Interpretation of IFRSs

The IASB has developed a procedure for issuing interpretations of its standards. In September 1996, the IASC Board approved the formation of a **Standards Interpretations Committee (SIC)** for this task. This has been renamed under the IASB as the **IFRS Interpretations Committee** (IFRSIC).

The duties of the Interpretations Committee are:

(a)     To interpret the application of International Financial Reporting Standards and provide timely guidance on financial reporting issues not specifically addressed in IFRSs or IASs in the context of the IASB's Framework, and undertake other tasks at the request of the Board.

(b)     To have regard to the Board's objective of working actively with national standard setters to bring about convergence of national accounting standards and IFRSs to high quality solutions.

(c)     To publish, after clearance by the Board, Draft Interpretations for public comment and consider comments made within a reasonable period before finalising an Interpretation.

(d)     To report to the Board and obtain Board approval for final Interpretations.

In developing interpretations, the IFRSIC will work closely with **similar national committees**. If no more than three of its members vote against an interpretation, the IFRSIC will ask the Board to approve the interpretation for issue. Interpretations will be formally published after approval by the Board.

## 3.7 Scope and application of IFRSs

### 3.7.1 Scope

Any limitation of the applicability of a specific IFRS is made clear within that standard. IFRSs are **not intended to be applied to immaterial items, nor are they retrospective**. Each individual IFRS lays out its scope at the beginning of the standard.

### 3.7.2 Application

Within each individual country **local regulations** govern, to a greater or lesser degree, the issue of financial statements. These local regulations include accounting standards issued by the national regulatory bodies and/or professional accountancy bodies in the country concerned.

The IASB **concentrated on essentials** when producing IFRSs. They tried not to make IFRSs too complex, because otherwise they would be impossible to apply on a worldwide basis.

## 3.8 World-wide effect of IFRSs and the IASB

The IASB, and before it the IASC, has now been in existence for around 25 years, and it is worth looking at the effect it has had in that time.

As far as **Europe** is concerned, the consolidated financial statements of many of Europe's top multinationals are now prepared in conformity with national requirements, EC directives and IFRSs. Furthermore, IFRSs are having a growing influence on national accounting requirements and practices. Many of these developments have been given added impetus by the internationalisation of capital markets. As mentioned previously, IFRSs have been implemented in the EU for listed companies since 2005.

In **Japan**, the influence of the IASC had, until recently, been negligible. This was mainly because of links in Japan between tax rules and financial reporting. The Japanese Ministry of Finance set up a working committee to consider whether to bring national requirements into line with IFRSs. The Tokyo Stock Exchange has announced that it will accept financial statements from foreign issuers that conform with home country standards, which would include IFRS.

This was widely seen as an attempt to attract foreign issuers, in particular companies from Hong Kong and Singapore. As these countries base their accounting on international standards, this action is therefore implicit acknowledgement by the Japanese Ministry of Finance of IFRS requirements.

In **America**, the Securities and Exchange Commission (SEC) agreed in 1993 to allow foreign issuers (of shares, etc) to follow IFRS treatments on certain issues, including cash flow statements under IAS 7. The overall effect is that, where an IFRS treatment differs from US GAAP, these treatments will now be acceptable. The SEC is now supporting the IASB because it wants to attract foreign listings. In October 2002, under the Norwalk Agreement the FASB and the IASB formally agreed that they would work towards convergence between US GAAP and IFRS and in February 2006 they released a 'roadmap' setting out the convergence projects.

## 3.9 Criticisms of the IASB

You need to be able to understand the problems that can arise.

We will begin by looking at some of the general problems created by **accounting standards**.

### 3.9.1 Accounting standards and choice

It is sometimes argued that companies should be given a choice in matters of financial reporting on the grounds that accounting standards are detrimental to the quality of such reporting. There are arguments on both sides.

**In favour of accounting standards** (both national and international), the following points can be made.

- They reduce or eliminate confusing variations in the methods used to prepare accounts.
- They provide a focal point for debate and discussions about accounting practice.
- They oblige companies to disclose the accounting policies used in the preparation of accounts.
- They are a less rigid alternative to enforcing conformity by means of legislation.
- They have obliged companies to **disclose more accounting information** than they would otherwise have done if accounting standards did not exist, for example IAS 33 *Earnings per share*.

Many companies are reluctant to disclose information which is not required by national legislation. However, the following arguments may be put forward **against standardisation** and **in favour of choice**.

- A set of rules which give backing to one method of preparing accounts might be **inappropriate in some circumstances**. For example, IAS 16 on depreciation is inappropriate for investment properties (properties not occupied by the entity but held solely for investment), which are covered by IAS 40 on investment property.
- Standards may be subject to **lobbying or government pressure** (in the case of national standards). For example, in the USA, the accounting standard FAS 19 on the accounts of oil and gas companies led to a powerful lobby of oil companies, which persuaded the SEC (Securities and Exchange Commission) to step in. FAS 19 was then suspended.
- Many national standards are not based on a **conceptual framework of accounting**, although IFRSs are.
- There may be a **trend towards rigidity**, and away from flexibility in applying the rules.

### 3.9.2 Political problems

Any international body, whatever its purpose or activity, faces enormous political difficulties in attempting to gain **international consensus** and the IASB is no exception to this. How can the IASB reconcile the financial reporting situation between economies as diverse as third-world developing countries and sophisticated first-world industrial powers?

**Developing countries** are suspicious of the IASB, believing it to be dominated by the **USA.** This arises because acceptance by the USA listing authority, the Securities and Exchange Commission (SEC), of IASs is seen as a major hurdle to be overcome. For all practical purposes it is the American market which must be persuaded to accept IFRSs.

Developing countries are being catered for to some extent by the issue of a standard on **agriculture**, which is generally of much more relevance to such countries.

There are also tensions between the **UK/US model** of financial reporting and the **European model**. The UK/US model is based around investor reporting, whereas the European model is mainly concerned with tax rules, so shareholder reporting has a much lower priority.

The break-up of the former USSR and the move in many **Eastern European countries** to free-market economies has also created difficulties. It is likely that these countries will have to 'catch up' to international standards as their economies stabilise.

You must keep up to date with the IASB's progress and the problems it encounters in the financial press. You should also be able to discuss:

- **Due process** of the IASB
- **Use and application** of IFRSs
- **Future work** of the IASB
- **Criticisms** of the IASB

One of the competences you require to fulfil performance objective 10 of the PER is the ability to recognise and apply the external legal and professional framework and regulations to financial reporting. The information in this chapter will give you knowledge to help you demonstrate this competence.

# Chapter Roundup

- A principles-based system works within a set of laid down principles. A rules-based system regulates for issues as they arise. Both of these have advantages and disadvantages.

- The organisational structure consists of:
  - the IFRS Foundation
  - the IASB
  - the IFRS Advisory Council
  - the IFRS Interpretations Committee

- IFRSs are developed through a formal system of due process and broad international consultation involving accountants, financial analysis and other users and regulatory bodies from around the world.

# Quick Quiz

1   What recent decisions will have a beneficial effect on global harmonisation of accounting?

2   One objective of the IASB is to promote the preparation of financial statements using the euro.

    True    ☐

    False   ☐

3   A conceptual framework is:
    A    A theoretical expression of accounting standards
    B    A list of key terms used by the IASB
    C    A statement of theoretical principles which form the frame of reference for financial reporting
    D    The proforma financial statements

4   What development at the IASB aided users' interpretation of IFRSs?

5   Which of the following arguments is not in favour of accounting standards, but is in favour of accounting choice?
    A    They reduce variations in methods used to produce accounts
    B    They oblige companies to disclose their accounting policies
    C    They are a less rigid alternative to legislation
    D    They may tend towards rigidity in applying the rules

# Answers to Quick Quiz

1    The IOSCO endorsement, and the EC requirement that listed companies should use IFRS from 2005.
2    False
3    C
4    The formation of the IFRS Interpretations Committee.
5    D    The other arguments are all in favour of accounting standards.

Now try the question below from the Exam Question Bank

| Number | Level | Marks | Time |
|--------|-------|-------|------|
| 2 | Examination | 10 | 18 mins |
| 3(a) | – | 5 | 9 mins |

# Presentation of published financial statements

| Topic list | Syllabus reference |
|---|---|
| 1 IAS 1 (revised) Presentation of financial statements | C10 |
| 2 Statement of financial position | C10 |
| 3 The current/non-current distinction | C10 |
| 4 Statement of profit or loss and other comprehensive income | C10 |
| 5 Statement of profit or loss | C10 |
| 6 Revision of basic accounts | C10 |
| 7 Changes in equity | C10 |
| 8 Notes to the financial statements | C10 |

## Introduction

The bulk of this Study Text looks at the accounts of limited liability companies, either single companies or groups of companies.

We begin in this chapter by looking at the overall **content and format** of company financial statements. These are governed by IAS 1 (revised) *Presentation of financial statements*.

# Study guide

| | | Intellectual level |
|---|---|---|
| **10** | **Regulatory requirements relating to the preparation of financial statements** | |
| (d) | describe the structure (format) and content of financial statements presented under IFRS. | 2 |
| (e) | prepare an entity's financial statements in accordance with the prescribed structure and content. | 2 |
| **11** | **Reporting financial performance** | |
| (d) | prepare and explain the contents and purpose of the statement of changes in equity. | 2 |
| (e) | describe and prepare a statement of changes in equity. | 2 |

# 1 IAS 1 (revised) Presentation of financial statements

**FAST FORWARD**

IAS 1 covers the form and content of financial statements. The main components are:

- Statement of financial position
- Statement of profit or loss and other comprehensive income
- Statement of changes in equity
- Statement of cash flows
- Notes to the financial statements

IMPORTANT NOTE

An amendment to IAS 1 was published in June 2011. This amendment changed the name of the full statement from 'statement of comprehensive income' to 'statement of profit or loss and other comprehensive income'. The statement down to 'Profit (loss) for the year', which had previously been referred to as the 'income statement', then became the 'statement of profit or loss'. We have used the revised terminology in this text, but you will still probably meet 'income statement' and 'statement of comprehensive income' in other publications or articles.

## 1.1 Profit or loss for the year

The statement of profit or loss and other comprehensive income is the most significant indicator of a company's financial performance. So it is important to ensure that it is not misleading.

IAS 1 stipulates that all items of income and expense recognised in a period shall be included in profit or loss unless a **Standard** or an **Interpretation** requires otherwise.

Circumstances where items may be excluded from profit or loss for the current year include the correction of errors and the effect of changes in accounting policies. These are covered in IAS 8.

## 1.2 How items are disclosed

IAS 1 specifies disclosures of certain items in certain ways.

- Some items must appear on the face of the statement of financial position or statement of profit or loss and other comprehensive income
- Other items can appear in a **note to the financial statements** instead
- **Recommended formats** are given which entities may or may not follow, depending on their circumstances

Obviously, disclosures specified by **other standards** must also be made, and we will mention the necessary disclosures when we cover each statement in turn. Disclosures in both IAS 1 and other standards must be made either on the face of the statement or in the notes unless otherwise stated, ie disclosures cannot be made in an accompanying commentary or report.

## 1.3 Identification of financial statements

As a result of the above point, it is most important that entities **distinguish the financial statements** very clearly from any other information published with them. This is because all IASs/IFRSs apply *only* to the financial statements (ie the main statements and related notes), so readers of the annual report must be able to differentiate between the parts of the report which are prepared under IFRSs, and other parts which are not.

The entity should **identify each** financial statement and the notes very clearly. IAS 1 also requires disclosure of the following information in a prominent position. If necessary it should be repeated wherever it is felt to be of use to the reader in his understanding of the information presented.

- **Name** of the reporting entity (or other means of identification)
- Whether the accounts cover the **single entity** only or a group of entities
- The **date of the end of the reporting period** or the period covered by the financial statements (as appropriate)
- The **presentation currency**
- The **level of rounding** used in presenting amounts in the financial statements

**Judgement** must be used to determine the best method of presenting this information. In particular, the standard suggests that the approach to this will be very different when the financial statements are communicated electronically.

The **level of rounding** is important, as presenting figures in thousands or millions of units makes the figures more understandable. The level of rounding must be disclosed, however, and it should not obscure necessary details or make the information less relevant.

## 1.4 Reporting period

It is normal for entities to present financial statements **annually** and IAS 1 states that they should be prepared at least as often as this. If (unusually) the end of an entity's reporting period is changed, for whatever reason, the period for which the statements are presented will be less or more than one year. In such cases the entity should also disclose:

(a)   the **reason(s) why** a period other than one year is used; and

(b)   the fact that the comparative figures given **are not in fact comparable**.

For practical purposes, some entities prefer to use a period which **approximates to a year**, eg 52 weeks, and the IAS allows this approach as it will produce statements not materially different from those produced on an annual basis.

## 1.5 Timeliness

If the publication of financial statements is delayed too long after the reporting period, their usefulness will be severely diminished. The standard states that entities should be able to produce their financial statements **within six months of the end of the reporting period.** An entity with consistently complex operations cannot use this as a reason for its failure to report on a timely basis. Local legislation and market regulation imposes specific deadlines on certain entities.

IAS 1 looks at the statement of financial position and statement of profit and other comprehensive income. We will not give all the detailed disclosures as some are outside the scope of your syllabus. Instead we will look at a **'proforma' set of accounts** based on the Standard.

# 2 Statement of financial position

IAS 1 suggests a format for the statement of financial position. Certain items are specified for **disclosure on the face of the financial statements**.

IAS 1 discusses the distinction between current and non-current items in some detail, as we shall see in the next section. First of all we can look at the **suggested format** of the statement of financial position (given in an appendix to the Standard) and then look at further disclosures required.

## 2.1 Statement of financial position example

The example given by IAS 1 is as follows.

XYZ GROUP – STATEMENT OF FINANCIAL POSITION AT 31 DECEMBER

| | 20X7 | 20X6 |
|---|---|---|
| | $'000 | $'000 |
| *Assets* | | |
| Non-current assets | | |
| Property, plant and equipment | 350,700 | 360,020 |
| Goodwill | 80,800 | 91,200 |
| Other intangible assets | 227,470 | 227,470 |
| Investments in associates | 100,150 | 110,770 |
| Investments in equity instruments | 142,500 | 156,000 |
| | 901,620 | 945,460 |
| Current assets | | |
| Inventories | 135,230 | 132,500 |
| Trade receivables | 91,600 | 110,800 |
| Other current assets | 25,650 | 12,540 |
| Cash and cash equivalents | 312,400 | 322,900 |
| | 564,880 | 578,740 |
| *Total assets* | 1,466,500 | 1,524,200 |
| *Equity and liabilities* | | |
| Equity attributable to owners of the parent | | |
| Share capital | 650,000 | 600,000 |
| Retained earnings | 243,500 | 161,700 |
| Other components of equity | 10,200 | 21,200 |
| | 903,700 | 782,900 |
| Non-controlling interest | 70,050 | 48,600 |
| *Total equity* | 973,750 | 831,500 |
| Non-current liabilities | | |
| Long-term borrowings | 120,000 | 160,000 |
| Deferred tax | 28,800 | 26,040 |
| Long-term provisions | 28,850 | 52,240 |
| *Total non-current liabilities* | 177,650 | 238,280 |
| Current liabilities | | |
| Trade and other payables | 115,100 | 187,620 |
| Short-term borrowings | 150,000 | 200,000 |
| Current portion of long-term borrowings | 10,000 | 20,000 |
| Current tax payable | 35,000 | 42,000 |
| Short-term provisions | 5,000 | 4,800 |
| *Total current liabilities* | 315,100 | 454,420 |
| *Total liabilities* | 492,750 | 692,700 |
| *Total equity and liabilities* | 1,466,500 | 1,524,200 |

IAS 1 (revised) specifies various items which must appear on the **face of the statement of financial position** as a minimum disclosure.

(a)  Property, plant and equipment (Chapter 4)
(b)  Investment property (Chapter 4)
(c)  Intangible assets (Chapter 5)
(d)  Financial assets (excluding amounts shown under (e), (h) and (i)) (Chapter 14)
(e)  Investments accounted for using the equity method (Chapter 11)
(f)  Biological assets (outside the scope of the syllabus)
(g)  Inventories (Chapter 12)
(h)  Trade and other receivables
(i)  Cash and cash equivalents (Chapter 21)
(j)  Assets classified as held for sale under IFRS 5 (Chapter 7)
(k)  Trade and other payables
(l)  Provisions (Chapter 13)
(m)  Financial liabilities (other than (j) and (k))
(n)  Current tax liabilities and assets as in IAS 12 (Chapter 17)
(o)  Deferred tax liabilities and assets (Chapter 17)
(p)  Liabilities included in disposal groups under IFRS 5 (Chapter 7)
(q)  Non-controlling interests (Chapter 9)
(r)  Issued capital and reserves

We will look at these items in the chapters marked.

Any **other line items**, headings or sub-totals should be shown on the face of the statement of financial position when it is necessary for an understanding of the entity's financial position.

The example shown above is for illustration only (although we will follow the format in this Study Text). The IAS, however, does not prescribe the order or format in which the items listed should be presented. It simply states that they **must be presented separately** because they are so different in nature or function from each other.

Whether additional items are presented separately depends on judgements based on the assessment of the following factors.

(a)  **Nature and liquidity of assets and their materiality**. Thus goodwill and assets arising from development expenditure will be presented separately, as will monetary/non-monetary assets and current/non-current assets.

(b)  **Function within the entity.** Operating and financial assets, inventories, receivables and cash and cash equivalents are therefore shown separately.

(c)  **Amounts, nature and timing of liabilities**. Interest-bearing and non-interest-bearing liabilities and provisions will be shown separately, classified as current or non-current as appropriate.

The standard also requires separate presentation where **different measurement bases** are used for assets and liabilities which differ in nature or function. According to IAS 16, for example, it is permitted to carry certain items of property, plant and equipment at cost or at a revalued amount.

## 2.2 Information presented either on the face of the statement of financial position or by note

Further **sub-classification** of the line items listed above should be disclosed either on the face of the statement of financial position or in the notes. The classification will depend upon the nature of the entity's operations. As well as each item being sub-classified by its nature, any amounts payable to or receivable from any **group company or other related party** should also be disclosed separately.

The sub-classification details will in part depend on the requirements of IFRSs. The size, nature and function of the amounts involved will also be important and the factors listed above should be considered. **Disclosures** will vary from item to item and IAS 1 gives the following examples.

(a)  **Property, plant and equipment** are classified by class as described in IAS 16, *Property, plant and equipment*

(b)     **Receivables** are analysed between amounts receivable from trade customers, other members of the group, receivables from related parties, prepayments and other amounts

(c)     **Inventories** are sub-classified, in accordance with IAS 2 *Inventories,* into classifications such as merchandise, production supplies, materials, work in progress and finished goods

(d)     **Provisions** are analysed showing separately provisions for employee benefit costs and any other items classified in a manner appropriate to the entity's operations

(e)     **Equity capital and reserves** are analysed showing separately the various classes of paid in capital, share premium and reserves

The standard then lists some **specific disclosures** which must be made, either on the face of the statement of financial position or in the related notes.

(a)     **Share capital disclosures** (for each class of share capital)

(i)     Number of shares authorised

(ii)    Number of shares issued and fully paid, and issued but not fully paid

(iii)   Par value per share, or that the shares have no par value

(iv)    Reconciliation of the number of shares outstanding at the beginning and at the end of the year

(v)     Rights, preferences and restrictions attaching to that class including restrictions on the distribution of dividends and the repayment of capital

(vi)    Shares in the entity held by the entity itself or by related group companies

(vii)   Shares reserved for issuance under options and sales contracts, including the terms and amounts

(b)     Description of the nature and purpose of **each reserve** within owners' equity

Some types of entity have no share capital, eg partnerships. Such entities should disclose information which is **equivalent** to that listed above. This means disclosing the movement during the period in each category of equity interest and any rights, preferences or restrictions attached to each category of equity interest.

# 3 The current/non-current distinction

FAST FORWARD
> You should appreciate the distinction between current and non-current assets and liabilities and their different treatments.

## 3.1 The current/non-current distinction

An entity must present **current** and **non-current** assets as separate classifications on the face of the statement of financial position. A presentation based on liquidity should only be used where it provides more relevant and reliable information, in which case all assets and liabilities must be presented broadly **in order of liquidity**.

In either case, the entity should disclose any portion of an asset or liability which is expected to be recovered or settled **after more than twelve months**. For example, for an amount receivable which is due in instalments over 18 months, the portion due after more than twelve months must be disclosed.

The IAS emphasises how helpful information on the **operating cycle** is to users of financial statements. Where there is a clearly defined operating cycle within which the entity supplies goods or services, then information disclosing those net assets that are continuously circulating as **working capital** is useful.

This distinguishes them from those net assets used in the long-term operations of the entity. Assets that are expected to be realised and liabilities that are due for settlement within the operating cycle are therefore highlighted.

The liquidity and solvency of an entity is also indicated by information about the **maturity dates** of assets and liabilities. As we will see later, IFRS 7 *Financial instruments: disclosures* requires disclosure of maturity dates of both financial assets and financial liabilities. (Financial assets include trade and other receivables; financial liabilities include trade and other payables.)

## 3.2 Current assets

**Key term**

> An asset should be classified as a **current asset** when it:
>
> - is expected to be realised in, or is held for sale or consumption in, the normal course of the entity's operating cycle; or
> - is held primarily for trading purposes or for the short-term and expected to be realised within twelve months of the end of the reporting period; or
> - is cash or a cash equivalent asset which is not restricted in its use.
>
> All other assets should be classified as non-current assets. *(IAS 1)*

**Non-current assets** includes tangible, intangible, operating and financial assets of a long-term nature. Other terms with the same meaning can be used (eg 'fixed', 'long-term').

The term 'operating cycle' has been used several times above and the standard defines it as follows.

**Key term**

> The **operating cycle** of an entity is the time between the acquisition of assets for processing and their realisation in cash or cash equivalents. *(IAS 1)*

Current assets therefore include inventories and trade receivables that are sold, consumed and realised as part of the normal operating cycle. **This is the case even where they are not expected to be realised within twelve months**.

Current assets will also include **marketable securities** if they are expected to be realised within twelve months after the reporting period. If expected to be realised later, they should be included in non-current assets.

## 3.3 Current liabilities

**Key term**

> A liability should be classified as a **current liability** when it:
>
> - is expected to be settled in the normal course of the entity's operating cycle; or
> - is held primarily for the purpose of trading; or
> - is due to be settled within twelve months after the end of the reporting period; or when
> - The entity does not have an unconditional right to defer settlement of the liability for at least twelve months after the end of the reporting period.
>
> All other liabilities should be classified as non-current liabilities. *(IAS 1)*

The categorisation of current liabilities is very similar to that of current assets. Thus, some current liabilities are part of the **working capital** used in the normal operating cycle of the business (ie trade payables and accruals for employee and other operating costs). Such items will be classed as current liabilities **even where they are due to be settled more than twelve months after the end of the reporting period.**

There are also current liabilities which are not settled as part of the normal operating cycle, but which are due to be settled within twelve months of the end of the reporting period. These include bank overdrafts, income taxes, other non-trade payables and the current portion of interest-bearing liabilities. Any interest-bearing liabilities that are used to finance working capital on a long-term basis, and that are not due for settlement within twelve months, should be classed as **non-current liabilities**.

A **non-current financial liability** due to be **settled within twelve months** of the end of the reporting period should be classified as a **current liability**, even if an agreement to refinance, or to reschedule payments, on a long-term basis is completed after the end of the reporting period and before the financial statements are authorised for issue.

| End of the reporting period | Agreement to refinance on long-term basis | Date financial statements authorised for issue | Settlement date <12 months after end of the reporting period therefore current liability |

A **non-current financial liability** that is payable on **demand** because the entity **breached** a **condition** of its loan agreement should be classified as **current** at the end of the reporting period even if the **lender** has agreed **after the end of the reporting period**, and **before** the financial statements are **authorised for issue**, **not** to **demand payment** as a consequence of the breach.

| Condition of loan agreement breached. Non-current liability becomes payable on demand | End of the reporting period | Lender agrees not to enforce payment resulting from breach | Date financial statements are authorised for issue. Loan shown as **current** liability |

However, if the **lender** has **agreed** by the **end of the reporting period** to provide a **period of grace** ending **at least twelve months after the end of the reporting period** within which the entity can rectify the breach and during that time the lender cannot demand immediate repayment, the liability is classified as **non-current.**

# 4 Statement of profit or loss and other comprehensive income

FAST FORWARD ▶▶

In June 2011 the IASB published an amendment to IAS 1 called 'Presentation of items of other comprehensive income'. This changed the name of the 'statement of comprehensive income' to the 'statement of profit or loss and other comprehensive income'.

## 4.1 Format

IAS 1 (revised) allows income and expense items to be presented either:

(a) in a single statement of profit or loss and other comprehensive income; or
(b) in two statements: a separate statement of profit or loss and statement of other comprehensive income.

The format for a single statement of profit or loss and other comprehensive income is shown as follows in the standard. The section down to 'profit for the year' can be shown as a separate 'statement of profit or loss' with an additional 'statement of other comprehensive income'. Note that not all of the items which would appear under 'other comprehensive income' are included in your syllabus.

Exam focus point

In the examinations, if a 'statement of profit or loss and other comprehensive income' is referred to, this will always relate to the single statement format. If 'statements of profit or loss' are referred to, this relates to the statement from 'revenue' to 'profit for the year'. Exams may refer to 'other comprehensive income' which relates to the 'other comprehensive income' section of the statement. In practice, the item of 'other comprehensive income' you are most likely to meet is a revaluation gain. Where we have used 'statement of profit or loss' in this text, this can be taken to refer to the profit or loss section of the full statement or separate statement of profit or loss.

XYZ GROUP – STATEMENT OF PROFIT OR LOSS AND OTHER COMPREHENSIVE INCOME FOR THE YEAR ENDED 31 DECEMBER 20X7

| | 20X7 | 20X6 |
|---|---|---|
| | $'000 | $'000 |
| Revenue | 390,000 | 355,000 |
| Cost of sales | (245,000) | (230,000) |
| Gross profit | 145,000 | 125,000 |
| Other income | 20,667 | 11,300 |
| Distribution costs | (9,000) | (8,700) |
| Administrative expenses | (20,000) | (21,000) |
| Other expenses | (2,100) | (1,200) |
| Finance costs | (8,000) | (7,500) |
| Share of profit of associates | 35,100 | 30,100 |
| Profit before tax | 161,667 | 128,000 |
| Income tax expense | (40,417) | (32,000) |
| Profit for the year from continuing operations | 121,250 | 96,000 |
| Loss for the year from discontinued operations | – | (30,500) |
| *Profit for the year* | 121,250 | 65,500 |
| Other comprehensive income: | | |
| Items that will not be reclassified to profit or loss: | | |
| Gains on property revaluation | 933 | 3,367 |
| Investments in equity instruments | (24,000) | 26,667 |
| *Actuarial gains (losses) on defined benefit pension plans | (667) | 1,333 |
| Share of gain(loss) on property revaluation of associates | 400 | (700) |
| Income tax relating to items that will not be reclassified | 5,834 | (7,667) |
| | (17,500) | 23,000 |
| Items that may be reclassified subsequently to profit or loss | | |
| * Exchange differences on translating foreign operations | 5,334 | 10,667 |
| *Cash flow hedges | (667) | (4,000) |
| Income tax relating to items that may be reclassified | (1,167) | (1,667) |
| | 3,500 | 5,000 |
| Other comprehensive income for the year, net of tax | (14,000) | 28,000 |
| *Total comprehensive income for the year* | 107,250 | 93,500 |
| Profit attributable to: | | |
| Owners of the parent | 97,000 | 52,400 |
| Non-controlling interest | 24,250 | 13,100 |
| | 121,250 | 65,500 |
| Total comprehensive income attributable to | | |
| Owners of the parent | 85,800 | 74,800 |
| Non-controlling interest | 21,450 | 18,700 |
| | 107,250 | 93,500 |
| Earnings per share (in currency units) | 0.46 | 0.30 |

*Not in the F7 syllabus

This is the full statement as issued by the IASB.

Note that the amendment to IAS 1 now splits items of other comprehensive income into those which can be reclassified to profit or loss and those which can not be reclassified. In practice, none of the items which can be reclassified are examinable at F7, so this is not an issue that you will encounter in your exam.

Companies are given the option of presenting this information in two statements as follows:

XYZ GROUP – STATEMENT OF PROFIT OR LOSS FOR THE YEAR ENDED 31 DECEMBER 20X7

|  | 20X7 | 20X6 |
|---|---|---|
|  | $'000 | $'000 |
| Revenue | 390,000 | 355,000 |
| Cost of sales | (245,000) | (230,000) |
| Gross profit | 145,000 | 125,000 |
| Other income | 20,667 | 11,300 |
| Distribution costs | (9,000) | (8,700) |
| Administrative expenses | (20,000) | (21,000) |
| Other expenses | (2,100) | (1,200) |
| Finance costs | (8,000) | (7,500) |
| Share of profit of associates | 35,100 | 30,100 |
| Profit before tax | 161,667 | 128,000 |
| Income tax expense | (40,417) | (32,000) |
| Profit for the year from continuing operations | 121,250 | 96,000 |
| Loss for the year from discontinued operations | – | (30,500) |
| *Profit for the year* | 121,250 | 65,500 |
| Profit attributable to: |  |  |
| Owners of the parent | 97,000 | 52,400 |
| Non-controlling interest | 24,250 | 13,100 |
|  | 121,250 | 65,500 |

XYZ GROUP STATEMENT OF PROFIT OR LOSS AND OTHER COMPREHENSIVE INCOME FOR THE YEAR
ENDED 31 DECEMBER 20X7 (TWO STATEMENT FORMAT)

|  | 20X7 | 20X6 |
|---|---|---|
|  | $'000 | $'000 |
| Profit for the year | 121,250 | 65,500 |
| *Other comprehensive income:* |  |  |
| *Items that will not be reclassified to profit or loss:* |  |  |
| Gains on property revaluation | 933 | 3,367 |
| Investments in equity instruments | (24,000) | 26,667 |
| *Actuarial gains (losses) on defined benefit pension plans | (667) | 1,333 |
| Share of gain(loss) on property revaluation of associates | 400 | (700) |
| Income tax relating to items that will not be reclassified | 5,834 | (7,667) |
|  | (17,500) | 23,000 |
| *Items that may be reclassified to profit or loss:* |  |  |
| *Exchange differences on translating foreign operations | 5,334 | 10,667 |
| *Cash flow hedges | (667) | (4,000) |
| Income tax relating to items that may be reclassified | (1,167) | (1,667) |
|  | 3,500 | 5,000 |
| Other comprehensive income for the year, net of tax | (14,000) | 28,000 |
| *Total comprehensive income for the year* | 107,250 | 93,500 |
| Total comprehensive income attributable to |  |  |
| Owners of the parent | 85,800 | 74,800 |
| Non-controlling interest | 21,450 | 18,700 |
|  | 107,250 | 93,500 |

*Not in the F7 syllabus

# 5 Statement of profit or loss

FAST FORWARD

> IAS 1 offers two possible formats for the statement of profit or loss or separate profit or loss section - by function or by nature. Classification by function is more common.

## 5.1 Examples of separate statements of profit or loss

XYZ GROUP
STATEMENT OF PROFIT OR LOSS FOR THE YEAR ENDED 31 DECEMBER 20X8

Illustrating the classification of expenses by function

|  | 20X8 $'000 | 20X7 $'000 |
|---|---|---|
| Revenue | X | X |
| Cost of sales | (X) | (X) |
| Gross profit | X | X |
| Other income | X | X |
| Distribution costs | (X) | (X) |
| Administrative expenses | (X) | (X) |
| Other expenses | (X) | (X) |
| Finance costs | (X) | (X) |
| Share of profit of associates | X | X |
| *Profit before tax* | X | X |
| Income tax expense | (X) | (X) |
| *Profit for the year* | X | X |
|  |  |  |
| Profit attributable to: |  |  |
| Owners of the parent | X | X |
| Non-controlling interest | X | X |
|  | X | X |

Illustrating the classification of expenses by nature

|  | 20X8 $'000 | 20X7 $'000 |
|---|---|---|
| Revenue | X | X |
| Other operating income | X | X |
| Changes in inventories of finished goods and work in progress | (X) | X |
| Work performed by the entity and capitalised | X | X |
| Raw material and consumables used | (X) | (X) |
| Employee benefits expense | (X) | (X) |
| Depreciation and amortisation expense | (X) | (X) |
| Impairment of property, plant and equipment | (X) | (X) |
| Other expenses | (X) | (X) |
| Finance costs | (X) | (X) |
| Share of profit of associates | X | X |
| Profit before tax | X | X |
| Income tax expense | (X) | (X) |
| Profit for the year | X | X |
|  |  |  |
| Profit attributable to: |  |  |
| Owners of the parent | X | X |
| Non-controlling interest | X | X |
|  | X | X |

*Note*: The usual method of presentation is expenses by function and this is the format likely to appear in your exam.

## 5.2 Information presented in the statement of profit or loss

The standard lists the following as the **minimum** to be disclosed on the face of the statement of profit or loss.

(a)   Revenue

(b)   Finance costs

(c)   Share of profits and losses of associates and joint ventures accounted for using the equity method

(d)   Pre-tax gain or loss recognised on the disposal of assets or settlement of liabilities attributable to discontinued operations

(e)   Tax expense

(f)   Profit or loss

The following items must be disclosed as allocations of profit or loss for the period.

(a)   Profit or loss attributable to non-controlling interest

(b)   Profit or loss attributable to owners of the parent

The allocated amounts must not be presented as items of income or expense. (These relate to group accounts, covered later in this text.)

Income and expense items can only be **offset** when, and only when:

(a)   It is permitted or required by an IFRS, or

(b)   Gains, losses and related expenses arising from the same or similar transactions and events are immaterial, in which case they can be aggregated.

## 5.3 Information presented either in the statement or in the notes

An analysis of expenses must be shown either in the profit or loss section (as above, which is encouraged by the standard) or by note, using a classification based on *either* the nature of the expenses or their function. This **sub-classification of expenses** indicates a range of components of financial performance; these may differ in terms of stability, potential for gain or loss and predictability.

### 5.3.1 Nature of expense method

Expenses are not reallocated amongst various functions within the entity, but are aggregated in the statement of profit or loss **according to their nature** (eg purchase of materials, depreciation, wages and salaries, transport costs). This is by far the easiest method, especially for smaller entities.

### 5.3.2 Function of expense/cost of sales method

You are likely to be more familiar with this method. Expenses are classified according to their function as part of cost of sales, distribution or administrative activities. This method often gives **more relevant information** for users, but the allocation of expenses by function requires the use of judgement and can be arbitrary. Consequently, perhaps, when this method is used, entities should disclose **additional information** on the nature of expenses, including staff costs, and depreciation and amortisation expense.

Which of the above methods is chosen by an entity will depend on **historical and industry factors**, and also the **nature of the organisation**. Under each method, there should be given an indication of costs which are likely to vary (directly or indirectly) with the level of sales or production. The choice of method should fairly reflect the main elements of the entity's performance. **This is the method you should expect to see in your exam**.

**Exam focus point**

Note that you get **no** marks for writing out the format for a financial statement. However, you must write out the format so that you can then fill in the numbers and earn the marks.

## 5.4 Dividends

IAS 1 also requires disclosure of the amount of **dividends per share** for the period covered by the financial statements. This may be shown either in the statement of profit or loss and other comprehensive income or in the statement of changes in equity.

**Further points**

(a)    All requirements previously set out in other Standards for the presentation of particular line items in the statement of financial position and statement of profit or loss and other comprehensive income are now dealt with in IAS 1. These line items are: biological assets; liabilities and assets for current tax and deferred tax; and pre-tax gain or loss recognised on the disposal of assets or settlement of liabilities attributable to discontinued operations.

(b)    An entity must disclose, in the summary of significant accounting policies and/or other notes, the **judgements** made by management in **applying** the **accounting policies** that have the **most significant effect** on the amounts of items recognised in the financial statements.

(c)    An entity must disclose in the notes information regarding **key assumptions** about the **future**, and other sources of **measurement uncertainty**, that have a significant **risk of** causing a **material adjustment** to the carrying amounts of assets and liabilities within the **next financial year**.

One of the competences you require to fulfil performance objection 10 of the PER is the ability to compile financial statements and accounts in line with appropriate standards and guidelines. You can apply the knowledge you obtain from this section of the text to help you demonstrate this competence.

# 6 Revision of basic accounts

**FAST FORWARD**

The Study Guide requires you to be able to prepare a basic set of company accounts from a trial balance.

In the next part of this text we move on to the mechanics of preparing financial statements. It would be useful at this point to refresh your memory of the basic accounting you have already studied and these questions will help you. Make sure that you understand everything before you go on.

Question                                                                      Basics

A friend has bought some shares in a company quoted on a local stock exchange and has received the latest accounts. There is one page he is having difficulty in understanding.

Briefly, but clearly, answer his questions.

(a)    What is a statement of financial position?
(b)    What is an asset?
(c)    What is a liability?
(d)    What is share capital?
(e)    What are reserves?
(f)    Why does the statement of financial position balance?
(g)    To what extent does the statement of financial position value my investment?

Answer

(a)    A **statement of financial position** is a statement of the assets, liabilities and capital of a business as at a stated date. It is laid out to show either total assets as equivalent to total liabilities and capital or net assets as equivalent to capital. Other formats are also possible but the top half (or left hand) total will always equal the bottom half (or right hand) total.

(b)    An **asset** is a resource controlled by a business and is expected to be of some future benefit. Its value is determined as the historical cost of producing or obtaining it (unless an attempt is being made to reflect rising prices in the accounts, in which case a replacement cost might be used). Examples of assets are:

(i)   Plant, machinery, land and other **non-current assets**

(ii)  **Current** assets such as inventories, cash and debts owed to the business with reasonable assurance of recovery: these are assets which are not intended to be held on a continuing basis in the business

(c)   A **liability** is an amount owed by a business, other than the amount owed to its proprietors (capital). Examples of liabilities are:

(i)   Amounts owed to the government (sales or other taxes)

(ii)  Amounts owed to suppliers

(iii) Bank overdraft

(iv)  Long-term loans from banks or investors

It is usual to differentiate between 'current' and 'long-term' liabilities. The former fall due within a year of the end of the reporting period.

(d)   **Share capital** is the permanent investment in a business by its owners. In the case of a limited company, this takes the form of *shares* for which investors subscribe on formation of the company. Each share has a **nominal** or **par** (ie face) **value** (say $1). In the statement of financial position, total issued share capital is shown at its par value.

(e)   If a company issues shares for more than their par value (at a **premium**) then (usually) by law this premium must be recorded separately from the par value in a 'share premium account'. This is an example of a reserve. It belongs to the shareholders but cannot be distributed to them, because it is a **capital reserve**. Other capital reserves include the revaluation surplus, which shows the surpluses arising on revaluation of assets which are still owned by the company.

Share capital and capital reserves are not distributable except on the winding up of the company, as a guarantee to the company's creditors that the company has enough assets to meet its debts. This is necessary because shareholders in limited liability companies have 'limited liability'; once they have paid the company for their shares they have no further liability to it if it becomes insolvent. The proprietors of other businesses are, by contrast, personally liable for business debts.

**Retained earnings** constitute accumulated profits (less losses) made by the company and can be distributed to shareholders as **dividends**. They too belong to the shareholders, and so are a claim on the resources of the company.

(f)   Statements of financial position do not always balance on the first attempt, as all accountants know! However, once errors are corrected, all statements of financial position balance. This is because in **double entry bookkeeping** every transaction recorded has a dual effect. Assets are always equal to liabilities plus capital and so capital is always equal to assets less liabilities. This makes sense as the owners of the business are entitled to the net assets of the business as representing their capital plus accumulated surpluses (or less accumulated deficit).

(g)   The statement of financial position is not intended as a statement of a business's worth at a given point in time. This is because, except where some attempt is made to adjust for the effects of rising prices, assets and liabilities are recorded at **historical cost** and on a prudent basis. For example, if there is any doubt about the recoverability of a debt, then the value in the accounts must be reduced to the likely recoverable amount. In addition, where non-current assets have a finite useful life, their cost is gradually written off to reflect the use being made of them.

Sometimes non-current assets are **revalued** to their market value but this revaluation then goes out of date as few assets are revalued every year.

The figure in the statement of financial position for capital and reserves therefore bears **no relationship** to the market value of shares. Market values are the product of a large number of factors, including general economic conditions, alternative investment returns (eg interest rates), likely future profits and dividends and, not least, market sentiment.

The accountant of Fiddles Co, a limited liability company, has begun preparing final accounts but the work is not yet complete. At this stage the items included in the list of account balances are as follows.

|  | $'000 |
|---|---|
| Land | 100 |
| Buildings | 120 |
| Plant and machinery | 170 |
| Depreciation provision | 120 |
| Ordinary shares of $1 | 100 |
| Retained earnings brought forward | 380 |
| Trade accounts receivable | 200 |
| Trade accounts payable | 110 |
| Inventory | 190 |
| Profit before tax | 80 |
| Allowance for receivables | 3 |
| Bank balance (asset) | 12 |
| Suspense | 1 |

Notes (i) to (v) below are to be taken into account.

(i)    The accounts receivable control account figure, which is used in the list of account balances, does not agree with the total of the sales ledger. A contra of $5,000 has been entered correctly in the individual ledger accounts but has been entered on the wrong side of both control accounts.

A batch total of sales of $12,345 had been entered in the double entry system as $13,345, although the individual ledger accounts entries for these sales were correct. The balance of $4,000 on the sales returns account has inadvertently been omitted from the trial balance though correctly entered in the ledger records.

(ii)   A standing order of receipt from a regular customer for $2,000, and bank charges of $1,000, have been completely omitted from the records.

(iii)  A receivable for $1,000 is to be written off. The allowance for receivables balance is to be adjusted to 1% of receivables.

(iv)   The opening inventory figure had been overstated by $1,000 and the closing inventory figure had been understated by $2,000.

(v)    Any remaining balance on the suspense account should be treated as purchases if a debit balance and as sales if a credit balance.

*Required*

(a)   Prepare journal entries to cover items in notes (i) to (v) above. You are not to open any new accounts and may use only those accounts included in the list of account balances as given.

(b)   Prepare final accounts for internal use within the limits of the available information. For presentation purposes all the items arising from notes (i) to (v) above should be regarded as material.

Answer

(a)   JOURNAL ENTRIES FOR ADJUSTMENTS

|  |  | Debit | Credit |
|---|---|---|---|
|  |  | $ | $ |
| (i) | Trade accounts payable | 10,000 |  |
|  | Trade accounts receivable |  | 10,000 |
|  | Profit before tax | 1,000 |  |
|  | Trade accounts receivable |  | 1,000 |
|  | Profit before tax | 4,000 |  |
|  | Suspense |  | 4,000 |

|   |   | | Debit | Credit |
|---|---|---|---|---|
|   |   | | $ | $ |
| (ii) | Bank | | 2,000 | |
|   | Trade accounts receivable | | | 2,000 |
|   | Profit before tax | | 1,000 | |
|   | Bank | | | 1,000 |
| (iii) | Profit before tax | | 1,000 | |
|   | Trade accounts receivable | | | 1,000 |
|   | Allowance for receivables (W1) | | 1,140 | |
|   | Profit before tax | | | 1,140 |
| (iv) | Inventories | | 2,000 | |
|   | Profit before tax | | | 2,000 |
|   | Retained earnings brought forward | | 1,000 | |
|   | Profit before tax | | | 1,000 |
| (v) | Suspense | | 3,000 | |
|   | Profit before tax | | | 3,000 |

(b)   FIDDLES CO
      STATEMENT OF FINANCIAL POSITION

|   | $ | $ | $ |
|---|---|---|---|
| *Assets* | | | |
| Non-current assets | | | |
| Land and buildings | | 220,000 | |
| Plant and machinery | | 170,000 | |
| Depreciation | | (120,000) | |
| | | | 270,000 |
| Current assets | | | |
| Inventories (190 + 2) | | 192,000 | |
| Accounts receivable (W1) | 186,000 | | |
| Less allowance | (1,860) | | |
| | | 184,140 | |
| Bank (12 + 2 – 1) | | 13,000 | |
| | | | 389,140 |
| *Total assets* | | | 659,140 |
| *Equity and liabilities* | | | |
| Equity | | | |
| Share capital | | 100,000 | |
| Retained earnings (see profit or loss) | | 459,140 | |
| | | | 559,140 |
| Current liabilities | | | |
| Accounts payable (110 – 10) | | | 100,000 |
| *Total equity and liabilities* | | | 659,140 |

FIDDLES CO
STATEMENT OF PROFIT OR LOSS (note: this is not as per IAS 1, it is purely for internal purposes)

|   | $ |
|---|---|
| Profit before tax (W2) | 80,140 |
| Retained earnings brought forward ($380,000 – 1,000) | 379,000 |
| Retained earnings carried forward | 459,140 |

*Workings*

|   |   | $ |
|---|---|---|
| 1 | *Accounts receivable* | |
|   | Per opening trial balance | 200,000 |
|   | Contra | (10,000) |
|   | Miscasting | (1,000) |
|   | Standing order | (2,000) |
|   | Written off | (1,000) |
|   | | 186,000 |

|  |  | $ |
|---|---|---|
| Allowance b/f |  | 3,000 |
| Allowance required |  | 1,860 |
| Journal |  | 1,140 |

2    *Profit before tax*

|  | $ |
|---|---|
| Per question | 80,000 |
| Wrong batch total | (1,000) |
| Returns | (4,000) |
| Bank charges | (1,000) |
| Irrecoverable debt | (1,000) |
| Allowance for receivables | 1,140 |
| Inventory (2,000 + 1,000) | 3,000 |
| Suspense (sales) | 3,000 |
|  | 80,140 |

Note:    This question dealt with accounts for **internal** purposes. In accounts produced for publication the statement of profit or loss would comply with the IAS 1 format. In the following chapter we will be dealing with all the issues involved in producing financial statements for publication.

# 7 Changes in equity

> **FAST FORWARD**
>
> IAS 1 requires a statement of changes in equity. This shows the movement in the equity section of the statement of financial position. A full set of financial statements includes a statement of changes in equity.

## 7.1 Format

This is the format of the statement of changes in equity as per IAS 1.

### XYZ GROUP – STATEMENT OF CHANGES IN EQUITY FOR THE YEAR ENDED 31 DECEMBER 20X7

|  | Share capital | Retained earnings | Investments in equity instruments | Revaluation surplus | Total | Non-controlling interest | Total equity |
|---|---|---|---|---|---|---|---|
|  | $'000 | $'000 | $'000 | $'000 | $'000 | $'000 | $'000 |
| **Balance at 1 January 20X6** | 600,000 | 118,100 | 1,600 | – | 719,700 | 29,800 | 749,500 |
| Changes in accounting policy | – | 400 | – | – | 400 | 100 | 500 |
| Restated balance | 600,000 | 118,500 | 1,600 | – | 720,100 | 29,900 | 750,000 |
| **Changes in equity** |  |  |  |  |  |  |  |
| Dividends | – | (10,000) | – | – | (10,000) | – | (10,000) |
| Total comprehensive income for the year | – | 53,200 | 16,000 | 1,600 | 70,800 | 18,700 | 89,500 |
| **Balance at 31 December 20X6** | 600,000 | 161,700 | 17,600 | 1,600 | 780,900 | 48,600 | 829,500 |
| **Changes in equity for 20X7** |  |  |  |  |  |  |  |
| Issue of share capital | 50,000 | – | – | – | 50,000 | – | 50,000 |
| Dividends | – | (15,000) | – | – | (15,000) | – | (15,000) |
| Total comprehensive income for the year | – | 96,600 | (14,400) | 800 | 83,000 | 21,450 | 104,450 |
| Transfer to retained earnings | – | 200 | – | (200) | – | – | – |
| **Balance at 31 December 20X7** | 650,000 | 243,500 | 3,200 | 2,200 | 898,900 | 70,050 | 968,950 |

Note that where there has been a change of accounting policy necessitating a retrospective restatement, the adjustment is disclosed for each period. So, rather than just showing an adjustment to the balance b/f on 1.1.X7, the balances for 20X6 are restated.

# 8 Notes to the financial statements

Some items need to be disclosed by way of note.

## 8.1 Contents of notes

The notes to the financial statements will **amplify** the information given in the statement of financial position, statement of profit or loss and other comprehensive income and statement of changes in equity. We have already noted above the information which the IAS allows to be shown by note rather than in the statements. To some extent, then, the contents of the notes will be determined by the level of detail shown on the **face of the statements**.

## 8.2 Structure

The notes to the financial statements should perform the following functions.

(a)   Provide information about the **basis on which the financial statements were prepared** and which **specific accounting policies** were chosen and applied to significant transactions/events

(b)   Disclose any information, not shown elsewhere in the financial statements, which is **required by IFRSs**

(c)   Show any additional information that is relevant to understanding which is not shown elsewhere in the financial statements

The way the notes are presented is important. They should be given in a **systematic manner** and **cross referenced** back to the related figure(s) in the statement of financial position, statement of comprehensive income or statement of cash flows.

Notes to the financial statements will amplify the information shown therein by giving the following.

(a)   More **detailed analysis** or breakdowns of figures in the statements

(b)   **Narrative information** explaining figures in the statements

(c)   **Additional information**, eg contingent liabilities and commitments

IAS 1 suggests a **certain order** for notes to the financial statements. This will assist users when comparing the statements of different entities.

(a)   Statement of **compliance** with IFRSs

(b)   Statement of the **measurement basis** (bases) and accounting policies applied

(c)   **Supporting information** for items presented in each financial statement in the same order as each line item and each financial statement is presented

(d)   Other disclosures, eg:

(i)    Contingent liabilities, commitments and other financial disclosures
(ii)   Non-financial disclosures

The order of specific items may have to be varied occasionally, but a systematic structure is still required.

## 8.3 Presentation of accounting policies

The accounting policies section should describe the following.

(a)   The **measurement basis** (or bases) used in preparing the financial statements

(b)   The **other accounting policies** used, as required for a proper understanding of the financial statements

This information may be shown in the notes or sometimes as a **separate component** of the financial statements.

The information on measurement bases used is obviously fundamental to an understanding of the financial statements. Where **more than one basis is used**, it should be stated to which assets or liabilities each basis has been applied.

Note: accounting policies are covered in Chapter 7.

## 8.4 Other disclosures

An entity must disclose in the notes:

(a)   The amount of dividends proposed or declared before the financial statements were authorised for issue but not recognised as a distribution to owners during the period, and the amount per share

(b)   The amount of any cumulative preference dividends not recognised

IAS 1 ends by listing some **specific disclosures** which will always be required if they are not shown elsewhere in the financial statements.

(a)   The domicile and legal form of the entity, its country of incorporation and the address of the registered office (or, if different, principal place of business)

(b)   A description of the nature of the entity's operations and its principal activities

(c)   The name of the parent entity and the ultimate parent entity of the group

**Exam focus point**

You will have to produce financial statements suitable for publication in your exam, so this chapter is important and you should refer back to it.

Question                                                          **Financial statements**

The accountant of Wislon Co has prepared the following list of account balances as at 31 December 20X7.

|  | $'000 |
|---|---|
| 50c ordinary shares (fully paid) | 450 |
| 10% debentures (secured) | 200 |
| Retained earnings 1.1.X7 | 242 |
| General reserve 1.1.X7 | 171 |
| Land and buildings 1.1.X7 (cost) | 430 |
| Plant and machinery 1.1.X7 (cost) | 830 |
| Accumulated depreciation | |
| Buildings 1.1.X7 | 20 |
| Plant and machinery 1.1.X7 | 222 |
| Inventory 1.1.X7 | 190 |
| Sales | 2,695 |
| Purchases | 2,152 |
| Ordinary dividend | 15 |
| Debenture interest | 10 |
| Wages and salaries | 254 |
| Light and heat | 31 |
| Sundry expenses | 113 |
| Suspense account | 135 |
| Trade accounts receivable | 179 |
| Trade accounts payable | 195 |
| Cash | 126 |

*Notes*

(a) Sundry expenses include $9,000 paid in respect of insurance for the year ending 1 September 20X8. Light and heat does not include an invoice of $3,000 for electricity for the three months ending 2 January 20X8, which was paid in February 20X8. Light and heat also includes $20,000 relating to salesmen's commission.

(b) The suspense account is in respect of the following items.

|  | $'000 |
|---|---|
| Proceeds from the issue of 100,000 ordinary shares | 120 |
| Proceeds from the sale of plant | 300 |
|  | 420 |
| Less consideration for the acquisition of Mary & Co | 285 |
|  | 135 |

(c) The net assets of Mary & Co were purchased on 3 March 20X7. Assets were valued as follows

|  | $'000 |
|---|---|
| Equity investments | 231 |
| Inventory | 34 |
|  | 265 |

All the inventory acquired was sold during 20X7. The equity investments were still held by Wislon at 31.12.X7. Goodwill has not been impaired in value.

(d) The property was acquired some years ago. The buildings element of the cost was estimated at $100,000 and the estimated useful life of the assets was fifty years at the time of purchase. As at 31 December 20X7 the property is to be revalued at $800,000.

(e) The plant which was sold had cost $350,000 and had a carrying amount of $274,000 as on 1.1.X7. $36,000 depreciation is to be charged on plant and machinery for 20X7.

(f) The management wish to provide for:
  (i) Debenture interest due
  (ii) A transfer to general reserve of $16,000
  (iii) Audit fees of $4,000

(g) Inventory as at 31 December 20X7 was valued at $220,000 (cost).

(h) Taxation is to be ignored.

*Required*

Prepare the financial statements of Wislon Co as at 31 December 20X7. You do not need to produce notes to the statements.

## Answer

(a) Normal adjustments are needed for accruals and prepayments (insurance, light and heat, debenture interest and audit fees). The debenture interest accrued is calculated as follows.

|  | $'000 |
|---|---|
| Charge needed in profit or loss (10% × $200,000) | 20 |
| Amount paid so far, as shown in list of account balances | 10 |
| Accrual: presumably six months' interest now payable | 10 |

The accrued expenses shown in the statement of financial position comprise:

|  | $'000 |
|---|---|
| Debenture interest | 10 |
| Light and heat | 3 |
| Audit fee | 4 |
|  | 17 |

(b)   The misposting of $20,000 to light and heat is also adjusted, by reducing the light and heat expense, but charging $20,000 to salesmen's commission.

(c)   Depreciation on the building is calculated as $\dfrac{\$100,000}{50} = \$2,000$.

The carrying amount of the building is then $430,000 – $20,000 – $2,000 = $408,000 at the end of the year. When the property is revalued a reserve of $800,000 – $408,000 = $392,000 is then created.

(d)   The profit on disposal of plant is calculated as proceeds $300,000 (per suspense account) less carrying amount $274,000, ie $26,000. The cost of the remaining plant is calculated at $830,000 – $350,000 = $480,000. The depreciation provision at the year end is:

|  | $'000 |
|---|---|
| Balance 1.1.X7 | 222 |
| Charge for 20X7 | 36 |
| Less depreciation on disposals (350 – 274) | (76) |
|  | 182 |

(e)   Goodwill arising on the purchase of Mary & Co is:

|  | $'000 |
|---|---|
| Consideration (per suspense account) | 285 |
| Assets at valuation | 265 |
| Goodwill | 20 |

This is shown as an asset in the statement of financial position. The equity investments, being owned by Wislon at the year end, are also shown on the statement of financial position, whereas Mary's inventory, acquired and then sold, is added to the purchases figure for the year.

(f)   The other item in the suspense account is dealt with as follows.

|  | $'000 |
|---|---|
| Proceeds of issue of 100,000 ordinary shares | 120 |
| Less nominal value 100,000 × 50c | 50 |
| Excess of consideration over par value (= share premium) | 70 |

(g)   The transfer to general reserve increases it to $171,000 + $16,000 = $187,000.

We can now prepare the financial statements.

WISLON CO
STATEMENT OF PROFIT OR LOSS AND OTHER COMPREHENSIVE INCOME FOR THE YEAR ENDED 31 DECEMBER 20X7

|  | $'000 |
|---|---|
| Revenue | 2,695 |
| Cost of sales (W1) | (2,156) |
| Gross profit | 539 |
| Other income (profit on disposal of plant) | 26 |
| Administrative expenses (W2) | (437) |
| Finance costs | (20) |
| Profit for the year | 108 |
| Other comprehensive income: |  |
| Gain on property revaluation | 392 |
| Total comprehensive income for the year | 500 |

**Note**

The only item of 'other comprehensive income' for the year was the revaluation gain. If there had been no revaluation gain, only a statement of profit or loss would have been required.

*Workings*

1    *Cost of sales*

|  | $'000 |
|---|---:|
| Opening inventory | 190 |
| Purchases (2,152 + 34) | 2,186 |
| Closing inventory | (220) |
|  | 2,156 |

2    *Administrative expenses*

|  | $'000 |
|---|---:|
| Wages, salaries and commission (254 + 20) | 274 |
| Sundry expenses (113 – 6) | 107 |
| Light and heat (31 – 20 + 3) | 14 |
| Depreciation:  buildings | 2 |
|                          plant | 36 |
| Audit fees | 4 |
|  | 437 |

WISLON CO
STATEMENT OF FINANCIAL POSITION AS AT 31 DECEMBER 20X7

|  | $'000 | $'000 |
|---|---:|---:|
| *Assets* | | |
| *Non-current assets* | | |
| Property, plant and equipment | | |
| Property at valuation | | 800 |
| Plant:    cost | 480 | |
|              Accumulated depreciation | (182) | |
|  | | 298 |
| Goodwill | | 20 |
| Equity investments | | 231 |
| *Current assets* | | |
| Inventory | 220 | |
| Trade accounts receivable | 179 | |
| Prepayments | 6 | |
| Cash | 126 | |
|  | | 531 |
| Total assets | | 1,880 |
| *Equity and liabilities* | | |
| Equity | | |
| 50c ordinary shares | 500 | |
| Share premium | 70 | |
| Revaluation surplus | 392 | |
| General reserve | 187 | |
| Retained earnings | 319 | |
|  | | 1,468 |
| *Non-current liabilities* | | |
| 10% loan stock (secured) | | 200 |
| *Current liabilities* | | |
| Trade accounts payable | 195 | |
| Accrued expenses | 17 | |
|  | | 212 |
| Total equity and liabilities | | 1,880 |

WISLON CO
STATEMENT OF CHANGES IN EQUITY
FOR THE YEAR ENDED 31 DECEMBER 20X7

| | Share capital $'000 | Share premium $'000 | Retained earnings $'000 | General reserve $'000 | Revaluation Surplus $'000 | Total $'000 |
|---|---|---|---|---|---|---|
| Balance at 1.1.X7 | 450 | – | 242 | 171 | - | 863 |
| Issue of share capital | 50 | 70 | | | | 120 |
| Dividends | | | (15) | | | (15) |
| Total comprehensive income for the year | | | 108 | | 392 | 500 |
| Transfer to reserve | | | (16) | 16 | | |
| Balance at 31.12.X7 | 500 | 70 | 319 | 187 | 392 | 1,468 |

Note that the total comprehensive income is analysed into its components.

# Chapter Roundup

- IAS 1 covers the **form and content of** financial statements. The main components are:

  - Statement of financial position
  - Statement of profit or loss and other comprehensive income
  - Statement of changes in equity
  - Statement of cash flows (see Chapter 20)
  - Notes to the financial statements

- Each component must be **identified clearly**.

- IAS 1 suggests **formats** for the statement of financial position and statement of profit or loss and other comprehensive income, but these are not rigid. Certain items are specified, however, for **disclosure on the face of the financial statements.**

- You should appreciate the distinction between **current and non-current** assets and liabilities and their different treatments.

- In June 2011 the IASB published an amendment to IAS 1 called 'Presentation of items of other comprehensive income'. This changed the name of the statement of comprehensive income to 'Statement of profit or loss and other comprehensive income'.

- IAS 1 offers **two** possible formats for the statement of profit or loss – by function or by nature. Classification by function is more common.

- IAS 1 requires a statement of changes in equity. This shows the movement in the equity section of the statement of financial position. A full set of financial statements includes a statement of changes in equity.

## Quick Quiz

1    Which of the following are examples of current assets?

    (a)    Property, plant and equipment
    (b)    Prepayments
    (c)    Cash equivalents
    (d)    Manufacturing licences
    (e)    Retained earnings

2    Provisions must be disclosed in the statement of financial position.

    True  ☐

    False  ☐

3    Which of the following must be disclosed on the face of the statement of profit or loss?

    (a)    Tax expense
    (b)    Analysis of expenses
    (c)    Net profit or loss for the period.

4    Where are revaluation gains shown in the financial statements?

## Answers to Quick Quiz

1    (b) and (c) only
2    True
3    (a) and (c) only. (b) may be shown in the notes.
4    In other comprehensive income and in the statement of changes in equity.

| Now try the questions below from the Exam Question Bank | | | |
|---|---|---|---|
| **Number** | **Level** | **Marks** | **Time** |
| 4 | Examination | 25 | 45 mins |

# Non-current assets

4

| Topic list | Syllabus reference |
|---|---|
| 1 IAS 16 Property, plant and equipment | C2 |
| 2 Depreciation accounting | C2 |
| 3 IAS 20 Government grants | C2 |
| 4 IAS 40 Investment property | C2 |
| 5 IAS 23 Borrowing costs | C2 |

## Introduction

**IAS 16** should be familiar to you from your earlier studies, as should the mechanics of accounting for depreciation, revaluations of non-current assets and disposals of non-current assets. Some questions are given here for revision purposes.

**IAS 20** on government grants is a straightforward standard and you should have few problems with it.

**IAS 40** deals with investment properties, which can be treated differently from other property under IAS 16.

# Study guide

| | | Intellectual level |
|---|---|---|
| **C2** | **Tangible non-current assets** | |
| (a) | define and compute the initial measurement of a non-current (including a self-constructed and borrowing costs) asset. | 2 |
| (b) | identify subsequent expenditure that may be capitalised, distinguishing between capital and revenue items. | 2 |
| (c) | discuss the requirements of relevant accounting standards in relation to the revaluation of non-current assets. | 2 |
| (d) | account for revaluation and disposal gains and losses for non-current assets. | 2 |
| (e) | compute depreciation based on the cost and revaluation models and on assets that have two or more significant parts (complex assets). | 2 |
| (f) | apply the provision of relevant accounting standards in relation to accounting for government grants. | 2 |
| (g) | discuss why the treatment of investment properties should differ from other properties. | 2 |
| (h) | apply the requirements of relevant accounting standards for investment property. | 2 |

# 1 IAS 16 Property, plant and equipment

**FAST FORWARD**

IAS 16 covers all aspects of accounting for property, plant and equipment. This represents the bulk of items which are **'tangible' non-current assets**..

## 1.1 Scope

IAS 16 should be followed when accounting for property, plant and equipment *unless* another international accounting standard requires a **different treatment**.

IAS 16 **does not apply** to the following.

(a)     Biological assets related to agricultural activity
(b)     Mineral rights and mineral reserves, such as oil, gas and other non-regenerative resources

However, the standard applies to property, plant and equipment used to develop these assets.

## 1.2 Definitions

The standard gives a large number of definitions.

**Key terms**

- **Property, plant and equipment** are tangible assets that:

    –     are held for use in the production or supply of goods or services, for rental to others, or for administrative purposes; and
    –     are expected to be used during more than one period.

- **Cost** is the amount of cash or cash equivalents paid or the fair value of the other consideration given to acquire an asset at the time of its acquisition or construction.

- **Residual value** is the net amount which the entity expects to obtain for an asset at the end of its useful life after deducting the expected costs of disposal.

- **Entity specific value** is the present value of the cash flows an entity expects to arise from the continuing use of an asset and from its disposal at the end of its useful life, or expects to incur when settling a liability.

- **Fair value** is the price that would be received to sell an asset or paid to transfer a liability in an orderly transaction between market participants at the measurement date. (IFRS 13)

- **Carrying amount** is the amount at which an asset is recognised in the statement of financial position after deducting any accumulated depreciation and accumulated impairment losses.

- An **impairment loss** is the amount by which the carrying amount of an asset exceeds its recoverable amount. (IAS 16)

Note that the definition of fair value has now been changed by IFRS 13.

## 1.3 Recognition

In this context, recognition simply means incorporation of the item in the business's accounts, in this case as a non-current asset. The recognition of property, plant and equipment depends on two criteria.

(a) It is probable that **future economic benefits** associated with the asset will flow to the entity
(b) The cost of the asset to the entity can be **measured reliably**

These recognition criteria apply to **subsequent expenditure** as well as costs incurred initially. There are no separate criteria for recognising subsequent expenditure.

Property, plant and equipment can amount to **substantial amounts** in financial statements, affecting the presentation of the company's financial position and the profitability of the entity, through depreciation and also if an asset is wrongly classified as an expense and taken to profit or loss.

### 1.3.1 First criterion: future economic benefits

The **degree of certainty** attached to the flow of future economic benefits must be assessed. This should be based on the evidence available at the date of initial recognition (usually the date of purchase). The entity should be assured that it will receive the rewards attached to the asset and it will incur the associated risks, which will only generally be the case when the rewards and risks have actually passed to the entity. Until then, the asset should not be recognised.

### 1.3.2 Second criterion: cost measured reliably

It is generally easy to measure the cost of an asset as the **transfer amount on purchase**, ie what was paid for it. **Self-constructed assets** can also be measured easily by adding together the purchase price of all the constituent parts (labour, material etc) paid to external parties.

## 1.4 Separate items

Most of the time assets will be identified individually, but this will not be the case for **smaller items**, such as tools, dies and moulds, which are sometimes classified as inventory and written off as an expense.

**Major components or spare parts**, however, should be recognised as property, plant and equipment.

For very **large and specialised items**, an apparently single asset should be broken down into its composite parts. This occurs where the different parts have different useful lives and different depreciation rates are applied to each part, eg an aircraft, where the body and engines are separated as they have different useful lives.

## 1.5 Safety and environmental equipment

These items may be necessary for the entity to **obtain future economic benefits** from its other assets. For this reason they are recognised as assets. However the original assets plus the safety equipment should be reviewed for impairment.

## 1.6 Initial measurement

Once an item of property, plant and equipment qualifies for recognition as an asset, it will initially be **measured at cost**.

### 1.6.1 Components of cost

The standard lists the components of the cost of an item of property, plant and equipment.

- **Purchase price**, less any trade discount or rebate

- **Import duties** and non-refundable purchase taxes

- **Directly attributable costs** of bringing the asset to working condition for its intended use, eg:

    - The cost of site preparation
    - Initial delivery and handling costs
    - Installation costs
    - Testing
    - Professional fees (architects, engineers)

- Initial estimate of the unavoidable cost of dismantling and removing the asset and restoring the site on which it is located

The revised IAS 16 provides **additional guidance on directly attributable** costs included in the cost of an item of property, plant and equipment.

(a) These costs bring the asset to the location and working conditions necessary for it to be capable of operating in the manner intended by management, including those costs to test whether the asset is functioning properly.

(b) They are determined after deducting the net proceeds from selling any items produced when bringing the asset to its location and condition.

The revised standard also states that income and related expenses of operations that are **incidental** to the construction or development of an item of property, plant and equipment should be **recognised** in profit or loss.

The following costs **will not be part of the cost** of property, plant or equipment unless they can be attributed directly to the asset's acquisition, or bringing it into its working condition.

- Administration and other general overhead costs
- Start-up and similar pre-production costs
- Initial operating losses before the asset reaches planned performance

All of these will be recognised as an **expense** rather than an asset.

In the case of **self-constructed assets**, the same principles are applied as for acquired assets. If the entity makes similar assets during the normal course of business for sale externally, then the cost of the asset will be the cost of its production under IAS 2 *Inventories*. This also means that abnormal costs (wasted material, labour or other resources) are excluded from the cost of the asset. An example of a self-constructed asset is when a building company builds its own head office.

### 1.6.2 Exchanges of assets

IAS 16 specifies that exchange of items of property, plant and equipment, regardless of whether the assets are similar, are measured at **fair value, unless the exchange transaction lacks commercial substance** or the fair value of neither of the assets exchanged can be **measured reliably**. If the acquired item is not measured at fair value, its cost is measured at the carrying amount of the asset given up.

**Expenditure incurred in replacing or renewing a component** of an item of property, plant and equipment must be **recognised in the carrying amount of the item**. The carrying amount of the replaced or renewed component must be derecognised. A similar approach is also applied when a separate component of an item of property, plant and equipment is identified in respect of a major inspection to enable the continued use of the item.

## 1.7 Measurement subsequent to initial recognition

The standard offers two possible treatments here, essentially a choice between keeping an asset recorded at **cost** or revaluing it to **fair value**.

(a) **Cost model.** Carry the asset at its cost less depreciation and any accumulated impairment loss.

(b) **Revaluation model.** Carry the asset at a revalued amount, being its fair value at the date of the revaluation less any subsequent accumulated depreciation and subsequent accumulated impairment losses. The revised IAS 16 makes clear that the **revaluation model is available only if the fair value of the item can be measured reliably.**

### 1.7.1 Revaluations

The **market value** of land and buildings usually represents fair value, assuming existing use and line of business. Such valuations are usually carried out by professionally qualified valuers.

In the case of **plant and equipment**, fair value can also be taken as **market value**. Where a market value is not available, however, depreciated replacement cost should be used. There may be no market value where types of plant and equipment are sold only rarely or because of their specialised nature (ie they would normally only be sold as part of an ongoing business).

The frequency of valuation depends on the **volatility of the fair values** of individual items of property, plant and equipment. The more volatile the fair value, the more frequently revaluations should be carried out. Where the current fair value is very different from the carrying value then a revaluation should be carried out.

Most importantly, when an item of property, plant and equipment is revalued, **the whole class of assets to which it belongs should be revalued.**

All the items within a class should be **revalued at the same time**, to prevent selective revaluation of certain assets and to avoid disclosing a mixture of costs and values from different dates in the financial statements. A rolling basis of revaluation is allowed if the revaluations are kept up to date and the revaluation of the whole class is completed in a short period of time.

How should any **increase in value** be treated when a revaluation takes place? The debit will be the increase in value in the statement of financial position, but what about the credit? IAS 16 requires the increase to be credited to a **revaluation surplus** (ie part of owners' equity), *unless* the increase is reversing a previous decrease which was recognised as an expense. To the extent that this offset is made, the increase is recognised as income; any excess is then taken to the revaluation surplus.

## 1.8 Example: revaluation surplus

Binkie Co has an item of land carried in its books at $13,000. Two years ago a slump in land values led the company to reduce the carrying value from $15,000. This was taken as an expense in profit or loss. There has been a surge in land prices in the current year, however, and the land is now worth $20,000.

Account for the revaluation in the current year.

## Solution

The double entry is:

| | | |
|---|---|---|
| DEBIT | Asset value (statement of financial position) $7,000 | |
| CREDIT | Profit or loss | $2,000 |
| | Revaluation surplus | $5,000 |

Note: the credit to the revaluation surplus will be shown under 'other comprehensive income'.

The case is similar for a **decrease in value** on revaluation. Any decrease should be recognised as an expense, except where it offsets a previous increase taken as a revaluation surplus in owners' equity. Any decrease greater than the previous upwards increase in value must be taken as an expense in the profit or loss.

## 1.9 Example: revaluation decrease

Let us simply swap round the example given above. The original cost was $15,000, revalued upwards to $20,000 two years ago. The value has now fallen to $13,000.

Account for the decrease in value.

## Solution

The double entry is:

| | | |
|---|---|---|
| DEBIT | Revaluation surplus | $5,000 |
| DEBIT | Profit or loss | $2,000 |
| CREDIT | Asset value (statement of financial position) | $7,000 |

There is a further complication when a **revalued asset is being depreciated**. As we have seen, an upward revaluation means that the depreciation charge will increase. Normally, a revaluation surplus is only realised when the asset is sold, but when it is being depreciated, part of that surplus is being realised as the asset is used. The amount of the surplus realised is the difference between depreciation charged on the revalued amount and the (lower) depreciation which would have been charged on the asset's original cost. **This amount can be transferred to retained (ie realised) earnings but** *not* **through profit or loss.**

## 1.10 Example: revaluation and depreciation

Crinckle Co bought an asset for $10,000 at the beginning of 20X6. It had a useful life of five years. On 1 January 20X8 the asset was revalued to $12,000. The expected useful life has remained unchanged (ie three years remain).

Account for the revaluation and state the treatment for depreciation from 20X8 onwards.

Solution

On 1 January 20X8 the carrying value of the asset is $10,000 − (2 × $10,000 ÷ 5) = $6,000. For the revaluation:

| | | |
|---|---|---|
| DEBIT | Accumulated depreciation | $4,000 |
| DEBIT | Asset value | $2,000 |
| CREDIT | Revaluation surplus | $6,000 |

The depreciation for the next three years will be $12,000 ÷ 3 = $4,000, compared to depreciation on cost of $10,000 ÷ 5 = $2,000. So each year, the extra $2,000 can be treated as part of the surplus which has become realised:

| | | |
|---|---|---|
| DEBIT | Revaluation surplus | $2,000 |
| CREDIT | Retained earnings | $2,000 |

This is a movement on owners' equity only, not an item in profit or loss.

**Exam focus point**

> Note that when a revaluation takes place, the depreciation for the period up to the date of revaluation should be deducted from the carrying value **before** calculating the revaluation surplus. The examiner has drawn attention to this as an error frequently made in exams.

## 1.11 Depreciation

The standard states:

- The **depreciable amount** of an item of property, plant and equipment should be allocated on a systematic basis over its useful life.

- The **depreciation method** used should reflect the pattern in which the asset's economic benefits are consumed by the entity.
- The **depreciation charge** for each period should be recognised as an expense unless it is included in the carrying amount of another asset.

**Land and buildings** are dealt with separately even when they are acquired together because land normally has an unlimited life and is therefore not depreciated. In contrast buildings do have a limited life and must be depreciated. Any increase in the value of land on which a building is standing will have no impact on the determination of the building's useful life.

### 1.11.1 Review of useful life

A review of the **useful life** of property, plant and equipment should be carried out **at least at each financial year end** and the depreciation charge for the current and future periods should be adjusted if expectations have changed significantly from previous estimates. Changes are changes in accounting estimates and are accounted for prospectively as adjustments to future depreciation.

### 1.11.2 Example: review of useful life

B Co acquired a non-current asset on 1 January 20X2 for $80,000. It had no residual value and a useful life of 10 years.

On 1 January 20X5 the remaining useful life was reviewed and revised to 4 years.

What will be the depreciation charge for 20X5?

## Solution

|  | $ |
|---|---|
| Original cost | 80,000 |
| Depreciation 20X2 – 20X4 (80,000 × 3/10) | (24,000) |
| Carrying amount at 31 December 20X4 | 56,000 |
| Remaining life | 4 years |
| Depreciation charge years 20X5 – 20X8 (56,000/4) | 14,000 |

### 1.11.3 Review of depreciation method

The **depreciation method** should also be reviewed **at least at each financial year end** and, if there has been a significant change in the expected pattern of economic benefits from those assets, the method should be changed to suit this changed pattern. When such a change in depreciation method takes place the change should be accounted for as a **change in accounting estimate** and the depreciation charge for the current and future periods should be adjusted.

### 1.11.4 Impairment of asset values

An **impairment loss** should be treated in the same way as a **revaluation decrease** ie the decrease should be **recognised as an expense**. However, a revaluation decrease (or impairment loss) should be charged directly against any related revaluation surplus to the extent that the decrease does not exceed the amount held in the revaluation surplus in respect of that same asset.

A **reversal of an impairment** loss should be treated in the same way as a **revaluation increase**, ie a revaluation increase should be recognised as income to the extent that it reverses a revaluation decrease or an impairment loss of the same asset previously recognised as an expense.

## 1.12 Complex assets

These are assets which are made up of separate components. Each component is separately depreciated over their useful life. An example which appeared in a recent examination was that of an aircraft. An aircraft could be considered as having the following components:

|  | Cost $'000 | Useful life |
|---|---|---|
| Fuselage | 20,000 | 20 years |
| Undercarriage | 5,000 | 500 landings |
| Engines | 8,000 | 1,600 flying hours |

Depreciation at the end of the first year , in which 150 flights totalling 400 hours were made would then be:

|  | $'000 |
|---|---|
| Exterior structure | 1,000 |
| Undercarriage (5,000 x 150/500) | 1,500 |
| Engines (8,000 x 400/1,600) | 2,000 |
|  | 4,500 |

## 1.13 Overhauls

Where an asset requires regular overhauls in order to continue to operate, the cost of the overhaul is treated as an additional component and depreciated over the period to the next overhaul.

In the case of the aircraft above, we will assume that an overhaul is required at the end of year 3 and every third year thereafter at a cost of $1.2m. This is capitalised as a separate component. The depreciation for year 4 (assuming 150 flights again) will therefore be:

|  | $'000 |
|---|---|
| Total as above | 4,500 |
| Overhaul ($1,200,000 / 3) | 400 |
|  | 4,900 |

## 1.14 Retirements and disposals

When an asset is permanently **withdrawn from use, or sold or scrapped**, and no future economic benefits are expected from its disposal, it should be withdrawn from the statement of financial position.

**Gains or losses** are the difference between the estimated net disposal proceeds and the carrying amount of the asset. They should be recognised as income or expense in profit or loss.

## 1.15 Derecognition

An entity is required to **derecognise the carrying amount** of an item of property, plant or equipment that it disposes of on the date the **criteria for the sale of goods** in IAS 18 *Revenue* would be met. This also applies to parts of an asset.

**An entity cannot classify as revenue a gain it realises on the disposal of an item of property, plant and equipment.**

## 1.16 Disclosure

The standard has a long list of disclosure requirements, for each class of property, plant and equipment.

(a) **Measurement bases** for determining the gross carrying amount (if more than one, the gross carrying amount for that basis in each category)

(b) **Depreciation methods** used

(c) **Useful lives** or depreciation rates used

(d) **Gross carrying amount** and accumulated depreciation (aggregated with accumulated impairment losses) at the beginning and end of the period

(e) **Reconciliation** of the carrying amount at the beginning and end of the period showing:

    (i)     Additions
    (ii)    Disposals
    (iii)   Acquisitions through business combinations
    (iv)   Increases/decreases during the period from revaluations and from impairment losses
    (v)    Impairment losses recognised in profit or loss
    (vi)   Impairment losses reversed in profit or loss
    (vii)  Depreciation
    (viii) Net exchange differences (from translation of statements of a foreign entity)
    (ix)   Any other movements.

The financial statements should also disclose the following.

(a) Any recoverable amounts of property, plant and equipment

(b) Existence and amounts of **restrictions on title**, and items pledged as security for liabilities

(c) Accounting policy for **the estimated costs of restoring the site**

(d) Amount of expenditures on account of **items in the course of construction**

(e) Amount of commitments to **acquisitions**

**Revalued assets** require further disclosures.

(a) Basis used to revalue the assets

(b) Effective date of the revaluation

(c) Whether an independent valuer was involved

(d) Nature of any indices used to determine replacement cost

(e) Carrying amount of each class of property, plant and equipment that would have been included in the financial statements had the assets been carried at cost less accumulated depreciation and accumulated impairment losses.

(f) Revaluation surplus, indicating the movement for the period and any restrictions on the distribution of the balance to shareholders.

The standard also **encourages disclosure** of additional information, which the users of financial statements may find useful.

(a) The carrying amount of temporarily idle property, plant and equipment

(b) The gross carrying amount of any fully depreciated property, plant and equipment that is still in use

(c) The carrying amount of property, plant and equipment retired from active use and held for disposal

(d) The fair value of property, plant and equipment when this is materially different from the carrying amount

The following format (with notional figures) is commonly used to disclose non-current assets movements.

| | Total $ | Land and buildings $ | Plant and equipment $ |
|---|---|---|---|
| Cost or valuation | | | |
| At 1 January 20X4 | 50,000 | 40,000 | 10,000 |
| Revaluation surplus | 12,000 | 12,000 | – |
| Additions in year | 4,000 | – | 4,000 |
| Disposals in year | (1,000) | – | (1,000) |
| At 31 December 20X4 | 65,000 | 52,000 | 13,000 |

| *Depreciation* | | | |
|---|---|---|---|
| At 1 January 20X4 | 16,000 | 10,000 | 6,000 |
| Charge for year | 4,000 | 1,000 | 3,000 |
| Eliminated on disposals | (500) | – | (500) |
| At 31 December 20X4 | 19,500 | 11,000 | 8,500 |
| *Net book value* | | | |
| At 31 December 20X4 | 45,500 | 41,000 | 4,500 |
| At 1 January 20X4 | 34,000 | 30,000 | 4,000 |

## Question

Non-current assets

(a) In a statement of financial position prepared in accordance with IAS 16, what does the carrying amount represent?

(b) In a set of financial statements prepared in accordance with IAS 16, is it correct to say that the carrying amount in a statement of financial position cannot be greater than the market (net realisable) value of the partially used asset as at the end of the reporting period? Explain your reasons for your answer.

## Answer

(a) In simple terms the carrying amount of an asset is the cost of an asset less the 'accumulated depreciation', that is, all depreciation charged so far. It should be emphasised that the main purpose of charging depreciation is to ensure that profits are fairly reported. Thus depreciation is concerned with the statement of profit or loss rather than the statement of financial position. In consequence the carrying amount in the statement of financial position can be quite arbitrary. In particular, it does not necessarily bear any relation to the market value of an asset and is of little use for planning and decision making.

An obvious example of the disparity between carrying amount and market value is found in the case of buildings, which may be worth more than ten times as much as their carrying amount.

(b) Carrying amount can in some circumstances be higher than market value (net realisable value). IAS 16 *Property, plant and equipment* states that the value of an asset cannot be greater than its 'recoverable amount'. However 'recoverable amount' as defined in IAS 16 is the amount recoverable from further use. This may be higher than the market value.

This makes sense if you think of a specialised machine which could not fetch much on the secondhand market but which will produce goods which can be sold at a profit for many years.

**Exam focus point**

Property and/or other non-current assets are likely to be tested as they have come up on a number of papers.

# 2 Depreciation accounting

**FAST FORWARD**

Where assets held by an entity have a **limited useful life** to that entity it is necessary to apportion the value of an asset over it's useful life.

## 2.1 Non-current assets

If an asset's life extends over more than one accounting period, it earns profits over more than one period. It is a **non-current asset**.

With the exception of land held on freehold or very long leasehold, **every non-current asset eventually wears out over time**. Machines, cars and other vehicles, fixtures and fittings, and even buildings do not last for ever. When a business acquires a non-current asset, it will have some idea about how long its useful life will be, and it might decide what to do with it.

(a)    Keep on using the non-current asset until it becomes **completely worn out**, useless, and worthless.

(b)    **Sell off** the non-current asset at the end of its useful life, either by selling it as a second-hand item or as scrap.

Since a non-current asset has a cost, and a limited useful life, and its value eventually declines, it follows that a charge should be made in profit or loss to reflect the use that is made of the asset by the business. This charge is called **depreciation**.

## 2.2 Scope

Depreciation accounting is governed by IAS 16 *Property, plant and equipment.* These are some of the IAS 16 definitions concerning depreciation.

<table>
<tr><td>**Key terms**</td><td>

- **Depreciation** is the result of systematic allocation of the depreciable amount of an asset over its estimated useful life. Depreciation for the accounting period is charged to net profit or loss for the period either directly or indirectly.

- **Depreciable assets** are assets which:
    - Are expected to be used during more than one accounting period
    - Have a limited useful life
    - Are held by an entity for use in the production or supply of goods and services, for rental to others, or for administrative purposes

- **Useful life** is one of two things.
    - The period over which a depreciable asset is expected to be used by the entity, or
    - The number of production or similar units expected to be obtained from the asset by the entity.

- **Depreciable amount** of a depreciable asset is the historical cost or other amount substituted for cost in the financial statements, less the estimated residual value.

*(IAS 16)*
</td></tr>
</table>

An 'amount substituted for cost' will normally be a **current market value** after a revaluation has taken place.

## 2.3 Depreciation

IAS 16 requires the depreciable amount of a depreciable asset to be allocated on a **systematic basis** to each accounting period during the useful life of the asset. **Every part of an item of property, plant and equipment with a cost that is significant in relation to the total cost of the item must be depreciated separately**.

One way of defining depreciation is to describe it as a means of **spreading the cost** of a non-current asset over its useful life, and so matching the cost against the full period during which it earns profits for the business. Depreciation charges are an example of the application of the accrual assumption to calculate profits.

There are situations where, over a period, an asset has **increased in value**, ie its current value is greater than the carrying value in the financial statements. You might think that in such situations it would not be necessary to depreciate the asset. The standard states, however, that this is irrelevant, and that depreciation should still be charged to each accounting period, based on the depreciable amount, irrespective of a rise in value.

An entity is required to begin depreciating an item of property, plant and equipment when it is available for use and to continue depreciating it until it is derecognised even if it is idle during the period.

## 2.4 Useful life

The following factors should be considered when **estimating the useful life** of a depreciable asset.

- Expected **physical wear and tear**
- **Obsolescence**
- Legal or other **limits** on the use of the assets

Once decided, the useful life should be **reviewed at least every financial year end** and depreciation rates adjusted for the current and future periods if expectations vary significantly from the original estimates. The effect of the change should be disclosed in the accounting period in which the change takes place.

The assessment of useful life requires **judgement** based on previous experience with similar assets or classes of asset. When a completely new type of asset is acquired (ie through technological advancement or through use in producing a brand new product or service) it is still necessary to estimate useful life, even though the exercise will be much more difficult.

The standard also points out that the physical life of the asset might be longer than its useful life to the entity in question. One of the main factors to be taken into consideration is the **physical wear and tear** the asset is likely to endure. This will depend on various circumstances, including the number of shifts for which the asset will be used, the entity's repair and maintenance programme and so on. Other factors to be considered include obsolescence (due to technological advances/improvements in production/reduction in demand for the product/service produced by the asset) and legal restrictions, eg length of a related lease.

## 2.5 Residual value

In most cases the residual value of an asset is **likely to be immaterial**. If it is likely to be of any significant value, that value must be estimated at the date of purchase or any subsequent revaluation. The amount of residual value should be estimated based on the current situation with other similar assets, used in the same way, which are now at the end of their useful lives. Any expected costs of disposal should be offset against the gross residual value.

## 2.6 Depreciation methods

**Consistency is important**. The depreciation method selected should be applied consistently from period to period unless altered circumstances justify a change. When the method *is* changed, the effect should be quantified and disclosed and the reason for the change should be stated.

Various methods of allocating depreciation to accounting periods are available, but whichever is chosen must be applied **consistently** (as required by IAS 1: see Chapter 1), to ensure comparability from period to period. Change of policy is not allowed simply because of the profitability situation of the entity.

You should be familiar with the various **accepted methods of allocating depreciation** and the relevant calculations and accounting treatments, which are revised in questions at the end of this section.

## 2.7 Disclosure

An accounting policy note should disclose the **valuation bases** used for determining the amounts at which depreciable assets are stated, along with the other accounting policies: see IAS 1.

IAS 16 also requires the following to be disclosed for each major class of depreciable asset.

- **Depreciation methods** used
- **Useful lives** or the depreciation rates used
- **Total depreciation** allocated for the period
- **Gross amount** of depreciable assets and the related accumulated depreciation

## 2.8 What is depreciation?

The need to depreciate non-current assets arises from the **accruals assumption**. If money is expended in purchasing an asset then the amount expended must at some time be charged against profits. If the asset is one which contributes to an entity's revenue over a number of accounting periods it would be inappropriate to charge any single period (eg the period in which the asset was acquired) with the whole of the expenditure. Instead, some method must be found of spreading the cost of the asset over its useful economic life.

This view of depreciation as a process of allocation of the cost of an asset over several accounting periods is the view adopted by IAS 16. It is worth mentioning here two **common misconceptions** about the purpose and effects of depreciation.

(a)     It is sometimes thought that the carrying amount of an asset is equal to its net realisable value and that the object of charging depreciation is to **reflect the fall in value of an asset over its life**. This misconception is the basis of a common, but incorrect, argument which says that freehold properties (say) need not be depreciated in times when property values are rising. It is true that historical cost statements of financial position often give a misleading impression when a property's carrying amount is much below its market value, but in such a case it is open to a business to incorporate a revaluation into its books, or even to prepare its accounts based on current costs. This is a separate problem from that of allocating the property's cost over successive accounting periods.

(b)     Another misconception is that depreciation is provided **so that an asset can be replaced at the end of its useful life**. This is not the case.

  (i)     If there is no intention of replacing the asset, it could then be argued that there is no need to provide for any depreciation at all.

  (ii)    If prices are rising, the replacement cost of the asset will exceed the amount of depreciation provided.

The following questions are for revision purposes only.

Question | Depreciation methods

A lorry bought for a business cost $17,000. It is expected to last for five years and then be sold for scrap for $2,000. Usage over the five years is expected to be:

Year 1                                                          200 days
Year 2                                                          100 days
Year 3                                                          100 days
Year 4                                                          150 days
Year 5                                                          40 days

*Required*

Work out the depreciation to be charged each year under:

(a)     The straight line method
(b)     The reducing balance method (using a rate of 35%)
(c)     The machine hour method
(d)     The sum-of-the digits method

Answer

(a)     Under the straight line method, depreciation for each of the five years is:

$$\text{Annual depreciation} = \frac{\$(17,000 - 2,000)}{5} = \$3,000$$

(b) Under the reducing balance method, depreciation for each of the five years is:

| Year | Depreciation | | |
|---|---|---|---|
| 1 | 35% × $17,000 | = | $5,950 |
| 2 | 35% × ($17,000 – $5,950) = 35% × $11,050 | = | $3,868 |
| 3 | 35% × ($11,050 – $3,868) = 35% × $7,182 | = | $2,514 |
| 4 | 35% × ($7,182 – $2,514) = 35% × $4,668 | = | $1,634 |
| 5 | Balance to bring book value down to $2,000 = $4,668 – $1,634 – $2,000 | = | $1,034 |

(c) Under the machine hour method, depreciation for each of the five years is calculated as follows.

Total usage (days) = 200 + 100 + 100 + 150 + 40 = 590 days

Depreciation per day = $\dfrac{\$(17,000 - 2,000)}{590}$ = $25.42

| Year | Usage (days) | Depreciation ($) (days × $25.42) |
|---|---|---|
| 1 | 200 | 5,084.00 |
| 2 | 100 | 2,542.00 |
| 3 | 100 | 2,542.00 |
| 4 | 150 | 3,813.00 |
| 5 | 40 | 1,016.80 |
| | | 14,997.80 |

*Note.* The answer does not come to exactly $15,000 because of the rounding carried out at the 'depreciation per day' stage of the calculation.

(d) The sum-of-the digits method begins by adding up the years of expected life. In this case, 5 + 4 + 3 + 2 + 1 = 15.

The depreciable amount of $15,000 will then be allocated as follows:

| Year | 1 | 15,000 × 5/15 = 5,000 |
|---|---|---|
| | 2 | 15,000 × 4/15 = 4,000 |
| | 3 | 15,000 × 3/15 = 3,000 |
| | 4 | 15,000 × 2/15 = 2,000 |
| | 5 | 15,000 × 1/15 = 1,000 |

**Exam focus point**

> The December 2008 exam had a question which included machine-hour depreciation. Some candidates failed to deduct the residual value before calculating the machine hour rate.

**Question**            **Depreciation discussion**

(a) What are the purposes of providing for depreciation?

(b) In what circumstances is the reducing balance method more appropriate than the straight-line method? Give reasons for your answer.

**Answer**

(a) The accounts of a business try to recognise that the cost of a non-current asset is gradually consumed as the asset wears out. This is done by gradually writing off the asset's cost to profit or loss over several accounting periods. This process is known as depreciation, and is an example of the accruals assumption. IAS 16 *Property, plant and equipment* requires that depreciation should be allocated on a systematic basis to each accounting period during the useful life of the asset.

With regard to the accrual principle, it is fair that the profits should be reduced by the depreciation charge; this is not an arbitrary exercise. Depreciation is not, as is sometimes supposed, an attempt to set aside funds to purchase new non-current assets when required. Depreciation is not generally provided on freehold land because it does not 'wear out' (unless it is held for mining etc).

(b)  The reducing balance method of depreciation is used instead of the straight line method when it is considered fair to allocate a greater proportion of the total depreciable amount to the earlier years and a lower proportion to the later years on the assumption that the benefits obtained by the business from using the asset decline over time.

In favour of this method it may be argued that it links the depreciation charge to the costs of maintaining and running the asset. In the early years these costs are low and the depreciation charge is high, while in later years this is reversed.

## Question

Depreciation accounting

A business purchased two rivet-making machines on 1 January 20X5 at a cost of $15,000 each. Each had an estimated life of five years and a nil residual value. The straight line method of depreciation is used.

Owing to an unforeseen slump in market demand for rivets, the business decided to reduce its output of rivets, and switch to making other products instead. On 31 March 20X7, one rivet-making machine was sold (on credit) to a buyer for $8,000.

Later in the year, however, it was decided to abandon production of rivets altogether, and the second machine was sold on 1 December 20X7 for $2,500 cash.

Prepare the machinery account, provision for depreciation of machinery account and disposal of machinery account for the accounting year to 31 December 20X7.

## Answer

### MACHINERY ACCOUNT

| | | $ | | | $ |
|---|---|---|---|---|---|
| *20X7* | | | *20X7* | | |
| 1 Jan | Balance b/f | 30,000 | 31 Mar | Disposal of machinery account | 15,000 |
| | | | 1 Dec | Disposal of machinery account | 15,000 |
| | | 30,000 | | | 30,000 |

### ACCUMULATED DEPRECIATION OF MACHINERY

| | | $ | | | $ |
|---|---|---|---|---|---|
| *20X7* | | | *20X7* | | |
| 31 Mar | Disposal of machinery account* | 6,750 | 1 Jan | Balance b/f | 12,000 |
| 1 Dec | Disposal of machinery account** | 8,750 | 31 Dec | Profit or loss*** | 3,500 |
| | | 15,500 | | | 15,500 |

\*      Depreciation at date of disposal = $6,000 + $750
\*\*    Depreciation at date of disposal = $6,000 + $2,750
\*\*\*  Depreciation charge for the year = $750 + $2,750

### DISPOSAL OF MACHINERY

| | | $ | | | $ |
|---|---|---|---|---|---|
| *20X7* | | | *20X7* | | |
| 31 Mar | Machinery account | 15,000 | 31 Mar | Account receivable (sale price) | 8,000 |
| | | | 31 Mar | Provision for depreciation | 6,750 |
| 1 Dec | Machinery | 15,000 | 1 Dec | Cash (sale price) | 2,500 |
| | | | 1 Dec | Provision for depreciation | 8,750 |
| | | | 31 Dec | Profit or loss (loss on disposal) | 4,000 |
| | | 30,000 | | | 30,000 |

You should be able to calculate that there was a loss on the first disposal of $250, and on the second disposal of $3,750, giving a total loss of $4,000.

*Workings*

1    At 1 January 20X7, accumulated depreciation on the machines will be:

2 machines × 2 years × $\dfrac{\$15,000}{5}$ per machine pa = $12,000, or $6,000 per machine

2    Monthly depreciation is $\dfrac{\$3,000}{12}$ = $250 per machine per month

3    The machines are disposed of in 20X7.

(a)    On 31 March – after 3 months of the year. Depreciation for the year on the machine = 3 months × $250 = $750.

(b)    On 1 December – after 11 months of the year. Depreciation for the year on the machine = 11 months × $250 = $2,750

# 3 IAS 20 Government grants

It is common for entities to receive government grants for various purposes (grants may be called subsidies, premiums, etc). They may also receive other types of assistance which may be in many forms. The treatment of government grants is covered by IAS 20 *Accounting for government grants and disclosure of government assistance*.

## 3.1 Scope

IAS 20 does *not* cover the following situations.

- Accounting for government grants in financial statements reflecting the effects of **changing prices**
- Government assistance given in the form of **'tax breaks'**
- Government acting as **part-owner** of the entity

## 3.2 Definitions

These definitions are given by the standard.

Key terms

- **Government.** Government, government agencies and similar bodies whether local, national or international.
- **Government assistance.** Action by government designed to provide an economic benefit specific to an entity or range of entities qualifying under certain criteria.
- **Government grants.** Assistance by government in the form of transfers of resources to an entity in return for past or future compliance with certain conditions relating to the operating activities of the entity. They exclude those forms of government assistance which cannot reasonably have a value placed upon them and transactions with government which cannot be distinguished from the normal trading transactions of the entity.
- **Grants related to assets.** Government grants whose primary condition is that an entity qualifying for them should purchase, construct or otherwise acquire non-current assets. Subsidiary conditions may also be attached restricting the type or location of the assets or the periods during which they are to be acquired or held.
- **Grants related to income**. Government grants other than those related to assets.
- **Forgivable loans.** Loans which the lender undertakes to waive repayment of under certain prescribed conditions.                                                                                          IAS 20

> • **Fair value.** The price that would be received to sell an asset or paid to transfer a liability in an orderly transaction between market participants at the measurement date. IFRS 13

You can see that there are many **different forms** of government assistance: both the type of assistance and the conditions attached to it will vary. Government assistance may have encouraged an entity to undertake something it otherwise would not have done.

How will the receipt of government assistance affect the financial statements?

(a) An appropriate method must be found to account for any **resources transferred**.

(b) The extent to which an entity has **benefited** from such assistance during the reporting period should be shown.

## 3.3 Government grants

An entity should not recognise government grants (including non-monetary grants at fair value) until it has **reasonable assurance** that:

- The entity will comply with any **conditions** attached to the grant
- The entity will **actually receive** the grant

Even if the grant has been received, this does not prove that the conditions attached to it have been or will be fulfilled.

It makes no difference in the treatment of the grant whether it is received in cash or given as a reduction in a liability to government, ie the **manner of receipt is irrelevant**.

Any related **contingency** should be recognised under IAS 37 Provisions, contingent liabilities and contingent assets, once the grant has been recognised.

In the case of a **forgivable loan** (as defined in key terms above) from government, it should be treated in the same way as a government grant when it is reasonably assured that the entity will meet the relevant terms for forgiveness.

### 3.3.1 Accounting treatment of government grants

IAS 20 requires grants to be recognised as income over the relevant periods to match them with related costs which they have been received to compensate. This should be done on a systematic basis. **Grants should not, therefore, be credited directly to equity.**

It would be against the accruals assumption to credit grants to income on a receipts basis, so a **systematic basis of matching** must be used. A receipts basis would only be acceptable if no other basis was available.

It will usually be easy to identify the **costs related to a government grant**, and thereby the period(s) in which the grant should be recognised as income, ie when the costs are incurred. Where grants are received in relation to a depreciating asset, the grant will be recognised over the periods in which the asset is depreciated *and* in the same proportions.

Question                                                                                                    Recognition

Arturo Co receives a government grant representing 50% of the cost of a depreciating asset which costs $40,000. How will the grant be recognised if Arturo Co depreciates the asset:

(a) over four years straight line; or

(b) at 40% reducing balance?

The residual value is nil. The useful life is four years.

The grant should be recognised in the same proportion as the depreciation.

(a)     Straight line

|  |  | Depreciation $ | Grant income $ |
|---|---|---|---|
| Year | 1 | 10,000 | 5,000 |
|  | 2 | 10,000 | 5,000 |
|  | 3 | 10,000 | 5,000 |
|  | 4 | 10,000 | 5,000 |

(b)     Reducing balance

|  |  | Depreciation $ | Grant income $ |
|---|---|---|---|
| Year | 1 | 16,000 | 8,000 |
|  | 2 | 9,600 | 4,800 |
|  | 3 | 5,760 | 2,880 |
|  | 4 (remainder) | 8,640 | 4,320 |

In the case of **grants for non-depreciable assets**, certain obligations may need to be fulfilled, in which case the grant should be recognised as income over the periods in which the cost of meeting the obligation is incurred. For example, if a piece of land is granted on condition that a building is erected on it, then the grant should be recognised as income over the building's life.

There may be a **series of conditions** attached to a grant, in the nature of a package of financial aid. An entity must take care to identify precisely those conditions which give rise to costs which in turn determine the periods over which the grant will be earned. When appropriate, the grant may be split and the parts allocated on different bases.

An entity may receive a grant as compensation for expenses or losses which it has **already incurred**. Alternatively, a grant may be given to an entity simply to provide immediate financial support where no future related costs are expected. In cases such as these, the grant received should be recognised as income of the period in which it becomes receivable.

### 3.3.2 Non-monetary government grants

A non-monetary asset may be transferred by government to an entity as a grant, for example a piece of land, or other resources. The **fair value** of such an asset is usually assessed and this is used to account for both the asset and the grant. Alternatively, both may be valued at a nominal amount.

### 3.3.3 Presentation of grants related to assets

There are two choices here for how government grants related to assets (including non-monetary grants at fair value) should be shown in the statement of financial position.

(a)     Set up the grant as **deferred income.**
(b)     **Deduct the grant** in arriving at the **carrying amount** of the asset.

These are considered to be acceptable alternatives and we can look at an example showing both.

### Example: accounting for grants related to assets

A company receives a 20% grant towards the cost of a new item of machinery, which cost $100,000. The machinery has an expected life of four years and a nil residual value. The expected profits of the company, before accounting for depreciation on the new machine or the grant, amount to $50,000 per annum in each year of the machinery's life.

# Solution

The results of the company for the four years of the machine's life would be as follows.

(a)  *Reducing the cost of the asset*

|  | Year 1 | Year 2 | Year 3 | Year 4 | Total |
|---|---|---|---|---|---|
|  | $ | $ | $ | $ | $ |
| Profit before depreciation | 50,000 | 50,000 | 50,000 | 50,000 | 200,000 |
| Depreciation* | 20,000 | 20,000 | 20,000 | 20,000 | 80,000 |
| Profit | 30,000 | 30,000 | 30,000 | 30,000 | 120,000 |

*The depreciation charge on a straight line basis, for each year, is ¼ of $(100,000 – 20,000) = $20,000.

*Statement of financial position at year end (extract)*

|  | $ | $ | $ | $ |
|---|---|---|---|---|
| Non-current asset | 80,000 | 80,000 | 80,000 | 80,000 |
| Depreciation 25% | 20,000 | 40,000 | 60,000 | 80,000 |
| Carrying amount | 60,000 | 40,000 | 20,000 | – |

(b)  *Treating the grant as deferred income*

|  | Year 1 | Year 2 | Year 3 | Year 4 | Total |
|---|---|---|---|---|---|
|  | $ | $ | $ | $ | $ |
| Profit as above | 50,000 | 50,000 | 50,000 | 50,000 | 200,000 |
| Depreciation | (25,000) | (25,000) | (25,000) | (25,000) | (100,000) |
| Grant | 5,000 | 5,000 | 5,000 | 5,000 | 20,000 |
| Profit | 30,000 | 30,000 | 30,000 | 30,000 | 120,000 |

*Statement of financial position at year end (extract)*

|  | | | | |
|---|---|---|---|---|
| Non-current asset at cost | 100,000 | 100,000 | 100,000 | 100,000 |
| Depreciation 25% | (25,000) | (50,000) | (75,000) | (100,000) |
| Carrying amount | 75,000 | 50,000 | 25,000 | – |
| Government grant deferred income | 15,000 | 10,000 | 5,000 | – |

Whichever of these methods is used, the **cash flows** in relation to the purchase of the asset and the receipt of the grant are often disclosed separately because of the significance of the movements in cash flow.

## 3.3.4 Presentation of grants related to income

These grants are a credit in profit or loss, but there is a choice in the method of disclosure.

(a)  Present as a **separate credit** or under a general heading, eg 'other income'

(b)  **Deduct from the related expense**

Some would argue that offsetting income and expenses in the statement of profit or loss is not good practice. Others would say that the expenses would not have been incurred had the grant not been available, so offsetting the two is acceptable. Although both methods are acceptable, disclosure of the grant may be necessary for a **proper understanding** of the financial statements, particularly the effect on any item of income or expense which is required to be separately disclosed.

## 3.3.5 Repayment of government grants

If a grant must be repaid it should be accounted for as a **revision of an accounting estimate** (see IAS 8).

(a)  **Repayment of a grant related to income:** apply first against any unamortised deferred income set up in respect of the grant; any excess should be recognised immediately as an expense.

(b)  **Repayment of a grant related to an asset**: increase the carrying amount of the asset or reduce the deferred income balance by the amount repayable. The cumulative additional depreciation that would have been recognised to date in the absence of the grant should be immediately recognised as an expense.

It is possible that the circumstances surrounding repayment may require a review of the **asset value** and an impairment of the new carrying amount of the asset.

## 3.4 Government assistance

Some forms of government assistance are excluded from the definition of government grants.

(a)    Some forms of government assistance **cannot reasonably have a value placed on them**, eg free technical or marketing advice, provision of guarantees.

(b)    There are transactions with government which **cannot be distinguished from the entity's normal trading transactions**, eg government procurement policy resulting in a portion of the entity's sales. Any segregation would be arbitrary.

Disclosure of such assistance may be necessary because of its significance; its nature, extent and duration should be disclosed. Loans at low or zero interest rates are a form of government assistance, but the imputation of interest does not fully quantify the benefit received.

## 3.5 Disclosure

Disclosure is required of the following.

• **Accounting policy** adopted, including method of presentation
• **Nature and extent** of government grants recognised and other forms of assistance received
• **Unfulfilled conditions and other contingencies** attached to recognised government assistance

## 3.6 SIC 10 Government assistance – no specific relation to operating activities

In some countries government assistance to entities may be aimed at encouragement or long-term support of business activities either in certain regions or industry sectors. Conditions to receive such assistance may not be specifically related to the operating activities of the entity. Examples of such assistance are transfers of resources by governments to entities which:

(a)    Operate in a particular industry
(b)    Continue operating in recently privatised industries
(c)    Start or continue to run their business in underdeveloped areas

The issue is whether such government assistance is a 'government grant' within the scope of IAS 20 and, therefore, should be accounted for in accordance with this Standard.

Government assistance to entities meets the definition of government grants in IAS 20, even if there are no conditions specifically relating to the operating activities of the entity other than the requirement to operate in certain regions or industry sectors. Such grants should therefore not be credited directly to equity.

# 4 IAS 40 Investment property

FAST FORWARD

An entity may own land or a building **as an investment** rather than for use in the business. It may therefore generate cash flows largely independently of other assets which the entity holds. The treatment of investment property is covered by IAS 40.

## 4.1 Definitions

Consider the following definitions.

**Investment property** is property (land or a building – or part of a building – or both) held (by the owner or by the lessee under a finance lease) to earn rentals or for capital appreciation or both, rather than for:

(a)     Use in the production or supply of goods or services or for administrative purposes, or

(b)     Sale in the ordinary course of business

**Owner-occupied property** is property held by the owner (or by the lessee under a finance lease) for use in the production or supply of goods or services or for administrative purposes.

**Fair value** is the price that would be received to sell an asset or paid to transfer a liability in an orderly transaction between market participants at the measurement date.

**Cost** is the amount of cash or cash equivalents paid or the fair value of other consideration given to acquire an asset at the time of its acquisition or construction.

**Carrying amount** is the amount at which an asset is recognised in the statement of financial position.

A property interest that is held by a lessee under an **operating lease** may be classified and accounted for as an **investment property**, if and only if the property would otherwise meet the definition of an investment property and the lessee uses the IAS 40 **fair value model**. This classification is available on a property-by-property basis.

**Examples** of investment property include:

(a)     **Land held for long-term capital appreciation** rather than for short-term sale in the ordinary course of business

(b)     A **building** owned by the reporting entity (or held by the entity under a finance lease) and **leased out under an operating lease**

(c)     A building held by a **parent** and leased to a **subsidiary**. Note, however, that while this is regarded as an investment property in the individual parent company financial statements, in the **consolidated** financial statements this property will be regarded as owner-occupied (because it is occupied by the group) and will therefore be treated in accordance with IAS 16.

(d)     Property that is being constructed or developed for future use as an investment property

Question                                                                                                    Investment

Rich Co owns a piece of land. The directors have not yet decided whether to build a factory on it for use in its business or to keep it and sell it when its value has risen.

Would this be classified as an investment property under IAS 40?

Answer

Yes. If an entity has not determined that it will use the land either as an owner-occupied property or for short-term sale in the ordinary course of business, the land is considered to be held for capital appreciation.

## 4.2 IAS 40

IAS 40 *Investment property* was published in March 2000 and has recently been revised. Its objective is to prescribe the accounting treatment for investment property and related disclosure requirements.

The standard includes investment property held under a finance lease or leased out under an operating lease. However, the current IAS 40 does not deal with matters covered in IAS 17 *Leases*.

You now know what **is** an investment property under IAS 40. Below are examples of items that are **not investment property.**

| Type of non-investment property | Applicable IAS |
|---|---|
| Property intended for sale in the ordinary course of business | IAS 2 *Inventories* |
| Property being constructed or developed on behalf of third parties | IAS 11 *Construction contracts* |
| Owner-occupied property | IAS 16 *Property, plant and equipment* |

## 4.3 Recognition

Investment property should be recognised as an asset when **two conditions** are met.

(a) It is **probable** that the **future economic benefits** that are associated with the investment property will **flow to the entity**.

(b) The **cost** of the investment property can be **measured reliably**.

## 4.4 Initial measurement

An investment property should be measured initially at its **cost,** including transaction costs.

A property interest held under a lease and classified as an investment property shall be accounted for **as if it were a finance lease**. The asset is recognised at the lower of the fair value of the property and the present value of the minimum lease payments. An equivalent amount is recognised as a liability.

## 4.5 Measurement subsequent to initial recognition

IAS 40 requires an entity to **choose between two models.**

- The fair value model
- The cost model

Whatever policy it chooses should be applied to **all of its investment property**.

Where an entity chooses to classify a property held under an **operating lease** as an investment property, there is **no choice**. The **fair value model must be used** for **all the entity's investment property**, regardless of whether it is owned or leased.

### 4.5.1 Fair value model

**Key terms**

(a) After initial recognition, an entity that chooses the **fair value model** should measure all of its investment property at fair value, except in the extremely rare cases where this cannot be measured reliably. In such cases it should apply the IAS 16 cost model.

(b) A gain or loss arising from a change in the fair value of an investment property should be recognised in net profit or loss for the period in which it arises.

(c) The fair value of investment property should reflect market conditions at the end of the reporting period.

This was the first time that the IASB has allowed a fair value model for non-financial assets. This is not the same as a revaluation, where increases in carrying amount above a cost-based measure are recognised as revaluation surplus. Under the fair-value model all changes in fair value are recognised in profit or loss.

The standard elaborates on **issues relating to fair value**.

(a) Fair value assumes that an orderly transaction has taken place between market participants, ie both buyer and seller are reasonably informed about the nature and characteristics of the investment property.

(b)    A buyer participating in an orderly transaction is **motivated but not compelled** to buy. A seller participating in an orderly transaction is neither an over-eager nor a forced seller, nor one prepared to sell at any price or to hold out for a price not considered reasonable in the current market.

(c)    **Fair value is not the same as 'value in use'** as defined in IAS 36 *Impairment of assets*. Value in use reflects factors and knowledge specific to the entity, while fair value reflects factors and knowledge relevant to the market.

(d)    In determining fair value an entity **should not double count assets**. For example, elevators or air conditioning are often an integral part of a building and should be included in the investment property, rather than recognised separately.

(e)    In those rare cases where the **entity cannot determine the fair value of an investment property reliably**, the cost model in **IAS 16** must be applied until the investment property is disposed of. The **residual value must be assumed to be zero**.

### 4.5.2 Cost model

The cost model is the **cost model in IAS 16**. Investment property should be measured at **depreciated cost, less any accumulated impairment losses**. An entity that chooses the cost model should **disclose the fair value of its investment property**.

### 4.5.3 Changing models

Once the entity has chosen the fair value or cost model, it should apply it to all its investment property. It **should not change from one model to the other unless the change will result in a more appropriate presentation**. IAS 40 states that it is highly unlikely that a change from the fair value model to the cost model will result in a more appropriate presentation.

## 4.6 Transfers

**Transfers** to or from investment property should **only** be made **when there is a change in use**. For example, owner occupation commences so the investment property will be treated under IAS 16 as an owner-occupied property.

When there is a transfer from investment property carried at fair value to owner-occupied property or inventories, the property's cost for subsequent accounting under IAS 16 or IAS 2 should be its fair value at the date of change of use.

Conversely, an owner-occupied property may become an investment property and need to be carried at fair value. An entity should apply IAS 16 up to the date of change of use. It should treat any difference at that date between the carrying amount of the property under IAS 16 and its fair value as a revaluation under IAS 16.

## 4.7 Worked example: Transfer to investment property

A business owns a building which it has been using as a head office. In order to reduce costs, on 30 June 20X9 it moved its head office functions to one of its production centres and is now letting out its head office. Company policy is to use the fair value model for investment property.

The building had an original cost on 1 January 20X0 of $250,000 and was being depreciated over 50 years. At 31 December 20X9 its fair value was judged to be $350,000.

How will this appear in the financial statements at 31 December 20X9?

## Solution

The building will be depreciated up to 30 June 20X9.

|  | $ |
|---|---|
| Original cost | 250,000 |
| Depreciation 1.1.X0 – 1.1.X9 (250/50 × 9) | (45,000) |
| Depreciation to 30.6.X9 (250/50 × 6/12) | (2,500) |

| | |
|---|---|
| Carrying amount at 30.6.X9 | 202,500 |
| Revaluation surplus | 147,500 |
| Fair value at 30.6.X9 | 350,000 |

The difference between the carrying amount and fair value is taken to a **revaluation surplus** in accordance with IAS 16.

**However** the building will be subjected to a fair value exercise at each year end and these gains or losses will go to **profit or loss**. If at the end of the following year the fair value of the building is found to be $380,000, $30,000 will be credited to profit or loss.

## 4.8 Disposals

**Derecognise** (eliminate from the statement of financial position) an investment property on disposal or when it is permanently withdrawn from use and no future economic benefits are expected from its disposal.

Any **gain or loss** on disposal is the difference between the net disposal proceeds and the carrying amount of the asset. It should generally be **recognised as income or expense in profit or loss.**

Compensation from third parties for investment property that was impaired, lost or given up shall be recognised in profit or loss when the compensation becomes receivable.

## 4.9 Disclosure requirements

These relate to:

- Choice of fair value model or cost model
- Whether property interests held as operating leases are included in investment property
- Criteria for classification as investment property
- Assumptions in determining fair value
- Use of independent professional valuer (encouraged but not required)
- Rental income and expenses
- Any restrictions or obligations

### 4.9.1 Fair value model – additional disclosures

An entity that adopts this must also disclose a **reconciliation** of the carrying amount of the investment property at the beginning and end of the period.

### 4.9.2 Cost model – additional disclosures

These relate mainly to the depreciation method. In addition, an entity which adopts the cost model **must disclose the fair value** of the investment property.

# 5 IAS 23 Borrowing costs

FAST FORWARD

IAS 23 looks at the treatment of **borrowing costs**, particularly where the related borrowings are applied to the construction of certain assets. These are what are usually called 'self-constructed assets', where an entity builds its own inventory or non-current assets over a substantial period of time.

## 5.1 Definitions

Only two definitions are given by the standard.

**Key terms**

> **Borrowing costs.** Interest and other costs incurred by an entity in connection with the borrowing of funds.
>
> **Qualifying asset.** An asset that necessarily takes a substantial period of time to get ready for its intended use or sale.
>
> *(IAS 23)*

The standard lists what may be **included in borrowing costs**.

- Interest on bank overdrafts and short-term and long-term borrowings
- Amortisation of discounts or premiums relating to borrowings
- Amortisation of ancillary costs incurred in connection with the arrangement of borrowings
- Finance charges in respect of finance leases recognised in accordance with IAS 17 (See Chapter 15)

The standard also gives examples of qualifying assets.

- Inventories that require a substantial period of time to bring them to a saleable condition
- Manufacturing plants
- Power generation facilities
- Investment properties

Inventories produced in bulk over short periods and on a regular basis are **not qualifying assets**, nor are assets ready for sale or their intended use when purchased.

## 5.2 Benchmark treatment

Prior to the revision of IAS 23 the benchmark treatment was to recognise borrowing costs as an expense. **This benchmark/allowed alternative has now been removed**.

## 5.3 IAS 23 revised: capitalisation

Under the revised treatment, all eligible borrowing costs must be **capitalised**.

Only borrowing costs that are **directly attributable** to the acquisition, construction or production of a qualifying asset can be capitalised as part of the cost of that asset. The standard lays out the criteria for determining which borrowing costs are eligible for capitalisation.

### 5.3.1 Borrowing costs eligible for capitalisation

Those borrowing costs directly attributable to the acquisition, construction or production of a qualifying asset must be identified. These are the borrowing costs that **would have been avoided** had the expenditure on the qualifying asset not been made. This is obviously straightforward where funds have been borrowed for the financing of one particular asset.

Difficulties arise, however, where the entity uses a **range of debt instruments** to finance a wide range of assets, so that there is no direct relationship between particular borrowings and a specific asset. For example, all borrowings may be made centrally and then lent to different parts of the group or entity. Judgement is therefore required, particularly where further complications can arise (eg foreign currency loans).

Once the relevant borrowings are identified, which relate to a specific asset, then the **amount of borrowing costs available for capitalisation** will be the actual borrowing costs incurred on those borrowings during the period, *less* any investment income on the temporary investment of those borrowings. It would not be unusual for some or all of the funds to be invested before they are actually used on the qualifying asset.

**Question**　　　　　　　　　　　　　　　　　　　　　　　　　　　　**Capitalisation**

On 1 January 20X6 Stremans Co borrowed $1.5m to finance the production of two assets, both of which were expected to take a year to build. Work started during 20X6. The loan facility was drawn down and incurred on 1 January 20X6, and was utilised as follows, with the remaining funds invested temporarily.

| | Asset A | Asset B |
| --- | --- | --- |
| | $'000 | $'000 |
| 1 January 20X6 | 250 | 500 |
| 1 July 20X6 | 250 | 500 |

The loan rate was 9% and Stremans Co can invest surplus funds at 7%.

*Required*

Ignoring compound interest, calculate the borrowing costs which may be capitalised for each of the assets and consequently the cost of each asset as at 31 December 20X6.

## Answer

| | | Asset A $ | Asset B $ |
|---|---|---|---|
| Borrowing costs | | | |
| To 31 December 20X6 | $500,000/$1,000,000 × 9% | 45,000 | 90,000 |
| Less investment income | | | |
| To 30 June 20X6 | $250,000/$500,000 × 7% × 6/12 | (8,750) | (17,500) |
| | | 36,250 | 72,500 |
| Cost of assets | | | |
| Expenditure incurred | | 500,000 | 1,000,000 |
| Borrowing costs | | 36,250 | 72,500 |
| | | 536,250 | 1,072,500 |

In a situation where **borrowings are obtained generally**, but are applied in part to obtaining a qualifying asset, then the amount of borrowing costs eligible for capitalisation is found by applying the 'capitalisation rate' to the expenditure on the asset.

The **capitalisation rate** is the weighted average of the borrowing costs applicable to the entity's borrowings that are outstanding during the period, *excluding* borrowings made specifically to obtain a qualifying asset. However, there is a cap on the amount of borrowing costs calculated in this way: it must not exceed actual borrowing costs incurred.

Sometimes one overall weighted average can be calculated for a group or entity, but in some situations it may be more appropriate to use a weighted average for borrowing costs for **individual parts of the group or entity**.

## Question

Construction

Acruni Co had the following loans in place at the beginning and end of 20X6.

| | 1 January 20X6 $m | 31 December 20X6 $m |
|---|---|---|
| 10% Bank loan repayable 20X8 | 120 | 120 |
| 9.5% Bank loan repayable 20X9 | 80 | 80 |
| 8.9% debenture repayable 20X7 | – | 150 |

The 8.9% debenture was issued to fund the construction of a qualifying asset (a piece of mining equipment), construction of which began on 1 July 20X6.

On 1 January 20X6, Acruni Co began construction of a qualifying asset, a piece of machinery for a hydro-electric plant, using existing borrowings. Expenditure drawn down for the construction was: $£30m on 1 January 20X6, $20m on 1 October 20X6.

*Required*

Calculate the borrowing costs that can be capitalised for the hydro-electric plant machine.

Capitalisation rate = weighted average rate = $(10\% \times \frac{120}{120+80}) + (9.5\% \times \frac{80}{120+80}) = 9.8\%$

Borrowing costs = ($30m × 9.8%) + ($20m × 9.8% × 3/12)
= $3.43m

### 5.3.2 Carrying amount exceeds recoverable amount

A situation may arise whereby the carrying amount (or expected ultimate cost) of the qualifying asset exceeds its recoverable amount or net realisable value. In these cases, the carrying amount must be **written down or written off**, as required by other IASs. In certain circumstances (again as allowed by other IASs), these amounts may be written back in future periods.

### 5.3.3 Commencement of capitalisation

**Three events or transactions** must be taking place for capitalisation of borrowing costs to be started.

(a)     Expenditure on the asset is being incurred
(b)     Borrowing costs are being incurred
(c)     Activities are in progress that are necessary to prepare the asset for its intended use or sale

**Expenditure** must result in the payment of cash, transfer of other assets or assumption of interest-bearing liabilities. **Deductions from expenditure** will be made for any progress payments or grants received in connection with the asset. IAS 23 allows the **average carrying amount** of the asset during a period (including borrowing costs previously capitalised) to be used as a reasonable approximation of the expenditure to which the capitalisation rate is applied in the period. Presumably more exact calculations can be used.

**Activities necessary to prepare the asset for its intended sale or use** extend further than physical construction work. They encompass technical and administrative work prior to construction, eg obtaining permits. They do *not* include holding an asset when no production or development that changes the asset's condition is taking place, eg where land is held without any associated development activity.

### 5.3.4 Suspension of capitalisation

If active development is **interrupted for any extended periods**, capitalisation of borrowing costs should be suspended for those periods.

Suspension of capitalisation of borrowing costs is not necessary for **temporary delays** or for periods when substantial technical or administrative work is taking place.

### 5.3.5 Cessation of capitalisation

Once substantially all the activities necessary to prepare the qualifying asset for its intended use or sale are complete, then capitalisation of borrowing costs should cease. This will normally be when **physical construction of the asset is completed**, although minor modifications may still be outstanding.

The asset may be completed in **parts or stages**, where each part can be used while construction is still taking place on the other parts. Capitalisation of borrowing costs should cease for each part as it is completed. The example given by the standard is a business park consisting of several buildings.

### 5.3.6 Disclosure

The following should be disclosed in the financial statements in relation to borrowing costs.
(a)     Amount of borrowing costs **capitalised during the period**
(b)     **Capitalisation rate** used to determine the amount of borrowing costs eligible for capitalisation

# Chapter Roundup

- IAS 16 covers all aspects of accounting for property, plant and equipment. This represents the bulk of items which are **'tangible' non-current assets**.

- Where assets held by an entity have a **limited useful life** it is necessary to apportion the value of an asset over its useful life.

- It is common for entities to receive government grants for various purposes. The treatment of these is covered by IAS 20 *Accounting for government grants and disclosure of government assistance.*

- An entity may own land or a building **as an investment** rather than for use in the business. It may therefore generate cash flows largely independently of other assets which the entity holds. The treatment of investment property is covered by IAS 40.

- IAS 23 looks at the treatment of **borrowing costs**, particularly where the related borrowings are applied to the construction of certain assets. These are what are usually called 'self-constructed assets,' where an entity builds its own inventory or non-current assets over a substantial period of time.

# Quick Quiz

1   Define depreciation.
2   Which of the following elements can be included in the production cost of a non-current asset?
    (i)     Purchase price of raw materials
    (ii)    Architect's fees
    (iii)   Import duties
    (iv)    Installation costs
3   Market value can usually be taken as fair value.

    True    ☐

    False   ☐

4   Investment properties must always be shown at fair value.

    True    ☐

    False   ☐

5   What is the correct treatment for property being constructed for future use as investment property?

1    See Para 2.2
2    All of them.
3    True
4    False. The cost model may be used, provided it is used consistently.
5    It is treated as an investment property under IAS 40.

Now try the question below from the Exam Question Bank

| Number | Level | Marks | Time |
|--------|-------|-------|------|
| 5 | Examination | 10 | 18 mins |

# Intangible assets

| Topic list | Syllabus reference |
| --- | --- |
| 1 IAS 38 Intangible assets | C3 |
| 2 Research and development costs | C3 |
| 3 Goodwill (IFRS 3) | C3 |

## Introduction

We begin our examination of intangible non-current assets with a discussion of the IAS on the subject (**IAS 38**).

**Goodwill** and its treatment is a controversial area, as is the accounting for items similar to goodwill, such as brands. Goodwill is very important in **group accounts** and we will look at it again in Chapter 9.

# Study guide

| | | Intellectual level |
|---|---|---|
| C | **Financial statements** | |
| 3 | **Intangible assets** | |
| (a) | discuss the nature and accounting treatment of internally generated and purchased intangibles. | 2 |
| (b) | distinguish between goodwill and other intangible assets. | 2 |
| (c) | describe the criteria for the initial recognition and measurement of intangible assets. | 2 |
| (d) | describe the subsequent accounting treatment, including the principle of impairment tests in relation to goodwill. | 2 |
| (e) | indicate why the value of purchase consideration for an investment may be less than the value of the acquired identifiable net assets and how the difference should be accounted for. | 2 |
| (f) | describe and apply the requirements of relevant accounting standards to research and development expenditure. | 2 |

# 1 IAS 38 Intangible assets

**FAST FORWARD**

> Intangible assets are defined by IAS 38 as non-monetary assets without physical substance.

IAS 38 *Intangible assets* was originally published in September 1998. It has recently been revised to reflect changes introduced by IFRS 3 *Business combinations*.

## 1.1 The objectives of the standard

(a) To establish the criteria for when an intangible asset may or should be **recognised**
(b) To specify how intangible assets should be **measured**
(c) To specify the **disclosure requirements** for intangible assets

## 1.2 Definition of an intangible asset

The definition of an intangible asset is a key aspect of the standard, because the rules for deciding whether or not an intangible asset may be **recognised** in the accounts of an entity are based on the definition of what an intangible asset is.

**Key term**

> An **intangible asset** is an identifiable non-monetary asset without physical substance The asset must be:
>
> (a) controlled by the entity as a result of events in the past, and
> (b) something from which the entity expects future economic benefits to flow.

Examples of items that might be considered as intangible assets include computer software, patents, copyrights, motion picture films, customer lists, franchises and fishing rights. An item should not be recognised as an intangible asset, however, unless it **fully meets the definition** in the standard. The guidelines go into great detail on this matter.

## 1.3 Intangible asset: must be identifiable

An intangible asset must be identifiable in order to distinguish it from goodwill. With non-physical items, there may be a problem with **'identifiability'**.

(a)     If an intangible asset is **acquired separately through purchase**, there may be a transfer of a legal right that would help to make an asset identifiable.

(b)     An intangible asset may be identifiable if it is **separable**, ie if it could be rented or sold separately. However, 'separability' is not an essential feature of an intangible asset.

## 1.4 Intangible asset: control by the entity

Another element of the definition of an intangible asset is that it must be under the control of the entity as a result of a past event. The entity must therefore be able to enjoy the future economic benefits from the asset, and prevent the access of others to those benefits. A **legally enforceable right** is evidence of such control, but is not always a *necessary* condition.

(a)     Control over **technical knowledge or know-how** only exists if it is protected by a **legal right**.

(b)     The skill of employees, arising out of the benefits of **training costs**, are most unlikely to be recognisable as an intangible asset, because an entity does not control the future actions of its staff.

(c)     Similarly, **market share and customer loyalty** cannot normally be intangible assets, since an entity cannot control the actions of its customers.

## 1.5 Intangible asset: expected future economic benefits

An item can only be recognised as an intangible asset if economic benefits are expected to flow in the future from ownership of the asset. Economic benefits may come from the **sale** of products or services, or from a **reduction in expenditures** (cost savings).

An intangible asset, when recognised initially, must be measured at **cost**. It should be recognised if, and only if **both** the following occur.

(a)     It is probable that the **future economic benefits** that are attributable to the asset will **flow to the entity**.

(b)     The **cost can be measured reliably**.

Management has to exercise its judgement in assessing the degree of certainty attached to the flow of economic benefits to the entity. External evidence is best.

(a)     If an intangible asset is **acquired separately**, its cost can usually be measured reliably as its purchase price (including incidental costs of purchase such as legal fees, and any costs incurred in getting the asset ready for use).

(b)     When an intangible asset is acquired as **part of a business combination** (ie an acquisition or takeover), the cost of the intangible asset is its fair value at the date of the acquisition.

IFRS 3 explains that the fair value of intangible assets acquired in business combinations can normally be measured with sufficient reliability to be **recognised separately** from goodwill.

**Quoted market prices** in an active market provide the most reliable estimate of the fair value of an intangible asset. If no active market exists for an intangible asset, its fair value is the amount that the entity would have paid for the asset, at the acquisition date, in an orderly transaction between market participants, on the basis of the best information available. In determining this amount, an entity should consider the outcome of recent transactions for similar assets. There are techniques for estimating the fair values of unique intangible assets (such as brand names) and these may be used to measure an intangible asset acquired in a business combination.

In accordance with IAS 20, intangible assets acquired by way of government grant and the grant itself may be recorded initially either at cost (which may be zero) or fair value.

## 1.6 Exchanges of assets

If one intangible asset is exchanged for another, the cost of the intangible asset is measured at fair value unless:

(a)    The exchange transaction lacks commercial substance, or

(b)    The fair value of neither the asset received nor the asset given up can be measured reliably.

Otherwise, its cost is measured at the carrying amount of the asset given up.

## 1.7 Internally generated goodwill

**Rule to Learn**

Internally generated goodwill may **not** be recognised as an **asset**.

The standard deliberately precludes recognition of internally generated goodwill because it requires that, for initial recognition, the cost of the asset rather than its fair value should be capable of being measured reliably and that it should be identifiable and controlled. Thus you do not recognise an asset which is subjective and cannot be measured reliably.

# 2 Research and development costs

**FAST FORWARD**

Development costs can be recognised as an asset if they meet certain criteria.

## 2.1 Research

Research activities by definition do not meet the criteria for recognition under IAS 38. This is because, at the research stage of a project, it cannot be certain that future economic benefits will probably flow to the entity from the project. There is too much uncertainty about the likely success or otherwise of the project. **Research costs should therefore be written off as an expense as they are incurred.**

### Examples of research costs

(a)    Activities aimed at obtaining new knowledge

(b)    The search for, evaluation and final selection of, applications of research findings or other knowledge

(c)    The search for alternatives for materials, devices, products, processes, systems or services

(d)    The formulation, design evaluation and final selection of possible alternatives for new or improved materials, devices, products, systems or services

## 2.2 Development

Development costs may qualify for recognition as intangible assets provided that the following strict criteria can be demonstrated.

(a)    The technical feasibility of completing the intangible asset so that it will be available for use or sale.

(b)    Its intention to complete the intangible asset and use or sell it.

(c)    Its ability to use or sell the intangible asset.

(d)    How the intangible asset will generate probable future economic benefits. Among other things, the entity should demonstrate the existence of a market for the output of the intangible asset or the intangible asset itself or, if it is to be used internally, the usefulness of the intangible asset.

(e)    Its ability to measure the expenditure attributable to the intangible asset during its development reliably.

In contrast with research costs development costs are incurred at a later stage in a project, and the probability of success should be more apparent. Examples of development costs include the following.

(a)    The design, construction and testing of pre-production or pre-use prototypes and models

(b)    The design of tools, jigs, moulds and dies involving new technology

(c) The design, construction and operation of a pilot plant that is not of a scale economically feasible for commercial production

(d) The design, construction and testing of a chosen alternative for new or improved materials, devices, products, processes, systems or services

## 2.3 Other internally generated intangible assets

The standard prohibits the recognition of internally generated brands, mastheads, publishing titles and customer lists and similar items as intangible assets. These all fail to meet one or more (in some cases all) the definition and recognition criteria and in some cases are probably indistinguishable from internally generated goodwill.

## 2.4 Cost of an internally generated intangible asset

 **FAST FORWARD**

Intangible assets should be initially be measured at cost, but subsequently they can be carried at **cost** or at a **revalued amount**.

The costs allocated to an internally generated intangible asset should be only costs that can be directly attributed or allocated on a reasonable and consistent basis to creating, producing or preparing the asset for its intended use. The principles underlying the costs which may or may not be included are similar to those for other non-current assets and inventory.

The cost of an internally generated intangible asset is the sum of the expenditure incurred from the date when the intangible asset first meets the recognition criteria. If, as often happens, considerable costs have already been recognised as expenses before management could demonstrate that the criteria have been met, this earlier expenditure should not be retrospectively recognised at a later date as part of the cost of an intangible asset.

### Question

### Treatment

Doug Co is developing a new production process. During 20X3, expenditure incurred was $100,000, of which $90,000 was incurred before 1 December 20X3 and $10,000 between 1 December 20X3 and 31 December 20X3. Doug Co can demonstrate that, at 1 December 20X3, the production process met the criteria for recognition as an intangible asset. The recoverable amount of the know-how embodied in the process is estimated to be $50,000.

How should the expenditure be treated?

### Answer

At the end of 20X3, the production process is recognised as an intangible asset at a cost of $10,000. This is the expenditure incurred since the date when the recognition criteria were met, that is 1 December 20X3. The $90,000 expenditure incurred before 1 December 20X3 is expensed, because the recognition criteria were not met. It will never form part of the cost of the production process recognised in the statement of financial position.

## 2.5 Recognition of an expense

All expenditure related to an intangible which does not meet the criteria for recognition either as an identifiable intangible asset or as goodwill arising on an acquisition should be **expensed as incurred**. The IAS gives examples of such expenditure.

- Start up costs
- Training costs
- Advertising costs
- Business relocation costs

**Prepaid costs for services**, for example advertising or marketing costs for campaigns that have been prepared but not launched, can still be recognised as a **prepayment**.

## 2.6 Measurement of intangible assets subsequent to initial recognition

The standard allows two methods of valuation for intangible assets after they have been first recognised.

Applying the **cost model**, an intangible asset should be **carried at its cost**, less any accumulated amortisation and less any accumulated impairment losses.

The **revaluation model** allows an intangible asset to be carried at a revalued amount, which is its **fair value** at the date of revaluation, less any subsequent accumulated amortisation and any subsequent accumulated impairment losses.

(a)     The fair value must be able to be measured reliably with reference to an **active market** in that type of asset.

(b)     The **entire class** of intangible assets of that type must be revalued at the same time (to prevent selective revaluations).

(c)     If an intangible asset in a class of revalued intangible assets cannot be revalued because there is **no active market** for this asset, the asset should be carried at its **cost less any accumulated amortisation and impairment losses**.

(d)     Revaluations should be made with such **regularity** that the carrying amount does not differ from that which would be determined using fair value at the end of the reporting period.

**Point to note**

> This treatment is not available for the initial recognition of intangible assets. This is because the cost of the asset must be reliably measured.

The guidelines state that there will not usually be an active market in an intangible asset; therefore the revaluation model will usually not be available. For example, although copyrights, publishing rights and film rights can be sold, each has a unique sale value. In such cases, revaluation to fair value would be inappropriate. A fair value might be obtainable however for assets such as fishing rights or quotas or taxi cab licences.

Where an intangible asset is revalued upwards to a fair value, the amount of the revaluation should be credited directly to equity under the heading of a **revaluation surplus**.

However, if a revaluation surplus is a **reversal of a revaluation decrease** that was previously charged against income, the increase can be recognised as income.

Where the carrying amount of an intangible asset is revalued downwards, the amount of the **downward revaluation** should be charged as an expense against income, unless the asset has previously been revalued upwards. A revaluation decrease should be first charged against any previous revaluation surplus in respect of that asset.

| Question | Downward revaluation |
| --- | --- |

An intangible asset is measured by a company at fair value. The asset was revalued by $400 in 20X3, and there is a revaluation surplus of $400 in the statement of financial position. At the end of 20X4, the asset is valued again, and a downward valuation of $500 is required.

*Required*

State the accounting treatment for the downward revaluation.

Answer

In this example, the downward valuation of $500 can first be set against the revaluation surplus of $400. The revaluation surplus will be reduced to $nil and a charge of $100 made as an expense in 20X4.

When the revaluation model is used, and an intangible asset is revalued upwards, the cumulative revaluation **surplus may be transferred to retained earnings** when the surplus is eventually realised. The surplus would be realised when the asset is disposed of. However, the surplus may also be realised over time as the **asset is used** by the entity. The amount of the surplus realised each year is the difference between the amortisation charge for the asset based on the revalued amount of the asset, and the amortisation that would be charged on the basis of the asset's historical cost. The realised surplus in such case should be transferred from revaluation surplus directly to retained earnings, and should not be taken through profit or loss.

## 2.7 Useful life

An entity should assess the useful life of an intangible asset, which may be **finite or indefinite**. An intangible asset has an indefinite useful life when there is **no foreseeable limit** to the period over which the asset is expected to generate net cash inflows for the entity.

Many factors are considered in determining the useful life of an intangible asset, including: expected usage; typical product life cycles; technical, technological, commercial or other types of obsolescence; the stability of the industry; expected actions by competitors; the level of maintenance expenditure required; and legal or similar limits on the use of the asset, such as the expiry dates of related leases. Computer software and many other intangible assets normally have short lives because they are susceptible to technological obsolescence. However, uncertainty does not justify choosing a life that is unrealistically short.

The useful life of an intangible asset that arises from **contractual or other legal rights** should not exceed the period of the rights, but may be shorter depending on the period over which the entity expects to use the asset.

## 2.8 Amortisation period and amortisation method

An intangible asset with a finite useful life should be amortised over its **expected useful life**.

(a) Amortisation should start when the asset is **available for use**.

(b) Amortisation should cease at the earlier of the date that the asset is classified **as held for sale** in accordance with IFRS 5 *Non-current assets held for sale and discontinued operations* and the date that the asset is **derecognised**.

(c) The amortisation method used should reflect the **pattern in which the asset's future economic benefits are consumed**. If such a pattern cannot be predicted reliably, the straight-line method should be used.

(d) The amortisation charge for each period should normally be recognised **in profit or loss**.

The **residual value** of an intangible asset with a finite useful life is **assumed to be zero** unless a third party is committed to buying the intangible asset at the end of its useful life or unless there is an active market for that type of asset (so that its expected residual value can be measured) and it is probable that there will be a market for the asset at the end of its useful life.

The amortisation period and the amortisation method used for an intangible asset with a finite useful life should be **reviewed at each financial year-end**.

## 2.9 Intangible assets with indefinite useful lives

An intangible asset with an indefinite useful life **should not be amortised**. (IAS 36 requires that such an asset is tested for impairment at least annually.)

The useful life of an intangible asset that is not being amortised should be **reviewed each year** to determine whether it is still appropriate to assess its useful life as indefinite. Reassessing the useful life of an intangible asset as finite rather than indefinite is an indicator that the asset may be impaired and therefore it should be tested for impairment.

Intangible assets could appear as part of the accounts preparation question or in Question 4 or 5. Make sure you know the capitalisation criteria.

## Question

Intangible asset

It may be difficult to establish the useful life of an intangible asset, and judgement will be needed. Consider how to determine the useful life of a *purchased* brand name.

## Answer

Factors to consider would include the following.

(a)   Legal protection of the brand name and the control of the entity over the (illegal) use by others of the brand name (ie control over pirating)

(b)   Age of the brand name

(c)   Status or position of the brand in its particular market

(d)   Ability of the management of the entity to manage the brand name and to measure activities that support the brand name (eg advertising and PR activities)

(e)   Stability and geographical spread of the market in which the branded products are sold

(f)   Pattern of benefits that the brand name is expected to generate over time

(g)   Intention of the entity to use and promote the brand name over time (as evidenced perhaps by a business plan in which there will be substantial expenditure to promote the brand name)

## 2.10 Disposals/retirements of intangible assets

An intangible asset should be eliminated from the statement of financial position when it is disposed of or when there is no further expected economic benefit from its future use. On disposal the gain or loss arising from the **difference between the net disposal proceeds and the carrying amount** of the asset should be taken to profit or loss as a gain or loss on disposal (ie treated as income or expense).

## 2.11 Section summary

- An intangible asset should be recognised if, and only if, it is probable that future economic benefits will flow to the entity and the cost of the asset can be measured reliably.
- An asset is initially recognised at cost and subsequently carried either at cost or revalued amount.
- Costs that do not meet the recognition criteria should be expensed as incurred.
- An intangible asset with a finite useful life should be amortised over its useful life. An intangible asset with an indefinite useful life should not be amortised.

## Question

R&D

As an aid to your revision, list the examples given in IAS 38 of activities that might be included in either research or development.

## Answer

IAS 38 gives these examples.

*Research*

- Activities aimed at obtaining new knowledge

- The search for applications of research findings or other knowledge
- The search for product or process alternatives
- The formulation and design of possible new or improved product or process alternatives

*Development*

- The evaluation of product or process alternatives
- The design, construction and testing of pre-production prototypes and models
- The design of tools, jigs, moulds and dies involving new technology
- The design, construction and operation of a pilot plant that is not of a scale economically feasible for commercial production

# 3 Goodwill (IFRS 3)

**FAST FORWARD**

Purchased goodwill arising on consolidation is retained in the statement of financial position as an intangible asset under IFRS 3. It must then be reviewed annually for impairment.

## 3.1 What is goodwill?

Goodwill is **created by good relationships** between a business and its customers.

(a)    By building up a **reputation** (by word of mouth perhaps) for high quality products or high standards of service

(b)    By **responding promptly and helpfully** to queries and complaints from customers

(c)    Through the **personality of the staff** and their attitudes to customers

The value of goodwill to a business might be considerable. However, goodwill is not usually valued in the accounts of a business at all, and we should not normally expect to find an amount for goodwill in its statement of financial position. For example, the welcoming smile of the bar staff may contribute more to a bar's profits than the fact that a new electronic cash register has recently been acquired. Even so, whereas the cash register will be recorded in the accounts as a non-current asset, the value of staff would be ignored for accounting purposes.

On reflection, we might agree with this omission of goodwill from the accounts of a business.

(a)    The goodwill is **inherent** in the business but it has not been paid for, and it does not have an 'objective' value. We can guess at what such goodwill is worth, but such guesswork would be a matter of individual opinion, and not based on hard facts.

(b)    Goodwill **changes** from day to day. One act of bad customer relations might damage goodwill and one act of good relations might improve it. Staff with a favourable personality might retire or leave to find another job, to be replaced by staff who need time to find their feet in the job, etc. Since goodwill is continually changing in value, it cannot realistically be recorded in the accounts of the business.

## 3.2 Purchased goodwill

There is one exception to the general rule that goodwill has no objective valuation. This is **when a business is sold**. People wishing to set up in business have a choice of how to do it – they can either buy their own long-term assets and inventory and set up their business from scratch, or they can buy up an existing business from a proprietor willing to sell it. When a buyer purchases an existing business, he will have to purchase not only its long-term assets and inventory (and perhaps take over its accounts payable and receivable too) but also the goodwill of the business.

**FAST FORWARD**

Purchased goodwill is shown in the statement of financial position because it has been paid for. It has no tangible substance, and so it is an **intangible non-current asset**

## 3.3 How is the value of purchased goodwill decided?

When a business is sold, there is likely to be some purchased goodwill in the selling price. But **how is the amount of this purchased goodwill decided**?

This is not really a problem for accountants, who must simply record the goodwill in the accounts of the new business. The value of the goodwill is a **matter for the purchaser and seller to agree upon in fixing the purchase/sale price**. However, two methods of valuation are worth mentioning here.

(a) The seller and buyer agree on a price for the business **without specifically quantifying the goodwill**. The purchased goodwill will then be the difference between the price agreed and the value of the identifiable net assets in the books of the new business.

(b) However, the calculation of goodwill often precedes the fixing of the purchase price and becomes a **central element of negotiation**. There are many ways of arriving at a value for goodwill and most of them are related to the profit record of the business in question.

No matter how goodwill is calculated within the total agreed purchase price, the goodwill shown by the purchaser in his accounts will be **the difference between the purchase consideration and his own valuation of the net assets acquired**. If A values his net assets at $40,000, goodwill is agreed at $21,000 and B agrees to pay $61,000 for the business but values the net assets at only $38,000, then the goodwill in B's books will be $61,000 – $38,000 = $23,000.

## 3.4 IFRS 3 Business combinations

IFRS 3 covers the accounting treatment of goodwill acquired in a business combination.

**Key terms**

> **Goodwill**. Future economic benefits arising from assets that are not capable of being individually identified and separately recognised.
> *(IFRS 3)*

Goodwill acquired in a business combination is **recognised as an asset** and is initially measured at **cost**. Cost is the excess of the cost of the combination over the acquirer's interest in the net fair value of the acquiree's identifiable assets, liabilities and contingent liabilities.

After initial recognition goodwill acquired in a business combination is measured **at cost less any accumulated impairment losses**. It is **not amortised**. Instead it is tested for impairment at least annually, in accordance with IAS 36 *Impairment of assets*.

**Negative goodwill** arises when the acquirer's interest in the net fair value of the acquiree's identifiable assets, liabilities and contingent liabilities exceeds the cost of the business combination. IFRS 3 refers to negative goodwill as the 'excess of acquirer's interest in the net fair value of acquiree's identifiable assets, liabilities and contingent liabilities over cost'.

Negative goodwill can arise as the result of **errors** in measuring the fair value of either the cost of the combination or the acquiree's identifiable net assets. It can also arise as the result of a **bargain purchase**.

Where there is negative goodwill, an entity should first **reassess** the amounts at which it has measured both the cost of the combination and the acquiree's identifiable net assets. This exercise should identify any errors.

Any negative goodwill remaining should be **recognised** immediately in profit or loss.

IFRS 3 requires extensive **disclosures**. These include a **reconciliation** of the carrying amount of goodwill at the beginning and end of the period, showing separately:

(a) The gross amount and accumulated impairment losses at the beginning of the period
(b) Additional goodwill recognised during the period
(c) Impairment losses recognised during the period
(d) Net exchange differences arising during the period, and
(e) The gross amount and accumulated impairment losses at the end of the period

## Question

What are the main characteristics of goodwill which distinguish it from other intangible non-current assets? To what extent do you consider that these characteristics should affect the accounting treatment of goodwill? State your reasons.

## Answer

Goodwill may be distinguished from other intangible non-current assets by reference to the following characteristics.

(a) It is incapable of realisation separately from the business as a whole.

(b) Its value has no reliable or predictable relationship to any costs which may have been incurred.

(c) Its value arises from various intangible factors such as skilled employees, effective advertising or a strategic location. These indirect factors cannot be valued.

(d) The value of goodwill may fluctuate widely according to internal and external circumstances over relatively short periods of time.

(e) The assessment of the value of goodwill is highly subjective.

It could be argued that, because goodwill is so different from other intangible non-current assets it does not make sense to account for it in the same way. Thus the capitalisation and amortisation treatment would not be acceptable. Furthermore, because goodwill is so difficult to value, any valuation may be misleading, and it is best eliminated from the statement of financial position altogether. However, there are strong arguments for treating it like any other intangible non-current asset. This issue remains controversial.

# Chapter Roundup

- Intangible assets are defined by IAS 38 as non-monetary assets without physical substance.

- Development costs can be recognised as an asset if they meet certain criteria.

- Intangible assets should initially be measured at cost, but subsequently they can be carried at **cost** or at a **revalued amount**.

- Purchased goodwill arising on consolidation is retained in the statement of financial position as an intangible asset under IFRS 3. It must then be reviewed annually for impairment.

- Purchased goodwill is shown in the statement of financial position because it has been paid for. It has no tangible substance and so it is an **intangible non-current asset**.

# Quick Quiz

1   Intangible assets can only be recognised in a company's accounts if:
    •   It is probable that ........................... will flow to the entity
    •   The cost can be .............................

2   What are the criteria which must be met before development expenditure can be deferred?

3   Start up costs must be expensed.

    True  ☐

    False ☐

4   Peggy buys Phil's business for $30,000. The business assets are a bar valued at $20,000, inventories at $3,000 and receivables of $3,000. How much is goodwill valued at?

5   What method of accounting for goodwill arising on consolidation is required by IFRS 3?

6   How should negative goodwill be accounted for under IFRS 3?

# Answers to Quick Quiz

1   Future economic benefits. Measured reliably.

2   See Para 2.2

3   True

4   $30,000 – $20,000 – $3,000 – $3,000 = $4,000

5   Cost less impairment losses

6   Recognised in profit or loss immediately

Now try the question below from the Exam Question Bank

| Number | Level | Marks | Time |
|--------|-------|-------|------|
| 6 | Introductory | 10 | 18 mins |

# Impairment
# of assets

| Topic list | Syllabus reference |
|---|---|
| 1 IAS 36 Impairment of assets | C8 |
| 2 Cash generating units | C8 |
| 3 Goodwill and the impairment of assets | C8 |
| 4 Accounting treatment of an impairment loss | C8 |

## Introduction

IAS 36 is an important standard. Impairment rules apply to both tangible and intangible assets.

# Study guide

| | | Intellectual level |
|---|---|---|
| 8 | **Impairment of assets** | |
| (a) | define an impairment loss. | 2 |
| (b) | identify the circumstances that may indicate impairments to assets. | 2 |
| (c) | describe what is meant by a cash generating unit. | 2 |
| (d) | state the basis on which impairment losses should be allocated, and allocate an impairment loss to the assets of a cash generating unit. | 2 |

# 1 IAS 36 Impairment of assets

Impairment is determined by comparing the carrying amount of the asset with its recoverable amount. This is the higher of its **fair value less costs to sell** and its **value in use**.

There is an established principle that assets should not be carried at above their recoverable amount. An entity should write down the carrying value of an asset to its recoverable amount if the carrying value of an asset is not recoverable in full. IAS 36 puts in place a detailed methodology for carrying out impairment reviews and related accounting treatments and disclosures.

## 1.1 Scope

IAS 36 applies to all tangible, intangible and financial assets except inventories, assets arising from construction contracts, deferred tax assets, assets arising under IAS 19 *Employee benefits* and financial assets within the scope of IAS 32 *Financial instruments: presentation.* This is because those IASs already have rules for recognising and measuring impairment. Note also that IAS 36 does not apply to non-current assets held for sale, which are dealt with under IFRS 5 *Non-current assets held for sale and discontinued operations*

**Key terms**

- **Impairment**: a fall in the value of an asset, so that its 'recoverable amount' is now less than its carrying value in the statement of financial position.
- **Carrying amount**: is the net value at which the asset is included in the statement of financial position (ie after deducting accumulated depreciation and any impairment losses).

*(IAS 36)*

The basic principle underlying IAS 36 is relatively straightforward. If an asset's value in the accounts is higher than its realistic value, measured as its 'recoverable amount', the asset is judged to have suffered an impairment loss. It should therefore be reduced in value, by the amount of the **impairment loss**. The amount of the impairment loss should be **written off against profit** immediately.

The main accounting issues to consider are therefore as follows.

(a) How is it possible to **identify when** an impairment loss may have occurred?
(b) How should the **recoverable amount** of the asset be measured?
(c) How should an 'impairment loss' be **reported in the accounts**?

## 1.2 Identifying a potentially impaired asset

An entity should assess at the end of each reporting period whether there are any indications of impairment to any assets. The concept of **materiality** applies, and only material impairment needs to be identified.

If there are indications of possible impairment, the entity is required to make a formal estimate of the **recoverable amount** of the assets concerned.

IAS 36 suggests how **indications of a possible impairment** of assets might be recognised. The suggestions are based largely on common sense.

(a) **External sources of information**

  (i) A fall in the asset's market value that is more significant than would normally be expected from passage of time over normal use.

  (ii) A significant change in the technological, market, legal or economic environment of the business in which the assets are employed.

  (iii) An increase in market interest rates or market rates of return on investments likely to affect the discount rate used in calculating value in use.

  (iv) The carrying amount of the entity's net assets being more than its market capitalisation.

(b) **Internal sources of information**: evidence of obsolescence or physical damage, adverse changes in the use to which the asset is put, or the asset's economic performance

Even if there are no indications of impairment, the following assets must **always** be tested for impairment annually.

(a) An intangible asset with an **indefinite useful life**
(b) **Goodwill** acquired in a business combination

## 1.3 Measuring the recoverable amount of the asset

What is an asset's recoverable amount?

**Key term**

> The **recoverable amount of an asset** should be measured as the *higher value* of:
>
> (a) the asset's fair value less costs to sell; and
> (b) its value in use.                                                                    *(IAS 36)*

An asset's fair value less costs to sell is the amount net of selling costs that could be obtained from the sale of the asset. Selling costs include sales transaction costs, such as legal expenses.

(a) If there is **an active market** in the asset, the net selling price should be based on the **market value**, or on the price of recent transactions in similar assets.

(b) If there is **no active market** in the assets it might be possible to **estimate** a net selling price using best estimates of what 'knowledgeable, willing parties' might pay in an arm's length transaction.

Net selling price **cannot** be reduced, however, by including within selling costs any **restructuring or reorganisation expenses**, or any costs that have already been recognised in the accounts as liabilities.

The concept of 'value in use' is very important.

**Key term**

> The **value in use** of an asset is measured as the present value of estimated future cash flows (inflows minus outflows) generated by the asset, including its estimated net disposal value (if any) at the end of its expected useful life.

## 1.4 Recognition and measurement of an impairment loss

The rule for assets at historical cost is:

**Rule to learn**

If the recoverable amount of an asset is lower than the carrying amount, the carrying amount should be reduced by the difference (ie the impairment loss) which should be charged as an expense in profit or loss.

The rule for assets held at a revalued amount (such as property revalued under IAS 16) is:

In practice this means:

- To the extent that there is a revaluation surplus held in respect of the asset, the impairment loss should be charged to revaluation surplus.
- Any excess should be charged to profit or loss.

# 2 Cash generating units

When it is not possible to calculate the recoverable amount of a single asset, then that of its **cash generating unit** should be measured instead.

## 2.1 Use of cash-generating unit

The IAS goes into quite a large amount of detail about the important concept of cash generating units. As a basic rule, the recoverable amount of an asset should be calculated for the **asset individually**. However, there will be occasions when it is not possible to estimate such a value for an individual asset, particularly in the calculation of value in use. This is because cash inflows and outflows cannot be attributed to the individual asset.

If it is not possible to calculate the recoverable amount for an individual asset, the recoverable amount of the asset's cash-generating unit should be measured instead.

**Key term**

A **cash-generating unit** is the smallest identifiable group of assets for which independent cash flows can be identified and measured.

## Question

Cash-generating unit I

Can you think of some examples of how a cash-generating unit would be identified?

## Answer

Here are two possibilities.

(a) A mining company owns a private railway that it uses to transport output from one of its mines. The railway now has no market value other than as scrap, and it is impossible to identify any separate cash inflows with the use of the railway itself. Consequently, if the mining company suspects an impairment in the value of the railway, it should treat the mine as a whole as a cash generating unit, and measure the recoverable amount of the mine as a whole.

(b) A bus company has an arrangement with a town's authorities to run a bus service on four routes in the town. Separately identifiable assets are allocated to each of the bus routes, and cash inflows and outflows can be attributed to each individual route. Three routes are running at a profit and one is running at a loss. The bus company suspects that there is an impairment of assets on the loss-making route. However, the company will be unable to close the loss-making route, because it is under an obligation to operate all four routes, as part of its contract with the local authority. Consequently, the company should treat all four bus routes together as a cash generating unit, and calculate the recoverable amount for the unit as a whole.

Minimart belongs to a retail store chain Maximart. Minimart makes all its retail purchases through Maximart's purchasing centre. Pricing, marketing, advertising and human resources policies (except for hiring Minimart's cashiers and salesmen) are decided by Maximart. Maximart also owns 5 other stores in the same city as Minimart (although in different neighbourhoods) and 20 other stores in other cities. All stores are managed in the same way as Minimart. Minimart and 4 other stores were purchased 5 years ago and goodwill was recognised.

What is the cash-generating unit for Minimart?

### Answer

In identifying Minimart's cash-generating unit, an entity considers whether, for example:

(a)   Internal management reporting is organised to measure performance on a store-by-store basis.
(b)   The business is run on a store-by-store profit basis or on a region/city basis.

All Maximart's stores are in different neighbourhoods and probably have different customer bases. So, although Minimart is managed at a corporate level, Minimart generates cash inflows that are largely independent from those of Maximart's other stores. Therefore, it is likely that Minimart is a cash-generating unit.

---

If an active market exists for the output produced by the asset or a group of assets, this asset or group should be identified as a cash generating unit, even if some or all of the output is used internally.

Cash-generating units should be identified consistently from period to period for the same type of asset unless a change is justified.

The group of net assets less liabilities that are considered for impairment should be the same as those considered in the calculation of the recoverable amount. (For the treatment of goodwill and corporate assets see below.)

## 2.2 Example: Recoverable amount and carrying amount

Fourways Co is made up of four cash generating units. All four units are being tested for impairment. Assets and liabilities will be allocated to them as follows:

(a)   Property, plant and equipment and separate intangibles will be allocated to the cash-generating units as far as possible.
(b)   Current assets such as inventories, receivables and prepayments will be allocated to the relevant cash-generating units.
(c)   Liabilities (eg payables) will be deducted from the net assets of the relevant cash-generating units.
(d)   The net figure for each cash-generating unit resulting from this exercise will be compared to the relevant recoverable amount, computed on the same basis.

# 3 Goodwill and the impairment of assets

## 3.1 Allocating goodwill to cash-generating units

Goodwill acquired in a business combination does not generate cash flows independently of other assets. It must be **allocated** to each of the acquirer's **cash-generating units** (or groups of cash-generating units) that are expected to benefit from the synergies of the combination. Each unit to which the goodwill is so allocated should:

(a) Represent the **lowest level** within the entity at which the goodwill is monitored for internal management purposes

(b) Not be **larger than a reporting segment** determined in accordance with IFRS 8 *Operating segments*.

It may be impracticable to complete the allocation of goodwill before the first reporting date after a business combination, particularly if the acquirer is accounting for the combination for the first time using provisional values. The initial allocation of goodwill must be completed before the end of the first reporting period after the acquisition date.

## 3.2 Testing cash-generating units with goodwill for impairment

A cash-generating unit to which goodwill has been allocated is tested for impairment annually. The **carrying amount** of the unit, including goodwill, is **compared with the recoverable amount**. If the carrying amount of the unit exceeds the recoverable amount, the entity must recognise an impairment loss.

The annual impairment test may be performed at any time during an accounting period, but must be performed at the **same time every year**.

## 3.3 Example: allocation of impairment loss

A cash-generating unit comprises the following:

|  | $m |
| --- | --- |
| Building | 30 |
| Plant and equipment | 6 |
| Goodwill | 10 |
| Current assets | 20 |
|  | 66 |

Following a recession, an impairment review has estimated the recoverable amount of the cash-generating unit to be $50m.

How do we allocate the impairment loss?

The loss will be applied first against the goodwill and then against the tangible non-current assets on a pro-rata basis.

|  | Carrying amount | Impairment loss | Carrying amount post- impairment |
| --- | --- | --- | --- |
|  | $m | $ | $ |
| Building | 30 | (5) | 25 |
| Plant and equipment | 6 | (1) | 5 |
| Goodwill | 10 | (10) | – |
| Current assets | 20 | – | 20 |
|  | 66 | (16) | 50 |

# 4 Accounting treatment of an impairment loss

If, and only if, the recoverable amount of an asset is less than its carrying amount in the statement of financial position, an impairment loss has occurred. This loss should be **recognised immediately**.

(a) The asset's **carrying amount** should be reduced to its recoverable amount in the statement of financial position.

(b) The **impairment loss** should be recognised immediately in profit or loss (unless the asset has been revalued in which case the loss is treated as a revaluation decrease).

After reducing an asset to its recoverable amount, the **depreciation charge** on the asset should then be based on its new carrying amount, its estimated residual value (if any) and its estimated remaining useful life.

An impairment loss should be recognised for a **cash - generating unit** if (and only if) the recoverable amount for the cash- generating unit is less than the carrying amount in the statement of financial position for all the assets in the unit. When an impairment loss is recognised for a cash- generating unit, the loss should be allocated between the assets in the unit in the following order.

(a) First, to any assets that are obviously damaged or destroyed
(b) Next, to the **goodwill** allocated to the cash generating unit
(c) Then to all other assets in the cash-generating unit, on a **pro rata basis**

In allocating an impairment loss, the carrying amount of an asset should not be reduced below the highest of:

(a) Its fair value less costs to sell
(b) Its value in use (if determinable)
(c) Zero

Any remaining amount of an impairment loss should be recognised as a liability if required by other IASs.

## 4.1 Example 1: impairment loss

A company that extracts natural gas and oil has a drilling platform in the Caspian Sea. It is required by legislation of the country concerned to remove and dismantle the platform at the end of its useful life. Accordingly, the company has included an amount in its accounts for removal and dismantling costs, and is depreciating this amount over the platform's expected life.

The company is carrying out an exercise to establish whether there has been an impairment of the platform.

(a) Its carrying amount in the statement of financial position is $3m.
(b) The company has received an offer of $2.8m for the platform from another oil company. The bidder would take over the responsibility (and costs) for dismantling and removing the platform at the end of its life.
(c) The present value of the estimated cash flows from the platform's continued use is $3.3m (before adjusting for dismantling costs).
(d) The carrying amount in the statement of financial position for the provision for dismantling and removal is currently $0.6m.

What should be the value of the drilling platform in the statement of financial position, and what, if anything, is the impairment loss?

## Solution

| | | |
|---|---|---|
| Fair value less costs to sell | = | $2.8m |
| Value in use | = | PV of cash flows from use less the carrying amount of the provision/liability = $3.3m – $0.6m = $2.7m |
| Recoverable amount | = | Higher of these two amounts, ie $2.8m |
| Carrying value | = | $3m |
| Impairment loss | = | $0.2m |

The carrying value should be reduced to $2.8m

## 4.2 Example 2: impairment loss

A company has acquired another business for $4.5m: tangible assets are valued at $4.0m and goodwill at $0.5m.

An asset with a carrying value of $1m is destroyed in a terrorist attack. The asset was not insured. The loss of the asset, without insurance, has prompted the company to assess whether there has been an impairment of assets in the acquired business and what the amount of any such loss is.

The recoverable amount of the business (a single cash generating unit) is measured as $3.1m.

## Solution

There has been an impairment loss of $1.4m ($4.5m – $3.1m).

The impairment loss will be recognised in profit or loss. The loss will be allocated between the assets in the cash generating unit as follows.

(a) A loss of $1m can be attributed directly to the uninsured asset that has been destroyed.
(b) The remaining loss of $0.4m should be allocated to goodwill.

The carrying value of the assets will now be $3m for tangible assets and $0.1m for goodwill.

## 4.3 Reversal of an impairment loss

The annual assessment to determine whether there may have been some impairment should be **applied to all assets**, including assets that have already been impaired in the past.

In some cases, the recoverable amount of an asset that has previously been impaired might turn out to be **higher** than the asset's current carrying value. In other words, there might have been a reversal of some of the previous impairment loss.

(a) The reversal of the impairment loss should be **recognised immediately** as income in profit or loss.
(b) The carrying amount of the asset should be increased to its **new recoverable amount**.

An exception to this rule is for **goodwill**. An impairment loss for goodwill should not be reversed in a subsequent period.

| Question | Reversal of impairment loss |
| --- | --- |

A cash generating unit comprising a factory, plant and equipment etc and associated purchased goodwill becomes impaired because the product it makes is overtaken by a technologically more advanced model produced by a competitor. The recoverable amount of the cash generating unit falls to $60m, resulting in an impairment loss of $80m, allocated as follows.

|  | Carrying amounts before impairment | Carrying amounts after impairment |
| --- | --- | --- |
|  | $m | $m |
| Goodwill | 40 | – |
| Patent (with no market value) | 20 | – |
| Tangible non-current assets (market value $60m) | 80 | 60 |
| Total | 140 | 60 |

After three years, the entity makes a technological breakthrough of its own, and the recoverable amount of the cash generating unit increases to $90m. The carrying amount of the tangible non-current assets had the impairment not occurred would have been $70m.

*Required*

Calculate the reversal of the impairment loss.

Answer

The reversal of the impairment loss is recognised to the extent that it increases the carrying amount of the tangible non-current assets to what it would have been had the impairment not taken place, ie a reversal of the impairment loss of $10m is recognised and the tangible non-current assets written back to $70m. Reversal of the impairment is not recognised in relation to the goodwill and patent because the effect of the external event that caused the original impairment has not reversed – the original product is still overtaken by a more advanced model.

## 4.4 Summary

The main aspects of IAS 36 to consider are:

- **Indications** of impairment of assets
- **Measuring recoverable amount**, as net selling price or value in use
- **Measuring value in use**
- **Cash generating units**
- **Accounting treatment** of an impairment loss, for individual assets and cash generating units
- **Reversal** of an impairment loss

# Chapter Roundup

- Impairment is determined by comparing the carrying amount of the asset with its **recoverable amount**. This is the higher of its **fair value less costs to sell** and its **value in use**.

- When it is not possible to calculate the recoverable amount of a single asset, then that of its **cash-generating unit** should be measured instead.

# Quick Quiz

1   Define **recoverable amount** of an asset.
2   How is an impairment loss on a revalued asset treated?
3   How is an impairment loss allocated to the assets in a cash-generating unit?

# Answers to Quick Quiz

1   Higher of **fair value less costs to sell** and **value in use**.
2   As a revaluation decrease.
3   In the following order: a) against any damaged or destroyed assets; then b) against goodwill; then c) against all other assets on a *pro rata* basis.

Now try the questions below from the Exam Question Bank

| Number | Level | Marks | Time |
|--------|-------|-------|------|
| 7 | Examination | 15 | 27 mins |

# 7

# Reporting financial performance

| Topic list | Syllabus reference |
|---|---|
| 1 IAS 8 Accounting policies, changes in accounting estimates and errors | A2 |
| 2 Changes in accounting polices | A2 |
| 3 Errors | A2 |
| 4 IFRS 5 Non-current assets held for sale and discontinued operations | C11 |
| 5 IAS 10 Events after the reporting period | C11 |

## Introduction

**IAS 8** deals with accounting policies. It also looks at certain circumstances and transactions which require different treatment to normal profit or loss items.

**IFRS 5** on assets held for sale and discontinued operations is an important standard which gives users additional information regarding the sources of the entity's profit and losses.

**IAS 10** sets out the treatment for events occurring after the accounting year end.

# Study guide

| | | Intellectual level |
|---|---|---|
| **A2** | **A conceptual framework for financial reporting** | |
| (d) | distinguish between changes in accounting policies and changes in accounting estimates and describe how accounting standards apply the principle of comparability where an entity changes its accounting policies. | 2 |
| (e) | recognise and account for changes in accounting policies and the correction of prior period errors. | 2 |
| **C11** | **Financial statements** | |
| (a) | discuss the importance of identifying and reporting the results of discontinued operations. | 2 |
| (b) | define and account for non-current assets held for sale and discontinued operations. | 2 |
| (c) | indicate the circumstances where separate disclosure of material items of income and expense is required. | 2 |
| (g) | Events after the reporting date: | |
| | i) distinguish between and account for adjusting and non-adjusting events after the reporting date | |
| | ii) identify items requiring separate disclosure, including their accounting treatment and required disclosures | 2 |

# 1 IAS 8 Accounting policies, changes in accounting estimates and errors

**FAST FORWARD**

IAS 8 deals with changes in accounting estimates, changes in accounting policies and errors.

## 1.1 Definitions

The following definitions are given in the standard.

**Key terms**

- **Accounting policies** are the specific principles, bases, conventions, rules and practices adopted by an entity in preparing and presenting financial statements.

- A **change in accounting estimate** is an adjustment of the carrying amount of an asset or a liability or the amount of the periodic consumption of an asset, that results from the assessment of the present status of, and expected future benefits and obligations associated with, assets and liabilities. Changes in accounting estimates result from new information or new developments and, accordingly, are not corrections of errors.

- **Material**: Omissions or misstatements of items are material if they could, individually or collectively, influence the economic decisions that users make on the basis of the financial statements.

- **Prior period errors** are omissions from, and misstatements in, the entity's financial statements for one or more prior periods arising from a failure to use, or misuse of, reliable information that:
  - Was available when financial statements for those periods were authorised for issue, and
  - Could reasonably be expected to have been obtained and taken into account in the preparation and presentation of those financial statements.

Such errors include the effects of mathematical mistakes, mistakes in applying accounting policies, oversights or misinterpretations of facts, and fraud.

- **Retrospective application** is applying a new accounting policy to transactions, other events and conditions as if that policy had always been applied.

- **Retrospective restatement** is correcting the recognition, measurement and disclosure of amounts of elements of financial statements as if a prior period error had never occurred.

- **Prospective application** of a change in accounting policy and of recognising the effect of a change in an accounting estimate, respectively, are:

    - Applying the new accounting policy to transactions, other events and conditions occurring after the date as at which the policy is changed; and
    - Recognising the effect of the change in the accounting estimate in the current and future periods affected by the change.

- **Impracticable.** Applying a requirement is impracticable when the entity cannot apply it after making every reasonable effort to do so. It is impracticable to apply a change in an accounting policy retrospectively or to make a retrospective restatement to correct an error if one of the following apply.

    - The effects of the retrospective application or retrospective restatement are not determinable.
    - The retrospective application or retrospective restatement requires assumptions about what management's intent would have been in that period.
    - The retrospective application or retrospective restatement requires significant estimates of amounts and it is impossible to distinguish objectively information about those estimates that: provides evidence of circumstances that existed on the date(s) at which those amounts are to be recognised, measured or disclosed; and would have been available when the financial statements for that prior period were authorised for issue, from other information.

(IAS 8)

## 1.2 Accounting policies

Accounting policies are determined by **applying the relevant IAS, IFRS or IFRS Interpretation** and considering any relevant Implementation Guidance issued by the IASB for that IFRS/Interpretation.

Where there is no applicable IFRS or Interpretation management should use its **judgement** in developing and applying an accounting policy that results in information that is **relevant** and **reliable**. Management should refer to:

(a)  The requirements and guidance in IFRSs and IFRICs dealing with **similar** and **related issues**

(b)  The definitions, recognition criteria and measurement concepts for assets, liabilities and expenses in the **Conceptual Framework**

Management may also consider the most recent pronouncements of **other standard setting bodies** that use a similar conceptual framework to develop standards, other accounting literature and accepted industry practices if these do not conflict with the sources above.

An entity must select and apply its accounting policies for a period **consistently** for similar transactions, other events and conditions, unless an IFRS or an IFRIC specifically requires or permits categorisation of items for which different policies may be appropriate. If an IFRS or an IFRIC requires or permits categorisation of items, an appropriate accounting policy must be selected and applied consistently to each category.

# 2 Changes in accounting policies

Changes in accounting policy are applied **retrospectively**.

## 2.1 Accounting for changes of policy

The same accounting policies are usually adopted from period to period, to allow users to analyse trends over time in profit, cash flows and financial position. **Changes in accounting policy will therefore be rare** and should be made only if :

(a)    The change is required by an IFRS; or

(b)    The change will result in a **more appropriate presentation** of events or transactions in the financial statements of the entity, providing more reliable and relevant information.

The standard highlights two types of event which do not constitute changes in accounting policy.

(a)    Adopting an accounting policy for a **new type of transaction** or event not dealt with previously by the entity.

(b)    Adopting a **new accounting policy** for a transaction or event which has not occurred in the past or which was not material.

In the case of tangible non-current assets, if a policy of revaluation is adopted for the first time then this is treated, not as a change of accounting policy under IAS 8, but as a revaluation under IAS 16 Property, plant and equipment (see Chapter 5). The following paragraphs do not therefore apply to a change in policy to adopt revaluations.

A change in accounting policy **must be applied retrospectively**. **Retrospective application** means that the new accounting policy is applied to transactions and events as if it had always been in use. In other words, at the earliest date such transactions or events occurred, the policy is applied from that date.

**Prospective application** is **no longer allowed** under the revised IAS 8 unless it is **impracticable** (see Key Terms) to determine the cumulative effect of the change.

## 2.2 Worked example: change of accounting policy

A company has always valued inventory on a FIFO (first in, first out) basis. In 20X9 it decides to switch to the weighted average method of valuation. Gross profit in the 20X8 financial statements was calculated as follows:

|  |  | $'000 |
|---|---|---|
| Revenue |  | 869 |
| Cost of sales: |  |  |
| Opening inventory | 135 |  |
| Purchases | 246 |  |
| Closing inventory | (174) | (207) |
| Gross profit |  | 662 |

In order to prepare comparative figures for 20X8 showing the change of accounting policy, it is necessary to recalculate the amounts for 20X7, so that the opening inventory for 20X8 is valued on a weighted average basis.

It is established that opening inventory for 20X8 based on the weighted average method would be $122,000 and closing inventory would be $143,000. So the 20X8 gross profit now becomes:

|  |  | $'000 |
|---|---|---|
| Revenue |  | 869 |
| Cost of sales: |  |  |
| Opening inventory | 122 |  |
| Purchases | 246 |  |
| Closing inventory | (143) | (225) |
|  |  | 644 |

This shows $18,000 lower gross profit for 20X8 which will reduce net profit and retained earnings by the same amount. The opening inventory for 20X9 will be $143,000 rather than $174,000 and the statement of changes in equity for 20X9 will show an $18,000 adjustment to opening retained earnings.

## 2.3 Adoption of an IFRS

Where a new IFRS is adopted, IAS 8 requires any transitional provisions in the new IFRS itself to be followed. If none are given in the IFRS which is being adopted, then you should follow the general principles of IAS 8.

## 2.4 Disclosure

Certain **disclosures** are required when a change in accounting policy has a material effect on the current period or any prior period presented, or when it may have a material effect in subsequent periods.

(a) Reasons for the change / nature of change
(b) Amount of the adjustment for the current period and for each period presented
(c) Amount of the adjustment relating to periods prior to those included in the comparative information
(d) The fact that comparative information has been restated or that it is impracticable to do so

An entity should also disclose information relevant to assessing the **impact of new IFRS** on the financial statements where these have **not yet come into force.**

## 2.5 Changes in accounting estimates

FAST FORWARD

Changes in accounting estimate are **not** applied retrospectively.

Estimates arise in relation to business activities because of the **uncertainties inherent within them**. Judgements are made based on the most up to date information and the use of such estimates is a necessary part of the preparation of financial statements. It does not undermine their reliability. Here are some examples of accounting estimates.

(a) A necessary **irrecoverable debt allowance**
(b) **Useful lives** of depreciable assets
(c) Provision for **obsolescence of inventory**

The rule here is that the **effect of a change in an accounting estimate** should be included in the determination of net profit or loss in one of:

(a) The period of the change, if the change affects that period only
(b) The period of the change and future periods, if the change affects both

Changes may occur in the circumstances which were in force at the time the estimate was calculated, or perhaps additional information or subsequent developments have come to light.

An example of a change in accounting estimate which affects only the **current period** is the bad debt estimate. However, a revision in the life over which an asset is depreciated would affect both the **current and future periods**, in the amount of the depreciation expense.

Reasonably enough, the effect of a change in an accounting estimate should be included in the **same expense classification** as was used previously for the estimate. This rule helps to ensure **consistency** between the financial statements of different periods.

The **materiality** of the change is also relevant. The nature and amount of a change in an accounting estimate that has a material effect in the current period (or which is expected to have a material effect in subsequent periods) should be disclosed. If it is not possible to quantify the amount, this impracticability should be disclosed.

# 3 Errors

FAST FORWARD

Prior period errors must be corrected **retrospectively.**

## 3.1 Introduction

Errors discovered during a current period which **relate to a prior period** may arise through:

(a) Mathematical mistakes
(b) Mistakes in the application of accounting policies
(c) Misinterpretation of facts
(d) Oversights
(e) Fraud

A more formal definition is given in the Key Terms in Paragraph 1.1.

Most of the time these errors can be **corrected through net profit or loss for the current period**. Where they are material prior period errors, however, this is not appropriate. The standard considers two possible treatments.

## 3.2 Accounting treatment

**Prior period errors: correct retrospectively**. There is no longer any allowed alternative treatment. This involves:

(a) Either restating the comparative amounts for the prior period(s) in which the error occurred,

(b) Or, when the error occurred before the earliest prior period presented, restating the opening balances of assets, liabilities and equity for that period

so that the financial statements are presented **as if the error had never occurred**.

Only where it is **impracticable** to determine the cumulative effect of an error on prior periods can an entity correct an error **prospectively**.

Various **disclosures** are required.

(a) **Nature** of the prior period error

(b) For each prior period, to the extent practicable, the **amount** of the correction.

   (i) For each financial statement line item affected
   (ii) If IAS 33 applies, for basic and diluted earnings per share

(c) The amount of the correction at the **beginning of the earliest prior period** presented

(d) If **retrospective restatement is impracticable** for a particular prior period, the **circumstances** that led to the existence of that condition and a description of how and from when the error has been corrected. Subsequent periods need not repeat these disclosures.

**Exam focus point**

> If you have to deal with a change of accounting policy or an error in an accounts preparation question, remember to adjust the balance of retained earnings brought forward.

**Question**        Error

During 20X7 Global discovered that certain items had been included in inventory at 31 December 20X6, valued at $4.2m, which had in fact been sold before the year end. The following figures for 20X6 (as reported) and 20X7 (draft) are available.

|  | 20X6 | 20X7 (draft) |
| --- | ---: | ---: |
|  | $'000 | $'000 |
| Sales | 47,400 | 67,200 |
| Cost of goods sold | (34,570) | (55,800) |
| Profit before taxation | 12,830 | 11,400 |
| Income taxes | (3,880) | (3,400) |
| Profit for the period | 8,950 | 8,000 |

Retained earnings at 1 January 20X6 were $13m. The cost of goods sold for 20X7 includes the $4.2m error in opening inventory. The income tax rate was 30% for 20X6 and 20X7. No dividends have been declared or paid.

*Required*

Show the statement of profit or loss for 20X7, with the 20X6 comparative, and retained earnings.

## Answer

STATEMENT OF PROFIT OR LOSS

|  | 20X6 | 20X7 |
|---|---|---|
|  | $'000 | $'000 |
| Sales | 47,400 | 67,200 |
| Cost of goods sold (W1) | (38,770) | (51,600) |
| Profit before tax | 8,630 | 15,600 |
| Income tax (W2) | (2,620) | (4,660) |
| Profit for the year | 6,010 | 10,940 |

RETAINED EARNINGS

|  | 20X6 | 20X7 |
|---|---|---|
|  | $'000 | $'000 |
| Opening retained earnings |  |  |
| As previously reported (13,000 + 8,950) | 13,000 | 21,950 |
| Correction of prior period error (4,200 – 1,260) | – | (2,940) |
| As restated | 13,000 | 19,010 |
| Profit for the year | 6,010 | 10,940 |
| Closing retained earnings | 19,010 | 29,950 |

*Workings*

| 1 | Cost of goods sold | 20X6 | 20X7 |
|---|---|---|---|
|  |  | $'000 | $'000 |
|  | As stated in question | 34,570 | 55,800 |
|  | Inventory adjustment | 4,200 | (4,200) |
|  |  | 38,770 | 51,600 |

| 2 | Income tax | 20X6 | 20X7 |
|---|---|---|---|
|  |  | $'000 | $'000 |
|  | As stated in question | 3,880 | 3,400 |
|  | Inventory adjustment (4,200 × 30%) | (1,260) | 1,260 |
|  |  | 2,620 | 4,660 |

# 4 IFRS 5 Non-current assets held for sale and discontinued operations

IFRS 5 requires assets 'held for sale' to be presented separately in the statement of financial position. It sets out the criteria for recognising a **discontinued operation**.

## 4.1 Background

IFRS 5 is the result of a short-term convergence project with the US Financial Accounting Standards Board (FASB). It replaced IAS 35 *Discontinuing operations*.

IFRS 5 requires assets and groups of assets that are 'held for sale' to be **presented separately** in the statement of financial position and the results of discontinued operations to be presented separately in the statement of profit or loss and other comprehensive income. This is required so that users of financial statements will be better able to make **projections** about the financial position, profits and cash flows of the entity.

> **Disposal group. A** group of assets to be disposed of, by sale or otherwise, together as a group in a single transaction, and liabilities directly associated with those assets that will be transferred in the transaction. (In practice a disposal group could be a subsidiary, a cash-generating unit or a single operation within an entity.)
>
> **Cash- generating unit**. The smallest identifiable group of assets for which independent cash flows can be identified and measured
>
> (IFRS 5)

IFRS 5 does not apply to certain assets covered by other accounting standards:

(a) Deferred tax assets (IAS 12)

(b) Assets arising from employee benefits (IAS 19)

(c) Financial assets (IFRS 9)

(d) Investment properties accounted for in accordance with the fair value model (IAS 40)

(e) Agricultural and biological assets (IAS 41)

(f) Insurance contracts (IFRS 4)

## 4.2 Classification of assets held for sale

A non-current asset (or disposal group) should be classified as **held for sale** if its carrying amount will be recovered **principally through a sale transaction** rather than **through continuing use**. A number of detailed criteria must be met:

(a) The asset must be **available for immediate sale** in its present condition.

(b) Its sale must be **highly probable** (ie significantly more likely than not).

For the sale to be highly probable, the following must apply.

(a) Management must be **committed** to a plan to sell the asset.

(b) There must be an active programme to **locate a buyer.**

(c) The asset must be marketed for sale at a **price that is reasonable** in relation to its current fair value.

(d) The sale should be expected to take place **within one year** from the date of classification.

(e) It is unlikely that significant changes to the plan will be made or that the plan will be withdrawn.

An asset (or disposal group) can still be classified as held for sale, even if the sale has not actually taken place within one year. However, the delay must have been **caused by events or circumstances beyond the entity's control** and there must be sufficient evidence that the entity is still committed to sell the asset or disposal group. Otherwise the entity must cease to classify the asset as held for sale.

If an entity acquires a disposal group (eg, a subsidiary) exclusively with a view to its subsequent disposal it can classify the asset as held for sale only if the sale is expected to take place within one year and it is highly probable that all the other criteria will be met within a short time (normally three months).

An asset that is to be **abandoned** should not be classified as held for sale. This is because its carrying amount will be recovered principally through continuing use. However, a disposal group to be abandoned may meet the definition of a discontinued operation and therefore separate disclosure may be required (see below).

Question

Held for sale

On 1 December 20X3, a company became committed to a plan to sell a manufacturing facility and has already found a potential buyer. The company does not intend to discontinue the operations currently carried out in the facility. At 31 December 20X3 there is a backlog of uncompleted customer orders. The company will not be able to transfer the facility to the buyer until after it ceases to operate the facility and has eliminated the backlog of uncompleted customer orders. This is not expected to occur until spring 20X4.

*Required*

Can the manufacturing facility be classified as 'held for sale' at 31 December 20X3?

The facility will not be transferred until the backlog of orders is completed; this demonstrates that the facility is not available for immediate sale in its present condition. The facility cannot be classified as 'held for sale' at 31 December 20X3. It must be treated in the same way as other items of property, plant and equipment: it should continue to be depreciated and should not be separately disclosed.

## 4.3 Measurement of assets held for sale

**Key terms**

**Fair value:** the price that would be received to sell an asset or paid to transfer a liability in an orderly transaction between market participants at the measurement date.

**Costs to sell:** the incremental costs directly attributable to the disposal of an asset (or disposal group), excluding finance costs and income tax expense.

**Recoverable amount:** the higher of an asset's fair value less costs to sell and its value in use.

**Value in use:** the present value of estimated future cash flows expected to arise from the continuing use of an asset and from its disposal at the end of its useful life.

A non-current asset (or disposal group) that is held for sale should be measured at the **lower of** its **carrying amount** and **fair value less costs to sell**. Fair value less costs to sell is equivalent to net realisable value.

An impairment loss should be recognised where fair value less costs to sell is lower than carrying amount. Note that this is an exception to the normal rule. IAS 36 *Impairment of assets* requires an entity to recognise an impairment loss only where an asset's recoverable amount is lower than its carrying value. Recoverable amount is defined as the higher of net realisable value and value in use. IAS 36 does not apply to assets held for sale. An impairment loss on an asset held under IFRS 5 is charged to **profit or loss**.

Non-current assets held for sale **should not be depreciated**, even if they are still being used by the entity. However, any impairment (arising for instance from an increase in costs to sell) is recognised and charged to profit or loss.

A non-current asset (or disposal group) that is **no longer classified as held for sale** (for example, because the sale has not taken place within one year) is measured at the **lower of**:

(a)     Its **carrying amount** before it was classified as held for sale, adjusted for any depreciation that would have been charged had the asset not been held for sale

(b)     Its **recoverable amount** at the date of the decision not to sell

## 4.4 Presentation of a non-current asset or disposal group classified as held for sale

Non-current assets and disposal groups classified as held for sale should be **presented separately** from other assets in the statement of financial position. The liabilities of a disposal group should be presented separately from other liabilities in the statement of financial position.

(a)     Assets and liabilities held for sale **should not be offset**.

(b)     The **major classes** of assets and liabilities held for sale should be **separately disclosed** either on the face of the statement of financial position or in the notes.

(c)     IFRS 5 requires non-current assets or disposal groups held for sale to be shown as a separate component of **current assets/current liabilities**.

For example (taken from standard)

| | |
|---|---|
| **ASSETS** | |
| *Non-current assets* | |
| AAA | X |
| *Current assets* | |
| BBB | X |
| CCC | X |
| | X |
| Non-current assets classified as held for sale | X |
| | X |
| Total assets | X |
| **EQUITY AND LIABILITIES** | |
| *Equity* | |
| DDD | X |
| *Non-current liabilities* | |
| EEE | X |
| *Current liabilities* | |
| FFF | X |
| GGG | X |
| Liabilities directly associated with non-current assets classified as held for sale | X |
| | X |
| Total equity and liabilities | X |

## 4.5 Additional disclosures

In the period in which a non-current asset (or disposal group) has been either classified as held for sale or sold the following should be disclosed.

(a)   A **description** of the non-current asset (or disposal group)

(b)   A description of the **facts and circumstances** of the disposal

(c)   Any **gain or loss** recognised when the item was classified as held for sale

Where an asset previously classified as held for sale is **no longer held for sale**, the entity should disclose a description of the facts and circumstances leading to the decision and its effect on results.

## 4.6 Presenting discontinued operations

Key terms

> **Discontinued operation:** a component of an entity that has either been disposed of, or is classified as held for sale, and:
>
> (a)   Represents a separate major line of business or geographical area of operations
>
> (b)   Is part of a single co-ordinated plan to dispose of a separate major line of business or geographical area of operations, or
>
> (c)   Is a subsidiary acquired exclusively with a view to resale.
>
> **Component of an entity:** operations and cash flows that can be clearly distinguished, operationally and for financial reporting purposes, from the rest of the entity.

An entity should **present and disclose information** that enables users of the financial statements to evaluate the financial effects of **discontinued operations** and disposals of non-current assets or disposal groups.

This allows users to distinguish between operations which will continue in the future and those which will not, and makes it more possible to predict future results.

An entity should disclose a **single amount** in the statement of profit or loss comprising the total of:

(a)    The **post-tax profit or loss** of discontinued operations and

(b)    The post-tax gain or loss recognised on the **measurement to fair value less costs to sell** or on the disposal of the assets or disposal group(s) constituting the discontinued operation.

An entity should also disclose an **analysis** of this single amount into:

(a)    The revenue, expenses and pre-tax profit or loss of discontinued operations

(b)    The related income tax expense

(c)    The gain or loss recognised on the measurement to fair value less costs to sell or on the disposal of the assets of the discontinued operation

(d)    The related income tax expense

This may be presented either in the statement of profit or loss or in the notes. If it is presented in the statement of profit or loss it should be presented in a section identified as relating to discontinued operations, ie separately from continuing operations. This analysis is not required where the discontinued operation is a newly acquired subsidiary that has been classified as held for sale.

An entity should disclose the **net cash flows** attributable to the operating, investing and financing activities of discontinued operations. These disclosures may be presented either on the face of the statement of cash flows or in the notes.

Gains and losses on the remeasurement of a disposal group that is not a discontinued operation but is held for sale should be included in profit or loss from continuing operations.

## 4.7 Illustration

The following illustration is taken from the implementation guidance to IFRS 5. Profit for the period from discontinued operations would be analysed in the notes.

XYZ GROUP
STATEMENT OF PROFIT OR LOSS FOR THE YEAR ENDED 31 DECEMBER 20X2

|  | 20X2 $'000 | 20X1 $'000 |
|---|---|---|
| **Continuing operations** |  |  |
| Revenue | X | X |
| Cost of sales | (X) | (X) |
| Gross profit | X | X |
| Other income | X | X |
| Distribution costs | (X) | (X) |
| Administrative expenses | (X) | (X) |
| Other expenses | (X) | (X) |
| Finance costs | (X) | (X) |
| Share of profit of associates | X | X |
| Profit before tax | X | X |
| Income tax expense | (X) | (X) |
| Profit for the year from continuing operations | X | X |
| **Discontinued operations** |  |  |
| Profit for the year from discontinued operations | X | X |
| Profit for the year | X | X |
|  |  |  |
| Profit attributable to: |  |  |
| Owners of the parent | X | X |
| Non-controlling interest | X | X |
|  | X | X |

Note that if there were items of 'other comprehensive income' this would be shown as a full 'statement of profit or loss and other comprehensive income' as per the format in Chapter 3.

## Question

On 20 October 20X3 the directors of a parent company made a public announcement of plans to close a steel works. The closure means that the group will no longer carry out this type of operation, which until recently has represented about 10% of its total revenue. The works will be gradually shut down over a period of several months, with complete closure expected in July 20X4. At 31 December output had been significantly reduced and some redundancies had already taken place. The cash flows, revenues and expenses relating to the steel works can be clearly distinguished from those of the subsidiary's other operations.

*Required*

How should the closure be treated in the financial statements for the year ended 31 December 20X3?

## Answer

Because the steel works is being closed, rather than sold, it cannot be classified as 'held for sale'. In addition, the steel works is not a discontinued operation. Although at 31 December 20X3 the group was firmly committed to the closure, this has not yet taken place nor can its assets be classified as held for sale, therefore the steel works must be included in continuing operations. Information about the planned closure could be disclosed in the notes to the financial statements.

# 5 IAS 10: Events after the reporting period

**FAST FORWARD**

IAS 10 sets out the criteria for recognising **events occurring after the reporting date**.

The standard gives the following definition.

**Key term**

**Events occurring after the reporting period** are those events, both favourable and unfavourable, that occur between the end of the reporting period and the date on which the financial statements are authorised for issue. Two types of events can be identified.

- Those that provide evidence of conditions that existed at the end of the reporting period – *adjusting*
- Those that are indicative of conditions that arose after the reporting period – *non-adjusting*

*(IAS 10)*

Between the end of the reporting period and the date the financial statements are authorised (ie for issue outside the organisation), **events may occur** which show that assets and liabilities at the end of the reporting period should be adjusted, or that disclosure of such events should be given.

## 5.1 Events requiring adjustment

The standard requires adjustment of assets and liabilities in certain circumstances.

An entity shall adjust the amounts recognised in its financial statements to reflect **adjusting events** after the reporting period. An entity shall not adjust the amounts recognised in its financial statements to reflect non-adjusting events after the reporting period. *(IAS 10)*

An **example** of additional evidence which becomes available after the reporting period is where a **customer goes bankrupt, thus confirming that the trade account receivable balance at the year end is uncollectable.** In relation to **going concern**, the standard states that, where operating results and the financial position have deteriorated after the reporting period, it may be necessary to reconsider whether the going concern assumption is appropriate in the preparation of the financial statements.

Examples of **adjusting events** would be:

- evidence of a permanent diminution in property value prior to the year end
- sale of inventory after the reporting period for less than its carrying value at the year end
- insolvency of a customer with a balance owing at the year end
- amounts received or paid in respect of legal or insurance claims which were in negotiation at the year end
- determination after the year end of the sale or purchase price of assets sold or purchased before the year end
- evidence of a permanent diminution in the value of a long-term investment prior to the year end
- discovery of error or fraud which shows that the financial statements were incorrect

## 5.2 Events not requiring adjustment

The standard then looks at events which do **not** require adjustment.

The standard gives the following examples of events which do **not** require adjustments:

- acquisition of, or disposal of, a subsidiary after the year end
- announcement of a plan to discontinue an operation
- major purchases and disposals of assets
- destruction of a production plant by fire after the reporting period
- announcement or commencing implementation of a major restructuring
- share transactions after the reporting period
- litigation commenced after the reporting period

But note that, while they may be non-adjusting, some events after the reporting period will require **disclosure**.

If non-adjusting events after the reporting period are material, non-disclosure could influence the economic decisions of users taken on the basis of the financial statements. Accordingly, an entity shall disclose the following for each material category of non-adjusting event after the reporting period:

(a) the nature of the event; and
(b) an estimate of its financial effect, or a statement that such an estimate cannot be made.

*(IAS 10)*

The **example** given by the standard of such an event is where the **value of an investment falls between the end of the reporting period and the date the financial statements are authorised** for issue. The fall in value represents circumstances during the current period, not conditions existing at the end of the previous reporting period, so it is not appropriate to adjust the value of the investment in the financial statements. Disclosure is an aid to users, however, indicating 'unusual changes' in the state of assets and liabilities after the reporting period.

The rule for **disclosure** of events occurring after the reporting period which relate to conditions that arose after that date, is that disclosure should be made if non-disclosure would hinder the user's ability to make **proper evaluations** and decisions based on the financial statements. An example might be the acquisition of another business.

One of the competences you require to fulfil performance objective 10 of the PER is the ability to provide supporting information to make statements and accounts more understandable to users. This chapter deals with important disclosures and you can apply the knowledge you obtain from this chapter to help to demonstrate this competence.

# Chapter Roundup

- IAS 8 deals with the treatment of changes in accounting estimates, changes in accounting policies and errors.

- Changes in accounting policy are applied **retrospectively**.

- Changes in accounting estimate are **not** applied retrospectively.

- Prior period errors must be corrected **retrospectively**.

- IFRS 5 requires assets 'held for sale' to be presented separately in the statement of financial position. It sets out the criteria for recognising a **discontinued operation**.

- IAS 10 sets out the criteria for recognising **events occurring after the reporting date**.

# Quick Quiz

1  How should a prior period error be corrected under IAS 8?
2  Give the circumstances when a change in accounting policy might be required.
3  When can a non-current asset be classified as held for sale?
4  How should an asset held for sale be measured?
5  How does IFRS 5 define a discontinued operation?

# Answers to Quick Quiz

1  By adjusting the opening balance of retained earnings (Para 3.2)

2  (a)  The change is required by an IFRS; or
   (b)  The change will result in a **more appropriate presentation** of events or transactions in the financial statements of the entity, providing more reliable and relevant information.

3  (a)  The asset must be **available for immediate sale** in its present condition
   (b)  Its sale must be **highly probable** (ie significantly more likely than not).

4  At the lower of carrying amount and fair value less costs to sell
5  See Key Term para 4.6

Now try the questions below from the Exam Question Bank

| Number | Level | Marks | Time |
|--------|-------|-------|------|
| 8 | Examination | 25 | 45 mins |

# Introduction
# to groups

| Topic list | Syllabus reference |
|---|---|
| 1 Group accounts | D1 |
| 2 Consolidated and separate financial statements | D1 |
| 3 Content of group accounts and group structure | D1 |
| 4 Group accounts: the related parties issue | D2 |

## Introduction

Consolidation is an extremely important area of your Paper 7 syllabus.

The key to consolidation questions in the examination is to adopt a logical approach and to practise as many questions as possible.

In this chapter we will look at the major definitions in consolidation. These matters are fundamental to your comprehension of group accounts, so make sure you can understand them and then **learn them**.

# Study guide

| | | Intellectual level |
|---|---|---|
| **D** | **BUSINESS COMBINATIONS** | |
| **1** | **The concept and principles of a group** | |
| (a) | describe the concept of a group as a single economic unit. | 2 |
| (b) | explain and apply the definition of a subsidiary within relevant accounting standards. | 2 |
| (c) | identify and outline using accounting standards and other applicable regulation the circumstances in which a group is required to prepare consolidated financial statements. | 2 |
| (d) | describe the circumstances when a group may claim exemption from the preparation of consolidated financial statements | 2 |
| (e) | explain why directors may not wish to consolidate a subsidiary and outline using accounting standards and other applicable regulation the circumstances where this is permitted | |
| (f) | explain the need for using coterminous year ends and uniform accounting policies when preparing consolidated financial statements | |
| **2** | **The concept of consolidated financial statements** | |
| (a) | explain the objective of consolidated financial statements. | 2 |
| (b) | indicate the effect that the related party relationship between a parent and subsidiary may have on the subsidiary's entity statements and the consolidated financial statements. | 2 |

# Exam guide

You will have a compulsory question on group accounts. Read this chapter carefully and refer back to it when needed.

# 1 Group accounts

**FAST FORWARD**

Many large businesses consist of several companies controlled by one central or administrative company. Together these companies are called a **group**. The controlling company, called the parent or **holding company**, will own some or all of the shares in the other companies, called subsidiaries.

## 1.1 Introduction

There are many reasons for businesses to operate as groups; for the goodwill associated with the names of the subsidiaries, for tax or legal purposes and so forth. In many countries, company law requires that the results of a group should be presented as a whole. Unfortunately, it is not possible simply to add all the results together and this chapter and those following will teach you how to **consolidate** all the results of companies within a group.

In traditional accounting terminology, a **group of companies** consists of a **parent company** and one or more **subsidiary companies** which are controlled by the parent company.

## 1.2 Accounting standards

We will be looking at five accounting standards in this and the next three chapters.

* IAS 27 *(revised) Separate financial statements*

- IFRS 3 *Business combinations*
- IFRS 10 *Consolidated financial statements*
- IAS 28 *Investments in associates*

These standards are all concerned with different aspects of group accounts, but there is some overlap between them, particularly between IFRS 10 and IAS 27.

In this and the next chapter we will concentrate on IAS 27 and IFRS 10, which cover the basic group definitions and consolidation procedures of a parent-subsidiary relationship. First of all, however, we will look at all the important definitions involved in group accounts, which **determine how to treat each particular type of investment** in group accounts.

## 1.3 Definitions

We will look at some of these definitions in more detail later, but they are useful here in that they give you an overview of all aspects of group accounts.

**Exam focus point**

> All the definitions relating to group accounts are extremely important. You must **learn them** and **understand** their meaning and application.

**Key terms**

> - **Control**. An investor controls an investee when the investor is exposed, or has rights, to variable returns from its involvement with the investee and has the ability to affect those returns through power over the investee. *(IFRS 10)*
>
> - **Power**. Existing rights that give the current ability to direct the relevant activities of the investee *(IFRS 10)*
>
> - **Subsidiary**. An entity that is controlled by another entity. *(IFRS 10)*
>
> - **Parent**. An entity that controls one or more subsidiaries. *(IFRS 10)*
>
> - **Group**. A parent and all its subsidiaries. *(IFRS 10)*
>
> - **Associate**. An entity over which an investor has significant influence and which is neither a subsidiary nor an interest in a joint venture. *(IFRS 10)*
>
> - **Significant influence** is the power to participate in the financial and operating policy decisions of an investee but is not control or joint control over those policies. *(IAS 28)*

We can summarise the different types of investment *and* the required accounting for them as follows.

| Investment | Criteria | Required treatment in group accounts |
|---|---|---|
| **Subsidiary** | Control | Full consolidation |
| **Associate** | Significant influence | Equity accounting (see Chapter 11) |
| **Investment** which is none of the above | Asset held for accretion of wealth | As for single company accounts per IFRS 9 |

## 1.4 Investments in subsidiaries

The important point here is **control**. In most cases, this will involve the holding company or parent owning a majority of the ordinary shares in the subsidiary (to which normal voting rights are attached). There are circumstances, however, when the parent may own only a minority of the voting power in the subsidiary, *but* the parent still has control.

IFRS 10 provides a definition of control and identifies three separate elements of control:

An investor controls an investee if and only if it has all of the following:

1) Power over the investee
2) Exposure to, or rights to, variable returns from its involvement with the investee; and
3) The ability to use its power over the investee to affect the amount of the investor's returns

If there are changes to one or more of these three elements of control, then an investor should reassess whether it controls an investee.

Power (as defined under Key Terms) can be obtained directly from ownership of the majority of voting rights or can be derived from other rights, such as:

- Rights to appoint, reassign or remove key management personnel who can direct the relevant activities
- Rights to appoint or remove another entity that directs the relevant activities
- Rights to direct the investee to enter into, or veto changes to, transactions for the benefit of the investor
- Other rights, such as those specified in a management contract

**Exam focus point**

You should learn the contents of the above paragraph as you may be asked to apply them in the exam.

### 1.4.1 Accounting treatment in group accounts

IFRS 10 requires a parent to present consolidated financial statements, in which the accounts of the parent and subsidiary (or subsidiaries) are combined and presented **as a single entity**.

## 1.5 Investments in associates

This type of investment is something less than a subsidiary, but more than a simple investment. The key criterion here is **significant influence**. This is defined as the 'power to participate', but *not* to 'control' (which would make the investment a subsidiary).

Significant influence can be determined by the holding of voting rights (usually attached to shares) in the entity. IAS 28 states that if an investor holds **20% or more** of the voting power of the investee, it can be presumed that the investor has significant influence over the investee, *unless* it can be clearly shown that this is not the case.

Significant influence can be presumed *not* to exist if the investor holds **less than 20%** of the voting power of the investee, unless it can be demonstrated otherwise.

The **existence of significant influence** is evidenced in one or more of the following ways.

(a) Representation on the **board of directors** (or equivalent) of the investee
(b) Participation in the **policy making process**
(c) **Material transactions** between investor and investee
(d) Interchange of management personnel
(e) Provision of essential technical information

IAS 28 requires the use of the **equity method** of accounting for investments in associates. This method will be explained in detail in Chapter 11.

Question

Treatments

The section summary after this question will give an augmented version of the table given in Paragraph 1.3 above. Before you look at it, see if you can write out the table yourself.

## 1.6 Section summary

| Investment | Criteria | Required treatment in group accounts |
|---|---|---|
| **Subsidiary** | Control (> 50% rule) | Full consolidation (IFRS 10) |
| **Associate** | Significant influence (20%+ rule) | Equity accounting (IAS 28) |
| **Investment** which is none of the above | Asset held for accretion of wealth | As for single company accounts (IFRS 9) |

# 2 Consolidated and separate financial statements

**FAST FORWARD** IFRS 10 requires a parent to present **consolidated** financial statements.

## 2.1 Introduction

**Key term**

*ccubara*

> **Consolidated financial statements**. The financial statements of a group in which the assets, liabilities, equity, income, expenses and cash flows of the parent and its subsidiaries are presented as those of a single economic entity.
>
> *(IFRS 10)*

When a parent issues consolidated financial statements, it should consolidate **all subsidiaries**, both foreign and domestic.

## 2.2 Exemption from preparing group accounts

A parent **need not present** consolidated financial statements if and only if all of the following hold:

(a)    The parent is itself a **wholly-owned subsidiary** or it is a **partially owned subsidiary** of another entity and its other owners, including those not otherwise entitled to vote, have been informed about, and do not object to, the parent not presenting consolidated financial statements

(b)    Its securities are **not publicly traded**

(c)    It is **not in the process of issuing securities** in public securities markets; and

(d)    The **ultimate or intermediate parent** publishes consolidated financial statements that comply with International Financial Reporting Standards

A parent that does not present consolidated financial statements must comply with the IAS 27 rules on separate financial statements (discussed later in this section).

## 2.3 Potential voting rights

An entity may own share warrants, share call options, or other similar instruments that are **convertible into ordinary shares** in another entity. If these are exercised or converted they may give the entity voting power or reduce another party's voting power over the financial and operating policies of the other entity (potential voting rights). The **existence and effect** of potential voting rights, including potential voting rights held by another entity, should be considered when assessing whether an entity has control over another entity (and therefore has a subsidiary).

## 2.4 Exclusion of a subsidiary from consolidation

The rules on exclusion of subsidiaries from consolidation are necessarily strict, because this is a common method used by entities to manipulate their results. If a subsidiary which carries a large amount of debt can be excluded, then the gearing of the group as a whole will be improved. In other words, this is a way of taking debt **out of the consolidated statement of financial position**.

IAS 27 did originally allow a subsidiary to be excluded from consolidation where **control is intended to be temporary**. This exclusion was then removed by IFRS 5.

Subsidiaries held for sale are accounted for in accordance with IFRS 5 *Non-current assets held for sale and discontinued operations*.

It has been argued in the past that subsidiaries should be excluded from consolidation on the grounds of **dissimilar activities**, ie the activities of the subsidiary are so different to the activities of the other companies within the group that to include its results in the consolidation would be misleading. IAS 27 and IFRS 10 both reject this argument: exclusion on these grounds is not justified because better (relevant) information can be provided about such subsidiaries by consolidating their results and then giving additional information about the different business activities of the subsidiary.

The previous version of IAS 27 permitted exclusion where the subsidiary operates under **severe long-term restrictions** and these significantly impair its ability to transfer funds to the parent. This exclusion has now been **removed**. Control must actually be lost for exclusion to occur.

## 2.5 Different reporting dates

In most cases, all group companies will prepare accounts to the same reporting date. One or more subsidiaries may, however, prepare accounts to a different reporting date from the parent and the bulk of other subsidiaries in the group.

In such cases the subsidiary may prepare additional statements to the reporting date of the rest of the group, for consolidation purposes. If this is not possible, the subsidiary's accounts may still be used for the consolidation, *provided that* the gap between the reporting dates is **three months or less**.

Where a subsidiary's accounts are drawn up to a different accounting date, **adjustments should be made** for the effects of significant transactions or other events that occur between that date and the parent's reporting date.

## 2.6 Uniform accounting policies

Consolidated financial statements should be prepared using **uniform accounting policies** for like transactions and other events in similar circumstances.

**Adjustments** must be made where members of a group use different accounting policies, so that their financial statements are suitable for consolidation.

## 2.7 Date of inclusion/exclusion

IFRS 10 requires the results of subsidiary undertakings to be included in the consolidated financial statements from:

(a)     the date of 'acquisition', ie the **date on which the investor obtains control of the investee**, to
(b)     the date of 'disposal', ie the **date the investor loses control of the investee**.

Once an investment is no longer a subsidiary, it should be treated as an associate under IAS 28 (if applicable) or as an investment under IFRS 9 (see Chapter 14).

## 2.8 Accounting for subsidiaries and associates in the parent's separate financial statements

A parent company will usually produce its own single company financial statements and these should be prepared in accordance with IAS 27(revised) *Separate financial statements*. In these statements, investments in subsidiaries and associates included in the consolidated financial statements should be *either*:

(a)     Accounted for at **cost**, *or*
(b)     In accordance with **IFRS 9** (see Chapter 14).

Where subsidiaries are **classified as held for sale** in accordance with IFRS 5 they should be accounted for in accordance with IFRS 5 (see Chapter 7) in the parent's separate financial statements.

## 2.9 Disclosure – individual financial statements

Where a parent chooses to take advantage of the exemptions from preparing consolidated financial statements (see above) under IAS 27 the **separate financial statements** must disclose:

(a)     The fact that the financial statements are separate financial statements; that the exemption from consolidation has been used; the name and country of incorporation of the entity whose consolidated financial statements that comply with IFRSs have been published; and the address where those consolidated financial statements are obtainable

(b) A list of significant investments in subsidiaries, jointly controlled entities and associates, including the name, country of incorporation, proportion of ownership interest and, if different, proportion of voting power held

(c) A description of the method used to account for the investments listed under (b)

When a parent prepares separate financial statements in addition to consolidated financial statements, the separate financial statements must disclose:

(a) The fact that the statements are separate financial statements and the reasons why they have been prepared if not required by law

(b) Information about investments and the method used to account for them, as above.

# 3 Content of group accounts and group structure

FAST FORWARD

> It is important to distinguish between the parent company individual accounts and the group accounts.

## 3.1 Introduction

The information contained in the individual financial statements of a parent company and each of its subsidiaries does not give a picture of the group's total activities. A **separate set of group statements** can be prepared from the individual ones. Remember that a group has no separate (legal) existence, except for accounting purposes.

**Consolidated accounts** are one form of group accounts which combines the information contained in the separate accounts of a holding company and its subsidiaries as if they were the accounts of a single entity. 'Group accounts' and 'consolidated accounts' are terms often used synonymously.

In simple terms a set of consolidated accounts is prepared by **adding together** the assets and liabilities of the parent company and each subsidiary. The **whole** of the assets and liabilities of each company are included, even though some subsidiaries may be only partly owned. The 'equity and liabilities' section of the statement of financial position will indicate how much of the net assets are attributable to the group and how much to outside investors in partly owned subsidiaries. These **outside investors** are known as the **non-controlling interest**.

**Key term**

> **Non-controlling interest**. The equity in a subsidiary not attributable, directly or indirectly, to a parent.
> *(IFRS 3, IAS 27)*

Non-controlling interest should be presented in the consolidated statement of financial position **within equity, separately from the parent shareholders' equity**.

Most parent companies present their own individual accounts and their group accounts in a single **package**. The package typically comprises the following.

- **Parent company financial statements**, which will include 'investments in subsidiary undertakings' as an asset in the statement of financial position, and income from subsidiaries (dividends) in the statement of profit or loss
- **Consolidated statement of financial position**
- **Consolidated statement of profit or loss and other comprehensive income**
- **Consolidated statement of cash flows**

It may not be necessary to publish all of the parent company's financial statements, depending on local or national regulations.

## 3.2 Group structure

With the difficulties of definition and disclosure dealt with, let us now look at group structures. The simplest are those in which a parent company has only a **direct interest** in the shares of its subsidiary companies. For example:

S₁ Co is a wholly owned subsidiary of P Co. S₂ Co, S₃ Co and S₄ Co are partly owned subsidiaries; a proportion of the shares in these companies is held by outside investors.

Often a parent will have **indirect holdings** in its subsidiary companies. This can lead to more complex group structures, involving sub-subsidiaries.

P Co owns 51% of the equity shares in S Co, which is therefore its subsidiary. S Co in its turn owns 51% of the equity shares in SS Co. SS Co is therefore a subsidiary of S Co and consequently a subsidiary of P Co. SS Co would describe S Co as its parent (or holding) company and P Co as its ultimate parent company.

Note that although P Co can control the assets and business of SS Co by virtue of the chain of control, its interest in the assets of SS Co is only 26%. This can be seen by considering a dividend of $100 paid by SS Co: as a 51% shareholder, S Co would receive $51; P Co would have an interest in 51% of this $51 = $26.01.

During the time until your examination you should obtain as many sets of the published accounts of large companies in your country as possible. Examine the accounting policies in relation to subsidiary and associated companies and consider how these policies are shown in the accounting and consolidation treatment. Also, look at all the disclosures made relating to fair values, goodwill etc and match them to the disclosure requirements outlined in this chapter and in subsequent chapters on IFRS 3 and IAS 28.

Alternatively (or additionally) you should attempt to obtain such information from the financial press.

**Exam focus point**

> You will not be tested on complex group structures at F7. Your exam will not feature sub-subsidiaries, but you will meet this topic again at P2.

# 4 Group accounts: the related parties issue

**FAST FORWARD**

> Parent companies and subsidiaries are **related parties** as per IAS 24. Bear in mind that this relationship can be exploited.

IAS 24 draws attention to the significance of related party relationships and transactions – that transactions between the parties may not be 'at arm's length' and that users of the accounts must be made aware of this, as it may affect their view of the financial statements.

## 4.1 Individual company accounts

The relationship between a parent and a subsidiary is the most obvious example of a related party relationship and it offers a number of opportunities for manipulating results. Some of these may be aimed at improving the parent's individual financial statements.

Any of the following could take place:

- The subsidiary sells goods to the parent company at an artificially low price. This increases parent company profit while reducing profit in the subsidiary, thus increasing profit available for distribution to parent company shareholders at the expense of the non-controlling interest.
- The parent sells goods to the subsidiary at an artificially high price. This has the same result as above.
- The subsidiary makes a loan to the parent at an artificially low rate of interest or the parent makes a loan to the subsidiary at an artificially high rate of interest. The loans will be cancelled on consolidation but the interest payments will transfer profits from the subsidiary to the parent.
- The parent can sell an asset to the subsidiary at an amount in excess of its carrying amount. This again serves to transfer profit (and cash) to the parent.

## 4.2 Consolidated financial statements

The transactions above seek to improve the **individual** parent company accounts at the expense of the individual subsidiary accounts. Dividends are paid to shareholders on the basis of these individual company financial statements, not the consolidated financial statements.

The tightening up of the opportunities for excluding a subsidiary from consolidation under IAS 27 have reduced the opportunities for improving the appearance of the **consolidated** financial statements. Prior to this, a number of possibilities could be exploited:

- A group could obtain loans via a subsidiary, which was not then consolidated. The loan would not appear in the consolidated statement of financial position and group gearing (% of capital provided by loans) would appear lower than it actually was.
- Sale and leaseback transactions could be carried out in which assets were sold to a non-consolidated subsidiary and leased back under an operating lease. This enabled the asset and its associated borrowings to be removed from the statement of financial position.

## 4.3 Disposal of subsidiaries

While the situations above are all concerned with improving the appearance of the parent company or group financial statements at the expense of those of the subsidiary, there may be occasions where the **opposite** is the intention.

For instance, when a parent company has decided to dispose of its shares in a poorly-performing subsidiary, it may seek to enhance the results of that subsidiary for the purpose of selling at a profit. In this case, transactions such as those at 4.1 above may be undertaken in the other direction – to transfer profit from the **parent** to the **subsidiary**.

## 4.4 Effect on trading

Even where no related party transactions have taken place, the parent/subsidiary relationship can still affect how the parties do business. For instance if, prior to acquisition by the parent, the subsidiary had a major customer or supplier who was a competitor of the parent, that trading arrangement can be expected to cease. The subsidiary may itself have been a competitor of the parent, in which case it may now have had to withdraw from certain markets in favour of the parent.

Look out for any of these issues in a consolidated accounts question.

# Chapter Roundup

- Many large businesses consist of several companies controlled by one central or administrative company. Together these companies are called a **group**. The controlling company, called the **parent** or **holding company** will own some or all of the shares in the other companies, called **subsidiaries**.

- IFRS 10 requires a parent to present consolidated financial statements.

- It is important to distinguish between the parent company **individual accounts** and the **group accounts**.

- Parent companies and subsidiaries are **related parties** as per IAS 24. Bear in mind that this relationship can be exploited.

1      Define a 'subsidiary'.

2      When can control be assumed?

3      What accounting treatment does IFRS 10 require of a parent company?

4      When is a parent exempted from preparing consolidated financial statements?

5      Under what circumstances should subsidiary undertakings be excluded from consolidation?

6      How should an investment in a subsidiary be accounted for in the separate financial statements of the parent?

7      What is a non-controlling interest?

# Answers to Quick Quiz

1   An entity that is controlled by another entity.

2   When the investor has rights to variable returns from the investee and is able to affect those returns by its power over the investee.

3   The accounts of parent and subsidiary are combined and presented as a single entity.

4   When the parent is itself a wholly owned subsidiary, or a partially owned subsidiary and the non-controlling interests do not object, when its securities are not publicly traded and when its ultimate or intermediate parent publishes IFRS-compliant financial statements

5   Very rarely, if at all. See section 2.4.

6   (a)   At cost, or
    (b)   In accordance with IFRS 9.

7   The equity in a subsidiary not attributable, directly or indirectly, to a parent.

# The consolidated statement of financial position

| Topic list | Syllabus reference |
|---|---|
| 1 IFRS 10 Summary of consolidation procedures | D1 |
| 2 Non-controlling interests | D3 |
| 3 Dividends paid by a subsidiary | D1 |
| 4 Goodwill arising on consolidation | D2 |
| 5 Non-controlling interest at fair value | D3 |
| 6 Intra-group trading | D1 |
| 7 Intra-group sales of non-current assets | D1 |
| 8 Summary: consolidated statement of financial position | D3 |
| 9 Acquisition of a subsidiary during its accounting period | D3 |
| 10 Fair values in acquisition accounting | D2 |

## Introduction

This chapter introduces the **basic procedures** required in consolidation and gives a formal step plan for carrying out a statement of financial position consolidation. This step procedure should be useful to you as a starting guide for answering any question, but remember that you cannot rely on it to answer the question for you.

Each question must be approached and **answered on its own merits**. Examiners often put small extra or different problems in because, as they are always reminding students, it is not possible to 'rote-learn' consolidation.

The **method of consolidation** shown here uses schedules for workings (retained earnings, non-controlling interest etc) rather than the ledger accounts used in some other texts. This is because we believe that ledger accounts lead students to 'learn' the consolidation journals without thinking about what they are doing - always a dangerous practice in consolidation questions.

There are plenty of questions in this chapter - work through *all* of them carefully.

# Study guide

| | | | Intellectual level |
|---|---|---|---|
| **D** | | **BUSINESS COMBINATIONS** | |
| **1** | (a) | explain why it is necessary to eliminate intra-group transactions. | 2 |
| **2** | (a) | describe and apply the required accounting treatment of consolidated goodwill. | 2 |
| | (b) | explain why it is necessary to use fair values for the consideration of an investment in a subsidiary together with the fair values of a subsidiary's identifiable assets and liabilities when preparing consolidated financial statements. | |
| **3** | (a) | prepare a consolidated statement of financial position for a simple group (parent and one subsidiary) dealing with pre and post acquisition profits, non-controlling interests and consolidated goodwill. | 2 |
| | (c) | explain and account for other reserves (eg share premium and revaluation reserves). | 1 |
| | (d) | account for the effects (in the financial statements) of intra-group trading. | 2 |
| | (e) | account for the effects of fair value adjustments (including their effect on consolidated goodwill) to: | 2 |
| | | (i) depreciating and non-depreciating non-current assets | |
| | | (ii) inventory | |
| | | (iii) monetary liabilities | |
| | | (iv) assets and liabilities not included in the subsidiary's own statement of financial position, including contingent assets and liabilities. | |
| | (f) | account for goodwill impairment. | 2 |

# 1 IFRS 10 Summary of consolidation procedures

IFRS 10 lays out the basic procedures for preparing consolidated financial statements.

## 1.1 Basic procedure

The financial statements of a parent and its subsidiaries are **combined on a line-by-line basis** by adding together like items of assets, liabilities, equity, income and expenses.

The following steps are then taken, in order that the consolidated financial statements should **show financial information about the group as if it was a single entity**.

(a)   The carrying amount of the parent's **investment in each subsidiary** and the parent's **portion of equity** of each subsidiary are **eliminated or cancelled**

(b)   **Non-controlling interests in the net income of consolidated subsidiaries** are adjusted against group income, to arrive at the net income attributable to the owners of the parent

(c)   **Non-controlling interests** in the net assets of consolidated subsidiaries should be presented separately in the consolidated statement of financial position

Other matters to be dealt with include the following.

(a)   **Goodwill on consolidation** should be dealt with according to IFRS 3

(b)  **Dividends paid** by a subsidiary must be accounted for

IFRS 10 states that all intragroup balances and transactions, and the resulting **unrealised profits**, should be **eliminated in full**. **Unrealised losses** resulting from intragroup transactions should also be eliminated *unless* cost can be recovered. This will be explained later in this chapter.

## 1.2 Cancellation and part cancellation

The preparation of a consolidated statement of financial position, in a very simple form, consists of two procedures.

(a)  Take the individual accounts of the parent company and each subsidiary and **cancel out items** which appear as an asset in one company and a liability in another.

(b)  Add together all the uncancelled assets and liabilities throughout the group.

Items requiring cancellation may include the following.

(a)  The asset **'shares in subsidiary companies'** which appears in the parent company's accounts will be matched with the liability 'share capital' in the subsidiaries' accounts.

(b)  There may be **intra-group trading** within the group. For example, S Co may sell goods on credit to P Co. P Co would then be a receivable in the accounts of S Co, while S Co would be a payable in the accounts of P Co.

## 1.3 Example: cancellation

P Co regularly sells goods to its one subsidiary company, S Co, which it has owned since S Co's incorporation. The statement of financial position of the two companies on 31 December 20X6 are given below.

STATEMENT OF FINANCIAL POSITION AS AT 31 DECEMBER 20X6

| | P Co $ | S Co $ |
|---|---|---|
| *Assets* | | |
| *Non-current assets* | | |
| Property, plant and equipment | 35,000 | 45,000 |
| Investment in 40,000 $1 shares in S Co at cost | 40,000 | |
| | 75,000 | |
| *Current assets* | | |
| Inventories | 16,000 | 12,000 |
| Receivables:  S Co | 2,000 | – |
| Other | 6,000 | 9,000 |
| Cash at bank | 1,000 | |
| Total assets | 100,000 | 66,000 |
| *Equity and liabilities* | | |
| *Equity* | | |
| 40,000 $1 ordinary shares | – | 40,000 |
| 70,000 $1 ordinary shares | 70,000 | – |
| Retained earnings | 16,000 | 19,000 |
| | 86,000 | 59,000 |
| *Current liabilities* | | |
| Bank overdraft | | 3,000 |
| Payables:  P Co | | 2,000 |
| Payables:  Other | 14,000 | 2,000 |
| | | |
| Total equity and liabilities | 100,000 | 66,000 |

*Required*

Prepare the consolidated statement of financial position of P Co at 31 December 20X6.

## Solution

The cancelling items are:

(a) P Co's asset 'investment in shares of S Co' ($40,000) cancels with S Co's liability 'share capital' ($40,000);

(b) P Co's asset 'receivables: S Co' ($2,000) cancels with S Co's liability 'payables: P Co' ($2,000).

The remaining assets and liabilities are added together to produce the following consolidated statement of financial position.

### P CO
### CONSOLIDATED STATEMENT OF FINANCIAL POSITION AS AT 31 DECEMBER 20X6

| | $ | $ |
|---|---|---|
| *Assets* | | |
| *Non-current assets* | | |
| Property, plant and equipment | | 80,000 |
| | | |
| *Current assets* | | |
| Inventories | 28,000 | |
| Receivables | 15,000 | |
| Cash at bank | 1,000 | |
| | | 44,000 |
| Total assets | | 124,000 |
| *Equity and liabilities* | | |
| *Equity* | | |
| 70,000 $1 ordinary shares | | 70,000 |
| Retained earnings | | 35,000 |
| | | 105,000 |
| Current liabilities | | |
| Bank overdraft | 3,000 | |
| Payables | 16,000 | |
| | | 19,000 |
| Total equity and liabilities | | 124,000 |

Note the following.

(a) P Co's bank balance is **not netted off** with S Co's bank overdraft. To offset one against the other would be less informative and would conflict with the principle that assets and liabilities should not be netted off.

(b) The share capital in the consolidated statement of financial position is the **share capital of the parent company alone**. This must *always* be the case, no matter how complex the consolidation, because the share capital of subsidiary companies must *always* be a wholly cancelling item.

## 1.4 Part cancellation

An item may appear in the statements of financial position of a parent company and its subsidiary, but not at the same amounts.

(a) The parent company may have acquired **shares in the subsidiary** at a price **greater or less than their par value**. The asset will appear in the parent company's accounts at cost, while the liability will appear in the subsidiary's accounts at par value. This raises the issue of **goodwill**, which is dealt with later in this chapter.

(b) Even if the parent company acquired shares at par value, it **may not** have **acquired all the shares of the subsidiary** (so the subsidiary may be only partly owned). This raises the issue of **non-controlling interests**, which are also dealt with later in this chapter.

(c) The inter-company trading balances may be out of step because of **goods or cash in transit**.

(d) One company may have **issued loan stock** of which a **proportion only** is taken up by the other company.

The following question illustrates the techniques needed to deal with items (c) and (d) above. The procedure is to **cancel as far as possible**. The remaining uncancelled amounts will appear in the consolidated statement of financial position.

(a) **Uncancelled loan stock** will appear as a **liability of the group**.

(b) **Uncancelled balances on intra-group accounts** represent **goods or cash in transit**, which will appear in the consolidated statement of financial position.

## Question                                                              Cancellation

The statements of financial position of P Co and of its subsidiary S Co have been made up to 30 June. P Co has owned all the ordinary shares and 40% of the loan stock of S Co since its incorporation.

STATEMENT OF FINANCIAL POSITION AS AT 30 JUNE

|  | P Co $ | S Co $ |
|---|---|---|
| *Assets* | | |
| *Non-current assets* | | |
| Property, plant and equipment | 120,000 | 100,000 |
| Investment in S Co, at cost | | |
| 80,000 ordinary shares of $1 each | 80,000 | |
| $20,000 of 12% loan stock in S Co | 20,000 | |
| | 220,000 | |
| *Current assets* | | |
| Inventories | 50,000 | 60,000 |
| Receivables | 40,000 | 30,000 |
| Current account with S Co | 18,000 | |
| Cash | 4,000 | 6,000 |
| | 112,000 | 96,000 |
| Total assets | 332,000 | 196,000 |
| *Equity and liabilities* | | |
| *Equity* | | |
| Ordinary shares of $1 each, fully paid | 100,000 | 80,000 |
| Retained earnings | 95,000 | 28,000 |
| | 195,000 | 108,000 |
| *Non-current liabilities* | | |
| 10% loan stock | 75,000 | |
| 12% loan stock | | 50,000 |
| *Current liabilities* | | |
| Payables | 47,000 | 16,000 |
| Taxation | 15,000 | 10,000 |
| Current account with P Co | | 12,000 |
| | 62,000 | 38,000 |
| Total equity and liabilities | 332,000 | 196,000 |

The difference on current account arises because of goods in transit.

*Required*

Prepare the consolidated statement of financial position of P Co.

P CO

CONSOLIDATED STATEMENT OF FINANCIAL POSITION AS AT 30 JUNE

|  | $ | $ |
|---|---|---|
| *Assets* | | |
| *Non-current assets* | | |
| Property, plant and equipment (120,000 + 100,000) | | 220,000 |
| *Current assets* | | |
| Inventories (50,000 + 60,000) | 110,000 | |
| Goods in transit (18,000 – 12,000) | 6,000 | |
| Receivables (40,000 + 30,000) | 70,000 | |
| Cash (4,000 + 6,000) | 10,000 | |
| | | 196,000 |
| *Total assets* | | 416,000 |
| *Equity and liabilities* | | |
| *Equity* | | |
| Ordinary shares of $1 each, fully paid (parent) | 100,000 | |
| Retained earnings (95,000 + 28,000) | 123,000 | |
| | | 223,000 |
| *Non-current liabilities* | | |
| 10% loan stock | 75,000 | |
| 12% loan stock (50,000 × 60%) | 30,000 | |
| | | 105,000 |
| *Current liabilities* | | |
| Payables (47,000 + 16,000) | 63,000 | |
| Taxation (15,000 + 10,000) | 25,000 | |
| | | 88,000 |
| *Total equity and liabilities* | | 416,000 |

*Note* especially how:

(a) The uncancelled loan stock in S Co becomes a liability of the group
(b) The goods in transit is the difference between the current accounts ($18,000 – $12,000)
(c) The investment in S Co's shares is cancelled against S Co's share capital

# 2 Non-controlling interests

**FAST FORWARD**

In the consolidated statement of financial position it is necessary to distinguish non-controlling interests from those net assets attributable to the group and financed by shareholders' equity.

## 2.1 Introduction

It was mentioned earlier that the total assets and liabilities of subsidiary companies are included in the consolidated statement of financial position, even in the case of subsidiaries which are only partly owned. A proportion of the net assets of such subsidiaries in fact belongs to investors from outside the group (**non-controlling interests**).

IFRS 3 allows two alternative ways of calculating non-controlling interest in the group statement of financial position. Non-controlling interest can be valued at:

(a) Its proportionate share of the fair value of the subsidiary's net assets; or
(b) Full (or fair) value (usually based on the market value of the shares held by the non-controlling interest).

You are required to be able to apply both of these methods in F7. The exam question will tell you which method to use. If you are required to use the 'full (or fair) value' method, then you will be given the share price or told what the fair value of the non-controlling interest is. You will normally be required to use the fair value method.

The following example shows non-controlling interest calculated at its proportionate share of the subsidiary's net assets.

## 2.2 Example: non-controlling interest

P Co has owned 75% of the share capital of S Co since the date of S Co's incorporation. Their latest statements of financial position are given below.

STATEMENT OF FINANCIAL POSITION

|  | P Co $ | S Co $ |
|---|---|---|
| Assets |  |  |
| Non-current assets |  |  |
| Property, plant and equipment | 50,000 | 35,000 |
| 30,000 $1 ordinary shares in S Co at cost | 30,000 |  |
|  | 80,000 |  |
| Current assets | 45,000 | 35,000 |
| Total assets | 125,000 | 70,000 |
| Equity and liabilities |  |  |
| Equity |  |  |
| $1 ordinary shares | 80,000 | 40,000 |
| Retained earnings | 25,000 | 10,000 |
|  | 105,000 | 50,000 |
| Current liabilities | 20,000 | 20,000 |
| Total equity and liabilities | 125,000 | 70,000 |

Required

Prepare the consolidated statement of financial position.

## Solution

All of S Co's net assets are consolidated despite the fact that the company is only 75% owned. The amount of net assets attributable to non-controlling interests is calculated as follows.

|  | $ |
|---|---|
| Non-controlling share of share capital (25% × $40,000) | 10,000 |
| Non-controlling share of retained earnings (25% × $10,000) | 2,500 |
|  | 12,500 |

Of S Co's share capital of $40,000, $10,000 is included in the figure for non-controlling interest, while $30,000 is cancelled with P Co's asset 'investment in S Co'.

The consolidated statement of financial position can now be prepared.

P GROUP
CONSOLIDATED STATEMENT OF FINANCIAL POSITION

|  | $ | $ |
|---|---|---|
| Assets |  |  |
| Property, plant and equipment |  | 85,000 |
| Current assets |  | 80,000 |
| Total assets |  | 165,000 |

*Equity and liabilities*
Equity attributable to owners of the parent

| | |
|---|---:|
| Share capital | 80,000 |
| Retained earnings $(25,000 + (75\% \times \$10,000))$ | 32,500 |
| | 112,500 |
| Non-controlling interest | 12,500 |
| | 125,000 |
| Current liabilities | 40,000 |
| *Total equity and liabilities* | 165,000 |

## 2.3 Procedure

(a)    Aggregate the assets and liabilities in the statement of financial position ie 100% P + 100% S irrespective of how much P actually owns.

This shows the amount of net assets **controlled** by the group.

(b)    Share capital is that of the parent only.

(c)    Balance of subsidiary's reserves are consolidated (after cancelling any intra-group items).

(d)    Calculate the non-controlling interest share of the subsidiary's net assets (share capital plus reserves).

**Exam focus point**

See *Student Accountant* July 2010 for an article by the examiner, Steve Scott, entitled 'IFRS 3 Business Combinations (revised)'.

# 3 Dividends paid by a subsidiary

When a subsidiary company pays a **dividend** during the year the accounting treatment is not difficult. Suppose S Co, a 60% subsidiary of P Co, pays a dividend of $1,000 on the last day of its accounting period. Its total reserves before paying the dividend stood at $5,000.

(a)    $400 of the dividend is paid to non-controlling shareholders. The cash leaves the group and will not appear anywhere in the consolidated statement of financial position.

(b)    The parent company receives $600 of the dividend, debiting cash and crediting profit or loss. This will be cancelled on consolidation.

(c)    The remaining balance of retained earnings in S Co's statement of financial position ($4,000) will be consolidated in the normal way. The group's share (60% × $4,000 = $2,400) will be included in group retained earnings in the statement of financial position; the non-controlling interest share (40% × $4,000 = $1,600) is credited to the non-controlling interest account in the statement of financial position.

# 4 Goodwill arising on consolidation

**FAST FORWARD**

**Goodwill** is the excess of the amount transferred plus the amount of non-controlling interests over the fair value of the net assets of the subsidiary.

## 4.1 Accounting

To begin with, **we will examine the entries made by the parent company in its own statement of financial position when it acquires shares.**

When a company P Co wishes to **purchase shares** in a company S Co it must pay the previous owners of those shares. The most obvious form of payment would be in **cash**. Suppose P Co purchases all 40,000 $1 shares in S Co and pays $60,000 cash to the previous shareholders in consideration. The entries in P Co's books would be:

| DEBIT | Investment in S Co at cost | $60,000 | |
|---|---|---|---|
| CREDIT | Bank | | $60,000 |

However, the previous shareholders might be prepared to accept some other form of consideration. For example, they might accept an agreed number of **shares** in P Co. P Co would then issue new shares in the agreed number and allot them to the former shareholders of S Co. This kind of deal might be attractive to P Co since it avoids the need for a heavy cash outlay. The former shareholders of S Co would retain an indirect interest in that company's profitability via their new holding in its parent company.

Continuing the example, suppose that instead of $60,000 cash the shareholders of S Co agreed to accept one $1 ordinary share in P Co for every two $1 ordinary shares in S Co. P Co would then need to issue and allot 20,000 new $1 shares. How would this transaction be recorded in the books of P Co?

The former shareholders of S Co have presumably agreed to accept 20,000 shares in P Co because they consider each of those shares to have a value of $3. This gives us the following method of recording the transaction in P Co's books.

| DEBIT | Investment in S Co | $60,000 | |
|---|---|---|---|
| CREDIT | Share capital | | $20,000 |
| | Share premium account | | $40,000 |

The amount which P Co records in its books as the cost of its investment in S Co may be more or less than the book value of the assets it acquires. Suppose that S Co in the previous example has nil reserves and nil liabilities, so that its share capital of $40,000 is balanced by tangible assets with a book value of $40,000. For simplicity, assume that the book value of S Co's assets is the same as their market or fair value.

Now when the directors of P Co agree to pay $60,000 for a 100% investment in S Co they must believe that, in addition to its tangible assets of $40,000, S Co must also have intangible assets worth $20,000. This amount of $20,000 paid over and above the value of the tangible assets acquired is called **goodwill arising on consolidation** (sometimes **premium on acquisition**).

Following the normal cancellation procedure the $40,000 share capital in S Co's statement of financial position could be cancelled against $40,000 of the 'investment in S Co' in the statement of financial position of P Co. This would leave a $20,000 debit uncancelled in the parent company's accounts and this $20,000 would appear in the consolidated statement of financial position under the caption 'Intangible non-current assets: goodwill arising on consolidation'.

## 4.2 Goodwill and pre-acquisition profits

Up to now we have assumed that S Co had nil retained earnings when its shares were purchased by P Co. Assuming instead that S Co had earned profits of $8,000 in the period before acquisition, its statement of financial position just before the purchase would look as follows.

| | $ |
|---|---|
| Total assets | 48,000 |
| | |
| Share capital | 40,000 |
| Retained earnings | 8,000 |
| | 48,000 |

If P Co now purchases all the shares in S Co it will acquire total assets worth $48,000 at a cost of $60,000. Clearly in this case S Co's intangible assets (goodwill) are being valued at $12,000. It should be apparent that any earnings retained by the subsidiary **prior to its acquisition** by the parent company must be **incorporated in the cancellation** process so as to arrive at a figure for goodwill arising on consolidation. In other words, not only S Co's share capital, but also its **pre-acquisition** retained earnings, must be cancelled against the asset 'investment in S Co' in the accounts of the parent company. The uncancelled balance of $12,000 appears in the consolidated statement of financial position.

The consequence of this is that **any pre-acquisition retained earnings of a subsidiary company are not aggregated with the parent company's retained earnings** in the consolidated statement of financial position. The figure of consolidated retained earnings comprises the retained earnings of the parent company plus the **post-acquisition retained earnings only of subsidiary companies**. The post-acquisition retained earnings are simply retained earnings now *less* retained earnings at acquisition.

## 4.3 Example: goodwill and pre-acquisition profits

Sing Co acquired the ordinary shares of Wing Co on 31 March when the draft statements of financial position of each company were as follows.

SING CO
STATEMENT OF FINANCIAL POSITION AS AT 31 MARCH

|  | $ |
|---|---|
| *Assets* | |
| Non-current assets | |
| Investment in 50,000 shares of Wing Co at cost | 80,000 |
| Current assets | 40,000 |
| *Total assets* | 120,000 |
| *Equity and liabilities* | |
| Equity | |
| Ordinary shares | 75,000 |
| Retained earnings | 45,000 |
| *Total equity and liabilities* | 120,000 |

WING CO
STATEMENT OF FINANCIAL POSITION AS AT 31 MARCH

|  | $ |
|---|---|
| Current assets | 60,000 |
| | |
| Equity | |
| 50,000 ordinary shares of $1 each | 50,000 |
| Retained earnings | 10,000 |
| | 60,000 |

Prepare the consolidated statement of financial position as at 31 March.

## Solution

The technique to adopt here is to produce a new working: 'Goodwill'. A proforma working is set out below.

*Goodwill*

|  | $ | $ |
|---|---|---|
| Consideration transferred | | X |
| Net assets acquired as represented by: | | |
| Ordinary share capital | X | |
| Share premium | X | |
| Retained earnings on acquisition | X | |
| | | (X) |
| Goodwill | | X |

Applying this to our example the working will look like this.

|  | $ | $ |
|---|---|---|
| Consideration transferred | | 80,000 |
| Net assets acquired as represented by: | | |
| Ordinary share capital | 50,000 | |
| Retained earnings on acquisition | 10,000 | |
| | | (60,000) |
| Goodwill | | 20,000 |

SING CO
CONSOLIDATED STATEMENT OF FINANCIAL POSITION AS AT 31 MARCH

|  | $ |
|---|---|
| *Assets* | |
| Non-current assets | |
|   Goodwill arising on consolidation (W) | 20,000 |
| Current assets (40,000 + 60,000) | 100,000 |
| Total assets | 120,000 |
| | |
| *Equity and liabilities* | |
| Ordinary shares | 75,000 |
| Retained earnings | 45,000 |
| Total equity and liabilities | 120,000 |

## 4.4 Goodwill and non-controlling interest

Now let us look at what would happen if Sing Co had obtained less than 100% of the shares of Wing Co.

If Sing Co had paid $70,000 for 40,000 shares in Wing Co, the goodwill working would be as follows:

|  | $ |
|---|---|
| Consideration transferred | 70,000 |
| Non-controlling interest (60,000 x 20%) | 12,000 |
| Net assets acquired | (60,000) |
| Goodwill | 22,000 |

## 4.5 Non-controlling interest at fair value

IFRS 3 (revised) gives entities the option of valuing non-controlling interest (NCI) at fair value. The thinking behind this is that the non-controlling interest also owns some of the goodwill in the subsidiary, and that the traditional method of consolidation does not show this goodwill.

IFRS 3 revised suggests that the closest approximation to fair value will be the market price of the shares held by non-controlling shareholders just before acquisition by the parent.

Continuing our example above, we will assume that the market price of the shares was $1.25. The goodwill calculation will then be as follows:

|  | $ |
|---|---|
| Consideration transferred | 70,000 |
| Fair value of NCI (10,000 × $1.25) | 12,500 |
| Net assets at acquisition | (60,000) |
| Goodwill | 22,500 |

Goodwill (total $22,500) is $500 higher than goodwill calculated measuring non-controlling interest at its share of the net assets of the subsidiary. This $500 represents the **goodwill attributable to the non-controlling interest**.

## 4.6 Non-controlling interest at year end

Where the option is used to value non-controlling interest at fair value, the goodwill attributable to the NCI will also be added to the NCI at the year end. The most straightforward way to calculate this is to start with the fair value of the NCI at acquisition and add the NCI share of post-acquisition retained earnings.

This is illustrated in the following worked example.

# 4.7 Worked example

P acquired 75% of the shares in S on 1 January 2007 when S had retained earnings of $15,000. The market price of S's shares just before the date of acquisition was $1.60. P values non-controlling interest at fair value. Goodwill is not impaired.

The statements of financial position of P and S at 31 December 20X7 were as follows:

|  | P | S |
|---|---|---|
|  | $ | $ |
| Property, plant and equipment | 60,000 | 50,000 |
| Shares in S | 68,000 | – |
|  | 128,000 | 50,000 |
| Current assets | 52,000 | 35,000 |
|  | 180,000 | 85,000 |
| Share capital – $1 shares | 100,000 | 50,000 |
| Retained earnings | 70,000 | 25,000 |
|  | 170,000 | 75,000 |
| Current liabilities | 10,000 | 10,000 |
|  | 180,000 | 85,000 |

Prepare the consolidated statement of financial position of the P Group.

# 4.8 Solution

## CONSOLIDATED STATEMENT OF FINANCIAL POSITION

|  | $ |
|---|---|
| *Assets* |  |
| Property plant and equipment (60,000 + 50,000) | 110,000 |
| Goodwill (W1) | 23,000 |
| Current assets (52,000 + 35,000) | 87,000 |
| Total assets | 220,000 |
| *Equity and liabilities* |  |
| Equity attributable to the owners of P |  |
| Share capital | 100,000 |
| Retained earnings (W2) | 77,500 |
|  | 177,500 |
| Non-controlling interest (W3) | 22,500 |
| Total equity | 200,000 |
| Current liabilities (10,000 + 10,000) | 20,000 |
|  | 220,000 |

*Workings*

1     *Goodwill*

|  | Group |
|---|---|
|  | $ |
| Consideration transferred | 68,000 |
| Fair value of NCI (12,500 × $1.60) | 20,000 |
| Net assets of S at acquisition (50,000 + 15,000) | (65,000) |
| Goodwill | 23,000 |

2    *Retained earnings*

|  | P | S |
|---|---|---|
|  | $ | $ |
| Per statement of financial position | 70,000 | 25,000 |
| Less pre- acquisition |  | (15,000) |
|  |  | 10,000 |
| Group share of S (10,000 × 75%) | 7,500 |  |
| Group retained earnings | 77,500 |  |

3    *Non-controlling interest at year end*

|  | $ |
|---|---|
| NCI at acquisition | 20,000 |
| Share of post-acquisition retained earnings (10,000 x 25%) | 2,500 |
|  | 22,500 |

## 4.9 Effect of non-controlling interest at fair value

You can see from the above example that the use of the fair value option increases goodwill and non-controlling interest by the same amount. That amount represents goodwill attributable to the shares held by non-controlling shareholders. It is not necessarily proportionate to the goodwill attributed to the parent. The parent may have paid proportionately more to acquire a controlling interest. If non-controlling interest was valued at share of net assets, goodwill and non-controlling interest in the example above would be as follows:

*W1 Goodwill*

|  | $ |
|---|---|
| Considered transferred | 68,000 |
| Non-controlling interest ((50,000 + 15,000) × 25%) | 16,250 |
| Net assets of S at acquisition (50,000 + 15,000) | (65,000) |
|  | 19,250 |

*W3 Non-controlling interest at year end*

|  | $ |
|---|---|
| NCI at acquisition | 16,250 |
| Share of post-acquisition retained earnings | 2,500 |
|  | 18,750 |

Compare these with goodwill and non-controlling interest in the solution above and you will see that both have been reduced by $3,750 – the goodwill attributable to the non-controlling interest. So whether non-controlling interest is valued at share of net assets or at fair value, the statement of financial position will still balance.

**Exam focus point**

> The option to value non-controlling interest at fair value is introduced by the revised IFRS 3, but it is just an **option**. Companies can choose to adopt it or to continue to value non-controlling interest at share of net assets. In the exam you will probably be directed to apply the fair value option. If you are required to use the fair value option, the examiner has stated that there are two possible options:
>
> (1)    You may be given the share price of the subsidiary just before acquisition.
>
> (2)    You may be told that the non-controlling interest is valued at a certain amount.
>
> **In the exam**, the consolidation question will tell you which method to use. It will state either:
>
> 'It is the group policy to value the non-controlling interest at full (or fair) value;' or
>
> 'It is the group policy to value the non-controlling interest at its proportionate share of the (fair value of the) subsidiary's identifiable net assets'.
>
> You are more likely to be tested on non-controlling interest at full (fair) value.

## 4.10 Impairment of goodwill

Goodwill arising on consolidation is subjected to an annual impairment review and impairment may be expressed as an amount or as a percentage. The double entry to write off the impairment is:

DEBIT  Group retained earnings                    CREDIT Goodwill

However, when non-controlling interest is valued at **fair value** the goodwill in the statement of financial position includes goodwill attributable to the non-controlling interest. In this case the double entry will reflect the non-controlling interest proportion based on their shareholding as follows:

DEBIT  Group retained earnings                    CREDIT  Goodwill
DEBIT  Non-controlling interest

In our solution above in 4.8 the non-controlling interest holds 25%. If the total goodwill of $23,000 was impaired by 20% the double entry for this would be:

|  | $ |  | $ |
|---|---|---|---|
| DEBIT  Retained earnings | 3,450 | CREDIT Goodwill | 4,600 |
| DEBIT Non-controlling interest | 1,150 | | |

Non-controlling interest at the year end would then be $21,350.

## 4.11 Gain on a bargain purchase

Goodwill arising on consolidation is one form of **purchased goodwill**, and is governed by IFRS 3. As explained in an earlier chapter IFRS 3 requires that goodwill arising on consolidation should **be capitalised in the consolidated statement of financial position** and **reviewed for impairment every year**.

Goodwill arising on consolidation is the difference between the cost of an acquisition and the value of the subsidiary's net assets acquired. This difference can be **negative**: the aggregate of the fair values of the separable net assets acquired may **exceed** what the parent company paid for them. This is often referred to as **negative** goodwill.  IFRS 3 refers to it as a **'gain on a bargain purchase'**. In this situation:

(a)     An entity should first **re-assess** the amounts at which it has measured both the cost of the combination and the acquiree's identifiable net assets. This exercise should **identify any errors.**

(b)     Any **excess remaining** should be **recognised immediately in profit or loss**.

## 4.12 Forms of consideration

The consideration paid by the parent for the shares in the subsidiary can take different forms and this will affect the calculation of goodwill. Here are some examples:

### 4.12.1 Contingent consideration

The parent acquired 60% of the subsidiary's $100m share capital on 1 Jan 20X6 for a cash payment of $150m and a further payment of $50m on 31 March 20X7 if the subsidiary's post acquisition profits have exceeded an agreed figure by that date.

In the financial statements for the year to 31 December 20X6 $50m will be added to the cost of the combination, discounted as appropriate.

IFRS 3 requires the acquisition-date **fair value** of contingent consideration to be recognised as part of the consideration for the acquiree.  In an examination question students will be told the acquisition-date fair value or told how to calculate it.

The acquirer may be required to pay contingent consideration in the form of equity or of a debt instrument or cash. A debt instrument should be presented as under IAS 32. Contingent consideration can also be an asset, if the consideration has already been transferred and the acquirer has the right to require the return of some of it, if certain considerations are met.

Note: The previous version of IFRS 3 only required contingent consideration to be recognised if it was **probable** that it would become payable. IFRS 3 (revised) dispenses with this requirement – **all contingent**

**consideration is now recognised**. It is possible that the fair value of the contingent consideration may change after the acquisition date. If this is due to additional information obtained that affects the position at acquisition date, goodwill should be remeasured. If the change is due to events after the acquisition date (such as a higher earnings target has been met, so more is payable) it should be accounted for under IFRS 9 if the consideration is in the form of a financial instrument (such as loan notes) or under IAS 37 as an increase in a provision if it is cash. Any equity instrument is not remeasured.

### 4.12.2 Deferred consideration

An agreement may be made that part of the consideration for the combination will be paid at a future date. This consideration will therefore be discounted to its present value using the acquiring entity's cost of capital.

### Example

The parent acquired 75% of the subsidiary's 80m $1 shares on 1 January 20X6. It paid $3.50 per share and agreed to pay a further $108m on 1 January 20X7.

The parent company's cost of capital is 8%.

In the financial statements for the year to 31 December 20X6 the cost of the combination will be as follows:

|  | $m |
|---|---|
| 80m shares × 75% × $3.50 | 210 |
| Deferred consideration: | |
| $108m × 1/1.08 | 100 |
| Total consideration | 310 |

At 31 December 20X6 $8m will be charged to finance costs, being the **unwinding of the discount** on the deferred consideration. The deferred consideration was discounted by $8m to allow for the time value of money. At 1 January 20X7 the full amount becomes payable.

### 4.12.3 Share exchange

The parent has acquired 12,000 $1 shares in the subsidiary by issuing 5 of its own $1 shares for every 4 shares in the subsidiary. The market value of the parent company's shares is $6.

Cost of the combination:

|  | $ |
|---|---|
| 12,000 × 5/4 × $6 | 90,000 |

Note that this is credited to the share capital and share premium of the parent company as follows:

|  | DR | CR |
|---|---|---|
| Investment in subsidiary | 90,000 | |
| Share capital ($12,000 × 5/4) | | 15,000 |
| Share premium ($12,000 × 5/4 × 5) | | 75,000 |

### 4.12.4 Expenses and issue costs

Expenses of the combination, such as lawyers and accountants fees are written off as incurred. However, IFRS 3 requires that the costs of issuing equity are treated as a deduction from the proceeds of the equity issue. Share issue costs will therefore be debited to the share premium account. Issue costs of financial instruments are deducted from the proceeds of the financial instrument.

## 4.13 Consolidation adjustments

At the date of acquisition the parent recognises the assets, liabilities and contingent liabilities of the subsidiary at their fair value at the date when control is acquired. It may be that some of these assets or liabilities had not previously been recognised by the acquiree.

For instance, the subsidiary may have tax losses brought forward, but had not recognised these as an asset because it could not foresee future profits against which they could be offset. If the tax losses can now be utilised by the acquirer they will be recognised as an identifiable asset and included in the goodwill calculation.

# 5 Non-controlling interest at fair value

Now we will look at a full consolidation question including non-controlling interest at fair value.

 **Question**                                      Consolidated statement of financial position

The draft statements of financial position of Ping Co and Pong Co on 30 June 20X8 were as follows.

STATEMENT OF FINANCIAL POSITION AS AT 30 JUNE 20X8

|  | PING CO $ | PONG CO $ |
|---|---|---|
| *Assets* | | |
| *Non-current assets* | | |
| Property, plant and equipment | 50,000 | 40,000 |
| 20,000 ordinary shares in Pong Co at cost | 30,000 | |
| | 80,000 | |
| *Current assets* | | |
| Inventory | 3,000 | 8,000 |
| Owed by Ping Co | | 10,000 |
| Receivables | 16,000 | 7,000 |
| Cash | 2,000 | – |
| | 21,000 | 25,000 |
| Total assets | 101,000 | 65,000 |
| *Equity and liabilities* | | |
| Equity | | |
| Ordinary shares of $1 each | 45,000 | 25,000 |
| Revaluation surplus | 12,000 | 5,000 |
| Retained earnings | 26,000 | 28,000 |
| | 83,000 | 58,000 |
| Current liabilities | | |
| Owed to Pong Co | 8,000 | – |
| Trade payables | 10,000 | 7,000 |
| | 18,000 | 7,000 |
| Total equity and liabilities | 101,000 | 65,000 |

Ping Co acquired its investment in Pong Co on 1 July 20X7 when the retained earnings of Pong Co stood at $6,000. The agreed consideration was $30,000 cash and a further $10,000 on 1 July 20X9. Ping Co's cost of capital is 7%. Pong Co has an internally-developed brand name – 'Pongo' – which was valued at $5,000 at the date of acquisition. There have been no changes in the share capital or revaluation surplus of Pong Co since that date. At 30 June 20X8 Pong Co had invoiced Ping Co for goods to the value of $2,000 and Ping Co had sent payment in full but this had not been received by Pong Co.

There is no impairment of goodwill. It is group policy to value non-controlling interest at full fair value. At the acquisition date the non-controlling interest was valued at $9,000.

Prepare the consolidated statement of financial position of Ping Co as at 30 June 20X8.

## 1 Calculate goodwill

*Goodwill*

|  | | Group $ |
|---|---|---|
| Consideration transferred (W2) | | 38,734 |
| Fair value of NCI | | 9,000 |
| Net assets acquired as represented by: | | |
| Ordinary share capital | 25,000 | |
| Revaluation surplus on acquisition | 5,000 | |
| Retained earnings on acquisition | 6,000 | |
| Intangible asset – brand name | 5,000 | |
|  | | (41,000) |
| Goodwill | | 6,734 |

This goodwill must be capitalised in the consolidated statement of financial position.

## 2 Consideration transferred

|  | $ |
|---|---|
| Cash paid | 30,000 |
| Fair value of deferred consideration $(10,000 \times 1/(1.07^{2*}))$ | 8,734 |
|  | 38,734 |

* Note that the deferred consideration has been discounted at 7% for two years (1 July 20X7 to 1 July 20X9).

However, at the date of the current financial statements, 30 June 20X8, the discount for one year has unwound. The amount of the discount unwound is

|  | $ |
|---|---|
| $(10,000 \times 1/1.07) - 8,734$ | 612 |

So this amount will be charged to finance costs in the consolidated financial statements and the deferred consideration under liabilities will be shown as $9,346 (8,734 + 612).

## 3 Calculate consolidated reserves.

*Consolidated revaluation surplus*

|  | $ |
|---|---|
| Ping Co | 12,000 |
| Share of Pong Co's post acquisition revaluation surplus | – |
|  | 12,000 |

*Consolidated retained earnings*

|  | Ping $ | Pong $ |
|---|---|---|
| Retained earnings per question | 26,000 | 28,000 |
| Less pre-acquisition | | (6,000) |
| Discount unwound – finance costs | (612) | 22,000 |
| Share of Pong: 80% × $22,000 | 17,600 | |
|  | 42,988 | |

## 4 Calculate non-controlling interest at year end

|  | $ |
|---|---|
| Fair value of non-controlling interest | 9,000 |
| Share of post-acquisition retained earnings (22,000 x 20%) | 4,400 |
|  | 13,400 |

## 5

**Agree current accounts**

Pong Co has cash in transit of $2,000 which should be added to cash and deducted from the amount owed by Ping Co.

Cancel common items: these are the current accounts between the two companies of $8,000 each.

6     **Prepare the consolidated statement of financial position.**

PING CO
CONSOLIDATED STATEMENT OF FINANCIAL POSITION AS AT 30 JUNE 20X8

|  | $ | $ |
|---|---|---|
| *Assets* | | |
| *Non-current assets* | | |
| Property, plant and equipment (50,000 + 40,000) | | 90,000 |
| Intangible assets: Goodwill (W1) | | 6,734 |
| Brand name (W1) | | 5,000 |
| *Current assets* | | |
| Inventories (3,000 + 8,000) | 11,000 | |
| Receivables (16,000 + 7,000) | 23,000 | |
| Cash (2,000 + 2,000) | 4,000 | |
| | | 38,000 |
| *Total assets* | | 139,734 |
| *Equity and liabilities* | | |
| *Equity* | | |
| Ordinary shares of $1 each | 45,000 | |
| Revaluation surplus (W3) | 12,000 | |
| Retained earnings (W3) | 42,988 | |
| | | 99,988 |
| Non-controlling interest (W4) | | 13,400 |
| | | 113,388 |
| Current liabilities | | |
| Trade payables (10,000 + 7,000) | | 17,000 |
| Deferred consideration (W2) | | 9,346 |
| *Total equity and liabilities* | | 139,734 |

**Exam focus point**

> The examiner has stated that he will usually examine the goodwill calculation in which non-controlling interest is stated at fair value, so make sure you understand how to do this.

# 6 Intra-group trading

**FAST FORWARD** ▶▶

> Intra-group trading can give rise to **unrealised profit** which is eliminated on consolidation.

## 6.1 Unrealised profit

Any receivable/payable balances outstanding between the companies are cancelled on consolidation. No further problem arises if all such intra-group transactions are **undertaken at cost**, without any mark-up for profit.

However, each company in a group is a separate trading entity and may wish to treat other group companies in the same way as any other customer. In this case, a company (say A Co) may buy goods at one price and sell them at a higher price to another group company (B Co). The accounts of A Co will quite properly include the profit earned on sales to B Co; and similarly B Co's statement of financial position will include inventories at their cost to B Co, ie at the amount at which they were purchased from A Co.

This gives rise to two problems.

(a) Although A Co makes a profit as soon as it sells goods to B Co, the group does not make a sale or achieve a profit until an outside customer buys the goods from B Co.

(b) Any purchases from A Co which remain unsold by B Co at the year end will be included in B Co's inventory. Their value in the statement of financial position will be their cost to B Co, which is not the same as their cost to the group.

The objective of consolidated accounts is to present the financial position of several connected companies as that of a single entity, the group. This means that **in a consolidated statement of financial position the only profits recognised should be those earned by the group** in providing goods or services to outsiders; and similarly, inventory in the consolidated statement of financial position should be valued at cost to the group.

Suppose that a parent company P Co buys goods for $1,600 and sells them to a wholly owned subsidiary S Co for $2,000. The goods are in S Co's inventory at the year end and appear in S Co's statement of financial position at $2,000. In this case, P Co will record a profit of $400 in its individual accounts, but from the group's point of view the figures are:

| | |
|---|---:|
| Cost | $1,600 |
| External sales | nil |
| Closing inventory at cost | $1,600 |
| Profit/loss | nil |

If we add together the figures for retained earnings and inventory in the individual statements of financial position of P Co and S Co the resulting figures for consolidated retained earnings and consolidated inventory will each be overstated by $400. A **consolidation adjustment** is therefore necessary as follows.

DEBIT        Group retained earnings
CREDIT     Group inventory (statement of financial position)

with the amount of **profit unrealised** by the group.

## 6.2 Non-controlling interests in unrealised intra-group profits

A further problem occurs where a subsidiary company which is **not wholly owned is involved in intra-group trading** within the group. If a subsidiary S Co is 75% owned and sells goods to the parent company for $16,000 cost plus $4,000 profit, ie for $20,000 and if these items are unsold by P Co at the end of the reporting period, the 'unrealised' profit of $4,000 earned by S Co and charged to P Co will be partly owned by the non-controlling interest of S Co.

The correct treatment of these intragroup profits is to remove the whole profit, charging the non-controlling interest with their proportion.

**Entries to learn**

| | |
|---|---|
| DEBIT | Group retained earnings |
| DEBIT | Non-controlling interest |
| CREDIT | Group inventory (statement of financial position) |

## 6.3 Example: non-controlling interests and intra-group profits

P Co has owned 75% of the shares of S Co since the incorporation of that company. During the year to 31 December 20X2, S Co sold goods costing $16,000 to P Co at a price of $20,000 and these goods were still unsold by P Co at the end of the year. Draft statements of financial position of each company at 31 December 20X2 were as follows.

| | P Co | | S Co | |
|---|---|---|---|---|
| Assets | $ | $ | $ | $ |
| Non-current assets | | | | |
| Property, plant and equipment | 125,000 | | 120,000 | |
| Investment: 75,000 shares in S Co at cost | 75,000 | | – | |
| | | 200,000 | | 120,000 |
| Current assets | | | | |
| Inventories | 50,000 | | 48,000 | |
| Trade receivables | 20,000 | | 16,000 | |
| | | 70,000 | | 64,000 |
| Total assets | | 270,000 | | 184,000 |
| Equity and liabilities | | | | |
| Equity | | | | |
| Ordinary shares of $1 each fully paid | 80,000 | | 100,000 | |
| Retained earnings | 150,000 | | 60,000 | |
| | | 230,000 | | 160,000 |
| Current liabilities | | 40,000 | | 24,000 |
| Total equity and liabilities | | 270,000 | | 184,000 |

Required

Prepare the consolidated statement of financial position of P Co at 31 December 20X2. The fair value of the non-controlling interest at acquisition was $25,000.

## Solution

The profit earned by S Co but unrealised by the group is $4,000 of which $3,000 (75%) is attributable to the group and $1,000 (25%) to the non-controlling interest.

| | P Co | S Co |
|---|---|---|
| | $ | $ |
| Retained earnings | | |
| Per question | 150,000 | 60,000 |
| Less unrealised profit | | (4,000) |
| | | 56,000 |
| Share of S Co: $56,000 × 75% | 42,000 | |
| | 192,000 | |
| Non-controlling interest | | |
| Fair value at acquisition | | 25,000 |
| Share of post-acquisition retained earnings (56,000 × 25%) | | 14,000 |
| | | 39,000 |

P CO
CONSOLIDATED STATEMENT OF FINANCIAL POSITION AS AT 31 DECEMBER 20X2

| | $ | $ |
|---|---|---|
| Assets | | |
| Property, plant and equipment | | 245,000 |
| Current assets | | |
| Inventories $(50,000 + 48,000 – 4,000) | 94,000 | |
| Trade receivables | 36,000 | |
| | | 130,000 |
| Total assets | | 375,000 |
| Equity and liabilities | | |
| Equity | | |
| Ordinary shares of $1 each | 80,000 | |
| Retained earnings | 192,000 | |
| | | 272,000 |
| Non-controlling interest | | 39,000 |

|  |  | 311,000 |
|---|---|---|
| Current liabilities |  | 64,000 |
| *Total equity and liabilities* |  | 375,000 |

**Unrealised profit**

P Co acquired 80% of the shares in S Co one year ago when the reserves of S Co stood at $10,000. Draft statements of financial position for each company are as follows.

|  | P Co | | S Co | |
|---|---|---|---|---|
|  | $ | $ | $ | $ |
| *Assets* |  |  |  |  |
| Non-current assets |  |  |  |  |
| Property, plant and equipment | 80,000 |  |  | 40,000 |
| Investment in S Co at cost | 46,000 |  |  |  |
|  |  | 126,000 |  |  |
| Current assets |  | 40,000 |  | 30,000 |
| *Total assets* |  | 166,000 |  | 70,000 |
| *Equity and liabilities* |  |  |  |  |
| Equity |  |  |  |  |
| Ordinary shares of $1 each | 100,000 |  | 30,000 |  |
| Retained earnings | 45,000 |  | 22,000 |  |
|  |  | 145,000 |  | 52,000 |
| Current liabilities |  | 21,000 |  | 18,000 |
| *Total equity and liabilities* |  | 166,000 |  | 70,000 |

During the year S Co sold goods to P Co for $50,000, the profit to S Co being 20% of selling price. At the end of the reporting period, $15,000 of these goods remained unsold in the inventories of P Co. At the same date, P Co owed S Co $12,000 for goods bought and this debt is included in the trade payables of P Co and the receivables of S Co. Non-controlling interest is valued at full fair value. It was valued at $9,000 at the date of acquisition.

*Required*

Prepare a draft consolidated statement of financial position for P Co.

P CO
CONSOLIDATED STATEMENT OF FINANCIAL POSITION

|  | $ | $ |
|---|---|---|
| *Assets* |  |  |
| Non-current assets |  |  |
| Property, plant and equipment (80,000 + 40,000) | 120,000 |  |
| Goodwill (W1) | 15,000 |  |
|  |  | 135,000 |
| Current assets (W3) |  | 55,000 |
| *Total assets* |  | 190,000 |
| *Equity and liabilities* |  |  |
| Equity |  |  |
| Ordinary shares of $1 each | 100,000 |  |
| Retained earnings (W2) | 52,200 |  |
|  |  | 152,200 |
| Non-controlling interest (W5) |  | 10,800 |
| Current liabilities (W4) |  | 27,000 |
| *Total equity and liabilities* |  | 190,000 |

*Workings*

1   *Goodwill*

|                                                    | $       | $        |
|----------------------------------------------------|---------|----------|
| Consideration transferred                          |         | 46,000   |
| Fair value of non-controlling interest             |         | 9,000    |
| Net assets acquired as represented by              |         |          |
|   Share capital                                    | 30,000  |          |
|   Retained earnings                                | 10,000  |          |
|                                                    |         | (40,000) |
| Goodwill                                           |         | 15,000   |

2   *Retained earnings*

|                                     | P Co    | S Co     |
|-------------------------------------|---------|----------|
|                                     | $       | $        |
| Retained earnings per question      | 45,000  | 22,000   |
| Unrealised profit: 20% × $15,000    |         | (3,000)  |
| Pre-acquisition                     |         | (10,000) |
|                                     |         | 9,000    |
| Share of S Co 80%                   | 7,200   |          |
|                                     | 52,200  |          |

3   *Current assets*

|                                                    | $        | $      |
|----------------------------------------------------|----------|--------|
| In P Co's statement of financial position          |          | 40,000 |
| In S Co's statement of financial position          | 30,000   |        |
| Less S Co's current account with P Co cancelled     | (12,000) |        |
|                                                    |          | 18,000 |
|                                                    |          | 58,000 |
| Less unrealised profit excluded from inventory valuation |    | (3,000) |
|                                                    |          | 55,000 |

4   *Current liabilities*

|                                                    | $        |
|----------------------------------------------------|----------|
| In P Co's statement of financial position          | 21,000   |
| Less P Co's current account with S Co cancelled     | (12,000) |
|                                                    | 9,000    |
| In S Co's statement of financial position          | 18,000   |
|                                                    | 27,000   |

5   *Non-controlling interest*

|                                                           | $      |
|-----------------------------------------------------------|--------|
| Fair value at date of acquisition                         | 9,000  |
| Share of post-acquisition retained earnings (9,000 × 20%) | 1,800  |
|                                                           | 10,800 |

# 7 Intra-group sales of non-current assets

FAST FORWARD ▶▶

> As well as engaging in trading activities with each other, group companies may on occasion wish to **transfer non-current assets**.

## 7.1 Accounting treatment

In their individual accounts the companies concerned will treat the transfer just like a sale between unconnected parties: the selling company will record a profit or loss on sale, while the purchasing company will record the asset at the amount paid to acquire it, and will use that amount as the basis for calculating depreciation.

On consolidation, the usual **'group entity' principle applies**. The consolidated statement of financial position must show assets at their cost to the group, and any depreciation charged must be based on that cost. Two consolidation adjustments will usually be needed to achieve this.

(a)    An adjustment to alter retained earnings and non-current assets cost so as to remove any element of unrealised profit or loss. This is similar to the adjustment required in respect of unrealised profit in inventory.

(b)    An adjustment to alter retained earnings and accumulated depreciation is made so that consolidated depreciation is based on the asset's cost to the group.

In practice, these steps are combined so that the retained earnings of the entity making the unrealised profit are debited with the unrealised profit less the additional depreciation.

The double entry is as follows.

(a)    Sale by parent

DEBIT        Group retained earnings
CREDIT    Non-current assets

with the profit on disposal, less the additional depreciation.

(b)    Sale by subsidiary

DEBIT        Group retained earnings (P's share of S)
DEBIT        Non-controlling interest (NCI's share of S)
CREDIT    Non-current assets

with the profit on disposal, less additional depreciation

## 7.2 Example: intra-group sale of non-current assets

P Co owns 60% of S Co and on 1 January 20X1 S Co sells plant costing $10,000 to P Co for $12,500. The companies make up accounts to 31 December 20X1 and the balances on their retained earnings at that date are:

| | |
|---|---|
| P Co    after charging depreciation of 10% on plant | $27,000 |
| S Co    including profit on sale of plant | $18,000 |

*Required*

Show the working for consolidated retained earnings.

## Solution

*Retained earnings*

| | P Co $ | S Co $ |
|---|---|---|
| Per question | 27,000 | 18,000 |
| Disposal of plant | | |
| Profit | | (2,500) |
| Depreciation: 10% × $2,500 | | 250 |
| | | 15,750 |
| Share of S Co: $15,750 × 60% | 9,450 | |
| | 36,450 | |

*Notes*

1    The non-controlling interest in the retained earnings of S Co is 40% × $15,750 = $6,300.

2    The asset is written down to cost and depreciation on the 'profit' element is removed. The group profit for the year is thus reduced by a net (($2,500 – $250) × 60%) = $1,350.

# 8 Summary: consolidated statement of financial position

| Purpose | To show the net assets which P controls and the ownership of those assets. |
|---|---|
| Net assets | Always 100% P plus 100% S providing P holds a majority of voting rights. |
| Share capital | P only. |
| *Reason* | Simply reporting to the parent company's shareholders in another form. |
| Retained earnings | 100% P plus group share of post-acquisition retained earnings of S less consolidation adjustments. |
| *Reason* | To show the extent to which the group actually owns total assets less liabilities. |
| Non-controlling interest | Fair value at acquisition plus share of post-acquisition retained profit (loss). |
| *Reason* | To show the equity in a subsidiary not attributable to the parent. |

# 9 Acquisition of a subsidiary during its accounting period

**FAST FORWARD**

> When a parent company acquires a subsidiary during its accounting period the only accounting entries made at the time will be those recording the **cost of acquisition in the parent company's books**. At the end of the accounting period the consolidation adjustments will be made.

## 9.1 Pre-acquisition profits

As we have already seen, at the end of the accounting year it will be necessary to prepare consolidated accounts.

The subsidiary company's accounts to be consolidated will show the subsidiary's profit or loss for the whole year. For consolidation purposes, however, it will be necessary to distinguish between:

(a)     Profits earned before acquisition
(b)     Profits earned after acquisition

In practice, a subsidiary company's profit may not accrue evenly over the year; for example, the subsidiary might be engaged in a trade, such as toy sales, with marked seasonal fluctuations. Nevertheless, the assumption can be made that **profits accrue evenly** whenever it is impracticable to arrive at an accurate split of pre– and post-acquisition profits.

Once the amount of pre-acquisition profit has been established the appropriate consolidation workings (goodwill, retained earnings) can be produced.

It is worthwhile to summarise what happens on consolidation to the retained earnings figures extracted from a subsidiary's statement of financial position. Suppose the accounts of S Co, a 60% subsidiary of P Co, show retained earnings of $20,000 at the end of the reporting period, of which $14,000 were earned prior to acquisition. The figure of $20,000 will appear in the consolidated statement of financial position as follows.

|  | $ |
|---|---|
| Non-controlling interests working: their share of post-acquisition retained earnings  (40% x 6,000) | 2,400 |
| Goodwill working: pre-acquisition retained earnings | 14,000 |
| Consolidated retained earnings working: group share of post-acquisition retained earnings  (60% × $6,000) | 3,600 |
|  | 20,000 |

The examiner has reported that many candidates fail to apportion the results of the subsidiary to include
only its post-acquisition results.

## Question

Hinge Co acquired 80% of the ordinary shares of Singe Co on 1 April 20X5. On 31 December 20X4 Singe
Co's accounts showed a share premium account of $4,000 and retained earnings of $15,000. The
statements of financial position of the two companies at 31 December 20X5 are set out below. Neither
company has paid any dividends during the year. Non-controlling interest should be valued at full fair
value. The market price of the subsidiary's shares was $2.50 prior to acquisition by the parent.

You are required to prepare the consolidated statement of financial position of Hinge Co at 31 December
20X5. There has been no impairment of goodwill.

STATEMENT OF FINANCIAL POSITION AS AT 31 DECEMBER 20X5

|  | HINGE CO $ | SINGE CO $ |
|---|---|---|
| *Assets* | | |
| Non-current assets | | |
| Property, plant and equipment | 32,000 | 30,000 |
| 16,000 ordinary shares of 50c each in Singe Co | 50,000 | |
|  | 82,000 | |
| Current assets | 85,000 | 43,000 |
| Total assets | 167,000 | 73,000 |
| *Equity and liabilities* | | |
| Equity | | |
| Ordinary shares of $1 each | 100,000 | |
| Ordinary shares of 50c each | | 10,000 |
| Share premium account | 7,000 | 4,000 |
| Retained earnings | 40,000 | 39,000 |
|  | 147,000 | 53,000 |
| Current liabilities | 20,000 | 20,000 |
| Total equity and liabilities | 167,000 | 73,000 |

## Answer

Singe Co has made a profit of $24,000 ($39,000 – $15,000) for the year. In the absence of any direction to
the contrary, this should be assumed to have arisen evenly over the year; $6,000 in the three months to 31
March and $18,000 in the nine months after acquisition. The company's pre-acquisition retained earnings
are therefore as follows.

|  | $ |
|---|---|
| Balance at 31 December 20X4 | 15,000 |
| Profit for three months to 31 March 20X5 | 6,000 |
| Pre-acquisition retained earnings | 21,000 |

The balance of $4,000 on share premium account is all pre-acquisition.

The consolidation workings can now be drawn up.

1    Goodwill

|  | $ | $ |
|---|---|---|
| Consideration transferred | | 50,000 |
| Non-controlling interest ($2.50 × 4,000) | | 10,000 |
| Net assets acquired | | |
| represented by | | |
| Ordinary share capital | 10,000 | |
| Retained earnings (pre-acquisition) | 21,000 | |
| Share premium | 4,000 | |
| | | (35,000) |
| Goodwill at acquisition | | 25,000 |

2    Retained earnings

|  | Hinge Co | Singe Co |
|---|---|---|
| | $ | $ |
| Per question | 40,000 | 39,000 |
| Pre-acquisition (see above) | | (21,000) |
| | | 18,000 |
| Share of Singe: $18,000 × 80% | 14,400 | |
| | 54,400 | |

3    Non-controlling interest at reporting date

|  | $ |
|---|---|
| NCI at acquisition | 10,000 |
| Share of post-acquisition retained earnings (18,000 x 20%) | 3,600 |
| | 13,600 |

HINGE CO
CONSOLIDATED STATEMENT OF FINANCIAL POSITION AS AT 31 DECEMBER 20X5

|  | $ | $ |
|---|---|---|
| Assets | | |
| Property, plant and equipment | | 62,000 |
| Goodwill (W1) | | 25,000 |
| Current assets | | 128,000 |
| Total assets | | 215,000 |
| Equity and liabilities | | |
| Equity | | |
| Ordinary shares of $1 each | 100,000 | |
| Share premium account | 7,000 | |
| Retained earnings (W2) | 54,400 | |
| | | 161,400 |
| Non-controlling interest (W3) | | 13,600 |
| | | 175,000 |
| Current liabilities | | 40,000 |
| Total equity and liabilities | | 215,000 |

## 9.2 Example: pre-acquisition losses of a subsidiary

As an illustration of the entries arising when a subsidiary has pre-acquisition *losses*, suppose P Co acquired all 50,000 $1 ordinary shares in S Co for $20,000 on 1 January 20X1 when there was a debit balance of $35,000 on S Co's retained earnings. In the years 20X1 to 20X4 S Co makes profits of $40,000 in total, leaving a credit balance of $5,000 on retained earnings at 31 December 20X4. P Co's retained earnings at the same date are $70,000.

## Solution

The consolidation workings would appear as follows.

| 1 | *Goodwill* | $ | $ |
|---|---|---|---|
| | Consideration transferred | | 20,000 |
| | Net assets acquired | | |
| | as represented by | | |
| | Ordinary share capital | 50,000 | |
| | Retained earnings | (35,000) | |
| | | | (15,000) |
| | Goodwill | | 5,000 |

| 2 | *Retained earnings* | P Co | S Co |
|---|---|---|---|
| | | $ | $ |
| | At the end of the reporting period | 70,000 | 5,000 |
| | Pre-acquisition loss | – | 35,000 |
| | | | 40,000 |
| | S Co – share of post-acquisition retained earnings | | |
| | (40,000 × 100%) | 40,000 | |
| | | 110,000 | |

# 10 Fair values in acquisition accounting

Fair values are very important in calculating goodwill.

## 10.1 Goodwill

To understand the importance of fair values in the acquisition of a subsidiary consider again what we mean by goodwill.

**Key term**

**Goodwill**. The excess of the fair value of the consideration transferred plus the amount of non-controlling interests over the fair value of the identifiable net assets of the acquiree on the acquisition date. (IFRS 3)

The **statement of financial position of a subsidiary company** at the date it is acquired may not be a guide to the fair value of its net assets. For example, the market value of a freehold building may have risen greatly since it was acquired, but it may appear in the statement of financial position at historical cost less accumulated depreciation.

## 10.2 What is fair value?

Fair value is defined as follows by IFRS 13. It is an important definition.

**Key term**

**Fair value**. The price that would be received to sell an asset or paid to transfer a liability in an orderly transaction between market participants at the measurement date.

We will look at the requirements of IFRS 3 regarding fair value in more detail below. First let us look at some practical matters.

## 10.3 Fair value adjustment calculations

Until now we have calculated goodwill as the difference between the consideration transferred and the **book value** of net assets acquired by the group. If this calculation is to comply with the definition above we must ensure that the book value of the subsidiary's net assets is the same as their **fair value**.

There are two possible ways of achieving this.

(a)  The **subsidiary company** might **incorporate any necessary revaluations** in its own books of account. In this case, we can proceed directly to the consolidation, taking asset values and reserves figures straight from the subsidiary company's statement of financial position.

(b)  The **revaluations** may be made as a **consolidation adjustment without being incorporated** in the subsidiary company's books. In this case, we must make the necessary adjustments to the subsidiary's statement of financial position as a working. Only then can we proceed to the consolidation.

*Note.* Remember that when depreciating assets are revalued there may be a corresponding alteration in the amount of depreciation charged and accumulated.

## 10.4 Example: fair value adjustments

P Co acquired 75% of the ordinary shares of S Co on 1 September 20X5. At that date the fair value of S Co's non-current assets was $23,000 greater than their net book value, and the balance of retained earnings was $21,000. The statements of financial position of both companies at 31 August 20X6 are given below. S Co has not incorporated any revaluation in its books of account. Non-controlling interest is valued at full fair value which was deemed to be $18,000 at the acquisition date.

P CO
STATEMENT OF FINANCIAL POSITION AS AT 31 AUGUST 20X6

|  | $ | $ |
|---|---|---|
| *Assets* | | |
| Non-current assets | | |
| Property, plant and equipment | 63,000 | |
| Investment in S Co at cost | 51,000 | |
| | | 114,000 |
| Current assets | | 82,000 |
| *Total assets* | | 196,000 |
| *Equity and liabilities* | | |
| Equity | | |
| Ordinary shares of $1 each | 80,000 | |
| Retained earnings | 96,000 | |
| | | 176,000 |
| Current liabilities | | 20,000 |
| *Total equity and liabilities* | | 196,000 |

S CO
STATEMENT OF FINANCIAL POSITION AS AT 31 AUGUST 20X6

|  | $ | $ |
|---|---|---|
| *Assets* | | |
| Property, plant and equipment | | 28,000 |
| Current assets | | 43,000 |
| *Total assets* | | 71,000 |
| *Equity and liabilities* | | |
| Equity | | |
| Ordinary shares of $1 each | 20,000 | |
| Retained earnings | 41,000 | |
| | | 61,000 |
| Current liabilities | | 10,000 |
| *Total equity and liabilities* | | 71,000 |

If S Co had revalued its non-current assets at 1 September 20X5, an addition of $3,000 would have been made to the depreciation charged for 20X5/X6.

*Required*

Prepare P Co's consolidated statement of financial position as at 31 August 20X6.

# Solution

## P CO CONSOLIDATED STATEMENT OF FINANCIAL POSITION AS AT 31 AUGUST 20X6

| | $ | $ |
|---|---|---|
| *Non-current assets* | | |
| Property, plant and equipment (63,000 + 28,000 + 23,000 – 3,000) | 111,000 | |
| Goodwill (W1) | 5,000 | |
| | | 116,000 |
| Current assets | | 125,000 |
| | | 241,000 |
| *Equity and liabilities* | | |
| Equity | | |
| Ordinary shares of $1 each | 80,000 | |
| Retained earnings (W2) | 108,750 | |
| | | 188,750 |
| Non-controlling interest (W3) | | 22,250 |
| | | 211,000 |
| Current liabilities | | 30,000 |
| | | 241,000 |

### 1 Goodwill

| | Group |
|---|---|
| | $ |
| Consideration transferred | 51,000 |
| Fair value of NCI | 18,000 |
| Net assets acquired as represented by | |
| Ordinary share capital | 20,000 |
| Retained earnings | 21,000 |
| Fair value adjustment | 23,000 |
| | (64,000) |
| Goodwill | 5,000 |

Ordinary share capital 20,000, Retained earnings 21,000, Fair value adjustment 23,000

### 2 Retained earnings

| | P Co | S Co |
|---|---|---|
| | $ | $ |
| Per question | 96,000 | 41,000 |
| Pre acquisition profits | | (21,000) |
| Depreciation adjustment | | (3,000) |
| Post acquisition S Co | | 17,000 |
| Group share in S Co | | |
| ($17,000 × 75%) | 12,750 | |
| Group retained earnings | 108,750 | |

### 3 Non-controlling interest at reporting date

| | $ |
|---|---|
| Fair value at acquisition | 18,000 |
| Share of post-acquisition retained earnings (17,000 × 25%) | 4,250 |
| | 22,250 |

## Question
**Fair value**

An asset is recorded in S Co's books at its historical cost of $4,000. On 1 January 20X5 P Co bought 80% of S Co's equity. Its directors attributed a fair value of $3,000 to the asset as at that date. It had been depreciated for two years out of an expected life of four years on the straight line basis. There was no expected residual value. On 30 June 20X5 the asset was sold for $2,600. What is the profit or loss on disposal of this asset to be recorded in S Co's accounts and in P Co's consolidated accounts for the year ended 31 December 20X5?

S Co:  Carrying amount at disposal (at historical cost) = $4,000 × 1½/4 = $1,500
∴ Profit on disposal = $1,100 (depreciation charge for the year = $500)

P Co:  Carrying amount at disposal (at fair value) = $3,000 × 1½/2 = $2,250
∴ Profit on disposal for consolidation = $350 (depreciation for the year = $750).

The non-controlling interest would be credited with 20% of both the profit on disposal and the depreciation charge as part of the one line entry in the consolidated statement of profit or loss.

## 10.5 IFRS 3 Fair values

IFRS 3 sets out **general principles** for arriving at the fair values of a subsidiary's assets and liabilities. The acquirer should recognise the acquiree's identifiable assets, liabilities and contingent liabilities at the acquisition date only if they satisfy the following criteria.

(a)    In the case of an **asset** other than an intangible asset, it is **probable** that any associated **future economic benefits** will flow to the acquirer, and its fair value can be **measured reliably**.

(b)    In the case of a **liability** other than a contingent liability, it is probable that an **outflow** of resources embodying economic benefits will be required to settle the obligation, and its fair value can be **measured reliably**.

(c)    In the case of an **intangible asset** or a **contingent liability**, its fair value can be **measured reliably**.

The acquiree's identifiable assets and liabilities might include assets and liabilities **not previously recognised** in the acquiree's financial statements. For example, a tax benefit arising from the acquiree's tax losses that was not recognised by the acquiree may be recognised by the group if the acquirer has future taxable profits against which the unrecognised tax benefit can be applied.

### 10.5.1 Restructuring and future losses

An acquirer **should not recognise liabilities for future losses** or other costs expected to be incurred as a result of the business combination.

IFRS 3 explains that a plan to restructure a subsidiary following an acquisition is not a present obligation of the acquiree at the acquisition date. Neither does it meet the definition of a contingent liability. Therefore an acquirer **should not recognise a liability for** such a **restructuring plan** as part of allocating the cost of the combination unless the subsidiary was already committed to the plan before the acquisition.

This **prevents creative accounting**. An acquirer cannot set up a provision for restructuring or future losses of a subsidiary and then release this to the profit or loss in subsequent periods in order to reduce losses or smooth profits.

### 10.5.2 Intangible assets

The acquiree may have **intangible assets**, such as development expenditure. These can be recognised separately from goodwill only if they are **identifiable**. An intangible asset is identifiable only if it:

(a)    Is **separable**, ie capable of being separated or divided from the entity and sold, transferred, or exchanged, either individually or together with a related contract, asset or liability, or

(b)    Arises from contractual or other legal rights

The acquiree may also have internally-generated assets such as brand names which have not been recognised as intangible assets. As the acquiring company is giving valuable consideration for these assets, they are now recognised as assets in the consolidated financial statements.

## 10.5.3 Contingent liabilities

Contingent liabilities of the acquirer are **recognised** if their **fair value can be measured reliably**. This is a departure from the normal rules in IAS 37; contingent liabilities are not normally recognised, but only disclosed.

After their initial recognition, the acquirer should measure contingent liabilities that are recognised separately at the higher of:

(a)     The amount that would be recognised in accordance with IAS 37
(b)     The amount initially recognised

## 10.5.4 Cost of a business combination

The general principle is that the acquirer should measure the cost of a business combination as the total of the **fair values**, at the date of exchange, **of assets given**, liabilities incurred or assumed, and equity instruments issued by the acquirer, in exchange for control of the acquiree.

Sometimes all or part of the cost of an acquisition is deferred (ie, does not become payable immediately). The fair value of any deferred consideration is determined by **discounting** the amounts payable to their **present value** at the date of exchange.

Where equity instruments (eg ordinary shares) of a quoted entity form part of the cost of a combination, the **published price** at the date of exchange normally provides the best evidence of the instrument's fair value and except in rare circumstances this should be used.

Future losses or other costs expected to be incurred as a result of a combination should not be included in the cost of the combination.

Costs **attributable** to the combination, for example professional fees and administrative costs, should not be included: they are recognised as an expense when incurred. **Costs of issuing debt instruments and equity shares** are covered by IAS 32 *Financial instruments: presentation*, which states that such costs should **reduce the proceeds from the debt issue or the equity issue**.

Question | Goodwill on consolidation

On 1 September 20X7 Tyzo Co acquired 6 million $1 shares in Kono Co at $2.00 per share. At that date Kono Co produced the following interim financial statements.

|  | $m |  | $m |
|---|---|---|---|
| Property, plant and equipment |  | Trade payables | 3.2 |
| (note 1) | 16.0 | Taxation | 0.6 |
| Inventories (note 2) | 4.0 | Bank overdraft | 3.9 |
| Receivables | 2.9 | Long-term loans | 4.0 |
| Cash in hand | 1.2 | Share capital ($1 shares) | 8.0 |
|  |  | Retained earnings | 4.4 |
|  | 24.1 |  | 24.1 |

*Notes*

1     The following information relates to the property, plant and equipment of Kono Co at 1 September 20X7.

|  | $m |
|---|---|
| Gross replacement cost | 28.4 |
| Net replacement cost (gross replacement cost less depreciation) | 16.6 |
| Economic value | 18.0 |
| Net realisable value | 8.0 |

2    The inventories of Kono Co which were shown in the interim financial statements are raw materials at cost to Kono Co of $4 million. They would have cost $4.2 million to replace at 1 September 20X7.

3    On 1 September 20X7 Tyzo Co took a decision to rationalise the group so as to integrate Kono Co. The costs of the rationalisation were estimated to total $3.0 million and the process was due to start on 1 March 20X8. No provision for these costs has been made in the financial statements given above.

4    It is group policy to recognise non-controlling interest at full (fair) value.

*Required*

Compute the goodwill on consolidation of Kono Co that will be included in the consolidated financial statements of the Tyzo Co group for the year ended 31 December 20X7, explaining your treatment of the items mentioned above. You should refer to the provisions of relevant accounting standards.

## Answer

Goodwill on consolidation of Kono Co

|  | $m | $m |
|---|---|---|
| Consideration transferred ($2.00 × 6m) |  | 12.0 |
| Non-controlling interest ($2.00 × 2m) |  | 4.0 |
| Fair value of net assets acquired |  |  |
| Share capital | 8.0 |  |
| Pre-acquisition reserves | 4.4 |  |
| *Fair value adjustments* |  |  |
| Property, plant and equipment (16.6 – 16.0) | 0.6 |  |
| Inventories (4.2 – 4.0) | 0.2 |  |
|  |  | (13.2) |
| Goodwill |  | 2.8 |

*Notes on treatment*

(a)    Share capital and pre-acquisition profits represent the book value of the net assets of Kono Co at the date of acquisition. Adjustments are then required to this book value in order to give the fair value of the net assets at the date of acquisition. For short-term monetary items, fair value is their carrying value on acquisition.

(b)    IFRS 3 states that the fair value of property, plant and equipment should be determined by market value or, if information on a market price is not available (as is the case here), then by reference to depreciated replacement cost, reflecting normal business practice. The net replacement cost (ie $16.6m) represents the gross replacement cost less depreciation based on that amount, and so further adjustment for extra depreciation is unnecessary.

(c)    IFRS 3 also states that raw materials should be valued at replacement cost. In this case that amount is $4.2m.

(d)    The rationalisation costs cannot be reported in pre-acquisition results under IFRS 3 as they are not a liability of Kono Co at the acquisition date.

One of the competences you require to fulfil performance objective 10 of the PER is the ability to prepare financial statements for single and combined entities. You can apply the knowledge you obtain from this chapter to help to demonstrate this competence.

# Chapter Roundup

- IFRS 10 lays out the basic procedures for preparing consolidated financial statements

- In the consolidated statement of financial position it is necessary to distinguish **non-controlling interests** from those net assets attributable to the group and financed by shareholders' equity.

- **Goodwill** is the excess of the amount transferred plus the amount of non-controlling interests over the fair value of the net assets of the subsidiary.

- Intra-group trading can give rise to **unrealised profit** which is eliminated on consolidation.

- As well as engaging in trading activities with each other, group companies may on occasion wish to **transfer non-current assets**.

- When a parent company acquires a subsidiary during its accounting period the only accounting entries made at the time will be those recording the **cost of the acquisition in the parent company's books**. At the end of the accounting period the consolidation adjustments will be made.

- **Fair values** are very important in calculating goodwill.

# Quick Quiz

1   Chicken Co owns 80% of Egg Co. Egg Co sells goods to Chicken Co at cost plus 50%. The total invoiced sales to Chicken Co by Egg Co in the year ended 31 December 20X9 were $900,000 and, of these sales, goods which had been invoiced at $60,000 were held in inventory by Chicken Co at 31 December 20X9. What is the reduction in aggregate group gross profit?

2   Major Co, which makes up its accounts to 31 December, has an 80% owned subsidiary Minor Co. Minor Co sells goods to Major Co at a mark-up on cost of 33.33%. At 31 December 20X8, Major had $12,000 of such goods in its inventory and at 31 December 20X9 had $15,000 of such goods in its inventory.

    What is the amount by which the consolidated profit attributable to Major Co's shareholders should be adjusted in respect of the above?

    Ignore taxation

    A    $1,000 Debit
    B    $800 Credit
    C    $750 Credit
    D    $600 Debit

3   Goodwill is always positive. True or false?

4   A parent company can assume that, for a subsidiary acquired during its accounting period, profits accrue evenly during the year. True or false?

5   What entries are made in the workings to record the pre-acquisition profits of a subsidiary?

6   Describe the requirement of IFRS 3 in relation to the revaluation of a subsidiary company's assets to fair value at the acquisition date.

7   What guidelines are given by IFRS 3 in relation to valuing land and buildings fairly?

# Answers to Quick Quiz

1.  $\$60,000 \times \dfrac{50}{150} = \$20,000$

2.  D $\quad (15,000 - 12,000) \times \dfrac{33.3}{133.3} \times 80\%$

3.  False. Goodwill can be negative if the purchaser has 'got a bargain'.

4.  Not necessarily – the examiner will advise you on this.

5.  See Para 4.2

6.  See Para 10.5

7.  Market value is the best guideline.

**Now try the question below from the Exam Question Bank**

| Number | Level | Marks | Time |
|--------|-------------|-------|---------|
| 9 | Examination | 15 | 27 mins |
| 10 | Examination | 15 | 27 mins |

# The consolidated statement of profit or loss and other comprehensive income

# 10

## Introduction

This chapter deals with the consolidated statement of profit or loss and the consolidated statement of profit or loss and other comprehensive income.

Most of the consolidation adjustments will involve the **statement of profit or loss**, so that is the focus of this chapter.

# Study guide

| | | Intellectual level |
|---|---|---|
| **D** | **BUSINESS COMBINATIONS** | |
| **3** | (b) prepare a consolidated income statement and consolidated statement of comprehensive income for simple group dealing with an acquisition in the period and non-controlling interest. | 2 |

# 1 The consolidated statement of profit or loss

**FAST FORWARD**

The source of the consolidated statement of profit or loss is the individual statements of profit or loss of the separate companies in the group.

## 1.1 Consolidation procedure

It is customary in practice to prepare a working paper (known as a **consolidation schedule**) on which the individual statements of profit or loss are set out side by side and totalled to form the basis of the consolidated statement of profit or loss.

**Exam focus point**

In an examination it is very much quicker not to do this. Use workings to show the calculation of complex figures such as the non-controlling interest and show the derivation of others on the face of the statement of profit or loss, as shown in our examples.

**FAST FORWARD**

In the consolidated statement of profit or loss non-controlling interest is brought in as a one-line adjustment at the end of the statement.

## 1.2 Simple example: consolidated statement of profit or loss

P Co acquired 75% of the ordinary shares of S Co on that company's incorporation in 20X3. The summarised statements of profit or loss and movement on retained earnings of the two companies for the year ending 31 December 20X6 are set out below.

| | P Co $ | S Co $ |
|---|---|---|
| Sales revenue | 75,000 | 38,000 |
| Cost of sales | (30,000) | (20,000) |
| Gross profit | 45,000 | 18,000 |
| Administrative expenses | (14,000) | (8,000) |
| Profit before tax | 31,000 | 10,000 |
| Income tax expense | (10,000) | (2,000) |
| Profit for the year | 21,000 | 8,000 |

*Note: Movement on retained earnings*

| | | |
|---|---|---|
| Retained earnings brought forward | 87,000 | 17,000 |
| Profit for the year | 21,000 | 8,000 |
| Retained earnings carried forward | 108,000 | 25,000 |

*Required*

Prepare the consolidated statement of profit or loss and extract from the statement of changes in equity showing retained earnings and non-controlling interest.

# Solution

P CO
CONSOLIDATED STATEMENT OF PROFIT OR LOSS
FOR THE YEAR ENDED 31 DECEMBER 20X6

| | $ |
|---|---:|
| Sales revenue (75 + 38) | 113,000 |
| Cost of sales (30 + 20) | (50,000) |
| Gross profit | 63,000 |
| Administrative expenses (14 + 8) | (22,000) |
| Profit before tax | 41,000 |
| Income tax expense | (12,000) |
| Profit for the year | 29,000 |
| | |
| Profit attributable to: | |
| Owners of the parent | 27,000 |
| Non-controlling interest ($8,000 × 25%) | 2,000 |
| | 29,000 |

STATEMENT OF CHANGES IN EQUITY (EXTRACT)

| | Retained Earnings $ | Non-controlling Interest $ | Total Equity $ |
|---|---:|---:|---:|
| Balance at 1 January 20X6 | 99,750 | 4,250 | 104,000 |
| Total comprehensive income for the year | 27,000 | 2,000 | 29,000 |
| Balance at 31 December 20X6 | 126,750 | 6,250 | 133,000 |

Notice how the non-controlling interest is dealt with.

(a) Down to the line **'profit for the year'** the **whole** of S Co's results is included without reference to group share or non-controlling share. A **one-line adjustment** is then inserted to deduct the non-controlling share of S Co's profit.

(b) The non-controlling share ($4,250) of S Co's retained earnings brought forward (17,000 × 25%) is **excluded** from group retained earnings. This means that the carried forward figure of $126,750 is the figure which would appear in the statement of financial position for group retained earnings.

This last point may be clearer if we construct the working for group retained earnings.

*Group retained earnings*

| | P Co $ | S Co $ |
|---|---:|---:|
| At year end | 108,000 | 25,000 |
| Less pre-acquisition retained earnings | | – |
| | | 25,000 |
| S Co – share of post acquisition retained earnings (25,000 × 75%) | 18,750 | |
| | 126,750 | |

The non-controlling share of S Co's retained earnings comprises the non-controlling interest in the $17,000 profits brought forward plus the non-controlling interest ($2,000) in $8,000 retained profits for the year.

We will now look at the complications introduced by **intra-group trading**, **intra-group dividends** and **pre-acquisition profits** in the subsidiary.

## 1.3 Intra-group trading

FAST FORWARD

Intra-group sales and purchases are eliminated from the consolidated statement of profit or loss.

Like the consolidated statement of financial position, the consolidated statement of profit or loss should deal with the results of the group as those of a single entity. When one company in a group sells goods to another the relevant amount is added to the sales revenue of the first company and to the cost of sales of the second. Yet as far as the entity's dealings with outsiders are concerned no sale has taken place.

The consolidated figures for sales revenue and cost of sales should represent **sales to**, and **purchases from, outsiders**. An adjustment is therefore necessary to reduce the sales revenue and cost of sales figures by the value of intra-group sales during the year.

We have also seen in an earlier chapter that any unrealised profits on intra-group trading should be excluded from the figure for group profits. This will occur whenever goods sold at a profit within the group remain in the inventory of the purchasing company at the year end. The best way to deal with this is to **calculate the unrealised profit on unsold inventories at the year end and reduce consolidated gross profit by this amount**. Cost of sales will be the balancing figure.

## 1.4 Example: intra-group trading

Suppose in our earlier example that S Co had recorded sales of $5,000 to P Co during 20X6. S Co had purchased these goods from outside suppliers at a cost of $3,000. One half of the goods remained in P Co's inventory at 31 December 20X6.

Prepare the revised consolidated statement of profit or loss.

## Solution

The consolidated statement of profit or loss for the year ended 31 December 20X6 would now be as follows.

|  | $ |
| --- | --- |
| Sales revenue (75 + 38 – 5) | 108,000 |
| Cost of sales (30 + 20 – 5 + 1*) | (46,000) |
| Gross profit (45 + 18 – 1*) | 62,000 |
| Administrative expenses | (22,000) |
| Profit before taxation | 40,000 |
| Income tax expense | (12,000) |
| Profit for the year | 28,000 |
|  |  |
| Profit attributable to : |  |
| Owners of the parent | 26,250 |
| Non-controlling interest (8,000 – 1,000) × 25% | 1,750 |
|  | 28,000 |

Note:

|  | $ |
| --- | --- |
| Retained earnings brought forward | 99,750 |
| Profit for the year | 26,250 |
| Retained earnings carried forward | 126,000 |

*Unrealised profit: ½ × ($5,000 – $3,000)

An adjustment will be made for the unrealised profit against the inventory figure in the consolidated statement of financial position.

## 1.5 Intra-group dividends

In our example so far we have assumed that S Co retains all of its after-tax profit. It may be, however, that S Co distributes some of its profits as dividends. As before, the **non-controlling interest** in the subsidiary's profit should be calculated immediately after the figure of after-tax profit. For this purpose, no account need be taken of how much of the non-controlling interest is to be distributed by S Co as dividend.

Note that group retained earnings are only adjusted for dividends paid to the parent company shareholders. Dividends paid by the subsidiary to the parent are cancelled on consolidation and dividends paid to the non-controlling interest are replaced by the allocation to the non-controlling interest of their share of the profit for the year of the subsidiary.

# 1.6 Pre-acquisition profits

> Only the **post-acquisition** profits of the subsidiary are brought into the consolidated profit or loss.

As explained above, the figure for retained earnings carried forward must be the same as the figure for retained earnings in the consolidated statement of financial position. We have seen in previous chapters that retained earnings in the consolidated statement of financial position comprise:

(a)     The **whole of the parent company's** retained earnings

(b)     A **proportion of the subsidiary company's** retained earnings. The proportion is the **group's share of post-acquisition retained earnings** in the subsidiary. From the total retained earnings of the subsidiary we must therefore **exclude** both the **non-controlling share** of total retained earnings and the **group's share of pre-acquisition** retained earnings.

A **similar procedure is necessary in the consolidated statement of profit or loss** if it is to link up with the consolidated statement of financial position. Previous examples have shown how the non-controlling share of profits is treated in the statement of profit or loss. Their share of profits for the year is deducted from profit after tax, while the figure for profits brought forward in the consolidation schedule includes only the group share of the subsidiary's profits.

In the same way, when considering examples which include pre-acquisition profits in a subsidiary, the figure for profits brought forward should include only the group share of the post-acquisition retained profits. If the subsidiary is **acquired during the accounting year**, it is therefore necessary to apportion its profit for the year between pre-acquisition and post-acquisition elements. The part-year method is used.

With the part-year method, the entire statement of profit or loss of the subsidiary is split between pre-acquisition and post-acquisition amounts. Only the post-acquisition figures are included in the consolidated statement of profit or loss.

## Question
Acquisition

P Co acquired 60% of the $100,000 equity of S Co on 1 April 20X5. The statements of profit or loss of the two companies for the year ended 31 December 20X5 are set out below.

|  | P Co | S Co | S Co ($^9/_{12}$) |
|---|---|---|---|
|  | $ | $ | $ |
| Sales revenue | 170,000 | 80,000 | 60,000 |
| Cost of sales | (65,000) | (36,000) | (27,000) |
| Gross profit | 105,000 | 44,000 | 33,000 |
| Other income – dividend received S Co | 3,600 |  |  |
| Administrative expenses | (43,000) | (12,000) | ( 9,000) |
| Profit before tax | 65,600 | 32,000 | 24,000 |
| Income tax expense | (23,000) | (8,000) | (6,000) |
| Profit for the year | 42,600 | 24,000 | 18,000 |
| | | | |
| *Note* | | | |
| Dividends (paid 31 December) | 12,000 | 6,000 | |
| Profit retained | 30,600 | 18,000 | |
| | | | |
| Retained earnings brought forward | 81,000 | 40,000 | |
| Retained earnings carried forward | 111,600 | 58,000 | |

Prepare the consolidated statement of profit or loss and the retained earnings and non-controlling interest extracts from the statement of changes in equity.

## Answer

The shares in S Co were acquired three months into the year. Only the post-acquisition proportion (9/12ths) of S Co's statement of profit or loss is included in the consolidated statement of profit or loss. This is shown above for convenience.

## P CO CONSOLIDATED STATEMENT OF PROFIT OR LOSS
## FOR THE YEAR ENDED 31 DECEMBER 20X5

|  | $ |
|---|---:|
| Sales revenue (170 + 60) | 230,000 |
| Cost of sales (65 + 27) | (92,000) |
| Gross profit | 138,000 |
| Administrative expenses (43 + 9) | (52,000) |
| Profit before tax | 86,000 |
| Income tax expense (23 + 6) | (29,000) |
| Profit for the year | 57,000 |
|  |  |
| Profit attributable to: |  |
| Owners of the parent | 49,800 |
| Non-controlling interest (18 × 40%) | 7,200 |
|  | 57,000 |

## STATEMENT OF CHANGES IN EQUITY

|  | Retained earnings $ | Non-controlling interest $ |
|---|---:|---:|
| Balance at 1 January 20X5 | 81,000 | – |
| Dividends paid (6,000 – 3,600) | (12,000) | (2,400) |
| Total comprehensive income for the year | 49,800 | 7,200 |
| Added on acquisition of subsidiary (W) | – | 58,400 |
| Balance at 31 December 20X5 | 118,800 | 63,200 |

Note: All of S Co's profits brought forward are pre-acquisition.

*Working*

|  | $ |
|---|---:|
| Added on acquisition of subsidiary: |  |
| Share capital | 100,000 |
| Retained earnings brought forward | 40,000 |
| Profits Jan-March 20X5 (24,000 – 18,000) | 6,000 |
|  | 146,000 |
| Non-controlling share 40% | 58,400 |

 ## Question

Non-controlling interest

The following information relates to Brodick Co and its subsidiary Lamlash Co for the year to 30 April 20X7.

|  | Brodick Co $'000 | Lamlash Co $'000 |
|---|---:|---:|
| Sales revenue | 1,100 | 500 |
| Cost of sales | (630) | (300) |
| Gross profit | 470 | 200 |
| Administrative expenses | (105) | (150) |
| Dividend from Lamlash Co | 24 | – |
| Profit before tax | 389 | 50 |
| Income tax expense | (65) | (10) |
| Profit for the year | 324 | 40 |
|  |  |  |
| *Note* |  |  |
| Dividends paid | 200 | 30 |
| Profit retained | 124 | 10 |
| Retained earnings brought forward | 460 | 106 |
| Retained earnings carried forward | 584 | 116 |

### Additional information

(a) The issued share capital of the group was as follows.

    Brodick Co   : 5,000,000 ordinary shares of $1 each.
    Lamlash Co   : 1,000,000 ordinary shares of $1 each.

(b) Brodick Co purchased 80% of the issued share capital of Lamlash Co in 20X0. At that time, the retained earnings of Lamlash stood at $56,000.

### Required

Insofar as the information permits, prepare the Brodick group consolidated statement of profit or loss for the year to 30 April 20X7, and extracts from the statement of changes in equity showing group retained earnings and the non-controlling interest.

## Answer

BRODICK GROUP
CONSOLIDATED STATEMENT OF PROFIT OR LOSS
FOR THE YEAR TO 30 APRIL 20X7

|  | $'000 |
|---|---:|
| Sales revenue (1,100 + 500) | 1,600 |
| Cost of sales (630 + 300) | (930) |
| Gross profit | 670 |
| Administrative expenses (105 + 150) | (255) |
| Profit before tax | 415 |
| Income tax expense (65 + 10) | (75) |
| Profit for the year | 340 |

| Profit attributable to: | $ |
|---|---:|
| Owners of the parent | 332 |
| Non-controlling interest (W1) | 8 |
|  | 340 |

STATEMENT OF CHANGES IN EQUITY

|  | Retained earnings $'000 | Non-controlling interest $'000 |
|---|---:|---:|
| Balance brought forward (W2), (W3) | 500 | 221 |
| Dividends paid (30,000 – 24,000) | (200) | (6) |
| Total comprehensive income for the year | 332 | 8 |
| Balance carried forward | 632 | 223 |

### Workings

1   *Non-controlling interests*

|  | $'000 |
|---|---:|
| In Lamlash (20% × 40) | 8 |

2   *Retained earnings brought forward*

|  | Brodick Co $'000 | Lamlash Co $'000 |
|---|---:|---:|
| Per question | 460 | 106 |
| Less pre-aqn |  | (56) |
|  |  | 50 |
| Share of Lamlash: 80% × 50 | 40 |  |
|  | 500 |  |

3    *Non-controlling interest b/f*

|  |  | $'000 |
|---|---|---:|
| Share capital | | 1,000 |
| Retained earnings | | 106 |
| | | 1,106 |
| | | |
| Non-controlling share 20% | | 221 |

## 1.7 Section summary

The table below summarises the main points about the consolidated statement of profit or loss.

| Purpose | To show the results of the group for an accounting period as if it were a single entity. |
|---|---|
| **Sales revenue to profit for year** | 100% P + 100% S (excluding adjustments for intra-group transactions). |
| *Reason* | To show the results of the group which were controlled by the parent company. |
| **Intra-group sales** | Strip out intra-group activity from both sales revenue and cost of sales. |
| **Unrealised profit on intra-group sales** | (a)  Goods sold by P. Increase cost of sales by unrealised profit.<br><br>(b)  Goods sold by S. Increase cost of sales by full amount of unrealised profit and decrease non-controlling interest by their share of unrealised profit. |
| **Depreciation** | If the value of S's non-current assets have been subjected to a fair value uplift then any additional depreciation must be charged to profit or loss. The non-controlling interest will need to be adjusted for their share. |
| **Transfer of non-current assets** | Expenses must be increased by any profit on the transfer and reduced by any additional depreciation arising from the increased carrying value of the asset. |
| **Non-controlling interests** | S's profit after tax (PAT) ............................................... X<br>Less:   * unrealised profit ........................................... (X)<br>         * profit on disposal of non-current assets .......... (X)<br>           additional depreciation following FV uplift ........ (X)<br>Add:   ** additional depreciation following disposal of<br>            non-current assets ...................................... X<br> ................................................................................ X<br><br>NCI% ........................................................................ X<br><br>* Only applicable if sales of goods and non-current assets made by subsidiary.<br><br>** Only applicable if sale of non-current assets made by subsidiary. |
| *Reason* | To show the extent to which profits generated through P's control are in fact owned by other parties. |

# 2 The consolidated statement of profit or loss and other comprehensive income

**FAST FORWARD**

> The consolidated statement of profit or loss and other comprehensive income is produced using the consolidated statement of profit or loss as a basis.

The only items of other comprehensive income that are included in your syllabus are revaluation gains and losses, so a consolidated statement of profit or loss and other comprehensive income will be easy to produce once you have done the consolidated statement of profit or loss.

We will take the last question and add an item of comprehensive income to illustrate this.

## 2.1 Example: Comprehensive income

The consolidated statement of profit or loss of the Brodrick Group is as in the answer to the last question. In addition, Lamlash made a $200,000 revaluation gain on one of its properties during the year.

## 2.2 Solution

BRODRICK GROUP
CONSOLIDATED STATEMENT OF PROFIT OR LOSS AND OTHER COMPREHENSIVE INCOME FOR THE YEAR TO 30 APRIL 20X7

|  | $'000 |
|---|---|
| Sales revenue | 1,600 |
| Cost of sales | (930) |
| Gross profit | 670 |
| Administrative expenses | (255) |
| Profit before tax | 415 |
| Income tax expense | (75) |
| Profit for the year | 340 |
| Other comprehensive income: |  |
| Gain on property revaluation | 200 |
| Total comprehensive income for the year | 540 |
|  |  |
| Profit attributable to: |  |
| Owners of the parent | 332 |
| Non-controlling interest | 8 |
|  | 340 |
|  |  |
| Total comprehensive income attributable to: |  |
| Owners of the parent (332 + (200 × 80%)) | 492 |
| Non-controlling interest (8 + (200 × 20%)) | 48 |
|  | 540 |

## 2.3 Consolidated statement of profit or loss and other comprehensive income (separate statement)

If we were using the two-statement format (as explained in Chapter 3) we would produce a separate statement of profit or loss and statement of other comprehensive income.

## 2.4 Example: Other comprehensive income

BRODRICK GROUP
CONSOLIDATED STATEMENT OF PROFIT OR LOSS AND OTHER COMPREHENSIVE INCOME

|  |  |
|---|---|
| Profit for the year | 340 |
| Other comprehensive income: |  |
| Gain on property revaluation | 200 |
| Total comprehensive income for the year | 540 |
|  |  |
| Total comprehensive income attributable to: |  |
| Owners of the parent (332 + (200 × 80%)) | 492 |
| Non-controlling interest (8 + (200 × 20%) | 48 |
|  | 540 |

## 2.5 Full worked example

On 1 July 20X8 Crystal acquired 60,000 of the 100,000 shares in Pebble, its only subsidiary. The draft statements of profit or loss and other comprehensive income of both companies at 31 December 20X8 are shown below:

|  | Crystal $'000 | Pebble $'000 |
|---|---|---|
| Revenue | 43,000 | 26,000 |
| Cost of sales | (28,000) | (18,000) |
| Gross profit | 15,000 | 8,000 |
| Other income – dividend received from Pebble | 2,000 | - |
| Distribution costs | (2,000) | (800) |
| Administrative expenses | (4,000) | (2,200) |
| Finance costs | (500) | (300) |
| Profit before tax | 10,500 | 4,700 |
| Income tax expense | (1,400) | (900) |
| Profit for the year | 9,100 | 3,800 |
| Other comprehensive income: |  |  |
| Gain on property revaluation (Note (i)) | - | 2,000 |
| Investment in equity instrument | 200 | - |
| Total comprehensive income for the year | 9,300 | 5,800 |

Additional information:

(i)     At the date of acquisition the fair values of Pebble's assets were equal to their carrying amounts with the exception of a building which had a fair value $1million in excess of its carrying amount. At the date of acquisition the building had a remaining useful life of 20 years. Building depreciation is charged to administrative expenses. The building was revalued again at 31 December 20X8 and its fair value had increased by an additional $1million.

(ii)    Sales from Crystal to Pebble were $6million during the post-acquisition period. Crystal marks up all sales by 20%.

(iii)   Despite the property revaluation, Crystal has concluded that goodwill in Pebble has been impaired by $500,000.

(iv)   It is Crystal's policy to value the non-controlling interest at full (fair) value.

(v)    Income and expenses can be assumed to have arisen evenly throughout the year.

Prepare the consolidated statement of profit or loss and other comprehensive income for the year ended 31 December 20X8.

## Solution

CONSOLIDATED STATEMENT OF PROFIT OR LOSS AND OTHER COMPREHENSIVE INCOME

|  | $'000 |
|---|---|
| Revenue (43,000 + (26,000 x 6/12) – 6,000 (W1)) | 50,000 |
| Cost of sales (28,000 + (18,000 x 6/12) – 6,000 + 1,000 (W1)) | (32,000) |
| Gross profit | 18,000 |
| Distribution costs (2,000 + (800 x 6/12)) | (2,400) |
| Administrative expenses (4,000 + (2,200 x 6/12) + 25 (W2) + 500 impairment) | (5,625) |
| Finance costs (500 + (300 x 6/12)) | (650) |
| Profit before tax | 9,325 |
| Income tax expense (1,400 + (900 x 6/12)) | (1,850) |
| Profit for the year | 7,475 |
| Other comprehensive income: |  |
| Gain on property revaluation(post-acquisition) | 1,000 |
| Investment in equity instrument | 200 |
| Total comprehensive income for the year | 8,675 |

Profit attributable to:
Owners of the parent 6,925
Non-controlling interest (W3) 550
7,475

Total comprehensive income attributable to:
Owners of the parent 7,725
Non-controlling interest (550 + (1,000 x 40%) 950
8,675

*Workings*

1 Unrealised profit

Remove intercompany trading:

DR Revenue $6m / CR Cost of sales $6m

Unrealised profit = 6,000 x 20/120 = 1,000 – add to cost of sales

2 Movement on fair value adjustment

The fair value adjustment of $1m will be depreciated over the remaining life of the building. The amount to be charged at 31 December is:

1,000,000/20 x 6/12 = 25,000

40% of this (10,000) will be charged to the NCI.

3 Non-controlling interest – share of profit for the year

| | $'000 |
|---|---|
| Share of post-acquisition profit (3,800 x 6/12 x 40%) | 760 |
| Movement on fair value adjustment (25 x 40%) | (10) |
| Share of goodwill impairment (500 x 40%) | (200) |
| | 550 |

# Chapter Roundup

- The source of the consolidated statement of profit or loss is the individual statements of profit or loss of the separate companies in the group.

- In the consolidated statement of profit or loss non-controlling interest is brought in as a one-line adjustment after 'profit for the year'.

- Intra-group sales and purchases are eliminated from the consolidated statement of profit or loss.

- Only the **post-acquisition** profits of the subsidiary are brought into the consolidated profit or loss.

- The consolidated statement of profit or loss and other comprehensive income is produced using the consolidated statement of profit or loss as a basis.

# Quick Quiz

1 Where does unrealised profit on intra-group trading appear in the statement of profit or loss?

2 At the beginning of the year a 75% subsidiary transfers a non-current asset to the parent for $500,000. It's carrying value was $400,000 and it has 4 years of useful life left. How is this accounted for at the end of the year in the consolidated statement of profit or loss?

1   As a deduction from consolidated gross profit.

2

|  | $ |
|---|---|
| Unrealised profit | 100,000 |
| Additional depreciation (100 ÷ 4) | (25,000) |
| Net charge to profit or loss | 75,000 |

|  | DR | CR |
|---|---|---|
|  | $ | $ |
| Non-current asset |  | 100,000 |
| Additional depreciation | 25,000 |  |
| Group profit (75%) | 56,250 |  |
| Non-controlling interest (25%) | 18,750 |  |
|  | 100,000 | 100,000 |

## Now try the questions below from the Exam Question Bank

| Number | Level | Marks | Time |
|---|---|---|---|
| 11 | Examination | 15 | 27 mins |
| 12 | – | 20 | 36 mins |

# Accounting for associates

**11**

| Topic list | Syllabus reference |
|---|---|
| 1 Accounting for associates | D3 |
| 2 The equity method | D3 |
| 3 Statement of profit or loss and statement of financial position | D3 |

## Introduction

In this chapter we deal with the treatment of associates in the consolidated financial statements. As the group's share of profit in the associate appears under profit or loss rather than other comprehensive income, we have concentrated on the separate statement of profit or loss.

# Study guide

| | | Intellectual level |
|---|---|---|
| **D** | **BUSINESS COMBINATIONS** | |
| **3** | (a) define an associate and explain the principle and reasoning for the use of equity accounting. | 2 |
| | (b) prepare consolidated financial statements to include a single subsidiary and an associate. | 2 |

# 1 Accounting for associates

FAST FORWARD

> This is covered by IAS 28 *Investments in associates*. The investing company does not have control, as it does with a subsidiary, but it does have **significant influence**.

## 1.1 Definitions

We looked at some of the important definitions in Chapter 8; these are repeated here with some additional important terms.

**Key terms**

- **Associate**. An entity, including an unincorporated entity such as a partnership, over which an investor has significant influence and which is neither a subsidiary nor an interest in a joint venture.
- **Significant influence** is the power to participate in the financial and operating policy decisions of the investee but is not control or joint control over those policies.
- **Equity method**. A method of accounting whereby the investment is initially recorded at cost and adjusted thereafter for the post-acquisition change in the investor's share of net assets of the investee. The profit or loss of the investor includes the investor's share of the profit or loss of the investee.

We have already looked at how the **status** of an investment in an associate should be determined. Go back to Section 1 of Chapter 8 to revise it. (Note that, as for an investment in a subsidiary, any **potential voting rights** should be taken into account in assessing whether the investor has **significant influence** over the investee.)

IAS 28 requires all investments in associates to be accounted for in the consolidated accounts using the equity method, *unless* the investment is classified as 'held for sale' in accordance with IFRS 5 in which case it should be accounted for under IFRS 5 (see Chapter 7), or the exemption in the paragraph below applies.

An investor is exempt from applying the equity method if:

(a) It is a parent exempt from preparing consolidated financial statements under IAS 27, or

(b) All of the following apply:

    (i) The investor is a **wholly-owned subsidiary** or it is a **partially owned subsidiary** of another entity and its other owners, including those not otherwise entitled to vote, have been informed about, and do not object to, the investor not applying the equity method;

    (ii) The investor's securities are **not publicly traded**

    (iii) It is **not in the process of issuing securities** in public securities markets; and

    (iv) The **ultimate or intermediate parent** publishes consolidated financial statements that comply with International Financial Reporting Standards.

The revised version of IAS 28 **no longer allows** an investment in an associate to be excluded from equity accounting when an investee operates under severe long-term restrictions that significantly impair its ability to transfer funds to the investor. Significant influence must be lost before the equity method ceases to be applicable.

The use of the equity method should be **discontinued** from the date that the investor **ceases to have significant influence.**

From that date, the investor shall account for the investment in accordance with IFRS 9 *Financial instruments*. The carrying amount of the investment at the date that it ceases to be an associate shall be regarded as its cost on initial measurement as a financial asset under IFRS 9.

## 1.2 Separate financial statements of the investor

If an investor **issues consolidated financial statements** (because it has subsidiaries), an investment in an associate should be *either*:

(a)    Accounted for at **cost**, or
(b)    In accordance with **IFRS 9** (at fair value)

in its separate financial statements.

If an investor that does *not* **issue consolidated financial statements** (ie it has no subsidiaries) but has an investment in an associate this should similarly be included in the financial statements of the investor either at cost, or in accordance with IFRS 9 (see Chapter 14).

# 2 The equity method

## 2.1 Application of the equity method: consolidated accounts

Many of the procedures required to apply the equity method are the same as are required for full consolidation. In particular, **intra-group unrealised profits** must be excluded.

### 2.1.1 Consolidated statement of profit or loss

The basic principle is that the investing company (X Co) should take account of its **share of the earnings** of the associate, Y Co, whether or not Y Co distributes the earnings as dividends. X Co achieves this by adding to consolidated profit the group's share of Y Co's profit after tax.

Notice the difference between this treatment and the **consolidation** of a subsidiary company's results. If Y Co were a subsidiary X Co would take credit for the whole of its sales revenue, cost of sales etc and would then make a one-line adjustment to remove any non-controlling share.

Under equity accounting, the associate's sales revenue, cost of sales and so on are *not* **amalgamated** with those of the group. Instead the group share only of the associate's profit after tax for the year is added to the group profit.

### 2.1.2 Consolidated statement of financial position

A figure for **investment in associates** is shown which at the time of the acquisition must be stated at cost. At the end of each accounting period the group share of the retained reserves of the associate is added to the original cost to get the total investment to be shown in the consolidated statement of financial position.

## 2.2 Example: associate

P Co, a company with subsidiaries, acquires 25,000 of the 100,000 $1 ordinary shares in A Co for $60,000 on 1 January 20X8. In the year to 31 December 20X8, A Co earns profits after tax of $24,000, from which it pays a dividend of $6,000.

How will A Co's results be accounted for in the individual and consolidated accounts of P Co for the year ended 31 December 20X8?

## Solution

In the **individual accounts** of P Co, the investment will be recorded on 1 January 20X8 at cost. Unless there is an impairment in the value of the investment (see below), this amount will remain in the individual statement of financial position of P Co permanently. The only entry in P Co's individual statement of profit or loss will be to record dividends received. For the year ended 31 December 20X8, P Co will:

| | | |
|---|---|---|
| DEBIT | Cash | $1,500 |
| CREDIT | Income from shares in associates | $1,500 |

In the **consolidated accounts** of P Co equity accounting principles will be used to account for the investment in A Co. Consolidated profit after tax will include the group's share of A Co's profit after tax (25% × $24,000 = $6,000). To the extent that this has been distributed as dividend, it is already included in P Co's individual accounts and will automatically be brought into the consolidated results. That part of the group's share of profit in the associate which has not been distributed as dividend ($4,500) will be brought into consolidation by the following adjustment.

| | | |
|---|---|---|
| DEBIT | Investment in associates | $4,500 |
| CREDIT | Share of profit of associates | $4,500 |

The asset 'Investment in associates' is then stated at $64,500, being cost plus the group share of post-acquisition retained profits.

# 3 Statement of profit or loss and statement of financial position

## 3.1 Consolidated statement of profit or loss

FAST FORWARD

> In the **consolidated statement of profit or loss** the investing group takes credit for its **share of the after-tax profits** of associates whether or not they are distributed as dividends.

A **consolidation schedule** may be used to prepare the consolidated statement of profit or loss of a group with associates. Note the treatment of the associate's profits in the following example.

## 3.2 Illustration

The following **consolidation schedule** relates to the P Co group, consisting of the parent company, an 80% owned subsidiary (S Co) and an associate (A Co) in which the group has a 30% interest.

CONSOLIDATION SCHEDULE

| | Group $'000 | P Co $'000 | S Co $'000 | A Co $'000 |
|---|---|---|---|---|
| Sales revenue | 1,400 | 600 | 800 | 300 |
| Cost of sales | 770 | 370 | 400 | 120 |
| Gross profit | 630 | 230 | 400 | 180 |
| Administrative expenses | 290 | 110 | 180 | 80 |
| | 340 | 120 | 220 | 100 |
| Interest receivable | 30 | 30 | – | – |
| | 370 | 150 | 220 | 100 |
| Interest payable | (20) | – | (20) | – |
| Share of profit of associate (57× 30%) | 17 | – | – | |
| | 367 | 150 | 200 | 100 |
| Income tax expense | | | | |
| Group | (145) | (55) | (90) | |
| Associate | – | – | – | (43) |
| Profit for the year | 222 | 95 | 110 | 57 |
| Non-controlling interest (110× 20%) | (22) | | | |
| | 200 | | | |

*Note the following*

(a)  Group sales revenue, group gross profit and costs such as depreciation etc exclude the sales revenue, gross profit and costs etc of associated companies.

(b)  The group share of the associated company profits is credited to group profit or loss. If the associated company has been acquired during the year, it would be necessary to deduct the pre-acquisition profits (remembering to allow for tax on current year profits).

(c)  The non-controlling interest will only ever apply to subsidiary companies.

## 3.3 Pro-forma consolidated statement of profit or loss

The following is a **suggested layout** (using the figures given in the illustration above) for the consolidated statement of profit or loss of a company having subsidiaries as well as associated companies.

|  | $'000 |
|---|---|
| Sales revenue | 1,400 |
| Cost of sales | (770) |
| Gross profit | 630 |
| Other income: interest receivable | 30 |
| Administrative expenses | (290) |
| Finance costs | (20) |
| Share of profit of associate | 17 |
| Profit before tax | 367 |
| Income tax expense | (145) |
| Profit for the year | 222 |
|  |  |
| Profit attributable to: |  |
| Owners of the parent | 200 |
| Non-controlling interest | 22 |
|  | 222 |

## 3.4 Consolidated statement of financial position

FAST FORWARD

In the consolidated statement of financial position the investment in associates should be shown as:

*  Cost of the investment in the associate; plus
*  Group share of post acquisition profits; less
*  Any amounts paid out as dividends; less
*  Any amount written off the investment

As explained earlier, the consolidated statement of financial position will contain an **asset 'Investment in associates'**. The amount at which this asset is stated will be its original cost plus the group's share of any **post-acquisition profits** which have not been distributed as dividends.

## 3.5 Example: consolidated statement of financial position

On 1 January 20X6 the net tangible assets of A Co amount to $220,000, financed by 100,000 $1 ordinary shares and revenue reserves of $120,000. P Co, a company with subsidiaries, acquires 30,000 of the shares in A Co for $75,000. During the year ended 31 December 20X6 A Co's profit after tax is $30,000, from which dividends of $12,000 are paid.

Show how P Co's investment in A Co would appear in the consolidated statement of financial position at 31 December 20X6.

## Solution

CONSOLIDATED STATEMENT OF FINANCIAL POSITION
AS AT 31 DECEMBER 20X6 (extract)

|  | $ |
|---|---|
| Non-current assets |  |
| Investment in associated company |  |
| Cost | 75,000 |
| Group share of post-acquisition retained profits |  |
| (30% × $18,000) | 5,400 |
|  | 80,400 |

## Question

Associate I

Set out below are the draft accounts of Parent Co and its subsidiaries and of Associate Co. Parent Co acquired 40% of the equity capital of Associate Co three years ago when the latter's reserves stood at $40,000.

SUMMARISED STATEMENTS OF FINANCIAL POSITION

|  | Parent Co & subsidiaries $'000 | Associate Co $'000 |
|---|---|---|
| Tangible non-current assets | 220 | 170 |
| Investment in Associate at cost | 60 | – |
| Loan to Associate Co | 20 | – |
| Current assets | 100 | 50 |
| Loan from Parent Co | – | (20) |
|  | 400 | 200 |
|  |  |  |
| Share capital ($1 shares) | 250 | 100 |
| Retained earnings | 150 | 100 |
|  | 400 | 200 |

SUMMARISED STATEMENTS OF PROFIT OR LOSS

|  | Parent Co & subsidiaries $'000 | Associate Co $'000 |
|---|---|---|
| Profit before tax | 95 | 80 |
| Income tax expense | 35 | 30 |
| Net profit for the year | 60 | 50 |

You are required to prepare the summarised consolidated accounts of Parent Co.

*Notes*

(1) Assume that the associate's assets/liabilities are stated at fair value.
(2) Assume that there are no non-controlling interests in the subsidiary companies.

## Answer

PARENT CO
CONSOLIDATED STATEMENT OF PROFIT OR LOSS

|  | $'000 |
|---|---|
| Net profit | 95 |
| Share of profits of associated company (50 × 40%) | 20 |
| Profit before tax | 115 |
| Income tax expense | (35) |
| Profit attributable to the members of Parent Co | 80 |

PARENT CO
CONSOLIDATED STATEMENT OF FINANCIAL POSITION

| | $'000 |
|---|---|
| *Assets* | |
| Tangible non-current assets | 220 |
| Investment in associate (see note) | 84 |
| Loan to associate | 20 |
| Current assets | 100 |
| *Total assets* | 424 |
| | |
| *Equity and liabilities* | |
| Share capital | 250 |
| Retained earnings (W) | 174 |
| *Total equity and liabilities* | 424 |

*Note*

| | $'000 |
|---|---|
| *Investment in associate* | |
| Cost of investment | 60 |
| Share of post-acquisition retained earnings (W) | 24 |
| | 84 |

*Working*

| Retained earnings | Parent & Subsidiaries $'000 | Associate $'000 |
|---|---|---|
| Per question | 150 | 100 |
| Pre-acquisition | | 40 |
| Post-acquisition | | 60 |
| | | |
| Group share in associate | | |
| ($60 × 40%) | 24 | |
| Group retained earnings | 174 | |

Question                                                                    Associate II

Alfred Co bought a 25% shareholding on 31 December 20X8 in Grimbald Co at a cost of $38,000.

During the year to 31 December 20X9 Grimbald Co made a profit before tax of $82,000 and the taxation charge on the year's profits was $32,000. A dividend of $20,000 was paid on 31 December out of these profits.

Calculate the entries for the associate which would appear in the consolidated accounts of the Alfred group, in accordance with the requirements of IAS 28.

Answer

CONSOLIDATED STATEMENT OF PROFIT OR LOSS

| | $ |
|---|---|
| Group share of profit of associate (82,000 × 25%) | 20,500 |
| Less taxation (32,000 × 25%) | (8,000) |
| Share of profit of associate | 12,500 |

CONSOLIDATED STATEMENT OF FINANCIAL POSITION

| | $ |
|---|---|
| Investment in associate (W) | 45,500 |

*Working*

| | $ |
|---|---|
| Cost of investment | 38,000 |
| Share of post-acquisition retained earnings ((82,000 – 32,000 – 20,000) × 25%) | 7,500 |
| | 45,500 |

The following points are also relevant and are similar to a parent-subsidiary consolidation situation.

(a) Use financial statements drawn up to the **same reporting date.**

(b) If this is impracticable, adjust the financial statements for **significant transactions/ events** in the intervening period. The difference between the reporting date of the associate and that of the investor must be no more than three months.

(c) Use **uniform accounting policies** for like transactions and events in similar circumstances, adjusting the associate's statements to reflect group policies if necessary.

## 3.6 'Upstream' and 'downstream' transactions

'Upstream' transactions are, for example, sales of assets from an associate to the investor. 'Downstream' transactions are, for example, sales of assets from the investor to an associate.

Profits and losses resulting from 'upstream' and 'downstream' transactions between an investor (including its consolidated subsidiaries) and an associate are eliminated to the extent of the investor's interest in the associate. This is very similar to the procedure for eliminating intra-group transactions between a parent and a subsidiary. The important thing to remember is that **only the group's share is eliminated**.

## 3.7 Example: downstream transaction

A Co, a parent with subsidiaries, holds 25% of the equity shares in B Co. During the year, A Co makes sales of $1,000,000 to B Co at cost plus a 25% mark-up. At the year-end, B Co has all these goods still in inventories.

## Solution

A Co has made an unrealised profit of $200,000 (1,000,000 × 25/125) on its sales to the associate. The group's share (25%) of this must be eliminated:

DEBIT     Cost of sales (consolidated profit or loss)                                    $50,000
CREDIT    Investment in associate (consolidated statement of financial position)  $50,000

Because the sale was made to the associate, the group's share of the unsold inventory forms part of the investment in the associate at the year-end. If the associate had made the sale to the parent, the adjustment would have been:

DEBIT     Cost of sales (consolidated profit or loss)                                    $50,000
CREDIT    Inventories (consolidated statement of financial position)             $50,000

## 3.8 Associate's losses

When the equity method is being used and the investor's share of losses of the associate equals or exceeds its interest in the associate, the investor should **discontinue** including its share of further losses. The investment is reported at nil value. After the investor's interest is reduced to nil, **additional losses** should only be recognised where the investor has incurred obligations or made payments on behalf of the associate (for example, if it has guaranteed amounts owed to third parties by the associate).

## 3.9 Impairment losses

IAS 39 sets out a list of indications that a financial asset (including an associate) may have become impaired. Any impairment loss is recognised in accordance with IAS 36 *Impairment of assets* for each associate individually.

In the case of an associate, any impairment loss will be deducted from the carrying value in the statement of financial position.

The working would be as follows.

|  | $ |
|---|---|
| Cost of investment | X |
| Share of post-acquisition retained earnings | X |
|  | X |
| Impairment loss | (X) |
| Investment in associate | X |

**Exam focus point**

It is not unusual in the exam to have both an associate and a subsidiary to account for in a consolidation.

**Question**                                                     Consolidated statement of financial position

The statements of financial position of J Co and its investee companies, P Co and S Co, at 31 December 20X5 are shown below.

STATEMENTS OF FINANCIAL POSITION AS AT 31 DECEMBER 20X5

|  | J Co | P Co | S Co |
|---|---|---|---|
|  | $'000 | $'000 | $'000 |
| *Non-current assets* |  |  |  |
| Freehold property | 1,950 | 1,250 | 500 |
| Plant and machinery | 795 | 375 | 285 |
| Investments | 1,500 | – | – |
|  | 4,245 | 1,625 | 785 |
| *Current assets* |  |  |  |
| Inventory | 575 | 300 | 265 |
| Trade receivables | 330 | 290 | 370 |
| Cash | 50 | 120 | 20 |
|  | 955 | 710 | 655 |
| Total assets | 5,200 | 2,335 | 1,440 |
| *Equity and liabilities* |  |  |  |
| *Equity* |  |  |  |
| Share capital – $1 shares | 2,000 | 1,000 | 750 |
| Retained earnings | 1,460 | 885 | 390 |
|  | 3,460 | 1,885 | 1,140 |
| *Non-current liabilities* |  |  |  |
| 12% loan stock | 500 | 100 |  |
| *Current liabilities* |  |  |  |
| Trade payables | 680 | 350 | 300 |
| Bank overdraft | 560 | – | – |
|  | 1,240 | 350 | 300 |
| Total equity and liabilities | 5,200 | 2,335 | 1,440 |

*Additional information*

(a)    J Co acquired 600,000 ordinary shares in P Co on 1 January 20X0 for $1,000,000 when the retained earnings of P Co were $200,000.

(b)    At the date of acquisition of P Co, the fair value of its freehold property was considered to be $400,000 greater than its value in P Co's statement of financial position. P Co had acquired the property in January 20W0 and the buildings element (comprising 50% of the total value) is depreciated on cost over 50 years.

(c)    J Co acquired 225,000 ordinary shares in S Co on 1 January 20X4 for $500,000 when the retained earnings of S Co were $150,000.

(d)    P Co manufactures a component used by both J Co and S Co. Transfers are made by P Co at cost plus 25%. J Co held $100,000 inventory of these components at 31 December 20X5. In the same period J Co sold goods to S Co of which S Co had $80,000 in inventory at 31 December 20X5. J Co had marked these goods up by 25%.

(e)    The goodwill in P Co is impaired and should be fully written off. An impairment loss of $92,000 is to be recognised on the investment in S Co.

(f)    Non-controlling interest is valued at full fair value. P Co shares were trading at $1.60 just prior to the acquisition by J Co.

*Required*

Prepare, in a format suitable for inclusion in the annual report of the J Group, the consolidated statement of financial position at 31 December 20X5.

## Answer

J GROUP CONSOLIDATED STATEMENT OF FINANCIAL POSITION AS AT 31 DECEMBER 20X5

|  | $'000 |
|---|---|
| *Non-current assets* |  |
| Freehold property (W2) | 3,570.00 |
| Plant and machinery (795 + 375) | 1,170.00 |
| Investment in associate (W7) | 475.20 |
|  | 5,215.20 |
| *Current assets* |  |
| Inventory (W3) | 855.00 |
| Receivables (330 + 290) | 620.00 |
| Cash (50 + 120) | 170.00 |
|  | 1,645.00 |
| Total assets | 6,860.20 |
| *Equity and liabilities* |  |
| *Equity* |  |
| Share capital | 2,000.00 |
| Retained earnings (W8) | 1,792.20 |
|  | 3,792.20 |
| Non-controlling interest (W9) | 878.00 |
|  | 4,670.20 |
| *Non-current liabilities* |  |
| 12% loan stock (500 + 100) | 600.00 |
| Current liabilities (680 + 560 + 350) | 1,590.00 |
| Total equity and liabilities | 6,860.20 |

*Workings*

1    Group structure

2    *Freehold property*

|  | $'000 |
|---|---|
| J Co | 1,950 |
| P Co | 1,250 |
| Fair value adjustment | 400 |
| Additional depreciation (400 × 50% ÷ 40) × 6 years (20X0–20X5) | (30) |
|  | 3,570 |

3    *Inventory*

|  | $'000 |
|---|---|
| J Co | 575 |
| P Co | 300 |
| PUP (100 × $^{25}/_{125}$) (W4) | (20) |
|  | 855 |

4    *Unrealised profit (PUP)*

|  | $'000 |
|---|---|
| On sales by P to J (parent co) 100 × 25/125 | 20.0 |
| On sales by J to S (associate) 80 × 25/125 × 30% | 4.8 |

5    *Fair value adjustments*

|  | Difference at acquisition | Difference now |
|---|---|---|
|  | $'000 | $'000 |
| Property | 400 | 400 |
| Additional depreciation: 200 × 6/40 | – | (30) |
|  | 400 | 370 |

∴ Charge $30,000 to retained earnings

6    *Goodwill*

|  | $'000 | $'000 |
|---|---|---|
| *P Co* |  |  |
| Consideration transferred |  | 1,000 |
| Non-controlling interest (400 × $1.60) |  | 640 |
| Net assets acquired |  |  |
|     Share capital | 1,000 |  |
|     Retained earnings | 200 |  |
|     Fair value adjustment | 400 |  |
|  |  | (1,600) |
| Goodwill at acquisition |  | 40 |
| Impairment loss |  | (40) |
|  |  | 0 |

7    *Investment in associate*

|  | $'000 |
|---|---|
| Cost of investment | 500.00 |
| Share of post-acquisition profit (390 – 150) × 30% | 72.00 |
| Less PUP | (4.80) |
| Less impairment loss | (92.00) |
|  | 475.20 |

8    Retained earnings

|  | J $'000 | P $'000 | S $'000 |
|---|---|---|---|
| Retained earnings per question | 1,460.0 | 885.0 | 390.0 |
| Adjustments |  |  |  |
| Unrealised profit (W4) | (4.8) | (20.0) |  |
| Fair value adjustments (W5) |  | (30.0) |  |
| Impairment loss (P) |  | (40.0) |  |
|  |  | 795.0 | 390.0 |
| Less pre-acquisition reserves |  | (200.0) | (150.0) |
|  | 1,455.20 | 595.0 | 240.0 |
| P:    60% × 595 | 357.00 |  |  |
| S:    30% × 240 | 72.00 |  |  |
| Impairment loss S | (92.00) |  |  |
|  | 1,792.20 |  |  |

9    Non-controlling interest at reporting date

|  | $'000 |
|---|---|
| NCI at acquisition (W6) | 640.00 |
| Share of post-acquisition retained earnings (595 x 40%) | 238.00 |
|  | 878.00 |

# Chapter Roundup

- A company investing in an associate does not have control but it does have **significant** influence. IAS 28 requires that, in consolidated financial statements, **associates** should be accounted for using **equity accounting principles**.

- In the **consolidated statement of profit or loss** the investing group takes credit for its **share of the after-tax profits** of associates, whether or not they are distributed as dividends.

- In the **consolidated statement of financial position**, the investment in associates should be shown as:

  - **Cost of the investment in the associate**; plus
  - Group share of post-acquisition profits; less
  - Any amounts paid out as dividends and any amounts written off.

# Quick Quiz

1    Define an associate.
2    How should associates be accounted for in the separate financial statements of the investor?
3    What is the effect of the equity method on the consolidated statement of profit or loss and statement of financial position?

# Answers to Quick Quiz

1   An entity in which an investor has a significant influence, but which is not a subsidiary or a joint venture of the investor.

2   Either at cost or in accordance with IFRS 9.

3   (a)   *Consolidated statement of profit or loss.* Investing company includes its share of the earnings of the associate, by adding its share of profit after tax.

    (b)   *Consolidated statement of financial position.* Investment in associates is initially included in assets at cost. This will increase or decrease each year according to whether the associated company makes a profit or loss.

Now try the questions below from the Exam Question Bank

| Number | Level | Marks | Time |
|--------|-------|-------|------|
| 13 | Examination | 25 | 45 mins |

# Inventories and construction contracts

| Topic list | Syllabus reference |
|---|---|
| 1 Inventories and short-term WIP (IAS 2) | C4 |
| 2 IAS 11 Construction contracts | C4 |

## Introduction

You have encountered inventory and its valuation in your earlier studies. Inventory and short-term work-in-progress valuation has a direct impact on a company's gross profit and it is usually a material item in any company's accounts. This is therefore an important subject area. If you have any doubts about accounting for inventories and methods of inventory valuation you would be advised to go back to your earlier study material and revise this topic.

Section 1 of this chapter goes over some of this ground again, concentrating on the effect of IAS 2. Section 2 goes on to discuss a new area, construction contracts, which are effectively long-term work in progress. You should find this topic fairly logical as long as you work through the examples and question carefully.

# Study guide

| | | | Intellectual level |
|---|---|---|:---:|
| **4** | **Inventory** | | |
| | (a) | describe and apply the principles of inventory valuation. | 2 |
| | (b) | define a construction contract and discuss the role of accounting concepts in the recognition of profit. | 2 |
| | (c) | describe the acceptable methods of determining the stage (percentage) of completion of a contract. | 2 |
| | (d) | prepare financial statement extracts for construction contracts. | 2 |

# Exam guide

Exams regularly contain a question on construction contracts. They are a good test of double entry. The examiner is likely to test them, if only because they do not feature at Paper P2.

# 1 Inventories and short-term WIP (IAS 2)

The use of LIFO is prohibited under the revised IAS 2.

## 1.1 Introduction

In most businesses the value put on inventory is an important factor in the determination of profit. Inventory valuation is, however, a highly subjective exercise and consequently there is a wide variety of different methods used in practice.

## 1.2 IAS 2 (revised) Inventories

IAS 2 was revised in December 2003. It lays out the required accounting treatment for inventories (sometimes called stocks) under the historical cost system. The major area of contention is the cost **value of inventory** to be recorded. This is recognised as an asset of the entity until the related revenues are recognised (ie the item is sold) at which point the inventory is recognised as an expense (ie cost of sales). Part or all of the cost of inventories may also be expensed if a write-down to **net realisable value** is necessary. The revised IAS also provides guidance on the cost formulas that are used to assign costs to inventories.

In other words, the fundamental accounting assumption of **accruals** requires costs to be matched with associated revenues. In order to achieve this, costs incurred for goods which remain unsold at the year end must be carried forward in the statement of financial position and matched against future revenues.

## 1.3 Scope

The following items are **excluded** from the scope of the standard.

- Work in progress under **construction contracts** (covered by IAS 11 *Construction contracts*, see Section 2)
- **Financial instruments** (ie shares, bonds)
- **Biological assets**

Certain inventories are exempt from the standard's **measurement rules**, ie those held by:

- Producers of **agricultural and forest products**
- **Commodity-broker traders**

## 1.4 Definitions

The following definitions are important.

> - **Inventories** are assets:
>   - held for sale in the ordinary course of business;
>   - in the process of production for such sale; or
>   - in the form of materials or supplies to be consumed in the production process or in the rendering of services.
>
> - **Net realisable value** is the estimated selling price in the ordinary course of business less the estimated costs of completion and the estimated costs necessary to make the sale.     (IAS 2)
>
> - **Fair value** is the price that would be received to sell an asset or paid to transfer a liability in an orderly transaction between market participants at the measurement date.     (IFRS 13)

Inventories can **include** any of the following.

- **Goods purchased and held for resale**, eg goods held for sale by a retailer, or land and buildings held for resale
- **Finished goods** produced
- **Work in progress** being produced
- Materials and supplies awaiting use in the production process (**raw materials**)

## 1.5 Measurement of inventories

The standard states that '**Inventories should be measured at the lower of cost and net realisable value.**'

> This is a very important rule and you will be expected to apply it in the exam.

## 1.6 Cost of inventories

The cost of inventories will consist of all costs of:

- **Purchase**
- **Costs of conversion**
- **Other costs** incurred in bringing the inventories to their **present location and condition**

### 1.6.1 Costs of purchase

The standard lists the following as comprising the costs of purchase of inventories:

- **Purchase price** *plus*
- **Import duties** and other taxes *plus*
- Transport, handling and any other cost **directly attributable** to the acquisition of finished goods, services and materials *less*
- **Trade discounts**, rebates and other similar amounts

### 1.6.2 Costs of conversion

Costs of conversion of inventories consist of two main parts.

(a)    Costs **directly related** to the units of production, eg direct materials, direct labour

(b)    Fixed and variable **production overheads** that are incurred in converting materials into finished goods, allocated on a systematic basis.

You may have come across the terms 'fixed production overheads' or 'variable production overheads' elsewhere in your studies. The standard defines them as follows.

> - **Fixed production overheads** are those indirect costs of production that remain relatively constant regardless of the volume of production, eg the cost of factory management and administration.
>
> - **Variable production overheads** are those indirect costs of production that vary directly, or nearly directly, with the volume of production, eg indirect materials and labour. *(IAS 2)*

The standard emphasises that fixed production overheads must be allocated to items of inventory on the basis of the **normal capacity of the production facilities**. This is an important point.

(a) **Normal capacity** is the expected achievable production based on the average over several periods/seasons, under normal circumstances.

(b) The above figure should take account of the capacity lost through **planned maintenance**.

(c) If it approximates to the normal level of activity then the **actual level of production** can be used.

(d) **Low production** or **idle plant** will *not* result in a higher fixed overhead allocation to each unit.

(e) **Unallocated overheads** must be recognised as an expense in the period in which they were incurred.

(f) When production is **abnormally high**, the fixed production overhead allocated to each unit will be reduced, so avoiding inventories being stated at more than cost.

(g) The allocation of variable production overheads to each unit is based on the **actual use** of production facilities.

### 1.6.3 Other costs

Any other costs should only be recognised if they are incurred in bringing the inventories to their **present location and condition**.

The standard lists types of cost which **would not be included** in cost of inventories. Instead, they should be recognised as an **expense** in the period they are incurred.

(a) **Abnormal amounts** of wasted materials, labour or other production costs

(b) **Storage costs** (except costs which are necessary in the production process before a further production stage)

(c) **Administrative overheads** not incurred to bring inventories to their present location and conditions

(d) **Selling costs**

### 1.6.4 Techniques for the measurement of cost

Two techniques are mentioned by the standard, both of which produce results which **approximate to cost**, and so both of which may be used for convenience.

(a) **Standard costs** are set up to take account of normal production values: amount of raw materials used, labour time etc. They are reviewed and revised on a regular basis.

(b) **Retail method**: this is often used in the retail industry where there is a large turnover of inventory items, which nevertheless have similar profit margins. The only practical method of inventory valuation may be to take the total selling price of inventories and deduct an overall average profit margin, thus reducing the value to an approximation of cost. The percentage will take account of reduced price lines. Sometimes different percentages are applied on a department basis.

## 1.7 Cost formulas

Cost of inventories should be assigned by **specific identification** of their individual costs for:

(a) Items that are **not ordinarily interchangeable**

(b) Goods or services produced and segregated for **specific projects**

Specific costs should be attributed to individual items of inventory when they are segregated for a specific project, but not where inventories consist of a large number of interchangeable (ie identical or very similar) items. In the latter case the rule is as specified below.

### 1.7.1 Interchangeable items

You should be familiar with these methods from your earlier studies. Under the weighted average cost method, a recalculation can be made after each purchase, **or alternatively only at the period end**.

## 1.8 Net realisable value (NRV)

As a general rule assets should not be carried at amounts greater than those expected to be realised from their sale or use. In the case of inventories this amount could fall below cost when items are **damaged or become obsolete**, or where the **costs to completion have increased** in order to make the sale.

In fact we can identify the principal situations in which **NRV is likely to be less than cost**, ie where there has been:

(a)   An **increase in costs** or a **fall in selling price**
(b)   A **physical deterioration** in the condition of inventory
(c)   **Obsolescence** of products
(d)   A decision as part of the company's marketing strategy to manufacture and sell products at a **loss**
(e)   **Errors in production or purchasing**

A write down of inventories would normally take place on an item by item basis, but similar or related items may be **grouped together**. This grouping together is acceptable for, say, items in the same product line, but it is not acceptable to write down inventories based on a whole classification (eg finished goods) or a whole business.

The assessment of NRV should take place **at the same time** as estimates are made of selling price, using the most reliable information available. Fluctuations of price or cost should be taken into account if they relate directly to **events after the reporting period,** which confirm conditions existing at the end of the period.

The reasons why inventory is held must also be taken into account. Some inventory, for example, may be held to satisfy a firm contract and its NRV will therefore be the **contract price**. Any additional inventory of the same type held at the period end will, in contrast, be assessed according to general sales prices when NRV is estimated.

Net realisable value must be reassessed at the end of each period and compared again with cost. If the NRV has risen for inventories held over the end of more than one period, then the previous write down must be **reversed** to the extent that the inventory is then valued at the lower of cost and the new NRV. This may be possible when selling prices have fallen in the past and then risen again.

On occasion a write down to NRV may be of such size, incidence or nature that it must be **disclosed separately**.

## 1.9 Recognition as an expense

The following treatment is required **when inventories are sold**.

(a)   The **carrying amount** is recognised as an expense in the period in which the related revenue is recognised
(b)   The amount of any **write-down of inventories** to NRV and all losses of inventories are recognised as an expense in the period the write-down or loss occurs
(c)   The amount of any **reversal of any write-down of inventories**, arising from an increase in NRV, is recognised as a reduction in the amount of inventories recognised as an expense in the period in which the reversal occurs

## Question

A company has inventory on hand at the end of the reporting period as follows:

| | Units | Raw material cost | Attributable production overheads | Attributable selling costs | Expected selling |
|---|---|---|---|---|---|
| | | $ | $ | $ | $ |
| Item A | 300 | 160 | 15 | 12 | 185 |
| Item B | 250 | 50 | 10 | 10 | 75 |

At what amount will inventories be stated in the statement of financial position in accordance with IAS 2?

## Answer

| | Units | Cost | NRV | Lower | Total |
|---|---|---|---|---|---|
| | | $ | $ | $ | $ |
| Item A | 300 | 175 | 173 | 173 | 51,900 |
| Item B | 250 | 60 | 65 | 60 | 15,000 |
| | | | | | 66,900 |

## 1.10 Consistency – different cost formulas for inventories

IAS 2 allows two cost formulas (FIFO or weighted average cost) for inventories that are ordinarily interchangeable or are not produced and segregated for specific projects. The issue is whether an entity may use different cost formulas for different types of inventories.

IAS 2 provides that an entity should use **the same cost formula for all inventories having similar nature and use to the entity.** For inventories with different nature or use (for example, certain commodities used in one business segment and the same type of commodities used in another business segment), different cost formulas may be justified. A difference in geographical location of inventories (and in the respective tax rules), by itself, is not sufficient to justify the use of different cost formulas.

# 2 IAS 11 Construction contracts

FAST FORWARD

Sales revenue on a construction contract is based upon stage of completion.

## 2.1 Introduction

Imagine that you are the accountant at a construction company. Your company is building a large tower block that will house offices, under a contract with an investment company. It will take three years to build the block and over that time you will obviously have to pay for building materials, wages of workers on the building, architects' fees and so on. You will receive periodic payments from the investment company at various predetermined stages of the construction. How do you decide, in each of the three years, **what to include as income and expenditure** for the contract in the statement of profit or loss?

This is the problem tackled by IAS 11 *Construction contracts*.

## 2.2 Example: construction contract

A numerical example might help to illustrate the problem. Suppose that a contract is started on 1 January 20X5, with an estimated completion date of 31 December 20X6. The final contract price is $1,500,000. In the first year, to 31 December 20X5:

(a)     Costs incurred amounted to $600,000.
(b)     Half the work on the contract was completed.

(c)    Certificates of work completed have been issued, to the value of $750,000. (*Note.* It is usual, in a construction contract, for a qualified person such as an architect or engineer to inspect the work completed, and if it is satisfactory, to issue certificates. This will then be the notification to the customer that progress payments are now due to the contractor. Progress payments are commonly the amount of valuation on the work certificates issued, minus a precautionary retention of 10%).

(d)    It is estimated with reasonable certainty that further costs to completion in 20X6 will be $600,000.

What is the contract profit in 20X5, and what entries would be made for the contract at 31 December 20X5 if:

(a)    Profits are deferred until the completion of the contract?

(b)    A proportion of the estimated revenue and profit is credited to profit or loss in 20X5?

## Solution

(a)    If profits were deferred until the completion of the contract in 20X6, the revenue and profit recognised on the contract in 20X5 would be nil, and the value of work in progress on 31 December 20X5 would be $600,000. IAS 11 takes the view that this policy is unreasonable, because in 20X6, the total profit of $300,000 would be recorded. Since the contract revenues are earned throughout 20X5 and 20X6, a profit of nil in 20X5 and $300,000 in 20X6 would be contrary to the accruals concept of accounting.

(b)    **It is fairer to recognise revenue and profit throughout the duration of the contract.**

As at 31 December 20X5 revenue of $750,000 should be matched with cost of sales of $600,000 in the statement of profit or loss, leaving an attributable profit for 20X5 of $150,000.

The only entry in the statement of financial position as at 31 December 20X5 is a receivable of $750,000 recognising that the company is owed this amount for work done to date. No balance remains for work in progress, the whole $600,000 having been recognised in cost of sales.

## 2.3 What is a construction contract?

A contract which needs IAS 11 treatment does not have to last for a period of more than one year. The main point is that the contract activity **starts in one financial period and ends in another**, thus creating the problem: to which of two or more periods should contract income and costs be allocated? In fact the definition given in the IAS of a construction contract is very straightforward.

**Key term**

> **Construction contract.** A contract specifically negotiated for the construction of an asset or a combination of assets that are closely interrelated or interdependent in terms of their design, technology and function or their ultimate purpose or use.                                                                                      *(IAS 11)*

The standard differentiates between fixed price contracts and cost plus contracts.

**Key terms**

> - **Fixed price contract.** A contract in which the contractor agrees to a fixed contract price, or a fixed rate per unit of output, which in some cases is subject to cost escalation clauses.
> - **Cost plus contract.** A construction contract in which the contractor is reimbursed for allowable or otherwise defined costs, plus a percentage of these costs or a fixed fee.

Construction contracts may involve the building of one asset, eg a bridge, or a series of interrelated assets eg an oil refinery. They may also include **rendering of services** (eg architects) or restoring or demolishing an asset.

## 2.4 Combining and segmenting construction contracts

The standard lays out the factors which determine whether the construction of a **series of assets** under one contract should be treated as several contracts.

- **Separate proposals** are submitted for each asset
- **Separate negotiations** are undertaken for each asset; the customer can accept/reject each individually
- **Identifiable costs and revenues** can be separated for each asset

There are also circumstances where a **group of** contracts should be treated as **one single construction contract**.

- The group of contracts are negotiated as a **single package**
- Contracts are **closely interrelated**, with an overall profit margin
- The contracts are performed **concurrently** or **in a single sequence**

## 2.5 Contract revenue

Contract revenue will be the **amount specified in the contract**, subject to variations in the contract work, incentive payments and claims *if* these will probably give rise to revenue and *if* they can be reliably measured. The result is that contract revenue is measured at the **fair value** of received or receivable revenue.

The standard elaborates on the types of uncertainty, which depend on the outcome of future events, that affect the **measurement of contract revenue**.

- An **agreed variation** (increase/decrease)
- **Cost escalation clauses** in a fixed price contract (increase)
- **Penalties** imposed due to delays by the contractor (decrease)
- **Number of units** varies in a contract for fixed prices per unit (increase/decrease)

In the case of any variation, claim or incentive payment, two factors should be assessed to determine whether contract revenue should be recognised.

- Whether it is **probable** that the customer will accept the variation/claim, or that the contract is sufficiently advanced that the performance criteria will be met
- Whether the amount of the revenue can be **measured reliably**

## 2.6 Contract costs

Contract costs consist of:

- Costs relating **directly** to the contract
- Costs attributable to general contract activity which can be **allocated** to the contract, such as insurance, cost of design and technical assistance not directly related to a specific contract and construction overheads
- Any other costs which can be **charged to the customer** under the contract, which may include general administration costs and development costs

Costs that **relate directly** to a specific contract include the following.

- **Site labour costs**, including site supervision
- Costs of **materials** used in construction
- **Depreciation** of plant and equipment used on the contract
- Costs of **moving** plant, equipment and materials to and from the contract site
- Costs of **hiring** plant and equipment
- Costs of **design and technical assistance** that are directly related to the contract
- Estimated costs of **rectification and guarantee work**, including expected warranty costs
- **Claims from third parties**

General contract activity costs should be **allocated systematically and rationally**, and all costs with similar characteristics should be treated **consistently**. The allocation should be based on the **normal level** of construction activity. Borrowing costs may be attributed in this way (see IAS 23: Chapter 4).

Some costs **cannot be attributed** to contract activity and so the following should be **excluded** from construction contract costs.

- **General administration costs** (unless reimbursement is specified in the contract)
- **Selling costs**
- **R&D** (unless reimbursement is specified in the contract)
- **Depreciation** of idle plant and equipment not used on any particular contract

## 2.7 Recognition of contract revenue and expenses

Revenue and costs associated with a contract should be recognised according to the stage of completion of the contract at the end of the reporting period, but *only when* the **outcome of the activity can be estimated reliably**. If a loss is predicted on a contract, then it should be recognised immediately. This is often known as the **percentage of completion method**.

A reliable estimate of the outcome of a construction contract can only be made when **certain conditions** have been met, and these conditions will be different for fixed price and cost plus contracts.

- **Fixed price contracts**
    - Probable that economic benefits of the contract will flow to the entity
    - Total contract revenue can be reliably measured
    - Stage of completion at the period end and costs to complete the contract can be reliably measured
    - Costs attributable to the contract can be identified clearly and be reliably measured (actual costs can be compared to previous estimates)

- **Cost plus contracts**
    - Probable that economic benefits of the contract will flow to the entity
    - Costs attributable to the contract (whether or not reimbursable) can be identified clearly and be reliably measured

The **percentage of completion method** is an application of the accruals assumption. Contract revenue is matched to the contract costs incurred in reaching the stage of completion, so revenue, costs and profit are attributed to the proportion of work completed.

We can **summarise** the treatment as follows.

- Recognise **contract revenue** as revenue in the accounting periods in which the work is performed
- Recognise **contract costs** as an expense in the accounting period in which the work to which they relate is performed
- Any **expected excess** of total contract costs over total contract revenue should be recognised as an expense immediately
- Any costs incurred which relate to **future activity** should be recognised as an asset if it is probable that they will be recovered (often called contract work in progress, ie amounts due from the customer)
- Where amounts have been recognised as contract revenue, but their **collectability** from the customer becomes doubtful, such amounts should be recognised as an expense, not a deduction from revenue

## 2.8 When can reliable estimates be made?

IAS 11 only allows contract revenue and costs to be recognised when the outcome of the contract can be predicted, ie when it is probable that the economic benefits attached to the contract will flow to the entity. IAS 11 states that this can only be when a contract has been agreed which establishes the following.

- The **enforceable rights** of each party in respect of the asset to be constructed
- The **consideration** that is to be exchanged
- **Terms and manner of settlement**

In addition, the entity should have an **effective internal financial budgeting and reporting system**, in order to review and revise the estimates of contract revenue and costs as the contract progresses.

## 2.9 Determining the stage of completion

How should you decide on the stage of completion of any contract? The standard lists several methods.

- **Proportion of contract costs incurred** for work carried out to date
- **Surveys** of work carried out
- **Physical proportion** of the contract work completed

## 2.10 Example: stage of completion

Centrepoint Co have a fixed price contract to build a tower block. The initial amount of revenue agreed is $220m. At the beginning of the contract on 1 January 20X6 the initial estimate of the contract costs is $200m. At the end of 20X6 the estimate of the total costs has risen to $202m.

During 20X7 the customer agrees to a variation which increases expected revenue from the contract by $5m and causes additional costs of $3m. At the end of 20X7 there are materials stored on site for use during the following period which cost $2.5m.

Centrepoint Co have decided to determine the stage of completion of the contract by calculating the proportion that contract costs incurred for work to date bear to the latest estimated total contract costs. The contract costs incurred at the end of each year were 20X6: $52.52m, 20X7: $154.2m (including materials in store), 20X8: $205m.

*Required*

Calculate the stage of completion for each year of the contract and show how revenues, costs and profits will be recognised in each year.

## Solution

We can summarise the financial data for each year end during the construction period as follows.

|  | 20X6 | 20X7 | 20X8 |
|---|---|---|---|
|  | $'000 | $'000 | $'000 |
| Initial amount of revenue agreed in the contract | 220,000 | 220,000 | 220,000 |
| Variation | – | 5,000 | 5,000 |
| Total contract revenue | 220,000 | 225,000 | 225,000 |
| Contract costs incurred to date | 52,520 | 154,200 | 205,000 |
| Contract costs to complete | 149,480 | 50,800 | – |
| Total estimated contract costs | 202,000 | 205,000 | 205,000 |
| Estimated profit | 18,000 | 20,000 | 20,000 |
| Stage of completion | 26% | 74% | 100% |

The stage of completion has been calculated using the formula:

$$\frac{\text{Contract costs incurred to date}}{\text{Total estimated contract costs}}$$

The stage of completion in 20X7 is calculated by deducting the $2.5m of materials held for the following period from the costs incurred up to that year end, ie $154.2m – $2.5m = $151.7m. $151.7m/$205m = 74%.

Revenue, expenses and profit will be recognised in profit or loss as follows.

| | To date $'000 | Recognised in prior years $'000 | Recognised in current year $'000 |
|---|---|---|---|
| **20X6** Revenue ($220m × 26%) | 57,200 | | |
| Costs ($202m × 26%) | 52,520 | | |
| | 4,680 | | |
| **20X7** Revenue ($225m × 74%) | 166,500 | 57,200 | 109,300 |
| Costs ($205m × 74%) | 151,700 | 52,520 | 99,180 |
| | 14,800 | 4,680 | 10,120 |
| **20X8** Revenue ($225m × 100%) | 225,000 | 166,500 | 58,500 |
| Costs ($205m × 100%) | 205,000 | 151,700 | 53,300 |
| | 20,000 | 14,800 | 5,200 |

You can see from the above example that, when the stage of completion is determined using the contract costs incurred to date, only contract costs reflecting the work to date should be included in costs incurred to date.

- Exclude costs relating to **future activity**, eg cost of materials delivered but not yet used
- Exclude payments made to subcontractors **in advance** of work performed

## 2.11 Outcome of the contract cannot be reliably estimated

When the contract's outcome cannot be reliably estimated the following treatment should be followed.

- Only recognise revenue to the extent of contract costs incurred which are expected to be **recoverable**
- Recognise contract costs as an **expense** in the period they are incurred

This **no profit/no loss approach** reflects the situation near the beginning of a contract, ie the outcome cannot be reliably estimated, but it is likely that costs will be recovered.

Contract costs which **cannot be recovered** should be recognised as an expense straight away. IAS 11 lists the following situations where this might occur.

- The contract is **not fully enforceable**, ie its validity is seriously questioned
- The completion of the contract is subject to the outcome of **pending litigation or legislation**
- The contract relates to properties which will probably be **expropriated or condemned**
- The customer is **unable to meet its obligations** under the contract
- The contractor **cannot complete** the contract or in any other way meet its obligations under the contract

Where these **uncertainties cease to exist,** contract revenue and costs should be recognised as normal, ie by reference to the stage of completion.

## 2.12 Recognition of expected losses

Any loss on a contract should be **recognised as soon as it is foreseen**. The loss will be the amount by which total expected contract revenue is exceeded by total expected contract costs. The loss amount is not affected by whether work has started on the contract, the stage of completion of the work or profits on other contracts (unless they are related contracts treated as a single contract).

## 2.13 Changes in estimates

The effect of any change in the estimate of contract revenue or costs or the outcome of a contract should be accounted for as a **change in accounting estimate** under IAS 8 *Accounting policies, changes in accounting estimates and errors.*

## 2.14 Example: changes in estimates

The example below shows the effect of a change in estimate of costs on the figures that appear in the statement of profit or loss and other comprehensive income and statement of financial position.

Battersby Co enters into a three-year contract.

Estimated revenue = $20,000
Estimated total cost = $16,000.

However, during Year 2, management revises its estimate of total costs incurred and thus the outcome of the contract. As a result, during Year 2, a loss is recognised on the contract for the year, even though the contract will still be profitable overall.

|  | Year 1 $ | Year 2 $ | Year 3 $ |
|---|---|---|---|
| Estimated revenue | 20,000 | 20,000 | 20,000 |
| Estimated total cost | 16,000 | 18,000 | 18,000 |
| Estimated total profit | 4,000 | 2,000 | 2,000 |
| Cost incurred to date | $8,000 | $13,500 | $18,000 |
| Percentage of completion | 50% | 75% | 100% |
| Recognised profit/(loss) for year | $2,000 | ($500) | $500 |
| Cumulative recognised profit | $2,000 | $1,500 | $2,000 |

Progress billings of $8,000, $8,000 and $4,000 are made on the last day of each year and are received in the first month of the following year. The asset at the end of each year is:

|  | Year 1 $ | Year 2 $ | Year 3 $ |
|---|---|---|---|
| Costs incurred | 8,000 | 13,500 | 18,000 |
| Recognised profits | 2,000 | 2,000 | 2,500 |
| (Recognised losses) |  | (500) | (500) |
| (Progress billings) | (8,000) | (16,000) | (20,000) |
| Amount recognised as an asset/(liability) | 2,000 | (1,000) | 0 |

In addition, at each year end, the entity recognises a trade receivable for the amount outstanding at the end of the year of $8,000, $8,000 and $4,000.

## 2.15 Section summary

In valuing long-term contracts and the other disclosures required under IAS 11, an organised approach is essential. The following suggested method breaks the process down into five logical steps.

**Step 1** **Compare the contract value** and the **total costs** expected to be incurred on the contract. If a loss is foreseen (that is, if the costs to date plus estimated costs to completion exceed the contract value) then it must be charged against profits. If a loss has already been charged in previous years, then only the difference between the loss as previously and currently estimated need be charged.

**Step 2** Using the percentage completed to date (or other formula given in the question), calculate sales revenue **attributable** to the contract for the period (for example percentage complete × total contract value, less of course, revenue taken in previous periods).

**Step 3** **Calculate the cost of sales** on the contract for the period.

|  | $ |
|---|---|
| Total contract costs × percentage complete (or follow instructions in question) | X |
| Less any costs charged in previous periods | (X) |
|  | X |
| Add foreseeable losses in full (not previously charged) | X |
| Cost of sales on contract for the period | X |

**Step 4**  **Deduct the cost of sales** for the period as calculated above (including any foreseeable loss) from the sales revenue calculated at step 2 to give profit (loss) recognised for the period.

**Step 5**  **Calculate amounts due to/from** customers as per the working on the previous page.

|  | $ |
|---|---|
| Contract costs incurred to date | X |
| Recognised profits/(losses) to date | X |
|  | X |
| Progress billings to date | (X) |
| Amounts due from/(to) customers | X/(X) |

Note: This represents unbilled revenue. Unpaid billed revenue will be included in trade receivables.

## 2.16 Summary of accounting treatment

The following summarises the accounting treatment for long-term contracts – **make sure that you understand it.**

### 2.16.1 Statement of profit or loss

(a)   **Revenue and costs**

   (i)   Sales revenue and associated costs should be recorded in profit or loss as the contract activity progresses.

   (ii)   Include an appropriate proportion of total contract value as sales revenue in the statement of profit or loss.

   (iii)   The costs incurred in reaching that stage of completion are matched with this sales revenue, resulting in the reporting of results which can be attributed to the proportion of work completed.

   (iv)   Sales revenue is the value of work carried out to date.

(b)   **Profit recognised in the contract**

   (i)   It must reflect the proportion of work carried out.

   (ii)   It should take into account any known inequalities in profitability in the various stages of a contract.

### 2.16.2 Statement of financial position

(a)   **Current asset/liability**

|  | $ |
|---|---|
| Costs incurred to date | X |
| Recognised profits/(losses) to date | (X) |
|  | X |
| Progress billings to date | (X) |
| Amount due from / (to)customers | X (X) |

(b)   **Receivables**

|  | $ |
|---|---|
| Unpaid progress billings | X |

(c)   **Payables**. Where (a) gives a net 'amount due to customers' this amount should be included in payables under 'payments on account'.

## Question

The main business of Santolina Co is construction contracts. At the end of September 20X3 there is an uncompleted contract on the books, details of which are as follows.

CONTRACT B

| | |
|---|---|
| Date commenced | 1.4.X1 |
| Expected completion date | 23.12.X3 |
| | $ |
| Final contract price | 290,000 |
| Costs to 30.9.X3 | 210,450 |
| Value of work certified to 30.9.X3 | 230,000 |
| Progress billings to 30.9.X3 | 210,000 |
| Cash received to 30.9.X3 | 194,000 |
| Estimated costs to completion at 30.9.X3 | 20,600 |

Santolina calculates % completion based on work certified/contract price.

*Required*

Prepare calculations showing the amount to be included in the statement of profit or loss and statement of financial position at 30 September 20X3 in respect of the above contract.

## Answer

*Contract B* is a construction contract and will be included in the statement of financial position at cost plus recognised profit less progress billings.

The estimated final profit is:

| | $ |
|---|---|
| Final contract price | 290,000 |
| Less: costs to date | (210,450) |
|     estimated future costs | (20,600) |
| Estimated final profit | 58,950 |

The recognised profit is found as follows.

$$\text{Estimated final profit} \times \frac{\text{Work certified}}{\text{Total contract price}}$$

$$\$58,950 \times \frac{230,000}{290,000} = \$58,950 \times 79.31\%$$

Profit recognised = $46,753

### Statement of profit or loss

| | $ |
|---|---|
| Revenue (290,000 × 79.31%) | 229,999 |
| Cost of sales ((210,450 + 20,600) × 79.31%) | (183,246) |
| Gross profit | 46,753 |

### Statement of financial position

*Gross amount due from customers for contract work*

| | $ |
|---|---|
| Costs to date | 210,450 |
| Attributable profit | 46,753 |
| | 257,203 |
| Progress billings | (210,000) |
| Amount due from customers | 47,203 |
| | |
| Trade receivables (210 – 194) | 16,000 |

**Exam focus point**

A question is more likely to be set on construction contracts than on inventory, simply because inventory is tested at the lower level.

## Question
IAS 11 calculations

Haggrun Co has two contracts in progress, the details of which are as follows.

|  | Happy (profitable) $'000 | Grumpy (loss-making) $'000 |
|---|---|---|
| Total contract price | 300 | 300 |
| Costs incurred to date | 90 | 150 |
| Estimated costs to completion | 135 | 225 |
| Progress payments invoiced and received | 116 | 116 |

*Required*

Show extracts from the statement of profit or loss and other comprehensive income and the statement of financial position for each contract, assuming they are both:

(a) 40% complete; and
(b) 36% complete.

## Answer

*Happy contract*

(a) *40% complete*

|  | $'000 |
|---|---|
| *Statement of profit or loss* | |
| Revenue (300 × 40%) | 120 |
| Cost of sales ((90+ 135) × 40%) | (90) |
| Profit to date (W) | 30 |

*Working*

*Profit to date*

|  | $'000 |
|---|---|
| Total contract price | 300 |
| Costs to date | (90) |
| Cost to completion | (135) |
| Total expected profit | 75 |
| Profit to date (75 × 40%) | 30 |

*Statement of financial position*

|  | $'000 |
|---|---|
| Costs to date | 90 |
| Profit recognised to date | 30 |
| Progress billings | (116) |
| Amount due from customers | 4 |

(b) *36% complete*

|  | $'000 |
|---|---|
| *Statement of profit or loss* | |
| Revenue (300 × 36%) | 108 |
| Cost of sales (((90 + 135) × 36%)) | (81) |
| Profit to date (75 × 36%) | 27 |

|  | $'000 |
|---|---|
| *Statement of financial position* | |
| Costs to date | 90 |
| Profit recognised to date | 27 |
| Progress billings | (116) |
| Amount due from customers | 1 |

## Grumpy contract

(a)    *40% complete*

|  | $'000 |
|---|---|
| *Statement of profit or loss* | |
| Revenue (300 × 40%) | 120 |
| Cost of sales* | (195) |
| Foreseeable loss (W) | (75) |

*Working*

|  | $'000 |
|---|---|
| Total contract revenue | 300 |
| Costs to date | (150) |
| Costs to complete | (225) |
| Foreseeable loss | (75) |
| *Statement of financial position* | |
| Costs to date | 150 |
| Foreseeable loss | (75) |
| Progress billings | (116) |
| Amounts due to customers | (41) |

|  | |
|---|---|
| * Costs to date (150 + 225) × 40% | 150 |
| Forseeable loss (75) × 60%** | 45 |
|  | 195 |

** The other 40% is taken into account in costs to date. We make this adjustment to bring in the **whole** of the foreseeable loss.

(b)    *36% complete*

|  | $'000 |
|---|---|
| *Statement of profit or loss* | |
| Revenue (300 × 36%) | 108 |
| Cost of sales* | (183) |
| Foreseeable loss | (75) |
| *Statement of financial position* | |
| Costs to date | 150 |
| Foreseeable loss | (75) |
| Progress billings | (116) |
| Amount due to customers | (41) |

|  | |
|---|---|
| * Costs to date (150 + 225) × 36% | 135 |
| Forseeable loss (75) × 64%** | 48 |
|  | 183 |

**Exam focus point**

See *Student Accountant* 18 November 2008 for an article by Bobbie Retallack entitled 'Construction Contracts'.

# Chapter roundup

- The use of **LIFO** is **prohibited** under the revised IAS 2.
- Sales revenue on a construction contract is based upon stage of completion

# Quick quiz

1    Net realisable value = Selling price **less** ........................ **less** .......................
2    Which inventory costing method is allowed under IAS 2?

    (a)    FIFO
    (b)    LIFO

3    Any expected loss on a construction contract must be recognised, in full, in the year it was identified.

    True    ☐

    False    ☐

4    List the five steps to be taken when valuing construction contracts.
5    Which items in the statement of profit or loss and other comprehensive income and statement of financial position are potentially affected by construction contracts?

# Answers to quick quiz

1    Net realisable value = selling price **less** costs to completion **less** costs necessary to make the sale.
2    (a) FIFO. LIFO is not allowed.
3    True
4    See paragraph 2.15
5    Statement of profit or loss and other comprehensive income: revenue and cost of sales.
    Statement of financial position: inventories, receivables, payables

Now try the question below from the Exam Question Bank

| Number | Level | Marks | Time |
|---|---|---|---|
| 14 | Examination | 15 | 27 mins |
| 15 | Examination | 15 | 27 mins |

# Provisions, contingent liabilities and contingent assets

# 13

| Topic list | Syllabus reference |
|---|---|
| 1 Provisions | C7 |
| 2 Provisions for restructuring | C7 |
| 3 Contingent liabilities and contingent assets | C7 |

## Introduction

You will have met this standard in your earlier studies. However, you will be asked in more detail about IAS 37 for Paper 7.

# Study guide

| | | Intellectual level |
|---|---|---|
| **C7** | **Provisions, contingent liabilities and contingent assets** | |
| (a) | explain why an accounting standard on provisions is necessary | 2 |
| (b) | distinguish between legal and constructive obligations. | 2 |
| (c) | state when provisions may and may not be made and demonstrate how they should be accounted for. | 2 |
| (d) | explain how provisions should be measured. | 1 |
| (e) | define contingent assets and liabilities and describe their accounting treatment. | 2 |
| (f) | identify and account for: | 2 |
| | (i)   warranties/guarantees | |
| | (ii)  onerous contracts | |
| | (iii) environmental and similar provisions | |
| | (iv)  provisions for future repairs or refurbishments | |

# 1 Provisions

**FAST FORWARD**

> Under IAS 37 a provision should be recognised when:
>
> - An entity has a **present obligation**, legal or constructive
> - It is probable that a **transfer of resources embodying economic benefits** will be required to settle it
> - A reliable estimate can be made of its amount.

## 1.1 Objective

IAS 37 *Provisions, contingent liabilities and contingent assets* aims to ensure that appropriate **recognition criteria** and **measurement bases** are applied to provisions, contingent liabilities and contingent assets and that **sufficient information** is disclosed in the **notes** to the financial statements to enable users to understand their nature, timing and amount.

## 1.2 Provisions

Before IAS 37, there was no accounting standard dealing with provisions. Companies wanting to show their results in the most favourable light used to make large 'one off' provisions in years where a high level of underlying profits was generated. These provisions, often known as 'big bath' provisions, were then available to shield expenditure in future years when perhaps the underlying profits were not as good.

In other words, provisions were used for profit smoothing. Profit smoothing is misleading.

**Important**

> The key aim of IAS 37 is to ensure that **provisions are made only** where there are valid grounds for them.

IAS 37 views a provision as a liability.

**Key terms**

> A **provision** is a **liability** of uncertain timing or amount.
>
> A **liability** is a present obligation of the entity arising from past events , the settlement of which is expected to result in an outflow from the entity of resources embodying economic benefits.     *(IAS 37)*

The IAS distinguishes provisions from other liabilities such as trade creditors and accruals. This is on the basis that for a provision there is **uncertainty** about the timing or amount of the future expenditure. Whilst uncertainty is clearly present in the case of certain accruals the uncertainty is generally much less than for provisions.

## 1.3 Recognition

IAS 37 states that a provision should be **recognised** as a liability in the financial statements when:

- An entity has a **present obligation** (legal or constructive) as a result of a past event
- It is probable that an **outflow of resources embodying economic benefits** will be required to settle the obligation
- A **reliable estimate** can be made of the amount of the obligation

## 1.4 Meaning of obligation

It is fairly clear what a legal obligation is. However, you may not know what a **constructive obligation** is.

**Key term**

IAS 37 defines a **constructive obligation** as

'An obligation that derives from an entity's actions where:

- by an established pattern of past practice, published policies or a sufficiently specific current statement the entity has indicated to other parties that it will accept certain responsibilities; and
- as a result, the entity has created a valid expectation on the part of those other parties that it will discharge those responsibilities.'

For instance, an oil company may have an established practice of always making good any environmental damage caused by drilling, even though it is not legally obliged to do so. In this way, it has created a valid expectation that it will do this and it will have to recognise the constructive obligation and make a corresponding provision each time it drills a new well.

### 1.4.1 Probable transfer of resources

For the purpose of the IAS, a transfer of resources embodying economic benefits is regarded as **'probable'** if the event is **more likely than not** to occur. This appears to indicate a probability of more than 50%. However, the standard makes it clear that where there is a number of similar obligations the probability should be based on considering the population as a whole, rather than one single item.

### 1.4.2 Example: transfer of resources

If a company has entered into a warranty obligation then the probability of transfer of resources embodying economic benefits may well be extremely small in respect of one specific item. However, when considering the population as a whole the probability of some transfer of resources is quite likely to be much higher. If there is a **greater than 50% probability** of some transfer of economic benefits then a **provision** should be made for the **expected amount**.

### 1.4.3 Measurement of provisions

**Important**

The amount recognised as a provision should be the best estimate of the expenditure required to settle the present obligation at the end of the reporting period.

The estimates will be determined by the **judgement** of the entity's management supplemented by the experience of similar transactions.

Allowance is made for **uncertainty**. Where the provision being measured involves a large population of items, the obligation is estimated by weighting all possible outcomes by their associated probabilities, ie **expected value**.

Where the provision involves a single item, such as the outcome of a legal case, provision is made **in full** for the most likely outcome.

## Question
Warranty

Parker Co sells goods with a warranty under which customers are covered for the cost of repairs of any manufacturing defect that becomes apparent within the first six months of purchase. The company's past experience and future expectations indicate the following pattern of likely repairs.

| % of goods sold | Defects | Cost of repairs if all items suffered from these defects |
|---|---|---|
| | | $m |
| 75 | None | – |
| 20 | Minor | 1.0 |
| 5 | Major | 4.0 |

What is the provision required?

## Answer

The cost is found using 'expected values' (75% × $nil) + (20% × $1.0m) + (5% × $4.0m) = $400,000.

Where the effect of the **time value of money** is material, the amount of a provision should be the **present value** of the expenditure required to settle the obligation. An appropriate **discount** rate should be used.

The discount rate should be a pre-tax rate that reflects current market assessments of the time value of money. The discount rate(s) should not reflect risks for which future cash flow estimates have been adjusted.

**Note:** You will be given any relevant discount rates in the exam.

# Example

A company knows that when it ceases a certain operation in 5 years time it will have to pay environmental cleanup costs of $5m.

The provision to be made now will be the present value of $5m in 5 years time.

The relevant discount rate in this case is 10%.

Therefore a provision will be made for:

| | $ |
|---|---|
| $5m × 0.62092* | 3,104,600 |

\* The discount rate for 5 years at 10%.

The following year the provision will be:

| | |
|---|---|
| $5m × 0.68301** | 3,415,050 |
| | 310,540 |

\*\* The discount rate for 4 years at 10%

The increase in the second year of $310,450 will be charged to profit or loss. It is referred to as the **unwinding** of the discount. This is accounted for as a finance cost. The original provision of $3,104,600 will be added to the cost of the assets involved in the operation and depreciated over 5 years.

## 1.4.4 Future events

**Future events** which are reasonably expected to occur (eg new legislation, changes in technology) may affect the amount required to settle the entity's obligation and should be taken into account.

### 1.4.5 Expected disposal of assets

Gains from the expected disposal of assets should not be taken into account in measuring a provision.

### 1.4.6 Reimbursements

Some or all of the expenditure needed to settle a provision may be expected to be recovered from a third party. If so, the reimbursement should be recognised only when it is virtually certain that reimbursement will be received if the entity settles the obligation.

- The reimbursement should be treated as a separate asset, and the amount recognised should not be greater than the provision itself.
- The provision and the amount recognised for reimbursement may be netted off in profit or loss.

### 1.4.7 Changes in provisions

Provisions should be reviewed at the end of each reporting period and adjusted to reflect the current best estimate. If it is no longer probable that a transfer of resources will be required to settle the obligation, the provision should be reversed.

### 1.4.8 Use of provisions

**A provision should be used only for expenditures for which the provision was originally recognised.** Setting expenditures against a provision that was originally recognised for another purpose would conceal the impact of two different events.

### 1.4.9 Future operating losses

**Provisions should not be recognised for future operating losses.** They do not meet the definition of a liability and the general recognition criteria set out in the standard.

### 1.4.10 Onerous contracts

If an entity has a contract that is onerous, the present obligation under the contract **should be recognised and measured** as a provision. An example might be vacant leasehold property. The entity holding the lease is under an obligation to maintain the property but is receiving no income or benefit from it.

Key term

> An **onerous contract** is a contract entered into with another party under which the unavoidable costs of fulfilling the terms of the contract exceed any revenues expected to be received from the goods or services supplied or purchased directly or indirectly under the contract and where the entity would have to compensate the other party if it did not fulfil the terms of the contract.

## 1.5 Examples of possible provisions

It is easier to see what IAS 37 is driving at if you look at examples of those items which are possible provisions under this standard. Some of these we have already touched on.

(a)  **Warranties.** These are argued to be genuine provisions as on past experience it is probable, ie more likely than not, that some claims will emerge. The provision must be estimated, however, on the basis of the class as a whole and not on individual claims. There is a clear legal obligation in this case.

(b)  **Major repairs.** In the past it has been quite popular for companies to provide for expenditure on a major overhaul to be accrued gradually over the intervening years between overhauls. Under IAS 37 this is no longer possible as IAS 37 would argue that this is a mere intention to carry out repairs, not an obligation. The entity can always sell the asset in the meantime. The only solution is to treat major assets such as aircraft, ships, furnaces etc as a series of smaller assets where each part is depreciated over shorter lives. Thus any major overhaul may be argued to be replacement and therefore capital rather than revenue expenditure.

(c) **Self insurance**. A number of companies have created a provision for self insurance based on the expected cost of making good fire damage etc instead of paying premiums to an insurance company. Under IAS 37 this provision is no longer justifiable as the entity has no obligation until a fire or accident occurs. No obligation exists until that time.

(d) **Environmental contamination**. If the company has an environmental policy such that other parties would expect the company to clean up any contamination or if the company has broken current environmental legislation then a provision for environmental damage must be made.

(e) **Decommissioning or abandonment costs**. When an oil company initially purchases an oilfield it is put under a legal obligation to decommission the site at the end of its life. Prior to IAS 37 most oil companies set up the provision gradually over the life of the field so that no one year would be unduly burdened with the cost.

IAS 37, however, insists that a legal obligation exists on the initial expenditure on the field and therefore a liability exists immediately. This would appear to result in a large charge to profit and loss in the first year of operation of the field. However, the IAS takes the view that the cost of purchasing the field in the first place is not only the cost of the field itself but also the costs of putting it right again. Thus all the costs of decommissioning may be capitalised.

(f) **Restructuring**. This is considered in detail below.

**Exam focus point**

These examples are the sort of situation you may get in the exam. The December 2008 exam had a question dealing with an oilfield and related clean-up costs, which had to be discounted.

# 2 Provisions for restructuring

**FAST FORWARD**

One of the main purposes of IAS 37 was to target abuses of provisions for restructuring. Accordingly, IAS 37 lays down **strict criteria** to determine when such a provision can be made.

**Key term**

IAS 37 defines a **restructuring** as:

A programme that is planned and is controlled by management and materially changes one of two things.

- The scope of a business undertaken by an entity
- The manner in which that business is conducted

The IAS gives the following **examples** of events that may fall under the definition of restructuring.

- The **sale or termination** of a line of business
- The **closure of business locations** in a country or region or the **relocation** of business activities from one country region to another
- **Changes in management structure**, for example, the elimination of a layer of management
- **Fundamental reorganisations** that have a material effect on the **nature and focus** of the entity's operations

The question is whether or not an entity has an obligation – legal or constructive – at the end of the reporting period. For this to be the case:

- An entity must have a **detailed formal plan** for the restructuring
- It must have **raised a valid expectation** in those affected that it will carry out the restructuring by starting to implement that plan or announcing its main features to those affected by it

**Important**

**A mere management decision is not normally sufficient.** Management decisions may sometimes trigger recognition, but only if earlier events such as negotiations with employee representatives and other interested parties have been concluded subject only to management approval.

Where the restructuring involves the **sale of an operation** then IAS 37 states that no obligation arises until the entity has entered into a **binding sale agreement**. This is because until this has occurred the entity will be able to change its mind and withdraw from the sale even if its intentions have been announced publicly.

## 2.1 Costs to be included within a restructuring provision

The IAS states that a restructuring provision should include only the **direct expenditures** arising from the restructuring, which are those that are both:

- **Necessarily entailed** by the restructuring; and
- Not associated with the **ongoing activities** of the entity.

The following costs should specifically **not** be included within a restructuring provision.

- **Retraining** or relocating continuing staff
- **Marketing**
- **Investment in new systems** and distribution networks

## 2.2 Disclosure

Disclosures for provisions fall into two parts.

- Disclosure of details of the **change in carrying value** of a provision from the beginning to the end of the year
- Disclosure of the **background** to the making of the provision and the uncertainties affecting its outcome

| Question | Provision |
|---|---|

In which of the following circumstances might a provision be recognised?

(a)    On 13 December 20X9 the board of an entity decided to close down a division. The accounting date of the company is 31 December. Before 31 December 20X9 the decision was not communicated to any of those affected and no other steps were taken to implement the decision.

(b)    The board agreed a detailed closure plan on 20 December 20X9 and details were given to customers and employees.

(c)    A company is obliged to incur clean up costs for environmental damage (that has already been caused).

(d)    A company intends to carry out future expenditure to operate in a particular way in the future.

## Answer

(a)    No provision would be recognised as the decision has not been communicated.

(b)    A provision would be made in the 20X9 financial statements.

(c)    A provision for such costs is appropriate.

(d)    No present obligation exists and under IAS 37 no provision would be appropriate. This is because the entity could avoid the future expenditure by its future actions, maybe by changing its method of operation.

# 3 Contingent liabilities and contingent assets

FAST FORWARD

> An entity should not **recognise** a contingent asset or liability, but they should be **disclosed**.

Now you understand provisions it will be easier to understand contingent assets and liabilities.

**Key term**

> IAS 37 defines a **contingent liability** as:
>
> - A possible obligation that arises from past events and whose existence will be confirmed only by the occurrence or non-occurrence of one or more uncertain future events not wholly within the control of the entity; or
>
> - A present obligation that arises from past events but is not recognised because:
>   - It is not probable that an outflow of resources embodying economic benefits will be required to settle the obligation; or
>   - The amount of the obligation cannot be measured with sufficient reliability.

As a rule of thumb, probable means more than 50% likely. If an obligation is probable, it is not a contingent liability – instead, a provision is needed.

## 3.1 Treatment of contingent liabilities

Contingent liabilities **should not be recognised in financial statements** but they **should be disclosed**. The required disclosures are:

- A brief description of the nature of the contingent liability
- An estimate of its financial effect
- An indication of the uncertainties that exist
- The possibility of any reimbursement

## 3.2 Contingent assets

**Key term**

> IAS 37 defines a **contingent asset** as:
>
> A possible asset that arises from past events and whose existence will be confirmed by the occurrence or non-occurrence of one or more uncertain future events not wholly within control of the entity.

**A contingent asset must not be recognised**. Only when the realisation of the related economic benefits is **virtually certain** should recognition take place. At that point, **the asset is no longer a contingent asset!**

## 3.3 Example

A company is engaged in a legal dispute. The outcome is not yet known. A number of possibilities arise:

- It expects to have to pay about $100,000. **A provision is recognised**.
- Possible damages are $100,000 but it is not expected to have to pay them. **A contingent liability is disclosed**.
- The company expects to have to pay damages but is unable to estimate the amount. **A contingent liability is disclosed**.
- The company expects to receive damages of $100,000 and this is virtually certain. **An asset is recognised**.
- The company expects to probably receive damages of $100,000. **A contingent asset is disclosed**.
- The company thinks it may receive damages, but it is not probable. **No disclosure**.

## 3.4 Disclosure

### 3.4.1 Disclosure: contingent liabilities

A **brief description** must be provided of all material contingent liabilities unless they are likely to be remote. In addition, provide

- An estimate of their **financial effect**
- Details of **any uncertainties**
- The possibility of any reimbursement

### 3.4.2 Disclosure: contingent assets

Contingent assets must only be disclosed in the notes if they are **probable**. In that case a brief description of the contingent asset should be provided along with an estimate of its likely financial effect.

## 3.5 'Let out'

IAS 37 permits reporting entities to avoid disclosure requirements relating to provisions, contingent liabilities and contingent assets if they would be expected to **seriously prejudice** the position of the entity in dispute with other parties. However, this should only be employed in **extremely rare** cases. Details of the general nature of the provision/contingencies must still be provided, together with an explanation of why it has not been disclosed.

## 3.6 Flow chart

You must practise the questions below to get the hang of IAS 37. But first, study the flow chart, taken from IAS 37, which is a good summary of its requirements concerning provisions and contingent liabilities.

**Exam focus point**

> If you learn this flow chart you should be able to deal with most questions you are likely to meet in an exam.

Question

**Accounting treatment**

During 20X0 Smack Co gives a guarantee of certain borrowings of Pony Co, whose financial condition at that time is sound. During 20X1, the financial condition of Pony Co deteriorates and at 30 June 20X1 Pony Co files for protection from its creditors.

What accounting treatment is required:

(a)     At 31 December 20X0?
(b)     At 31 December 20X1?

Answer

(a)     *At 31 December 20X0*

There is a present obligation as a result of a past obligating event. The obligating event is the giving of the guarantee, which gives rise to a legal obligation. However, at 31 December 20X0 no transfer of resources is probable in settlement of the obligation.

No provision is recognised. The guarantee is disclosed as a contingent liability unless the probability of any transfer is regarded as remote.

(b)     *At 31 December 20X1*

As above, there is a present obligation as a result of a past obligating event, namely the giving of the guarantee.

At 31 December 20X1 it is probable that a transfer of resources will be required to settle the obligation. A provision is therefore recognised for the best estimate of the obligation.

Question

**Recognition of provision**

Warren Co gives warranties at the time of sale to purchasers of its products. Under the terms of the warranty the manufacturer undertakes to make good, by repair or replacement, manufacturing defects that become apparent within a period of three years from the date of the sale. Should a provision be recognised?

Answer

Warren Co **cannot avoid** the cost of repairing or replacing all items of product that manifest manufacturing defects in respect of which warranties are given before the end of the reporting period, and a provision for the cost of this should therefore be made.

Warren Co is obliged to repair or replace items that fail within the entire warranty period. Therefore, in respect of **this year's sales**, the obligation provided for at the end of the reporting period should be the cost of making good items for which defects have been notified but not yet processed, **plus** an estimate of costs in respect of the other items sold for which there is sufficient evidence that manufacturing defects **will** manifest themselves during their remaining periods of warranty cover.

Question

**Accounting treatment**

After a wedding in 20X0 ten people died, possibly as a result of food poisoning from products sold by Callow Co. Legal proceedings are started seeking damages from Callow but it disputes liability. Up to the date of approval of the financial statements for the year to 31 December 20X0, Callow's lawyers advise that it is probable that it will not be found liable. However, when Callow prepares the financial statements for the year to 31 December 20X1 its lawyers advise that, owing to developments in the case, it is probable that it will be found liable.

What is the required accounting treatment:

(a)    At 31 December 20X0?
(b)    At 31 December 20X1?

## Answer

(a)    *At 31 December 20X0*

On the basis of the evidence available when the financial statements were approved, there is no obligation as a result of past events. No provision is recognised. The matter is disclosed as a contingent liability unless the probability of any transfer is regarded as remote.

(b)    *At 31 December 20X1*

On the basis of the evidence available, there is a present obligation. A transfer of resources in settlement is probable.

A provision is recognised for the best estimate of the amount needed to settle the present obligation.

## 3.7 Summary

- The objective of IAS 37 is to ensure that appropriate recognition criteria and measurement bases are applied to provisions and contingencies and that sufficient information is disclosed.
- The IAS seeks to ensure that provisions are **only recognised** when a **measurable obligation** exists. It includes detailed rules that can be used to ascertain when an obligation exists and how to measure the obligation.
- The standard attempts to **eliminate** the **'profit smoothing'** which has gone on before it was issued.

# Chapter Roundup

- Under **IAS 37**, a **provision** should be recognised
    - When an entity has a **present obligation**, legal or constructive
    - It is probable that a **transfer of resources embodying economic benefits** will be required to settle it
    - A **reliable estimate** can be made of its amount
- One the main purposes of IAS 37 was to target abuses of provisions for restructuring. Accordingly, IAS 37 lays down **strict criteria** to determine when such a provision can be made.
- An entity **should not recognise a contingent asset or liability**, but they **should be disclosed**.

# Quick Quiz

1    A provision is a ......................... of ................. timing or amount.
2    A programme is undertaken by management which converts the previously wholly owned chain of restaurants they ran into franchises. Is this restructuring?
3    Define contingent asset and contingent liability.
4    How should decommissioning costs on an oilfield be accounted for under IAS 37?
5    'Provisions for major overhauls should be accrued for over the period between overhauls'. Is this correct?

# Answers to Quick Quiz

1     Liability of uncertain timing or amount
2     Yes. The manner in which the business is conducted has changed
3     Refer to paragraphs 3.1 and 3.2
4     They should be capitalised as part of the initial expenditure on the oilfield.
5     No. It is not correct. See paragraph 1.5.

Now try the questions below from the Exam Question Bank

| Number | Level | Marks | Time |
|--------|-------|-------|------|
| 16 | Examination | 25 | 45 mins |

# Financial assets and liabilities

| Topic list | Syllabus reference |
|---|---|
| 1 Financial instruments | C5 |
| 2 Presentation of financial instruments | C5 |
| 3 Disclosure of financial instruments | C5 |
| 4 Recognition of financial instruments | C5 |
| 5 Measurement of financial instruments | C5 |

## Introduction

IAS 32: *Financial instruments: presentation,* IFRS 9: *Financial instruments* and
IFRS 7: *Financial instruments: disclosure* are the relevant standards. IAS 32
and IAS 39 were introduced to regulate the accounting treatment of financial
instruments, especially derivatives which had previously been 'off balance
sheet'.

IFRS 9 was brought in to simplify the treatment of financial instruments. It
has replaced those sections of IAS 39 relevant to the F7 syllabus.

# Study guide

| | | Intellectual level |
|---|---|---|
| **C5** | **Financial assets and financial liabilities** | |
| | (a)    explain the need for an accounting standard on financial instruments. | 1 |
| | (b)    define financial instruments in terms of financial assets and financial liabilities. | 1 |
| | (c)    indicate for the following categories of financial instruments how they should be measured and how any gains and losses from subsequent measurement should be treated in the financial statements: | 1 |
| |     (i)    amortised cost | |
| |     (ii)   fair value (including option to classify equity instruments through other comprehensive income) | |
| | (d)    distinguish between debt and equity capital. | 2 |
| | (e)    apply the requirements of relevant accounting standards to the issue and finance costs of: | 2 |
| |     (i)    equity | |
| |     (ii)   redeemable preference shares and debt instruments with no conversion rights (principle of amortised cost) | |
| |     (iii)  convertible debt | |

# Exam guide

Financial instruments are generally tested as part of a question rather than as a full question.

**Exam focus point**

Financial instruments are a complex area. You should concentrate on the essential points. To date, financial instruments have mainly been examined within a larger scenario based question. However they did come up as a 10-mark question in June 2008

# 1 Financial instruments

**FAST FORWARD**

A financial instrument gives rise to a financial asset of one entity and a financial liability or equity instrument of another.

## 1.1 Introduction

If you read the financial press you will probably be aware of **rapid international expansion** in the use of financial instruments. These vary from straightforward, traditional instruments, eg bonds, through to various forms of so-called 'derivative instruments'.

We can perhaps summarise the reasons why a project on accounting for financial instruments was considered necessary as follows.

(a)    The **significant growth of financial instruments** over recent years has outstripped the development of guidance for their accounting.

(b)    The topic is of **international concern**, other national standard-setters are involved as well as the IASB.

(c)    There have been recent **high-profile disasters** involving derivatives which, while not caused by accounting failures, have raised questions about accounting and disclosure practices.

Four accounting standards deal with financial instruments:

(a) IAS 32 *Financial instruments: presentation*, which deals with:

    (i) The classification of financial instruments between liabilities and equity

    (ii) Presentation of certain compound instruments (instruments combining debt and equity)

(b) IAS 39 *Financial instruments: recognition and measurement*, which deals with:

    (i) Recognition and derecognition

    (ii) The measurement of financial instruments

    (iii) Hedge accounting

The provisions of IAS 39 for hedging and impairment (both not in the F7 syllabus) are still currently in force. The recognition and measurement provisions are now replaced by IFRS 9.

(c) IFRS 7 *Financial instruments: disclosure*

(d) IFRS 9 *Financial instruments*. IFRS 9 deals with recognition, derecognition and measurement of financial assets and liabilities.

## 1.2 Definitions

The most important definitions are common to all four standards.

- **Financial instrument.** Any contract that gives rise to both a financial asset of one entity and a financial liability or equity instrument of another entity.

- **Financial asset.** Any asset that is:

    (a) cash

    (b) an equity instrument of another entity

    (c) a contractual right to receive cash or another financial asset from another entity; or to exchange financial instruments with another entity under conditions that are potentially favourable to the entity

- **Financial liability.** Any liability that is:

    (a) a contractual obligation:

        (i) to deliver cash or another financial asset to another entity, or

        (ii) to exchange financial instruments with another entity under conditions that are potentially unfavourable

- **Equity instrument.** Any contract that evidences a residual interest in the assets of an entity after deducting all of its liabilities.

- **Fair value** is price that would be received to sell an asset or paid to transfer a liability in an orderly transaction between market participants at the measurement date.

These definitions are very important – so learn them.

We should clarify some points arising from these definitions. Firstly, one or two terms above should be themselves defined.

(a) A '**contract**' need not be in writing, but it must comprise an agreement that has 'clear economic consequences' and which the parties to it cannot avoid, usually because the agreement is enforceable in law.

(b) An '**entity**' here could be an individual, partnership, incorporated body or government agency.

The definitions of **financial assets** and **financial liabilities** may seem rather circular, referring as they do to the terms financial asset and financial instrument. The point is that there may be a chain of contractual rights and obligations, but it will lead ultimately to the receipt or payment of cash *or* the acquisition or issue of an equity instrument.

Examples of **financial assets** include:

(a)　Trade receivables
(b)　Options
(c)　Shares (when held as an investment)

Examples of **financial liabilities** include:

(a)　Trade payables
(b)　Debenture loans payable
(c)　Redeemable preference (non-equity) shares

IAS 32 makes it clear that the following items are *not* financial instruments.

(a)　**Physical assets**, eg inventories, property, plant and equipment, leased assets and **intangible assets** (patents, trademarks etc)
(b)　**Prepaid expenses**, deferred revenue and most warranty obligations
(c)　Liabilities or assets that are **not contractual** in nature

## Question

Definitions

Can you give the reasons why physical assets and prepaid expenses do not qualify as financial instruments?

## Answer

Refer to the definitions of financial assets and liabilities given above.

(a)　**Physical assets**: control of these creates an opportunity to generate an inflow of cash or other assets, but it does not give rise to a present right to receive cash or other financial assets.
(b)　**Prepaid expenses, etc**: the future economic benefit is the receipt of goods/services rather than the right to receive cash or other financial assets.

**Contingent rights and obligations** meet the definition of financial assets and financial liabilities respectively, even though many do not qualify for recognition in financial statements. This is because the contractual rights or obligations exist because of a past transaction or event (eg assumption of a guarantee).

# 2 Presentation of financial instruments

FAST FORWARD

The objective of IAS 32 is to help users understand how financial instruments may have affected the entity's financial position, financial performance and cash flows.

## 2.1 Scope

IAS 32 should be applied in the presentation and disclosure of **all types of financial instruments**.

Certain items are **excluded** for example subsidiaries, associates and joint ventures, pensions and insurance contracts.

## 2.2 Liabilities and equity

The main thrust of IAS 32 is that financial instruments should be presented according to their **substance**, **not merely their legal form**. In particular, entities which issue financial instruments should classify them (or their component parts) as **either financial liabilities, or equity**.

The classification of a financial instrument as a liability or as equity depends on the following.

- The **substance of the contractual arrangement** on initial recognition
- The definitions of a **financial liability** and an **equity instrument**

How should a **financial liability be distinguished from an equity instrument**? The critical feature of a **liability** is an **obligation** to transfer economic benefit. Therefore a financial instrument is a financial liability if there is a **contractual obligation** on the issuer either to deliver cash or another financial asset to the holder or to exchange another financial instrument with the holder under potentially unfavourable conditions to the issuer.

Where the above critical feature is *not* met, then the financial instrument is an **equity instrument**. IAS 32 explains that although the holder of an equity instrument may be entitled to a *pro rata* share of any distributions out of equity, the issuer does *not* have a contractual obligation to make such a distribution. For instance, a company is not obliged to pay a dividend to its ordinary shareholders. Although substance and legal form are often **consistent with each other**, this is not always the case. In particular, a financial instrument may have the legal form of equity, but in substance it is in fact a liability. Other instruments may combine features of both equity instruments and financial liabilities.

For example, many entities issue **preference shares** which must be **redeemed** by the issuer for a fixed (or determinable) amount at a fixed (or determinable) future date. Alternatively, the holder may have the right to require the issuer to redeem the shares at or after a certain date for a fixed amount. In such cases, the issuer has an **obligation**. Therefore the instrument is a **financial liability** and should be classified as such.

The distinction between redeemable and non-redeemable preference shares is important. Most preference shares are redeemable and are therefore classified as a **financial liability**. Expect to see this in your exam.

## 2.3 Compound financial instruments

Some financial instruments contain both a liability and an equity element. In such cases, IAS 32 requires the component parts of the instrument to be **classified separately**, according to the substance of the contractual arrangement and the definitions of a financial liability and an equity instrument.

One of the most common types of compound instrument is **convertible debt**. This creates a primary financial liability of the issuer and grants an option to the holder of the instrument to convert it into an equity instrument (usually ordinary shares) of the issuer. This is the economic equivalent of the issue of conventional debt plus a warrant to acquire shares in the future.

Although in theory there are several possible ways of calculating the split, IAS 32 requires the following method:

(a)    Calculate the value for the liability component.
(b)    Deduct this from the instrument as a whole to leave a residual value for the equity component.

The reasoning behind this approach is that an entity's equity is its residual interest in its assets amount after deducting all its liabilities.

The **sum of the carrying amounts** assigned to liability and equity will always be equal to the carrying amount that would be ascribed to the instrument **as a whole**.

## 2.4 Example: valuation of compound instruments

Rathbone Co issues 2,000 convertible bonds at the start of 20X2. The bonds have a three year term, and are issued at par with a face value of $1,000 per bond, giving total proceeds of $2,000,000. Interest is payable annually in arrears at a nominal annual interest rate of 6%. Each bond is convertible at any time up to maturity into 250 ordinary shares.

When the bonds are issued, the prevailing market interest rate for similar debt without conversion options is 9%.

*Required*

What is the value of the equity component in the bond?

# Solution

The liability component is valued first, and the **difference** between the proceeds of the bond issue and the fair value of the liability is assigned to the **equity component**. The present value of the liability component is calculated using a discount rate of 9%, the market interest rate for similar bonds having no conversion rights, as shown.

|  | $ |
|---|---:|
| Present value of the principal: $2,000,000 payable at the end of three years ($2m × 0.772183)* | 1,544,367 |
| Present value of the interest: $120,000 payable annually in arrears for three years ($120,000 × 2.5313)* | 303,755 |
| Total liability component | 1,848,122 |
| Equity component (balancing figure) | 151,878 |
| Proceeds of the bond issue | 2,000,000 |

\* These figures can be obtained from discount and annuity tables or simply calculated arithmetically as follows.

|  |  | $ |
|---|---:|---:|
| **Principal** |  |  |
| $2,000,000 discounted at 9% over 3 years: |  |  |
| 2,000,000 ÷ 1.09 ÷ 1.09 ÷ 1.09 (or 2,000,000 x 1/1.09³) |  | 1,544,367 |
| **Interest** |  |  |
| Year 1 120,000 ÷ 1.09 | 110,091 |  |
| Year 2 110,091 ÷ 1.09 | 101,002 |  |
| Year 3 101,002 ÷ 1.09 | 92,662 |  |
|  |  | 303,755 |
| Value of liability component |  | 1,848,122 |
| Equity component (balancing figure) |  | 151,878 |
| Proceeds of bond issue |  | 2,000,000 |

The split between the liability and equity components remains the same throughout the term of the instrument, even if there are changes in the **likelihood of the option being exercised.** This is because it is not always possible to predict how a holder will behave. The issuer continues to have an obligation to make future payments until conversion, maturity of the instrument or some other relevant transaction takes place.

## Question
Convertible debt

A company issues $20m of 4% convertible loan notes at par on 1 January 2009. The loan notes are redeemable for cash or convertible into equity shares on the basis of 20 shares per $100 of debt at the option of the loan note holder on 31 December 2011. Similar but non-convertible loan notes carry an interest rate of 9%.

The present value of $1 receivable at the end of the year based on discount rates of 4% and 9% can be taken as:

|  |  | 4% | 9% |
|---|---|---:|---:|
|  |  | $ | $ |
| End of year | 1 | 0.96 | 0.92 |
|  | 2 | 0.93 | 0.84 |
|  | 3 | 0.89 | 0.77 |
| Cumulative |  | 2.78 | 2.53 |

Show how these loan notes should be accounted for in the financial statements at 31 December 2009.

| | $ |
|---|---|
| *Statement of profit or loss* | |
| Finance costs (W2) | 1,568 |
| *Statement of financial position* | |
| Equity – option to convert (W1) | 2,576 |
| *Non-current liabilities* | |
| 4% convertible loan notes (W2) | 18,192 |

*Workings*

1   *Equity and liability elements*

| | $'000 |
|---|---|
| 3 years interest (20,000 × 4% × 2.53) | 2,024 |
| Redemption (20,000 × 0.77) | 15,400 |
| Liability element | 17,424 |
| Equity element (β) | 2,576 |
| Proceeds of loan notes | 20,000 |

2   *Loan note balance*

| | $'000 |
|---|---|
| Liability element (W1) | 17,424 |
| Interest for the year at 9% | 1,568 |
| Less interest paid (20,000 × 4%) | (800) |
| Carrying value at 31 December 2009 | 18,192 |

## 2.5 Interest, dividends, losses and gains

As well as looking at presentation in the statement of financial position, IAS 32 considers how financial instruments affect the statement of profit or loss and other comprehensive income (and changes in equity). The treatment varies according to whether interest, dividends, losses or gains relate to a **financial liability** or an **equity instrument**.

(a)   Interest, dividends, losses and gains relating to a financial instrument (or component part) classified as a **financial liability** should be recognised as **income or expense** in profit or loss.

(b)   Distributions to holders of a financial instrument classified as an **equity instrument** (dividends to ordinary shareholders) should be **debited directly to equity** by the issuer. These will appear in the statement of changes in equity.

(c)   **Transaction costs** of an equity transaction should be accounted for as a **deduction from equity**, usually debited to the share premium account.

## 2.6 Section summary

- Issuers of financial instruments must classify them as **liabilities** or **equity**
- The **substance** of the financial instrument is more important than its **legal form**
- The **critical feature of a financial liability** is the contractual obligation to deliver cash or another financial asset
- **Compound instruments** are split into equity and liability parts and presented accordingly
- **Interest, dividends, losses and gains** are treated according to whether they relate to a financial liability or an equity instrument

# 3 Disclosure of financial instruments

FAST FORWARD

IFRS 7 replaces the disclosure requirements which were previously in IAS 32.

## 3.1 IFRS 7

As well as specific monetary disclosures, **narrative commentary** by issuers is encouraged by the Standard. This will enable users to understand management's attitude to risk, whatever the current transactions involving financial instruments are at the period end.

The standard does not prescribe the **format or location** for disclosure of information. A combination of narrative descriptions and specific quantified data should be given, as appropriate.

The **level of detail** required is a matter of judgement. Where a large number of very similar financial instrument transactions are undertaken, these may be grouped together. Conversely, a single significant transaction may require full disclosure.

**Classes of instruments** will be grouped together by management in a manner appropriate to the information to be disclosed.

Exam focus
point

> The examiner has indicated that he will not set questions about the **risks** of financial instruments.

# 4 Recognition of financial instruments

FAST FORWARD

IFRS 9 *Financial instruments* establishes principles for recognising and measuring financial assets and liabilities.

## 4.1 Scope

IFRS 9 applies to **all entities** and to **all types of financial instruments except** those specifically excluded, for example investments in subsidiaries, associates, joint ventures and other joint arrangements.

## 4.2 Initial recognition

A financial asset or financial liability should be recognised in the statement of financial position when the reporting entity becomes a party to the contractual provisions of the instrument.

Notice that this is **different** from the recognition criteria in the *Conceptual Framework* and in most other standards. Items are normally recognised when there is a probable inflow or outflow of resources and the item has a cost or value that can be measured reliably.

## 4.3 Derecognition

Derecognition is the removal of a previously recognised financial instrument from an entity's statement of financial position.

An entity should derecognise a **financial asset** when:

(a)     the **contractual rights** to the cash flows from the financial asset **expire**; or
(b)     it transfers substantially all the risks and rewards of ownership of the financial asset to another party.

An entity should derecognise a **financial liability** when it is **extinguished** – ie, when the obligation specified in the contract is discharged or cancelled or expires.

It is possible for only **part** of a financial asset or liability to be derecognised. This is allowed if the part comprises:

(a)     only specifically identified cash flows; or

(b)     only a fully proportionate (pro rata) share of the total cash flows.

For example, if an entity holds a bond it has the right to two separate sets of cash inflows: those relating to the principal and those relating to the interest. It could sell the right to receive the interest to another party while retaining the right to receive the principal.

On derecognition, the amount to be included in net profit or loss for the period is calculated as follows:

|  | $ | $ |
|---|---|---|
| Carrying amount of asset/liability (or the portion of asset/liability) transferred | | X |
| Less:   Proceeds received/paid | | (X) |
| Difference to profit or loss | | X |

Where only part of a financial asset is derecognised, the carrying amount of the asset should be allocated between the part retained and the part transferred based on their relative fair values on the date of transfer. A gain or loss should be recognised based on the proceeds for the portion transferred.

## 4.4  Classification of financial assets

On **recognition**, IFRS 9 requires that financial assets are **classified as measured** at either:

*   **Amortised cost**, or
*   **Fair value**

### 4.4.1 Comparison table

The following table shows the extent to which IFRS 9 simplifies the IAS 39 definitions.

| Old IAS 39 Category | Measured at | Gains and losses |
|---|---|---|
| Financial asset at fair value through profit or loss | Fair value | Profit or loss |
| Available for sale financial asset | Fair value | Other comprehensive income |
| Financial asset held to maturity | Amortised cost | Profit or loss |
| Loans and receivables | Amortised cost | Profit or loss |

### 4.4.2 Classification basis

The IFRS 9 classification is made on the basis of both:

(a)     The **entity's business model** for managing the financial assets, and

(b)     The **contractual cash flow** characteristics of the financial asset.

A financial asset is classified as measured at amortised cost where:

(a)     The objective of the business model within which the asset is held is to hold assets in order to collect contractual cash flows and

(b)     The contractual terms of the financial asset give rise on specified dates to cash flows that are solely payments of principal and interest on the principal outstanding.

An application of these rules means that **equity investments may not be classified as measured at amortised cost** and must be measured at fair value. This is because contractual cash flows on specified dates are not a characteristic of equity instruments.  They are held at fair value with changes going through profit or loss unless the entity makes an **irrevocable election at initial recognition to recognise all changes through other comprehensive income.**

 A **debt instrument** may be classified as measured at either amortised cost or fair value **depending on whether it meets the criteria above.** Even where the criteria are met at initial recognition, a debt instrument may in certain circumstances be classified as measured at fair value through profit or loss.

### 4.4.3 Business model test in more detail

IFRS 9 introduces a business model test that requires an entity to assess whether its **business objective for a debt instrument is to collect the contractual cash flows of the instrument as opposed to realising any change in its fair value by selling it prior to its contractual maturity**. Note the following key points:

(a)    The assessment of a 'business model' is not made at an individual financial instrument level.

(b)    The assessment is based on how key management personnel actually manage the business, rather than management's intentions for specific financial assets.

(c)    An entity may have more than one business model for managing its financial assets and the classification need not be determined at the reporting entity level. For example, it may have one portfolio of investments that it manages with the objective of collecting contractual cash flows and another portfolio of investments held with the objective of trading to realise changes in fair value. It would be appropriate for entities like these to carry out the assessment for classification purposes at portfolio level, rather than at entity level.

(d)    Although the objective of an entity's business model may be to hold financial assets in order to collect contractual cash flows, the entity need not hold all of those assets until maturity. Thus an entity's business model can be to hold financial assets to collect contractual cash flows even when sales of financial assets occur.

### 4.4.4 Contractual cash flow test in more detail

The requirement in IFRS 9 to assess the contractual cash flow characteristics of a financial asset is based on the concept that **only instruments with contractual cash flows of principal and interest on principal may qualify for amortised cost measurement.** By interest, IFRS 9 means consideration for the time value of money and the credit risk associated with the principal outstanding during a particular period of time.

## Question

Contractual cash flows

Would an investment in a convertible loan qualify to be measured at amortised cost under IFRS 9?

## Answer

No because of the inclusion of the conversion option which is not deemed to represent payments of principal and interest

## 4.5 Re-classification of financial assets

Although on initial recognition financial instruments must be classified in accordance with the requirements of IFRS 9, in some cases they may be subsequently reclassified. IFRS 9 requires that **when an entity changes its business model for managing financial assets, it should reclassify all affected financial assets.** This reclassification applies only to **debt instruments**, as equity instruments must be classified as measured at fair value.

## 4.6 Classification of financial liabilities

On **recognition**, IFRS 9 requires that financial liabilities are **classified as measured** at either:

(a)    **At fair value through profit or loss**, or

(b)    Financial liabilities at **amortised cost**

A financial liability is classified at fair value through profit or loss if:

(a)    It is **held for trading**, or

(b)    Upon initial recognition it is **designated at fair value through profit or loss**.

**Derivatives are always measured at fair value through profit or loss.**

These classification rules are unchanged from those previously contained within IAS 39.

**Exam focus point**

A financial instrument is likely to appear as an item in question 2 of the exam.

# 5 Measurement of financial instruments

Under IFRS 9 all financial assets should be initially measured at cost = fair value plus transaction costs. Financial liabilities should be measured at transaction price ie fair value of the consideration received.

## 5.1 Initial measurement

Financial instruments are initially measured at the **fair value** of the consideration given or received (ie, **cost**) **plus** (or minus in the case of financial liabilities) **transaction costs** that are **directly attributable** to the acquisition or issue of the financial instrument.

The **exception** to this rule is where a financial instrument is designated as **at fair value through profit or loss** (this term is explained below). In this case, **transaction costs** are **not** added to fair value at initial recognition.

The fair value of the consideration is normally the transaction price or market prices. If market prices are not reliable, the fair value may be **estimated** using a valuation technique (for example, by discounting cash flows).

## 5.2 Subsequent measurement of financial assets

After initial recognition, IFRS 9 requires an entity to measure financial assets at either **amortised cost** or **fair value**, based on:

(a)     the entity's business model for managing the financial assets; and
(b)     the contractual cash flow characteristics of the financial asset

A financial asset is measured at **amortised cost** if both of the following conditions are met:

(a)     the asset is held within a business model whose objective is to hold assets in order to collect contractual cash flows
(b)     the contractual terms of the financial asset give rise on specified dates to cash flows that are solely payments of principal and interest on the principal amount outstanding.

After initial recognition, all financial assets other than those held at fair value through profit or loss should be remeasured to either **fair value** or **amortised cost**.

IFRS 9 allows the option to **initially** measure a financial asset at **fair value through profit or loss** where a mismatch would otherwise arise between the asset and a related liability. In this case, the asset will also be **subsequently** measured at fair value through profit or loss.

**Key terms**

A **financial asset or liability at fair value through profit or loss** meets either of the following conditions:

(a)     It is classified as held for trading. A financial instrument is classified as held for trading if it is:

    (i)     acquired or incurred principally for the purpose of selling or repurchasing it in the near term;
    (ii)    part of a portfolio of identified financial instruments that are managed together and for which there is evidence of a recent actual pattern of short-term profit-taking

(b)     Upon initial recognition it is **designated** by the entity as at fair value through profit or loss.

## 5.3 Amortised cost

Assets held at **amortised cost** are measured using the **effective interest method**.

**Amortised cost of a financial asset or financial liability** is the amount at which the financial asset or liability is measured at initial recognition minus principal repayments, plus or minus the cumulative amortisation of any difference between that initial amount and the maturity amount, and minus any write-down for impairment or uncollectability.

The **effective interest method** is a method of calculating the amortised cost of a financial instrument and of allocating the interest income or interest expense over the relevant period.

The **effective interest rate** is the rate that exactly discounts estimated future cash payments or receipts through the expected life of the financial instrument to the net carrying amount.　　　　(*IFRS 9, IAS 39*)

## 5.4 Example: amortised cost

On 1 January 20X1 Abacus Co purchases a debt instrument for its fair value of $1,000. The debt instrument is due to mature on 31 December 20X5. The instrument has a principal amount of $1,250 and the instrument carries fixed interest at 4.72% that is paid annually. The effective rate of interest is 10%.

How should Abacus Co account for the debt instrument over its five year term?

## Solution

Abacus Co will receive interest of $59 (1,250 × 4.72%) each year and $1,250 when the instrument matures.

Abacus must allocate the discount of $250 and the interest receivable over the five year term at a constant rate on the carrying amount of the debt. To do this, it must apply the effective interest rate of 10%. The following table shows the allocation over the years:

| Year | Amortised cost at beginning of year | Profit or loss: Interest income for year (@10%) | Interest received during year (cash inflow) | Amortised cost at end of year |
|---|---|---|---|---|
| | $ | $ | $ | $ |
| 20X1 | 1,000 | 100 | (59) | 1,041 |
| 20X2 | 1,041 | 104 | (59) | 1,086 |
| 20X3 | 1,086 | 109 | (59) | 1,136 |
| 20X4 | 1,136 | 113 | (59) | 1,190 |
| 20X5 | 1,190 | 119 | (1,250+59) | – |

Each year the carrying amount of the financial asset is increased by the interest income for the year and reduced by the interest actually received during the year.

## 5.5 Subsequent measurement of financial liabilities

After initial recognition all financial liabilities should be measured at **amortised cost**, with the exception of financial liabilities at fair value through profit or loss. These should be measured at **fair value**, but where the fair value **is not capable of reliable measurement**, they should be measured at **cost**.

Question　　　　　　　　　　　　　　　　　　　　　　　　　　　　　　Bond

Galaxy Co issues a bond for $503,778 on 1 January 20X2. No interest is payable on the bond, but it will be held to maturity and redeemed on 31 December 20X4 for $600,000. The bond has **not** been designated as at fair value through profit or loss. The effective interest rate is 6%.

*Required*

Calculate the charge to profit or loss in the financial statements of Galaxy Co for the year ended 31 December 20X2 and the balance outstanding at 31 December 20X2.

The bond is a 'deep discount' bond and is a financial liability of Galaxy Co. It is measured at amortised cost. Although there is no interest as such, the difference between the initial cost of the bond and the price at which it will be redeemed is a finance cost. This must be allocated over the term of the bond at a constant rate on the carrying amount. This is done by applying the effective interest rate.

The charge to profit or loss is $30,226 (503,778 × 6%)

The balance outstanding at 31 December 20X2 is $534,004 (503,778 + 30,226)

## 5.6 Gains and losses

Instruments at **fair value through profit or loss**: gains and losses are recognised **in profit or loss**.

**Financial instruments held at fair value**: gains and losses are recognised in **profit or loss** unless the financial asset is an **equity instrument** and the entity made an election upon initial recognition to present gains and losses **directly in equity** through other comprehensive income. Dividends from the investment will be recognised in profit or loss.

Financial instruments carried at **amortised cost**: gains and losses are recognised **in profit or loss** as a result of the amortisation process **and** when the asset is derecognised.

## 5.7 Impairment and uncollectability of financial assets

At the end of each reporting period, an entity should assess whether there is any objective evidence that a financial asset or group of assets is impaired.

Where there is objective evidence of impairment, the entity should **determine the amount** of any impairment loss.

### 5.7.1 Financial assets carried at amortised cost

The impairment loss is the **difference** between the asset's **carrying amount** and its **recoverable amount**. The asset's recoverable amount is the present value of estimated future cash flows, discounted at the financial instrument's **original** effective interest rate.

The amount of the loss should be **recognised in profit or loss**.

### 5.7.2 Financial assets carried at fair value

On financial assets carried at fair value gains and losses are recognised in **profit or loss**. Any impairment loss should be **recognised in net profit or loss for the year** even though the financial asset has not been derecognised.

The impairment loss is the difference between its **acquisition cost** (net of any principal repayment and amortisation) and **current fair value** (for equity instruments) or recoverable amount (for debt instruments), less any impairment loss on that asset previously recognised in profit or loss.

# Chapter Roundup

- A financial instrument gives rise to a financial asset of one entity and a financial liability or equity instrument of another.

- The objective of IAS 32 is to help users understand how financial instruments may have affected the entity's financial position, financial performance and cash flows.

- IFRS 7 replaces the disclosure requirements which were previously in IAS 32.

- IFRS 9 *Financial instruments* establishes principles for recognising and measuring financial assets and liabilities.

- Under IFRS 9 all financial assets should be initially measured at cost = fair value plus transaction costs. Financial liabilities should be measured at transaction price ie fair value of the consideration received.

# Quick Quiz

1   Which issues are dealt with by IAS 32?
2   Define the following.
    (a)   Financial asset
    (b)   Financial liability
    (c)   Equity instrument
3   What is the critical feature used to identify a financial liability?
4   How should compound instruments be classified by the issuer?
5   When should a financial asset be de-recognised?
6   How are financial instruments initially measured?
7   Where should redeemable preference shares appear in the statement of financial position?

# Answers to Quick Quiz

1   Classification between liabilities and equity; presentation
2   See Key Terms, paragraph 1.2
3   The contractual obligation to deliver cash or another financial asset to the holder
4   By calculating the present value of the liability component and then deducting this from the instrument as a whole to leave a residual value for the equity component.
5   Financial assets should be derecognised when the rights to the cash flows from the asset expire or where substantially all the risks and rewards of ownership are transferred to another party.
6   At fair value plus transaction costs.
7   Under non-current liabilities (not equity).

Now try the questions below from the Exam Question Bank

| Number | Level | Marks | Time |
| --- | --- | --- | --- |
| 17 | – | 10 | 18 mins |

# The legal versus the commercial view of accounting

## Introduction

This is a very topical area and has been for some time. Companies (and other entities) have in the past used the **legal form** of a transaction to determine its accounting treatment, when in fact the **substance** of the transaction has been very different. We will look at the question of **substance over form** and the kind of transactions undertaken by entities trying to avoid reporting true substance in Sections 1 and 2.

The main weapon in tackling these abuses is the IASB's *Conceptual Framework for Financial Reporting* because it applies **general definitions** to the elements that make up financial statements. We will look at how this works in Section 3.

# Study guide

| | | Intellectual level |
|---|---|---|
| **A** | **CONCEPTUAL FRAMEWORK FOR FINANCIAL REPORTING** | |
| **3** | (d)  demonstrate the role of the principle of substance over form in relation to recognising sales revenue. | 2 |
| **4** | **The legal versus the commercial view of accounting** | |
| | (a)  explain the importance of recording the commercial substance rather than the legal form of transactions – give examples where recording the legal form of transactions may be misleading. | 2 |
| | (b)  describe the features which may indicate that the substance of transactions differs from their legal form. | 2 |
| | (c)  apply the principle of substance over form to the recognition and derecognition of assets and liabilities. | 2 |
| | (d)  recognise the substance of transactions in general, and specifically account for the following types of transactions: | 2 |
| | (i)   goods sold on sale or return/consignment inventory | |
| | (ii)  sale and repurchase/leaseback agreements | |
| | (iii)  factoring of receivables. | |

# 1 Off-balance sheet finance explained

**Key term**

> **Off-balance sheet finance** is the funding or refinancing of a company's operations in such a way that, under legal requirements and traditional accounting conventions, some or all of the finance may not be shown in its statement of financial position.

'Off-balance sheet transactions' are transactions which meet the above objective. These transactions may involve the **removal of assets** from the statement of financial position, as well as liabilities, and they are also likely to have a significant impact on profit or loss.

## 1.1 Why off-balance sheet finance exists

Why might company managers wish to enter into such transactions?

(a)   In some countries, companies traditionally have a lower level of gearing (ratio of debt to equity) than companies in other countries. Off balance sheet finance is used to **keep gearing low**, probably because of the views of analysts and brokers.

(b)   A company may need to keep its gearing down in order to stay within the terms of **loan covenants** imposed by lenders.

(c)   A quoted company with high borrowings is often expected (by analysts and others) to declare a **rights issue** in order to reduce gearing. This has an adverse effect on a company's share price and so off-balance sheet financing is used to reduce gearing *and* the expectation of a rights issue.

(d)   Analysts' short term views are a problem for companies **developing assets** which are not producing income during the development stage. Such companies will match the borrowings associated with such developing assets, along with the assets themselves, off-balance sheet. They are brought back into the statement of financial position once income is being generated by the assets. This process keeps return on capital employed higher than it would have been during the development stage.

(e)   In the past, groups of companies have excluded **subsidiaries** from consolidation in an off-balance sheet transaction because they carry out completely different types of business and have different characteristics. The usual example is a leasing company (in say a retail group) which has a high level of gearing. This exclusion is now disallowed.

You can see from this brief list of reasons that the overriding motivation is to avoid **misinterpretation**. In other words, the company does not trust the analysts or other users to understand the reasons for a transaction and so avoids any effect such transactions might have by taking them off-balance sheet. Unfortunately, the position of the company is then misstated and the user of the accounts is misled.

You must understand that not all forms of 'off-balance sheet finance' are undertaken for cosmetic or accounting reasons. Some transactions are carried out to **limit or isolate risk**, to reduce interest costs and so on. In other words, these transactions are in the best interests of the company, not merely a cosmetic repackaging of figures which would normally appear in the statement of financial position.

## 1.2 The off-balance sheet finance problem

The result of the use of increasingly sophisticated off-balance sheet finance transactions is a situation where the users of financial statements do not have a proper or clear view of the **state of the company's affairs**. The disclosures required by national company law and accounting standards did not in the past provide sufficient rules for disclosure of off-balance sheet finance transactions and so very little of the true nature of the transaction was exposed.

Whatever the purpose of such transactions, **insufficient disclosure** creates a problem. This problem has been debated over the years by the accountancy profession and other interested parties and some progress has been made (see the later sections of this chapter). However, company collapses during recessions have often revealed much higher borrowings than originally thought, because part of the borrowing was off-balance sheet.

The main argument used for banning off-balance sheet finance is that the true **substance** of the transactions should be shown, not merely the **legal form**, particularly when it is exacerbated by poor disclosure.

# 2 Substance over form

Key term

> **Substance over form.** The principle that transactions and other events are accounted for and presented in accordance with their substance and economic reality and not merely their legal form.

This is a very important concept. It is used to **determine accounting treatment** in financial statements through accounting standards and so prevent off-balance sheet transactions. The following paragraphs give examples of where the principle of substance over form is enforced in various accounting standards.

## 2.1 IAS 17 Leases

In IAS 17, there is an explicit requirement that if the lessor transfers substantially all the **risks and rewards of ownership** to the lessee then, even though the legal title has not necessarily passed, the item being leased should be shown as an asset in the statement of financial position of the lessee and the amount due to the lessor should be shown as a liability. (This will be covered in Chapter 16.)

## 2.2 IAS 24 Related party disclosures

IAS 24 requires financial statements to disclose fully any material transactions undertaken with a related party by the reporting entity, **regardless of any price charged**.

## 2.3 IAS 11 Construction contracts

In IAS 11 there is a requirement to account for **attributable profits** on construction contracts under the accruals convention. However, there may be a problem with realisation, since it is arguable whether we should account for profit which, although attributable to the work done, may not have yet been invoiced to the customer. It is argued that the convention of substance over form is applied to justify ignoring the strict legal position.

## 2.4 IAS 27 and quasi-subsidiaries

This is perhaps the most important area of off-balance sheet finance which has been prevented by the application of the substance over form concept. The use of **quasi-subsidiaries** was very common in the 1980s. These may be defined as follows.

> A **quasi-subsidiary** of a reporting entity is a company, trust, partnership or other vehicle that, though not fulfilling the definition of a subsidiary, is directly or indirectly controlled by the reporting entity and gives rise to benefits for that entity that are in substance no different from those that would arise were the vehicle a subsidiary.

IAS 27 brought in the definition of a subsidiary based on **control** rather than just ownership rights, thus substantially reducing the effectiveness of this method of off-balance sheet finance. (The definition of control has now been amended by IFRS 10, as explained in Chapter 8.)

IAS 27 therefore **curtailed drastically** the use of quasi-subsidiaries for off-balance sheet finance.

You may also hear the term **creative accounting** used in the context of reporting the substance of transactions. This can be defined simply as the manipulation of figures for a desired result. Remember, however, that it is very rare for a company, its directors or employees to manipulate results for the purpose of fraud. The major consideration is usually the effect the results will have on the company's share price. Some areas open to abuse (although some of these loopholes have been closed) are given below and you should by now understand how these can distort a company results.

(a) Income recognition and cut-off

(b) Impairment of purchased goodwill

(c) Manipulation of reserves

(d) Revaluations and depreciation

(e) Window dressing – transactions undertaken, eg loans repaid just before the year end and then reversed in the following period.

(f) Changes in accounting policy

> Articles on creative accounting appear fairly regularly in *Student Accountant*. Although often based on UK accounting, most of the points can be applied to international accounting.

Question                                                                                          Creative accounting

Creative accounting, off-balance sheet finance and related matters (in particular how ratio analysis can be used to discover these practices) often come up in articles in the financial press. Find a library, preferably a good technical library, which can provide you with copies of back issues of such newspapers or journals and look for articles on creative accounting.

# 3 The IASB Conceptual Framework

The 1989 *Framework* included substance over form as a qualitative characteristic. The 2011 *Conceptual Framework* does not mention substance over form but the IASB considers it to be implied in the concept of 'faithful representation'. To account for an item according to its legal form but not its economic substance would not be a faithful representation.

(a) For the majority of transactions there is **no difference** between the two and therefore no issue.

(b) For other transactions **substance and form diverge** and the choice of treatment can give different results due to non-recognition of an asset or liability even though benefits or obligations result.

Full disclosure is not enough: all transactions must be **accounted for** correctly, with full disclosure of related details as necessary to give the user of accounts a full understanding of the transactions.

## 3.1 Relationship to IFRSs

The interaction of the *Conceptual Framework* **with other standards** is also an important issue. Whichever rules are the more specific should be applied, given that IFRSs should be consistent with the *Conceptual Framework*. Leasing provides a good example: straightforward leases which fall squarely within the terms of IAS 17 should be accounted for without any need to refer to the *Conceptual Framework*, but where their terms are more complex, or the lease is only one element in a larger series of transactions, then the *Conceptual Framework* comes into play.

## 3.2 Basic principles

How else does the *Conceptual Framework* enforce the substance over form rule? Its main method is to define the elements of financial statements and therefore to give rules for their recognition. The key considerations are whether a transaction has **given rise to new assets and liabilities**, and whether it has **changed any existing assets and liabilities**.

The characteristics of transactions whose substance is not readily apparent are as follows.

(a) The **legal title** to an item is separated from the ability to enjoy the principal benefits, and the exposure to the main risks associated with it.

(b) The transaction is **linked to one or more others** so that the commercial effect of the transaction cannot be understood without reference to the complete series.

(c) The transaction includes **one or more options**, under such terms that it makes it highly likely that the option(s) will be exercised.

## 3.3 Definitions

These are perhaps the most important definitions.

**Key terms**

> - An **asset** is a resource controlled by the entity as a result of past events and from which future economic benefits are expected to flow to the entity.
>
> - A **liability** is a present obligation of the entity arising from past events, the settlement of which is expected to result in an outflow from the entity of resources embodying economic benefits.
>
> *(Conceptual Framework)*

Identification of **who has the risks** relating to an asset will generally indicate **who has the benefits** and hence **who has the asset**. If an entity is in certain circumstances unable to avoid an **outflow of benefits**, this will provide evidence that it has a liability.

The definitions given in the IASB *Conceptual Framework* of income and expenses are not as important as those of assets and liabilities. This is because income and expenses are **described in terms of changes in assets and liabilities**, ie they are secondary definitions.

**Key terms**

> - **Income** is increases in economic benefits during the accounting period in the form of inflows or enhancements of assets or decreases of liabilities that result in increases in equity, other than those relating to contributions from equity participants.
>
> - **Expenses** are decreases in economic benefits during the accounting period in the form of outflows or depletions of assets or incurrences of liabilities that result in decreases in equity, other than those relating to distributions to equity participants. *(Conceptual Framework)*

The real importance, then, is the way the *Conceptual Framework* defines assets and liabilities. This forces entities to acknowledge their assets and liabilities regardless of the legal status.

It is not sufficient, however, that the asset or liability fulfils the above definitions; it must also satisfy **recognition criteria** in order to be shown in an entity's accounts.

## 3.4 Recognition

Key term

**Recognition** is the process of incorporating in the statement of financial position or statement of profit or loss and other comprehensive income an item that meets the definition of an element and satisfies the criteria for recognition set out below. It involves the depiction of the item in words and by a monetary amount and the inclusion of that amount in the statement of financial position or statement of profit or loss and other comprehensive income totals.

The next key question is deciding **when** something which satisfies the definition of an asset or liability has to be recognised in the statement of financial position. Where a transaction results in an item that meets the definition of an asset or liability, that item should be recognised in the statement of financial position if:

(a) it is **probable that a future inflow or outflow** of benefit to or from the entity will occur, and
(b) the item can be **measured at a monetary amount with sufficient reliability.**

This effectively prevents entities abusing the definitions of the elements by recognising items that are vague in terms of likelihood of occurrence and measurability. If this were not in force, entities could **manipulate the financial statements** in various ways, eg recognising assets when the likely future economic benefits cannot yet be determined.

**Probability** is assessed based on the situation at the end of the reporting period. For example, it is usually expected that some customers of an entity will not pay what they owe. The expected level of non-payment is based on past experience and the receivables asset is reduced by a percentage (the general bad debt provision).

**Measurement** must be reliable, but it does not preclude the use of **reasonable estimates**, which is an essential part of the financial statement preparation.

Even if something does not qualify for recognition now, it may meet the criteria **at a later date**.

## 3.5 Other standards

The IASB has developed guidance for specific transactions. These were mentioned in Section 2 and they are covered in various parts of this text. You should consider the particular off balance sheet finance problem they tackle as you study them.

- IAS 17 Leases (see Chapter 16)
- IAS 32 Financial instruments (see Chapter 14)
- IAS 27 Separate financial statements (see Chapter 8)
- IAS 24 Related party disclosures (see Chapter 8)
- IAS 18 Revenue (see Section 5)

## 3.6 Section summary

Important points to remember from the *Conceptual Framework* are:

- **Substance over form** as implied in faithful representation
- Definitions of **assets** and **liabilities**
- Definition of **recognition**
- **Criteria** for recognition

# 4 Common forms of off-balance sheet finance

FAST FORWARD

> The subject of **off-balance sheet finance** is a complex one and off-balance sheet finance schemes are often very sophisticated.

We will consider how the principles of the *Conceptual Framework* would be applied to the following transactions.

- Consignment inventory
- Sale and repurchase agreements/sale and leaseback agreements
- Factoring of receivables/debts

## 4.1 Consignment inventory

Consignment inventory is an arrangement where inventory is held by one party (say a distributor) but is owned by another party (for example a manufacturer or a finance company). Consignment inventory is common in the motor trade and is similar to goods sold on a 'sale or return' basis.

To identify the correct treatment, it is necessary to identify the point at which the distributor or dealer acquired the benefits of the asset (the inventory) rather than the point at which legal title was acquired. If the manufacturer has the right to require the return of the inventory, and if that right is likely to be exercised, then the inventory is *not* an asset of the dealer. If the dealer is rarely required to return the inventory, then this part of the transaction will have little commercial effect in practice and should be ignored for accounting purposes. The potential liability would need to be disclosed in the accounts.

### 4.1.1 Summary of indications of asset status

The following analysis summarises the range of possibilities in such a transaction.

| Indications that the inventory is *not an asset* of the dealer at delivery | Indications that the inventory *is an asset* of the dealer at delivery |
|---|---|
| Manufacturer can require dealer to **return inventory** (or transfer inventory to another dealer) without compensation. | Manufacturer cannot require dealer to **return or transfer inventory**. |
| **Penalty paid** by the dealer to prevent returns/transfers of inventory at the manufacturer's request. | **Financial incentives** given to persuade dealer to transfer inventory at manufacturer's request. |
| Dealer has unfettered **right to return inventory** to the manufacturer without penalty and actually exercises the right in practice. | Dealer has **no right to return inventory** or is commercially compelled not to exercise its right of return. |
| Manufacturer bears **obsolescence risk**, eg:<br>• obsolete inventory is returned to the manufacturer without penalty, or<br>• financial incentives given by manufacturer to prevent inventory being returned to it (eg on a model change or if it becomes obsolete). | Dealer bears **obsolescence risk**, eg:<br>• penalty charged if dealer returns inventory to manufacturer, or<br>• obsolete inventory cannot be returned to the manufacturer and no compensation is paid by manufacturer for losses due to obsolescence. |
| Inventory **transfer price** charged by manufacturer is based on manufacturer's list price at date of transfer of legal title. | Inventory **transfer price** charged by manufacturer is based on manufacturer's list price at date of delivery. |
| Manufacturer bears **slow movement risk**, eg: transfer price set independently of time for which dealer holds inventory, and there is no deposit. | Dealer bears **slow movement risk**, eg:<br>• dealer is effectively charged interest as transfer price or other payments to manufacturer vary with time for which dealer holds inventory, or<br>• dealer makes a substantial interest-free deposit that varies with the levels of inventory held. |

### 4.1.2 Required accounting

The following apply where it is concluded that the inventory **is in substance an asset** of the dealer.

(a)     The inventory should be recognised as such in the dealer's statement of financial position, together with a corresponding liability to the manufacturer.

(b)     Any deposit should be deducted from the liability and the excess classified as a trade payable.

Where it is concluded that the inventory is **not in substance an asset** of the dealer, the following apply.

(a)     The inventory should not be included in the dealer's statement of financial position until the transfer of risks and rewards has crystallised.

(b)     Any deposit should be included under 'other receivables'.

| Question | | Recognition |
|---|---|---|

Daley Motors Co owns a number of car dealerships throughout a geographical area. The terms of the arrangement between the dealerships and the manufacturer are as follows.

(a)     Legal title passes when the cars are either used by Daley Co for demonstration purposes or sold to a third party.

(b)     The dealer has the right to return vehicles to the manufacturer without penalty. (Daley Co has rarely exercised this right in the past.)

(c)     The transfer price is based on the manufacturer's list price at the date of delivery.

(d)     Daley Co makes a substantial interest-free deposit based on the number of cars held.

Should the asset and liability be recognised by Daley Co at the date of delivery?

| Answer | |
|---|---|

(a)     Legal form is irrelevant

(b)     Yes: only because rarely exercised (otherwise 'no')

(c)     Yes

(d)     Yes: the dealership is effectively forgoing the interest which could be earned on the cash sum

## 4.2 Sale and repurchase agreements

These are arrangements under which the company sells an asset to another person on terms that allow the company to **repurchase the asset** in certain circumstances. A common example is the sale and repurchase of maturing whisky inventories. The key question is whether the transaction is a **straightforward sale**, or whether it is, in effect, a **secured loan**. It is necessary to look at the arrangement to determine who has the rights to the economic benefits that the asset generates, and the terms on which the asset is to be repurchased.

If the seller has the right to the benefits of the **use of the asset**, and the repurchase terms are such that the **repurchase is likely** to take place, the transaction should be accounted for as a **loan**.

### 4.2.1 Summary of indications of the sale of the asset

The following summary is helpful.

| Indications of *sale* of original asset to buyer (nevertheless, the seller may retain a different asset) | Indications of *no sale* of original asset to buyer (secured loan) |
|---|---|
| | Sale price does not equal **market value** at date of sale. |
| No commitment for **seller to repurchase** asset, eg call option where there is a real possibility the option will fail to be exercised. | Commitment for **seller to repurchase** asset, eg:<br>• put and call option with the same exercise price<br>• either a put or a call option with no genuine commercial possibility that the option will fail to be exercised, or<br>• seller requires asset back to use in its business, or asset is in effect the only source of seller's future sales |
| Risk of **changes in asset value** borne by buyer such that buyer does not receive solely a lender's return, eg both sale and repurchase price equal market value at date of sale/repurchase. | Risk of **changes in asset value** borne by seller such that buyer receives solely a lender's return, eg:<br>• repurchase price equals sale price plus costs plus interest<br>• original purchase price adjusted retrospectively to pass variations in the value of the asset to the seller<br>• seller provides residual value guarantee to buyer or subordinated debt to protect buyer from falls in the value of the asset |
| Nature of the asset is such that it will be used over the life of the agreement, and seller has no rights to **determine its use**. Seller has no rights to determine asset's development or future sale. | Seller retains right to **determine asset's use**, development or sale, or rights to profits therefrom. |

### 4.2.2 Required accounting

Where the substance of the transaction is that of a **secured loan**:

(a) The seller should continue to recognise the original asset and record the proceeds received from the buyer as a liability.

(b) Interest, however designated, should be accrued.

(c) The carrying amount of the asset should be reviewed for impairment and written down if necessary.

### 4.2.3 Sale and leaseback transactions

A sale and leaseback transaction involves the sale of an asset and the leasing back of the same asset. The lease payment and the sale price are usually negotiated as a package.

The accounting treatment depends upon the type of lease involved. If the transaction results in a **finance lease**, then it is in substance a loan from the lessor to the lessee (the lessee has sold the asset and then leased it back), with the asset as security. In this case, any 'profit' on the sale should not be recognised as such, but should be deferred and amortised over the lease term.

If the transaction results in an **operating lease** and the transaction has been conducted at **fair value**, then it can be regarded as a normal sale transaction. The asset is derecognised and any profit on the sale is recognised. The operating lease instalments are treated as lease payments, rather than repayments of capital plus interest.

If the result is an operating lease and the sale price was **below fair value**, this may be being **compensated for by lower rentals** in the future. If this is the case, any loss on sale should be amortised over the period for which the asset is expected to be used. If the sale price was **above fair value** any excess is deferred and amortised over the period for which the asset is expected to be used.

This will become clearer when you have covered Chapter 16 and you may want to return to it at that point.

## Question

**Recognition and sales proceeds**

A construction company, Mecanto Co, agrees to sell to Hamlows Bank some of the land within its landbank. The terms of the sale are as follows.

(a)     The sales price is to be at open market value.

(b)     Mecanto Co has the right to develop the land on the basis that it will pay all the outgoings on the land plus an annual fee of 5% of the purchase price.

(c)     Mecanto has the option to buy back the land at any time within the next five years. The repurchase price is based on:

(i)      original purchase price
(ii)     expenses relating to the purchase
(iii)    an interest charge of base rate + 2%
(iv)    less amounts received from Mecanto by Hamlows

(d)     At the end of five years Hamlows Bank may offer the land for sale generally. Any shortfall on the proceeds relative to the agreed purchase price agreed with Mecanto has to be settled by Mecanto in cash.

Should the asset continue to be recognised by Mecanto Co and the sales proceeds treated as a loan?

## Answer

(a)     No: the sales price is as for an arm's length transaction.

(b)     Yes: Mecanto has control over the asset.
        Yes: Mecanto has to pay a fee based on cash received.

(c)     Yes: interest is charged on the proceeds paid by Mecanto.
        Yes: the repurchase price is based on the lender's return

(d)     Yes: options ensure that Mecanto bears all the risk (both favourable and unfavourable) of changes in the market value of the land.

In this case the evidence overwhelmingly suggests that Mecanto has obtained a loan from Hamlows using the land as security. So the asset should continue to be recognised and the sales proceeds should be treated as a loan.

## 4.3 Factoring of receivables/debts

Where debts or receivables are factored, the original creditor **sells the debts to the factor**. The sales price may be fixed at the outset or may be adjusted later. It is also common for the factor to offer a credit facility that allows the seller to draw upon a proportion of the amounts owed.

In order to determine the correct accounting treatment it is necessary to consider whether the benefit of the debts has been passed on to the factor, or whether the factor is, in effect, providing a loan on the security of the receivable balances. If the seller has to **pay interest** on the difference between the amounts advanced to him and the amounts that the factor has received, and if the seller bears the **risks of non-payment** by the debtor, then the indications would be that the transaction is, in effect, a loan.

### 4.3.1 Summary of indications of appropriate treatment

The following is a summary of indicators of the appropriate treatment.

| Indications the debts are *not an asset* of the seller | Indications that the debts are an *asset* of the seller |
|---|---|
| Transfer is for a single non-returnable fixed sum. | Finance cost varies with speed of collection of debts, eg: <br> • by adjustment to consideration for original transfer, or <br> • subsequent transfers priced to recover costs of earlier transfers. |
| There is no recourse to the seller for losses. | There is full recourse to the seller for losses. |
| Factor is paid all amounts received from the factored debts (and no more). Seller has no rights to further sums from the factor. | Seller is required to repay amounts received from the factor on or before a set date, regardless of timing or amounts of collections from debtors. |

### 4.3.2 Required accounting

Where the seller has retained no significant benefits and risks relating to the debts and has no obligation to repay amounts received from the factors, the receivables should be removed from its statement of financial position and no liability shown in respect of the proceeds received from the factor. A profit or loss should be recognised, calculated as the difference between the carrying amount of the debts and the proceeds received.

Where the seller does retain significant benefits and risks, a gross asset (equivalent in amount to the gross amount of the receivables) should be shown in the statement of financial position of the seller within assets, and a corresponding liability in respect of the proceeds received from the factor should be shown within liabilities. The interest element of the factor's charges should be recognised as it accrues and included in profit or loss with other interest charges. Other factoring costs should be similarly accrued.

# 5 Revenue recognition

FAST FORWARD

Revenue recognition is straightforward in most business transactions, but some situations are more complicated and some give opportunities for manipulation.

## 5.1 Introduction

Accruals accounting is based on the **matching of costs with the revenue they generate**. It is crucially important under this convention that we can establish the point at which revenue may be recognised so that the correct treatment can be applied to the related costs. For example, the costs of producing an item of finished goods should be carried as an asset in the statement of financial position until such time as it is sold; they should then be written off as a charge to the trading account. Which of these two treatments should be applied cannot be decided until it is clear at what moment the sale of the item takes place.

The decision has a **direct impact on profit** since under the prudence concept it would be unacceptable to recognise the profit on sale until a sale had taken place in accordance with the criteria of revenue recognition.

Revenue is generally recognised as **earned at the point of sale**, because at that point four criteria will generally have been met.

- The product or service has been **provided to the buyer**.
- The buyer has **recognised his liability** to pay for the goods or services provided. The converse of this is that the seller has recognised that ownership of goods has passed from himself to the buyer.
- The buyer has indicated his **willingness to hand over cash** or other assets in settlement of his liability.
- The **monetary value** of the goods or services has been established.

At earlier points in the business cycle there will not in general be **firm evidence** that the above criteria will be met. Until work on a product is complete, there is a risk that some flaw in the manufacturing process will necessitate its writing off; even when the product is complete there is no guarantee that it will find a buyer.

At later points in the business cycle, for example when cash is received for the sale, the recognition of revenue may occur in a period later than that in which the related costs were charged. Revenue recognition would then depend on fortuitous circumstances, such as the cash flow of a company's customers, and might fluctuate misleadingly from one period to another.

However, there are times when revenue is **recognised at other times than at the completion of a sale**. For example, in the recognition of profit on long-term construction contracts. Under IAS 11 *Construction contracts* (see Chapter 12) contract revenue and contract costs associated with the construction contract should be recognised as revenue and expenses respectively by reference to the stage of completion of the contract activity at the end of the reporting period.

(a) Owing to the length of time taken to complete such contracts, to defer taking profit into account until completion may result in the statement of profit and loss reflecting not so much a fair view of the activity of the company during the year, but rather the results relating to contracts which have been completed by the year end.

(b) Revenue in this case is recognised when production on, say, a section of the total contract is complete, even though no sale can be made until the whole is complete.

## 5.2 IAS 18 Revenue

IAS 18 governs the recognition of revenue in specific (common) types of transaction. Generally, recognition should be when it is probable that **future economic benefits** will flow to the entity and when these benefits can be **measured reliably**.

Income, as defined by the IASB *Conceptual Framework* includes both revenues and gains. Revenue is income arising in the ordinary course of an entity's activities and it may be called different names, such as sales, fees, interest, dividends or royalties.

## 5.3 Scope

IAS 18 covers the revenue from specific types of transaction or events.

- **Sale of goods** (manufactured products and items purchased for resale)
- **Rendering of services**
- Use by others of entity assets yielding **interest, royalties and dividends**

Interest, royalties and dividends are included as income because they arise from the use of an entity's assets by other parties.

**Key terms**

> **Interest** is the charge for the use of cash or cash equivalents or amounts due to the entity.
>
> **Royalties** are charges for the use of non-current assets of the entity, eg patents, computer software and trademarks.

> **Dividends** are distributions of profit to holders of equity investments, in proportion with their holdings, of each relevant class of capital.

The Standard specifically **excludes** various types of revenue arising from leases, insurance contracts, changes in value of financial instruments or other current assets, natural increases in agricultural assets and mineral ore extraction.

## 5.4 Definitions

The following definitions are relevant.

**Key terms**

> **Revenue** is the gross inflow of economic benefits during the period arising in the course of the ordinary activities of an entity when those inflows result in increases in equity, other than increases relating to contributions from equity participants. (IAS 18)
>
> **Fair value** is the price that would be received to sell an asset or paid to transfer a liability in an orderly transaction between market participants at the measurement date. (IFRS 13)

Revenue **does not include** sales taxes, value added taxes or goods and service taxes which are only collected for third parties, because these do not represent an economic benefit flowing to the entity. The same is true for revenues collected by an agent on behalf of a principal. Revenue for the agent is only the commission received for acting as agent.

## 5.5 Measurement of revenue

When a transaction takes place, the amount of revenue is usually decided by the **agreement of the buyer and seller**. The revenue is actually measured, however, as the **fair value of the consideration received**, which will take account of any trade discounts and volume rebates.

## 5.6 Identification of the transaction

Normally, each transaction can be looked at **as a whole**. Sometimes, however, transactions are more complicated, and it is necessary to break a transaction down into its **component parts**. For example, a sale may include the transfer of goods and the provision of future servicing, the revenue for which should be deferred over the period the service is performed.

At the other end of the scale, **seemingly separate transactions must be considered together** if apart they lose their commercial meaning. An example would be to sell an asset with an agreement to buy it back at a later date. The second transaction cancels the first and so both must be considered together. We looked at sale and repurchase in Section 4.2.

## 5.7 Sale of goods

Revenue from the sale of goods should only be recognised when *all* these conditions are satisfied.

(a) The entity has transferred the **significant risks and rewards** of ownership of the goods to the buyer

(b) The entity has **no continuing managerial involvement** to the degree usually associated with ownership, and no longer has effective control over the goods sold

(c) The amount of revenue can be **measured reliably**

(d) It is probable that the **economic benefits** associated with the transaction will flow to the entity

(e) The **costs incurred** in respect of the transaction can be measured reliably

The transfer of risks and rewards can only be decided by examining each transaction. Mainly, the transfer occurs at the same time as either the **transfer of legal title**, or the **passing of possession** to the buyer – this is what happens when you buy something in a shop.

If **significant risks and rewards remain with the seller**, then the transaction is *not* a sale and revenue cannot be recognised, for example if the receipt of the revenue from a particular sale depends on the buyer receiving revenue from his own sale of the goods.

It is possible for the seller to retain only an **'insignificant' risk of ownership** and for the sale and revenue to be recognised. The main example here is where the seller retains title only to ensure collection of what is owed on the goods. This is a common commercial situation, and when it arises the revenue should be recognised on the date of sale.

The probability of the entity receiving the revenue arising from a transaction must be assessed. It may only become probable that the economic benefits will be received when an uncertainty is removed, for example government permission for funds to be received from another country. Only when the uncertainty is removed should the revenue be recognised. This is in contrast with the situation where revenue has already been recognised but where the **collectability of the cash** is brought into doubt. Where recovery has ceased to be probable, the amount should be recognised as an expense, *not* an adjustment of the revenue previously recognised. These points also refer to services and interest, royalties and dividends below.

**Matching** should take place, ie the revenue and expenses relating to the same transaction should be recognised at the same time. It is usually easy to estimate expenses at the date of sale (eg warranty costs, shipment costs, etc). Where they cannot be estimated reliably, then revenue cannot be recognised; any consideration which has already been received is treated as a liability.

## 5.8 Example

A washing machine sells for $500 with a one-year warranty. The dealer knows from experience that 15% of these machines develop a fault in the first year and that the average cost of repair is $100. He sells 200 machines. How does he account for this sale?

## Solution

He will recognise revenue of $100,000 ($500 × 200) and an associated provision of $3,000 ($100 × 200 × 15%).

## 5.9 Servicing fees included in the price

The sales price of a product may include an identifiable amount for subsequent servicing. In this case, that amount is deferred and recognised as revenue over the period during which the service is performed. The amount deferred must cover the cost of those services together with a reasonable profit on those services.

## 5.10 Example

A computerised accountancy package is sold with one year's after sales support. The cost of providing support to one customer for one year is calculated to be $50. The company has a mark-up on cost of 15%. The product is sold for $350. How is this sale accounted for?

## Solution

$57.50 (50 + (50 × 15%)) will be treated as deferred income and recognised over the course of the year.

The remaining $292.50 will be treated as revenue.

## 5.11 Rendering of services

When the outcome of a transaction involving the rendering of services can be estimated reliably, the associated revenue should be recognised by reference to the **stage of completion of the transaction** at the end of the reporting period. The outcome of a transaction can be estimated reliably when *all* these conditions are satisfied.

(a)     The amount of revenue can be **measured reliably**

(b)     It is probable that the **economic benefits** associated with the transaction will flow to the entity

(c)     The **stage of completion** of the transaction at the end of the reporting period can be measured reliably

(d)     The **costs incurred** for the transaction and the costs to complete the transaction can be measured reliably

The parties to the transaction will normally have to agree the following before an entity can make reliable estimates.

(a)     Each party's **enforceable rights** regarding the service to be provided and received by the parties

(b)     The **consideration** to be exchanged

(c)     The **manner and terms of settlement**

There are various methods of determining the stage of completion of a transaction, but for practical purposes, when services are performed by an indeterminate number of acts over a period of time, revenue should be recognised on a **straight line basis** over the period, unless there is evidence for the use of a more appropriate method. If one act is of more significance than the others, then the significant act should be carried out *before* revenue is recognised.

In uncertain situations, when the outcome of the transaction involving the rendering of services cannot be estimated reliably, the standard recommends a **no loss/no gain approach**. Revenue is recognised only to the extent of the expenses recognised that are recoverable.

This is particularly likely during the **early stages of a transaction**, but it is still probable that the entity will recover the costs incurred. So the revenue recognised in such a period will be equal to the expenses incurred, with no profit.

Obviously, if the costs are not likely to be reimbursed, then they must be recognised as an expense immediately. **When the uncertainties cease to exist**, revenue should be recognised as laid out in the first paragraph of this section.

## 5.12 Interest, royalties and dividends

When others use the entity's assets yielding interest, royalties and dividends, the revenue should be recognised on the bases set out below when:

(a)     it is probable that the **economic benefits** associated with the transaction will flow to the entity; and

(b)     the amount of the revenue can be **measured reliably**.

The revenue is recognised on the following bases.

(a)     **Interest** is recognised on a time proportion basis that takes into account the effective yield on the asset

(b)     **Royalties** are recognised on an accruals basis in accordance with the substance of the relevant agreement

(c)     **Dividends** are recognised when the shareholder's right to receive payment is established

It is unlikely that you would be asked about anything as complex as this in the exam, but you should be aware of the basic requirements of the Standard. The **effective yield** on an asset mentioned above is the rate of interest required to discount the stream of future cash receipts expected over the life of the asset to equate to the initial carrying amount of the asset.

Royalties are usually recognised on the same basis that they accrue **under the relevant agreement**. Sometimes the true substance of the agreement may require some other systematic and rational method of recognition.

Once again, the points made above about **probability and collectability** on sale of goods also apply here.

## 5.13 Disclosure

The following items should be disclosed.

(a)    The **accounting policies** adopted for the recognition of revenue, including the methods used to determine the stage of completion of transactions involving the rendering of services

(b)    The amount of each **significant category of revenue** recognised during the period including revenue arising from:

    (i)     The sale of goods
    (ii)    The rendering of services
    (iii)   Interest
    (iv)    Royalties
    (v)     Dividends

(c)    The amount of revenue arising from **exchanges of goods or services** included in each significant category of revenue

Any **contingent gains or losses**, such as those relating to warranty costs, claims or penalties should be treated according to IAS 37 *Provisions, contingent liabilities and contingent assets* (covered in Chapter 13).

## Question
Recognition

Discuss under what circumstances, if any, revenue might be recognised at the following stages of a sale.

(a)    Goods are acquired by the business which it confidently expects to resell very quickly.
(b)    A customer places a firm order for goods.
(c)    Goods are delivered to the customer.
(d)    The customer is invoiced for goods.
(e)    The customer pays for the goods.
(f)    The customer's cheque in payment for the goods has been cleared by the bank.

## Answer

(a)    A sale must never be recognised before the goods have even been ordered by a customer. There is no certainty about the value of the sale, nor when it will take place, even if it is virtually certain that goods will be sold.

(b)    A sale must never be recognised when the customer places an order. Even though the order will be for a specific quantity of goods at a specific price, it is not yet certain that the sale transaction will go through. The customer may cancel the order, the supplier might be unable to deliver the goods as ordered or it may be decided that the customer is not a good credit risk.

(c)    A sale will be recognised when delivery of the goods is made only when:

    (i)     the sale is for cash, and so the cash is received at the same time; or
    (ii)    the sale is on credit and the customer accepts delivery (eg by signing a delivery note).

(d)    The critical event for a credit sale is usually the despatch of an invoice to the customer. There is then a legally enforceable debt, payable on specified terms, for a completed sale transaction.

(e)    The critical event for a cash sale is when delivery takes place and when cash is received; both take place at the same time.

It would be too cautious or 'prudent' to await cash payment for a credit sale transaction before recognising the sale, unless the customer is a high credit risk and there is a serious doubt about his ability or intention to pay.

(f)    It would again be over-cautious to wait for clearance of the customer's cheques before recognising sales revenue. Such a precaution would only be justified in cases where there is a very high risk of the bank refusing to honour the cheque.

- The subject of **off-balance sheet finance** is a complex one and off-balance sheet finance schemes are often very sophisticated.

- Revenue recognition is straightforward in most business transactions, but some situations are more complicated and give some opportunities for manipulation.

# Quick Quiz

1    Why do companies want to use off-balance sheet finance?

2    What is meant by the concept of substance over form?

3    What is a quasi-subsidiary?

4    How has the use of quasi-subsidiaries been curtailed?

5    What are the common features of transactions whose substance is not readily apparent?

6    When should a transaction be recognised?

# Answers to Quick Quiz

1   The overriding motivation is to avoid misinterpretation. However the result is that users are misled.

2   The principle that transactions and other events are accounted for and presented in accordance with their substance and economic reality rather than merely their legal form.

3   An entity that does not fulfil the definition of a subsidiary but is directly or indirectly controlled by the reporting entity and gives rise to benefits that are in substance no different from those arising if it were a subsidiary.

4   By IAS 27 – the definition of a subsidiary based on **control** rather than ownership.

5   (a)    The legal title is separated from the ability to enjoy benefits.

  (b)   The transaction includes one or more options under such terms that it is likely the option(s) will be exercised.

6   When it is probable that a future inflow or outflow of economic benefit to the entity will occur and the item can be measured in monetary terms with sufficient reliability.

Now try the questions below from the Exam Question Bank

| Number | Level | Marks | Time |
|--------|-------|-------|------|
| 18 | Examination | 25 | 45 mins |
| 19 | Examination | 25 | 45 mins |

# 16

# Leasing

| Topic list | Syllabus reference |
|---|---|
| 1 Types of lease | C6 |
| 2 Lessees | C6 |

# Introduction

Leasing transactions are extremely common so this is an important practical subject. **Lease accounting is regulated by IAS 17**, which was introduced because of abuses in the use of lease accounting by companies.

These companies effectively 'owned' an asset and 'owed' a debt for its purchase, but showed neither the asset nor the liability in the statement of financial position because they were not required to do so. This is called **'off-balance sheet finance'**, as explained in Chapter 15.

# Study guide

| | | Intellectual level |
|---|---|---|
| 6 | **Leases** | |
| (a) | explain why recording the legal form of a finance lease can be misleading to users (referring to the commercial substance of such leases). | 2 |
| (b) | describe and apply the method of determining a lease type (ie an operating or finance lease). | 2 |
| (c) | discuss the effect on the financial statements of a finance lease being incorrectly treated as an operating lease. | 2 |
| (d) | account for assets financed by finance leases in the records of the lessee. | 2 |
| (e) | account for operating leases in the records of the lessee. | 2 |

# Exam guide

You are quite likely to meet a finance lease in an accounts preparation question.

# 1 Types of lease

**FAST FORWARD**

A finance lease is a means of acquiring the long-term use of an asset whereas an operating lease is a short-term rental agreement. Substance over form is important in distinguishing between them.

## 1.1 IAS 17 *Leases*

IAS 17 *Leases* standardises the accounting treatment and disclosure of assets held under lease.

In a leasing transaction there is a **contract** between the lessor and the lessee for the hire of an asset. The lessor retains legal ownership but conveys to the lessee the right to use the asset for an agreed period of time in return for specified rentals. IAS 17 defines a lease and recognises two types.

**Key terms**

> **Lease.** An agreement whereby the lessor conveys to the lessee in return for rent the right to use an asset for an agreed period of time.
>
> **Finance lease.** A lease that transfers substantially all the risks and rewards incident to ownership of an asset. Title may or may not eventually be transferred.
>
> **Operating lease.** A lease other than a finance lease. *(IAS 17)*

In this chapter the **user** of an asset will often be referred to simply as the **lessee**, and the **supplier** as the **lessor**. You should bear in mind that identical requirements apply in the case of hirers and vendors respectively under hire purchase agreements.

To expand on the definition above, a finance lease should be presumed if at the inception of a lease the **present value of the minimum lease payments** is approximately equal to the **fair value of the leased asset**.

The present value should be calculated by using the **interest rate implicit in the lease**.

- **Minimum lease payments**. The payments over the lease term that the lessee is or can be required to make.

- **Interest rate implicit in the lease**.

  The discount rate that, at the inception of the lease, causes the aggregate present value of

  (a)    the minimum lease payments, and
  (b)    the unguaranteed residual value

  to be equal to the sum of

  (a)    the fair value of the leased asset, and
  (b)    any initial direct costs.

- **Lease term**. The non-cancellable period for which the lessee has contracted to lease the asset together with any further terms for which the lessee has the option to continue to lease the asset, with or without further payment, when at the inception of the lease it is reasonably certain that the lessee will exercise the option.

**Note**

In an exam question you will be given the interest rate implicit in the lease.

## 1.2 Accounting for operating leases

**Operating leases** do not really pose an accounting problem. The lessee pays amounts periodically to the lessor and these are **charged to the statement of profit or loss**.

Where the lessee is offered an incentive such as a **rent-free period** or **cashback incentive**, this is effectively a **discount**, which will be spread over the period of the operating lease in accordance with the accruals principle. For instance, if a company entered into a 4-year operating lease but was not required to make any payments until year 2, the total payments to be made over years 2-4 should be charged evenly over years 1-4.

Where a cashback incentive is received, the total amount payable over the lease term, less the cashback, should be charged evenly over the term of the lease. This can be done by crediting the cashback received to deferred income and releasing it to profit or loss over the lease term.

## 1.3 Accounting for finance leases

For assets held under **finance leases or hire purchase** this accounting treatment would not disclose the reality of the situation. If a **lessor** leases out an asset on a finance lease, the asset will probably never be seen on his premises or used in his business again. It would be inappropriate for a lessor to record such an asset as a non-current asset. In reality, what he owns is a **stream of cash flows receivable** from the lessee. **The asset is an amount receivable rather than a non-current asset.**

Similarly, a **lessee** may use a finance lease to fund the 'acquisition' of a major asset which he will then use in his business perhaps for many years. **The substance of the transaction is that he has acquired a non-current asset**, and this is reflected in the accounting treatment prescribed by IAS 17, even though in law the lessee never becomes the owner of the asset.

The following summary diagram should help you when deciding whether a lease is an operating lease or a finance lease.

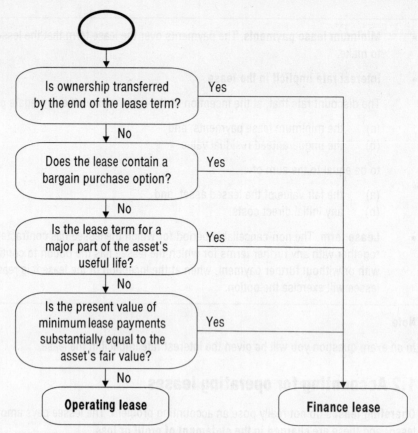

Note that a finance lease can also be presumed if the leased assets are of such a specialised nature that only the lessee can use them without major modifications.

## 1.4 Land and buildings

Under IAS 17 the land and buildings elements of a lease of land and buildings are considered separately for the purposes of lease classification.

A lease of land is normally treated as an operating lease, unless title is expected to pass at the end of the lease term. A lease of buildings will be treated as a finance lease if it satisfies the requirements in paragraph 1.1 above. The minimum lease payments are allocated between the land and buildings elements in proportion to the relative fair values of the leasehold interests in the land and the buildings. If the value of the land is immaterial, classification will be according to the buildings.

If payments cannot be reliably allocated, the entire lease is classified as a finance lease, unless both elements are operating leases, in which case the entire lease is classified as an operating lease.

## 1.5 Example

A business has taken out a new lease on a factory building and surrounding land. The fair value of the building is $5m and the fair value of the land is $3m. The lease is for 20 years with annual payments in arrears of $500,000.

## Solution

The lease payments will be split in line with the fair values of the land and the building. $187,500 (500,000 × 3/8) will be treated as payment on an operating lease for the land and $312,500 will be treated as payment on a finance lease for the building. The building will be capitalised and depreciated.

# 2 Lessees

> **FAST FORWARD**
>
> Under finance leases:
>
> - Assets acquired should be capitalised
> - The interest element of instalments should be charged against profit

## 2.1 Accounting treatment

**IAS 17** requires that, when an asset changes hands under a **finance lease, lessor and lessee should account for the transaction as though it were a credit sale**. In the lessee's books therefore:

DEBIT      Asset account
CREDIT     Lessor (liability) account

The amount to be recorded in this way is the **lower of** the **fair value** and the **present value** of the **minimum lease payments**.

IAS 17 states that it is not appropriate to show liabilities for leased assets as deductions from the leased assets. A distinction should be made between **current and non-current** lease liabilities, if the entity makes this distinction for other liabilities.

The asset should be **depreciated** (on the bases set out in IASs 16 and 38) over the shorter of:

- The lease term
- The asset's useful life

**If there is reasonable certainty of eventual ownership of the asset, then it should be depreciated over its useful life.**

## 2.2 Apportionment of rental payments

When the lessee makes a rental payment it will comprise two elements.

(a)   An **interest charge** on the finance provided by the lessor. This proportion of each payment is interest payable in the statement of profit or loss of the lessee.

(b)   A repayment of part of the **capital cost** of the asset. In the lessee's books this proportion of each rental payment must be debited to the lessor's account to reduce the outstanding liability.

The accounting problem is to decide what proportion of each instalment paid by the lessee represents interest, and what proportion represents a repayment of the capital advanced by the lessor. There are two usual apportionment methods:

- The **actuarial method**
- The **sum-of-the-digits method**

**Exam focus point**

> The examiner will not examine the **sum-of-the-digits method**, so we are not covering it.

The **actuarial method** is the best and most scientific method. It derives from the common-sense assumption that the interest charged by a lessor company will equal the rate of return desired by the company, multiplied by the amount of capital it has invested.

(a)   At the beginning of the lease the capital invested is equal to the fair value of the asset (less any initial deposit paid by the lessee).

(b)   This amount reduces as each instalment is paid. It follows that the interest accruing is greatest in the early part of the lease term, and gradually reduces as capital is repaid. In this section, we will look at a simple example of the actuarial method.

## 2.3 Example

On 1 January 20X0 Bacchus Co, wine merchants, buys a small bottling and labelling machine from Silenus Co under a finance lease. The cash price of the machine was $7,710 while the amount to be paid was $10,000. The agreement required the immediate payment of a $2,000 deposit with the balance being settled in four equal annual instalments commencing on 31 December 20X0. The charge of $2,290 represents interest of 15% per annum, calculated on the remaining balance of the liability during each accounting period. Depreciation on the plant is to be provided for at the rate of 20% per annum on a straight line basis assuming a residual value of nil.

## Solution

Interest is calculated as 15% of the outstanding *capital* balance at the beginning of each year. The outstanding capital balance reduces each year by the capital element comprised in each instalment. The outstanding capital balance at 1 January 20X0 is $5,710 ($7,710 fair value less $2,000 deposit).

|  | $ |
|---|---|
| Balance 1 January 20X0 | 5,710 |
| Interest 15% | 856 |
| Instalment 31 December 20X0 | (2,000) |
| Balance outstanding 31 December 20X0 | 4,566 |
| Interest 15% | 685 |
| Instalment 31 December 20X1 | (2,000) |
| Balance outstanding 31 December 20X1 | 3,251 |
| Interest 15% | 488 |
| Instalment 31 December 20X2 | (2,000) |
| Balance outstanding 31 December 20X2 | 1,739 |
| Interest 15% | 261 |
| Instalment 31 December 20X3 | (2,000) |
|  | – |

### Note

You will not be required to do this whole calculation in an exam. You will probably have to calculate the first few instalments in order to obtain figures for current and non-current liabilities (as in Section 2.5).

## 2.4 Disclosure requirements for lessees

IAS 17 (revised) requires the following disclosures by lessees in respect of finance leases:

- The **net carrying amount** at the end of the reporting period for each class of asset

- A **reconciliation** between the total of minimum lease payments at the end of the reporting period, and their present value. In addition, an entity should disclose the total of minimum lease payments at the end of the reporting period, and their present value, for each of the following periods:

  - Not later than one year
  - Later than one year and not later than five years
  - Later than five years

## 2.5 Example: lessee disclosures

These disclosure requirements will be illustrated for Bacchus Co (above example). We will assume that Bacchus Co makes up its accounts to 31 December and uses the actuarial method to apportion finance charges.

## Solution

The company's accounts for the first year of the lease, the year ended 31 December 20X0, would include the information given below.

STATEMENT OF FINANCIAL POSITION AS AT 31 DECEMBER 20X0 (EXTRACTS)

| | $ | $ |
|---|---:|---:|
| *Non-current assets* | | |
| Assets held under finance leases | | |
| Plant and machinery at cost | 7,710 | |
| Less accumulated depreciation (20% × $7,710) | (1,542) | |
| | | 6,168 |
| *Non-current liabilities* | | |
| Obligations under finance leases | | |
| (Balance at 31 December 20X1) | | 3,251 |
| *Current liabilities* | | |
| Obligations under finance leases (4,566 – 3,251) | | 1,315 |

(Notice that only the outstanding **capital** element is disclosed under liabilities, ie the total of the minimum lease payments with future finance charges separately deducted.)

STATEMENT OF PROFIT OR LOSS
FOR THE YEAR ENDED 31 DECEMBER 20X0 (EXTRACT)

| | $ |
|---|---:|
| Interest payable and similar charges | |
| Interest on finance leases | 856 |

## 2.6 Example: 6-monthly payments

Now let us see what would change if Bacchus was not required to pay a deposit but had to pay $1,250 every 6 months for 4 years. We will use the same interest rate and calculate the amounts for the first year's financial statements.

| | $ |
|---|---:|
| Balance 1 January 20X0 | 7,710 |
| Interest to 30 June 20X0 (7,710 × 15% × 6/12) | 578 |
| Instalment paid 30 June 20X0 | (1,250) |
| Balance 30 June 20X0 | 7,038 |
| Interest to 31 December 20X0 (7,038 × 15% × 6/12) | 528 |
| Instalment paid 31 December 20X0 | (1,250) |
| Balance 31 December 20X0 | 6,316 |
| Interest to 30 June 20X1 (6,316 × 15% × 6/12) | 474 |
| Instalment paid 30 June 20X1 | (1,250) |
| Balance 30 June 20X1 | 5,540 |
| Interest to 31 December 20X0 (5,544 × 15% × 6/12) | 416 |
| Instalment paid 31 December 20X1 | (1,250) |
| Balance 31 December 20X1 | 4,706 |

*Financial statement extracts at 31 December 20X0:*

| | $ |
|---|---:|
| *Non-current assets* (as above) | 6,168 |
| *Non-current liabilities* | |
| Obligations under finance leases | 4,706 |
| *Current liabilities* | |
| Obligations under finance leases (6,316 – 4,706) | 1,610 |
| *Profit or loss: interest payable* (578 + 528) | 1,106 |

## 2.7 Operating leases: disclosures

For **operating leases** the disclosures are as follows.

The total of future minimum lease payments under non-cancellable operating leases for each of the following periods:

(a)  Not later than one year
(b)  Later than one year and not later than five years
(c)  Later than five years

## 2.8 Classification of leases

A final issue to consider is the importance of correctly classifying a lease.

A finance lease gives rise to a non-current asset and a lease liability in the statement of financial position. If it is treated as an operating lease, there will be no asset or liability in the statement of financial position. All that will be shown is the lease payments going through as an expense in the statement of profit or loss. If the asset is not shown, assets will be understated and return on capital employed (ROCE) will be overstated. If the lease liability is not shown, gearing (ratio of debt to equity) will be understated. [These ratios are covered in Chapter 19]. This is why finance leases must be accounted for according to their 'substance', rather than their legal form (under which the asset is treated as being owned by the lessor).

# Chapter Roundup

- A finance lease is a means of acquiring the long-term use of an asset whereas an operating lease is a short-term rental agreement. Substance over form is important in distinguishing between them.

- Under **finance leases**:
    - Assets acquired should be capitalised
    - Interest element of instalments should be charged against profit.

- **Operating leases** are **rental agreements** and all instalments are charged against profit.

# Quick Quiz

1   (a)   ....................leases transfer substantially all the risks and rewards of ownership.

    (b)   ....................leases are usually short-term rental agreements with the lessor being responsible for the repairs and maintenance of the asset.

2   A business acquires an asset under a finance lease. What is the double entry?

3   List the disclosures required under IAS 17 for lessees in respect of finance leases.

4   A lorry has an expected useful life of six years. It is acquired under a four year finance lease. Over which period should it be depreciated?

5   A company leases a photocopier under an operating lease which expires in June 20X2. Its office is leased under an operating lease due to expire in January 20X3. How should past and future operating leases be disclosed in its 31 December 20X1 accounts?

# Answers to Quick Quiz

1   (a)   Finance leases
    (b)   Operating leases

2   DEBIT  Asset account
    CREDIT   Lessor account

3   See Para 2.4.

4   The four year term, being the shorter of the lease term and the useful life.

5   The total operating lease rentals charged though profit or loss should be disclosed. The payments committed to should be disclosed analysing them between those falling due in the next year and the second to fifth years.

Now try the questions below from the Exam Question Bank

| Number | Level | Marks | Time |
|---|---|---|---|
| 20 | Examination | 10 | 18 mins |
| 21 | Examination | 10 | 18 mins |
| 22 | Examination | 25 | 45 mins |

# 17

# Accounting for taxation

| Topic list | Syllabus reference |
|---|---|
| 1 Current tax | C9 |
| 2 Deferred tax | C9 |
| 3 Taxable temporary differences | C9 |
| 4 Deductible temporary differences | C9 |
| 5 Measurement and recognition of deferred tax | C9 |
| 6 Taxation in company accounts | C9 |

## Introduction

In almost all countries entities are taxed on the basis of their trading income. In some countries this may be called corporation or corporate tax, but we will follow the terminology of IAS 12 *Income taxes* and call it income tax.

There are two aspects of income tax which must be accounted for: **current tax** and **deferred tax**. These will be discussed in Sections 1 and 2 respectively.

# Study guide

| | | Intellectual level |
|---|---|---|
| **9** | **Taxation** | |
| (a) | account for current taxation in accordance with relevant accounting standards. | 2 |
| (b) | record entries relating to income tax in the accounting records. | 2 |
| (c) | explain the effect of taxable temporary differences on accounting and taxable profits. | 2 |
| (d) | compute and record deferred tax amounts in the financial statements. | 2 |

# 1 Current tax

**FAST FORWARD**

Current tax is the amount payable to the tax authorities in relation to the trading activities of the period. It is generally straightforward.

## 1.1 Introduction

You may have assumed until now that accounting for income tax was a very simple matter for companies. You would calculate the amount of tax due to be paid on the company's taxable profits and you would:

DEBIT     Tax charge (statement of profit or loss)
CREDIT    Tax liability (statement of financial position)

with this amount.

Indeed, this aspect of corporate taxation – **current tax** – *is* ordinarily straightforward. Complexities arise, however, when we consider the future tax consequences of what is going on in the accounts now. This is an aspect of tax called **deferred tax**, which we will look at in the next section.

## 1.2 IAS 12 Income taxes

IAS 12 covers both current and deferred tax. The parts relating to current tax are fairly brief, because this is the simple and uncontroversial area of tax.

## 1.3 Definitions

These are some of the definitions given in IAS 12. We will look at the rest later.

**Key terms**

> - **Accounting profit**. Net profit or loss for a period before deducting tax expense.
> - **Taxable profit (tax loss)**. The profit (loss) for a period, determined in accordance with the rules established by the taxation authorities, upon which income taxes are payable (recoverable).
> - **Tax expense (tax income)**. The aggregate amount included in the determination of net profit or loss for the period in respect of current tax and deferred tax.
> - **Current tax**. The amount of income taxes payable (recoverable) in respect of the taxable profit (tax loss) for a period.
>   *(IAS 12)*

Before we go any further, let us be clear about the difference between current and deferred tax.

(a)  **Current tax** is the amount *actually payable* to the tax authorities in relation to the trading activities of the entity during the period.

(b)  **Deferred tax** is an *accounting measure*, used to match the tax effects of transactions with their accounting impact and thereby produce less distorted results.

You should understand this a little better after working through Section 2.

## 1.4 Recognition of current tax liabilities and assets

IAS 12 requires any **unpaid tax** in respect of the current or prior periods to be recognised as a **liability**.

Conversely, any **excess tax** paid in respect of current or prior periods over what is due should be recognised as an **asset**.

| Question | Current tax |
|---|---|

In 20X8 Darton Co had taxable profits of $120,000. In the previous year (20X7) income tax on 20X7 profits had been estimated as $30,000. The corporate income tax rate is 30%.

*Required*

Calculate tax payable and the charge for 20X8 if the tax due on 20X7 profits was subsequently agreed with the tax authorities as:

(a) $35,000; or
(b) $25,000.

Any under or over payments are not settled until the following year's tax payment is due.

### Answer

(a)

|  | $ |
|---|---|
| Tax due on 20X8 profits ($120,000 × 30%) | 36,000 |
| Underpayment for 20X7 | 5,000 |
| Tax charge and liability | 41,000 |

(b)

|  | $ |
|---|---|
| Tax due on 20X8 profits (as above) | 36,000 |
| Overpayment for 20X7 | (5,000) |
| Tax charge and liability | 31,000 |

Alternatively, the rebate due could be shown separately as income in the statement of comprehensive income and as an asset in the statement of financial position. An offset approach like this is, however, most likely.

Taking this a stage further, IAS 12 also requires recognition as an asset of the benefit relating to any tax loss that can be **carried back** to recover current tax of a previous period. This is acceptable because it is probable that the benefit will flow to the entity *and* it can be reliably measured.

## 1.5 Example: tax losses carried back

In 20X7 Eramu Co paid $50,000 in tax on its profits. In 20X8 the company made tax losses of $24,000. The local tax authority rules allow losses to be carried back to offset against current tax of prior years. The tax rate is 30%.

*Required*

Show the tax charge and tax liability for 20X8.

### Solution

Tax repayment due on tax losses = 30% × $24,000 = $7,200.

The double entry will be:

| | | |
|---|---|---|
| DEBIT | Tax receivable (statement of financial position) | $7,200 |
| CREDIT | Tax repayment (statement of profit or loss) | $7,200 |

The tax receivable will be shown as an asset until the repayment is received from the tax authorities.

## 1.6 Measurement

Measurement of current tax liabilities (assets) for the current and prior periods is very simple. They are measured at the **amount expected to be paid to (recovered from) the tax authorities**.

## 1.7 Recognition of current tax

Normally, current tax is recognised as income or expense and included in the net profit or loss for the period, except in two cases.

(a)     Tax arising from a **business combination** is treated differently (tax assets or liabilities of the acquired subsidiary will form part of the goodwill calculation).

(b)     Tax arising from a transaction or event which is recognised **directly in equity** (in the same or a different period).

The rule in (b) is logical. If a transaction or event is charged or credited directly to equity, rather than to profit or loss, then the related tax should be also. An example of such a situation is where, under IAS 8, an adjustment is made to the **opening balance of retained earnings** due to either a change in accounting policy that is applied retrospectively, or to the correction of a material prior period error (see Chapter 7).

## 1.8 Presentation

In the statement of financial position, **tax assets and liabilities** should be shown separately from other assets and liabilities.

Current tax assets and liabilities can be **offset**, but this should happen only when certain conditions apply.

(a)     The entity has a **legally enforceable right** to set off the recognised amounts.

(b)     The entity intends to settle the amounts on a **net basis**, or to realise the asset and settle the liability at the same time.

The **tax expense (income)** related to the profit or loss from ordinary activities should be shown in the statement of profit or loss.

The **disclosure requirements** of IAS 12 are extensive and we will look at these later in the chapter.

# 2 Deferred tax

FAST FORWARD

Deferred tax is an accounting measure used to match the tax effects of transactions with their accounting impact. It is quite complex.

**Exam focus point**

Students invariably find deferred tax very confusing. You are unlikely to be asked any very complicated questions on deferred tax in Paper 7, so concentrate on understanding and being able to explain the purpose of deferred tax and to carry out basic calculations.

## 2.1 What is deferred tax?

When a company recognises an asset or liability, it expects to **recover or settle the carrying amount** of that asset or liability. In other words, it expects to sell or use up assets, and to pay off liabilities. What happens if that recovery or settlement is likely to make future tax payments larger (or smaller) than they would otherwise have been if the recovery or settlement had no tax consequences? In these circumstances, IAS 12 requires companies to recognise a **deferred tax liability** (or **deferred tax asset**).

## 2.2 Definitions

Don't worry too much if you don't understand the concept of deferred tax yet; things should become clearer as you work through this section. First of all, here are the definitions relating to deferred tax given in IAS 12.

**Key terms**

> **Deferred tax liabilities** are the amounts of income taxes payable in future periods in respect of taxable temporary differences.
>
> **Deferred tax assets** are the amounts of income taxes recoverable in future periods in respect of:
>
> - Deductible temporary differences
> - The carry forward of unused tax losses
> - The carry forward of unused tax credits
>
> **Temporary differences** are differences between the carrying amount of an asset or liability in the statement of financial position and its tax base. Temporary differences may be either:
>
> - **Taxable temporary differences**, which are temporary differences that will result in taxable amounts in determining taxable profit (tax loss) of future periods when the carrying amount of the asset or liability is recovered or settled
>
> - **Deductible temporary differences**, which are temporary differences that will result in amounts that are deductible in determining taxable profit (tax loss) of future periods when the carrying amount of the asset or liability is recovered or settled
>
> The **tax base** of an asset or liability is the amount attributed to that asset or liability for tax purposes.
>
> *(IAS 12)*

We need to look at some of these definitions in more detail.

## 2.3 Tax base

We can expand on the definition given above by stating that the **tax base of an asset** is the amount that will be <u>deductible</u> for tax purposes against any taxable economic benefits that will flow to the entity when it recovers the carrying value of the asset. Where those economic benefits are not taxable, the tax base of the asset is the same as its carrying amount.

**Question**                                                                                      Tax base (1)

State the tax base of each of the following assets.                              $10,000 - $3,000 = $7,000

(a)    A machine cost $10,000. For tax purposes, depreciation of $3,000 has already been deducted in the current and prior periods and the remaining cost will be deductible in future periods, either as depreciation or through a deduction on disposal. Revenue generated by using the machine is taxable, any gain on disposal of the machine will be taxable and any loss on disposal will be deductible for tax purposes.

(b)    Interest receivable has a carrying amount of $1,000. The related interest revenue will be taxed on a cash basis.

(c)    Trade receivables have a carrying amount of $10,000. The related revenue has already been included in taxable profit (tax loss).

(d)    A loan receivable has a carrying amount of $1m. The repayment of the loan will have no tax consequences.

(a)    The tax base of the machine is $7,000.
(b)    The tax base of the interest receivable is nil.
(c)    The tax base of the trade receivables is $10,000.
(d)    The tax base of the loan is $1m.

In the case of a **liability**, the tax base will be its carrying amount, less any amount that will be deducted for tax purposes in relation to the liability in future periods. For revenue received in advance, the tax base of the resulting liability is its carrying amount, less any amount of the revenue that will *not* be taxable in future periods.

Question

Tax base (2)

State the tax base of each of the following liabilities.

(a)    Current liabilities include accrued expenses with a carrying amount of $1,000. The related expense will be deducted for tax purposes on a cash basis.

(b)    Current liabilities include interest revenue received in advance, with a carrying amount of $10,000. The related interest revenue was taxed on a cash basis.

(c)    Current liabilities include accrued expenses with a carrying amount of $2,000. The related expense has already been deducted for tax purposes.

(d)    Current liabilities include accrued fines and penalties with a carrying amount of $100. Fines and penalties are not deductible for tax purposes.

(e)    A loan payable has a carrying amount of $1m. The repayment of the loan will have no tax consequences.

Answer

(a)    The tax base of the accrued expenses is nil.
(b)    The tax base of the interest received in advance is nil.
(c)    The tax base of the accrued expenses is $2,000.
(d)    The tax base of the accrued fines and penalties is $100.
(e)    The tax base of the loan is $1m.

IAS 12 gives the following examples of circumstances in which the carrying amount of an asset or liability will be **equal to its tax base**.

•    **Accrued expenses** which have already been deducted in determining an enterprise's current tax liability for the current or earlier periods.

•    A **loan payable** is measured at the amount originally received and this amount is the same as the amount repayable on final maturity of the loan.

•    **Accrued expenses** which will never be deductible for tax purposes.

•    **Accrued income** will never be taxable.

## 2.4 Temporary differences

You may have found the definition of temporary differences somewhat confusing. Remember that accounting profits form the basis for computing **taxable profits**, on which the tax liability for the year is calculated; however, accounting profits and taxable profits are different. There are two reasons for the differences.

(a) **Permanent differences**. These occur when certain items of revenue or expense are excluded from the computation of taxable profits (for example, entertainment expenses may not be allowable for tax purposes).

(b) **Temporary differences**. These occur when items of revenue or expense are included in both accounting profits and taxable profits, but not for the same accounting period. For example, an expense which is allowable as a deduction in arriving at taxable profits for 20X7 might not be included in the financial accounts until 20X8 or later. In the long run, the total taxable profits and total accounting profits will be the same (except for permanent differences) so that timing differences originate in one period and are capable of reversal in one or more subsequent periods. Deferred tax is the tax attributable to **temporary differences.**

The distinction made in the definition between **taxable temporary differences** and **deductible temporary differences** can be made clearer by looking at the explanations and examples given in the standard and its appendices.

## 2.5 Section summary

- Deferred tax is an **accounting device**. It does *not* represent tax payable to the tax authorities.
- The **tax base** of an asset or liability is the value of that asset or liability for tax purposes.
- You should understand the difference between **permanent and temporary differences**.
- Deferred tax is the tax attributable to **temporary differences**.

# 3 Taxable temporary differences

**FAST FORWARD** ▶ Deferred tax assets and liabilities arise from taxable and deductible temporary differences.

**Exam focus point**

The rule to remember here is that:

'All taxable temporary differences give rise to a deferred tax liability.'

## 3.1 Examples

The following are examples of circumstances that give rise to taxable temporary differences.

### 3.1.1 Transactions that affect the statement of profit or loss

(a) **Interest revenue** received in arrears and included in accounting profit on the basis of time apportionment. It is included in taxable profit, however, on a cash basis.

(b) **Sale of goods revenue** is included in accounting profit when the goods are delivered, but only included in taxable profit when cash is received.

(c) **Depreciation** of an asset is accelerated for tax purposes. When new assets are purchased, allowances may be available against taxable profits which exceed the amount of depreciation chargeable on the assets in the financial accounts for the year of purchase.

(d) **Development costs** which have been capitalised will be amortised in the statement of profit or loss, but they were deducted in full from taxable profit in the period in which they were incurred.

(e) **Prepaid expenses** have already been deducted on a cash basis in determining the taxable profit of the current or previous periods.

### 3.1.2 Transactions that affect the statement of financial position

(a) **Accounting depreciation of an asset** is not deductible for tax purposes. Deduction for tax purposes will be allowed through tax depreciation.

(b) A borrower records a **loan** at proceeds received (amount due at maturity) less transaction costs. The carrying amount of the loan is subsequently increased by amortisation of the transaction costs against accounting profit. The transaction costs were, however, deducted for tax purposes in the period when the loan was first recognised.

### 3.1.3 Fair value adjustments and revaluations

(a)  **Current investments** or financial instruments are carried at fair value. This exceeds cost, but no equivalent adjustment is made for tax purposes.

(b)  Property, plant and equipment can be **revalued** by an entity (under IAS 16), but no equivalent adjustment is made for tax purposes. This also applies to long-term investments. As the tax base remains at the original value, there will be a difference between the carrying value and the tax base, leading to an increase in the deferred tax provision.

## 3.2 Taxable temporary differences

Try to **understand the reasoning** behind the recognition of deferred tax liabilities on taxable temporary differences.

(a)  When an **asset is recognised**, it is expected that its carrying amount will be recovered in the form of economic benefits that flow to the entity in future periods.

(b)  If the carrying amount of the asset is **greater than** its tax base, then taxable economic benefits will also be greater than the amount that will be allowed as a deduction for tax purposes.

(c)  The difference is therefore a **taxable temporary difference** and the obligation to pay the resulting income taxes in future periods is a **deferred tax liability**.

(d)  As the entity recovers the carrying amount of the asset, the taxable temporary difference will **reverse** and the enterprise will have taxable profit.

(e)  It is then probable that economic benefits will flow from the entity in the form of **tax payments**, and so the recognition of all deferred tax liabilities (except those excluded above) is required by IAS 12.

## 3.3 Example: taxable temporary differences

A company purchased an asset costing $1,500. At the end of 20X8 the carrying amount is $1,000. The cumulative depreciation for tax purposes is $900 and the current tax rate is 25%.

*Required*

Calculate the deferred tax liability for the asset.

## Solution

Firstly, what is the tax base of the asset? It is $1,500 – $900 = $600.

In order to recover the carrying value of $1,000, the entity must earn taxable income of $1,000, but it will only be able to deduct $600 as a taxable expense. The entity must therefore pay income tax of $400 × 25% = $100 when the carrying value of the asset is recovered.

The entity must therefore recognise a deferred tax liability of $400 × 25% = $100, recognising the difference between the carrying amount of $1,000 and the tax base of $600 as a taxable temporary difference.

## 3.4 Timing differences

Some temporary differences are often called **timing differences**, when income or expense is included in accounting profit in one period, but is included in taxable profit in a different period. The main types of taxable temporary differences which are timing differences and which result in deferred tax liabilities are:

• **Interest received** which is accounted for on an accruals basis, but which for tax purposes is included on a cash basis.

• **Accelerated depreciation** for tax purposes.

• Capitalised and amortised **development costs**.

## 3.5 Revalued assets

Under IAS 16 assets may be revalued. This changes the carrying amount of the asset but the tax base of the asset is not adjusted. Consequently, the taxable flow of economic benefits to the entity as the carrying value of the asset is recovered will differ from the amount that will be deductible for tax purposes.

The difference between the carrying amount of a revalued asset and its tax base is a temporary difference and gives rise to a **deferred tax liability or asset**.

The following question on accelerated depreciation should clarify some of the issues and introduce you to the calculations which may be necessary in the exam.

### Question
Current and deferred tax

Jonquil Co buys equipment for $50,000 and depreciates it on a straight line basis over its expected useful life of five years. For tax purposes, the equipment is depreciated at 25% per annum on a straight line basis. Tax losses may be carried back against taxable profit of the previous five years. In year 20X0, the entity's taxable profit was $25,000. The tax rate is 40%.

*Required*

Assuming nil profits/losses after depreciation in years 20X1 to 20X5 show the current and deferred tax impact in years 20X1 to 20X5 of the acquisition of the equipment.

### Answer

Jonquil Co will recover the carrying amount of the equipment by using it to manufacture goods for resale. Therefore, the entity's current tax computation is as follows.

|  | Year | | | | |
|---|---|---|---|---|---|
|  | *20X1* | *20X2* | *20X3* | *20X4* | *20X5* |
|  | $ | $ | $ | $ | $ |
| Taxable income* | 10,000 | 10,000 | 10,000 | 10,000 | 10,000 |
| Depreciation for tax purposes | 12,500 | 12,500 | 12,500 | 12,500 | 0 |
| Taxable profit (tax loss) | (2,500) | (2,500) | (2,500) | (2,500) | 10,000 |
| Current tax expense (income) at 40% | (1,000) | (1,000) | (1,000) | (1,000) | 4,000 |

\* ie nil profit plus $50,000 ÷ 5 depreciation add-back.

The entity recognises a current tax asset at the end of years 20X1 to 20X4 because it recovers the benefit of the tax loss against the taxable profit of year 20X0.

The temporary differences associated with the equipment and the resulting deferred tax asset and liability and deferred tax expense and income are as follows.

|  | Year | | | | |
|---|---|---|---|---|---|
|  | *20X1* | *20X2* | *20X3* | *20X4* | *20X5* |
|  | $ | $ | $ | $ | $ |
| Carrying amount | 40,000 | 30,000 | 20,000 | 10,000 | 0 |
| Tax base | 37,500 | 25,000 | 12,500 | 0 | 0 |
| Taxable temporary difference | 2,500 | 5,000 | 7,500 | 10,000 | 0 |
| Opening deferred tax liability | 0 | 1,000 | 2,000 | 3,000 | 4,000 |
| Deferred tax expense (income): bal fig | 1,000 | 1,000 | 1,000 | 1,000 | (4,000) |
| Closing deferred tax liability @ 40% | 1,000 | 2,000 | 3,000 | 4,000 | 0 |

The entity recognises the deferred tax liability in years 20X1 to 20X4 because the reversal of the taxable temporary difference will create taxable income in subsequent years. The entity's statement of profit or loss is as follows.

| | | | Year | | |
|---|---|---|---|---|---|
| | 20X1 | 20X2 | 20X3 | 20X4 | 20X5 |
| | $ | $ | $ | $ | $ |
| Income | 10,000 | 10,000 | 10,000 | 10,000 | 10,000 |
| Depreciation | 10,000 | 10,000 | 10,000 | 10,000 | 10,000 |
| Profit before tax | 0 | 0 | 0 | 0 | 0 |
| Current tax expense (income) | (1,000) | (1,000) | (1,000) | (1,000) | 4,000 |
| Deferred tax expense (income) | 1,000 | 1,000 | 1,000 | 1,000 | (4,000) |
| Total tax expense (income) | 0 | 0 | 0 | 0 | 0 |
| Net profit for the year | 0 | 0 | 0 | 0 | 0 |

## 3.6 Section summary

- Taxable temporary differences give rise to a **deferred tax liability**.
- Many taxable temporary differences are **timing differences**.
- Timing differences arise when income or an expense is included in accounting profit in one period, but in taxable profit in a **different period**.

# 4 Deductible temporary differences

## 4.1 Definition

Refer again to the definition given in Section 2 above.

**Exam focus point**

The rule to remember here is that:

'All deductible temporary differences give rise to a deferred tax asset.'

There is a proviso, however. The deferred tax asset must also satisfy the **recognition criteria** given in IAS 12. This is that a deferred tax asset should be recognised for all deductible temporary differences to the extent that it is **probable that taxable profit will be available** against which it can be utilised. This is an application of prudence. Before we look at this issue in more detail, let us consider the examples of deductible temporary differences given in the standard.

## 4.2 Transactions that affect the statement of profit or loss

(a) **Retirement benefit costs** (pension costs) are deducted from accounting profit as service is provided by the employee. They are not deducted in determining taxable profit until the entity pays either retirement benefits or contributions to a fund. (This may also apply to similar expenses.)

(b) **Accumulated depreciation** of an asset in the financial statements is greater than the accumulated depreciation allowed for tax purposes up to the end of the reporting period.

(c) The **cost of inventories** sold before the end of the reporting period is deducted from accounting profit when goods/services are delivered, but is deducted from taxable profit when the cash is received. (*Note.* There is also a taxable temporary difference associated with the related trade receivable, as noted in Section 3 above.)

(d) The **NRV** of inventory, or the **recoverable amount** of an item of property, plant and equipment falls and the carrying value is therefore **reduced**, but that reduction is ignored for tax purposes until the asset is sold.

(e) **Research costs** (or organisation/other start-up costs) are recognised as an expense for accounting purposes but are not deductible against taxable profits until a later period.

(f) Income is **deferred** in the statement of financial position, but has already been included in taxable profit in current/prior periods.

(g)    A **government grant** is included in the statement of financial position as deferred income, but it will not be taxable in future periods. (*Note.* A deferred tax asset may *not* be recognised here according to the standard.)

## 4.3 Fair value adjustments and revaluations

**Current investments** or **financial instruments** may be carried at fair value which is less than cost, but no equivalent adjustment is made for tax purposes.

## 4.4 Recognition of deductible temporary differences

Let us lay out the reasoning behind the recognition of deferred tax assets arising from deductible temporary differences.

(a)    When a **liability is recognised**, it is assumed that its carrying amount will be settled in the form of outflows of economic benefits from the entity in future periods.

(b)    When these resources flow from the entity, part or all may be deductible in determining taxable profits of a **period later** than that in which the liability is recognised.

(c)    A **temporary tax difference** then exists between the carrying amount of the liability and its tax base.

(d)    A **deferred tax asset** therefore arises, representing the income taxes that will be recoverable in future periods when that part of the liability is allowed as a deduction from taxable profit.

(e)    Similarly, when the carrying amount of an asset is **less than its tax base**, the difference gives rise to a deferred tax asset in respect of the income taxes that will be recoverable in future periods.

## 4.5 Example: deductible temporary differences

Pargatha Co recognises a liability of $10,000 for accrued product warranty costs on 31 December 20X7. These product warranty costs will not be deductible for tax purposes until the entity pays claims. The tax rate is 25%.

*Required*

State the deferred tax implications of this situation.

## Solution

What is the tax base of the liability? It is nil (carrying amount of $10,000 less the amount that will be deductible for tax purposes in respect of the liability in future periods).

When the liability is settled for its carrying amount, the entity's future taxable profit will be reduced by $10,000 and so its future tax payments by $10,000 × 25% = $2,500.

The difference of $10,000 between the carrying amount ($10,000) and the tax base (nil) is a deductible temporary difference. The entity should therefore recognise a deferred tax asset of $10,000 × 25% = $2,500 **provided that** it is probable that the entity will earn sufficient taxable profits in future periods to benefit from a reduction in tax payments.

## 4.6 Taxable profits in future periods

When can we be sure that sufficient taxable profit will be available against which a deductible temporary difference can be utilised? IAS 12 states that this will be assumed when sufficient **taxable temporary differences** exist which relate to the same taxation authority and the same taxable entity. These should be expected to reverse:

(a)    In the same period as the expected reversal of the deductible temporary difference, *or*

(b)    In periods into which a tax loss arising from the deferred tax asset can be carried back or forward.

Only in these circumstances is the deferred tax asset **recognised**, in the period in which the deductible temporary differences arise.

### 4.7 Unused tax losses and unused tax credits

An entity may have unused tax losses or credits (ie which it can offset against taxable profits) at the end of a period. Should a deferred tax asset be recognised in relation to such amounts? IAS 12 states that a deferred tax asset may be recognised in such circumstances **to the extent that it is probable future taxable profit will be available against which the unused tax losses/credits can be utilised.**

### 4.8 Section summary

- Deductible temporary differences give rise to a **deferred tax asset**.
- **Prudence** dictates that deferred tax assets can only be recognised when **sufficient future taxable profits** exist against which they can be utilised.

# 5 Measurement and recognition of deferred tax

## 5.1 Basis of provision of deferred tax

IAS 12 adopts the **full provision** method of accounting for deferred tax.

The **full provision method** has the **advantage** that it recognises that each timing difference at the end of the reporting period has an effect on future tax payments. If a company claims an accelerated tax allowance on an item of plant, future tax assessments will be bigger than they would have been otherwise. Future transactions may well affect those assessments still further, but that is not relevant in assessing the position at the end of the reporting period.

## 5.2 Example

Suppose that Girdo Co begins trading on 1 January 20X7. In its first year it makes profits of $5m, the depreciation charge is $1m and the tax allowances on those assets is $1.5m. The rate of income tax is 30%.

### Solution

The tax liability is $1.35m (30% × $m(5.0 + 1.0 −1.5), but the debit to profit or loss is increased by the deferred tax liability of 30% × $0.5m = $150,000. The total charge to profit or loss is therefore $1.5m which is an effective tax rate of 30% on accounting profits (ie 30% × $5.0m).

## 5.3 Changes in tax rates

Where the corporate rate of income tax **fluctuates from one year to another**, a problem arises in respect of the amount of deferred tax to be credited (debited) to the statement of profit or loss in later years.

IAS 12 requires deferred tax assets and liabilities to be measured at the tax rates expected to apply in the period **when the asset is realised or liability settled**, based on tax rates and laws enacted (or substantively enacted) at the end of the reporting period. In other words, IAS 12 requires the **liability method** to be used.

## 5.4 Discounting

Discounting is used to allow for the effect of the time value of money.

IAS 12 states that deferred tax assets and liabilities **should not be discounted** because of the complexities and difficulties involved. Discounting is applied to other non-current liabilities such as provisions and deferred payments.

## 5.5 Carrying amount of deferred tax assets

The carrying amount of deferred tax assets should be **reviewed at the end of each reporting period** and reduced where appropriate (insufficient future taxable profits). Such a reduction may be reversed in future years.

## 5.6 Recognition

As with current tax, deferred tax should normally be recognised as income or an expense and included in the net profit or loss for the year in the **statement of profit or loss**. Current and deferred tax will together make up the tax charge. The exception is where the tax arises from a transaction or event which is recognised (in the same or a different period) **directly in equity**.

The figures shown for deferred tax in the statement of profit or loss will consist of **two components**.

(a)   Deferred tax relating to **timing differences**.

(b)   Adjustments relating to **changes in the carrying amount of deferred tax assets/liabilities** (where there is no change in timing differences), eg changes in tax rates/laws, reassessment of the recoverability of deferred tax assets, or a change in the expected recovery of an asset.

Items in (b) will be recognised in profit or loss, *unless* they relate to items previously charged/credited to equity.

Deferred tax (and current tax) should be **charged/credited directly to equity** if the tax relates to items also charged/credited directly to equity (in the same or a different period).

Examples of IASs which allow certain items to be credited/charged directly to equity include:

(a)   **Revaluations** of property, plant and equipment (IAS 16), and

(b)   The effect of a **change in accounting policy** (applied retrospectively) or correction of a **material error** (IAS 8)

Revaluations will appear under 'other comprehensive income' in the statement of profit or loss and other comprehensive income and the tax element will be shown separately as 'Income tax relating to components of other comprehensive income'.

### 5.6.1 Example

Z Co owns a property which has a carrying value at the beginning of 20X9 of $1,500,000. At the year end it has entered into a contract to sell the property for $1,800,000. The tax rate is 30%. How will this be shown in the financial statements?

### Solution

STATEMENT OF PROFIT OR LOSS AND OTHER COMPREHENSIVE INCOME (EXTRACT)

|  | $'000 |
|---|---|
| Profit for the year | X |
| Other comprehensive income: |  |
| Gains on property revaluation | 300 |
| Income tax relating to components of other comprehensive income (300 × 30%) | (90) |
| Other comprehensive income for the year net of tax | 210 |

The amounts will be posted as follows:

|  | Dr | Cr |
|---|---|---|
|  | $'000 | $'000 |
| Property, plant and equipment | 300 |  |
| Deferred tax |  | 90 |
| Revaluation surplus |  | 210 |

## 5.7 Why do we recognise deferred tax?

(a) Adjustments for deferred tax are made in accordance with the **accruals concept** and in accordance with the definition of a **liability** in the Conceptual Framework, ie a past event has given rise to an obligation in the form of increased taxation which will be payable in the future. The amount can be reliably estimated. A deferred tax asset similarly meets the definition of an **asset**.

(b) If the future tax consequences of transactions are not recognised, profit can be overstated, leading to overpayment of dividends and distortion of share price and EPS.

# 6 Taxation in company accounts

In the statement of financial position the liability for tax payable is the tax on the current year profits. In the statement of profit or loss the tax on the current year profits is adjusted for transfers to or from the deferred tax balance and for prior year under– or over-provisions.

We have now looked at the 'ingredients' of taxation in company accounts. There are two aspects to be learned:

(a) Taxation on profits in the statement of profit or loss.
(b) Taxation payments due, shown as a liability in the statement of financial position.

## 6.1 Taxation in the statement of profit or loss

The tax on profit on ordinary activities is calculated by **aggregating**:

(a) **Income tax** on taxable profits
(b) **Transfers to or from deferred taxation**
(c) Any **under provision or overprovision** of income tax on profits of previous years

When income tax on profits is calculated, **the calculation is only an estimate of what the company thinks its tax liability will be. In subsequent dealings with the tax authorities, a different income tax charge might eventually be agreed.**

The difference between the estimated tax on profits for one year and the actual tax charge finally agreed for the year is made as an adjustment to taxation on profits in the following year, **resulting in the disclosure of either an underprovision or an overprovision of tax.**

### Question

Tax payable

In the accounting year to 31 December 20X3, Neil Down Co made an operating profit before taxation of $110,000.

Income tax on the operating profit has been estimated as $45,000. In the previous year (20X2) income tax on 20X2 profits had been estimated as $38,000 but it was subsequently agreed at $40,500.

A transfer to the credit of the deferred taxation account of $16,000 will be made in 20X3.

*Required*

(a) Calculate the tax on profits for 20X3 for disclosure in the accounts.
(b) Calculate the amount of tax payable.

### Answer

(a)

| | $ |
|---|---|
| Income tax on profits (liability in the statement of FP) | 45,000 |
| Deferred taxation | 16,000 |
| Underprovision of tax in previous year $(40,500 – 38,000) | 2,500 |
| Tax on profits for 20X3 (profit or loss charge) | 63,500 |

(b)

| | $ |
|---|---|
| Tax payable on 20X3 profits (liability) | 45,000 |

## 6.2 Taxation in the statement of financial position

It should already be apparent from the previous examples that the income tax charge in the statement of profit or loss will not be the same as income tax liabilities in the statement of financial position.

In the statement of financial position, there are several items which we might expect to find.

(a) **Income tax may be payable** in respect of (say) interest payments paid in the last accounting return period of the year, or accrued.

(b) If no tax is payable (or very little), then there might be an **income tax recoverable asset** disclosed in current assets (income tax is normally recovered by offset against the tax liability for the year).

(c) There will usually be a **liability for tax**, possibly including the amounts due in respect of previous years but not yet paid.

(d) We may also find a **liability on the deferred taxation account**. Deferred taxation is shown under 'non-current liabilities' in the statement of financial position.

Question                                                                 Tax charge

For the year ended 31 July 20X4 Norman Kronkest Co made taxable trading profits of $1,200,000 on which income tax is payable at 30%.

(a) A transfer of $20,000 will be made to the deferred taxation account. The balance on this account was $100,000 before making any adjustments for items listed in this paragraph.

(b) The estimated tax on profits for the year ended 31 July 20X3 was $80,000, but tax has now been agreed at $84,000 and fully paid.

(c) Tax on profits for the year to 31 July 20X4 is payable on 1 May 20X5.

(d) In the year to 31 July 20X4 the company made a capital gain of $60,000 on the sale of some property. This gain is taxable at a rate of 30%.

*Required*

(a) Calculate the tax charge for the year to 31 July 20X4.

(b) Calculate the tax liabilities in the statement of financial position of Norman Kronkest as at 31 July 20X4.

Answer

(a) *Tax charge for the year*

| | | $ |
|---|---|---|
| (i) | Tax on trading profits (30% of 1,200,000) | 360,000 |
| | Tax on capital gain (30% of 60,000) | 18,000 |
| | Deferred taxation | 20,000 |
| | | 398,000 |
| | Underprovision of taxation in previous years $(84,000 – 80,000) | 4,000 |
| | Tax charge on profit for the period | 402,000 |

(ii) *Note.* The statement of profit or loss will show the following.

| | $ |
|---|---|
| Profit before tax (1,200,000 + 60,000) | 1,260,000 |
| Income tax expense | (402,000) |
| Profit for the year | 858,000 |

(b)

| | $ |
|---|---:|
| *Deferred taxation* | |
| Balance brought forward | 100,000 |
| Transferred from profit or loss | 20,000 |
| Deferred taxation in the statement of financial position | 120,000 |

The tax liability is as follows.

| | $ |
|---|---:|
| Payable on 1 May 20X5 | |
| Tax on profits (30% of $1,200,000) | 360,000 |
| Tax on capital gain (30% of $60,000) | 18,000 |
| Due on 1 May 20X5 | 378,000 |

| | $ |
|---|---:|
| *Summary* | |
| *Current liabilities* | |
| Tax, payable on 1 May 20X5 | 378,000 |
| *Non-current liabilities* | |
| Deferred taxation | 120,000 |

*Note.* It may be helpful to show the journal entries for these items.

| | | $ | $ |
|---|---|---:|---:|
| DEBIT | Tax charge (statement of profit or loss) | 402,000 | |
| CREDIT | Tax payable | | *382,000 |
| | Deferred tax | | 20,000 |

\* This account will show a debit balance of $4,000 until the underprovision is recorded, since payment has already been made: (360,000 + 18,000 + 4,000). The closing balance will therefore be $378,000.

## 6.3 Presentation of tax assets and liabilities

These should be **presented separately** from other assets and liabilities in the statement of financial position. Deferred tax assets and liabilities should be distinguished from current tax assets and liabilities.

In addition, deferred tax assets/liabilities should *not* be classified as current assets/liabilities, where an entity makes such a distinction.

There are only limited circumstances where **current tax** assets and liabilities may be **offset**. This should only occur if two things apply

(a) The entity has a legally enforceable right to set off the recognised amounts.
(b) The entity intends either to settle on a net basis, or to realise the asset and settle the liability simultaneously.

Similar criteria apply to the **offset of deferred tax assets and liabilities**.

## 6.4 Presentation of tax expense

The tax expense or income related to the profit or loss for the year should be presented in the statement of profit or loss.

# Chapter roundup

- **Current tax** is the amount payable to the tax authorities in relation to the trading activities during the period. It is generally straightforward.

- **Deferred tax** is an accounting measure, used to match the tax effects of transactions with their accounting impact. It is quite complex.

- **Deferred tax assets and liabilities** arise from deductible and taxable temporary differences.

- In the statement of financial position the liability for tax payable is the tax on the current year profits. In the statement of profit or loss the tax on current year profits is adjusted for transfers to or from the deferred tax balance and for prior year under- and over-provisions.

# Quick quiz

1   The tax expense related to the profit for the year should be shown in the statement of profit or loss.

    True    ☐

    False   ☐

2   Deferred tax liabilities are the amounts of income taxes payable in future periods in respect of
    ....................

3   Give three examples of temporary differences.

4   An entity has a tax overprovision relating to the prior year of $3,000. Taxable temporary differences have increased by $6,000 and profit for the year is $150,000. Tax is at 30%.
What is the charge to profit or loss?

# Answers to quick quiz

1    True

2    Taxable temporary differences

3    Any three of:

- Interest revenue received in arrears
- Depreciation accelerated for tax purposes
- Development costs capitalised in the statement of financial position
- Prepayments
- Sale of goods revenue recognised before the cash is received

4    $43,800

|  | $ |
|---|---|
| Tax on profit (150,000 × 30%) | 45,000 |
| Overprovision | (3,000) |
| Deferred tax increase (6,000 × 30%) | 1,800 |
|  | 43,800 |

Now try the question below from the Exam Question Bank

| Number | Level | Marks | Time |
|---|---|---|---|
| 23 | Examination | 15 | 27 mins |

# Earnings per share

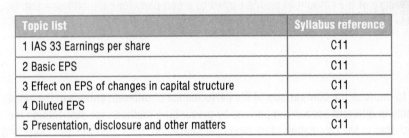

| Topic list | Syllabus reference |
|---|---|
| 1 IAS 33 Earnings per share | C11 |
| 2 Basic EPS | C11 |
| 3 Effect on EPS of changes in capital structure | C11 |
| 4 Diluted EPS | C11 |
| 5 Presentation, disclosure and other matters | C11 |

## Introduction

**Earnings per share** (EPS) is widely used by investors as a measure of a company's performance and is of particular importance in:

(a) **Comparing the results** of a company over a **period of time**

(b) **Comparing the performance** of one company's equity against the performance of **another company's equity**, and also against the returns obtainable from loan stock and other forms of investment.

The purpose of any earnings yardstick is to achieve as far as possible clarity of meaning, comparability between one company and another, one year and another, and attributability of profits to the equity shares. IAS 33 *Earnings per share* goes some way to ensuring that all these aims are achieved.

# Study guide

| | | Intellectual level |
|---|---|---|
| **C** | **FINANCIAL STATEMENTS** | |
| **11** | **Reporting financial performance** | |
| (f) | earning per share (eps) | |
| | (i) calculate the eps in accordance with relevant accounting standards (dealing with bonus issues, full market value issues and rights issues) | 2 |
| | (ii) explain the relevance of the diluted eps and calculate the diluted eps involving convertible debt and share options (warrants) | 2 |
| | (iii) explain why the trend of eps may be a more accurate indicator of performance than a company's profit trend and the importance of eps as a stock market indicator. | 2 |
| | (iv) discuss the limitations of using eps as a performance measure. | 2 |

# 1 IAS 33 Earnings per share

FAST FORWARD

**Earnings per share** is a measure of the amount of profits earned by a company for each ordinary share. Earnings are profits after tax and preference dividends.

## 1.1 Objective

The objective of IAS 33 is to improve the **comparison** of the performance of different entities in the same period and of the same entity in different accounting periods by prescribing methods for determining the number of shares to be included in the calculation of earnings per share and other amounts per share and by specifying their presentation.

## 1.2 Definitions

The following definitions are given in IAS 33 and IAS 32.

**Key terms**

- **Ordinary shares**: an equity instrument that is subordinate to all other classes of equity instruments.
- **Potential ordinary share:** a financial instrument or other contract that may entitle its holder to ordinary shares.
- **Options, warrants and their equivalents**: financial instruments that give the holder the right to purchase ordinary shares.
  *(IAS 33)*
- **Financial instrument**: any contract that gives rise to both a financial asset of one entity and a financial liability or equity instrument of another entity.
- **Equity instrument**: any contract that evidences a residual interest in the assets of an entity after deducting all of its liabilities.
  *(IAS 32)*

### 1.2.1 Ordinary shares

There may be more than one class of ordinary shares, but ordinary shares of the same class will have the same rights to receive dividends. Ordinary shares participate in the net profit for the period **only after other types of shares**, eg preference shares.

### 1.2.2 Potential ordinary shares

IAS 33 identifies the following examples of financial instruments and other contracts generating potential ordinary shares.

(a) **Debt or equity instruments**, including preference shares, that are convertible into ordinary shares

(b) **Share warrants and options**

(c) **Employee plans** that allow employees to receive ordinary shares as part of their remuneration and other share purchase plans

(d) Shares that would be issued upon the satisfaction of **certain conditions** resulting from contractual arrangements, such as the purchase of a business or other assets

## 1.3 Scope

IAS 33 has the following scope restrictions.

(a) Only companies with (potential) ordinary shares which are **publicly traded** need to present EPS (including companies in the process of being listed).

(b) EPS need only be presented on the basis of **consolidated results** where the parent's results are shown as well.

(c) Where companies **choose** to present EPS, even when they have no (potential) ordinary shares which are traded, they must do so in accordance with IAS 33.

# 2 Basic EPS

**Basic EPS** is calculated by dividing the net profit or loss for the period attributable to ordinary shareholders by the weighted average number of ordinary shares outstanding during the period.

## 2.1 Measurement

**Basic EPS** should be calculated by dividing the **net profit** or loss for the period attributable to ordinary shareholders by the **weighted average number of ordinary shares** outstanding during the period.

$$\text{Basic EPS} = \frac{\text{Net profit /(loss) attributable to ordinary shareholders}}{\text{Weighted average number of ordinary shares outstanding during the period}}$$

## 2.2 Earnings

Earnings includes **all items of income and expense** (including tax and non-controlling interests) *less* the results of discontinued operations where these are presented, *less* net profit attributable to **preference shareholders**, including preference dividends.

**Preference dividends** deducted from net profit consist of:

(a) Preference dividends on non-cumulative preference shares declared in respect of the period

(b) The full amount of the required preference dividends for cumulative preference shares for the period, *whether or not* they have been declared (*excluding* those paid/declared during the period in respect of previous periods)

*Note.* In an exam question any preference shares will be redeemable and the dividend will already have been accounted for under finance costs.

## 2.3 Per share

The number of ordinary shares used should be the weighted average number of ordinary shares during the period. This figure (for all periods presented) should be **adjusted for events**, other than the conversion of potential ordinary shares, that have changed the number of shares outstanding without a corresponding change in resources.

The **time-weighting factor** is the number of days the shares were outstanding compared with the total number of days in the period; a reasonable approximation is usually adequate.

## 2.4 Example: weighted average number of shares

Justina Co, a listed company, has the following share transactions during 20X7.

| Date | Details | Shares issued |
|---|---|---|
| 1 January 20X7 | Balance at beginning of year | 170,000 |
| 31 May 20X7 | Issue of new shares for cash | 80,000 |
| 31 December 20X7 | Balance at year end | 250,000 |

*Required*

Calculate the weighted average number of shares outstanding for 20X7.

## Solution

The weighted average number of shares can be calculated in two ways.

(a)  $(170,000 \times 5/12) + (250,000 \times 7/12) = 216,666$ shares
(b)  $(170,000 \times 12/12) + (80,000 \times 7/12) = 216,666$ shares

## 2.5 Consideration

Shares are usually included in the weighted average number of shares from the **date consideration is receivable** which is usually the date of issue. The treatment for the issue of ordinary shares in different circumstances is as follows.

Ordinary shares issued as **purchase consideration** in an acquisition should be included as of the date of acquisition because the acquired entity's results will also be included from that date.

If ordinary shares are **partly paid**, they are treated as a fraction of an ordinary share to the extent they are entitled to dividends relative to fully paid ordinary shares.

**Contingently issuable shares** (including those subject to recall) are included in the computation when all necessary conditions for issue have been satisfied.

Question

Basic EPS

Flame Co is a company with a called up and paid up capital of 100,000 ordinary shares of $1 each and 20,000 10% redeemable preference shares of $1 each.

The gross profit was $200,000 and trading expenses were $50,000. Flame Co paid the required preference share dividend and an ordinary dividend of 42c per share. The tax charge for the year was estimated at $40,000.

Calculate basic EPS for the year.

FLAME CO
TRADING RESULTS FOR YEAR TO 31 DECEMBER

|  | $ |
|---|---|
| Gross profit | 200,000 |
| Expense (50,000 + 2,000 preference dividend) | (52,000) |
| Profit before tax | 148,000 |
| Income tax expense | (40,000) |
| Profit for the year | 108,000 |

EARNINGS PER SHARE

$$\frac{108,000}{100,000} = 108c$$

# 3 Effect on EPS of changes in capital structure

**FAST FORWARD**

You should know how to calculate **basic EPS** and how to deal with related complications (issue of shares for cash, bonus issues, rights issues).

## 3.1 Introduction

We looked at the effect of issues of new shares on basic EPS above. In these situations, the corresponding figures for EPS for the previous year will be comparable with the current year because, as the weighted average number of shares has risen, there has been a **corresponding increase in resources**. Money has been received when shares were issued. It is assumed that shares are issued at full market price.

## 3.2 Example: earnings per share with a new issue

On 30 September 20X2, Boffin Co made an issue at full market price of 1,000,000 ordinary shares. The company's accounting year runs from 1 January to 31 December. Relevant information for 20X1 and 20X2 is as follows.

|  | 20X2 | 20X1 |
|---|---|---|
| Shares in issue as at 31 December | 9,000,000 | 8,000,000 |
| Profits after tax and preference dividend | $3,300,000 | $3,280,000 |

*Required*

Calculate the EPS for 20X2 and the corresponding figure for 20X1.

## Solution

|  | 20X2 | 20X1 |
|---|---|---|
| Weighted average number of shares |  |  |
| 8 million × 9/12 | 6,000,000 |  |
| 9 million × 3/12 | 2,250,000 |  |
|  | 8,250,000 | 8,000,000 |
| Earnings | $3,300,000 | $3,280,000 |
| EPS | 40 cents | 41 cents |

In spite of the increase in total earnings by $20,000 in 20X2, the EPS is not as good as in 20X1, because there was extra capital employed for the final 3 months of 20X2.

There are other events, however, which change the number of shares outstanding, **without a corresponding change in resources**. In these circumstances it is necessary to make adjustments so that the current and prior period EPS figures are comparable.

Four such events are considered by IAS 33.

(a) **Capitalisation or bonus issue** (sometimes called a stock dividend)
(b) Bonus element in any other issue, eg a **rights issue** to existing shareholders
(c) **Share split**
(d) **Reverse share split** (consolidation of shares)

## 3.3 Capitalisation/bonus issue and share split/reverse share split

These two types of event can be considered together as they have a similar effect. In both cases, ordinary shares are issued to existing shareholders for **no additional consideration**. The number of ordinary shares has increased without an increase in resources.

This problem is solved by **adjusting the number of ordinary shares outstanding before the event** for the proportionate change in the number of shares outstanding as if the event had occurred at the beginning of the earliest period reported.

## 3.4 Example: earnings per share with a bonus issue

Greymatter Co had 400,000 shares in issue, until on 30 September 20X2 it made a bonus issue of 100,000 shares. Calculate the EPS for 20X2 and the corresponding figure for 20X1 if total earnings were $80,000 in 20X2 and EPS for 20X1 was 18.75c. The company's accounting year runs from 1 January to 31 December.

## Solution

|                    | 20X2         |
|--------------------|--------------|
| Earnings           | $80,000      |
| Shares at 1 January | 400,000     |
| Bonus issue        | 100,000      |
|                    | 500,000 shares |
| EPS                | 16c          |

The number of shares for 20X1 must also be adjusted if the figures for EPS are to remain comparable.

The EPS for 20X1 is therefore restated as:

$$18.75c \times \frac{400}{500} = 15c$$

## 3.5 Rights issue

A rights issue of shares is an issue of new shares to existing shareholders **at a price below the current market value**. The offer of new shares is made on the basis of x new shares for every y shares currently held; eg a 1 for 3 rights issue is an offer of 1 new share at the offer price for every 3 shares currently held. This means that there is a bonus element included.

To arrive at figures for EPS when a rights issue is made, we need to calculate first of all the **theoretical ex-rights price**. This is a weighted average value per share, and is perhaps explained most easily with a numerical example.

## 3.6 Example: theoretical ex-rights price

Suppose that Egghead Co has 10,000,000 shares in issue. It now proposes to make a 1 for 4 rights issue at a price of $3 per share. The market value of existing shares on the final day before the issue is made is $3.50 (this is the 'with rights' value). What is the theoretical ex-rights price per share?

## Solution

|                                          | $        |
|------------------------------------------|----------|
| Before issue 4 shares, value $3.50 each  | 14.00    |
| Rights issue 1 share, value $3           | 3.00     |
| Theoretical value of 5 shares            | 17.00    |

Theoretical ex-rights price = $\dfrac{\$17.00}{5}$ = $3.40 per share

Note that this calculation can alternatively be performed using the total value and number of outstanding shares.

### 3.7 Procedures

The procedures for calculating the EPS for the current year and a corresponding figure for the previous year are now as follows.

(a) The **EPS for the corresponding previous period** should be multiplied by the following fraction. (*Note.* The market price on the last day of quotation is taken as the fair value immediately prior to exercise of the rights, as required by the standard.)

**Formula to learn**

$$\dfrac{\text{Theoretical ex - rights fair value per share}}{\text{Fair value per share immediately before the exercise of rights (cum rights price)}}$$

(b) To obtain the **EPS for the current year** you should:

   (i) Multiply the number of shares before the rights issue by the fraction of the year before the date of issue and by the following fraction

**Formula to learn**

$$\dfrac{\text{Fair value per share immediately before the exercise of rights (cum rights price)}}{\text{Theoretical ex - rights fair value per share}}$$

   (ii) Multiply the number of shares after the rights issue by the fraction of the year after the date of issue and add to the figure arrived at in (i)

The total earnings should then be divided by the total number of shares so calculated.

### 3.8 Example: earnings per share with a rights issue

Brains Co had 100,000 shares in issue, but then makes a 1 for 5 rights issue on 1 October 20X2 at a price of $1. The market value on the last day of quotation with rights was $1.60.

Calculate the EPS for the year ended 31 December 20X2 and the corresponding figure for 20X1 given total earnings of $50,000 in 20X2 and $40,000 in 20X1.

### Solution

Calculation of theoretical ex-rights price:

|                                          | $        |
|------------------------------------------|----------|
| Before issue 5 shares, value × $1.60     | 8.00     |
| Rights issue 1 share, value × $1.00      | 1.00     |
| Theoretical value of 6 shares            | 9.00     |

Theoretical ex-rights price = $\dfrac{\$9}{6}$ = $1.50

*EPS for 20X1*

EPS as calculated before taking into account the rights issue = 40c ($40,000 divided by 100,000 shares).

$$EPS = \frac{1.50}{1.60} \times 40c = 37\frac{1}{2}c$$

(Remember: this is the corresponding value for 20X1 which will be shown in the financial statements for Brains Co at the end of 20X2.)

*EPS for 20X2*

Number of shares before the rights issue was 100,000. 20,000 shares were issued.

| | | |
|---|---|---:|
| Stage 1: | $100,000 \times {}^9/_{12} \times \dfrac{1.60}{1.50}$ | 80,000 |
| Stage 2: | $120,000 \times {}^3/_{12}$ | 30,000 |
| | | 110,000 |

$$EPS = \frac{\$50,000}{110,000} = 45\frac{1}{2}c$$

The figure for total earnings is the actual earnings for the year.

## Question

**Rights issue**

Marcoli Co has produced the following net profit figures for the years ending 31 December.

| | $m |
|---|---:|
| 20X6 | 1.1 |
| 20X7 | 1.5 |
| 20X8 | 1.8 |

On 1 January 20X7 the number of shares outstanding was 500,000. During 20X7 the company announced a rights issue with the following details.

| | |
|---|---|
| Rights: | 1 new share for each 5 outstanding (100,000 new shares in total) |
| Exercise price: | $5.00 |
| Last date to exercise rights: | 1 March 20X7 |

The market (fair) value of one share in Marcoli immediately prior to exercise on 1 March 20X7 = $11.00.

*Required*

Calculate the EPS for 20X6, 20X7 and 20X8.

## Answer

*Computation of theoretical ex-rights price*

This computation uses the total fair value and number of shares.

$$\frac{\text{Fair value of all outstanding shares} + \text{total received from exercise of rights}}{\text{No shares outstanding prior to exercise} + \text{no shares issued in exercise}}$$

$$= \frac{(\$11.00 \times 500,000) + (\$5.00 \times 100,000)}{500,000 + 100,000} = \$10.00$$

*Computation of EPS*

|  | | 20X6 $ | 20X7 $ | 20X8 $ |
|---|---|---|---|---|
| 20X6 | EPS as originally reported $$\frac{\$1,100,000}{500,000}$$ | 2.20 | | |
| 20X6 | EPS restated for rights issue $$\frac{\$1,100,000}{500,000} \times \frac{10}{11}$$ | 2.00 | | |
| 20X7 | EPS including effects of rights issue $$\frac{\$1,500,000}{(500,000 \times 2/12 \times 11/10) + (600,000 \times 10/12)}$$ | | 2.54 | |
| 20X8 | $$EPS = \frac{\$1,800,000}{600,000}$$ | | | 3.00 |

**Exam focus point**

You should know how to deal with the effect on EPS of bonus and rights issues and be able to calculate diluted EPS.

# 4 Diluted EPS

**FAST FORWARD**

**Diluted EPS** is calculated by adjusting the net profit due to continuing operations attributable to ordinary shareholders and the weighted average number of shares outstanding for the effects of all dilutive potential ordinary shares.

## 4.1 Introduction

At the end of an accounting period, a company may have in issue some **securities** which do not (at present) have any 'claim' to a share of equity earnings, but **may give rise to such a claim in the future**. These securities include:

(a) A **separate class of equity shares** which at present is not entitled to any dividend, but will be entitled after some future date

(b) **Convertible loan stock** or **convertible preferred shares** which give their holders the right at some future date to exchange their securities for ordinary shares of the company, at a pre-determined conversion rate

(c) **Options** or **warrants**

In such circumstances, the future number of ordinary shares in issue might increase, which in turn results in a fall in the EPS. In other words, a **future increase** in the **number of ordinary shares will cause a dilution or 'watering down' of equity**, and it is possible to calculate a **diluted earnings per share** (ie the EPS that would have been obtained during the financial period if the dilution had already taken place). This will indicate to investors the possible effects of a future dilution.

## 4.2 Earnings

The earnings calculated for basic EPS should be based on **continuing operations** and adjusted by the **post-tax** (including deferred tax) effect of:

(a) Any **dividends** on dilutive potential ordinary shares that were deducted to arrive at earnings for basic EPS

(b) **Interest recognised** in the period for the dilutive potential ordinary shares (convertible debt)

(c) Any **other changes in income or expenses** (fees or discount) that would result from the conversion of the dilutive potential ordinary shares

The conversion of some potential ordinary shares may lead to changes in **other income or expenses**. For example, the reduction of interest expense related to potential ordinary shares and the resulting increase in net profit for the period may lead to an increase in the expense relating to a non-discretionary employee profit-sharing plan. When calculating diluted EPS, the net profit or loss for the period is adjusted for any such consequential changes in income or expense.

## 4.3 Per share

The number of ordinary shares is the weighted average number of ordinary shares calculated for basic EPS plus the weighted average number of ordinary shares that would be issued on the conversion of all the **dilutive potential ordinary shares** into ordinary shares.

It should be assumed that dilutive ordinary shares were converted into ordinary shares at the **beginning of the period** or, if later, at the actual date of issue. There are two other points.

(a) The computation assumes the most **advantageous conversion rate** or exercise rate from the standpoint of the holder of the potential ordinary shares.

(b) **Contingently issuable** (potential) ordinary shares are treated as for basic EPS; if the conditions have not been met, the number of contingently issuable shares included in the computation is based on the number of shares that would be issuable if the end of the reporting period was the end of the contingency period. Restatement is not allowed if the conditions are not met when the contingency period expires.

## 4.4 Example: diluted EPS

In 20X7 Farrah Co had a basic EPS of 105c based on earnings of $105,000 and 100,000 ordinary $1 shares. It also had in issue $40,000 15% convertible loan stock which is convertible in two years' time at the rate of 4 ordinary shares for every $5 of stock. The rate of tax is 30%.

*Required*

Calculate the diluted EPS.

## Solution

Diluted EPS is calculated as follows.

**Step 1**    **Number of shares**: the additional equity on conversion of the loan stock will be 40,000 × 4/5 = 32,000 shares

**Step 2**    **Earnings**: Farrah Co will save interest payments of $6,000 (40,000 × 15%) but this increase in profits will be taxed. Hence the earnings figure may be recalculated:

$(105,000 + (6,000 \times 70\%)) = \$109,200$

**Step 3**    **Calculation**: Diluted EPS $= \dfrac{\$109,200}{132,000} = 82.7c$

**Step 4**    **Dilution**: the dilution in earnings would be 105c − 82.7c = 22.3c per share.

Question

Diluted EPS

Ardent Co has 5,000,000 ordinary shares of 25 cents each in issue, and also had in issue in 20X4:

(a) $1,000,000 of 14% convertible loan stock, convertible in three years' time at the rate of 2 shares per $10 of stock;

(b) $2,000,000 of 10% convertible loan stock, convertible in one year's time at the rate of 3 shares per $5 of stock.

The total earnings in 20X4 were $1,750,000.

The rate of income tax is 35%.

*Required*

Calculate the basic EPS and diluted EPS.

## Answer

(a) Basic EPS = $\dfrac{\$1,750,000}{5 \text{ million}}$ = 35 cents

(b) We must decide which of the potential ordinary shares (ie the loan stocks) are dilutive (ie would decrease the EPS if converted).

For the 14% loan stock, incremental EPS = $\dfrac{0.65 \times \$140,000}{200,000 \text{ shares}}$

$= 45.5c$

For the 10% loan stock, incremental EPS $= \dfrac{0.65 \times \$200,000}{1.2m \text{ shares}}$

$= 10.8c$

The effect of converting the 14% loan stock is therefore to **increase** the EPS figure, since the incremental EPS of 45.5c is greater than the basic EPS of 35c. The 14% loan stock is not dilutive and is therefore excluded from the diluted EPS calculation.

The 10% loan stock is dilutive.

Diluted EPS = $\dfrac{\$1.75m + \$0.13m}{5m + 1.2m}$ = 30.3c

## 4.5 Treatment of options

It should be assumed that options are exercised and that the assumed proceeds would have been received from the issue of shares at **fair value**. Fair value for this purpose is calculated on the basis of the average price of the ordinary shares during the period. Options are brought into the dilution calculation in the year in which they are issued.

Options and other share purchase arrangements are dilutive when they would result in the issue of ordinary shares for **less than fair value**. The amount of the dilution is fair value less the issue price. In order to calculate diluted EPS, each transaction of this type is treated as consisting of two parts.

(a) A contract to issue a certain number of ordinary shares at their **average market price** during the period. These shares are fairly priced and are assumed to be neither dilutive nor antidilutive. They are ignored in the computation of diluted earnings per share.

(b) A contract to issue the remaining ordinary shares for **no consideration**. Such ordinary shares generate no proceeds and have no effect on the net profit attributable to ordinary shares outstanding. Therefore such shares are dilutive and they are added to the number of ordinary shares outstanding in the computation of diluted EPS.

To the extent that **partly paid shares** are not entitled to participate in dividends during the period, they are considered the equivalent of **warrants** or **options**.

Brand Co has the following results for the year ended 31 December 20X7.

| | |
|---|---|
| Net profit for year | $1,200,000 |
| Weighted average number of ordinary shares outstanding during year | 500,000 shares |
| Average fair value of one ordinary share during year | $20.00 |
| Weighted average number of shares under option during year | 100,000 shares |
| Exercise price for shares under option during year | $15.00 |

*Required*

Calculate both basic and diluted earnings per share.

### Answer

| | Per share | Earnings $ | Shares |
|---|---|---|---|
| Net profit for year | | 1,200,000 | |
| Weighted average shares outstanding during 20X7 | | | 500,000 |
| *Basic earnings per share* | 2.40 | | |
| Number of shares under option | | | 100,000 |
| Number of shares that would have been issued At fair value: (100,000 × $15.00/$20.00) | | | (75,000) * |
| *Diluted earnings per share* | 2.29 | 1,200,000 | 525,000 |

\* The earnings have not been increased as the total number of shares has been increased only by the number of shares (25,000) deemed for the purpose of the computation to have been issued for no consideration.

## 4.6 Dilutive potential ordinary shares

According to IAS 33, potential ordinary shares should be treated as dilutive when, and only when, their conversion to ordinary shares would **decrease net profit per share** from continuing operations. This point was illustrated in the question above.

# 5 Presentation, disclosure and other matters

**FAST FORWARD**

IAS 33 contains a number of requirements on presentation and disclosure.

## 5.1 Presentation

Basic and diluted EPS should be presented by an entity in the statement of profit or loss and other comprehensive income for each class of ordinary share that has a different right to share in the net profit for the period. The basic and diluted EPS should be presented with **equal prominence** for all periods presented.

Disclosure must still be made where the EPS figures (basic and/or diluted) are **negative** (ie a loss per share).

## 5.2 Disclosure

An entity should disclose the following.

(a)   The amounts used as the **numerators** in calculating basic and diluted EPS, and a **reconciliation** of those amounts to the net profit or loss for the period

(b)   The weighted average number of ordinary shares used as the **denominator** in calculating basic and diluted EPS, and a **reconciliation** of these denominators to each other.

## 5.3 Alternative EPS figures

An entity may present **alternative EPS figures if it wishes**. However, IAS 33 lays out certain rules where this takes place.

(a)   The weighted average number of shares as calculated under IAS 33 **must** be used.

(b)   A **reconciliation** must be given if necessary between the component of profit used in the alternative EPS and the line item for profit reported in the statement of profit or loss and other comprehensive income.

(c)   Basic and diluted EPS must be shown with **equal prominence**.

## 5.4 Significance of earnings per share

Earnings per share (EPS) is one of the most frequently quoted statistics in financial analysis. Because of the widespread use of the price earnings **(P/E) ratio** as a yardstick for investment decisions, it became increasingly important. It is certainly true that EPS gives a more accurate picture of the actual return to investors than reported profits, which do not show the dilutive effect of share issues.

Reported and forecast EPS can, through the P/E ratio, have a **significant effect on a company's share price**. Thus, a share price might fall if it looks as if EPS is going to be low.

There are a number of reasons why EPS should not be used to determine the value of a company's shares. IAS 33 concentrates on the **denominator** of EPS – ie. the number of shares. However, it is more difficult to regulate the **numerator** – earnings. Reported earnings can be affected by a number or factors – choice of accounting policy, asset valuation, taxation issues. Directors who want to present favourable EPS can find ways to boost reported earnings, as happened with Enron.

EPS has also served as a means of assessing the **stewardship and management** role performed by company directors and managers. Remuneration packages might be linked to EPS growth, thereby increasing the pressure on management to improve EPS. The danger of this, however, is that management effort may go into distorting results to produce a favourable EPS.

It should also be noted that EPS takes no account of other issues that affect whether a company is worth investing in, such as its risk profile and its investment requirements. Nevertheless, the market is sensitive to EPS.

# Chapter roundup

- **Earnings per share** is a measure of the amount of profits earned by a company for each ordinary share. Earnings are profits after tax and preferred dividends.

- **Basic EPS** is calculated by dividing the net profit or loss for the period attributable to ordinary shareholders by the weighted average number of ordinary shares outstanding during the period.

- You should know how to calculate **basic EPS** and how to deal with related complications (issue of shares for cash, bonus issues, rights issues).

- **Diluted EPS** is calculated by adjusting the net profit attributable to ordinary shareholders and the weighted average number of shares outstanding for the effects of all dilutive potential ordinary shares.

- **IAS 33** contains a number of requirements on presentation and disclosure.

# Quick quiz

1. How is basic EPS calculated?
2. Give the formula for the 'bonus element' of a rights issue.
3. Define 'dilutive potential ordinary share'.
4. Which numerator is used to decide whether potential ordinary shares are dilutive?
5. Why is the numerator adjusted for convertible bonds when calculating diluted EPS?

# Answers to quick quiz

1.
$$\frac{\text{Net profit /(loss) attributable to ordinary shareholders}}{\text{Weighted average number of ordinary shares outstanding during the period}}$$

2.
$$\frac{\text{Actual cum} - \text{rights price}}{\text{Theoretical ex} - \text{rights price}}$$

3. See Para 4.1

4. Net profit from continuing operations only.

5. Because the issue of shares will affect earnings (the interest will no longer have to be paid).

Now try the question below from the Exam Question Bank

| Number | Level | Marks | Time |
|--------|-------|-------|------|
| 24 | – | 15 | 27 mins |

# Analysing and interpreting financial statements

19

| Topic list | Syllabus reference |
|---|---|
| 1 The broad categories of ratio | E2 |
| 2 Profitability and return on capital | E2 |
| 3 Liquidity, gearing/leverage and working capital | E2 |
| 4 Shareholders' investment ratios | E2 |
| 5 Presentation of financial performance | E2 |

## Introduction

This chapter looks at **interpretation of accounts**. We deal here with the calculation of ratios, how they can be analysed and interpreted, and how the results should be presented to management.

# Study guide

| | | Intellectual level |
|---|---|:---:|
| **E2** | **Calculation and interpretation of accounting ratios and trends to address users' and stakeholders' needs** | |
| (a) | define and compute relevant financial ratios. | 2 |
| (b) | explain what aspects of performance specific ratios are intended to assess. | 2 |
| (c) | analyse and interpret ratios to give an assessment of an entity's performance and financial position in comparison with: | 2 |
| | (i)   an entity's previous periods' financial statements | |
| | (ii)  another similar entity for the same reporting period | |
| | (iii)  industry average ratios. | |
| (d) | interpret an entity's financial statements to give advice from the perspectives of different stakeholders. | 2 |
| (e) | discuss how the interpretation of current value based financial statements would differ from those using historical cost based accounts. | 1 |

# 1 The broad categories of ratio

FAST FORWARD

> You must be able to **appraise and communicate** the position and prospects of a business based on given and prepared statements and ratios.

If you were to look at a statement of financial position or statement of profit or loss and other comprehensive income, how would you decide whether the company was doing well or badly? Or whether it was financially strong or financially vulnerable? And what would you be looking at in the figures to help you to make your judgement?

Ratio analysis involves **comparing one figure against another** to produce a ratio, and assessing whether the ratio indicates a weakness or strength in the company's affairs.

## 1.1 The broad categories of ratios

Broadly speaking, basic ratios can be grouped into five categories.

- Profitability and return
- Long-term solvency and stability
- Short-term solvency and liquidity
- Efficiency (turnover ratios)
- Shareholders' investment ratios

Within each heading we will identify a number of standard measures or ratios that are normally calculated and generally accepted as meaningful indicators. One must stress however that each individual business must be considered separately, and a ratio that is meaningful for a manufacturing company may be completely meaningless for a financial institution. **Try not to be too mechanical** when working out ratios and constantly think about what you are trying to achieve.

The key to obtaining meaningful information from ratio analysis is **comparison**. This may involve comparing ratios over time within the same business to establish whether things are improving or declining, and comparing ratios between similar businesses to see whether the company you are analysing is better or worse than average within its specific business sector.

It must be stressed that ratio analysis on its own is not sufficient for interpreting company accounts, and that there are **other items of information** which should be looked at, for example:

(a) The content of any **accompanying commentary** on the accounts and other statements

(b) The age and nature of the **company's assets**

(c) **Current and future developments** in the company's markets, at home and overseas, recent acquisitions or disposals of a subsidiary by the company

(d) **Unusual** items separately disclosed in the financial statements

(e) Any other **noticeable features** of the report and accounts, such as events after the end of the reporting period, contingent liabilities, a qualified auditors' report, the company's taxation position, and so on

## 1.2 Example: calculating ratios

To illustrate the calculation of ratios, the following **draft** statement of financial position and statement of profit or loss figures will be used. We are using a separate statement of profit or loss for this example as no items of other comprehensive income are involved.

FURLONG CO STATEMENT OF PROFIT OR LOSS
FOR THE YEAR ENDED 31 DECEMBER 20X8

|  | Notes | 20X8 $ | 20X7 $ |
|---|---|---|---|
| Revenue | 1 | 3,095,576 | 1,909,051 |
| Operating profit | 1 | 359,501 | 244,229 |
| Interest | 2 | 17,371 | 19,127 |
| Profit before taxation |  | 342,130 | 225,102 |
| Income tax expense |  | 74,200 | 31,272 |
| Profit for the year |  | 267,930 | 193,830 |
| Earnings per share |  | 12.8c | 9.3c |

FURLONG CO STATEMENT OF FINANCIAL POSITION
AS AT 31 DECEMBER 20X8

|  | Notes | 20X8 $ | 20X7 $ |
|---|---|---|---|
| *Assets* |  |  |  |
| Non-current assets |  |  |  |
| Property, plant and equipment |  | 802,180 | 656,071 |
| Current assets |  |  |  |
| Inventory |  | 64,422 | 86,550 |
| Receivables | 3 | 1,002,701 | 853,441 |
| Cash at bank and in hand |  | 1,327 | 68,363 |
|  |  | 1,068,450 | 1,008,354 |
| Total assets |  | 1,870,630 | 1,664,425 |
| *Equity and liabilities* |  |  |  |
| Equity |  |  |  |
| Ordinary shares 10c each | 5 | 210,000 | 210,000 |
| Share premium account |  | 48,178 | 48,178 |
| Retained earnings |  | 651,721 | 410,591 |
|  |  | 909,899 | 668,769 |
| Non-current liabilities |  |  |  |
| 10% loan stock 20X4/20Y0 |  | 100,000 | 100,000 |
| Current liabilities | 4 | 860,731 | 895,656 |
| Total equity and liabilities |  | 1,870,630 | 1,664,425 |

## NOTES TO THE ACCOUNTS

| | | 20X8 | 20X7 |
|---|---|---:|---:|
| 1 | *Sales revenue and profit* | $ | $ |
| | Sales revenue | 3,095,576 | 1,909,051 |
| | Cost of sales | 2,402,609 | 1,441,950 |
| | Gross profit | 692,967 | 467,101 |
| | Administration expenses | 333,466 | 222,872 |
| | Operating profit | 359,501 | 244,229 |
| | | | |
| | Depreciation charged | 151,107 | 120,147 |
| | | | |
| 2 | *Interest* | | |
| | Payable on bank overdrafts and other loans | 8,115 | 11,909 |
| | Payable on loan stock | 10,000 | 10,000 |
| | | 18,115 | 21,909 |
| | Receivable on short-term deposits | 744 | 2,782 |
| | Net payable | 17,371 | 19,127 |
| | | | |
| 3 | *Receivables* | | |
| | Amounts falling due within one year | | |
| |   Trade receivables | 905,679 | 807,712 |
| |   Prepayments and accrued income | 97,022 | 45,729 |
| | | 1,002,701 | 853,441 |
| | | | |
| 4 | *Current liabilities* | | |
| | Trade payables | 627,018 | 545,340 |
| | Accruals and deferred income | 81,279 | 280,464 |
| | Corporate taxes | 108,000 | 37,200 |
| | Other taxes | 44,434 | 32,652 |
| | | 860,731 | 895,656 |
| 5 | *Called-up share capital* | | |
| | Authorised ordinary shares of 10c each | 1,000,000 | 1,000,000 |
| | Issued and fully paid ordinary shares of 10c each | 210,000 | 210,000 |
| | | | |
| 6 | Dividends paid | 20,000 | – |

# 2 Profitability and return on capital

Return on capital employed (ROCE) may be used by the shareholders or the Board to assess the performance of management.

In our example, the company made a profit in both 20X8 and 20X7, and there was an increase in profit between one year and the next:

(a) Of 52% before taxation
(b) Of 39% after taxation

**Profit before taxation** is generally thought to be a better figure to use than profit after taxation, because there might be unusual variations in the tax charge from year to year which would not affect the underlying profitability of the company's operations.

Another profit figure that should be calculated is PBIT, **profit before interest and tax**. This is the amount of profit which the company earned before having to pay interest to the providers of loan capital, such as loan notes and medium-term bank loans, which will be shown in the statement of financial position as non-current liabilities.

**Formula to learn**

**Profit before interest and tax** is therefore:

(a) the profit on ordinary activities before taxation; **plus**
(b) interest charges on loan capital.

Published accounts do not always give sufficient detail on interest payable to determine how much is interest on long-term finance. We will assume in our example that the whole of the interest payable ($18,115, note 2) relates to long-term finance.

PBIT in our example is therefore:

|  | 20X8 | 20X7 |
|---|---|---|
|  | $ | $ |
| Profit on ordinary activities before tax | 342,130 | 225,102 |
| Interest payable | 18,115 | 21,909 |
| PBIT | 360,245 | 247,011 |

This shows a 46% growth between 20X7 and 20X8.

## 2.1 Return on capital employed (ROCE)

It is impossible to assess profits or profit growth properly without relating them to the **amount of funds (capital) that were employed in making the profits**. The most important profitability ratio is therefore return on capital employed (ROCE), which states the profit as a percentage of the amount of capital employed.

**Formula to learn**

$$\text{ROCE} = \frac{\text{Profit before interest and taxation}}{\text{Total assets less current liabilities}} \times 100\%$$

| Capital employed | = | Shareholders' equity plus non-current liabilities (*or* total assets less current liabilities) |
|---|---|---|

The underlying principle is that we must **compare like with like**, and so if capital means share capital and reserves plus non-current liabilities and debt capital, profit must mean the profit earned by all this capital together. This is PBIT, since interest is the return for loan capital.

In our example, capital employed = 20X8 $1,870,630 − $860,731 = $1,009,899
20X7 $1,664,425 − $895,656 = $768,769

These total figures are the total assets less current liabilities figures for 20X8 and 20X7 in the statement of financial position.

|  | 20X8 | 20X7 |
|---|---|---|
| ROCE | $\dfrac{\$360,245}{\$1,009,899} = 35.7\%$ | $\dfrac{\$247,011}{\$768,769} = 32.1\%$ |

What does a company's ROCE tell us? What should we be looking for? There are three comparisons that can be made.

(a) The **change in ROCE from one year to the next** can be examined. In this example, there has been an increase in ROCE by about 4 percentage points from its 20X7 level.

(b) The **ROCE being earned by other companies**, if this information is available, can be compared with the ROCE of this company. Here the information is not available.

(c) A comparison of the ROCE with **current market borrowing rates** may be made.

  (i) What would be the cost of extra borrowing to the company if it needed more loans, and is it earning a ROCE that suggests it could make profits to make such borrowing worthwhile?

  (ii) Is the company making a ROCE which suggests that it is getting value for money from its current borrowing?

  (iii) Companies are in a risk business and commercial borrowing rates are a good independent yardstick against which company performance can be judged.

In this example, if we suppose that current market interest rates, say, for medium-term borrowing from banks, are around 10%, then the company's actual ROCE of 36% in 20X8 would not seem low. On the contrary, it might seem high.

However, it is easier to spot a low ROCE than a high one, because there is always a chance that the company's non-current assets, especially property, are **undervalued** in its statement of financial position, and so the capital employed figure might be unrealistically low. If the company had earned a ROCE, not of 36%, but of, say only 6%, then its return would have been below current borrowing rates and so disappointingly low.

## 2.2 Return on equity (ROE)

Return on equity gives a more restricted view of capital than ROCE, but it is based on the same principles.

**Formula to learn**

$$ROE = \frac{\text{Profit after tax and preference dividend}}{\text{Equity shareholders funds}} \times 100\%$$

In our example, ROE is calculated as follows.

|  | 20X8 | 20X7 |
|---|---|---|
| ROE | $\dfrac{\$267,930}{\$909,899} = 29.4\%$ | $\dfrac{\$193,830}{\$668,769} = 29\%$ |

ROE is **not a widely-used ratio**, however, because there are more useful ratios that give an indication of the return to shareholders, such as earnings per share, dividend per share, dividend yield and earnings yield, which are described later.

## 2.3 Analysing profitability and return in more detail: the secondary ratios

We often sub-analyse ROCE, to find out more about why the ROCE is high or low, or better or worse than last year. There are two factors that contribute towards a return on capital employed, both related to sales revenue.

(a) **Profit margin**. A company might make a high or low profit margin on its sales. For example, a company that makes a profit of 25c per $1 of sales is making a bigger return on its revenue than another company making a profit of only 10c per $1 of sales.

(b) **Asset turnover**. Asset turnover is a measure of how well the assets of a business are being used to generate sales. For example, if two companies each have capital employed of $100,000 and Company A makes sales of $400,000 per annum whereas Company B makes sales of only $200,000 per annum, Company A is making a higher revenue from the same amount of assets (twice as much asset turnover as Company B) and this will help A to make a higher return on capital employed than B. Asset turnover is expressed as 'x times' so that assets generate x times their value in annual sales. Here, Company A's asset turnover is 4 times and B's is 2 times.

Profit margin and asset turnover together explain the ROCE and if the ROCE is the primary profitability ratio, these other two are the secondary ratios. The relationship between the three ratios can be shown mathematically.

**Formula to learn**

Profit margin × Asset turnover = ROCE

$$\therefore \quad \frac{\text{PBIT}}{\text{Sales}} \times \frac{\text{Sales}}{\text{Capital employed}} = \frac{\text{PBIT}}{\text{Capital employed}}$$

In our example:

|  |  | Profit margin | | Asset turnover | | ROCE |
|---|---|---|---|---|---|---|
| (a)2 | 0X8 | $\dfrac{\$360,245}{\$3,095,576}$ | × | $\dfrac{\$3,095,576}{\$1,009,899}$ | = | $\dfrac{\$360,245}{\$1,009,899}$ |
|  |  | 11.64% | × | 3.07 times | = | 35.7% |

| | | Profit margin | | Asset turnover | | ROCE |
|---|---|---|---|---|---|---|
| (b) | 20X7 | $\dfrac{\$247,011}{\$1,909,051}$ | × | $\dfrac{\$1,909,051}{\$768,769}$ | = | $\dfrac{\$247,011}{\$768,769}$ |
| | | 12.94% | × | 2.48 times | = | 32.1% |

In this example, the company's improvement in ROCE between 20X7 and 20X8 is attributable to a higher asset turnover. Indeed the profit margin has fallen a little, but the higher asset turnover has more than compensated for this.

It is also worth commenting on the change in sales revenue from one year to the next. You may already have noticed that Furlong achieved sales growth of over 60% from $1.9 million to $3.1 million between 20X7 and 20X8. This is very strong growth, and this is certainly one of the most significant items in the statement of profit or loss and statement of financial position.

### 2.3.1 A warning about comments on profit margin and asset turnover

It might be tempting to think that a high profit margin is good, and a low asset turnover means sluggish trading. In broad terms, this is so. But there is a trade-off between profit margin and asset turnover, and you cannot look at one without allowing for the other.

(a)     A **high profit margin** means a high profit per $1 of sales, but if this also means that sales prices are high, there is a strong possibility that sales revenue will be depressed, and so asset turnover lower.

(b)     A **high asset turnover** means that the company is generating a lot of sales, but to do this it might have to keep its prices down and so accept a low profit margin per $1 of sales.

Consider the following.

| Company A | | Company B | |
|---|---|---|---|
| Sales revenue | $1,000,000 | Sales revenue | $4,000,000 |
| Capital employed | $1,000,000 | Capital employed | $1,000,000 |
| PBIT | $200,000 | PBIT | $200,000 |

These figures would give the following ratios.

| ROCE | = | $\dfrac{\$200,000}{\$1,000,000}$ | = 20% | ROCE | = | $\dfrac{\$200,000}{\$1,000,000}$ | = 20% |
|---|---|---|---|---|---|---|---|
| Profit margin | = | $\dfrac{\$200,000}{\$1,000,000}$ | = 20% | Profit margin | = | $\dfrac{\$200,000}{\$4,000,000}$ | = 5% |
| Asset turnover | = | $\dfrac{\$1,000,000}{\$1,000,000}$ | = 1 | Asset turnover | = | $\dfrac{\$4,000,000}{\$1,000,000}$ | = 4 |

The companies have the same ROCE, but it is arrived at in a very different fashion. Company A operates with a low asset turnover and a comparatively high profit margin whereas company B carries out much more business, but on a lower profit margin. Company A could be operating at the luxury end of the market, whilst company B is operating at the popular end of the market.

## 2.4 Gross profit margin, net profit margin and profit analysis

Depending on the format of the statement of profit or loss, you may be able to calculate the gross profit margin as well as the net profit margin. **Looking at the two together** can be quite informative.

For example, suppose that a company has the following summarised statement of profit or loss for two consecutive years.

| | Year 1 | Year 2 |
|---|---|---|
| | $ | $ |
| Revenue | 70,000 | 100,000 |
| Cost of sales | 42,000 | 55,000 |
| Gross profit | 28,000 | 45,000 |
| Expenses | 21,000 | 35,000 |
| Profit for the year | 7,000 | 10,000 |

Although the net profit margin is the same for both years at 10%, the gross profit margin is not.

In year 1 it is: $\dfrac{\$28,000}{\$70,000}$ = 40%

and in year 2 it is: $\dfrac{\$45,000}{\$100,000}$ = 45%

The improved gross profit margin has not led to an improvement in the net profit margin. This is because expenses as a percentage of sales have risen from 30% in year 1 to 35% in year 2.

## 2.5 Historical vs current cost

In this chapter we are dealing with interpretation of financial statements based on historical cost accounts.

It is worth considering how the analysis would change if we were dealing with financial statements based on some form of current value accounting (which we will go on to look at in Chapter 22).

These are some of the issues that would arise:

- Non-current asset values would probably be stated at fair value. This may be higher than depreciated historical cost. Therefore capital employed would be higher. This would lead to a reduction in ROCE.
- Higher asset values would lead to a higher depreciation charge, which would reduce net profit.
- If opening inventory were shown at current value, this would increase cost of sales and reduce net profit.

So you can see that ROCE based on historical cost accounts is probably overstated in real terms.

# 3 Liquidity, gearing/leverage and working capital

FAST FORWARD

Banks and other lenders will be interested in a company's gearing level.

## 3.1 Long-term solvency: debt and gearing ratios

Debt ratios are concerned with **how much the company owes in relation to its size**, whether it is getting into heavier debt or improving its situation, and whether its debt burden seems heavy or light.

(a) When a company is heavily in debt banks and other potential lenders may be unwilling to advance further funds.

(b) When a company is earning only a modest profit before interest and tax, and has a heavy debt burden, there will be very little profit left over for shareholders after the interest charges have been paid. And so if interest rates were to go up (on bank overdrafts and so on) or the company were to borrow even more, it might soon be incurring interest charges in excess of PBIT. This might eventually lead to the liquidation of the company.

These are two big reasons why companies should keep their debt burden under control. There are four ratios that are particularly worth looking at, the debt ratio, gearing ratio, interest cover and cash flow ratio.

## 3.2 Debt ratio

**Formula to learn**

The **debt ratio** is the ratio of a company's total debts to its total assets.

(a) Assets consist of non-current assets at their carrying value, plus current assets.

(b) Debts consist of all payables, whether they are due within one year or after more than one year.

You can ignore other non-current liabilities, such as deferred taxation.

There is no absolute guide to the maximum safe debt ratio, but as a very general guide, you might regard 50% as a safe limit to debt. In practice, many companies operate successfully with a higher debt ratio than this, but 50% is nonetheless a helpful benchmark. In addition, if the debt ratio is over 50% and getting worse, the company's debt position will be worth looking at more carefully.

In the case of Furlong the debt ratio is as follows.

|  | 20X8 | 20X7 |
|---|---|---|
| Total debts | $ (860,731 + 100,000) | $ (895,656 + 100,000) |
| Total assets | $1,870,630 | $1,664,425 |
|  | = 51% | = 60% |

In this case, the debt ratio is quite high, mainly because of the large amount of current liabilities. However, the debt ratio has fallen from 60% to 51% between 20X7 and 20X8, and so the company appears to be improving its debt position.

## 3.3 Gearing/leverage

**Gearing or leverage** is concerned with a company's **long-term capital structure**. We can think of a company as consisting of non-current assets and net current assets (ie working capital, which is current assets minus current liabilities). These assets must be financed by long-term capital of the company, which is one of two things.

(a)     Issued share capital which can be divided into:

   (i)     Ordinary shares plus other equity (eg reserves)
   (ii)    Non-redeemable preference shares (unusual)

(b)     Long-term debt including redeemable preference shares.

Preference share capital is normally classified as a non-current liability in accordance with IAS 32, and preference dividends (paid or accrued) are included in finance costs in profit or loss.

The **capital gearing ratio** is a measure of the proportion of a company's capital that is debt. It is measured as follows.

**Formula to learn**

$$\text{Gearing} = \frac{\text{Interest bearing debt}}{\text{Shareholders' equity} + \text{interest bearing debt}} \times 100\%$$

As with the debt ratio, there is **no absolute limit** to what a gearing ratio ought to be. A company with a gearing ratio of more than 50% is said to be high-geared (whereas low gearing means a gearing ratio of less than 50%). Many companies are high geared, but if a high geared company is becoming increasingly high geared, it is likely to have difficulty in the future when it wants to borrow even more, unless it can also boost its shareholders' capital, either with retained profits or by a new share issue.

**Leverage** is an alternative term for gearing; the words have the same meaning. Note that leverage (or gearing) can be looked at conversely, by calculating the proportion of total assets financed by equity, and which may be called the equity to assets ratio. It is calculated as follows.

**Formula to learn**

$$\text{Equity to assets ratio} = \frac{\text{Shareholders' equity}}{\text{Shareholders' equity} + \text{interest bearing debt}} \times 100\%$$

$$\text{or} \quad \frac{\text{Shareholders' equity}}{\text{Total assets less current liabilities}} \times 100\%$$

In the example of Furlong, we find that the company, although having a high debt ratio because of its current liabilities, has a low gearing ratio. It has no preference share capital and its only long-term debt is the 10% loan stock. The equity to assets ratio is therefore high.

| | | 20X8 | 20X7 |
|---|---|---|---|
| Gearing ratio | = | $100,000 | $100,000 |
| | | $1,009,899 | $768,769 |
| | | = 10% | = 13% |
| Equity to assets ratio | = | $909,899 | $668,769 |
| | | $1,009,899 | $768,769 |
| | | = 90% | = 87% |

As you can see, the equity to assets ratio is the mirror image of gearing.

## 3.4 The implications of high or low gearing/leverage

We mentioned earlier that **gearing or leverage** is, amongst other things, an attempt to **quantify the degree of risk involved in holding equity shares in a company**, risk both in terms of the company's ability to remain in business and in terms of expected ordinary dividends from the company. The problem with a highly geared company is that by definition there is a lot of debt. Debt generally carries a fixed rate of interest (or fixed rate of dividend if in the form of preference shares), hence there is a given (and large) amount to be paid out from profits to holders of debt before arriving at a residue available for distribution to the holders of equity. The riskiness will perhaps become clearer with the aid of an example.

| | Company A | Company B | Company C |
|---|---|---|---|
| | $'000 | $'000 | $'000 |
| Ordinary shares | 600 | 400 | 300 |
| Retained earnings | 200 | 200 | 200 |
| Revaluation surplus | 100 | 100 | 100 |
| | 900 | 700 | 600 |
| 6% preference shares (redeemable) | – | – | 100 |
| 10% loan stock | 100 | 300 | 300 |
| Capital employed | 1,000 | 1,000 | 1,000 |
| Gearing ratio | 10% | 30% | 40% |
| Equity to assets ratio | 90% | 70% | 60% |

Now suppose that each company makes a profit before interest and tax of $50,000, and the rate of tax on company profits is 30%. Amounts available for distribution to equity shareholders will be as follows.

| | Company A | Company B | Company C |
|---|---|---|---|
| | $'000 | $'000 | $'000 |
| Profit before interest and tax | 50 | 50 | 50 |
| Interest/preference dividend | 10 | 30 | 36 |
| Taxable profit | 40 | 20 | 14 |
| Taxation at 30% | 12 | 6 | 4 |
| Profit for the period | 28 | 14 | 10 |

If in the subsequent year profit before interest and tax falls to $40,000, the amounts available to ordinary shareholders will become as follows.

| | Company A | Company B | Company C |
|---|---|---|---|
| | $'000 | $'000 | $'000 |
| Profit before interest and tax | 40 | 40 | 40 |
| Interest/preference dividend | 10 | 30 | 36 |
| Taxable profit | 30 | 10 | 4 |
| Taxation at 30% | 9 | 3 | 1 |
| Profit for the period | 21 | 7 | 3 |

Note the following.

| | | | |
|---|---|---|---|
| Gearing ratio | 10% | 30% | 40% |
| Equity to assets ratio | 90% | 70% | 60% |
| Change in PBIT | –20% | –20% | –20% |
| Change in profit available for ordinary shareholders | –25% | –50% | –70% |

**The more highly geared the company, the greater the risk that little (if anything) will be available to distribute by way of dividend to the ordinary shareholders.** The example clearly displays this fact in so far as the more highly geared the company, the greater the percentage change in profit available for ordinary shareholders for any given percentage change in profit before interest and tax. The relationship similarly holds when profits increase, and if PBIT had risen by 20% rather than fallen, you would find that once again the largest percentage change in profit available for ordinary shareholders (this means an increase) will be for the highly geared company. This means that there will be greater *volatility* of amounts available for ordinary shareholders, and presumably therefore greater volatility in dividends paid to those shareholders, where a company is highly geared. That is the risk: you may do extremely well or extremely badly without a particularly large movement in the PBIT of the company.

The risk of a company's ability to remain in business was referred to earlier. Gearing or leverage is relevant to this. A highly geared company has a large amount of interest to pay annually (assuming that the debt is external borrowing rather than preference shares). If those borrowings are **'secured'** in any way (and loan notes in particular are secured), then the **holders of the debt are perfectly entitled to force the company** to **realise assets to pay their interest** if funds are not available from other sources. Clearly the more highly geared a company the more likely this is to occur when and if profits fall.

## 3.5 Interest cover

The interest cover ratio shows whether a company is earning enough profits before interest and tax to pay its interest costs comfortably, or whether its interest costs are high in relation to the size of its profits, so that a fall in PBIT would then have a significant effect on profits available for ordinary shareholders.

**Formula to learn**

$$\text{Interest cover} = \frac{\text{Profit before interest and tax}}{\text{Interest charges}}$$

An interest cover of 2 times or less would be low, and should really exceed 3 times before the company's interest costs are to be considered within acceptable limits.

Returning first to the example of Companies A, B and C, the interest cover was as follows.

| | | Company A | Company B | Company C |
|---|---|---|---|---|
| (a) | When PBIT was $50,000 = | $\dfrac{\$50,000}{\$10,000}$ | $\dfrac{\$50,000}{\$30,000}$ | $\dfrac{\$50,000}{\$36,000}$ |
| | | 5 times | 1.67 times | 1.39 times |
| (b) | When PBIT was $40,000 = | $\dfrac{\$40,000}{\$10,000}$ | $\dfrac{\$40,000}{\$30,000}$ | $\dfrac{\$40,000}{\$36,000}$ |
| | | 4 times | 1.33 times | 1.11 times |

Both B and C have a low interest cover, which is a warning to ordinary shareholders that their profits are highly vulnerable, in percentage terms, to even small changes in PBIT.

Question                                                                 Interest cover

Returning to the example of Furlong in Paragraph 1.2, what is the company's interest cover?

Interest payments should be taken gross, from the note to the accounts, and not net of interest receipts as shown in the statement of profit or loss.

|  | 20X8 | 20X7 |
|---|---|---|
| PBIT | 360,245 | 247,011 |
| Interest payable | 18,115 | 21,909 |
|  | = 20 times | = 11 times |

Furlong has more than sufficient interest cover. In view of the company's low gearing, this is not too surprising and so we finally obtain a picture of Furlong as a company that does not seem to have a debt problem, in spite of its high (although declining) debt ratio.

## 3.6 Cash flow ratio

The cash flow ratio is the ratio of a company's **net cash inflow to its total debts**.

(a) **Net cash inflow** is the amount of cash which the company has coming into the business from its operations. A suitable figure for net cash inflow can be obtained from the statement of cash flows.

(b) **Total debts** are short-term and long-term payables, including provisions. A distinction can be made between debts payable within one year and other debts and provisions.

Obviously, a company needs to be earning enough cash from operations to be able to meet its foreseeable debts and future commitments, and the cash flow ratio, and changes in the cash flow ratio from one year to the next, provide a **useful indicator of a company's cash position**.

## 3.7 Short-term solvency and liquidity

Profitability is of course an important aspect of a company's performance and gearing or leverage is another. Neither, however, addresses directly the key issue of *liquidity*.

**Key term**

> **Liquidity** is the amount of cash a company can put its hands on quickly to settle its debts (and possibly to meet other unforeseen demands for cash payments too).

**Liquid funds** consist of:

(a) Cash

(b) Short-term investments for which there is a ready market

(c) Fixed-term deposits with a bank or other financial institution, for example, a six month high-interest deposit with a bank

(d) Trade receivables (because they will pay what they owe within a reasonably short period of time)

(e) Bills of exchange receivable (because like ordinary trade receivables, these represent amounts of cash due to be received within a relatively short period of time)

In summary, **liquid assets are current asset items that will or could soon be converted into cash, and cash itself.** Two common definitions of liquid assets are:

- All current assets without exception
- All current assets with the exception of inventories

A company can obtain liquid assets from sources other than sales of goods and services, such as the issue of shares for cash, a new loan or the sale of non-current assets. But a company cannot rely on these at all times, and in general, obtaining liquid funds depends on making sales revenue and profits. Even so, profits do not always lead to increases in liquidity. This is mainly because funds generated from trading may be immediately invested in non-current assets or paid out as dividends.

The reason why a company needs liquid assets is so that it can meet its debts when they fall due. Payments are continually made for operating expenses and other costs, and so there is a **cash cycle** from trading activities of cash coming in from sales and cash going out for expenses.

## 3.8 The cash cycle

To help you to understand liquidity ratios, it is useful to begin with a brief explanation of the cash cycle. The cash cycle describes **the flow of cash out of a business and back into it again as a result of normal trading operations.**

Cash goes out to pay for supplies, wages and salaries and other expenses, although payments can be delayed by taking some credit. A business might hold inventory for a while and then sell it. Cash will come back into the business from the sales, although customers might delay payment by themselves taking some credit.

The main points about the cash cycle are as follows.

(a) The timing of cash flows in and out of a business does not coincide with the time when sales and costs of sales occur. **Cash flows out can be postponed by taking credit. Cash flows in can be delayed by having receivables.**

(b) **The time between making a purchase and making a sale also affects cash flows**. If inventories are held for a long time, the delay between the cash payment for inventory and cash receipts from selling it will also be a long one.

(c) **Holding inventories and having receivables can therefore be seen as two reasons why cash receipts are delayed.** Another way of saying this is that if a company invests in working capital, its cash position will show a corresponding decrease.

(d) Similarly, **taking credit from creditors can be seen as a reason why cash payments are delayed**. The company's liquidity position will worsen when it has to pay the suppliers, unless it can get more cash in from sales and receivables in the meantime.

The liquidity ratios and working capital turnover ratios are used to test a company's liquidity, length of cash cycle, and investment in working capital.

## 3.9 Liquidity ratios: current ratio and quick ratio

The 'standard' test of liquidity is the **current ratio**. It can be obtained from the statement of financial position.

**Formula to learn**

$$\text{Current ratio} = \frac{\text{Current assets}}{\text{Current liabilities}}$$

The idea behind this is that a company should have enough current assets that give a promise of 'cash to come' to meet its future commitments to pay off its current liabilities. Obviously, a **ratio in excess of 1 should be expected**. Otherwise, there would be the prospect that the company might be unable to pay its debts on time. In practice, a ratio comfortably in excess of 1 should be expected, but what is 'comfortable' varies between different types of businesses.

Companies are not able to convert all their current assets into cash very quickly. In particular, some manufacturing companies might hold large quantities of raw material inventories, which must be used in production to create finished goods inventory. These might be warehoused for a long time, or sold on lengthy credit. In such businesses, where inventory turnover is slow, most inventories are not very 'liquid' assets, because the cash cycle is so long. For these reasons, we calculate an additional liquidity ratio, known as the quick ratio or acid test ratio.

The **quick ratio**, or **acid test ratio**, is calculated as follows.

**Formula to learn**

$$\text{Quick ratio} = \frac{\text{Current assets less inventory}}{\text{Current liabilities}}$$

This ratio should ideally be **at least 1** for companies with a slow inventory turnover. For companies with a fast inventory turnover, a quick ratio can be comfortably less than 1 without suggesting that the company could be in cash flow trouble.

Both the current ratio and the quick ratio offer an indication of the company's liquidity position, but the absolute figures **should not be interpreted too literally**. It is often theorised that an acceptable current ratio is 1.5 and an acceptable quick ratio is 0.8, but these should only be used as a guide. Different businesses operate in very different ways. A supermarket group for example might have a current ratio of 0.52 and a quick ratio of 0.17. Supermarkets have low receivables (people do not buy groceries on credit), low cash (good cash management), medium inventories (high inventories but quick turnover, particularly in view of perishability) and very high payables.

Compare this with a manufacturing and retail organisation, with a current ratio of 1.44 and a quick ratio of 1.03. Such businesses operate with liquidity ratios closer to the standard.

What is important is the **trend** of these ratios. From this, one can easily ascertain whether liquidity is improving or deteriorating. If a supermarket has traded for the last 10 years (very successfully) with current ratios of 0.52 and quick ratios of 0.17 then it should be supposed that the company can continue in business with those levels of liquidity. If in the following year the current ratio were to fall to 0.38 and the quick ratio to 0.09, then further investigation into the liquidity situation would be appropriate. It is the relative position that is far more important than the absolute figures.

Don't forget the other side of the coin either. A current ratio and a quick ratio can get **bigger than they need to be**. A company that has large volumes of inventories and receivables might be over-investing in working capital, and so tying up more funds in the business than it needs to. This would suggest poor management of receivables (credit) or inventories by the company.

## 3.10 Efficiency ratios: control of receivables and inventories

A rough measure of the average length of time it takes for a company's customers to pay what they owe is the **accounts receivable collection period**.

**Formula to learn**

> The estimated average accounts receivable collection period is calculated as:
>
> $$\frac{\text{Trade receivables}}{\text{Sales}} \times 365 \text{ days}$$

The figure for sales should be taken as the sales revenue figure in the statement of profit or loss. Note that any **cash sales should be excluded** – this ratio only uses credit sales. The trade receivables are not the total figure for receivables in the statement of financial position, which includes prepayments and non-trade receivables. The trade receivables figure will be itemised in an analysis of the receivable total, in a note to the accounts.

The estimate of the accounts receivable collection period is **only approximate**.

(a)   The value of receivables in the statement of financial position might be abnormally high or low compared with the 'normal' level the company usually has.

(b)   Sales revenue in the statement of profit or loss is exclusive of sales taxes, but receivables in the statement of financial position are inclusive of sales tax. We are not strictly comparing like with like.

Sales are usually made on 'normal credit terms' of payment within 30 days. A collection period significantly in excess of this might be representative of poor management of funds of a business. However, some companies must allow generous credit terms to win customers. Exporting companies in particular may have to carry large amounts of receivables, and so their average collection period might be well in excess of 30 days.

The **trend of the collection period over time** is probably the best guide. If the collection period is increasing year on year, this is indicative of a poorly managed credit control function (and potentially therefore a poorly managed company).

## 3.11 Accounts receivable collection period: examples

Using the same types of company as examples, the collection period for each of the companies was as follows.

| Company | Trade receivables Sales | Collection period (× 365) | Previous year | Collection period (× 365) |
|---|---|---|---|---|
| Supermarket | $\dfrac{\$5,016K}{\$284,986K} =$ | 6.4 days | $\dfrac{\$3,977K}{\$290,668K} =$ | 5.0 days |
| Manufacturer | $\dfrac{\$458.3m}{\$2,059.5m} =$ | 81.2 days | $\dfrac{\$272.4m}{\$1,274.2m} =$ | 78.0 days |
| Sugar refiner and seller | $\dfrac{\$304.4m}{\$3,817.3m} =$ | 29.1 days | $\dfrac{\$287.0m}{\$3,366.3m} =$ | 31.1 days |

The differences in collection period reflect the differences between the types of business. Supermarkets have hardly any trade receivables at all, whereas the manufacturing companies have far more. The collection periods are fairly constant from the previous year for all three companies.

## 3.12 Inventory turnover period

Another ratio worth calculating is the inventory turnover period. This is another estimated figure, obtainable from published accounts, which indicates the average number of days that items of inventory are held for. As with the average receivable collection period, however, it is only an approximate estimated figure, but one which should be reliable enough for comparing changes year on year.

**Formula to learn**

> The inventory turnover period is calculated as:
>
> $$\dfrac{\text{Inventory}}{\text{Cost of sales}} \times 365 \text{ days}$$

This is another measure of how vigorously a business is trading. A lengthening inventory turnover period from one year to the next indicates:

(a)     a slowdown in trading; or

(b)     a build-up in inventory levels, perhaps suggesting that the investment in inventories is becoming excessive.

Generally the **higher the inventory turnover the better**, ie the lower the turnover period the better, but several aspects of inventory holding policy have to be balanced.

(a)     Lead times
(b)     Seasonal fluctuations in orders
(c)     Alternative uses of warehouse space
(d)     Bulk buying discounts
(e)     Likelihood of inventory perishing or becoming obsolete

Presumably if we add together the inventory turnover period and receivables collection period, this should give us an indication of how soon inventory is converted into cash. Both receivables collection period and inventory turnover period therefore give us a further indication of the company's liquidity.

## 3.13 Inventory turnover period: example

The estimated inventory turnover periods for a supermarket are as follows.

| Company | Inventory Cost of sales | Inventory turnover period (days× 365) | Previous year |
|---|---|---|---|
| Supermarket | $\dfrac{\$15,554K}{\$254,571K}$ | 22.3 days | $\dfrac{\$14,094K}{\$261,368K} \times 365 = 19.7$ days |

## 3.14 Accounts payable payment period

Formula to learn

**Accounts payable payment period** is ideally calculated by the formula:

$$\frac{\text{Trade accounts payable}}{\text{Purchases}} \times 365 \text{ days}$$

It is rare to find purchases disclosed in published accounts and so **cost of sales serves as an approximation**. The payment period often helps to assess a company's liquidity; an increase is often a sign of lack of long-term finance or poor management of current assets, resulting in the use of extended credit from suppliers, increased bank overdraft and so on.

### Question

Liquidity and working capital

Calculate liquidity and working capital ratios from the accounts of TEB Co, a business which provides service support (cleaning etc) to customers worldwide. Comment on the results of your calculations.

|  | 20X7 $m | 20X6 $m |
|---|---|---|
| Sales revenue | 2,176.2 | 2,344.8 |
| Cost of sales | 1,659.0 | 1,731.5 |
| Gross profit | 517.2 | 613.3 |
| Current assets |  |  |
| Inventories | 42.7 | 78.0 |
| Receivables (note 1) | 378.9 | 431.4 |
| Short-term deposits and cash | 205.2 | 145.0 |
|  | 626.8 | 654.4 |
| Current liabilities |  |  |
| Loans and overdrafts | 32.4 | 81.1 |
| Tax on profits | 67.8 | 76.7 |
| Accruals | 11.7 | 17.2 |
| Payables (note 2) | 487.2 | 467.2 |
|  | 599.1 | 642.2 |
| Net current assets | 27.7 | 12.2 |
| Notes |  |  |
| 1  Trade receivables | 295.2 | 335.5 |
| 2  Trade payables | 190.8 | 188.1 |

### Answer

|  | 20X7 | 20X6 |
|---|---|---|
| Current ratio | $\frac{626.8}{599.1} = 1.05$ | $\frac{654.4}{642.2} = 1.02$ |
| Quick ratio | $\frac{584.1}{599.1} = 0.97$ | $\frac{576.4}{642.2} = 0.90$ |
| Accounts receivable collection period | $\frac{295.2}{2,176.2} \times 365 = 49.5$ days | $\frac{335.5}{2,344.8} \times 365 = 52.2$ days |
| Inventory turnover period | $\frac{42.7}{1,659.0} \times 365 = 9.4$ days | $\frac{78.0}{1,731.5} \times 365 = 16.4$ days |
| Accounts payable payment period | $\frac{190.8}{1,659.0} \times 365 = 42.0$ days | $\frac{188.1}{1,731.5} \times 365 = 39.7$ days |

The company's current ratio is a little lower than average but its quick ratio is better than average and very little less than the current ratio. This suggests that inventory levels are strictly controlled, which is reinforced by the low inventory turnover period. It would seem that working capital is tightly managed, to avoid the poor liquidity which could be caused by a long receivables collection period and comparatively high payables.

The company in the exercise is a service company and hence it would be expected to have very low inventory and a very short inventory turnover period. The similarity of receivables collection period and payables payment period means that the company is passing on most of the delay in receiving payment to its suppliers.

## Question
Operating cycle

(a) Calculate the operating cycle for Moribund plc for 20X2 on the basis of the following information.

|  |  | $ |
|---|---|---|
| Inventory: | raw materials | 150,000 |
|  | work in progress | 60,000 |
|  | finished goods | 200,000 |
| Purchases |  | 500,000 |
| Trade accounts receivable |  | 230,000 |
| Trade accounts payable |  | 120,000 |
| Sales |  | 900,000 |
| Cost of goods sold |  | 750,000 |

*Tutorial note.* You will need to calculate inventory turnover periods (total year end inventory over cost of goods sold), receivables as daily sales, and payables in relation to purchases, all converted into 'days'.

(b) List the steps which might be taken in order to improve the operating cycle.

## Answer

(a) The operating cycle can be found as follows.

Inventory turnover period: $\dfrac{\text{Total closing inventory} \times 365}{\text{Cost of goods sold}}$

*plus*

Accounts receivable collection period: $\dfrac{\text{Closing trade receivables} \times 365}{\text{Sales}}$

*less*

Accounts payable payment period: $\dfrac{\text{Closing trade payables} \times 365}{\text{Purchases}}$

|  | 20X2 |
|---|---|
| Total closing inventory ($) | 410,000 |
| Cost of goods sold ($) | 750,000 |
| Inventory turnover period | 199.5 days |
| Closing receivables ($) | 230,000 |
| Sales ($) | 900,000 |
| Receivables collection period | 93.3 days |
| Closing payables ($) | 120,000 |
| Purchases ($) | 500,000 |
| Payables payment period | (87.6 days) |
| Length of operating cycle (199.5 + 93.3 – 87.6) | 205.2 days |

(b) The steps that could be taken to reduce the operating cycle include the following.

(i) Reducing the raw material inventory turnover period.

(ii) Reducing the time taken to produce goods. However, the company must ensure that quality is not sacrificed as a result of speeding up the production process.

(iii) Increasing the period of credit taken from suppliers. The credit period already seems very long – the company is allowed three months credit by its suppliers, and probably could not be increased. If the credit period is extended then the company may lose discounts for prompt payment.

(iv) Reducing the finished goods inventory turnover period.

(v) Reducing the receivables collection period. The administrative costs of speeding up debt collection and the effect on sales of reducing the credit period allowed must be evaluated. However, the credit period does already seem very long by the standards of most industries. It may be that generous terms have been allowed to secure large contracts and little will be able to be done about this in the short term.

# 4 Shareholders' investment ratios

Ratios such as EPS and dividend per share help equity shareholders and other investors to **assess the value and quality of an investment in the ordinary shares of a company.**

They are:

(a) Earnings per share
(b) Dividend per share
(c) Dividend cover
(d) P/E ratio
(e) Dividend yield

The value of an investment in ordinary shares in a company **listed on a stock exchange** is its market value, and so investment ratios must have regard not only to information in the company's published accounts, but also to the current price, and the fourth and fifth ratios involve using the share price.

## 4.1 Earnings per share

It is possible to calculate the return on each ordinary share in the year. This is the earnings per share (EPS). Earnings per share is the amount of net profit for the period that is attributable to each ordinary share which is outstanding during all or part of the period (see Chapter 18).

## 4.2 Dividend per share and dividend cover

The **dividend per share** in cents is self-explanatory, and clearly an item of some interest to shareholders.

**Formula to learn**

**Dividend cover** is a ratio of: $\dfrac{\text{Earnings per share}}{\text{Dividend per (ordinary) share}}$

It shows the **proportion of profit for the year that is available for distribution to shareholders that has been paid (or proposed) and what proportion will be retained in the business to finance future growth.** A dividend cover of 2 times would indicate that the company had paid 50% of its distributable profits as dividends, and retained 50% in the business to help to finance future operations. Retained profits are an important source of funds for most companies, and so the dividend cover can in some cases be quite high.

A **significant change** in the dividend cover from one year to the next would be worth looking at closely. For example, if a company's dividend cover were to fall sharply between one year and the next, it could be that its profits had fallen, but the directors wished to pay at least the same amount of dividends as in the previous year, so as to keep shareholder expectations satisfied.

## 4.3 P/E ratio

Formula to learn

> The **Price/Earnings (P/E) ratio** is the ratio of a company's current share price to the earnings per share.

A high P/E ratio indicates strong shareholder **confidence** in the company and its future, eg in profit growth, and a lower P/E ratio indicates lower confidence.

The P/E ratio of one company can be compared with the P/E ratios of:

- Other companies in the same business sector
- Other companies generally

It is often used in **stock exchange reporting** where prices are readily available.

## 4.4 Dividend yield

Dividend yield is the return a shareholder is currently expecting on the shares of a company.

Formula to learn

> $$\text{Dividend yield} = \frac{\text{Dividend on the share for the year}}{\text{Current market value of the share (ex div)}} \times 100\%$$

(a) The dividend per share is taken as the dividend for the previous year.
(b) Ex-div means that the share price does *not* include the right to the most recent dividend.

Shareholders look for **both dividend yield and capital growth**. Obviously, dividend yield is therefore an important aspect of a share's performance.

### Question
Dividend yield

In the year to 30 September 20X8, an advertising agency declares an interim ordinary dividend of 7.4c per share and a final ordinary dividend of 8.6c per share. Assuming an ex div share price of 315 cents, what is the dividend yield?

### Answer

The total dividend per share is (7.4 + 8.6) = 16 cents

$$\frac{16}{315} \times 100 = 5.1\%$$

# 5 Presentation of financial performance

FAST FORWARD

> However many ratios you can find to calculate **numbers alone will not answer a question**. You **must** interpret all the information available to you and support your interpretation with ratio calculations.

Exam focus point

> Examination questions on financial performance may try to simulate a real life situation. A set of accounts could be presented and you may be asked to prepare a report on them, addressed to a specific interested party, such as a bank.

You should begin your report with a heading showing who it is from, the name of the addressee, the subject of the report and a suitable date.

A good approach is often to head up a **'schedule of ratios and statistics'** which will form an appendix to the main report. Calculate the ratios in a logical sequence, dealing in turn with operating and profitability ratios, use of assets (eg turnover period for inventories, collection period for receivables), liquidity and gearing/leverage.

As you calculate the ratios you are likely to be struck by **significant fluctuations and trends**. These will form the basis of your comments in the body of the report. The report should begin with some introductory comments, setting out the scope of your analysis and mentioning that detailed figures have been included in an appendix. You should then go on to present your analysis under any categories called for by the question (eg separate sections for management, shareholders and creditors, or separate sections for profitability and liquidity).

Finally, look out for opportunities to **suggest remedial action** where trends appear to be unfavourable. Questions sometimes require you specifically to set out your advice and recommendations.

## 5.1 Planning your answers

This is as good a place as any to stress the importance of planning your answers. This is particularly important for 'wordy' questions. While you may feel like breathing a sigh of relief after all that number crunching, you should not be tempted to 'waffle'. The best way to avoid going off the point is to **prepare an answer plan**. This has the advantage of making you think before you write and structure your answer logically.

The following approach may be adopted when preparing an answer plan.

(a)     Read the question **requirements**.

(b)     **Skim through the question** to see roughly what it is about.

(c)     Read through the question carefully, **underlining any key words**.

(d)     Set out the **headings** for the main parts of your answer. Leave space to insert points within the headings.

(e)     **Jot down points** to make within the main sections, underlining points on which you wish to expand.

(f)     Write your **full answer**.

You should allow yourself the full time allocation for written answers, that is 1.8 minutes per mark. If, however, you run out of time, a clear answer plan with points in note form will earn you more marks than an introductory paragraph written out in full.

Question                                                                                                    Ratios

The following information has been extracted from the recently published accounts of DG.

EXTRACTS FROM THE STATEMENTS OF PROFIT OR LOSS TO 30 APRIL

|  | 20X9 | 20X8 |
|---|---|---|
|  | $'000 | $'000 |
| Sales | 11,200 | 9,750 |
| Cost of sales | 8,460 | 6,825 |
| Net profit before tax | 465 | 320 |
| This is after charging: |  |  |
| Depreciation | 360 | 280 |
| Loan note interest | 80 | 60 |
| Interest on bank overdraft | 15 | 9 |
| Audit fees | 12 | 10 |

## STATEMENTS OF FINANCIAL POSITION AS AT 30 APRIL

|  | 20X9 | | 20X8 | |
|---|---|---|---|---|
|  | $'000 | $'000 | $'000 | $'000 |
| *Assets* |  |  |  |  |
| Non-current assets |  | 1,850 |  | 1,430 |
| Current assets |  |  |  |  |
| Inventory | 640 |  | 490 |  |
| Receivables | 1,230 |  | 1,080 |  |
| Cash | 80 |  | 120 |  |
|  |  | 1,950 |  | 1,690 |
| Total assets |  | 3,800 |  | 3,120 |
| *Equity and liabilities* |  |  |  |  |
| Equity |  |  |  |  |
| Ordinary share capital | 800 |  | 800 |  |
| Retained earnings | 1,310 |  | 930 |  |
|  |  | 2,110 |  | 1,730 |
| Non-current liabilities |  |  |  |  |
| 10% loan stock |  | 800 |  | 600 |
| Current liabilities |  |  |  |  |
| Bank overdraft | 110 |  | 80 |  |
| Payables | 750 |  | 690 |  |
| Taxation | 30 |  | 20 |  |
|  |  | 890 |  | 790 |
| Total equity and liabilities |  | 3,800 |  | 3,120 |

The following ratios are those calculated for DG, based on its published accounts for the previous year, and also the latest industry average ratios:

|  | DG 30 April 20X8 | Industry average |
|---|---|---|
| ROCE (capital employed = equity and debentures) | 16.30% | 18.50% |
| Profit/sales | 3.90% | 4.73% |
| Asset turnover | 4.19 | 3.91 |
| Current ratio | 2.14 | 1.90 |
| Quick ratio | 1.52 | 1.27 |
| Gross profit margin | 30.00% | 35.23% |
| Accounts receivable collection period | 40 days | 52 days |
| Accounts payable payment period | 37 days | 49 days |
| Inventory turnover (times) | 13.90 | 18.30 |
| Gearing | 26.75% | 32.71% |

*Required*

(a)  Calculate comparable ratios (to two decimal places where appropriate) for DG for the year ended 30 April 20X9. All calculations must be clearly shown.

(b)  Write a report to your board of directors analysing the performance of DG, comparing the results against the previous year and against the industry average.

## Answer

|  | 20X8 | 20X9 | Industry average |
|---|---|---|---|
| (a) |  |  |  |
| ROCE | $\frac{320+60}{2,330}=16.30\%$ | $\frac{465+80}{2,910}=18.72\%$ | 18.50% |
| Profit/sales | $\frac{320+60}{9,750}=3.90\%$ | $\frac{465+80}{11,200}=4.87\%$ | 4.73% |

| | 20X8 | 20X9 | Industry average |
|---|---|---|---|
| Asset turnover | $\dfrac{9{,}750}{2{,}330}=4.18x$ | $\dfrac{11{,}200}{2{,}910}=3.85x$ | 3.91x |
| Current ratio | $\dfrac{1{,}690}{790}=2.10$ | $\dfrac{1{,}950}{890}=2.20$ | 1.90 |
| Quick ratio | $\dfrac{1{,}080+120}{790}=1.52$ | $\dfrac{1{,}230+80}{890}=1.47$ | 1.27 |
| Gross profit margin | $\dfrac{9{,}750-6{,}825}{9{,}750}=30.00\%$ | $\dfrac{11{,}200-8{,}460}{11{,}200}=24.46\%$ | 35.23% |
| Accounts receivable collection period | $\dfrac{1{,}080}{9{,}750}\times365=40\text{days}$ | $\dfrac{1{,}230}{11{,}200}\times365=40\text{days}$ | 52 days |
| Accounts payable payment period | $\dfrac{690}{6{,}825}\times365=37\text{days}$ | $\dfrac{750}{8{,}460}\times365=32\text{days}$ | 49 days |
| Inventory turnover (times) | $\dfrac{6{,}825}{490}=13.9x$ | $\dfrac{8{,}460}{640}=13.2x$ | 18.30x |
| Gearing | $\dfrac{600}{2{,}330}=25.75\%$ | $\dfrac{800}{2{,}910}=27.5\%$ | 32.71% |

(b) (i) REPORT

To: Board of Directors
From: Accountant
Subject: Analysis of performance of DG
Date: xx/xx/xx

This report should be read in conjunction with the appendix attached which shows the relevant ratios (from part (a)).

Trading and profitability

Return on capital employed has improved considerably between 20X8 and 20X9 and is now higher than the industry average.

Net income as a proportion of sales has also improved noticeably between the years and is also now marginally ahead of the industry average. Gross margin, however, is considerably lower than in the previous year and is only some 70% of the industry average. This suggests either that there has been a change in the cost structure of DG or that there has been a change in the method of cost allocation between the periods. Either way, this is a marked change that requires investigation. The company may be in a period of transition as sales have increased by nearly 15% over the year and it would appear that new non-current assets have been purchased.

Asset turnover has declined between the periods although the 20X9 figure is in line with the industry average. This reduction might indicate that the efficiency with which assets are used has deteriorated or it might indicate that the assets acquired in 20X9 have not yet fully contributed to the business. A longer term trend would clarify the picture.

(ii) Liquidity and working capital management

The current ratio has improved slightly over the year and is marginally higher than the industry average. It is also in line with what is generally regarded as satisfactory (2:1).

The quick ratio has declined marginally but is still better than the industry average. This suggests that DG has no short term liquidity problems and should have no difficulty in paying its debts as they become due.

Receivables as a proportion of sales is unchanged from 20X8 and are considerably lower than the industry average. Consequently, there is probably little opportunity to reduce this further and there may be pressure in the future from customers to increase the period of credit given. The period of credit taken from suppliers has fallen from 37 days' purchases to

32 days' and is much lower than the industry average; thus, it may be possible to finance any additional receivables by negotiating better credit terms from suppliers.

Inventory turnover has fallen slightly and is much slower than the industry average and this may partly reflect stocking up ahead of a significant increase in sales. Alternatively, there is some danger that the inventory could contain certain obsolete items that may require writing off. The relative increase in the level of inventory has been financed by an increased overdraft which may reduce if the inventory levels can be brought down.

The high levels of inventory, overdraft and receivables compared to that of payables suggests a labour intensive company or one where considerable value is added to bought-in products.

(iii)    Gearing

The level of gearing has increased only slightly over the year and is below the industry average. Since the return on capital employed is nearly twice the rate of interest on the loan stock, profitability is likely to be increased by a modest increase in the level of gearing.

Signed: Accountant

One of the competences you require to fulfil performance objective 11 of the PER is the ability to interpret the relationship between the elements within financial statements. You can apply the knowledge you obtain from this chapter to help to demonstrate this competence.

**Exam focus point**

Analysis questions require the exercise of a certain amount of critical judgement. Questions are often set in which the directors propose a course of action and the examiner reports that candidates often agree with the directors' proposals. In which case, why was the question set??

# Chapter roundup

- You must be able to **appraise and communicate** the position and prospects of a business based on given and prepared statements and ratios.

- Return on capital employed (ROCE) may be used by shareholders or the Board to assess the performance of management.

- Banks and other lenders will be interested in a company's gearing level.

- Ratios such as EPS and dividend per share help equity shareholders and other investors to **assess the value and quality** of an investment in the ordinary shares of a company.

- However many ratios you can find to calculate, **numbers alone will not answer a question**. You *must* interpret all the information available to you and support your interpretation with ratio calculations.

# Quick quiz

1 List the main categories of ratio.

2 ROCE is $\dfrac{\text{Profit before interest and tax}}{\text{Capital employed}} \times 100\%$

    True ☐

    False ☐

3 Company Q has a profit margin of 7%. Briefly comment on this.

4 The debt ratio is a company's long-term debt divided by its net assets.

    True ☐

    False ☐

5 The cash flow ratio is the ratio of:

    A    Gross cash inflow to total debt
    B    Gross cash inflow to net debt
    C    Net cash inflow to total debt
    D    Net cash inflow to net debt

6 List the formulae for:

    (a)    Current ratio    (c)    Accounts receivable collection period
    (b)    Quick ratio    (d)    Inventory turnover period

1    See Section 1.1.

2    True

3    You should be careful here. You have very little information. This is a low margin but you need to know what industry the company operates in. 7% may be good for a major retailer.

4    False (see Section 3.2)

5    C (see Section 3.6)

6    See Sections 3.9, 3.10 and 3.12.

Now try the questions below from the Exam Question Bank

| Number | Level | Marks | Time |
|--------|-------|-------|------|
| 25 | Examination | 25 | 45 mins |

# 20

# Limitations of financial statements and interpretation techniques

| Topic list | Syllabus reference |
|---|---|
| 1 Limitations of financial statements | E1 |
| 2 Accounting polices and the limitations of ratio analysis | E3 |

## Introduction

In the least chapter we looked at how we interpret financial statements. In this chapter we take a look at how far we can rely on such interpretation.

# Study guide

| | | | Intellectual level |
|---|---|---|---|
| **E** | **ANALYSING AND INTERPRETING FINANCIAL STATEMENTS** | | |
| **1** | **Limitations of financial statements** | | |
| | (a) | indicate the problems of using historic information to predict future performance and trends. | 2 |
| | (b) | discuss how financial statements may be manipulated to produce a desired effect (creative accounting, window dressing) | 2 |
| | (c) | recognise how related party relationships have the potential to mislead users. | 2 |
| | (d) | explain why figures in the statement of financial position may not be representative of average values throughout the period for example, due to: | 2 |
| | | (i)   seasonal trading | |
| | | (ii)   major asset acquisitions near the end of the accounting period. | |
| **3** | **Limitations of interpretation techniques** | | |
| | (a) | discuss the limitations in the use of ratio analysis for assessing corporate performance. | 2 |
| | (b) | discuss the effect that changes in accounting policies or the use of different accounting policies between entities can have on the ability to interpret performance. | 2 |
| | (c) | indicate other information, including non-financial information, that may be of relevance to the assessment of an entity's performance. | 1 |

# Exam guide

These issues are unlikely to form a whole question but could well appear in a question on interpretation of accounts.

# 1 Limitations of financial statements

**FAST FORWARD**

> Financial statements are affected by the obvious shortcomings of historical cost information and are also subject to manipulation.

Financial statements are intended to give a fair presentation of the financial performance of an entity over a period and its financial position at the end of that period. The IASB *Conceptual Framework* and the IFRSs are there to ensure as far as possible that they do. However, there are a number of reasons why the information in financial statements should not just be taken at its face value.

## 1.1 Problems of historical cost information

Historical cost information is reliable and can be verified, but it becomes less relevant as time goes by. The value shown for assets carried in the statement of financial position at historical cost may bear no relation whatever to what their current value is and what it may cost to replace them. The corresponding depreciation charge will also be low, leading to the overstatement of profits in real terms. The financial statements do not show the real cost of using such assets.

This is particularly misleading when attempting to predict future performance. It could be that a major asset will need to be replaced in two years time, at vastly more than the original cost of the asset currently shown in the statement of financial position. This will then entail much higher depreciation and interest payments (if a loan or finance lease is used). In addition, overstatement of profit due to the low depreciation charge could have led to too much profit having been distributed, increasing the likelihood of new asset purchases having to be financed by loans. This information could not have been obtained just from looking at the financial statements.

In a period of inflation, financial statements based on historical cost are subject to an additional distortion. Sales revenue will be keeping pace with inflation and so will the cost of purchases. However, using FIFO (and to some degree the weighted average method) inventory being used will be valued as the earliest (and therefore cheapest) purchases. This leads to understatement of cost of sales and overstatement of profits. This is the result of inventory carried at historical cost.

## 1.2 Creative accounting

Listed companies produce their financial statements with one eye on the stock market and, where possible, they like to produce financial statements which show analysts what they are expecting to see. For instance, a steady rise in profits, with no peaks or troughs, is reassuring to potential investors. Companies could sometimes achieve this by using provisions to smooth out the peaks and troughs. This has been largely outlawed by IAS 37 (see Chapter 13), but companies can still achieve similar effects by delaying or advancing invoicing or manipulating cut-offs or accruals. Directors who are paid performance bonuses will favour the steady rise (enough to secure the bonus each year, rather than up one year, down the next) while those who hold share options may be aiming for one spectacular set of results just before they sell.

An important aspect of improving the appearance of the statement of financial position is keeping gearing as low as possible. Investors know that interest payments reduce the amount available for distribution and potential lenders will be less willing to lend to a company which is already highly geared.

A number of creative accounting measures are aimed at reducing gearing. In the past parent companies could find reasons to exclude highly-geared subsidiaries from the consolidation and could obtain loans in the first place via such 'quasi subsidiaries', so that the loan never appeared in the consolidated statement of financial position. This loophole was effectively closed by IAS 27, but other means of keeping debt out of the statement of financial position exist. Finance leases can be treated as operating leases, so that the asset and the loan are kept off-balance sheet. Assets can be 'sold' under a sale and leaseback agreement, which is in effect a disguised loan. And if all else fails, a last minute piece of 'window dressing' can be undertaken. For instance, a loan can be repaid just before the year end and taken out again at the beginning of the next year.

## 1.3 The effect of related parties

The objective of IAS 24 is to "ensure that an entity's financial statements contain the disclosures necessary to draw attention to the possibility that its financial position and profit or loss may have been affected by the existence of related parties and by transactions and outstanding balances with such parties".

Related parties are a normal feature of business. It is common for entities to carry on activities with or through subsidiaries and associates, or occasionally to engage in transactions with directors or their families. The point is that such transactions cannot be assumed to have been engaged in 'at arm's length' or in the best interests of the entity itself, which is why investors and potential investors need to be made aware of them. Transfer pricing can be used to transfer profit from one company to another and inter-company loans and transfers of non-current assets can also be used in the same way.

Despite IAS 24, companies which wish to disguise a related party relationship can probably still find complex ways to do it (the Enron scandal revealed the existence of numerous related party transactions) and financial statements do not show the unseen effects of such a relationship. For instance, a subsidiary may not have been allowed to tender for a contract in competition with another group company. Its shareholders will never know about such missed opportunities.

## 1.4 Seasonal trading

This is another issue that can distort reported results. Many companies whose trade is seasonal position their year end after their busy period, to minimise time spent on the inventory count. At this point in time, the statement of financial position will show a healthy level of cash and/or receivables and a low level of trade payables, assuming most of them have been paid. Thus the position is reported at the moment when the company is at its most solvent. A statement of financial position drawn up a few months earlier, or even perhaps a few months later, when trade is still slack but fixed costs still have to be paid, may give a very different picture.

## 1.5 Asset acquisitions

Major asset acquisitions just before the end of an accounting period can also distort results. The statement of financial position will show an increased level of assets and corresponding liabilities (probably a loan or lease payable), but the income which will be earned from utilisation of the asset will not yet have materialised. This will adversely affect the company's return on capital employed.

# 2 Accounting policies and the limitations of ratio analysis

> We discussed the disclosure of accounting policies in our examination of IAS 1. The choice of accounting policy and the effect of its implementation are almost as important as its disclosure in that the results of a company can be altered significantly by the choice of accounting policy.

## 2.1 The effect of choice of accounting policies

Where accounting standards allow alternative treatment of items in the accounts, then the accounting policy note should declare which policy has been chosen. It should then be applied consistently.

You should be able to think of examples of how the choice of accounting policy can affect the financial statements eg whether to revalue property in IAS 16, or whether to capitalise the cost of interest in self-constructed assets in IAS 23.

## 2.2 Changes in accounting policy

The effect of a change of accounting policy is treated as a prior year adjustment according to IAS 8 (see Chapter 7). This just means that the comparative figures are adjusted for the change in accounting policy for comparative purposes and an adjustment is put through retained earnings.

Under **consistency of presentation** in IAS 1, any change in policy may only be made if it can be justified on the grounds that the new policy is preferable to the one it replaces because it will give a fairer presentation of the result and of the financial position of a reporting entity.

The problem with this situation is that the directors may be able to **manipulate the results** through change(s) of accounting policies. This would be done to avoid the effect of an old accounting policy or gain the effect of a new one. It is likely to be done in a sensitive period, perhaps when the company's profits are low or the company is about to announce a rights issue. The management would have to convince the auditors that the new policy was much better, but it is not difficult to produce reasons in such cases.

The effect of such a change is very **short-term**. Most analysts and sophisticated users will discount its effect immediately, except to the extent that it will affect any dividend (because of the effect on distributable profits). It may help to avoid breaches of banking covenants because of the effect on certain ratios.

Obviously, the accounting policy for any item in the accounts could only be changed once in quite a long period of time. Auditors would not allow another change, even back to the old policy, unless there was a wholly exceptional reason.

The managers of a company can choose accounting policies **initially** to suit the company or the type of results they want to get. Any changes in accounting policy must be justified, but some managers might try to change accounting policies just to manipulate the results.

## 2.3 Limitations of ratio analysis

The consideration of how accounting policies may be used to manipulate company results leads us to some of the other limitations of ratio analysis.

The most important ones are:

- In a company's first year of trading there will be no comparative figures. So there will be no indication of whether or not a ratio is improving.
- Comparison against industry averages may not be that revealing. A business may be subject to factors which are not common in the industry.
- Ratios based on historic cost accounts are subject to the distortions described in 1.1 above. In particular, undervalued assets will distort ROCE and exaggerate gearing.
- Ratios are influenced by the choice of accounting policy. For instance, a company seeking to maintain or increase its ROCE may choose not to revalue its assets.
- Financial statements are subject to manipulation and so are the ratios based on them. Creative accounting is undertaken with key ratios in mind.
- Inflation over a period will distort results and ratios. Net profit, and therefore ROCE, can be inflated where FIFO is applied during an inflationary period.
- No two companies, even operating in the same industry, will have the same financial and business risk profile. For instance, one may have better access to cheap borrowing than the other and so may be able to sustain a higher level of gearing.

## 2.4 Other issues

Are there other issues which should be looked at when assessing an entity's performance? Factors to consider are:

- How technologically advanced is it? If it is not using the latest equipment and processes it risks being pushed out of the market at some point or having to undertake a high level of capital expenditure.
- What are its environmental policies? Is it in danger of having to pay for cleanup if the law is tightened? Does it appeal to those seeking 'ethical investment'?
- What is the reputation of its management? If it has attracted good people and kept them, that is a positive indicator.
- What is its mission statement? To what degree does it appear to be fulfilling it?
- What is its reputation as an employer? Do people want to work for this company? What are its labour relations like?
- What is the size of its market? Does it trade in just one or two countries or worldwide?
- How strong is its competition? Is it in danger of takeover?

You can probably think of other factors that you would consider important. In some cases you can also look at the quality of the product that a company produces.

Question | Company analysis
---

Analyse a company that you know something about against these criteria.

In any interpretation of accounts question, bear the issues in this chapter in mind. The examiner expects you to be able to look critically at financial information.

One of the competences you require to fulfil performance objective 11 of the PER is the ability to draw valid conclusions from the information contained within financial statements or other financial data. You can apply the knowledge you obtain from this chapter to help to demonstrate this competence.

# Chapter Roundup

- Financial statements are affected by the obvious shortcoming of historic cost information and are also subject to manipulation.

- The choice of accounting policy and the effect of its implementation are almost as important as its disclosure, in that the results of a company can be altered significantly by the choice of accounting policy.

# Quick Quiz

1 What is the effect of inventory carried at historical cost in a period of inflation?
2 What is 'window dressing'?
3 How can companies attempt to transfer profits from one group company to another?
4 Will two companies in the same industry have the same ROCE?

# Answers to Quick Quiz

1    Overstatement of profits (see 1.1).
2    An accounting adjustment made just before the year end to improve the appearance of the financial statements (1.2).
3    Transfer pricing, intercompany loans, transfers of fixed assets (1.3).
4    Probably not, there may be many other differences between them.

Now try the questions below from the Exam Question Bank

| Number | Level | Marks | Time |
|--------|-------|-------|------|
| 26 | Examination | 25 | 45 mins |

# Statements of cash flows

| Topic list | Syllabus reference |
|---|---|
| 1 IAS 7 Statement of cash flows | C1 |
| 2 Preparing a statement of cash flows | C1 |
| 3 Interpretation of statements of cash flows | C1 |

## Introduction

You have already covered much of the material on statements of cash flows in your earlier studies. Much of this is repeated here for revision.

The importance of the distinction between cash and profit and the scant attention paid to this by the statement of profit or loss has resulted in the development of statements of cash flows.

This chapter adopts a systematic approach to the preparation of statements of cash flows in examinations; you should learn this method and you will then be equipped for any problems in the exam.

The third section of the chapter looks at the information which is provided by statements of cash flows and how it should be analysed.

# Study guide

| | | Intellectual level |
|---|---|---|
| C1 | FINANCIAL STATEMENTS | |
| | Statements of cash flows | |
| (a) | prepare a statement of cash flows for a single entity (not a group) in accordance with relevant accounting standards using the direct and the indirect method. | 2 |
| (b) | compare the usefulness of cash flow information with that of an income statement or statement of comprehensive income. | 2 |
| (c) | interpret a statement of cash flows (together with other financial information) to assess the performance and financial position of an entity. | 2 |

# Exam guide

Statements of cash flows appear regularly as Question 3 in the F7 paper, sometimes combined with interpretation of the financial statements.

# 1 IAS 7 Statement of cash flows

**Statements of cash flows** are a useful addition to the financial statements because it is recognised that accounting profit is not the only indicator of a company's performance.

## 1.1 Introduction

It has been argued that 'profit' does not always give a useful or meaningful picture of a company's operations. Readers of a company's financial statements might even be **misled by a reported profit figure**.

(a) Shareholders might believe that if a company makes a profit after tax, of say, $100,000 then this is the amount which it could afford to **pay as a dividend**. Unless the company has **sufficient cash** available to stay in business and also to pay a dividend, the shareholders' expectations would be wrong.

(b) Employees might believe that if a company makes profits, it can afford to **pay higher wages** next year. This opinion may not be correct: the ability to pay wages depends on the **availability of cash**.

(c) Survival of a business entity depends not so much on profits as on its **ability to pay its debts when they fall due**. Such payments might include 'revenue' items such as material purchases, wages, interest and taxation etc, but also capital payments for new non-current assets and the repayment of loan capital when this falls due (for example on the redemption of debentures).

From these examples, it may be apparent that a company's performance and prospects depend not so much on the 'profits' earned in a period, but more realistically on liquidity or **cash flows**.

## 1.2 Funds flow and cash flow

Some countries, either currently or in the past, have required the disclosure of additional statements based on **funds flow** rather than cash flow. However, the definition of 'funds' can be very vague and such statements often simply require a rearrangement of figures already provided in the statement of financial position and statement of profit or loss. By contrast, a statement of cash flows is unambiguous and provides information which is additional to that provided in the rest of the accounts. It also lends itself to organisation by activity and not by classification in the statement of financial position.

Statements of cash flows are frequently given as an **additional statement**, supplementing the statement of financial position, statement of profit or loss and other comprehensive income and related notes. The group aspects of statements of cash flows (and certain complex matters) have been excluded as they are beyond the scope of your syllabus.

## 1.3 Objective of IAS 7

The aim of IAS 7 is to provide information to users of financial statements about the entity's **ability to generate cash and cash equivalents**, as well as indicating the cash needs of the entity. The statement of cash flows provides *historical* information about cash and cash equivalents, classifying cash flows between operating, investing and financing activities.

## 1.4 Scope

A statement of cash flows should be presented as an **integral part** of an entity's financial statements. All types of entity can provide useful information about cash flows as the need for cash is universal, whatever the nature of their revenue-producing activities. Therefore **all entities are required by the standard to produce a statement of cash flows**.

## 1.5 Benefits of cash flow information

The use of statements of cash flows is very much **in conjunction** with the rest of the financial statements. Users can gain further appreciation of the change in net assets, of the entity's financial position (liquidity and solvency) and the entity's ability to adapt to changing circumstances by affecting the amount and timing of cash flows. Statements of cash flows **enhance comparability** as they are not affected by differing accounting policies used for the same type of transactions or events.

Cash flow information of a historical nature can be used as an indicator of the amount, timing and certainty of future cash flows. Past forecast cash flow information can be **checked for accuracy** as actual figures emerge. The relationship between profit and cash flows can be analysed as can changes in prices over time.

## 1.6 Definitions

The standard gives the following definitions, the most important of which are **cash** and **cash equivalents**.

**Key terms**

> - **Cash** comprises cash on hand and demand deposits.
> - **Cash equivalents** are short-term, highly liquid investments that are readily convertible to known amounts of cash and which are subject to an insignificant risk of changes in value.
> - **Cash flows** are inflows and outflows of cash and cash equivalents.
> - **Operating activities** are the principal revenue-producing activities of the entity and other activities that are not investing or financing activities.
> - **Investing activities** are the acquisition and disposal of non-current assets and other investments not included in cash equivalents.
> - **Financing activities** are activities that result in changes in the size and composition of the equity capital and borrowings of the entity.
>                                                                                                           *(IAS 7)*

## 1.7 Cash and cash equivalents

The standard expands on the definition of cash equivalents: they are not held for investment or other long-term purposes, but rather to meet short-term cash commitments. To fulfil the above definition, an investment's **maturity date should normally be within three months from its acquisition date**. It would usually be the case then that equity investments (ie shares in other companies) are *not* cash equivalents. An exception would be where preferred shares were acquired with a very close maturity date.

**Loans and other borrowings** from banks are classified as financing activities. In some countries, however, **bank overdrafts** are repayable on demand and are treated as part of an entity's total cash management system. In these circumstances an overdrawn balance will be included in cash and cash equivalents. Such banking arrangements are characterised by a balance which fluctuates between overdrawn and credit.

**Movements** between different types of cash and cash equivalent are not included in cash flows. The investment of surplus cash in cash equivalents is part of cash management, not part of operating, investing or financing activities.

## 1.8 Presentation of a statement of cash flows

IAS 7 requires statements of cash flows to report cash flows during the period classified by **operating, investing and financing activities**.

The manner of presentation of cash flows between operating, investing and financing activities **depends on the nature of the entity**. By classifying cash flows between different activities in this way users can see the impact on cash and cash equivalents of each one, and their relationships with each other. We can look at each in more detail.

### 1.8.1 Operating activities

This is perhaps the key part of the statement of cash flows because it shows whether, and to what extent, companies can **generate cash from their operations**. It is these operating cash flows which must, in the end pay for all cash outflows relating to other activities, ie paying loan interest, dividends and so on.

Most of the components of cash flows from operating activities will be those items which **determine the net profit or loss of the entity**, ie they relate to the main revenue-producing activities of the entity. The standard gives the following as examples of cash flows from operating activities.

(a)     Cash receipts from the sale of goods and the rendering of services
(b)     Cash receipts from royalties, fees, commissions and other revenue
(c)     Cash payments to suppliers for goods and services
(d)     Cash payments to and on behalf of employees

Certain items may be included in the net profit or loss for the period which do *not* relate to operational cash flows, for example the profit or loss on the sale of a piece of plant will be included in net profit or loss, but the cash flows will be classed as **investing**.

### 1.8.2 Investing activities

The cash flows classified under this heading show the extent of new investment in **assets which will generate future profit and cash flows**. The standard gives the following examples of cash flows arising from investing activities.

(a)     Cash payments to acquire property, plant and equipment, intangibles and other non-current assets, including those relating to capitalised development costs and self-constructed property, plant and equipment
(b)     Cash receipts from sales of property, plant and equipment, intangibles and other non-current assets
(c)     Cash payments to acquire shares or debentures of other entities
(d)     Cash receipts from sales of shares or debentures of other entities
(e)     Cash advances and loans made to other parties
(f)     Cash receipts from the repayment of advances and loans made to other parties

### 1.8.3 Financing activities

This section of the statement of cash flows shows the share of cash which the entity's capital providers have claimed during the period. This is an indicator of **likely future interest and dividend payments**. The standard gives the following examples of cash flows which might arise under this heading.

(a) Cash proceeds from issuing shares

(b) Cash payments to owners to acquire or redeem the entity's shares

(c) Cash proceeds from issuing debentures, loans, notes, bonds, mortgages and other short or long-term borrowings

(d) Principal repayments of amounts borrowed under finance leases

Item (d) needs more explanation. Where the reporting entity uses an asset held under a finance lease, the amounts to go in the statement of cash flows as **financing activities** are repayments of the **principal (capital)** rather than the **interest**. The interest paid will be shown under **operating activities**.

## 1.9 Example: finance lease rental

The notes to the financial statements of Hayley Co show the following in respect of obligations under finance leases.

| Year ended 30 June | 20X5 | 20X4 |
|---|---|---|
| | $'000 | $'000 |
| Amounts payable within one year | 12 | 8 |
| Within two to five years | 110 | 66 |
| | 122 | 74 |
| Less finance charges allocated to future periods | (14) | (8) |
| | 108 | 66 |

Additions to tangible non-current assets acquired under finance leases were shown in the non-current asset note at $56,000.

*Required*

Calculate the capital repayment to be shown in the statement of cash flows of Hayley Co for the year to 30 June 20X5.

## Solution

OBLIGATIONS UNDER FINANCE LEASES

| | $'000 | | $'000 |
|---|---|---|---|
| Capital repayment (bal fig) | 14 | Bal 1.7.X4 | 66 |
| Bal 30.6.X5 | 108 | Additions | 56 |
| | 122 | | 122 |

## 1.10 Reporting cash flows from operating activities

The standard offers a choice of method for this part of the statement of cash flows.

(a) **Direct method:** disclose major classes of gross cash receipts and gross cash payments

(b) **Indirect method:** net profit or loss is adjusted for the effects of transactions of a non-cash nature, any deferrals or accruals of past or future operating cash receipts or payments, and items of income or expense associated with investing or financing cash flows

The **direct method is the preferred method** because it discloses information, not available elsewhere in the financial statements, which could be of use in estimating future cash flows. The example below shows both methods.

### 1.10.1 Using the direct method

There are different ways in which the **information about gross cash receipts and payments** can be obtained. The most obvious way is simply to extract the information from the accounting records. This may be a laborious task, however, and the indirect method below may be easier. The example and question above used the direct method.

## 1.10.2 Using the indirect method

This method is undoubtedly **easier** from the point of view of the preparer of the statement of cash flows. The net profit or loss for the period is adjusted for the following.

(a) Changes during the period in inventories, operating receivables and payables
(b) Non-cash items, eg depreciation, provisions, profits/losses on the sales of assets
(c) Other items, the cash flows from which should be classified under investing or financing activities.

A **proforma** of such a calculation, taken from the IAS, is as follows and this method may be more common in the exam. (The proforma has been amended to reflect changes to IFRS.)

|  | $ |
|---|---:|
| *Cash flows from operating activities* | |
| Profit before taxation | X |
| Adjustments for: | |
| Depreciation | X |
| Foreign exchange loss | X |
| Investment income | (X) |
| Interest expense | X |
|  | X |
| Increase in trade and other receivables | (X) |
| Decrease in inventories | X |
| Decrease in trade payables | (X) |
| Cash generated from operations | X |
| Interest paid | (X) |
| Income taxes paid | (X) |
| *Net cash from operating activities* | X |

It is important to understand why **certain items are added and others subtracted**. Note the following points.

(a) Depreciation is not a cash expense, but is deducted in arriving at profit. It makes sense, therefore, to eliminate it by adding it back.
(b) By the same logic, a loss on a disposal of a non-current asset (arising through underprovision of depreciation) needs to be added back and a profit deducted.
(c) An increase in inventories means less cash – you have spent cash on buying inventory.
(d) An increase in receivables means the company's debtors have not paid as much, and therefore there is less cash.
(e) If we pay off payables, causing the figure to decrease, again we have less cash.

## 1.10.3 Indirect versus direct

The direct method is encouraged where the necessary information is not too costly to obtain, but IAS 7 does not require it. In practice the indirect method is more commonly used, since it is quicker and easier.

## 1.11 Interest and dividends

Cash flows from interest and dividends received and paid should each be **disclosed separately**. Each should be classified in a consistent manner from period to period as either operating, investing or financing activities.

Dividends paid by the entity can be classified in **one of two ways**.

(a) As a **financing cash flow**, showing the cost of obtaining financial resources.
(b) As a component of **cash flows from operating activities** so that users can assess the entity's ability to pay dividends out of operating cash flows.

## 1.12 Taxes on income

Cash flows arising from taxes on income should be **separately disclosed** and should be classified as cash flows from operating activities *unless* they can be specifically identified with financing and investing activities.

Taxation cash flows are often **difficult to match** to the originating underlying transaction, so most of the time all tax cash flows are classified as arising from operating activities.

## 1.13 Components of cash and cash equivalents

The components of cash and cash equivalents should be disclosed and a **reconciliation** should be presented, showing the amounts in the statement of cash flows reconciled with the equivalent items reported in the statement of financial position.

It is also necessary to disclose the **accounting policy** used in deciding the items included in cash and cash equivalents, in accordance with IAS 1 *Presentation of Financial Statements*, but also because of the wide range of cash management practices worldwide.

## 1.14 Other disclosures

All entities should disclose, together with a **commentary by management**, any other information likely to be of importance, for example:

(a) Restrictions on the use of or access to any part of cash equivalents
(b) The amount of undrawn borrowing facilities which are available
(c) Cash flows which increased operating capacity compared to cash flows which merely maintained operating capacity
(d) Cash flows arising from each reported industry and geographical segment

## 1.15 Example of a statement of cash flows

In the next section we will look at the procedures for preparing a statement of cash flows. First, look at this **example**, adapted from the example given in the standard (which is based on a group and therefore beyond the scope of your syllabus).

### 1.15.1 Direct method

STATEMENT OF CASH FLOWS (DIRECT METHOD)
YEAR ENDED 31 DECEMBER 20X7

|  | $m | $m |
|---|---|---|
| *Cash flows from operating activities* | | |
| Cash receipts from customers | 30,330 | |
| Cash paid to suppliers and employees | (27,600) | |
| Cash generated from operations | 2,730 | |
| Interest paid | (270) | |
| Income taxes paid | (900) | |
| *Net cash from operating activities* | | 1,560 |
| *Cash flows from investing activities* | | |
| Purchase of property, plant and equipment | (900) | |
| Proceeds from sale of equipment | 20 | |
| Interest received | 200 | |
| Dividends received | 200 | |
| *Net cash used in investing activities* | | (480) |

|                                                  | $m      | $m    |
|--------------------------------------------------|---------|-------|
| *Cash flows from financing activities*           |         |       |
| Proceeds from issue of share capital             | 250     |       |
| Proceeds from long-term borrowings               | 250     |       |
| Dividends paid*                                   | (1,290) |       |
| *Net cash used in financing activities*          |         | (790) |
| *Net increase in cash and cash equivalents*      |         | 290   |
| *Cash and cash equivalents at beginning of period (Note)* |   | 120   |
| *Cash and cash equivalents at end of period (Note)* |      | 410   |

\* This could also be shown as an operating cash flow

## 1.15.2 Indirect method

STATEMENT OF CASH FLOWS (INDIRECT METHOD)
YEAR ENDED 31 DECEMBER 20X7

|                                                  | $m      | $m    |
|--------------------------------------------------|---------|-------|
| *Cash flows from operating activities*           |         |       |
| Profit before taxation                           | 3,570   |       |
| Adjustments for:                                 |         |       |
| Depreciation                                     | 450     |       |
| Investment income                                | (500)   |       |
| Interest expense                                 | 400     |       |
|                                                  | 3,920   |       |
| Increase in trade and other receivables          | (500)   |       |
| Decrease in inventories                          | 1,050   |       |
| Decrease in trade payables                       | (1,740) |       |
| Cash generated from operations                   | 2,730   |       |
| Interest paid                                    | (270)   |       |
| Income taxes paid                                | (900)   |       |
| *Net cash from operating activities*             |         | 1,560 |
| *Cash flows from investing activities*           |         |       |
| Purchase of property, plant and equipment        | (900)   |       |
| Proceeds from sale of equipment                  | 20      |       |
| Interest received                                | 200     |       |
| Dividends received                               | 200     |       |
| *Net cash used in investing activities*          |         | (480) |
| *Cash flows from financing activities*           |         |       |
| Proceeds from issue of share capital             | 250     |       |
| Proceeds from long-term borrowings               | 250     |       |
| Dividends paid*                                   | (1,290) |       |
| *Net cash used in financing activities*          |         | (790) |
| *Net increase in cash and cash equivalents*      |         | 290   |
| *Cash and cash equivalents at beginning of period* |      | 120   |
| *Cash and cash equivalents at end of period*     |         | 410   |

\* This could also be shown as an operating cash flow

# 2 Preparing a statement of cash flows

FAST FORWARD

> You need to be aware of the **format** of the statement as laid out in **IAS 7**; setting out the format is an essential first stage in preparing the statement, so this format must be learnt.

## 2.1 Introduction

In essence, preparing a statement of cash flows is very straightforward. You should therefore simply learn the format and apply the steps noted in the example below. Note that the following items are treated in a way that might seem confusing, but the treatment is logical if you **think in terms of cash**.

(a)  **Increase in inventory** is treated as **negative** (in brackets). This is because it represents a cash **outflow**; cash is being spent on inventory.

(b)  An **increase in receivables** would be treated as **negative** for the same reasons; more receivables means less cash.

(c)  By contrast an **increase in payables is positive** because cash is being retained and not used to settle accounts payable. There is therefore more of it.

## 2.2 Example: preparation of a statement of cash flows

Kane Co's statement of profit or loss for the year ended 31 December 20X2 and statements of financial position at 31 December 20X1 and 31 December 20X2 were as follows.

KANE CO
STATEMENT OF PROFIT OR LOSS FOR THE YEAR ENDED 31 DECEMBER 20X2

|  | $'000 | $'000 |
|---|---|---|
| Sales |  | 720 |
| Raw materials consumed | 70 |  |
| Staff costs | 94 |  |
| Depreciation | 118 |  |
| Loss on disposal of non-current asset | 18 |  |
|  |  | 300 |
| Operating profit |  | 420 |
| Interest payable |  | 28 |
| Profit before tax |  | 392 |
| Taxation |  | 124 |
| Profit for the year |  | 268 |

KANE CO
STATEMENTS OF FINANCIAL POSITION AS AT 31 DECEMBER

|  | 20X2 | 20X1 |
|---|---|---|
|  | $'000 | $'000 |
| Non-current assets |  |  |
| Cost | 1,596 | 1,560 |
| Depreciation | (318) | (224) |
|  | 1,278 | 1,336 |
| Current assets |  |  |
| Inventory | 24 | 20 |
| Trade receivables | 76 | 58 |
| Bank | 48 | 56 |
|  | 148 | 134 |
| Total assets | 1,426 | 1,470 |

|                            | 20X2 $'000 | 20X1 $'000 |
|----------------------------|-----------|-----------|
| Equity and liabilities     |           |           |
| Equity                     |           |           |
| Share capital              | 360       | 340       |
| Share premium              | 36        | 24        |
| Retained earnings          | 716       | 514       |
|                            | 1,112     | 878       |
| Non-current liabilities    |           |           |
| Long-term loans            | 200       | 500       |
| Current liabilities        |           |           |
| Trade payables             | 12        | 6         |
| Taxation                   | 102       | 86        |
|                            | 114       | 92        |
| Total equity and liabilities | 1,426   | 1,470     |

Dividends paid were $66,000

During the year, the company paid $90,000 for a new piece of machinery.

*Required*

Prepare a statement of cash flows for Kane Co for the year ended 31 December 20X2 in accordance with the requirements of IAS 7, using the indirect method.

## Solution

**Step 1**   **Set out the proforma statement of cash flows** with the headings required by IAS 7. You should leave plenty of space. Ideally, use three or more sheets of paper, one for the main statement, one for the notes and one for your workings. It is obviously essential to know the formats very well.

**Step 2**   Begin with the **cash flows from operating activities** as far as possible. When preparing the statement from statements of financial position, you will usually have to calculate such items as depreciation, loss on sale of non-current assets, profit for the year and tax paid (see Step 4). Note that you may not be given the tax charge in the statement of profit or loss. You will then have to assume that the tax paid in the year is last year's year-end provision and calculate the charge as the balancing figure.

**Step 3**   Calculate the cash flow figures for **purchase or sale of non-current assets, issue of shares and repayment of loans** if these are not already given to you (as they may be).

**Step 4**   If you are not given the profit figure, open up a **working for profit or loss**. Using the opening and closing balances of retained earnings, the taxation charge and dividends paid and proposed, you will be able to calculate profit for the year as the balancing figure to put in the cash flows from operating activities section.

**Step 5**   You will now be able to **complete the statement** by slotting in the figures given or calculated.

KANE CO
STATEMENT OF CASH FLOWS FOR THE YEAR ENDED 31 DECEMBER 20X2

| | $'000 | $'000 |
|---|---|---|
| *Cash flows from operating activities* | | |
| Profit before tax | 392 | |
| Depreciation charges | 118 | |
| Loss on sale of tangible non-current assets | 18 | |
| Interest expense | 28 | |
| Increase in inventories | (4) | |
| Increase in receivables | (18) | |
| Increase in payables | 6 | |
| Cash generated from operations | 540 | |
| Interest paid | (28) | |
| Dividends paid | (66) | |
| Tax paid (86 + 124 − 102) | (108) | |
| *Net cash from operating activities* | | 338 |
| *Cash flows from investing activities* | | |
| Payments to acquire tangible non-current assets | (90) | |
| Receipts from sales of tangible non-current assets (W) | 12 | |
| *Net cash used in investing activities* | | (78) |
| *Cash flows from financing activities* | | |
| Issues of share capital (360 + 36 − 340 − 24) | 32 | |
| Long-term loans repaid (500 − 200) | (300) | |
| *Net cash used in financing activities* | | (268) |
| Decrease in cash and cash equivalents | | (8) |
| Cash and cash equivalents at 1.1.X2 | | 56 |
| Cash and cash equivalents at 31.12.X2 | | 48 |

*Working: non-current asset disposals*

COST

| | $'000 | | $'000 |
|---|---|---|---|
| At 1.1.X2 | 1,560 | At 31.12.X2 | 1,596 |
| Purchases | 90 | Disposals (balance) | 54 |
| | 1,650 | | 1,650 |

ACCUMULATED DEPRECIATION

| | $'000 | | $'000 |
|---|---|---|---|
| At 31.12.X2 | 318 | At 1.1.X2 | 224 |
| Depreciation on disposals | | Charge for year | 118 |
| (balance) | 24 | | |
| | 342 | | 342 |

| | |
|---|---|
| NBV of disposals | 30 |
| Net loss reported | (18) |
| Proceeds of disposals | 12 |

## Question

**Prepare a statement of cash flows**

Set out below are the financial statements of Emma Co. You are the financial controller, faced with the task of implementing IAS 7 *Statement of cash flows*.

EMMA CO
STATEMENT OF PROFIT OR LOSS FOR THE YEAR ENDED 31 DECEMBER 20X2

|  | $'000 |
|---|---|
| Revenue | 2,553 |
| Cost of sales | (1,814) |
| Gross profit | 739 |
| Other income: interest received | 25 |
| Distribution costs | (125) |
| Administrative expenses | (264) |
| Finance costs | (75) |
| Profit before tax | 300 |
| Income tax expense | (140) |
| Profit for the year | 160 |

EMMA CO
STATEMENTS OF FINANCIAL POSITION AS AT 31 DECEMBER

|  | 20X2 | 20X1 |
|---|---|---|
|  | $'000 | $'000 |
| **Assets** | | |
| Non-current assets | | |
| Property, plant and equipment | 380 | 305 |
| Intangible assets | 250 | 200 |
| Investments | – | 25 |
| Current assets | | |
| Inventories | 150 | 102 |
| Receivables | 390 | 315 |
| Short-term investments | 50 | – |
| Cash in hand | 2 | 1 |
| Total assets | 1,222 | 948 |
| **Equity and liabilities** | | |
| Equity | | |
| Share capital ($1 ordinary shares) | 200 | 150 |
| Share premium account | 160 | 150 |
| Revaluation surplus | 100 | 91 |
| Retained earnings | 260 | 180 |
| Non-current liabilities | | |
| Long-term loan | 170 | 50 |
| Current liabilities | | |
| Trade payables | 127 | 119 |
| Bank overdraft | 85 | 98 |
| Taxation | 120 | 110 |
| Total equity and liabilities | 1,222 | 948 |

The following information is available.

(a) The proceeds of the sale of non-current asset investments amounted to $30,000.

(b) Fixtures and fittings, with an original cost of $85,000 and a net book value of $45,000, were sold for $32,000 during the year.

(c) The following information relates to property, plant and equipment.

|  | 31.12.20X2 | 31.12.20X1 |
|---|---|---|
|  | $'000 | $'000 |
| Cost | 720 | 595 |
| Accumulated depreciation | 340 | 290 |
| Net book value | 380 | 305 |

(d) 50,000 $1 ordinary shares were issued during the year at a premium of 20c per share.

(e) The short-term investments are highly liquid and are close to maturity.

(f) Dividends of $80,000 were paid during the year.

*Required*

Prepare a statement of cash flows for the year to 31 December 20X2 using the format laid out in IAS 7.

Answer

EMMA CO
STATEMENT OF CASH FLOWS FOR THE YEAR ENDED 31 DECEMBER 20X2

|  | $'000 | $'000 |
|---|---|---|
| *Cash flows from operating activities* | | |
| Profit before tax | 300 | |
| Depreciation charge (W1) | 90 | |
| Loss on sale of property, plant and equipment (45 – 32) | 13 | |
| Profit on sale of non-current asset investments | (5) | |
| Interest expense (net) | 50 | |
| (Increase)/decrease in inventories | (48) | |
| (Increase)/decrease in receivables | (75) | |
| Increase/(decrease) in payables | 8 | |
| | 333 | |
| Interest paid | (75) | |
| Dividends paid | (80) | |
| Tax paid (110 + 140 – 120) | (130) | |
| *Net cash from operating activities* | | 48 |
| *Cash flows from investing activities* | | |
| Payments to acquire property, plant and equipment (W2) | (201) | |
| Payments to acquire intangible non-current assets | (50) | |
| Receipts from sales of property, plant and equipment | 32 | |
| Receipts from sale of non-current asset investments | 30 | |
| Interest received | 25 | |
| *Net cash flows from investing activities* | | (164) |
| *Cash flows from financing activities* | | |
| Issue of share capital | 60 | |
| Long-term loan | 120 | |
| *Net cash flows from financing* | | 180 |
| Increase in cash and cash equivalents | | 64 |
| Cash and cash equivalents at 1.1.X2 | | (97) |
| Cash and cash equivalents at 31.12.X2 | | (33) |

*Workings*

1   *Depreciation charge*

|  | $'000 | $'000 |
|---|---|---|
| Depreciation at 31 December 20X2 | | 340 |
| Depreciation 31 December 20X1 | 290 | |
| Depreciation on assets sold (85 – 45) | 40 | |
| | | 250 |
| Charge for the year | | 90 |

2   *Purchase of property, plant and equipment*

PROPERTY, PLANT AND EQUIPMENT (COST)

|  | $'000 |  | $'000 |
|---|---|---|---|
| 1.1.X2 Balance b/d | 595 | Disposals | 85 |
| Revaluation (100 – 91) | 9 | | |
| Purchases (bal fig) | 201 | 31.12.X2 Balance c/d | 720 |
| | 805 | | 805 |

BPP

*Note.* In the exam you may have a number of issues to deal with in the statement of cash flows. Examples are:

- Share capital issues. The proceeds will be split between share capital and share premium.
- Bonus issues. These do *not* involve cash.
- Revaluation of non-current assets. This must be taken into account in calculating acquisitions and disposals.
- Movement on deferred tax. This must be taken into account in calculating tax paid.
- Finance leases. Assets acquired under finance leases must be adjusted for in non-current asset calculations and the amount paid under the finance lease must appear as a cash flow.

Make sure you attempt Question 27 in the question bank which includes a finance lease.

# 3 Interpretation of statements of cash flows

FAST FORWARD

IAS 7 was introduced to provide users with an evaluation of the ability of an entity to generate cash and cash equivalents and of its needs to utilise those cash flows.

## 3.1 Introduction

So what kind of information does the statement of cash flows, along with its notes, provide?

Some of the main areas where IAS 7 should provide information not found elsewhere in the financial statements are as follows.

(a)     The **relationships between profit and cash** can be seen clearly and analysed accordingly.
(b)     **Cash equivalents** are highlighted, giving a better picture of the liquidity of the company.
(c)     **Financing inflows and outflows must be shown, rather than simply passed through reserves**.

One of the most important things to realise at this point is that it is wrong to try to assess the health or predict the death of a reporting entity solely on the basis of a single indicator. When analysing cash flow data, the **comparison should not just be between cash flows and profit, but also between cash flows over a period of time** (say three to five years).

Cash is not synonymous with profit on an annual basis, but you should also remember that the 'behaviour' of profit and cash flows will be very different. **Profit is smoothed out** through accruals, prepayments, provisions and other accounting conventions. This does not apply to cash, so the **cash flow figures** are likely to be **'lumpy'** in comparison. You must distinguish between this 'lumpiness' and the trends which will appear over time.

The **relationship between profit and cash flows will vary constantly**. Note that healthy companies do not always have reported profits exceeding operating cash flows. Similarly, unhealthy companies can have operating cash flows well in excess of reported profit. The value of comparing them is in determining the extent to which earned profits are being converted into the necessary cash flows.

Profit is not as important as the extent to which a company can **convert its profits into cash on a continuing basis.** This process should be judged over a period longer than one year. The cash flows should be compared with profits over the same periods to decide how successfully the reporting entity has converted earnings into cash.

Cash flow figures should also be considered in terms of their specific relationships with each other over time. A form of **'cash flow gearing'** can be determined by comparing operating cash flows and financing flows, particularly borrowing, to establish the extent of dependence of the reporting entity on external funding.

**Other relationships** can be examined.

(a)     Operating cash flows and investment flows can be related to match cash recovery from investment to investment.

(b)    Investment can be compared to distribution to indicate the proportion of total cash outflow designated specifically to investor return and reinvestment.

(c)    A comparison of tax outflow to operating cash flow minus investment flow will establish a 'cash basis tax rate'.

The 'ratios' mentioned above can be monitored **inter– and intra-firm** and the analyses can be undertaken in monetary, general price-level adjusted, or percentage terms.

## 3.2 Worked example

Here is a full example of how the position and performance of a company can be analysed using the statement of financial position, profit or loss extracts and the statement of cash flows.

The following draft financial statements relate to Tabba, a private company.

| Statements of financial position as at: | 30 September 20X5 | | 30 September 20X4 | |
|---|---|---|---|---|
| | $'000 | $'000 | $'000 | $'000 |
| Property, plant and equipment (note (ii)) | | 10,600 | | 15,800 |
| Current assets | | | | |
| Inventories | 2,550 | | 1,850 | |
| Trade receivables | 3,100 | | 2,600 | |
| Insurance claim (note (iii)) | 1,500 | | 1,200 | |
| Cash and bank | 850 | | nil | |
| | | 8,000 | | 5,650 |
| Total assets | | 18,600 | | 21,450 |
| | | | | |
| Equity | | | | |
| Share capital ($1 each) | | 6,000 | | 6,000 |
| Reserves: | | | | |
| Revaluation (note (ii)) | nil | | 1,600 | |
| Retained earnings | 2,550 | | 850 | |
| | | 2,550 | | 2,450 |
| | | 8,550 | | 8,450 |
| Non–current liabilities | | | | |
| Finance lease obligations (note (ii)) | 2,000 | | 1,700 | |
| 6% loan notes | 800 | | nil | |
| 10% loan notes | nil | | 4,000 | |
| Deferred tax | 200 | | 500 | |
| Government grants (note (ii)) | 1,400 | | 900 | |
| | | 4,400 | | 7,100 |
| Current liabilities | | | | |
| Bank overdraft | nil | | 550 | |
| Trade payables | 4,050 | | 2,950 | |
| Government grants (note (ii)) | 600 | | 400 | |
| Finance lease obligations (note (ii)) | 900 | | 800 | |
| Current tax payable | 100 | | 1,200 | |
| | | 5,650 | | 5,900 |
| Total equity and liabilities | | 18,600 | | 21,450 |

The following additional information is relevant:

(i)    Profit or loss extract for the year ended 30 September 20X5:

| | $'000 |
|---|---|
| Operating profit before interest and tax | 270 |
| Interest expense | (260) |
| Interest receivable | 40 |
| Profit before tax | 50 |
| Net income tax credit | 50 |
| Profit for the year | 100 |

*Note.* The interest expense includes finance lease interest.

(ii)     The details of the property, plant and equipment are:

|  | Cost $'000 | Acc'd depreciation $'000 | Carrying amount $'000 |
|---|---|---|---|
| At 30 September 20X4 | 20,200 | 4,400 | 15,800 |
| At 30 September 20X5 | 16,000 | 5,400 | 10,600 |

During the year Tabba sold its factory for its fair value $12 million and agreed to rent it back, under an operating lease, for a period of five years at $1 million per annum. At the date of sale it had a carrying value of $7.4 million based on a previous revaluation of $8.6 million less depreciation of $1.2 million since the revaluation. The profit on the sale of the factory has been included in operating profit. The surplus on the revaluation reserve related entirely to the factory. No other disposals of non–current assets were made during the year.

Plant acquired under finance leases during the year was $1.5 million. Other purchases of plant during the year qualified for government grants of $950,000.

Amortisation of government grants has been credited to cost of sales.

(iii)     The insurance claim related to flood damage to the company's inventories which occurred in September 20X4. The original estimate has been revised during the year after negotiations with the insurance company. The claim is expected to be settled in the near future.

*Required*

(a)     Prepare a statement of cash flows using the indirect method for Tabba in accordance with IAS 7 *Statement of Cash Flows* for the year ended 30 September 20X5.

(b)     Using the information in the question and your statement of cash flows, comment on the change in the financial position of Tabba during the year ended 30 September 20X5.

*Note.* You are not required to calculate any ratios.

## Solution

(a)   TABBA: STATEMENT OF CASH FLOWS FOR THE YEAR ENDED 30 SEPTEMBER 20X5

|  | $'000 | $'000 |
|---|---|---|
| *Cash flows from operating activities* | | |
| Profit before taxation | | 50 |
| Adjustments for: | | |
| Depreciation (W2) | | 2,200 |
| Profit on disposal of PPE (12,000 – 7,400) | | (4,600) |
| Release of grant (W3) | | (250) |
| Increase in insurance claim receivable (1,500 – 1,200) | | (300) |
| Interest expense | | 260 |
| Investment income | | (40) |
| | | (2,680) |
| (Increase) decrease in inventories (2,550 – 1,850) | | (700) |
| (Increase) decrease in trade & other receivables (3,100 – 2,600) | | (500) |
| Increase (decrease) in trade payables (4,050 – 2,950) | | 1,100 |
| Cash used in operations | | (2,780) |
| Interest paid | | (260) |
| Income taxes paid (W4) | | (1,350) |
| Net cash outflow from operating activities | | (4,390) |
| | | |
| *Cash flows from investing activities* | | |
| Interest received | 40 | |
| Proceeds of grants (From question) | 950 | |
| Proceeds of disposal of property (From question) | 12,000 | |
| Purchase of property, plant and equipment (W1) | (2,900) | |
| Net cash from investing activities | | 10,090 |

*Cash flows from financing activities*
Proceeds of loan (6% loan received)                                         800
Repayment of loan (10% loan repaid)                                      (4,000)
Payments under finance leases (W5)                                       (1,100)
*Net cash used in financing activities*                                                    (4,300)

*Net increase in cash and cash equivalents*                                                 1,400
*Opening cash and cash equivalents*                                                          (550)
*Closing cash and cash equivalents*                                                           850

*Workings*

1

### PROPERTY, PLANT AND EQUIPMENT – COST

|  | $'000 |  | $'000 |
|---|---|---|---|
| Bal b/d | 20,200 | Factory disposal | 8,600 |
| Plant acquired under finance | | | |
| Leases | 1,500 | | |
| Other acquisitions | | | |
| (balancing figure) | 2,900 | Bal c/d: | 16,000 |
| | 24,600 | | 24,600 |

2

### PROPERTY, PLANT AND EQUIPMENT – DEPRECIATION

|  | $'000 |  | $'000 |
|---|---|---|---|
| Depreciation on | | | |
| factory disposal | 1,200 | Bal b/f | 4,400 |
| | | Charge for | |
| Bal c/f | 5,400 | year (balancing figure) | 2,200 |
| | 6,600 | | 6,600 |

3

### GOVERNMENT GRANT

|  | $'000 |  | $'000 |
|---|---|---|---|
| Grant released (balancing figure) | 250 | Bal b/f (400 + 900) | 1,300 |
| Bal c/f (1,400 + 600) | 2,000 | Received | 950 |
| | 2,250 | | 2,250 |

4

### TAX

|  |  | $'000 |  |  | $'000 |
|---|---|---|---|---|---|
| C/f | Current | 100 | B/f | Current | 1,200 |
| | Deferred | 200 | | Deferred | 500 |
| Credit  P or L | | 50 | | | |
| Cash paid | balance | 1,350 | | | – |
| | | 1,700 | | | 1,700 |

## 5

## MOVEMENT ON FINANCE LEASE

|  |  | $'000 |  |  | $'000 |
|---|---|---|---|---|---|
| C/f | Current | 2,000 | B/f | Current | 1,700 |
|  | Non-current | 900 |  | Non-current | 800 |
|  |  |  | New |  | 1,500 |
| Cash paid | balance | 1,100 |  |  | – |
|  |  | 4,000 |  |  | 4,000 |

(b)   **Changes in Tabba's financial position**

The last section of the statement of cash flows reveals a healthy increase in cash of $1.4m. However, Tabba is losing cash on its operating activities and its going concern status must be in doubt.

To survive and thrive businesses must generate cash from their operations; but Tabba has absorbed $2.68m. Whereas most companies report higher operating cash inflows than profits, Tabba has reported the reverse. The only reason Tabba was able to report a profit was because of the one-off $4.6m surplus on disposal. There were two other items that inflated profits without generating cash; a $300,000 increase in the insurance claim receivable and a $250,000 release of a government grant. Without these three items Tabba would have reported a $5.1m loss before tax.

Were it not for the disposal proceeds Tabba would be reporting a $10.6m net decrease in cash. Tabba has no other major assets to sell and so the coming year will see a large outflow of cash unless Tabba's trading position improves. When the current operating lease expires in four years time there will probably be a rent hike, further damaging Tabba's profitability and cash flows.

The high tax bill for the previous year suggests that Tabba's fall from profitability has been swift and steep. Despite this downturn in trade Tabba's inventories and receivables have increased, suggesting poor financial management. This in turn damages cash flow, which is indicated by the increase in the level of payables.

There are some good signs though. Investment in non-current assets has continued, although $1.5m of this was on finance leases which are often a sign of cash shortages. Some of the disposal proceeds have been used to redeem the expensive $4m 10% loan and replace it with a smaller and cheaper $800,000 6% loan. This will save $352,000 per annum.

Tabba's recovery may depend on whether the circumstances causing the slump in profits and cash flow will either disappear of their own accord or whether Tabba can learn to live with them. The statement of cash flows has however highlighted some serious issues for the shareholders to discuss with the directors at the annual general meeting.

## 3.3 The advantages of cash flow accounting

The advantages of cash flow accounting are as follows.

(a)   Survival in business depends on the **ability to generate** cash. Cash flow accounting directs attention towards this critical issue.

(b)   Cash flow is **more comprehensive** than 'profit' which is dependent on accounting conventions and concepts.

(c)   **Creditors** (long and short-term) are more interested in an entity's ability to repay them than in its profitability. Whereas 'profits' might indicate that cash is likely to be available, cash flow accounting is more direct with its message.

(d)   Cash flow reporting provides a better means of **comparing the results** of different companies than traditional profit reporting.

(e)   Cash flow reporting **satisfies the needs of all users** better.

(i)     For **management**, it provides the sort of information on which decisions should be taken (in management accounting, 'relevant costs' to a decision are future cash flows); traditional profit accounting does not help with decision-making.

(ii)    For **shareholders and auditors**, cash flow accounting can provide a satisfactory basis for stewardship accounting.

(iii)   As described previously, the information needs of **creditors and employees** will be better served by cash flow accounting.

(f)     Cash flow forecasts are **easier to prepare**, as well as more useful, than profit forecasts.

(g)     They can in some respects be **audited more easily** than accounts based on the accruals concept.

(h)     The accruals concept is confusing, and cash flows are **more easily understood**.

(i)     Cash flow accounting should be both retrospective, and also include a forecast for the future. This is of **great information value** to all users of accounting information.

(j)     **Forecasts** can subsequently be **monitored** by the publication of variance statements which compare actual cash flows against the forecast.

## Question                                                                 Disadvantages

Can you think of some possible disadvantages of cash flow accounting?

## Answer

The main disadvantages of cash accounting are essentially the advantages of accruals accounting (proper matching of related items). There is also the practical problem that few businesses keep historical cash flow information in the form needed to prepare a historical statement of cash flows and so extra record keeping is likely to be necessary.

**Exam focus point**

> A statement of cash flows is very likely to come up as Question 3 in your exam. In this chapter we give you the basics, but you should also do as many as possible of the statement of cash flows questions in the Practice and Revision Kit. These will give you practice at the various items that you may have to deal with in a cash flow question.

## 3.4 Criticisms of IAS 7

The inclusion of **cash equivalents** has been criticised because it does not reflect the way in which businesses are managed: in particular, the requirement that to be a cash equivalent an investment has to be within three months of maturity is considered **unrealistic**.

The management of assets similar to cash (ie 'cash equivalents') is not distinguished from other investment decisions.

# Chapter roundup

- **Statements of cash flows** are a useful addition to the financial statements because it is recognised that accounting profit is not the only indicator of a company's performance.

- You need to be aware of the **format** of the statement as laid out in **IAS 7**; setting out the format is an essential first stage in preparing the statement, so this format must be learnt.

- IAS 7 was introduced to provide users with an evaluation of the ability of an entity to generate cash and cash equivalents and of its needs to utilise those cash flows.

# Quick quiz

1   What is the aim of a statement of cash flows?

2   The standard headings in IAS 7 *Statement of cash flows* are:

- O................. a.................
- I................... a......................
- F.................... a.....................
- Net.................. in C...................... and ...................

3   Cash equivalents are current asset investments which will mature or can be redeemed within three months of the year end.

   True  ☐

   False ☐

4   Why are you more likely to encounter the indirect method as opposed to the direct method?

5   List five advantages of cash flow accounting.

# Answers to quick quiz

1   To indicate an entity's ability to generate cash and cash equivalents.

2   - Operating activities
    - Investing activities
    - Financing activities
    - Net increase (decrease) in cash and cash equivalents

3   False. See the definition in paragraph 1.6 if you are not sure about this.

4   The indirect method utilises figures which appear in the financial statements. The figures required for the direct method may not be readily available.

5   See paragraph 3.3

Now try the question below from the Exam Question Bank

| Number | Level | Marks | Time |
|--------|-------|-------|------|
| 27 | – | 14 | 25 mins |
| 28 | Examination | 25 | 45 mins |

# 22

# Alternative models and practices

| Topic list | Syllabus reference |
|---|---|
| 1 Historical cost versus current value | A5 |
| 2 Concepts of capital and capital maintenance | A5 |
| 3 Current purchasing power (CPP) | A5 |
| 4 Current cost accounting (CCA) | A5 |

## Introduction

In this chapter we look at the alternatives to historical cost accounting.

# Study guide

| | | | Intellectual level |
|---|---|---|---|
| 5 | **Alternative models and practices** | | |
| | (a) | describe the advantages and disadvantages of the use of historical cost accounting. | 2 |
| | (b) | discuss whether the use of current value accounting overcomes the problems of historical cost accounting. | 2 |
| | (c) | describe the concept of financial and physical capital maintenance and how this affects the determination of profits. | 1 |

# Exam guide

This is a topical issue which could come up as part of a discussion question.

# 1 Historical cost versus current value

**FAST FORWARD**

A number of alternatives to historical cost accounting have come under discussion in the past, mainly during periods of high inflation.

## 1.1 Advantages of historical cost accounting

As we are still using historical cost accounting, it may be supposed to have a number of advantages. The most important ones are:

- Amounts used are objective and free from bias.
- Amounts are reliable, they can always be verified, they exist on invoices and documents.
- Amounts in the statement of financial position can be matched perfectly with amounts in the statement of cash flows.
- Opportunities for creative accounting are less than under systems which allow management to apply their judgement to the valuation of assets.
- It has been used for centuries and is easily understood.

## 1.2 Disadvantages of historical cost accounting

Historical cost accounting has a number of disadvantages. They arise as particular problems in periods of inflation. The main ones are:

- It can lead to understatement of assets in the statement of financial position. A building purchased 50 years ago will appear at the price that was paid for it 50 years ago.
- Because assets are understated, depreciation will also be understated. While the purpose of depreciation is not to set aside funds for replacement of assets, if an asset has to be replaced at twice the price that was paid for its predecessor, the company may decide that it may have been prudent to make some provision for this in earlier years.
- When inventory prices are rising, and when the company is operating a FIFO system, the cheapest inventories are being charged to cost of sales and the most expensive are being designated as closing inventory in the statement of financial position. This leads to understatement of cost of sales.
- An organisation selling in an inflationary market will see its revenue and profits rise, but this is 'paper profit', distorted by the understated depreciation and cost of sales.

From these disadvantages various issues arise:

- Understatement of assets will depress a company's share price and make it vulnerable to takeover. In practice, listed companies avoid this by revaluing land and buildings in line with market values.
- Understated depreciation and understated cost of sales lead to overstatement of profits, compounded by price inflation.
- Overstated profits can lead to too much being distributed to shareholders, leaving insufficient amounts for investment.
- Overstated profits will lead shareholders to expect higher dividends and employees to demand higher wages.
- Overstated profits lead to overstated tax bills.

During periods where price inflation is low, profit overstatement will be marginal. The disadvantages of historical cost accounting become most apparent in periods of inflation. It was during the inflationary period of the 70s that alternatives were sought and that an attempt was made to introduce Current Cost Accounting (CCA). As inflation came back under control, the debate died down, but it is becoming increasingly recognised that historical cost accounting has shortcomings which need to be addressed.

## 1.3 Current value accounting

The move towards current value accounting has already taken a number of steps. Entities are now permitted to revalue non-current assets such as land and buildings in line with market value and financial assets and liabilities such as securities and investments can be carried at **fair value**, defined in IFRS 13 as: 'the price that would be received to sell an asset or paid to transfer a liability in an orderly transaction between market participants at the measurement date'.

These developments, and the use of fair values in acquisition accounting (to measure the assets of the subsidiary and thus arrive at a realistic goodwill valuation) are relatively uncontroversial. However, there are those who would like fair value to be used more widely as a system of current value. The European Central Bank recently produced a paper on the possible use of Full Fair Value Accounting (FFVA) in the banking industry.

In the US a similar move is being advocated towards Current Value Accounting (CVA). Under CVA the original cost of an asset would be replaced with its discounted present value ie. the present value of its future cash flows. This is obviously suitable for monetary items such as receivables and payables. The expected inflows and outflows would be discounted to present value using an interest rate which reflects the current time value of money. For assets such as vehicles, which do not yield a pre-determined future cash flow, current cost would be a more applicable measure – based either on the current cost of the original asset or on its replacement by a more up-to-date version. For inventories, current replacement cost or NRV would be indicated. Under this measurement basis, the LIFO/FIFO distinction would no longer apply.

## 1.4 Historical cost accounting; does it have a future?

Investment analysts have argued that historical cost information is out of date and not relevant and that fair value information, where based on active market prices, is the best available measure of future cash flows which an asset can be expected to generate.

This is heard increasingly in the US, where investors are the most highly-regarded user group for financial information, and the issue is likely to arise in the context of the IASB/FASB convergence discussions .

We will now go on to look at two alternative systems which have sought in the past to address the shortcomings of historical cost accounting - **current purchasing power (CPP)** and **Current cost accounting (CCA)**. We begin by looking at the fundamental difference between these two systems - a different concept of capital maintenance and therefore of profit.

# 2 Concepts of capital and capital maintenance

**Measurement of profit** depends on the methods used to value capital and on the method, if any, of accounting for price level changes.

Most entities use a **financial concept of capital** when preparing their financial statements.

## 2.1 Concepts of capital maintenance and the determination of profit

First of all, we need to define the different concepts of capital.

**Key term**

> **Capital.** Under a **financial concept of capital**, such as invested money or invested purchasing power, capital is the net assets or equity of the entity. The financial concept of capital is adopted by most entities.
>
> Under a **physical concept of capital**, such as operating capability, capital is the productive capacity of the entity based on, for example, units of output per day. *(Conceptual Framework)*

The definition of profit is also important.

**Key term**

> **Profit.** The residual amount that remains after expenses (including capital maintenance adjustments, where appropriate) have been deducted from income. Any amount over and above that required to maintain the capital at the beginning of the period is profit. *(Conceptual Framework)*

The main difference between the two concepts of capital maintenance is the treatment of the **effects of changes in the prices of assets and liabilities** of the entity. In general terms, an entity has maintained its capital if it has as much capital at the end of the period as it had at the beginning of the period. Any amount over and above that required to maintain the capital at the beginning of the period is profit.

(a) **Financial capital maintenance**: profit is the increase in nominal money capital over the period. This is the concept used in CPP, and used under historical cost accounting.

(b) **Physical capital maintenance**: profit is the increase in the physical productive capacity over the period. This is the concept used in CCA.

## 2.2 Capital maintenance in times of inflation

**Profit** can be measured as the **difference between how wealthy a company is at the beginning and at the end of an accounting period.**

(a) This wealth can be expressed in terms of the capital of a company as shown in its opening and closing statements of financial position.

(b) A business which maintains its capital unchanged during an accounting period can be said to have broken even.

(c) Once **capital has been maintained**, **anything** achieved **in excess represents profit.**

For this analysis to be of any use, we must be able to draw up a company's statement of financial position at the beginning and at the end of a period, so as to place a value on the opening and closing capital. There are particular difficulties in doing this during a **period of rising prices**.

In conventional historical cost accounts, assets are stated in the statement of financial position at the amount it cost to acquire them (less any amounts written off in respect of depreciation or impairment in value). Capital is simply the **difference between assets and liabilities**.

**Exam focus point**

> If prices are rising, it is possible for a company to show a profit in its historical cost accounts despite having identical physical assets and owing identical liabilities at the beginning and end of its accounting period.

For example, consider the following opening and closing statements of financial position of a company.

|  | Opening | Closing |
|---|---|---|
|  | $ | $ |
| Inventory (100 items at cost) | 500 | 600 |
| Other net assets | 1,000 | 1,000 |
| Capital | 1,500 | 1,600 |

Assuming that no new capital has been introduced during the year, and no capital has been distributed as dividends, the profit shown in historical cost accounts would be $100, being the excess of closing capital over opening capital. And yet in physical terms the company is no better off: it still has 100 units of inventory (which cost $5 each at the beginning of the period, but $6 each at the end) and its other net assets are identical. The 'profit' earned has merely enabled the company to keep pace with inflation.

An alternative to the concept of capital maintenance based on historical costs is to express capital in **physical** terms. On this basis, no profit would be recognised in the example above because the physical substance of the company is unchanged over the accounting period. Capital is maintained if at the end of the period the company is in a position to achieve the same physical output as it was at the beginning of the period. You should bear in mind that financial definitions of capital maintenance are not the only ones possible; in theory at least, there is no reason why profit should not be measured as the increase in a company's *physical* capital over an accounting period.

# 3 Current purchasing power (CPP)

FAST FORWARD **CPP accounting** is a method of accounting for general (not specific) inflation. It does so by expressing asset values in a stable monetary unit, the $ of current purchasing power.

## 3.1 The unit of measurement

Another way to tackle the problems of capital maintenance in times of rising prices is to look at the **unit of measurement** in which accounting values are expressed.

It is an axiom of conventional accounting, as it has developed over the years, that value should be measured in terms of money. It is also **implicitly assumed** that **money values are stable**, so that $1 at the start of the financial year has the same value as $1 at the end of that year. But when **prices are rising**, this assumption is invalid: **$1 at the end of the year has less value (less purchasing power) than it had one year previously**.

This leads to problems when aggregating amounts which have arisen at different times. For example, a company's non-current assets may include items bought at different times over a period of many years. They will each have been recorded in $s, but the value of $1 will have varied over the period. In effect the **non-current asset figure in a historical cost statement of financial position is an aggregate of a number of items expressed in different units**. It could be argued that such a figure is **meaningless**.

Faced with this argument, one possibility would be to re-state all accounts items in terms of a stable monetary unit. There would be difficulties in practice, but in theory there is no reason why a stable unit ($ CPP = $s of current purchasing power) should not be devised. In this section we will look at a system of accounting (current purchasing power accounting, or CPP) based on precisely this idea.

## 3.2 Specific and general price changes

We can identify two different types of price inflation.

When prices are rising, it is likely that the **current value of assets will also rise**, but not necessarily by the general rate of inflation. For example, if the replacement cost of a machine on 1 January 20X2 was $5,000, and the general rate of inflation in 20X2 was 8%, we would not necessarily expect the replacement cost of the machine at 31 December 20X2 to be $5,000 plus 8% = $5,400. The rate of price increase on the machinery might have been less than 8% or more than 8%. (Conceivably, in spite of general inflation, the replacement cost of the machinery might have gone down.)

(a) There is **specific price inflation**, which measures price changes over time for a specific asset or group of assets.

(b) There is **general price inflation**, which is the average rate of inflation, which reduces the general purchasing power of money.

To counter the problems of specific price inflation some system of current value accounting may be used (such as current cost accounting). The capital maintenance concepts underlying current value systems do not attempt to allow for the maintenance of real value in money terms.

**Current purchasing power (CPP) accounting** is based on a different concept of capital maintenance.

> **CPP** measures profits as the increase in the current purchasing power of equity. Profits are therefore stated after allowing for the declining purchasing power of money due to price inflation.

When applied to historical cost accounting, CPP is a system of accounting which makes adjustments to income and capital values to allow for the general rate of price inflation.

## 3.3 Monetary and non-monetary items

It is obvious that during a period of inflation borrowers benefit at the expense of lenders. A sum borrowed at the beginning of the year will cost less to repay at the end of the year (although lenders will seek to allow for this in higher interest charges). Similarly, customers with balances owing benefit at the expense of suppliers. CPP accounting seeks to remove this element of 'holding gain'.

Monetary items (cash, receivables, payables) cannot be restated as their amount is fixed. Non-monetary items (not-current assets and inventories) are restated in line with the general price index (at $c) and the balancing figure is equity.

Question                                                                                               CPP profits

Rice and Price set up in business on 1 January 20X5 with no non-current assets, and cash of $5,000. On 1 January they acquired inventories for the full $5,000, which they sold on 30 June 20X5 for $6,000. On 30 November they obtained a further $2,100 of inventory on credit. The index of the general price level gives the following index figures.

| Date | Index |
|---|---|
| 1 January 20X5 | 300 |
| 30 June 20X5 | 330 |
| 30 November 20X5 | 350 |
| 31 December 20X5 | 360 |

Calculate the CPP profits (or losses) of Rice and Price for the year to 31 December 20X5.

Answer

The approach is to prepare a CPP statement of profit or loss.

|  | $c | $c |
|---|---|---|
| Sales (6,000 × 360/330) |  | 6,545 |
| Less cost of goods sold (5,000 × 360/300) |  | 6,000 |
|  |  | 545 |
| Loss on holding cash for 6 months* | (545) |  |
| Gain by owing payables for 1 month** | 60 |  |
|  |  | (485) |
| CPP profit |  | 60 |

\* ($6,000 × 360/330) – $6,000 = $c 545
\*\*($2,100 × 360/350) – $2,100 = $c 60

Note that under historic cost accounting the gross profit would be $1,000 ($6,000 – $5,000).

## 3.4 The advantages and disadvantages of CPP accounting

### 3.4.1 Advantages

(a) The restatement of asset values in terms of a **stable money value** provides **a more meaningful basis of comparison** with other companies. Similarly, provided that previous years' profits are re-valued into CPP terms, it is also possible to compare the current year's results with past performance.

(b) **Profit** is measured in **'real' terms** and excludes 'inflationary value increments'. This enables better forecasts of future prospects to be made.

(c) CPP **avoids the subjective valuations** of current value accounting, because a single price index is applied to all non-monetary assets.

(d) CPP **provides a stable monetary** unit with which to value profit and capital; ie $c.

(e) Since it is based on historical cost accounting, **raw data is easily verified**, and measurements of value can be readily audited.

### 3.4.2 Disadvantages

(a) It is not **clear what $c means**. 'Generalised purchasing power' as measured by a retail price index, or indeed any other general price index, has no obvious practical significance.

'Generalised purchasing power has no relevance to any person or entity because no such thing exists in reality, except as a statistician's computation.' (T A Lee)

(b) The use of indices inevitably involves **approximations** in the measurements of value.

(c) The value **of assets in a CPP statement of financial position has less meaning than a current value statement of financial position**. It cannot be supposed that the CPP value of net assets reflects:

(i) The general goods and services that could be bought if the assets were released

(ii) The consumption of general goods and services that would have to be forgone to replace those assets

In this respect, a CPP statement of financial position has similar drawbacks to an historical cost statement of financial position.

# 4 Current cost accounting (CCA)

FAST FORWARD CCA is based on a **physical concept of capital maintenance**. Profit is recognised after the operating capability of the business has been maintained.

## 4.1 Value to the business (deprival value)

Current cost accounting (CCA) reflects an approach to capital maintenance based on maintaining the **operating capability** of a business. The conceptual basis of CCA is that the value of assets consumed or sold, and the value of assets in the statement of financial position, should be stated at their **value to the business** (also known as 'deprival value').

**Key term**

> The **deprival value** of an asset is the loss which a business entity would suffer if it were deprived of the use of the asset.

(a) A basic assumption in CCA is that 'capital maintenance' should mean maintenance of the 'business substance' or 'operating capability' of the business entity. As we have seen already, it is generally accepted that profit is earned only after a sufficient amount has been charged against sales to ensure that the capital of the business is maintained. In CCA, a **physical** rather than financial definition of capital is used: capital maintenance is measured by the ability of the business entity to keep up the same level of operating capability.

(b) 'Value to the business' is the required method of valuation in current cost accounting, because it reflects the extra funds which would be required to maintain the operating capability of the business entity if it suddenly lost the use of an asset.

**Value to the business**, or deprival value, can be any of the following values.

(a) **Replacement cost**: in the case of non-current assets, it is assumed that the replacement cost of an asset would be its net replacement cost (NRC), its gross replacement cost minus an appropriate provision for depreciation to reflect the amount of its life already 'used up'.

(b) **Net realisable value** (NRV): what the asset could be sold for, net of any disposal costs.

(c) **Economic value** (EV), or value in use: what the existing asset will be worth to the company over the rest of its useful life.

The choice of deprival value from one of the three values listed will depend on circumstances. In simple terms you should remember that in **CCA deprival value is nearly always replacement cost.**

**If the asset is worth replacing, its deprival value will always be net replacement cost**. If the asset is not worth replacing, it might have been disposed of straight away, or else it might have been kept in operation until the end of its useful life.

You may therefore come across a statement that deprival value is the **lower of**:

- **Net replacement cost (NRC)**
- The **higher of net realisable value and economic value**

We have already seen that if an asset is not worth replacing, the deprival value will be NRV or EV. However, there are many assets which will not be replaced either:

(a) Because the asset is **technologically obsolete**, and has been (or will be) superseded by more modern equipment

(b) Because the business is **changing the nature of its operations** and will not want to continue in the same line of business once the asset has been used up

Such assets, even though there are reasons not to replace them, would still be valued (usually) at net replacement cost, because this 'deprival value' still provides an estimate of the **operating capability** of the company.

## 4.2 CCA profits and deprival value

The deprival value of assets is reflected in the CCA statement of profit or loss by the following means.

(a) **Depreciation** is charged on non-current assets on the basis of **gross replacement cost** of the asset (where NRC is the deprival value).

(b) Where **NRV or EV** is the deprival value, the charge against CCA profits will be the **loss in value of the asset** during the accounting period; ie from its previous carrying value to its current NRV or EV.

(c) **Goods sold** are charged at their **replacement cost**. Thus if an item of inventory cost $15 to produce, and sells for $20, by which time its replacement cost has risen to $17, the CCA profit would be $3.

|  | $ |
|---|---|
| Sales | 20 |
| Less replacement cost of goods sold | 17 |
| Current cost profit | 3 |

## 4.3 Example: CCA v accounting for inflation

Suppose that Arthur Smith Co buys an asset on 1 January for $10,000. The estimated life of the asset is 5 years, and straight line depreciation is charged. At 31 December the gross replacement cost of the asset is $10,500 (5% higher than on 1 January) but general inflation during the year, as measured by the retail price index, has risen 20%.

(a)     To maintain the value of the business against inflation, the asset should be revalued as follows.

|                                                     | $      |
| --------------------------------------------------- | ------ |
| Gross ($10,000 × 120%)                              | 12,000 |
| Depreciation charge for the year (@ 20%)            | 2,400  |
| Net value in the statement of financial position    | 9,600  |

(b)     In CCA, the business maintains its operating capability if we revalue the asset as follows.

|                                                     | $      |
| --------------------------------------------------- | ------ |
| Gross replacement cost                              | 10,500 |
| Depreciation charge for the year (note)             | 2,100  |
| NRC; value in the statement of financial position   | 8,400  |

| Note                                | $     |
| ----------------------------------- | ----- |
| Historical cost depreciation        | 2,000 |
| CCA depreciation adjustment (5%)     | 100   |
| Total CCA depreciation cost          | 2,100 |

**CCA preserves the operating capability of the company but does not necessarily preserve it against the declining value in the purchasing power of money** (against inflation). As mentioned previously, CCA is a system which takes account of specific price inflation (changes in the prices of specific assets or groups of assets) but **not of general price inflation.**

A strict view of current cost accounting might suggest that a set of CCA accounts should be prepared from the outset on the basis of deprival values. In practice, current cost accounts are usually prepared by **starting from historical cost accounts and making appropriate adjustments.**

## 4.4 CCA accounts

CAC accounts will include the following adjustments:

(1)     Depreciation adjustment – to amend depreciation in line with the gross replacement cost of the asset.

(2)     Cost of sales adjustment – to take account of increases in inventory prices and remove any element of profit based on this.

(3)     Working capital adjustment – to remove any element of profit or loss based on holding payables or receivables in a period of inflation.

You do not need to know how to do these adjustment, but you can see that they attempt to deal with the areas where inflation can lead to 'holding gains'.

## 4.5 The advantages and disadvantages of current cost accounting

### 4.5.1 Advantages

(a)     By excluding holding gains from profit, CCA can be used to indicate whether the dividends paid to shareholders will **reduce the operating capability** of the business.

(b)     Assets are valued after management has considered the **opportunity cost** of holding them, and the expected benefits from their future use. CCA is therefore a useful guide for management in deciding whether to hold or sell assets.

(c)     It is **relevant** to the needs of information users in:

   (i)     Assessing the stability of the business entity

   (ii)    Assessing the vulnerability of the business (eg to a takeover), or the liquidity of the business

   (iii)   Evaluating the performance of management in maintaining and increasing the business substance

   (iv)    Judging future prospects

(d)     It can be **implemented fairly easily** in practice, by making simple adjustments to the historical cost accounting profits. A current cost statement of financial position can also be prepared with reasonable simplicity.

### 4.5.2 Disadvantages

(a)     It is impossible to make valuations of EV or NRV without **subjective judgements**. The measurements used are therefore not objective.

(b)     There are several problems to be overcome in deciding how to provide an **estimate of replacement** costs for non-current assets.

(c)     The mixed value approach to valuation means that some assets will be valued at replacement cost, but others will be valued at net realisable value or economic value. It is arguable that the **total assets** will, therefore, have an **aggregate value** which is **not particularly meaningful** because of this mixture of different concepts.

(d)     It can be argued that **'deprival value'** is an **unrealistic concept**, because the business entity has not been deprived of the use of the asset. This argument is one which would seem to reject the fundamental approach to 'capital maintenance' on which CCA is based.

## Chapter Roundup

- A number of alternatives to historical cost accounting have come under discussion in the past, mainly during periods of high inflation.

- **Measurement of profit** depends on the methods used to value capital and on the method, if any, of accounting for price level changes.

- **CPP accounting** is a method of accounting for general (not specific) inflation. It does so by expressing asset values in a stable monetary unit, the $ of current purchasing power.

- CCA is based on a **physical concept of capital maintenance**. Profit is recognised after the operating capability of the business has been maintained.

## Quick Quiz

1       Can methods of current value accounting be described as systems for accounting for inflation?

2       Distinguish between specific price inflation and general price inflation.

3       What is an asset's deprival value if it is not worth replacing?

## Answers to Quick Quiz

1       No

2       • Specific price inflation measures price changes over time for a specific asset or group of assets

        • General price inflation measures the continual reduction in the general purchasing power of money

3       The higher of net realisable value and economic value

Now try the questions below from the Exam Question Bank

| Number | Level | Marks | Time |
|--------|-------|-------|------|
| 29 | Examination | 15 | 27 mins |

# Specialised, not-for-profit and public sector entities

| Topic list | Syllabus reference |
|---|---|
| 1 Primary aims | |
| 2 Regulatory framework | |
| 3 Performance measurement | |

## Introduction

In this chapter we look at the application of financial reporting requirements to not-for-profit and public sector entities.

# Study guide

| | | | Intellectual level |
|---|---|---|---|
| **B3** | **Specialised, not-for-profit and public sector entities** | | |
| | (a) | distinguish between the primary aims of not-for-profit and public sector entities and those of profit oriented entities. | 1 |
| | (b) | discuss the extent to which International Financial Reporting Standards (IFRSs) are relevant to specialised, not-for-profit and public sector entities. | 1 |
| **E4** | **Specialised, not-for-profit and public sector entities** | | |
| | (a) | discuss the different approaches that may be required when assessing the performance of specialised, not-for-profit and public sector organisations. | 1 |

# Exam guide

In the pilot paper, there was a 5-mark part of a question on this topic.

# 1 Primary aims

**FAST FORWARD**

The accounting requirements for not-for-profit and public sector entities are moving closer to those required for profit-making entities. However, they do have different goals and purposes.

What organisations do we have in mind when we refer to **Not-for-profit and public sector entities**? These are the most obvious examples:

(a) Central government departments and agencies
(b) Local or federal government departments
(c) Publicly-funded bodies providing healthcare (in the UK this would be the NHS) and social housing
(d) Further and higher education institutions
(e) Charitable bodies

The first four are **public sector entities**. Charities are **private** not-for-profit entities.

Not-for-profit entities have different goals and purposes to profit-making entities and are responsible to different stakeholders. However, they are dealing in very large sums of money and it is important that they are properly managed and that their accounts present fairly the results of their operations.

Until recently, **public sector** accounts were prepared on a **cash basis**. A transition is still in progress which will get them operating on an **accruals basis**, in line with normal practice in the private sector.

## 1.1 Conceptual framework for not-for profit entities

The new IASB/FASB *Conceptual Framework for Financial Reporting* is being undertaken in phases. Phase G is entitled *Application to not-for-profit entities in the private and public sector*. A monitoring group, including ASB members, set up to advise on this has made the following points:

(a) Not-for profit entities have different objectives, different operating environments and other different characteristics to private sector businesses.

(b) The following issues exist regarding application of the proposals to not-for-profit entities:

- Insufficient emphasis on accountability/stewardship
- A need to broaden the definition of users and user groups
- The emphasis on future cash flows is inappropriate to not-for-profit entities
- Insufficient emphasis on budgeting

## 1.2 Accountability/stewardship

Not-for-profit entities are not reporting to shareholders, but it is very important that they can account for funds received and show how they have been spent. In some cases, resources may be contributed for specific purposes and management is required to show that they have been utilised for that purpose. Perhaps most importantly, taxpayers are entitled to see how the government is spending their money.

## 1.3 Users and user groups

The primary user group for not-for-profit entities is providers of funds. In the case of public bodies, such as government departments, this primary group will consist of taxpayers. In the case of private bodies such as charities it will be financial supporters, and also potential future financial supporters. There is also a case for saying that a second primary user group should be recognised, being the recipients of the goods and services provided by the not-for-profit entity.

## 1.4 Cash flow focus

The Conceptual Framework, emphasises the need to provide information which will enable users to assess an entity's ability to generate net cash inflows. Not-for-profit entities also need to generate cash flows, but other aspects are generally more significant – for instance, the resources the entity has available to deliver future goods and services, the cost and effectiveness of those it has delivered in the past and the degree to which it is meeting its objectives.

## 1.5 Budgeting

The IASB has decided to leave consideration of whether financial reporting should include forecast information until later in the project. However, for not-for-profit entities, budgets and variance analyses are more important. In some cases, funding is supplied on the basis of a formal, published budget.

# 2 Regulatory framework

FAST FORWARD

There is a general move to get public bodies reporting under the accruals system. Many private not-for-profit organisations still use cash accounting.

Regulation of public not-for-profit entities, principally local and national governments and governmental agencies, is by the International Public Sector Accounting Standards Board (IPSAB), which comes under the International Federation of Accountants (IFAC).

## 2.1 International public sector accounting standards

The IPSASB is developing a set of International Public Sector Accounting Standards (IPSASs), based on IFRSs. To date the following IPSASs have been issued:

1       Presentation of Financial Statements
2       Cash Flow Statements
3       Net Surplus or Deficit for the Period, Fundamental Errors and Changes in Accounting Policies
4       The Effect of Changes in Foreign Exchange Rates
5       Borrowing Costs
6       Consolidated Financial Statements and Accounting for Controlled Entities
7       Accounting for investments in Associates
8       Financial Reporting of Interests in Joint Ventures
9       Revenue from Exchange Transactions
10      Financial Reporting in Hyperinflationary Economies
11      Construction Contracts
12      Inventories
13      Leases

| 14 | Events After the Reporting Date |
|---|---|
| 15 | Financial Instruments: Disclosure and Presentation |
| 16 | Investment Property |
| 17 | Property, Plant and Equipment |
| 18 | Segment Reporting |
| 19 | Provisions, Contingent Liabilities and Contingent Assets |
| 10 | Related Party Disclosures |
| 21 | Impairment of Non-Cash-Generating Assets |

You are not required to remember this list of IPSAs, or know any of their detailed provisions, but you can see that they closely mirror the IAS/IFRSes and each one is based on the relevant Standard.

The IPSAs are all based on the **accrual method** of accounting and one of the aims of the IPSAB is to move public sector organisations from the cash to the accruals basis of accounting.

## 2.2 Characteristics of Not-for-profit Entities

As part of its preliminary report on the *Conceptual Framework*, the IASB set out some of the characteristics of not-for-profit entities as follows:

### 2.2.1 Private Sector

Not-for-profit entities in the private sector have the following characteristics:

- Their objective is to provide goods and services to various recipients and not to make a profit
- They are generally characterised by the absence of defined ownership interests (shares) that can be sold, transferred or redeemed
- They may have a wide group of stakeholders to consider (including the public at large in some cases)
- Their revenues generally arise from contributions (donations or membership dues) rather than sales
- Their capital assets are typically acquired and held to deliver services without the intention of earning a return on them

### 2.2.2 Public Sector

Nor-for-profit entities in the public sector have similar key characteristics to those in the private sector. They are typically established by legislation and:

- Their objective is to provide goods and services to various recipients or to develop or implement policy on behalf of governments and not to make a profit
- They are characterised by the absence of defined ownership interests that can be sold, transferred or redeemed
- They typically have a wide group of stakeholders to consider (including the public at large)
- Their revenues are generally derived from taxes or other similar contributions obtained through the exercise of coercive powers
- Their capital assets are typically acquired and held to deliver services without the intention of earning a return on them

## 2.3 Not-for-profit entities – specific issues

While the general trend is to get not-for-profit entities producing accounts which are based as far as possible on the provisions of IFRS and which are generally comparable to those produced for profit-making entities, there are two issues which have yet to be resolved.

### 2.3.1 Cost of transition

While there has been a general assumption that for public sector entities the move to the accruals basis will result in more relevant and better quality financial reporting, no actual cost-benefit analysis has been undertaken on this.

One of the arguments in favour of the adoption of the accruals basis is that it will be possible to compare the cost of providing a service against the same cost in the private sector. It will then be possible to see how goods and services can be most cheaply sourced.

### 2.3.2 Definition of a liability

The *Conceptual Framework* defines a liability as 'a present obligation of the entity arising from past events, the settlement of which is expected to result in an outflow from the entity of resources embodying economic benefits'. A liability is recognised when the amount of the outflow can be reliably measured.

Public benefit entities are subject to a commitment to provide public benefits, but there is an issue to be resolved over whether this commitment meets the definition of a liability. In this situation there has been no 'exchange'. The entity has not received any goods or services for which it is required to make 'settlement'. A distinction can be drawn between 'general commitments to provide public benefits' and 'specific commitments to provide public benefits'. The specific commitment can be regarded as a 'present obligation', but it can be argued that the obligation only arises when the entity formally undertakes to provide something such as a non-performance-related grant. (If the grant were performance-related, the entity would be able to withdraw from the agreement if the performance targets were not reached.)

There is also the issue of 'reliable measurement'. Governments in particular often find themselves funding projects which go a long way over budget, suggesting that reliable measurement was not obtained at the outset.

This issue is still being debated by the IPSAB. It is of major importance in the financial reporting of the social policies of governments.

# 3 Performance measurement

> Not-for-profit and public sector entities are required to manage their funds efficiently but are not expected to show a profit. Their performance is measured in terms of achievement of their stated purpose.

Not-for-profit and public sector entities produce financial statements in the same way as profit-making entities do but, while they are expected to remain solvent, their performance cannot be measured simply by the bottom line.

A public sector entity is not expected to show a profit or to underspend its budget. In practice, central government and local government departments know that if they underspend the budget, next year's allocation will be correspondingly reduced. This leads to a rash of digging up the roads and other expenditure just before the end of the financial year as councils strive to spend any remaining funds.

Private and public sector entities are judged principally on the basis of what they have achieved, not how much or how little they have spent in achieving it. So how is performance measured?

## 3.1 Public sector entities

These will have performance measures laid down by government. The emphasis is on economy, efficiency and effectiveness. Departments and local councils have to show how they have spent public money and what level of service they have achieved. Performance measurement will be based on Key Performance Indicators (KPIs). Examples of these for a local council could be:

- Number of homeless people rehoused
- % of rubbish collections made on time
- Number of children in care adopted

Public sector entities use the services of outside contractors for a variety of functions. They then have to be able to show that they have obtained the best possible value for what they have spent on outside services. This principle is usually referred to as Value For Money (VFM). In the UK, local authorities are required to report under a system known as Best Value. They have to show that they applied 'fair competition' in awarding contracts.

Best Value is based on the principle of the 'four Cs':

1   **Challenging** why, how and by whom a service is provided
2   **Comparing** performance against other local authorities
3   **Consulting** service users, the local community etc.
4   Using fair **Competition** to secure efficient and effective services

**Exam focus point**

> You will not be asked anything detailed or specific on this topic. The examiner has said that the question in the pilot paper (3(c)) is typical of what he will ask.

# Chapter Roundup

- The accounting requirements for not-for-profit and public sector entities are moving closer to those required for profit-making entities. However, they do have different goals and purposes.

- There is a general move to get public bodies reporting under the accruals system. Many private not-for-profit organisations still use cash accounting.

- Not-for-profit and public sector entities are required to manage their funds efficiently but are not expected to show a profit. Their performance is measured in terms of achievement of their stated purpose.

# Quick Quiz

1   Give some examples of not-for-profit and public sector entities.

2   What are some of the characteristics of **private sector** not-for-profit entities?

3   What are the 'four Cs'?

# Answers to Quick Quiz

1   Central and local government departments, schools, hospitals, charities.

2   See paragraph 2.2.1.

3   See paragraph 3.1

Now try the questions below from the Exam Question Bank

| Number | Level | Marks | Time |
|--------|-------|-------|------|
| 3(b) | – | 5 | 9 mins |

# Exam question and answer bank

# 1 Conceptual framework                                           18 mins

(a)  Explain and give an example of the effect on a set of published financial statements if the going concern convention is held not to apply.

(b)  Explain in general terms what the IASB *Conceptual Framework* is trying to achieve.      **(10 marks)**

# 2 Regulators                                                     18 mins

State three different regulatory influences on the preparation of the published accounts of quoted companies and briefly explain the role of each one. Comment briefly on the effectiveness of this regulatory system.                                                           **(10 marks)**

# 3 Standard setters                                               18 mins

There are those who suggest that any standard setting body is redundant because accounting standards are unnecessary. Other people feel that such standards should be produced, but by the government, so that they are a legal requirement.

*Required*

(a)  Discuss the statement that accounting standards are unnecessary for the purpose of regulating financial statements.

(b)  Discuss whether or not the financial statements of not-for-profit entities should be subject to regulation.                                                        **(10 marks)**

# 4 Polymer

The following list of account balances has been prepared by Polymer, plastics manufacturers, on 31 May 20X8, which is the end of the company's accounting period:

|  | $ | $ |
|---|---|---|
| Authorised and issued 300,000 ordinary shares of $1 each, fully paid | | 300,000 |
| 100,000 8.4% cumulative redeemable preference shares of $1 each, fully paid | | 100,000 |
| Revaluation surplus | | 50,000 |
| Share premium reserve | | 100,000 |
| General reserve | | 50,000 |
| Retained earnings – 31 May 20X7 | | 283,500 |
| Patents and trademarks | 215,500 | |
| Freehold land at cost | 250,000 | |
| Leasehold property at cost | 75,000 | |
| Amortisation of leasehold property – 31 May 20X7 | | 15,000 |
| Factory plant and equipment at cost | 150,000 | |
| Accumulated depreciation – plant and equipment – 31 May 20X7 | | 68,500 |
| Furniture and fixtures at cost | 50,000 | |
| Accumulated depreciation – furniture and fixtures – 31 May 20X7 | | 15,750 |
| Motor vehicles at cost | 75,000 | |
| Accumulated depreciation – motor vehicles – 31 May 20X7 | | 25,000 |
| 10% loan notes (20Y0 – 20Y5) | | 100,000 |
| Trade receivables/ trade payables | 177,630 | 97,500 |
| Bank overdraft | | 51,250 |
| Inventories – raw materials at cost – 31 May 20X7 | 108,400 | |
| Purchases – raw materials | 750,600 | |
| Carriage inwards – raw materials | 10,500 | |
| Manufacturing wages | 250,000 | |
| Manufacturing overheads | 125,000 | |

| | $ | $ |
|---|---|---|
| Cash | 5,120 | |
| Work in progress – 31 May 20X7 | 32,750 | |
| Sales | | 1,526,750 |
| Administrative expenses | 158,100 | |
| Selling and distribution expenses | 116,800 | |
| Legal and professional expenses | 54,100 | |
| Allowance for receivables – 31 May 20X8 | | 5,750 |
| Inventories – finished goods – 31 May 20X7 | 184,500 | |
| | 2,789,000 | 2,789,000 |

Additional information:

(1)  Inventories at 31 May 20X8 were:

|  | $ |
|---|---|
| Raw materials | 112,600 |
| Finished goods | 275,350 |
| Work in progress | 37,800 |

(2)  Depreciation for the year is to be charged as follows:

| | |
|---|---|
| Plant and equipment | 8% on cost – charged to production |
| Furniture and fixtures | 10% on cost – charged to admin |
| Motor vehicles | 20% on reducing value  – 25% admin |
| | – 75% selling and distribution |

(3)  Financial, legal and professional expenses include:

|  | $ |
|---|---|
| Solicitors' fees for purchase of freehold land during year | 5,000 |

(4)  Provision is to be made for a full year's interest on the loan notes.

(5)  Income tax on the profits for the year is estimated at $40,000 and is due for payment on 28 February 20X9.

(6)  The directors recommended on 30 June that a dividend of 3.5c per share be paid on the ordinary share capital. No ordinary dividend was paid during the year ended 31 May 20X7.

(7)  The leasehold land and buildings are held on a 50 year lease, acquired ten years ago.

*Required*

From the information given above, prepare the statement of profit or loss and other comprehensive income of Polymer for the year to 31 May 20X8 and a statement of financial position at that date for publication in accordance with International Financial Reporting Standards.

Notes to the financial statements are not required.                                        **(25 marks)**

# 5 Gains

*Required*

Using the information below prepare the Statement of changes in equity for Gains for the year ended 31 December 20X9.                                        **(10 marks)**

(a)  **Gains**
     **Statement of profit or loss and other comprehensive income (extract)**

|  | $'000 |
|---|---:|
| Profit before interest and tax | 792 |
| Finance income | 24 |
| Finance cost | (10) |
| **Profit before tax** | 806 |
| Income tax expense | (240) |
| **PROFIT FOR THE YEAR** | 566 |
| **Other comprehensive income:** | |
| Gain on property revaluation | 120 |
| **TOTAL COMPREHENSIVE INCOME FOR THE YEAR** | 686 |

(b)  *Non-current assets*

(i)   Assets held at cost were impaired by $25,000.
(ii)  Freehold land and buildings were revalued to $500,000 (Book value $380,000).
(iii) A previously revalued asset was sold for $60,000.

Details of the revaluation are as follows:

|  | $ |
|---|---:|
| Book value at revaluation | 30,000 |
| Revaluation | 50,000 |
|  | 80,000 |
| Depreciation (80,000/10) × 3 | 24,000 |
|  | 56,000 |

Gains has been following paragraph 41 of IAS 16 which allows a reserve transfer of the realised revaluation surplus (the difference between depreciation based on revalued amount and depreciation based on cost) as the asset is used to retained earnings.

Revaluations during the year related to land.

(iv)  Details of investment properties are as follows:

|  | $ |
|---|---:|
| Original cost | 120,000 |
| Revaluation surplus | 40,000 |
| Value at 1.1.20X9 | 160,000 |

The properties had a valuation on 31 December 20X9 of $110,000. Gains previously accounted for its investment properties by crediting gains to a revaluation surplus as allowed by local GAAP. Gains now wishes to apply the fair value model of IAS 40 which states that gains and losses should be accounted for in profit or loss. The elimination of the previous revaluation surplus is to be treated as a change in accounting policy in accordance with IAS 8. No adjustment has yet been made for the change in accounting policy or subsequent fall in value.

(c)  *Share capital*

During the year the company had the following changes to its capital structure:

(i)   An issue of $200,000 $1 ordinary bonus shares capitalising its share premium reserve
(ii)  An issue of 400,000 $1 ordinary shares (issue price $1.40 per share).

(d)  *Equity*

The book value of equity at the start of the year was as follows:

|  | $ |
|---|---:|
| Share capital | 2,800,000 |
| Share premium | 1,150,000 |
| Retained earnings | 2,120,000 |
| Revaluation surplus | 750,000 |
|  | 6,820,000 |

(e)   *Dividends*

Dividends paid during the year amounted to $200,000.

# 6 Biogenics

(a)   Over the last 20 years many companies have spent a great deal of money internally developing new intangible assets such as software. The treatment for these assets is prescribed by IAS 38 *Intangible assets.*

*Required*

In accordance with IAS 38, discuss whether internally-developed intangible assets should be recognised, and if so how they should be initially recorded and subsequently accounted for.    **(3 marks)**

(b)   Biogenics is a publicly listed pharmaceutical company. During the year to 31 December 20X9 the following transactions took place:

(i)    $6m was spent on developing a new obesity drug which received clinical approval on 1 July 20X9 and is proving commercially successful. The directors expect the project to be in profit within 12 months of the approval date. The patent was registered on 1 July 20X9. It cost $1.5m and remains in force for three years.

(ii)   A research project was set up on 1 October 20X9 which is expected to result in a new cancer drug. $200,000 was spent on computer equipment and $400,000 on staff salaries. The equipment has an expected life of four years.

(iii)  On 1 September 20X9 Biogenics acquired an up-to-date list of GPs at a cost of $500,000 and has been visiting them to explain the new obesity drug. The list is expected to generate sales throughout the life-cycle of the drug.

*Required*

Prepare extracts from the statement of financial position of Biogenics at 31 December 20X9 relating to the above items and summarise the costs to be included in the statement of profit or loss for that year.

**(7 marks)**

**(Total = 10 marks)**

# 7 Multiplex                                                                27 mins

**(Adapted from past ACCA exam paper 2.5 Pilot paper)**

On 1 January 20X0 Multiplex acquired Steamdays, a company that operates a scenic railway along the coast of a popular tourist area. The summarised statement of financial position at fair values of Steamdays on 1 January 20X0, reflecting the terms of the acquisition was:

|                                  | $'000 |
|----------------------------------|------:|
| Goodwill                         | 200   |
| Operating licence                | 1,200 |
| Property – train stations and land | 300 |
| Rail track and coaches           | 300   |
| Two steam engines                | 1,000 |
| Purchase consideration           | 3,000 |

The operating licence is for ten years. It was renewed on 1 January 20X0 by the transport authority and is stated at the cost of its renewal. The carrying values of the property and rail track and coaches are based on their value in use. The engines are valued at their net selling prices.

On 1 February 20X0 the boiler of one of the steam engines exploded, completely destroying the whole engine. Fortunately no one was injured, but the engine was beyond repair. Due to its age a replacement could not be obtained. Because of the reduced passenger capacity the estimated value in use of the whole of the business after the accident was assessed at $2 million.

Passenger numbers after the accident were below expectations even allowing for the reduced capacity. A market research report concluded that tourists were not using the railway because of their fear of a similar accident occurring to the remaining engine. In the light of this the value in use of the business was re-assessed on 31 March 20X0 at $1.8 million. On this date Multiplex received an offer of $900,000 in respect of the operating licence (it is transferable). The realisable value of the other net assets has not changed significantly.

*Required*

Calculate the carrying value of the assets of Steamdays (in Multiplex's consolidated statement of financial position) at 1 February 20X0 and 31 March 20X0 after recognising the impairment losses.

# 8 Hewlett

Hewlett is a quoted company reporting under IFRSs. During the year end 31 December 20X2, the company changed its accounting policy with respect to property valuation. There are also a number of other issues that need to be finalised before the financial statements can be published.

Hewlett's trial balance from the general ledger at 31 December 20X2 showed the following balances:

|  | $'m | $'m |
|---|---|---|
| Revenue |  | 2,648 |
| Purchases | 1,669 |  |
| Inventories at 1 January 20X2 | 444 |  |
| Distribution costs | 514 |  |
| Administrative expenses | 345 |  |
| Loan note interest paid | 3 |  |
| Rental income |  | 48 |
| Land and buildings: cost (including $90m land) | 840 |  |
| accumulated depreciation at 1 January 20X2 |  | 120 |
| Plant and equipment: cost | 258 |  |
| accumulated depreciation at 1 January 20X2 |  | 126 |
| Investment property at 1 January 20X2 | 548 |  |
| Trade receivables | 541 |  |
| Cash and cash equivalents | 32 |  |
| 50c ordinary shares |  | 100 |
| Share premium |  | 244 |
| Retained earnings at 1 January 20X2 |  | 753 |
| Interim dividend paid | 6 |  |
| General reserve |  | 570 |
| 4% loan note repayable 20X8 (issued 20X0) |  | 150 |
| Trade payables |  | 434 |
| Proceeds from sale of equipment |  | 7 |
|  | 5,200 | 5,200 |

Further information to be taken into account:

(i) Closing inventories were counted and amounted to $388m at cost. However, shortly after the year end out-of-date inventories with a cost of $21m were sold for $14m.

(ii) At the beginning of the year, Hewlett disposed of some malfunctioning equipment for $7m. The equipment had cost $15m and had accumulated depreciation brought forward at 1 January 20X2 of $3m.

There were no other additions or disposal to property, plant and equipment in the year.

(iii) The company treats depreciation on plant and equipment as a cost of sale and on land and buildings as an administrative cost. Depreciation rates as per the company's accounting policy note are as follows:

| Buildings | Straight line over 50 years |
|---|---|
| Plant and equipment | 20% reducing balance |

Hewlett's accounting policy is to charge a full year's depreciation in the year of an asset's purchase and none in the year of disposal. Hewlett's land and buildings were 8 year old on 1 January 20X2.

(iv) On 31 December 20X2 the company revalued its land and buildings to $760m (including $100m for the land). The company follows the revaluation model of IAS 16 for its land and buildings, but no revaluations had previously been necessary. The company wishes to treat the revaluation surplus as being realised on disposal of the assets.

(v) Due to a change in the company's product portfolio plans, an item of plant with a carrying value $22m at 31 December 20X2 (after adjusting for depreciation for the year) may be impaired due to a change in use. An impairment test conducted at 31 December, revealed its fair value less costs to sell to be $16m. The asset is now expected to generate an annual net income stream of $3.8m for the next 5 years at which point the asset would be disposed of for $4.2m. An appropriate discount rate is 8%. 5 year discount factors at 8% are:

| | Simple | Cumulative |
|---|---|---|
| | 0.677 | 3.993 |

(vi) The income tax charge (current and deferred tax) for the year is estimated at $45m (of which $17m relates to future payable tax on the revaluation, to be charged to other comprehensive income (and the revaluation surplus)).

(vii) An interim dividend of 3c per share was paid on 30 June 20X2. A final dividend of 1.5c per share was declared by the directors on 28 January 20X3. No dividends were paid or declared in 20X1.

(viii) During the year on 1 July 20X2, Hewlett made a 1 for 4 bonus issue, capitalising its general reserve. This transaction had not yet been accounted for. The fair value of the company's shares on the date of the bonus issue was $7.50 each.

(ix) Hewlett uses the fair value model of IAS 40. The fair value of the investment property at 31 December 20X2 was $588m.

*Required*

Prepare the statement of profit or loss and other comprehensive income and statement of changes in equity for Hewlett for the year to 31 December 20X2 and a statement of financial position at that date in accordance with IFRSs insofar as the information permits.

Notes to the financial statements are not required, but all workings should be clearly shown.

Work to the nearest $1m. Comparative information is not required.

# 9 Barcelona and Madrid
22 mins

Barcelona acquired 60% of Madrid's ordinary share capital on 1 October 20X2 at a price of $1.06 per share. The balance on Madrid's retained earnings at that date was $104m and the general reserve stood at $11m.

Their respective statements of financial position as at 30 September 20X6 are as follows:

| | Barcelona $m | Madrid $m |
|---|---|---|
| **Non-current assets** | | |
| Property, plant & equipment | 2,848 | 354 |
| Patents | 45 | – |
| Investment in Madrid | 159 | – |
| | 3,052 | 354 |
| **Current assets** | | |
| Inventories | 895 | 225 |
| Trade and other receivables | 1,348 | 251 |
| Cash and cash equivalents | 212 | 34 |
| | 2,455 | 510 |
| | 5,507 | 864 |

## Equity

|  |  |  |
|---|---|---|
| Share capital (20c ordinary shares) | 920 | 50 |
| Retained earnings | 2,086 | 394 |
| General reserve | 775 | 46 |
|  | 3,781 | 490 |

## Non-current liabilities

|  |  |  |
|---|---|---|
| Long-term borrowings | 558 | 168 |

## Current liabilities

|  |  |  |
|---|---|---|
| Trade and other payables | 1,168 | 183 |
| Current portion of long-term borrowings | – | 23 |
|  | 1,168 | 206 |
|  | 5,507 | 864 |

At the date of acquisition the fair values of some of Madrid's assets were greater than their carrying amounts. One line of Madrid's inventory had a fair value of $8m above its carrying amount. This inventory had all been sold by 30 September 20X6. Madrid's land and buildings had a fair value $26m above their carrying amount. $20 of this is attributable to the buildings, which had a remaining useful life of 10 years at the date of acquisition.

It is group policy to value non-controlling interests at full (or fair) value. The fair value of the non-controlling interests at acquisition was $86m.

Annual impairment tests have revealed cumulative impairment losses relating to recognised goodwill of $20m to date.

*Required*

Produce the consolidated statement of financial position for the Barcelona Group as at 30 September 20X6.

**(12 marks)**

# 10 Reprise
**36 mins**

Reprise purchased 75% of Encore for $2,000,000 10 years ago when the balance on its retained earnings was $1,044,000. The statements of financial position of the two companies as at 31 March 20X4 are as follows:

|  | Reprise | Encore |
|---|---|---|
|  | $'000 | $'000 |
| **Non-current assets** |  |  |
| Investment in Encore | 2,000 | – |
| Land and buildings | 3,350 | – |
| Plant and equipment | 1,010 | 2,210 |
| Motor vehicles | 510 | 345 |
|  | 6,870 | 2,555 |
| **Current assets** |  |  |
| Inventories | 890 | 352 |
| Trade receivables | 1,372 | 514 |
| Cash and cash equivalents | 89 | 51 |
|  | 2,351 | 917 |
|  | 9,221 | 3,472 |
| **Equity** |  |  |
| Share capital - $1 ordinary shares | 1,000 | 500 |
| Retained earnings | 4,225 | 2,610 |
| Revaluation surplus | 2,500 | – |
|  | 7,725 | 3,110 |

| | Reprise $'000 | Encore $'000 |
|---|---|---|
| **Non-current liabilities** | | |
| 10% debentures | 500 | – |
| **Current liabilities** | | |
| Trade payables | 996 | 362 |
| | 9,221 | 3,472 |

The following additional information is available:

(1)    Included in trade receivables of Reprise are amounts owed by Encore of $75,000. The current accounts do not at present balance due to a payment for $39,000 being in transit at the year end from Encore.

(2)    Included in the inventories of Encore are items purchased from Reprise during the year for $31,200. Reprise marks up its goods by 30% to achieve its selling price.

(3)    $180,000 of the recognised goodwill arising is to be written off due to impairment losses.

(4)    Encore shares were trading at $4.40 just prior to acquisition by Reprise.

*Required*

Prepare the consolidated statement of financial position for the Reprise group of companies as at 31 March 20X4. It is the group policy to value the non-controlling interests at full (or fair) value.   **(14 marks)**

# 11 Fallowfield and Rusholme                                          27 mins

Fallowfield acquired a 60% holding in Rusholme three years ago when Rusholme's retained earnings balance stood at $16,000. Both businesses have been very successful since the acquisition and their respective statements of profit or loss for the year ended 30 June 20X8 are as follows:

| | Fallowfield $ | Rusholme $ |
|---|---|---|
| **Revenue** | 403,400 | 193,000 |
| Cost of sales | (201,400) | (92,600) |
| Gross profit | 202,000 | 100,400 |
| Distribution costs | (16,000) | (14,600) |
| Administrative expenses | (24,250) | (17,800) |
| Dividends from Rusholme | 15,000 | |
| **Profit before tax** | 176,750 | 68,000 |
| Income tax expense | (61,750) | (22,000) |
| **PROFIT FOR THE YEAR** | 115,000 | 46,000 |

**Statement of changes in equity (extract)**

| | Fallowfield Retained earnings $ | Rusholme Retained earnings $ |
|---|---|---|
| Balance at 1 July 20X7 | 163,000 | 61,000 |
| Dividends | (40,000) | (25,000) |
| Profit for the year | 115,000 | 46,000 |
| Balance at 30 June 20X8 | 238,000 | 82,000 |

*Additional information:*

During the year Rusholme sold some goods to Fallowfield for $40,000, including 25% mark up. Half of these items were still in inventories at the year-end.

*Required*

Produce the consolidated statement of profit or loss of Fallowfield and its subsidiary for the year ended 30 June 20X8, and an extract from the statement of changes in equity, showing retained earnings. Goodwill is to be ignored.   **(10 marks)**

# 12 Panther Group

Panther operated as a single company, but in 20X4 decided to expand its operations. Panther acquired a 60% interest in Sabre on 1 July 20X4 for $2,000,000.

The statements of profit or loss and other comprehensive income of Panther and Sabre for the year ended 31 December 20X4 are as follows:

|  | Panther $'000 | Sabre $'000 |
|---|---|---|
| **Revenue** | 22,800 | 4,300 |
| Cost of sales | (13,600) | (2,600) |
| Gross profit | 9,200 | 1,700 |
| Distribution costs | (2,900) | (500) |
| Administrative expenses | (1,800) | (300) |
| Finance costs | (200) | (70) |
| Finance income | 50 | – |
| **Profit before tax** | 4,350 | 830 |
| Income tax expense | (1,300) | (220) |
| **PROFIT FOR THE YEAR** | 3,050 | 610 |
| Other comprehensive income for the year, net of tax | 1,600 | 180 |
| **TOTAL COMPREHENSIVE INCOME FOR THE YEAR** | 4,650 | 790 |

Historically, Sabre had been a significant trading partner of Panther. During 20X4, Panther purchased $640,000 of goods from Sabre. Of these, $60,000 remained in inventories at the year end. Sabre makes a mark-up on cost of 20% under the transfer pricing agreement between the two companies. The fair value of the identifiable net assets of Sabre on purchase were $200,000 greater than their book value. The difference relates to properties with a remaining useful life of 20 years.

On 1 January 20X4 (to protect its supply lines), Panther had advanced a loan to Sabre amounting to $800,000 at a market interest rate of 5%. The loan is due for repayment in 20X9.

Statement of changes in equity (extracts) for the two companies:

|  | Panther Reserves $'000 | Sabre Reserves $'000 |
|---|---|---|
| Balance at 1 January 20X4 | 12,750 | 2,480 |
| Dividend paid | (900) | – |
| Total comprehensive income for the year | 4,650 | 790 |
| Balance at 31 December 20X4 | 16,500 | 3,270 |

Panther and Sabre had $400,000 and $150,000 of share capital in issue throughout the period respectively.

*Required*

Prepare the consolidated statement of profit or loss and other comprehensive income and statement of changes in equity (extract for reserves) for the Panther Group for the year ended 31 December 20X4.

No adjustments for impairment losses were necessary in the group financial statements.

Assume income and expenses (other than intragroup items) accrue evenly. **(15 marks)**

# 13 Hever
**45 mins**

Hever has held shares in two companies, Spiro and Aldridge, for a number of years. As at 31 December 20X4 they have the following statements of financial position:

|  | Hever $'000 | Spiro $'000 | Aldridge $'000 |
|---|---|---|---|
| **Non-current assets** |  |  |  |
| Property, plant & equipment | 370 | 190 | 260 |
| Investments | 218 | – | – |
|  | 588 | 190 | 260 |

## Current assets

|  |  |  |  |
|---|---|---|---|
| Inventories | 160 | 100 | 180 |
| Trade receivables | 170 | 90 | 100 |
| Cash | 50 | 40 | 10 |
|  | 380 | 230 | 290 |
|  | 968 | 420 | 550 |

## Equity

|  |  |  |  |
|---|---|---|---|
| Share capital ($1 ords) | 200 | 80 | 50 |
| Share premium | 100 | 80 | 30 |
| Retained earnings | 568 | 200 | 400 |
|  | 868 | 360 | 480 |

## Current liabilities

|  |  |  |  |
|---|---|---|---|
| Trade payables | 100 | 60 | 70 |
|  | 968 | 420 | 550 |

You ascertain the following additional information:

(1) The 'investments' in the statement of financial position comprise solely Hever's investment in Spiro ($128,000) and in Aldridge ($90,000).

(2) The 48,000 shares in Spiro were acquired when Spiro's retained earnings balance stood at $20,000.

The 15,000 shares in Aldridge were acquired when that company had a retained earnings balance of $150,000.

(3) When Hever acquired its shares in Spiro the fair value of Spiro's net assets equalled their book values with the following exceptions:

|  | $'000 |
|---|---|
| Property, plant and equipment | 50 higher |
| Inventories | 20 lower (sold during 20X4) |

Depreciation arising on the fair value adjustment to non-current assets since this date is $5,000.

(4) During the year, Hever sold inventories to Spiro for $16,000, which originally cost Hever $10,000. Three-quarters of these inventories have subsequently been sold by Spiro.

(5) No impairment losses on goodwill had been necessary by 31 December 20X4.

(6) It is group policy to value non-controlling interests at full (or fair) value. The fair value of the non-controlling interests at acquisition was $90,000.

*Required*

Produce the consolidated statement of financial position for the Hever group (incorporating the associate).

**(20 marks)**

# 14 Trontacc
**18 mins**

Trontacc is a company whose activities are in the field of major construction projects. During the year ended 30 September 20X7, it enters into three separate construction contracts, each with a fixed contract price of $1,000,000. The following information relates to these contracts at 30 September 20X7:

|  | Contract | | |
|---|---|---|---|
|  | A | B | C |
|  | $'000 | $'000 | $'000 |
| Payments on account (including amounts receivable) | 540 | 475 | 400 |
| Costs incurred to date | 500 | 550 | 320 |
| Estimate costs to complete the contract | 300 | 550 | 580 |
| Estimate percentage of work completed | 60% | 50% | 35% |

*Required*

(a) Show how each contract would be reflected in the statement of financial position of Trontacc at 30 September 20X7 under IAS 11.

(b) Show how each contract would be reflected in the statement of profit or loss of Trontacc for the year ended 30 September 20X7 under IAS 11. **(10 marks)**

# 15 C Co                                                                    27 mins

C Co is a civil engineering company. It started work on two construction projects during the year ended 31 December 20X0. The following figures relate to those projects at the end of the reporting period.

|  | *Maryhill bypass* | *Rottenrow Centre* |
|---|---|---|
|  | *$'000* | *$'000* |
| Contract price | 9,000 | 8,000 |
| Costs incurred to date | 1,400 | 2,900 |
| Estimated costs to completion | 5,600 | 5,200 |
| Value of work certified to date | 2,800 | 3,000 |
| Progress billings | 2,600 | 3,400 |

An old mineshaft has been discovered under the site for the Rottenrow Centre and the costs of dealing with this have been taken into account in the calculation of estimated costs to completion. C Co's lawyers are reasonably confident that the customer will have to bear the additional costs which will be incurred in stabilising the land. If negotiations are successful then the contract price will increase to $10m.

C Co recognises revenues and profits on construction contracts on the basis of work certified to date.

*Required*

(a) Calculate the figures which would appear in C Co's financial statements in respect of these two projects.

(b) It has been suggested that profit on construction contracts should not be recognised until the contract is completed. Briefly explain whether you believe that this suggestion would improve the quality of financial reporting for long-term contracts. **(15 marks)**

# 16 Provisions                                                             45 mins

IAS 37 *Provisions, contingent liabilities and contingent assets* was issued in 1998. Prior to its publication, there was no International Accounting Standard that dealt with the general subject of accounting for provisions.

Extract prepares its financial statements to 31 December each year. During the years ended 31 December 20X0 and 31 December 20X1, the following event occurred.

Extract is involved in extracting minerals in a number of different countries. The process typically involves some contamination of the site from which the minerals are extracted. Extract makes good this contamination only where legally required to do so by legislation passed in the relevant country.

The company has been extracting minerals in Copperland since January 20W8 and expects its site to produce output until 31 December 20X5. On 23 December 20X0, it came to the attention of the directors of Extract that the government of Copperland was virtually certain to pass legislation requiring the making good of mineral extraction sites. The legislation was duly passed on 15 March 20X1. The directors of Extract estimate that the cost of making good the site in Copperland will be $2 million. This estimate is of the actual cash expenditure that will be incurred on 31 December 20X5.

*Required*

(a) Explain why there was a need for an accounting standard dealing with provisions, and summarise the criteria that need to be satisfied before a provision is recognised. **(12 marks)**

(b) Compute the effect of the estimated cost of making good the site on the financial statements of Extract for BOTH of the years ended 31 December 20X0 and 20X1. Give full explanations of the figures you compute.

The annual discount rate to be used in any relevant calculations is 10%.

The relevant discount factors at 10% are:

Year 4 at 10%    0.683
Year 5 at 10%    0.621

(13 marks)

(Total = 25 marks)

# 17 Financial assets and liabilities          18 mins

(a)    On 1 January 2005, an entity issued a debt instrument with a coupon rate of 3.5% at a par value of
       $6,000,000. The directly attributable costs of issue were $120,000. The debt instrument is
       repayable on 31 December 2011 at a premium of $1,100,000.

       What is the total amount of the finance cost associated with the debt instrument?          (3 marks)

(b)    On 1 January 20X3 Deferred issued $600,000 loan notes. Issue costs were $200. The loan notes
       do not carry interest, but are redeemable at a premium of $152,389 on 31 December 20X4. The
       effective finance cost of the loan notes is 12%.

       What is the finance cost in respect of the loan notes for the year ended 31 December 20X4?

       (3 marks)

(c)    On 1 January 20X1, EFG issued 10,000 5% convertible bonds at their par value of $50 each. The
       bonds will be redeemed on 1 January 20X6. Each bond is convertible to equity shares at the option
       of the holder at any time during the five year period. Interest on the bond will be paid annually in
       arrears.

       The prevailing market interest rate for similar debt without conversion options at the date of issue
       was 6%.

       The discount factors for 6% at year 5 is 0.747.

       The cumulative discount factor for years 1-5 at 6% is 4.212.

       At what value should the equity element of the hybrid financial instrument be recognised in the
       financial statements at EFG at the date of issue?          (4 marks)

       (Total = 10 marks)

# 18 Alpha          45 mins

In producing the Conceptual Framework for Financial Reporting and some of the current IFRSs, the IASB
has had to address the potential problem that the management of some companies may choose to adopt
inappropriate accounting policies. These could have the effect of portraying an entity's financial position in
a favourable manner. In some countries this is referred to as 'creative accounting'. A common feature of
many IFRSs, is the application of the principle of 'substance over form'.

*Required*

(a)    Describe in broad terms common ways in which management can manipulate financial statements
       to indulge in 'creative accounting' and why they would wish to do so.          (7 marks)

(b)    Explain the principle of substance over form and how it limits the above practice; and for each of
       the following areas of accounting describe an example of the application of substance over form.

       (i)    Group accounting
       (ii)   Financing non-current assets
       (iii)  Measurement and disclosure of current assets          (8 marks)

(c)    Alpha, a public listed corporation, is considering how it should raise $10 million of finance which is
       required for a major and vital non-current asset renewal scheme that will be undertaken during the
       current year to 31 December 20X6. Alpha is particularly concerned about how analysts are likely to
       react to its financial statements for the year to 31 December 20X6. Present forecasts suggest that
       Alpha's earnings per share and its financial gearing ratios may be worse than market expectations.

Mr Wong, Alpha's Finance Director, is in favour of raising the finance by issuing a convertible loan. He has suggested that the coupon (interest) rate on the loan should be 5%; this is below the current market rate of 9% for this type of loan. In order to make the stock attractive to investors the terms of conversion into equity would be very favourable to compensate for the low interest rate.

*Required*

(i)  Explain why the Finance Director believes the above scheme may favourably improve Alpha's earnings per share and gearing.

(ii)  Describe how the requirements of IAS 33 *Earnings per share* and IAS 32 *Financial instruments: presentation* are intended to prevent the above effects.  **(10 marks)**

**(Total = 25 marks)**

# 19 Jenson                                                    45 mins

**(Adapted from past ACCA exam paper 2.5 Pilot paper)**

The timing of revenue (income) recognition has long been an area of debate and inconsistency in accounting. Industry practice in relation to revenue recognition varies widely, the following are examples of different points in the operating cycle of businesses that revenue and profit can be recognised.

(a)  On the acquisition of goods
(b)  During the manufacture or production of goods
(c)  On delivery/acceptance of goods
(d)  When certain conditions have been satisfied after the goods have been delivered
(e)  Receipt of payment for credit sales
(f)  On the expiry of a guarantee or warranty

In the past the 'critical event' approach has been used to determine the timing of revenue recognition. The IASB in the Conceptual Framework has defined the 'elements' of financial statements, and it uses these to determine when a gain or loss occurs.

*Required*

(a)  Explain what is meant by the critical event in relation to revenue recognition and discuss the criteria used in the Conceptual Framework for determining when a gain or loss arises.  **(5 marks)**

(b)  For each of the stages of the operating cycle identified above, explain why it may be an appropriate point to recognise revenue and, where possible, give a practical example of an industry where it occurs.  **(12 marks)**

(c)  Jenson has entered into the following transactions/agreements in the year to 31 March 20X5.

(i)  Goods, which had a cost of $20,000, were sold to Wholesaler for $35,000 on 1 June 20X4. Jenson has an option to repurchase the goods from Wholesaler at any time within the next two years. The repurchase price will be $35,000 plus interest charged at 12% per annum from the date of sale to the date of repurchase. It is expected that Jenson will repurchase the goods.

(ii)  Jenson owns the rights to a fast food franchise. On 1 April 20X4 it sold the right to open a new outlet to Mr Cody. The franchise is for five years. Jenson received an initial fee of $50,000 for the first year and will receive $5,000 per annum thereafter. Jenson has continuing service obligations on its franchise for advertising and product development that amount to approximately $8,000 per annum for each franchised outlet. A reasonable profit margin on the provision of the continuing services is deemed to be 20% of revenues received.

(iii)  On 1 September 20X4 Jenson received subscriptions in advance of $240,000. The subscriptions are for 24 monthly publications of a magazine produced by Jenson. At the year end Jenson had produced and despatched six of the 24 publications. The total cost of producing the magazine is estimated at $192,000 with each publication costing a broadly similar amount.

## Required

Describe how Jenson should treat each of the above examples in its financial statements in the year to 31 March 20X5.

**(8 marks)**

**(Total = 25 marks)**

# 20 Bulwell

**18 mins**

Bulwell Aggregates Co wish to expand their transport fleet and purchased three heavy lorries with a list price of $18,000 each. Robert Bulwell has negotiated lease finance to fund this expansion, and the company has entered into a finance lease agreement with Granby Garages Co on 1 January 20X1. The agreement states that Bulwell Aggregates will pay a deposit of $9,000 on 1 January 20X1, and two annual instalments of $24,000 on 31 December 20X1, 20X2 and a final instalment of $20,391 on 31 December 20X3.

Interest is to be calculated at 25% on the balance outstanding on 1 January each year and paid on 31 December each year.

The depreciation policy of Bulwell Aggregates Co is to write off the vehicles over a four year period using the straight line method and assuming a scrap value of $1,333 for each vehicle at the end of its useful life.

*Required*

Show the entries in the statement of profit or loss and statement of financial position for the years 20X1, 20X2, 20X3. This is the only lease transaction undertaken by this company.

Calculations to the nearest $.

**(10 marks)**

# 21 Lis

**18 mins**

On 1 January 20X3 Lis entered into a lease agreement to rent an asset for a 6 year period, at which point it will be returned to the lessor and scrapped, with annual payments of $18,420 made in advance. The market price of the asset on the same date was $86,000. The present value of minimum lease payments amounts to $84,000, discounted at the implicit interest rate shown in the lease agreement of 12.5%.

Lis expects to sell goods produced by the asset during the first 5 years of the lease term, but has leased the asset for 6 years as this is the requirement of the lessor, and in case this expectation changes.

*Required*

Explain how the above lease would be accounted for the year ending 31 December 20X3 including producing relevant extracts from the statement of profit or loss and statement of financial position.

You are not required to prepare the notes to the financial statements.

**(10 marks)**

# 22 Winger

**45 mins**

**(Adapted from past ACCA exam paper 2.5 Pilot paper)**

The following list of account balances relates to Winger at 31 March 20X1.

|  | $'000 | $'000 |
|---|---|---|
| Sales revenue (note a) |  | 358,450 |
| Cost of sales | 185,050 |  |
| Distribution costs | 28,700 |  |
| Administration expenses | 15,000 |  |
| Lease rentals (note b) | 20,000 |  |
| Loan note interest paid | 2,000 |  |
| Dividend paid | 12,000 |  |
| Property at cost (note c) | 200,000 |  |
| Plant and equipment cost | 154,800 |  |
| Depreciation 1 April 20X0 – plant and equipment |  | 34,800 |

| | | |
|---|---:|---:|
| Development expenditure (note d) | 30,000 | |
| Profit on disposal of non-current assets (note c) | | 45,000 |
| Trade accounts receivable | 55,000 | |
| Inventories: 31 March 20X1 | 28,240 | |
| Cash and bank | 10,660 | |
| Trade accounts payable | | 29,400 |
| Taxation: over provision in year to 31 March 20X0 | | 2,200 |
| Equity shares of 25c each | | 150,000 |
| 8% loan note (issued in 20W9) | | 50,000 |
| Retained earnings 1 April 20X0 | | 71,600 |
| | 741,450 | 741,450 |

The following notes are relevant.

(a) Included in sales revenue is $27 million, which relates to sales made to customers under sale or return agreements. The expiry date for the return of these goods is 30 April 20X1. Winger has charged a mark-up of 20% on cost for these sales.

(b) A lease rental of $20 million was paid on 1 April 20X0. It is the first of five annual payments in advance for the rental of an item of equipment that has a cash purchase price of $80 million. The auditors have advised that this is a finance lease and have calculated the implicit interest rate in the lease as 12% per annum. Leased assets should be depreciated on a straight-line basis over the life of the lease.

(c) On 1 April 20X0 Winger acquired a new property at a cost of $200 million. For the purpose of calculating depreciation only, the asset has been separated into the following elements.

| Separate asset | Cost | Life |
|---|---:|---|
| | $'000 | |
| Land | 50,000 | freehold |
| Heating system | 20,000 | 10 years |
| Lifts | 30,000 | 15 years |
| Building | 100,000 | 50 years |

The depreciation of the elements of the property should be calculated on a straight-line basis. The new property replaced an existing one that was sold on the same date for $95 million. It had cost $50 million and had a carrying value of $80 million at the date of sale. The profit on this property has been calculated on the original cost. It had not been depreciated on the basis that the depreciation charge would not be material.

Plant and machinery is depreciated at 20% on the reducing balance basis.

(d) The figure for development expenditure in the list of account balances represents the amounts deferred in previous years in respect of the development of a new product. Unfortunately, during the current year, the government has introduced legislation which effectively bans this type of product. As a consequence of this the project has been abandoned. The directors of Winger are of the opinion that writing off the development expenditure, as opposed to its previous deferment, represents a change of accounting policy and therefore wish to treat the write off as a prior period adjustment.

(e) A provision for income tax for the year to 31 March 20X1 of $15 million is required.

*Required*

(a) Prepare the statement of profit or loss of Winger for the year to 31 March 20X1. **(9 marks)**

(b) Prepare a statement of financial position as at 31 March 20X1 in accordance with International Accounting Standards as far as the information permits. **(11 marks)**

(c) Discuss the acceptability of the company's previous policy in respect of non-depreciation of property and the proposed treatment of the deferred development expenditure. **(5 marks)**

**(Total = 25 marks)**

# 23 Carpati

The following information relates to Carpati:

(1) The carrying amount of plant and equipment at 30 September 20X6 is $1,185,000.

(2) The tax written down value of plant and equipment at 1 October 20X5 was $405,000.

(3) During the year ended 30 September 20X6, the company bought plant and equipment of $290,000, which is eligible for tax depreciation.

(4) Carpati bought its freehold property in 20W5 for $600,000. It was revalued in the 20X6 accounts to $1,500,000. Ignore depreciation on buildings. No tax allowances were available to Carpati on the buildings.

*Required*

Draft the note to the statement of financial position at 30 September 20X6 omitting comparatives, in respect of deferred tax. Work to the nearest $'000. Assume a current income tax rate of 30%. Tax depreciation is at 25% on a reducing balance basis. The income tax rate enacted for 20X7 is 28%. **(6 marks)**

# 24 Pilum                                                                 18 mins

A statement showing the retained profit of Pilum for the year ended 31 December 20X4 is set out below:

|  | $ | $ |
|---|---|---|
| Profit before tax |  | 2,530,000 |
| Less: income tax expense |  | (1,127,000) |
|  |  | 1,403,000 |
| Transfer to reserves |  | (230,000) |
| Dividends: |  |  |
| Paid preference interim dividend | 138,000 |  |
| Paid ordinary interim divided | 414,000 |  |
| Declared preference final dividend | 138,000 |  |
|  |  | (690,000) |
| Retained |  | 483,000 |

On 1 January 20X4 the issued share capital of Pilum was 4,600,000 6% preference shares of $1 each and 4,120,000 ordinary shares of $1 each.

*Required*

Calculate the earnings per share (on basic and diluted basis) in respect of the year ended 31 December 20X4 for each of the following circumstances. (Each of the three circumstances (a) to (c) is to be dealt with separately):

(a) On the basis that there was no change in the issued share capital of the company during the year ended 31 December 20X4.

(b) On the basis that the company made a rights issue of $1 ordinary shares on 1 October 20X4 in the proportion of 1 for every 5 shares held, at a price of $1.20. The market price for the shares at close of trade on the last day of quotation cum rights was $1.78 per share.

(c) On the basis that the company made no new issue of shares during the year ended 31 December 20X4 but on that date it had in issue $1,500,000 10% convertible loan stock 20X8 – 20Y1. This loan stock will be convertible into ordinary $1 shares as follows:

      20X8  90 $1 shares for $100 nominal value loan stock
      20X9  85 $1 shares for $100 nominal value loan stock
      20Y0  80 $1 shares for $100 nominal value loan stock
      20Y1  75 $1 shares for $100 nominal value loan stock

Assume where appropriate that the income tax rate is 30%. **(10 marks)**

# 25 Biggerbuys

45 mins

Biggerbuys has carried on business for a number of years as a retailer of a wide variety of consumer products. The entity operates from a number of stores around the country. In recent years the entity has found it necessary to provide credit facilities to its customers in order to maintain growth in revenue. As a result of this decision the liability to its bankers has increased substantially. The statutory financial statements for the year ended 30 June 20X9 have recently been published and extracts are provided below, together with comparative figures for the previous two years.

## STATEMENTS OF PROFIT OR LOSS FOR THE YEARS ENDED 30 JUNE

|  | 20X7 | 20X8 | 20X9 |
|---|---|---|---|
|  | $m | $m | $m |
| Revenue | 1,850 | 2,200 | 2,500 |
| Cost of sales | (1,250) | (1,500) | (1,750) |
| Gross profit | 600 | 700 | 750 |
| Other operating costs | (550) | (640) | (700) |
| Operating profit | 50 | 60 | 50 |
| Interest from credit sales | 45 | 60 | 90 |
| Interest payable | (25) | (60) | (110) |
| Profit before taxation | 70 | 60 | 30 |
| Tax payable | (23) | (20) | (10) |
| Profit for the year | 47 | 40 | 20 |

## STATEMENTS OF FINANCIAL POSITION AT 30 JUNE

|  | 20X7 | 20X8 | 20X9 |
|---|---|---|---|
|  | $m | $m | $m |
| Property, plant and equipment | 278 | 290 | 322 |
| Inventories | 400 | 540 | 620 |
| Trade receivables | 492 | 550 | 633 |
| Cash | 12 | 12 | 15 |
|  | 1,182 | 1,392 | 1,590 |
|  |  |  |  |
| Share capital | 90 | 90 | 90 |
| Reserves | 282 | 292 | 282 |
|  | 372 | 382 | 372 |
| Bank loans | 320 | 520 | 610 |
| Other interest bearing borrowings | 200 | 200 | 320 |
| Trade payables | 270 | 270 | 280 |
| Tax payable | 20 | 20 | 8 |
|  | 1,182 | 1,392 | 1,590 |

## Other information

(a) Depreciation charged for the three years in question was as follows.

| Year ended 30 June | 20X7 | 20X8 | 20X9 |
|---|---|---|---|
|  | $m | $m | $m |
|  | 55 | 60 | 70 |

(b) The other interest bearing borrowings are secured by a floating charge over the assets of Biggerbuys. Their repayment is due on 30 June 20Y9.

(c) Dividends of $30m were paid in 20X7 and 20X8. A dividend of $20m has been proposed.

(d) The bank loans are unsecured. The maximum lending facility the bank will provide is $630m.

(e) Over the past three years the level of credit sales has been:

| Year ended 30 June | 20X7 | 20X8 | 20X9 |
|---|---|---|---|
|  | $m | $m | $m |
|  | 300 | 400 | 600 |

The entity offers extended credit terms for certain products to maintain market share in a highly competitive environment.

Given the steady increase in the level of bank loans which has taken place in recent years, the entity has recently written to its bankers to request an increase in the lending facility. The request was received by the bank on 15 October 20X9, two weeks after the financial statements were published. The bank is concerned at the steep escalation in the level of the loans and has asked for a report on the financial performance of Biggerbuys for the last three years.

*Required*

As a consultant management accountant employed by the bankers of Biggerbuys, prepare a report to the bank which analyses the financial performance of the company for the period covered by the financial statements. Your report may take any form you wish, but you are aware of the particular concern of the bank regarding the rapidly increasing level of lending. Therefore it may be appropriate to include aspects of prior performance that could have contributed to the increase in the level of bank lending. **(25 marks)**

# 26 Webster                                                                            45 mins

**(Adapted from past ACCA exam paper 2.5 Pilot paper)**

Webster is a publicly listed diversified holding company that is looking to acquire a suitable engineering company. Two private limited engineering companies, Cole and Darwin, are available to purchase. The summarised financial statements for the year to 31 March 20X9 of both companies are as follows.

STATEMENT OF PROFIT OR LOSS

| | Cole | | Darwin | |
|---|---|---|---|---|
| | $'000 | $'000 | $'000 | $'000 |
| Sales revenue (note (a)) | | 3,000 | | 4,400 |
| Opening inventory | 450 | | 720 | |
| Purchases (note (b)) | 2,030 | | 3,080 | |
| | 2,480 | | 3,800 | |
| Closing inventory | (540) | | (850) | |
| | | (1,940) | | (2,950) |
| Gross profit | | 1,060 | | 1,450 |
| Operating expenses | | (480) | | (964) |
| Profit from operations | | 580 | | 486 |
| Loan note interest | | (80) | | – |
| Overdraft interest | | – | | (10) |
| Net profit for year | | 500 | | 476 |

STATEMENT OF FINANCIAL POSITION

| | Cole | | Darwin | |
|---|---|---|---|---|
| | $'000 | $'000 | $'000 | $'000 |
| Non-current assets | | | | |
| Property, plant and equipment (note (c) and (d)) | | 2,340 | | 3,100 |
| | | | | |
| Current assets | | | | |
| Inventory | 540 | | 850 | |
| Accounts receivable | 522 | | 750 | |
| Bank | 20 | | – | |
| | | 1,082 | | 1,600 |
| Total assets | | 3,422 | | 4,700 |

|  | Cole |  | Darwin |  |
|---|---|---|---|---|
|  | $'000 | $'000 | $'000 | $'000 |
| **Equity and liabilities** |  |  |  |  |
| **Equity** |  |  |  |  |
| Equity shares of $1 each |  | 1,000 |  | 500 |
| Reserves |  |  |  |  |
| Revaluation surplus |  | – |  | 700 |
| Retained earnings – 1 April 20X8 |  | 684 |  | 1,912 |
| Profit – year to 31 March 20X9 |  | 500 |  | 476 |
|  |  | 2,184 |  | 3,588 |
| **Non-current liabilities** |  |  |  |  |
| 10% Loan note |  | 800 |  | – |
| **Current liabilities** |  |  |  |  |
| Accounts payable | 438 |  | 562 |  |
| Overdraft | – |  | 550 |  |
|  |  | 438 |  | 1,112 |
| Total equity and liabilities |  | 3,422 |  | 4,700 |

Webster bases its preliminary assessment of target companies on certain key ratios. These are listed below together with the relevant figures for Cole and Darwin calculated from the above financial statements:

|  |  | Cole |  | Darwin |
|---|---|---|---|---|
| Return on capital employed | (500+80)/(2,184+800) |  | (476/3,588) |  |
|  | ×100 | 19·4 % | × 100 | 13·3 % |
| Asset turnover | (3,000/2,984) | 1·01 times | (4,400/3,588) | 1·23 times |
| Gross profit margin |  | 35·3 % |  | 33·0 % |
| Net profit margin |  | 16·7 % |  | 10·8 % |
| Accounts receivable collection period |  | 64 days |  | 62 days |
| Accounts payable payment period |  | 79 days |  | 67 days |

Note. Capital employed is defined as shareholders' funds plus non-current debt at the year end; asset turnover is sales revenues divided by gross assets less current liabilities.

The following additional information has been obtained.

(a) Cole is part of the Velox Group. On 1 March 20X9 it was permitted by its holding company to sell goods at a price of $500,000 to Brander, a fellow subsidiary. The sale gave Cole a gross profit margin of 40% instead of its normal gross margin of only 20% on these types of goods. In addition Brander was instructed to pay for the goods immediately. Cole normally allows three months credit.

(b) On 1 January 20X9 Cole purchased $275,000 (cost price to Cole) of its materials from Advent, another member of the Velox Group. Advent was also instructed by Velox to depart from its normal trading terms, which would have resulted in a charge of $300,000 to Cole for these goods. The Group's finance director also authorised a four-month credit period on this sale. Cole normally receives two months credit from its suppliers. Cole had sold all of these goods at the year-end.

(c) Non-current assets:

Details relating to the two companies' non-current assets are:

|  | Cost/revaluation | Depreciation | Book value |
|---|---|---|---|
|  | $'000 | $'000 | $'000 |
| Cole:  property | 3,000 | 1,860 | 1,140 |
| plant | 6,000 | 4,800 | 1,200 |
|  |  |  | 2,340 |
| Darwin: property | 2,000 | 100 | 1,900 |
| plant | 3,000 | 1,800 | 1,200 |
|  |  |  | 3,100 |

The two companies own very similar properties. Darwin's property was revalued to $2,000,000 at the beginning of the current year (ie 1 April 20X8). On this date Cole's property, which is carried at cost less depreciation, had a book value of $1,200,000. Its current value (on the same basis as Darwin's property) was also $2,000,000. On this date (1 April 20X8) both properties had the same remaining life of 20 years.

(d)     Darwin purchased new plant costing $600,000 in February 20X9. In line with company policy a full year's depreciation at 20% per annum has been charged on all plant owned at year-end. The equipment is still being tested and will not come on-stream until next year. The purchase of the plant was largely financed by an overdraft facility, which resulted in the interest cost shown in the statement of profit or loss. Both companies depreciate plant over a five-year life and treat all depreciation as an operating expense.

(e)     The bank overdraft that would have been required but for the favourable treatment towards Cole in respect of items in (a) and (b) above, would have attracted interest of $15,000 in the year to 31 March 20X9.

*Required*

(a)     Restate the financial statements of Cole and Darwin in order that they may be considered comparable for decision making purposes. State any assumptions you make.     **(10 marks)**

(b)     Recalculate the key ratios used by Webster and, referring to any other relevant points, comment on how the revised ratios may affect the assessment of the two companies.     **(10 marks)**

**(Total = 20 marks)**

# 27 Dundee                                                                        25 mins

The summarised accounts of Dundee for the year ended 31 March 20X7 are as follows:

**Statements of financial position at 31 March**

|  | 20X7<br>$m | 20X6<br>$m |
|---|---|---|
| **Non-current assets** | | |
| Property, plant and equipment | 4,200 | 3,700 |
| **Current assets** | | |
| Inventories | 1,500 | 1,600 |
| Trade receivables | 2,200 | 1,800 |
|  | 3,700 | 3,400 |
|  | 7,900 | 7,100 |
| **Equity** | | |
| Share capital | 1,200 | 1,200 |
| Retained earnings | 2,200 | 1,900 |
|  | 3,400 | 3,100 |
| **Non-current liabilities** | | |
| Deferred tax | 1,070 | 850 |
| Finance lease liabilities | 1,300 | 1,200 |
|  | 2,370 | 2,050 |
| **Current liabilities** | | |
| Trade payables | 1,250 | 1,090 |
| Current tax | 225 | 205 |
| Finance lease liabilities | 500 | 450 |
| Bank overdraft | 155 | 205 |
|  | 2,130 | 1,950 |
|  | 7,900 | 7,100 |

**Statement of profit or loss for the year ended 31 March 20X7**

|                      | $m      |
|----------------------|---------|
| Revenue              | 4,300   |
| Cost of sales        | (2,000) |
| Gross profit         | 2,300   |
| Operating expenses   | (1,000) |
| Finance costs        | (250)   |
| **Profit before tax**| 1,050   |
| Income tax expense   | (450)   |
| **PROFIT FOR THE YEAR** | 600  |

| Dividends paid in the year | 300 |
|----------------------------|-----|

*Notes*

(1)    Depreciation charged for the year totalled $970 million. There were no disposals of property, plant and equipment in the period.

(2)    There was no accrual of interest at the beginning or at the end of the year.

(3)    Dundee finances a number (but not all) of its property, plant and equipment purchases using finance leases. In the period, property, plant and equipment which would have cost $600 million to purchase outright was acquired under finance leases.

*Required*

Prepare the statement of cash flows for Dundee for the year ended 31 March 20X7 as per IAS 7 using the indirect method.    **(14 marks)**

# 28 Elmgrove    45 mins

As financial accountant for Elmgrove, you are responsible for the preparation of a statement of cash flows for the year ended 31 March 20X9.

The following information is available.

ELMGROVE
STATEMENT OF FINANCIAL POSITION AS AT 31 MARCH 20X9

|                               | 20X9 $m | 20X8 $m |
|-------------------------------|---------|---------|
| *Non-current assets*          |         |         |
| Property, plant and equipment | 327     | 264     |
| *Current assets*              |         |         |
| Inventories                   | 123     | 176     |
| Trade receivables             | 95      | 87      |
| Short term investments        | 65      | 30      |
| Cash at bank and in hand      | 29      | –       |
|                               | 312     | 293     |
|                               | 639     | 557     |
| *Equity*                      |         |         |
| Share capital – $1 shares     | 200     | 120     |
| Share premium                 | 30      | –       |
| Revaluation surplus           | 66      | 97      |
| Retained earnings             | 71      | 41      |
|                               | 367     | 258     |
| *Non-current liabilities*     |         |         |
| 10% Debentures                | 100     | 150     |
| *Current liabilities*         | 172     | 149     |
|                               | 639     | 557     |

ELMGROVE
STATEMENT OF PROFIT OR LOSS FOR THE YEAR ENDED 31 MARCH 20X9

|  | $m |
|---|---|
| Revenue | 473 |
| Cost of sales | (229) |
| Gross profit | 244 |
| Distribution costs | (76) |
| Administrative expenses | (48) |
| Finance income | 6 |
| Finance costs | (17) |
| Profit before tax | 109 |
| Income tax expense | (47) |
| Profit for the year | 62 |
|  |  |
| Dividends paid in the period | 32 |

The following notes are also relevant.

1    *Property, plant and equipment*

Property, plant and equipment held by Elmgrove are items of plant and equipment and freehold premises. During 20X9 items of plant and equipment which originally cost $40m were disposed of, resulting in a loss of $6m. These items have a net book value of $28m at the date of disposal.

2    *Short term investments*

The short-term investments meet the definition of cash equivalents per IAS 7 *Statement of cash flows.*

3    *Current liabilities*

Current liabilities consist of the following.

|  | 20X9 | 20X8 |
|---|---|---|
|  | $m | $m |
| Bank overdraft | – | 22 |
| Trade payables | 126 | 70 |
| Interest payable | 7 | 3 |
| Income tax payable | 39 | 54 |
|  | 172 | 149 |

4    *10% debentures*

On 1 August 20X8 $50m of 10% debentures was converted into $50m of $1 ordinary shares.

5    *Depreciation*

The depreciation charge for the year included in the statement of profit or loss was $43m.

*Required*

(a)    Using the information provided, prepare a statement of cash flows for Elmgrove for the year ended 31 March 20X9 using the indirect method.    **(20 marks)**

(b)    Write a memorandum to a director of Elmgrove summarising the major benefits a user receives from a published statement of cash flows.    **(5 marks)**

**(Total = 25 marks)**

# 29 CPP and CCA

**27 mins**

(a)   'It is important that management and other users of financial accounts should be in a position to appreciate the effects of inflation on the business with which they are concerned.'

*Required*

Consider the above statement and explain how inflation obscures the meaning of accounts prepared by the traditional historical cost convention, and discuss the contribution which CPP accounting could make to providing a more satisfactory system of accounting for inflation.

(b)   Compare the general principles underlying CPP and CCA accounting.

(c)   Define the term 'realised holding gain'.                                          **(15 marks)**

# 1 Conceptual framework

(a) The **going concern assumption** is that an entity will continue in operational existence for the foreseeable future. This means that the financial statements of an entity are prepared on the assumption that the entity will **continue** trading. If this were not the case, various adjustments would have to be made to the accounts: provisions for losses; revaluation of assets to their possible market value; all non-current assets and liabilities would be reclassified as current; and so forth.

**Unless it can be assumed that the business is a going concern, other accounting assumptions cannot apply.**

For example, it is meaningless to speak of consistency from one accounting period to the next when this is the final accounting period.

The **accruals basis** of accounting states that items are recognised as assets, liabilities, equity, income and expenses when they satisfy the definitions and recognition criteria in the *Conceptual Framework*. The effect of this is that revenue and expenses which are related to each other are matched, so as to be dealt with in the same accounting period, without regard to when the cash is actually paid or received. This is particularly relevant to the purchase of non-current assets. The cost of a non-current asset is spread over the accounting periods expected to benefit from it, thus matching costs and revenues. In the absence of the going concern convention, this cannot happen, as an example will illustrate.

Suppose a company has a machine which cost $10,000 two years ago and now has a carrying amount of $6,000. The machine can be used for another three years, but as it is highly specialised, there is no possibility of selling it, and so it has no market value.

If the going concern assumption applies, the machine will be shown at **cost less depreciation** in the accounts (ie $6,000), as it still has a part to play in the continued life of the entity. However, if the assumption cannot be applied, the machine will be given a nil value and other assets and liabilities will be similarly revalued on the basis of winding down the company's operations.

(b) One of the ideas behind the *Conceptual Framework* is to **avoid the fire-fighting approach**, which has characterised the development of accounting standards in the past, and instead develop an underlying philosophy as a basis for consistent accounting principles so that each standard fits into the whole framework. Research began from an analysis of the fundamental objectives of accounting and their relationship to the information needs of accounts users. The *Conceptual Framework* has gone behind the requirements of existing accounting standards, which define accounting treatments for particular assets, liabilities, income and expenditure, to define the nature of assets, liabilities, income and expenditure.

# 2 Regulators

> **Tutorial note**. It is best to use headings to divide up your answer, as we do here.

*Stock Exchange*

A quoted company is a company whose shares are bought and sold on a stock exchange. This involves the signing of an agreement which requires compliance with the rules of that stock exchange. This would normally contain amongst other things the stock exchange's detailed rules on the information to be disclosed in quoted companies' accounts. This, then, is one regulatory influence on a quoted company's accounts. The stock exchange may enforce compliance by monitoring accounts and reserving the right to withdraw a company's shares from the stock exchange: ie the company's shares would no longer be traded through the stock exchange. In many countries there is, however, no statutory requirement to obey these rules.

*Local legislation*

In most countries, companies have to comply with the local companies legislation, which lays down detailed requirements on the preparation of accounts. Company law is often quite detailed, partly because of external influences such as EU Directives. Another reason to increase statutory regulation is that quoted companies are under great pressure to show profit growth and an obvious way to achieve this is to manipulate accounting policies. If this involves breaking the law, as opposed to ignoring professional guidance, company directors may think twice before bending the rules – or, at least, this is often a government's hope.

*Standard-setters*

Professional guidance is given by the national and international standard-setters. Prescriptive guidance is given in accounting standards which must be applied in all accounts intended to show a 'true and fair view' or 'present fairly in all material respects'. International Financial Reporting Standards and national standards are issued after extensive consultation and are revised as required to reflect economic or legal changes. In some countries, legislation requires details of non-compliance to be disclosed in the accounts. 'Defective' accounts can be revised under court order if necessary and directors signing such accounts can be prosecuted and fined (or even imprisoned).

The potential for the IASB's influence in this area is substantial. It must pursue excellence in standards with absolute rigour to fulfil that potential.

# 3 Standard setters

(a)  The users of financial information – creditors, management, employees, business contacts, financial specialists, government and the general public – are entitled to information about a business entity to a greater or lesser degree. However, the needs and expectations of these groups will vary.

The preparers of the financial information often find themselves in the position of having to reconcile the interests of different groups in the best way for the business entity. For example whilst shareholders are looking for increased profits to support higher dividends, employees will expect higher wage increases; and yet higher profits without corresponding higher tax allowances (increased capital allowances for example) will result in a larger tax bill.

Without accounting standards to prescribe how certain transactions should be treated, preparers would be tempted to produce financial information which meets the expectations of the favoured user group. For example creative accounting methods, such as off balance sheet finance could be used to enhance a company's statement of financial position to make it more attractive to investors/lenders.

The aim of accounting standards is that they should regulate financial information in order that it is relevant and a faithful representation. It should also exhibit the following enhancing characteristics.

(i)    Comparability
(ii)   Verifiability
(iii)  Timeliness
(iv)   Understandability

Comparability is a good example of why accounting standards are necessary. In the absence of regulation, entities would be able to present items in the financial statements in whatever form would produce the most favourable result for that reporting period. Different entities would therefore be using different accounting policies and could change them from one period to the next. Analysts and investors would be unable to meaningfully compare the performance of an entity over time or to compare the performance and results of one entity again the performance and results of another entity.

(b)  A number of reasons could be advanced why the financial statements of not-for-profit entities should not be subject to regulation.

- They do not have shares that are being traded, so their financial statements are not produced with a share price in mind.
- They do not have chief executives with share options seeking to present favourable figures to the market.
- They are not seeking to make a profit, so whether they have or not is perhaps irrelevant.
- They are perceived to be on slightly higher moral ground than profit-making entities, so are less in need of regulation.

However a closer look at this brings up the following points.

- Public sector bodies, such as local government organisations, are spending taxpayers' money and should be required to account for it.
- The chief executives of public sector bodies are often highly rewarded and their performance should be verified.
- Charities may not be invested in by the general public, but they are funded by the public, often through direct debits.
- Charities are big business. In addition to regular public donations they receive large donations from high-profile backers.
- They employ staff and executives at market rates and have heavy administrative costs. Supporters are entitled to know how much of their donation has gone on administration.
- Any misappropriation of funds is serious in two ways. It is taking money from the donating public, who thought they were donating to a good cause, and it is diverting resources from the people who should have been helped.
- Not all charities are *bona fide*. For instance, some are thought to be connected to terrorism.

For these reasons, it is important that the financial statements of not-for-profit entities are subject to regulation.

# 4 Polymer

**POLYMER CO: STATEMENT OF PROFIT OR LOSS FOR THE YEAR ENDED 31 MAY 20X8**

|  | $ |
|---|---|
| Revenue | 1,526,750 |
| Cost of sales (W3) | (1,048,000) |
| Gross profit | 478,750 |
| Distribution costs (W4) | (124,300) |
| Administrative expenses (W5) | (216,200) |
| Finance costs (W6) | (18,400) |
| Profit before tax | 119,850 |
| Income tax expense | (40,000) |
| PROFIT FOR THE YEAR | 79,850 |

**POLYMER CO: STATEMENT OF FINANCIAL POSITION AS AT 31 MAY 20X8**

|  | $ |
|---|---|
| ASSETS |  |
| Non-current assets |  |
| Property, plant and equipment (W7) | 452,250 |
| Intangible assets | 215,500 |
|  | 667,750 |
| Current assets |  |
| Inventories (W8) | 425,750 |
| Receivables (W9) | 171,880 |
| Cash and cash equivalents | 5,120 |
|  | 602,750 |
| Total assets | 1,270,500 |

|  |  | $ |
|---|---|---:|
| **EQUITY AND LIABILITIES** | | |
| **Equity** | | |
| Share capital | | 300,000 |
| Share premium reserve | | 100,000 |
| Retained earnings (283,500 + 79,850) | | 363,350 |
| General reserve | | 50,000 |
| Revaluation surplus | | 50,000 |
| | | 863,350 |
| **Non-current liabilities** | | |
| 10% debentures | | 100,000 |
| 8.4% cumulative redeemable preference shares* | | 100,000 |
| | | 200,000 |
| **Current liabilities** | | |
| Trade and other payables (W10) | | 115,900 |
| Short-term borrowings | | 51,250 |
| Current tax payable | | 40,000 |
| | | 207,150 |
| **Total equity and liabilities** | | 1,270,500 |

\* **Tutorial note:**

Redeemable preference shares are presented under IAS 32 *Financial Instruments: Presentation* as a loan payable, and dividends on them as interest payable. This point is covered in Chapter 14.

*Workings*

1    *Depreciation*

| | | $ |
|---|---|---:|
| Cost of sales: | 8% × 150,000 | 12,000 |
| Administration: | 10% × 50,000 | 5,000 |
| | 1/4 × 20% × 50,000 | 2,500 |
| | | 7,500 |
| Distribution: | 3/4 × 20% × 50,000 | 7,500 |

2    *Depreciation (amortisation) of lease*

$75,000 × 1/50                      1,500

3    *Cost of sales*

| | $ |
|---|---:|
| Opening inventories (108,400 + 32,750 + 184,500) | 325,650 |
| Purchases | 750,600 |
| Carriage inwards | 10,500 |
| Manufacturing wages | 250,000 |
| Manufacturing overheads | 125,000 |
| Depreciation of plant (W1) | 12,000 |
| Closing inventories (W9) | (425,750) |
| | 1,048,000 |

4    *Distribution costs*

| | $ |
|---|---:|
| Per question | 116,800 |
| Depreciation (W1) | 7,500 |
| | 124,300 |

## 5 Administrative expenses

| | | $ |
|---|---:|---:|
| Per question | | 158,100 |
| Legal expenses | 54,100 | |
| less: solicitors' fees capitalised | (5,000) | |
| | | 49,100 |
| Depreciation (W1) | | 7,500 |
| Amortisation of lease (W2) | | 1,500 |
| | | 216,200 |

## 6 Finance costs

| | $ |
|---|---:|
| Interest expense on loan notes ($100,000 × 10%) | 10,000 |
| Dividend on redeemable preference shares ($100,000 × 8.4%) | 8,400 |
| | 18,400 |

## 7 Property, plant and equipment

| | Freehold land $ | Leasehold property $ | Plant & equipment $ | Furniture & fixtures $ | Motor vehicles $ | Total $ |
|---|---:|---:|---:|---:|---:|---:|
| NBV per TB | | | | | | |
| Cost or valuation | 250,000 | 75,000 | 150,000 | 50,000 | 75,000 | |
| Accumulated dep'n | – | (15,000) | (68,500) | (15,750) | (25,000) | |
| Net book value | 250,000 | 60,000 | 81,500 | 34,250 | 50,000 | |
| Solicitor's fees | 5,000 | | | | | |
| Depreciation charge | – | (1,500) | (12,000) | (5,000) | (10,000) | |
| NBV 31 May 20X8 | 255,000 | 58,500 | 69,500 | 29,250 | 40,000 | 452,250 |

## 8 Inventories

| | $ |
|---|---:|
| Raw materials | 112,600 |
| Work in progress | 37,800 |
| Finished goods | 275,350 |
| | 425,750 |

## 9 Receivables

| | $ |
|---|---:|
| Trade receivables (177,630 – 5,750 allowance for receivables) | 171,880 |

## 10 Trade and other payables

| | $ |
|---|---:|
| Trade payables | 97,500 |
| Loan interest payable | 10,000 |
| Preference dividend payable | 8,400 |
| | 115,900 |

# 5 Gains

**Gains – Statement of changes in equity for the year ended 31 December 20X9**

| | Share capital $'000 | Share premium $'000 | Retained earnings $'000 | Revaluation surplus $'000 | Total $'000 |
|---|---:|---:|---:|---:|---:|
| Balance at 1 January 20X9 | 2,800 | 1,150 | 2,120 | 750 | 6,820 |
| Change in accounting policy | | | 40 | (40) | – |
| Restated balance | 2,800 | 1,150 | 2,160 | 710 | 6,820 |

**Changes in equity for 20X9**

| | | | | | |
|---|---|---|---|---|---|
| Issue of share capital | 600 | (40) | – | – | 560 |
| Dividends | | | (200) | | (200) |
| Total comprehensive income for the year (566 – (W1) 50) | – | – | 516 | 120 | 636 |
| Transfer to retained earnings (W2) | | | 35 | (35) | – |
| **Balance at 31 December 20X9** | 3,400 | 1,110 | 2,511 | 795 | 7,816 |

*Workings*

1   Loss on investment property (160 – 110)   (50)

2   *Calculation of profit realised on sale of revalued asset*

| | $ |
|---|---|
| Revaluation recognised in past | 50,000 |
| Less: amounts transferred to retained earnings: | |
| (80,000/10 – 30,000/10) × 3 | (15,000) |
| | 35,000 |

# 6 Biogenics

(a)   To be recognised, an intangible asset must first of all meet the definition of an intangible asset in IAS 38. It must be controlled by the entity, it must be separately identifiable and it must be something from which the entity expects future economic benefits to flow. It must then meet the recognition criteria of having a cost that can be measured reliably.

For this reason internally-generated intangibles are not normally recognised as assets. They have not been acquired for a consideration and therefore do not have a cost or value that can be measured reliably. For this reason, a brand name that has been acquired can be capitalised, a brand name that has been internally developed can not be capitalised. The exception to this is development costs which can be capitalised if/when they meet the IAS 38 criteria. They are initially recognised at cost.

After initial recognition development costs are amortised over the life cycle of the product. If at any point it becomes apparent that the development costs no longer meet the capitalisation criteria, they should be written off. Intangible assets with an indefinite useful life are not amortised but tested annually for impairment.

(b)

STATEMENT OF FINANCIAL POSITION (extracts)

| | $ |
|---|---|
| *Non-current assets* | |
| Property, plant and equipment (W1) | 187,500 |
| Intangible assets (W2) | 6,691,000 |

COSTS CHARGED TO PROFIT OR LOSS

| | $ |
|---|---|
| Depreciation (W1) | 12,500 |
| Amortisation (W2) | 1,309,000 |
| Staff salaries | 400,000 |

*Workings*

| | $ |
|---|---|
| 1   Computer equipment | |
| Cost | 200,000 |
| Depreciation (200 x 3/48) | (12,500) |
| Carrying amount | 187,500 |

## 2 Intangible assets

| | Patent $'000 | Development costs $'000 | Customer list $'000 | Total $'000 |
|---|---|---|---|---|
| Cost | 1,500 | 6,000 | 500 | 8,000 |
| Amortisation: | | | | |
| (6/36) | (250) | (1,000) | – | – |
| (4/34) | – | – | (59) | (1,309) |
| | 1,250 | 5,000 | 441 | 6,691 |

# 7 Multiplex

The impairment losses are allocated as required by IAS 36 *Impairment of assets*.

| | Asset @ 1.1.20X0 $'000 | 1st loss (W1) $'000 | Assets @ 1.2.20X0 $'000 | 2nd loss (W2) $'000 | Revised asset $'000 |
|---|---|---|---|---|---|
| Goodwill | 200 | (200) | – | – | – |
| Operating licence | 1,200 | (200) | 1,000 | (100) | 900 |
| Property: stations/land | 300 | (50) | 250 | (50) | 200 |
| Rail track/coaches | 300 | (50) | 250 | (50) | 200 |
| Steam engines | 1,000 | (500) | 500 | – | 500 |
| | 3,000 | (1,000) | 2,000 | (200) | 1,800 |

*Workings*

1   *First impairment loss*

$500,000 relates directly to an engine and its recoverable amount can be assessed directly (ie zero) and it is no longer part of the cash generating unit.

IAS 36 then requires goodwill to be written off. Any further impairment must be written off the remaining assets pro rata, except the engine which must not be reduced below its net selling price of $500,000.

2   *Second impairment loss*

The first $100,000 of the impairment loss is applied to the operating licence to write it down to net selling price.

The remainder is applied pro rata to assets carried at other than their net selling prices, ie $50,000 to both the property and the rail track and coaches.

# 8 Hewlett

**HEWLETT**
**STATEMENT OF PROFIT OR LOSS AND OTHER COMPREHENSIVE INCOME FOR THE YEAR ENDED 31 DECEMBER 20X2**

| | $'m |
|---|---|
| Revenue | 2,648 |
| Cost of sales (W1) | (1,765) |
| Gross profit | 883 |
| Distribution costs (W1) | (514) |
| Administrative expenses (W1) | (360) |
| Finance costs (150 × 4%) | (6) |
| Fair value gain on investment properties (588 – 548) | 40 |
| Rental income | 48 |
| Profit before tax | 91 |
| Income tax expense (note vi) (45 – 17) | (28) |
| **PROFIT FOR THE YEAR** | 63 |

**Other comprehensive income:**

| | |
|---|---:|
| Gain on property revaluation (W2) | 55 |
| Income tax relating to gain on property revaluation | (17) |
| **Other comprehensive income, net of tax** | 38 |
| **TOTAL COMPREHENSIVE INCOME FOR THE YEAR** | 101 |

**HEWLETT**

**STATEMENT OF FINANCIAL POSITION AS AT 31 DECEMBER 20X2**

| | $'m |
|---|---:|
| **ASSETS** | |
| **Non-current assets** | |
| Property, plant and equipment (W2) | 852 |
| Investment properties (note ix) | 588 |
| | 1,440 |
| **Current assets** | |
| Inventories (388 – (21 – 14)) | 381 |
| Trade receivables | 541 |
| Cash and cash equivalents | 32 |
| | 954 |
| | 2,394 |
| **EQUITY AND LIABILITIES** | |
| **Equity** | |
| Share capital | 125 |
| Share premium | 244 |
| Retained earnings | 810 |
| General reserve | 545 |
| Revaluation surplus ((W2) 55 – 17) | 38 |
| | 1,762 |
| **Non-current liabilities** | |
| 4% loan notes 20X8 | 150 |
| **Current liabilities** | |
| Trade payables | 434 |
| Income tax payable (note vi) | 45 |
| Interest payable ((4% × 150) – 3) | 3 |
| | 482 |
| | 2,394 |

**HEWLETT**

**STATEMENT OF CHANGES IN EQUITY FOR THE YEAR ENDED 31 DECEMBER 20X2**

| | Share capital $'m | Share premium $'m | Retained earnings $'m | General reserve $'m | Revaluation surplus $'m | Total $'m |
|---|---:|---:|---:|---:|---:|---:|
| **Balance at 1 January 20X2** | 100 | 244 | 753 | 570 | - | 1,667 |
| **Changes in equity for 20X2** | | | | | | |
| Issue of share capital (W4) | 25 | | | (25) | | - |
| Dividends (W5) | | | (6) | | | (6) |
| Total comprehensive income for the year | | | 63 | | 38 | 101 |
| **Balance at 31 December 20X2** | 125 | 244 | 810 | 545 | 38 | 1,762 |

**Workings**

1    Expenses

| | Cost of sales $'m | Distribution $'m | Admin $'m |
|---|---|---|---|
| Per TB | 1,669 | 514 | 345 |
| Opening inventories | 444 | | |
| Depreciation of buildings (W2) | | | 15 |
| Depreciation of plant and equipment (W2) | 24 | | |
| Impairment loss on plant (W3) | 4 | | |
| Loss on sale of equipment ((15 – 3) – 7) | 5 | | |
| Closing inventories (388 – (21 – 14)) | (381) | | |
| | 1,765 | 514 | 360 |

2    Property, plant and equipment

| | Land $'m | Buildings $'m | Plant & equipment $'m | Total $'m |
|---|---|---|---|---|
| Cost | 90 | 750 | 258 | |
| Accumulated depreciation b/d | – | (120) | (126) | |
| NBV b/d at 1 January 20X2 | 90 | 630 | 132 | |
| Disposal of equipment (15 – 3) | | | (12) | |
| | 90 | 630 | 120 | |
| Depreciation during year | | | | |
|   Buildings ($750m/50 years) | | (15) | | |
|   Plant & equipment ($120m × 20%) | | | (24) | |
| Impairment loss on plant (W3) | | | (4) | |
| | 90 | 615 | 92 | |
| Revaluation (balancing figure) | 10 | 45 | | 55 |
| NBV c/d at 31 December 20X2 (Buildings 760 – 100) | 100 | 660 | 92 | 852 |

3    Impairment loss on plant

| | $'m |
|---|---|
| Carrying value | 22 |
| Recoverable amount (Value in use: (3.8m × 3.993) + (4.2m × 0.677)) | (18) |
| | (4) |

Recoverable amount is the higher of value in use ($18m) and fair value less costs to sell ($16m).

4    Bonus issue

| | |
|---|---|
| Dr General reserve ($100m /$0.50 × 1/4 = 50m shares × $0.50) | $25m |
| Cr Share capital | $25m |

5    Dividends (proof)

| | $'m |
|---|---|
| Interim ($100m /$0.50 = 200m shares × $0.03) | 6 per trial balance |

The final dividend has not been paid and is not a liability of the company at the year end.

# 9 Barcelona and Madrid

**BARCELONA GROUP**
**CONSOLIDATED STATEMENT OF FINANCIAL POSITION AS AT 30 SEPTEMBER 20X6**

|  | $m |
|---|---|
| **Non-current assets** | |
| Property, plant & equipment (2,848 + 354 + (W6) 18) | 3,220 |
| Patents | 45 |
| Goodwill (W2) | 26 |
| | 3,291 |
| **Current assets** | |
| Inventories (895 + 225) | 1,120 |
| Trade and other receivables (1,348 + 251) | 1,599 |
| Cash and cash equivalents (212 + 34) | 246 |
| | 2,965 |
| | 6,256 |
| **Equity attributable to owners of the parent** | |
| Share capital | 920 |
| Retained earnings (W3) | 2,238 |
| General reserve (W4) | 796 |
| | 3,954 |
| **Non-controlling interests** (W5) | 202 |
| | 4,156 |
| **Non-current liabilities** | |
| Long-term borrowings (558 + 168) | 726 |
| **Current liabilities** | |
| Trade and other payables (1,168 + 183) | 1,351 |
| Current portion of long-term borrowings | 23 |
| | 1,374 |
| | 6,256 |

## Workings

### 1 Group structure

Barcelona

60% (1.10.X2)

Madrid

### 2 Goodwill

|  | $m | $m |
|---|---|---|
| Consideration transferred (250m x 60% × $1.06) | | 159 |
| Non-controlling interests at fair value | | 86 |
| Net assets at acquisition as represented by: | | |
| Share capital | 50 | |
| Retained earnings | 104 | |
| General reserve | 11 | |
| Fair value adjustments (W6) | 34 | |
| | | (199) |
| Goodwill at acquisition | | 46 |
| Impairment losses to date | | (20) |
| Goodwill at year end | | 26 |

3    *Retained earnings*

|                                          | *Barcelona* | *Madrid* |
|------------------------------------------|-------------|----------|
|                                          | $m          | $m       |
| Per question                             | 2,086       | 394      |
| Pre-acquisition                          |             | (104)    |
| Movement on fair value adjustment (W6)   |             | (16)     |
|                                          |             | 274      |

|                                                    |       |
|----------------------------------------------------|-------|
| Group share of post acquisition retained earnings: |       |
| Madrid (274 × 60%)                                 | 164   |
| Less: group impairment losses to date (20 x 60%)   | (12)  |
|                                                    | 2,238 |

4    *General reserve*

|                 | *Barcelona* | *Madrid* |
|-----------------|-------------|----------|
|                 | $m          | $m       |
| Per question    | 775         | 46       |
| Pre-acquisition |             | (11)     |
|                 |             | 35       |

|                                                 |     |
|-------------------------------------------------|-----|
| Group share of post acquisition general reserve:|     |
| Madrid (35 × 60%)                               | 21  |
|                                                 | 796 |

5    *Non-controlling interests*

|                                          | $m   |
|------------------------------------------|------|
| NCI at acquisition (W2)                  | 86   |
| NCI share of post acquisition:           |      |
| Retained earnings ((W3) 274 × 40%)       | 110  |
| General reserve ((W4) 35 × 40%)          | 14   |
| Goodwill impairment (20 x 40%)           | (8)  |
|                                          | 202  |

6    Fair value adjustments

|             | Acquisition date | Movement | Year end |
|-------------|------------------|----------|----------|
|             | $m               | $m       | $m       |
| Inventories | 8                | (8)      | -        |
| Land        | 6                | -        | 6        |
| Buildings   | 20               | (8)*     | 12       |
|             | 34               | (16)     | 18       |

\* 20 / 10 years x 4

# 10 Reprise

**Reprise Group – Consolidated statement of financial position as at 31 March 20X4**

|  | $'000 |
|---|---|
| **Non-current assets** | |
| Land and buildings | 3,350 |
| Plant and equipment (1,010 + 2,210) | 3,220 |
| Motor vehicles (510 + 345) | 855 |
| Goodwill (W2) | 826 |
|  | 8,251 |
| **Current assets** | |
| Inventories (890 + 352 – (W5) 7.2) | 1,234.8 |
| Trade receivables (1,372 + 514 – 39 – (W6) 36) | 1,811 |
| Cash and cash equivalents (89 + 39 + 51) | 179 |
|  | 3,224.8 |
|  | 11,475.8 |
| **Equity attributable to owners of the parent** | |
| Share capital | 1,000 |
| Retained earnings (W3) | 5,257.3 |
| Revaluation surplus | 2,500 |
|  | 8,757.3 |
| **Non-controlling interests** (W4) | 896.5 |
|  | 9,653.8 |
| **Non-current liabilities** | |
| 10% debentures | 500 |
| **Current liabilities** | |
| Trade payables (996 + 362 – (W6) 36) | 1,322 |
|  | 11,475.8 |

*Workings*

1   Group structure

R
|
E

75%   ∴ non-controlling interests = 25%

2   Goodwill

|  | $'000 | $'000 |
|---|---|---|
| Consideration transferred |  | 2,000 |
| Non-controlling interests (at 'full' FV) (125k shares × $4.40) |  | 550 |
| Net assets at acquisition as represented by: |  | |
| Share capital | 500 | |
| Retained earnings | 1,044 | |
|  |  | (1,544) |
|  |  | 1,006 |
| Impairment losses to date |  | (180) |
|  |  | 826 |

3    Consolidated retained earnings

|  | Reprise $'000 | Encore $'000 |
|---|---|---|
| Per question | 4,225 | 2,610 |
| PUP (W5) | (7.2) | |
| Pre-acquisition retained earnings | | (1,044) |
| | | 1,566 |
| Group share of post acquisition retained earnings: | | |
| Encore (1,566 × 75%) | 1,174.5 | |
| Group share of impairment losses (180 × 75%) | (135) | |
| | 5,257.3 | |

4    Non-controlling interests

| | $'000 |
|---|---|
| NCI at acquisition (W2) | 550 |
| NCI share of post acquisition retained earnings ((W3) 1,566 × 25%) | 391.5 |
| NCI share of impairment losses (180 × 25%) | (45) |
| | 896.5 |

5    Unrealised profit on inventories

Unrealised profit included in inventories is:

$$\$31,200 \times \frac{30}{130} = \$7,200$$

6    Trade receivables/trade payables

Intragroup balance of $75,000 is reduced to $36,000 once cash-in-transit of $39,000 is followed through to its ultimate destination.

# 11 Fallowfield and Rusholme

**Fallowfield Group**
**Consolidated statement of profit or loss for the year ended 30 June 20X8**

| | $ |
|---|---|
| **Revenue** (403,400 + 193,000 – 40,000) | 556,400 |
| Cost of sales (201,400 + 92,600 – 40,000 + 4,000) | (258,000) |
| Gross profit | 298,400 |
| Distribution costs (16,000 + 14,600) | (30,600) |
| Administrative expenses (24,250 + 17,800) | (42,050) |
| **Profit before tax** | 225,750 |
| Income tax expense (61,750 + 22,000) | (83,750) |
| **PROFIT FOR THE YEAR** | 142,000 |
| | |
| Profit attributable to: | |
| Owners of the parent | 125,200 |
| Non-controlling interests (W2) | 16,800 |
| | 142,000 |

**Statement of changes in equity (extract)**

| | Retained earnings $ |
|---|---|
| Balance at 1 July 20X7 (W3) | 190,000 |
| Dividends | (40,000) |
| Profit for the year | 125,200 |
| Balance at 30 June 20X8 (W4) | 275,200 |

*Workings*

1   *Group structure*

Fallowfield
|
| 60%  3 years ago
| Pre-acquisition ret'd earnings: $16,000
|
Rusholme

2   *Non-controlling interests*

|   | $ |
|---|---|
| Rusholme – profit for the year | 46,000 |
| Less: PUP (40,000 × ½ × 25/125) | 4,000 |
|   | 42,000 |
| Non-controlling interest share 40% | 16,800 |

3   *Retained earnings brought forward*

|   | *Fallowfield* | *Rusholme* |
|---|---|---|
|   | $ | $ |
| Per question | 163,000 | 61,000 |
| Pre-acquisition retained earnings |   | (16,000) |
|   |   | 45,000 |
| Group share of post acquisition retained earnings: |   |   |
| Rusholme (45,000 × 60%) | 27,000 |   |
|   | 190,000 |   |

4   *Retained earnings carried forward*

|   | *Fallowfield* | *Rusholme* |
|---|---|---|
|   | $ | $ |
| Per question | 238,000 | 82,000 |
| PUP | – | (4,000) |
| Pre-acquisition retained earnings |   | (16,000) |
|   |   | 62,000 |
| Group share of post acquisition retained earnings: |   |   |
| Rusholme (62,000 × 60%) | 37,200 |   |
|   | 275,200 |   |

# 12  Panther Group

**PANTHER GROUP**
**CONSOLIDATED STATEMENT OF PROFIT OR LOSS AND OTHER COMPREHENSIVE INCOME FOR THE YEAR ENDED 31 DECEMBER 20X4**

|   | $'000 |
|---|---|
| **Revenue** [22,800 + (4,300 × 6/12) − (640 × 6/12)] | 24,630 |
| Cost of sales [13,600 + (2,600 × 6/12) − (640 × 6/12) + (W3) 10 + (W5) 5] | (14,595) |
| Gross profit | 10,035 |
| Distribution costs (2,900 + (500 × 6/12)) | (3,150) |
| Administrative expenses (1,800 + (300 × 6/12)) | (1,950) |
| Finance costs [200 + (70 × 6/12) − (W4) 20 cancellation] | (215) |
| Finance income (50 − (W4) 20 cancellation) | 30 |
| **Profit before tax** | 4,750 |
| Income tax expense [1,300 + (220 × 6/12)] | (1,410) |
| **PROFIT FOR THE YEAR** | 3,340 |
| **Other comprehensive income for the year, net of tax** [1,600 + (180 × 6/12)] | 1,690 |
| **TOTAL COMPREHENSIVE INCOME FOR THE YEAR** | 5,030 |

Profit attributable to:
Owners of the parent (3,340 – 116)                                    3,224
Non-controlling interests (W2)                                          116
                                                                      3,340

Total comprehensive income attributable to:
Owners of the parent (5,030 – 152)                                    4,878
Non-controlling interests (W2)                                         152
                                                                      5,030

## CONSOLIDATED STATEMENT OF CHANGES IN EQUITY FOR THE YEAR ENDED 31 DECEMBER 20X4 (EXTRACT)

|  | $'000 Reserves |
|---|---|
| Balance at 1 January 20X4 (Panther only) | 12,750 |
| Dividend paid | (900) |
| Total comprehensive income for the year | 4,878 |
| Balance at 31 December 20X4 (W6) | 16,728 |

*Workings*

1    Timeline

| | 1.1.X4 | 1.7.X4 | 31.12.X4 |
|---|---|---|---|
| | | Panther – all year | |
| | | Sabre – Income & expenses & NCI × 6/12 | |
| | | Sabre acquired | PUP |

2    *Non-controlling interests*

|  | PFY $'000 | TCI $'000 |
|---|---|---|
| Profit/TCI for the year (610 × 6/12)/(790 × 6/12) | 305 | 395 |
| Less: PUP (W3) | (10) | (10) |
| Additional depreciation on fair value adjustment (W5) | (5) | (5) |
|  | 290 | 380 |
| NCI share (× 40%) | 116 | 152 |

3    *Unrealised profit on intragroup trading*

Sabre to Panther $= \$60,000 \times \dfrac{20\%}{120\%} = \$10,000$

Adjust cost of sales and non-controlling interests in books of seller (Sabre).

4    *Interest on intragroup loan*

The loan is an intragroup item for the last 6 months of the year (i.e. only since Sabre's acquisition by Panther):

$\$800,000 \times 5\% \times 6/12 = \$20,000$

Cancel in books of Panther and Sabre.

5    *Fair value adjustments*

|  | At acq'n 1.7.X4 $'000 | Movement $'000 |  | At year end 31.12.X4 $'000 |
|---|---|---|---|---|
| Property | 200 | (200/20 × 6/12) | (5) | 195 |

6  *Group reserves carried forward (proof)*

|  | Panther $'000 | Sabre $'000 |
|---|---|---|
| Reserves per question | 16,500 | 3,270 |
| PUP (W3) |  | (10) |
| Fair value movement (W5) |  | (5) |
| Pre acquisition reserves [2,480 + ((610 + 180) × 6/12)] |  | (2,875) |
|  |  | 380 |
| Group share of post acquisition reserves: |  |  |
| Sabre (380 × 60%) | 228 |  |
|  | 16,728 |  |

# 13  Hever

## Consolidated statement of financial position as at 31 December 20X4

|  | $'000 |
|---|---|
| **Non-current assets** |  |
| Property, plant & equipment (370 + 190 + (W7) 45) | 605 |
| Goodwill (W2) | 8 |
| Investment in associate (W3) | 165 |
|  | 778 |
| **Current assets** |  |
| Inventories (160 + 100 – (W6) 1.5) | 258.5 |
| Trade receivables (170 + 90) | 260 |
| Cash (50 + 40) | 90 |
|  | 608.5 |
|  | 1,386.5 |
| **Equity attributable to owners of the parent** |  |
| Share capital | 200 |
| Share premium reserve | 100 |
| Retained earnings (W4) | 758.5 |
|  | 1,058.5 |
| **Non-controlling interests** (W5) | 168 |
|  | 1,226.5 |
| **Current liabilities** |  |
| Trade payables (100 + 60) | 160 |
|  | 1,386.5 |

*Workings*

1  *Group structure*

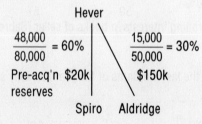

∴ In the absence of information to the contrary, Spiro is a subsidiary, and Aldridge an associate of Hever.

2  *Goodwill on consolidation - Spiro*

|                                          | $'000 | $'000 |
|------------------------------------------|-------|-------|
| Consideration transferred                |       | 128   |
| Non-controlling interests (at 'full' fair value) |       | 90    |
| Net assets at acquisition:               |       |       |
| Share capital                            | 80    |       |
| Retained earnings                        | 20    |       |
| Share premium                            | 80    |       |
| Fair value adjustments (W7)              | 30    |       |
|                                          |       | (210) |
| Goodwill arising on consolidation        |       | 8     |

3    *Investment in associate*

|                                          | $'000 |
|------------------------------------------|-------|
| Cost of associate                        | 90    |
| Share of post-acquisition retained reserves (W4) | 75    |
|                                          | 165   |

4    *Retained earnings*

|                          | Hever $'000 | Spiro $'000 | Aldridge $'000 |
|--------------------------|-------------|-------------|----------------|
| Per question             | 568         | 200         | 400            |
| PUP (W6)                 | (1.5)       | –           | –              |
| Fair value movement (W7) |             | 15          |                |
| Pre-acquisition retained earnings |    | (20)        | (150)          |
|                          |             | 195         | 250            |
| Group share of post acquisition ret'd earnings: |  |  |  |
| Spiro (195 × 60%)        | 117         |             |                |
| Aldridge (250 × 30%)     | 75          |             |                |
| Less: group share of impairment losses to date | (0) |  |  |
| Less: impairment losses on associate to date | (0) |  |  |
|                          | 758.5       |             |                |

5    *Non-controlling interests*

|                                          | $'000 |
|------------------------------------------|-------|
| NCI at acquisition (W2)                   | 90    |
| NCI share of post acquisition ret'd earnings ((W4) 195 × 40%) | 78    |
|                                          | 168   |

6    *Unrealised profit on inventories*

Mark-up: $16,000 – $10,000 = $6,000 ∴ ¼ × $6,000 = $1,500

7    *Fair values – adjustment to net assets*

|                            | At acquisition | Movement | At year end |
|----------------------------|----------------|----------|-------------|
| Property, plant and equipment | 50          | (5)      | 45          |
| Inventories                | (20)           | 20       | 0           |
|                            | 30             | 15       | 45          |

# 14 Trontacc

(a)    Treatment of construction contracts in the statement of financial position of Trontacc at 30 September 20X7

|                                       | A $'000 | B $'000 | C $'000 | Total $'000 |
|---------------------------------------|---------|---------|---------|-------------|
| Gross amounts due from customers (Note 1) | 80      | –       | –       | 80          |
| Trade receivables (Note 2)            | –       | –       | –       | –           |
| Gross amounts due to customers (Note 1) | –       | (25)    | (45)    | (70)        |

## Note 1

| | A $'000 | B $'000 | C $'000 |
|---|---:|---:|---:|
| **Gross amounts due from/to customers** | | | |
| Contract costs incurred | 500 | 550 | 320 |
| Recognised profits less losses | 120 | (100) | 35 |
| | 620 | 450 | 355 |
| Less: progress billings to date | (540) | (475) | (400) |
| | 80 | (25) | (45) |

## Note 2

| | A $'000 | B $'000 | C $'000 |
|---|---:|---:|---:|
| **Trade receivables** | | | |
| Progress billings to date | 540 | 475 | 400 |
| Less: cash received | (540) | (475) | (400) |
| | – | – | – |

(b) Treatment of construction contracts in the statement of profit or loss of Trontacc for the year ended 30 September 20X7

| | Contract A $'000 (W1) | B $'000 (W2) | C $'000 (W3) | Total $'000 |
|---|---:|---:|---:|---:|
| Revenue | 600 | 500 | 350 | 1,450 |
| Expenses | (480) | (550) | (315) | (1,345) |
| Expected loss | – | (50) | – | (50) |
| Gross profit/(loss) | 120 | (100) | 35 | 55 |

**Workings**

1   Contract A

| | $'000 |
|---|---:|
| Statement of profit or loss | |
| Revenue (60% × 1,000) | 600 |
| Expenses (60% of 800) | (480) |
| Gross profit | 120 |

2   Contract B

| | $'000 |
|---|---:|
| Statement of profit or loss | |
| Revenue (50% × 1,000) | 500 |
| Expenses (all costs to date) | (550) |
| Expected losses | (50) |
| Gross profit | (100) |

3   Contract C

| | $'000 |
|---|---:|
| Statement of profit or loss | |
| Revenue (35% × 1,000) | 350 |
| Expenses (35% × 900) | (315) |
| Gross profit | 35 |

## 15 C Co

(a)

| | Maryhill bypass $'000 | Rottenrow centre $'000 |
|---|---|---|
| Revenue | 2,800 | 3,000 |
| Profit/(loss) (W1) | 622 | (100) |
| Cost of sales | 2,178 | 3,100 |
| *Current liabilities* | | |
| Gross amounts due to customers (W2) | 578 | 600 |

*Workings*

1    Maryhill: $(9{,}000 - (1{,}400 + 5{,}600)) \times \dfrac{2{,}800}{9{,}000} = 622$

Rottenrow: $8{,}000 - (2{,}900 + 5{,}200) = (100)$

| 2 | Maryhill $'000 | Rottenrow $'000 |
|---|---|---|
| Costs incurred to date | 1,400 | 2,900 |
| Recognised profits/(losses) | 622 | (100) |
| Progress billings | (2,600) | (3,400) |
| | (578) | (600) |

(b)    Construction contracts are recognised as such when they cover at **least two accounting periods**. If they were not to be treated as they are under IAS 11, then the costs incurred during the early years of the contract would be recognised but with no corresponding revenue. This would lead to several years of losses then one year of high profits regardless of how profitable the contract really was. The advantage of this approach however would be that there would be no need to use estimates and forecasts.

The current treatment **matches an element of the revenue to the costs incurred**. There is an attempt to maintain **prudence** by ensuring that any **foreseeable** losses are **accounted for immediately**. This gives a fairer representation of the underlying financial substance of the transaction and makes it easier for the user of the accounts to assess the financial position of the company.

# 16 Provisions

(a)    **Why there was a need for an accounting standard dealing with provisions**

IAS 37 *Provisions, contingent liabilities and contingent assets* was issued to prevent entities from using provisions for creative accounting. It was common for entities to recognise material provisions for items such as future losses, restructuring costs or even expected future expenditure on repairs and maintenance of assets. These could be combined in one large provision (sometimes known as the 'big bath'). Although these provisions reduced profits in the period in which they were recognised (and were often separately disclosed on grounds of materiality), they were then released to enhance profits in subsequent periods. To make matters worse, provisions were often recognised where there was no firm commitment to incur expenditure. For example, an entity might set up a provision for restructuring costs and then withdraw from the plan, leaving the provision available for profit smoothing.

**The criteria that need to be satisfied before a provision is recognised**

IAS 37 states that a provision should not be recognised unless:

(i)    An entity has a present obligation (legal or constructive) as a result of a past event, and

(ii)   It is probable that an outflow of resources embodying economic benefits will be required to settle the obligation, and

(iii)  A reliable estimate can be made of the amount of the obligation.

An obligation can be legal or constructive. An entity has a constructive obligation if:

(i)    It has indicated to other parties that it will accept certain responsibilities (by an established pattern of past practice or published policies), and

(ii)   As a result, it has created a valid expectation on the part of those other parties that it will discharge those responsibilities.

(b)  Extract should recognise a provision for the estimated costs of making good the site because:

(i)    It has a present obligation to incur the expenditure as a result of a past event. In this case the obligating event occurred when it became virtually certain that the legislation would be passed. Therefore the obligation existed at 31 December 20X0, and

(ii)   An outflow of resources embodying economic benefits is probable, and

(iii)  It is possible to make a reliable estimate of the amount.

### Effect on the financial statements

*For the year ended 31 December 20X0:*

- A provision of $1,242,000 (2,000,000 × 0.621) is reported as a liability.
- A non-current asset of $1,242,000 is also recognised. The provision results in a corresponding asset because the expenditure gives the company access to an inflow of resources embodying future economic benefits; there is no effect on profit or loss for the year.

*For the year ended 31 December 20X1:*

- Depreciation of $248,400 (1,242,000 × 20%) is charged to profit or loss. The non-current asset is depreciated over its remaining useful economic life of 5 years from 31 December 20X0 (the site will cease to produce output on 31 December 20X5).
- Therefore at 31 December 20X1 the net book value of the non-current asset will be $993,600 (1,242,000 – 248,400).
- At 31 December 20X1 the provision will be $1,366,000 (2,000,000 × 0.683).
- The increase in the provision of $124,000 (1,366,000 – 1,242,000) is recognised in profit or loss as a finance cost. This arises due to the unwinding of the discount.

# 17 Financial assets and liabilities

(a)

|  | $ |
|---|---|
| Issue costs | 120,000 |
| Interest $6,000,000 × 3.5% × 7 | 1,470,000 |
| Premium on redemption | 1,100,000 |
| Total finance cost | 2,690,000 |

(b)  The premium on redemption of the loan notes represents a finance cost. The effective rate of interest must be applied so that the debt is measured at amortised cost (IFRS 9).

At the time of issue, the loan notes are recognised at their net proceeds of $599,800 (600,000 – 200).

The finance cost for the year ended 31 December 20X4 is calculated as follows:

|  | $ |
|---|---|
| 1.1.20X3 Proceeds of issue (600,000 – 200) | 599,800 |
| Interest at 12% | 71,976 |
| Balance 31.12.20X3 | 671,776 |
| Interest at 12% | 80,613 |
| Balance at 31.12.210X4 | 752,389 |

The finance cost for the year ended 31.12.20X4 is $80,613.

(c)

> **Top tip.** The method to use here is to find the present value of the principal value of the bond, $500,000 (10,000 × $50) and the interest payments of $25,000 annually (5% × $500,000) at the market rate for non-convertible bonds of 6%, using the discount factors. The difference between this total and the principal amount of $500,000 is the equity element.

|  | $ |
|---|---|
| Present value of principal $500,000 × 0.747 | 373,500 |
| Present value of interest $25,000 × 4.212 | 105,300 |
| Liability value | 478,800 |
| Principal amount | 500,000 |
| Equity element | 21,200 |

# 18 Alpha

> **Tutorial note.** Creative accounting and substance over form are important concepts. You must relate your answer to the situation given in part (c) of the question and not just write a general essay. One or two examples would be enough in (a).

(a) **Creative accounting**, the manipulation of figures for a desired result, takes many forms. Off-balance sheet finance is a major type of creative accounting and it probably has the most serious implications.

It is very rare for a company, its directors or employees to manipulate results for the purpose of fraud. The major consideration is usually the effect the results will have on the share price of the company. If the share price falls, the company becomes vulnerable to takeover. Analysts, brokers and economists, whose opinions affect the stock markets, are often perceived as having an outlook which is both short-term and superficial. Consequently, companies will attempt to produce the results the market expects or wants. The companies will aim for steady progress in a few key numbers and ratios and they will aim to meet the market's stated expectation.

The number of methods available for creative accounting and the determination and imagination of those who wish to perpetrate such acts are endless. It has been seen in the past that, wherever an accounting standard or law closes a loophole, another one is found. This has produced a change of approach in regulators and standard setters, towards general principles rather than detailed rules.

Here are a few examples of creative accounting.

(i) **Income recognition and cut-off**
Manipulation of cut-off is relatively straightforward. For instance a company may delay invoicing in order to move revenue into the following year.

(ii) **Revaluations**
The optional nature of the revaluation of non-current assets leaves such practices open to manipulation. The choice of whether to revalue can have a significant impact on a company's statement of financial position.

(iii) **Window dressing**
This is where transactions are passed through the books at the year end to make figures look better, but in fact they have not taken place and are often reversed after the year end. An example is where cheques are written to creditors, entered in the cash book, but not sent out until well after the year end.

(iv) **Change of accounting policies**
This tends to be a last resort because companies which change accounting policies know they will not be able to do so again for some time. The effect in the year of change can be substantial and prime candidates for such treatment are depreciation, inventory valuation, changes from current cost to historical cost (practised frequently by privatised public utilities) and foreign currency losses.

(v)  **Manipulation of accruals, prepayments and contingencies**

These figures can often be very subjective, particularly contingencies. In the case of impending legal action, for example, a contingent liability is difficult to estimate, the case may be far off and the lawyers cannot give any indication of likely success, or failure. In such cases companies will often only disclose the possibility of such a liability, even though the eventual costs may be substantial.

(b)  The phrase 'substance over form' has been described as follows.

'Transactions and other events should be accounted for and presented in accordance with their substance and financial reality and not merely with their legal form.'

This is a very important concept and it has been used to determine accounting treatment in financial statements through accounting standards and so prevent off balance sheet transactions.

(i)  **Group accounting** is perhaps the most important area of off balance sheet finance which has been prevented by the application of the substance over form concept. A number of IASs have tackled abuses by enforcing the substance over form concept.

The most important point is that the definition of a subsidiary (under IAS 27 and IFRS 10) is based upon the **principle of control rather than purely ownership.** Where an entity is controlled by another, the controlling entity can ensure that the benefits accrue to itself and not to other parties. Similarly, one of the circumstances where a subsidiary may be excluded from consolidation is where there are severe long-term restrictions that prevent effective control.

(ii)  Finance leases and their accounting treatment under IAS 17 *Leases* are an example of the application of substance over form.

**Operating leases** do not really pose an accounting problem. The lessee pays amounts periodically to the lessor and these are charged to profit or loss. The lessor treats the leased asset as a non-current asset and depreciates it in the normal way. Rentals received from the lessee are credited to profit or loss in the lessor's books.

For assets held under **finance leases** this accounting treatment would not disclose the reality of the situation. If a lessor leases out an asset on a finance lease, the asset will probably never be seen on his premises or used in his business again. It would be inappropriate for a lessor to record such an asset as a non-current asset. In reality, what he owns is a stream of cash flows receivable from the lessee. The asset is a receivable rather than a non-current asset.

Similarly, a lessee may use a finance lease to fund the 'acquisition' of a major asset which he will then use in his business perhaps for many years. The substance of the transaction is that he has acquired a non-current asset, and this is reflected in the accounting treatment prescribed by IAS 17, even though in law the lessee may never become the owner of the asset.

(iii)  With regard to **measurement or disclosure of current assets**, a common example where substance over form is relevant are sale and repurchase agreements. These are arrangements under which the company sells an asset to another person on terms that allow the company to repurchase the asset in certain circumstances. A common example of such a transaction is the sale and repurchase of maturing whisky inventories. The key question is whether the transaction is a straightforward sale, or whether it is, in effect, a secured loan. It is necessary to look at the arrangement to determine who has the rights to the economic benefits that the asset generates, and the terms on which the asset is to be repurchased.

If the seller has the right to the benefits of the use of the asset, and the repurchase terms are such that the repurchase is likely to take place, the transaction should be accounted for as a loan.

Another example is the factoring of **trade receivables**. Where debts are factored, the original creditor sells the receivables to the factor. The sales price may be fixed at the outset or may be adjusted later. It is also common for the factor to offer a credit facility that allows the seller to draw upon a proportion of the amounts owed.

In order to determine the correct accounting treatment it is necessary to consider whether the benefit of the receivables has been passed on to the factor, or whether the factor is, in effect, providing a loan on the security of the receivables. If the seller has to pay interest on the difference between the amounts advanced to him and the amounts that the factor has received, and if the seller bears the risks of non-payment by the debtor, then the indications would be that the transaction is, in effect, a loan.

(c)   (i)   The Finance Director may be right in believing that renewing the non-current assets of the company will contribute to generating higher earnings and hence improved earnings per share. However, this will not happen immediately as the assets will need to have been in operation for at least a year for results to be apparent. Earnings will be higher because of the loan being at a commercially unrealistic rate, namely 5% instead of 9%.

As regards gearing, the Finance Director may well wish to classify the convertible loan stock as equity rather than debt; thus gearing will be lower. He may argue that because the loan is very likely to be converted into shares, the finance should be treated as equity rather than as debt.

(ii)   IAS 33 *Earnings per share* requires the calculation of **basic earnings per share**. The Finance Director believes that the convertible loan he is proposing will not affect EPS and that an interest cost of 5% will not impact heavily on gearing.

However, IAS 32 will require the interest cost to be based on 9% and IAS 33 also requires the calculation and disclosure of **diluted EPS**.

The need to disclose diluted earnings per share arose because of the limited value of a basic EPS figure when a company is financed partly by convertible debt. Because the right to convert carries benefits, it is usual that the interest rate on the debt is lower than on straight debt. Calculation of EPS on the assumption that the debt is non-convertible can, therefore, be misleading since:

(1)   Current EPS is higher than it would be under straight debt

(2)   On conversion, EPS will fall – diluted EPS provides some information about the extent of this future reduction, and warning shareholders of the reduction which will happen in the future

IAS 32 *Financial instruments: presentation* affects the proposed scheme in that IAS 32 requires that convertible loans such as this should be split in the statement of financial position and presented partly as equity and partly as debt. Thus the company's gearing will probably increase as the convertible loan cannot be 'hidden' in equity.

# 19 Jenson

**Tutorial note.** This is an important subject and it is closely linked with the IASB's *Conceptual Framework*, which you should have discussed, rather than IAS 18, the accounting standard on revenue recognition. You need to use your imagination to come up with examples in (b).

(a)   In revenue recognition, the 'critical event' is the point in the earnings process or operating cycle at which the transaction is deemed to have been **sufficiently completed** to allow the **profit** arising from the transaction, or a distinct component part of it, to be **recognised** in income in a particular period. This has to be addressed in order to allocate transactions and their effects to different accounting periods and is a direct result of the episodic nature of financial reporting. For most companies the **normal earnings cycle** is the purchase of raw materials which are transformed through a manufacturing process into saleable goods, for which orders are subsequently received, delivery is made and then payment received.

In the past the approach has been to **match costs with revenues** and record both once the critical event has passed; in most systems this critical event has been full or **near full performance of the transaction**, so that no material uncertainties surround either the transaction being completed or the amounts arising from the transaction. This is encompassed in the notion of prudence, so that revenue is recognised only in cash or near cash form. However, any point in the cycle could be deemed to be the critical event. This approach leaves the statement of financial position as a statement of uncompleted transaction balances, comprising unexpired costs and undischarged liabilities.

In contrast, the IASB's **Conceptual Framework** defines income and expenses in terms of increases in economic benefits (income) and outflow or depletion of assets (expenses), not in terms of an earnings or matching process. The statement of financial position thus assumes primary importance in the recognition of earnings and profits. Income **can only be recognised** if there is an **increase** in the equity (ie net assets) of an entity not resulting from contributions from owners. Similarly, an expense is recognised if there is a **decrease** in the ownership interest of an entity not resulting from distributions to owners. Thus income arises from recognition of assets and derecognition of liabilities, and expenses arise from derecognition of assets and recognition of liabilities. The IASB explains that it is not possible to reverse this definitional process, ie by defining assets and liabilities in terms of income and expenses, because it has not been possible to formulate robust enough base definitions of income and expenses (partly because the choice of critical event can be subjective). Nevertheless commentators often attempt to link the two approaches by asserting that **sufficient evidence** for recognition or derecognition will be met at the critical event in the operating cycle.

(b)    *On the acquisition of goods*

This would be **unlikely** to be a critical event for most businesses. However, for some the acquisition of the raw materials is the most important part of the process, eg extraction of gold from a mine, or the harvesting of coffee beans. Only where the goods in question could **be sold immediately in a liquid market** would it be appropriate to recognise revenue, ie they would have to have a **commodity value.**

*During the manufacture or production of goods*

This is also **unlikely** to be the critical event for most businesses because **too many uncertainties** remain, eg of damaged goods or overproduction leading to obsolete inventory. An **exception** would be **long-term contracts** for the construction of specific assets, which tend to earn the constructing company revenues over the length of the contract, usually in stages, ie there is a **series of critical events** in the operating cycle. It would **not** be appropriate to recognise all the revenue at the end of the contract, because this would reflect profit earned in past periods as well as the present period. Profit is therefore recognised during manufacture or production, usually through certification by a qualified valuer. Some would argue that this is not really a critical event approach, but rather an 'accretion approach'.

*On delivery/acceptance of goods*

Goods are frequently sold on **credit**, whereby the vendor hands over the inventory asset and receives in its place **a financial asset of a debt** due for the price of the goods. At that point legal title passes and **full performance** has taken place. In general, the bulk of the risks of the transaction have gone and the only ones remaining relate to the creditworthiness of the purchaser and any outstanding warranty over the goods. Many trade sales take place in this way, with periods of credit allowed for goods delivered, eg 30 days. This therefore tends to be the critical event for many types of business operating cycles.

*Where certain conditions have been satisfied after the goods have been delivered*

In these situations the customer has a right of return of the goods without reason or penalty, but usually within a time and non-use condition. A good example is clothes retailers who **allow non-faulty goods to be returned.** Another example is where the goods need only be paid for once they are sold on to a third party. Traditionally, recognition of revenue is delayed until, eg **the deadline to allowed return passes.** However, in circumstances where goods are never returned, it might be argued that the substance of the transaction is a sale on delivery.

*Receipt of payment for credit sales*

Once payment is received, only warranty risk remains. A company may wait until this point to recognise income if receipt is considered uncertain, eg when goods have been sold to a company resident in a country that has exchange controls. It would otherwise be **rare** to delay recognition until payment.

*On the expiry of a guarantee or warranty*

Many businesses may feel unable to recognise revenue in full because of **outstanding warranties,** eg a construction company which is subject to fee retention until some time after completion of the contract. Other businesses, such as car manufacturers, may make a **general provision** for goods returned under warranty as it will not be possible to judge likely warranty costs under individual contracts.

(c) (i) This agreement is worded as a **sale**, but it is fairly obvious from the terms and assessed substance that it is in fact a **secured loan.** Jenson should therefore continue to recognise the inventory in the statement of financial position and should treat the receipt from Wholesaler as a loan, not revenue. Finance costs will be charged to profit or loss of $35,000 × 12% × 9/12 = $3,150.

(ii) The initial fee of $50,000 should be spread evenly over the term of the franchise. This will give revenue of $10,000 in year 1 and $15,000 thereafter. The profit will therefore be 20% for year 1 and approximately 46% for years 2 – 5.

(iii) The cost of the first 6 months' publications is $192,000 ÷ 24 × 6 = $48,000. On an accruals basis, income of $240,000 ÷ 24 × 6 = $60,000 should be recognised. This would leave deferred income of $240,000 – $60,000 = $180,000 in Jenson's statement of financial position (ie as a liability). As in (ii), however, this may not represent a liability. In fact, the liability of the company may only extend to the cost of the future publications, ie $192,000 – $48,000 = $144,000. This would allow Jenson to **recognise all the profit** on the publications **immediately.** In the absence of an updated accounting standard on revenue recognition, it will be necessary to consider the extent of Jenson's commitments under this arrangement.

# 20 Bulwell

STATEMENTS OF PROFIT OR LOSS (EXTRACTS)

|  | 20X1 | 20X2 | 20X3 | 20X4 |
|---|---|---|---|---|
|  | $ | $ | $ | $ |
| Finance cost | 11,250 | 8,063 | 4,078 |  |
| Depreciation on lorries | 12,500 | 12,500 | 12,500 | 12,500 |

STATEMENTS OF FINANCIAL POSITION AT 31 DECEMBER (EXTRACTS)

|  | 20X1 | 20X2 | 20X3 | 20X4 |
|---|---|---|---|---|
|  | $ | $ | $ | $ |
| **Non-current assets** |  |  |  |  |
| Lorries: at cost | 54,000 | 54,000 | 54,000 | 54,000 |
| Depreciation | 12,500 | 25,000 | 37,500 | 50,000 |
|  | 41,500 | 29,000 | 16,500 | 4,000 |

|  | 20X1 $ | 20X2 $ | 20X3 $ | 20X4 $ |
|---|---|---|---|---|
| *Current liabilities* | | | | |
| Finance lease obligations | 15,937* | 16,313 | – | – |
| *Non-current liabilities* | | | | |
| Finance lease obligations | 16,313 | – | – | – |

* (24,000 – 8,063)

*Working*

|  | $ |
|---|---|
| **Finance lease** | |
| Original cost ($18,000 × 3) | 54,000 |
| Deposit | (9,000) |
| Balance 1.1.20X1 | 45,000 |
| Interest 25% | 11,250 |
| Payment 31.12.20X1 | (24,000) |
| Balance 31.12.20X1 | 32,250 |
| Interest 25% | 8,063 |
| Payment 31.12.20X2 | (24,000) |
| Balance 31.12.20X2 | 16,313 |
| Interest 25% | 4,078 |
| Payment 31.12.20X3 | (20,391) |
|  | – |

# 21 Lis

The lease appears to be a finance lease for the following reasons:

- the present value of minimum lease payments amounts to 98% ($84,000/$86,000) of the fair value of the asset at inception of the lease, which can be regarded as 'substantially all'

- the asset will be used by Lis for the whole of its useful life, as it will be scrapped by the lessor at the end of the lease.

Consequently the asset should be capitalised in the statement of financial position. The asset should be depreciated over the shorter of its useful life (5 years) and the lease term (6 years).

A lease liability will be shown in the statement of financial position reduced by lease payments made in advance and increased by interest calculated using the interest rate implicit in the lease, 12.5%.

Both the asset and lease liability will initially be recognised at $84,000, the present value of minimum lease payments, as this is lower than the fair value of the asset. In present value terms the lessor is making a $2,000 loss by not selling the asset at its market value of $86,000, but may have reasons for doing so or the market may be illiquid.

*FINANCIAL STATEMENT EXTRACTS*

|  | $ |
|---|---|
| **Statement of profit or loss (extract)** | |
| Depreciation (W1) | 16,800 |
| Finance costs (W2) | 8,198 |
| **Statement of financial position (extract)** | |
| *Non-current assets* | |
| Leasehold assets (W1) | 67,200 |
| *Non-current liabilities* | |
| Finance lease liability (W2) | 55,358 |
| *Current liabilities* | |
| Finance lease liability (W2) (73,778 – 55,358) | 18,420 |

*Workings*

1   *Carrying amount of leased asset*

|  | $ |
|---|---:|
| Depreciation of asset: $84,000/5 years useful life | 16,800 |
| Carrying amount at year end ($84,000 – $16,800) | 67,200 |

The asset is depreciated over the shorter of its useful life (5 years) and lease term (6 years).

2   *Finance lease*

|  |  | $ |
|---|---|---:|
| 1.1.X3 | Present value of minimum lease payments | 84,000 |
| 1.1.X3 | Payment in advance | (18,420) |
|  |  | 65,580 |
| 1.1.X3 – 31.12.X3 | Interest at 12.5% ($65,580 × 12.5%) | 8,198 |
| **31.12.X3** | **Finance lease liability c/d** | **73,778** |
| 1.1.X4 | Payment in advance | (18,420) |
| **1.1.X4** | **Finance lease liability c/d after next instalment** | **55,358** |

The interest element ($8,198) of the current liability can also be shown separately as interest payable.

# 22 Winger

> **Tutorial note.** As with consolidated accounts questions, a question on the preparation of a single company's accounts needs a methodical approach. Lay out proformas and fill the numbers in gradually by systematically working through the question. Points are as follows
>
> (a)   Exclude 'sale or return' goods from both sales and cost of sales.
>
> (b)   The profit on sale of property needs to be correctly accounted for.
>
> (c)   Exclude from the finance lease interest charge the $20m down payment – interest does not accrue on this.
>
> (d)   When calculating the lease payable, you need to accrue one year's interest but no more. You know that $20m is due within one year, so the non-current liability is the balance of the total amount due.

(a)   WINGER
      STATEMENT OF PROFIT OR LOSS FOR THE YEAR ENDED 31 MARCH 20X1

|  | $'000 |
|---|---:|
| Sales revenues (358,450 – 27,000) | 331,450 |
| Cost of sales (W1) | (208,550) |
| Gross profit | 122,900 |
| Distribution expenses | (28,700) |
| Administration expenses | (15,000) |
| Profit on disposal of land and buildings (95,000 – 80,000) | 15,000 |
| Loss on abandonment of research project | (30,000) |
| Finance cost (W3) | (11,200) |
| Profit before tax | 53,000 |
| Income tax (15,000 – 2,200) | (12,800) |
| Profit for the year | 40,200 |

(b)   STATEMENT OF FINANCIAL POSITION
      AS AT 31 MARCH 20X1

|  | $'000 | $'000 |
|---|---:|---:|
| *Assets* |  |  |
| Tangible non current assets |  |  |
| Property (200,000 – 6,000 (W2)) |  | 194,000 |
| Plant and equipment (W4) |  | 160,000 |
|  |  | 354,000 |

|  | $'000 | $'000 |
|---|---|---|
| Current assets | | |
| Inventories (28,240 + 22,500 (W1)) | 50,740 | |
| Accounts receivable (55,000 − 27,000 (W1)) | 28,000 | |
| Cash | 10,660 | |
| | | 89,400 |
| *Total assets* | | 443,400 |
| *Equity and liabilities* | | |
| Equity | | |
| Equity shares 25c each | | 150,000 |
| Retained earnings (W5) | | 129,800 |
| | | 279,800 |
| Non-current liabilities | | |
| Leasing obligations (W6) | 47,200 | |
| 8% loan notes | 50,000 | |
| | | 97,200 |
| Current liabilities | | |
| Trade and other accounts payable (W7) | 51,400 | |
| Income tax payable | 15,000 | |
| | | 66,400 |
| *Total equity and liabilities* | | 443,400 |

*Workings*

| 1 | *Cost of sales* | $'000 |
|---|---|---|
| | Per question | 185,050 |
| | Less sale/return goods (27,000 × 100/120) | (22,500) |
| | Add depreciation (W2) | 46,000 |
| | | 208,550 |

| 2 | *Depreciation* | $'000 |
|---|---|---|
| | Building (100,000 ÷ 50) | 2,000 |
| | Heating system (20,000 ÷ 10) | 2,000 |
| | Lifts (30,000 ÷ 15) | 2,000 |
| | | 6,000 |
| | Leased plant (80,000 × 20%) | 16,000 |
| | Owned plant (154,800 − 34,800) × 20% | 24,000 |
| | | 46,000 |

| 3 | *Finance cost* | $'000 |
|---|---|---|
| | Loan note interest (50,000 × 8%) | 4,000 |
| | Finance lease (80,000 − 20,000) × 12% | 7,200 |
| | | 11,200 |

| 4 | *Plant and equipment* | $'000 |
|---|---|---|
| | Cost: owned plant | 154,800 |
| | leased plant | 80,000 |
| | | 234,800 |
| | Depreciation: owned plant (34,800 + 24,000 (W2)) | (58,800) |
| | Leased plant (80,000 × 20%) | (16,000) |
| | | 160,000 |

| 5 | *Retained earnings* | $'000 |
|---|---|---|
| | Balance b/f | 71,600 |
| | Profit for the year | 40,200 |
| | Profit on disposal of property (45,000 – 15,000) | 30,000 |
| | Dividend paid | (12,000) |
| | | 129,800 |

| 6 | *Leasing obligations* | $'000 |
|---|---|---|
| | Total payments due | 80,000 |
| | Less amount paid | (20,000) |
| | | 60,000 |
| | Add accrued interest (60,000 × 12%) | 7,200 |
| | Total creditor | 67,200 |
| | Due within one year | 20,000 |
| | Due after one year | 47,200 |

| 7 | *Trade and other payables* | $'000 |
|---|---|---|
| | Trial balance | 29,400 |
| | Lease creditor (W6) | 20,000 |
| | Accrued loan note interest | 2,000 |
| | | 51,400 |

(c) Companies often used to justify the non-depreciation of buildings on several grounds, including:

(i) That the current value of the buildings was **higher than cost**.

(ii) That the level of **maintenance** meant that no deterioration or consumption had taken place.

(iii) That the depreciation charge would **not be material.**

However, IAS 16 requires the **depreciable amount** of an asset to be charged against profit over its useful life. That depreciable amount is obtained by comparing the cost of the asset with its **estimated residual value** at the end of its useful life. By requiring the residual value to be estimated at **current prices**, the standard removes any **potential inflationary effects** which would otherwise increase the residual value and hence reduce, even to zero, the depreciable amount. This overcomes the argument that high residual values remove the need for depreciation, unless the value of a second-hand asset has greater value than the same asset new – an unlikely proposition.

The argument regarding **immateriality** of the depreciation charge because of a long life may have some validity. Although it is not addressed directly by IAS 16, accounting standards generally only apply to **material items,** according to the *Conceptual Framework*. However, under this principle, it will be necessary to consider not only each year's potential depreciation charge, but also the **accumulated depreciation** that would need to be provided against the asset. Over time, this amount would inevitably become material and the 'long life' argument would cease to hold.

Thus, Winger's **previous policy** was not appropriate and the change to depreciate assets was necessary to comply with IAS 16.

The directors' proposed treatment of the deferred development expenditure is also incorrect. It needs to be written off because its **value** has become **impaired due to adverse legislation, not a change of accounting policy**. It now has no effective value. There has therefore not been a change of accounting policy, so it cannot be treated as a prior period adjustment. It must be written off to profit or loss.

# 23 Carpati

*Deferred tax liability*

|  | 20X6 |
|---|---|
|  | $'000 |
| Accelerated tax depreciation (W1) | 186 |
| Revaluation (W2) * | 252 |
|  | 438 |

* The deferred tax on the revaluation gain will be charged to the revaluation surplus as IAS 12 requires deferred tax on gains recognised in other comprehensive income to be charged or credited to other comprehensive income.

*Workings*

1    *Tax depreciation*

|  | $'000 | $'000 |
|---|---|---|
| At 30 September 20X6: |  |  |
| Carrying value |  | 1,185 |
| Tax base: |  |  |
|     At 1 October 20X5 | 405 |  |
|     Expenditure in year | 290 |  |
|  | 695 |  |
|     Less: tax depreciation (25%) | (174) |  |
|  |  | (521) |
| Cumulative temporary difference |  | 664 |
|  | @ 28%= | 186 |

2    *Revaluation surplus*

Temporary difference ($1,500,000 – $600,000) @ 28%. = $252,000

> **Tutorial note**. IAS 12 requires the deferred tax liability on revaluations to be recognised *even if* the entity does not intend to dispose of the asset since the value of the asset is recovered through use which generates taxable income in excess of tax depreciation allowable.

# 24 Pilum

(a)    **Earnings per share**

|  | $ |
|---|---|
| Profit before tax | 2,530,000 |
| Less: income tax expense | (1,127,000) |
| Profit for the year | 1,403,000 |
| Less: preference dividends | (276,000) |
| Earnings | 1,127,000 |
| Earnings per share = | 1,127,000 |
|  | 4,120,000 |
|  | 27.4c |

(b)    The first step is to calculate the theoretical ex-rights price.  Consider the holder of 5 shares.

|  | No | $ |
|---|---|---|
| Before rights issue | 5 | 8.90 |
| Rights issue | 1 | 1.20 |
| After rights issue | 6 | 10.10 |

The theoretical ex-rights price is therefore $10.10/6 = $1.68.

The number of shares in issue before the rights issue must be multiplied by the fraction:

$$\frac{\text{Fair value immediately before exercise of rights}}{\text{theoretical ex-rights price}} = \frac{\$1.78}{\$1.68}$$

Weighted average number of shares in issue during the year:

| Date | Narrative | Shares | Time period | Bonus fraction | Total |
|------|-----------|--------|-------------|----------------|-------|
| 1.1.X4 | b/d | 4,120,000 | × 9/12 | 1.78/1.68 | 3,273,929 |
| 1.10.X4 | Rights issue | 824,000 | | | |
| | | 4,944,000 | × 3/12 | | 1,236,000 |
| | | | | | 4,509,929 |

$$\text{EPS} = \frac{\$1,127,000}{4,509,929}$$

$$= 25.0\text{c}$$

(c) The maximum number of shares into which the loan stock could be converted is 90% × 1,500,000 = 1,350,000. The calculation of diluted EPS should be based on the assumption that such a conversion actually took place on 1 January 20X4. Shares in issue during the year would then have numbered (4,120,000 + 1,350,000) = 5,470,000 and revised earnings would be as follows:

|  | $ | $ |
|--|---|---|
| Earnings from (a) above | | 1,127,000 |
| Interest saved by conversion (1,500,000 × 10%) | 150,000 | |
| Less: attributable tax (150,000 × 30%) | (45,000) | |
| | | 105,000 |
| | | 1,232,000 |

$$\therefore \text{Diluted EPS} = \frac{1,232,000}{5,470,000}$$

$$= 22.5\text{c}$$

# 25 Biggerbuys

**REPORT**

To:        The bankers of Biggerbuys
From:      Consultant management accountant
Subject:   Financial performance 20X7 – 20X9
Date:      30 October 20X9

## 1 Introduction

1.1 In accordance with your instructions, I set out below a review of the entity's financial performance over the last three years.

1.2 The main focus of this report is on the reasons for the increase in the level of bank loans.

1.3 Appropriate accounting ratios are included in the attached appendix.

## 2 Bank lending

2.1 The main reason for the steep increase in bank lending is due to the entity not generating sufficient cash from its operating activities over the past three years.

2.2 For the year ended 30 June 20X8, the entity had a **net cash deficiency on operating activities** of $18m.

2.3 In addition, for at least the past two years, the cash generated from operating activities has not been sufficient to cover interest payable. Therefore those payments, together with tax and dividends, have had to be covered by borrowings.

2.4 As at 30 June 20X9, bank borrowings were $610m out of a total facility of $630m. Payment of the proposed dividends alone would increase the borrowings to the limit.

**3    Operating review**

3.1 Although revenue has been rising steadily over the period, operating profit has remained almost static.

3.2 Over this period the profit margin has risen, but not as much as would be expected. The cost of sales have risen in almost the same proportion as sales. This may be due to increased costs of raw materials, as inventories have risen steeply; but the turnover of inventory has been falling or static over the same period.

3.3 There has also been a large increase in trade receivables. Both the increase in inventories and trade receivables have had to be financed out of operating activities leading to the present pressure on borrowings.

3.4 Although the number of days sales in trade receivables has fallen steadily over the period, the trade receivables at the end of June 20X9 still represent nearly a year's credit sales. This is excessive and seems to imply a poor credit control policy, even taking into account the extended credit terms being granted by the company.

**4    Recommendations**

4.1 The entity needs to undertake an urgent review of its credit terms in order to reduce the levels of trade receivables.

4.2 Inventory levels are also extremely high (representing over four months' sales) and should be reviewed.

4.3 Operating costs also need to be kept under control in order to generate more cash from sales.

Please contact me if you need any further information.

Signed: An Accountant

Appendix: Accounting ratios

| | | 20X7 | 20X8 | 20X9 |
|---|---|---|---|---|
| 1 | *Profit margin* | | | |

1 *Profit margin*

$$\frac{\text{Profit before interest}}{\text{Revenue}} \times 100$$

$\dfrac{(50+45)}{1,850} \times 100\% = 5.1\%$    $\dfrac{(60+60)}{2,200} \times 100\% = 5.5\%$    $\dfrac{(50+90)}{2,500} \times 100\% = 5.6\%$

2 *Operating costs*

$$\frac{\text{Other operating costs}}{\text{Revenue}} \times 100$$

$\dfrac{550}{1,850} \times 100\% = 29.7\%$    $\dfrac{640}{2,200} \times 100\% = 29.1\%$    $\dfrac{700}{2,500} \times 100\% = 28.0\%$

3 *Inventory turnover*

$$\frac{\text{Cost of sales}}{\text{Inventory}}$$

$\dfrac{1,250}{400} = 3.1 \text{ times}$    $\dfrac{1,500}{540} = 2.8 \text{ times}$    $\dfrac{1,750}{620} = 2.8 \text{ times}$

4 *Trade receivables turnover*

$$\frac{\text{Trade receivables}}{\text{Credit sales}} \times 365$$

$\dfrac{492}{(300+45)} \times 365 = 523 \text{ days}$    $\dfrac{550}{(400+60)} \times 365 = 436 \text{ days}$    $\dfrac{633}{(600+90)} \times 365 = 334 \text{ days}$

5 *Cash generated from operations*

| | 20X8 $m | 20X9 $m |
|---|---|---|
| Profit before interest | 120 | 140 |
| Depreciation | 60 | 70 |
| Increase in inventory | (140) | (80) |
| Increase in trade receivables | (58) | (83) |
| Increase in trade payables | – | 10 |
| | (18) | 57 |

6 *ROCE*

$$\frac{\text{Profit before interest}}{\text{Net assets} + \text{borrowings}} \times 100\%$$

20X7: $\dfrac{95}{(372+520)} \times 100\% = 10.6\%$    20X8: $\dfrac{120}{(382+720)} \times 100\% = 10.9\%$    20X9: $\dfrac{140}{(372+930)} \times 100\% = 10.7\%$

7 *Interest cover*

$$\frac{\text{Profit before interest}}{\text{Interest payable}}$$

$\dfrac{95}{25} = 3.8$    $\dfrac{120}{60} = 2.0$    $\dfrac{140}{110} = 1.3$

8 *Gearing*

$$\frac{\text{Borrowings}}{\text{Net assets} + \text{borrowings}}$$

$\dfrac{520}{892} = 58.3\%$    $\dfrac{720}{1,102} = 65.3\%$    $\dfrac{930}{1,302} = 71.4\%$

9 *Asset turnover*

$$\frac{\text{Revenue}}{\text{Net assets} + \text{borrowings}}$$

$\dfrac{1,850}{892} = 2.1 \text{ times}$    $\dfrac{2,200}{1,102} = 2.0 \text{ times}$    $\dfrac{2,500}{1,302} = 1.9 \text{ times}$

# 26 Webster

> **Top tip.** This question is at the upper end of the scale of difficulty which you are likely to encounter, particularly part (a). Study the answer carefully.

(a)    STATEMENTS OF PROFIT OR LOSS (RESTATED)

|  | Cole | | Darwin | |
|---|---|---|---|---|
|  | $'000 | $'000 | $'000 | $'000 |
| Revenue (3,000 – 125) (Note 1) |  | 2,875 |  | 4,400 |
| Opening inventory | 450 |  | 720 |  |
| Purchases (Note 2) | 2,055 |  | 3,080 |  |
| Closing inventory | (540) |  | (850) |  |
|  |  | 1,965 |  | 2,950 |
| Gross profit |  | 910 |  | 1,450 |
| Operating expenses | 480 |  | 964 |  |
| Depreciation (Note 3) | 40 |  | (120) |  |
| Loan interest | 80 |  | – |  |
| Overdraft interest (W3) | 15 |  | – |  |
|  |  | (615) |  | (844) |
| Profit for the year |  | 295 |  | 606 |

STATEMENT OF FINANCIAL POSITION (RESTATED)

|  | Cole | | Darwin | |
|---|---|---|---|---|
|  | $'000 | $'000 | $'000 | $'000 |
| *Assets* |  |  |  |  |
| Non current assets |  |  |  |  |
| Property, plant, equipment (W1) |  | 3,100 |  | 2,620 |
| Current assets |  |  |  |  |
| Inventory | 540 |  | 850 |  |
| Receivables (W2) | 897 |  | 750 |  |
| Bank (W3) | – |  | 60 |  |
|  |  | 1,437 |  | 1,660 |
|  |  | 4,537 |  | 4,280 |
| *Equity and liabilities* |  |  |  |  |
| Equity shares ($1) |  | 1,000 |  | 500 |
| Revaluation surplus (800 – 40) |  | 760 |  | 700 |
| Retained earnings to 31 March 20X9 |  |  |  |  |
| (684 + 295 + 40)/(1,912 + 606) |  | 1,019 |  | 2,518 |
|  |  | 2,779 |  | 3,718 |
| Non current liabilities |  |  |  |  |
| 10% loan note |  | 800 |  | – |
| Current liabilities |  |  |  |  |
| Trade payables (W4) |  | 163 |  | 562 |
| Overdraft (W3) |  | 795 |  | – |
|  |  | 4,537 |  | 4,280 |

*Workings*

1    Non-current assets

|  |  | Cost/valuation | Depreciation | NBV |
|---|---|---|---|---|
|  |  | $'000 | $'000 | $'000 |
| Cole: | property | 2,000 | 100 | 1,900 |
|  | plant | 6,000 | 4,800 | 1,200 |
|  |  |  |  | 3,100 |
| Darwin: | property | 2,000 | 100 | 1,900 |
|  | plant (3,000 – 600) | 2,400 | 1,680 | 720 |
|  |  |  |  | 2,620 |

2    *Receivables*
    Cole:  522 + 375 (Note 1) = 897

3    *Bank*

|  | Cole | Darwin |
|---|---|---|
|  | $'000 | $'000 |
| As stated | 20 | (550) |
| Reversal of sale (Note 1) | (500) |  |
| Payment for purchases (Note 2) | (300) |  |
| Payment for plant  (Note 3) |  | 600 |
| Payment/saving of interest to statement of |  |  |
| financial position | 15 | 10 |
|  | (795) | 60 |

4    *Payables*
    Cole 438 −275 (Note 2) = 163

---

**Tutorial notes**

1    Sale to Brander is at gross margin 40%, therefore the cost of sale is $500 × 60% = $300.

   Had a normal margin of 20% applied, the cost of this sale would represent 80% of the selling price. The normal selling price would be $\dfrac{300}{0.8}$ = $375.

   Sales and receivables would reduce  by $125 and the proceeds of $500 would not have been received.

2    Purchase of goods from Advent on normal terms would have increased purchases by $25. Using the normal credit period would mean these goods would have been paid for by the year end, increasing the overdraft and reducing trade payables.

3    The plant bought in February 20X9 has not yet generated income for Darwin, so it is sensible to ignore it in the acquisition comparison.

   The effects are:

   - Cost of plant – $600, overdraft affected
   - Depreciation reduced $600 × 20% = $120

   The depreciation charged changes:

|  | Cole | Darwin |
|---|---|---|
|  | $'000 | $'000 |
| As stated for property | (60) |  |
| Depreciation on revaluation | 100 |  |
| Reduction (above) |  | (120) |
|  | 40 increase | (120) (decrease) |

---

(b)

| Ratios | Cole | | Darwin | |
|---|---|---|---|---|
| Return on capital employed: | (295+80)/(2,779+800) | = 10.5% | 606/3,718 | = 16.3% |
| Asset turnover | 2,875/(4,537 – 958) | = 0.8 times | 4,400/(4,280 – 562) | =1.2 times |
| Gross profit % | 910/2,875 | = 31.7% | (unchanged) | = 33% |
| Net profit % | 295/2,875 | = 10.3% | 606/4,400 | = 13.8% |
| Receivables collection (days) | 897/2,875 ×365 | = 114 | (unchanged) | = 62 |
| Payables period (days) | 163/2,055 ×365 | = 29 | (unchanged) | = 67 |

Using the unadjusted figures, Cole would be preferred, as its key ratios given are better than those of Darwin. Cole achieves better profitability due to greater unit margins. Both companies have poor asset turnover implying under-utilisation or inefficient methods.

Both companies manage working capital in a similar fashion. Webster should examine liquidity ratios:

Cole:     1,082/438 = 2.5
Darwin:   1,600/1,112 = 1.4

The acid test ratio of Cole is 1.23 whereas Darwin's is 0.67.

Using the adjusted accounts, the above position is reversed showing Darwin to be more profitable and to manage its assets more efficiently. Cole's true liquidity position is not so healthy – Cole controls receivables poorly and appears to pay suppliers earlier.

Darwin's poor liquidity position is probably due to financing non-current assets from its overdraft. Alternative refinancing would be beneficial.

Cole's parent company has produced an initially favourable set of ratios by creating favourable payment terms and trading conditions, and Darwin's original ratios were distorted by revaluations and the timing of new plant purchases.

Other factors to consider include:

(i)     The asking price
(ii)    The future prospects, profits and cash flow forecasts
(iii)   The state of forward order books
(iv)    The quality of the management and labour force
(v)     Other possible acquisitions

# 27 Dundee

**Dundee**
**Statement of cash flows for the year ended 31 March 20X7**

|  | $m | $m |
|---|---:|---:|
| **Cash flows from operating activities** | | |
| Profit before taxation | 1,050 | |
| Adjustments for: | | |
| Depreciation | 970 | |
| Interest expense | 250 | |
| | 2,270 | |
| Decrease in inventories (1,500 – 1,600) | 100 | |
| Increase in trade receivables (2,200 – 1,800) | (400) | |
| Increase in trade payables (1,250 – 1,090) | 160 | |
| Cash generated from operations | 2,130 | |
| Interest paid | (250) | |
| Income taxes paid (W2) | (210) | |
| *Net cash from operating activities* | | 1,670 |
| **Cash flow from investing activities** | | |
| Purchase of property, plant and equipment (W1) | (870) | |
| *Net cash used in investing activities* | | (870) |
| **Cash flows from financing activities** | | |
| Payment of finance lease liabilities (W3) | (450) | |
| Dividends paid | (300) | |
| *Net cash used in financing activities* | | (750) |
| **Net increase in cash and cash equivalents** | | 50 |
| **Cash and cash equivalents at beginning of year** | | (205) |
| **Cash and cash equivalents at end of year** | | (155) |

*Workings*

1    *Purchase of property, plant and equipment*

### PROPERTY, PLANT AND EQUIPMENT

|  | $ |  | $ |
|---|---|---|---|
| b/d | 3,700 | Depreciation | 970 |
| Addition – finance leases | 600 |  |  |
| ∴ Additions – cash | 870 | c/d | 4,200 |
|  | 5,170 |  | 5,170 |

2    *Income taxes paid*

### INCOME TAX PAYABLE

|  |  | $ |  |  | $ |
|---|---|---|---|---|---|
| ∴ paid |  | 210 | b/d | DT | 850 |
| c/d | DT | 1,070 |  | CT | 205 |
|  | CT | 225 | P/L | | 450 |
|  |  | 1,505 |  |  | 1,505 |

3    *Payments under finance leases*

### FINANCE LEASE LIABILITIES

|  |  | $ |  |  | $ |
|---|---|---|---|---|---|
| ∴ paid |  | 450 | b/d | > 1 yr | 1,200 |
| c/d | > 1 yr | 1,300 |  | < 1 yr | 450 |
|  | < 1 yr | 500 | Property, plant & equipment | | 600 |
|  |  | 2,250 |  |  | 2,250 |

# 28 Elmgrove

**Marking scheme**                                                                      **Marks**

| (a) | Format/presentation | 2 |
|---|---|---|
|  | Cash generated from operations (½ per item) | 4 |
|  | Interest paid | 2 |
|  | Income taxes paid | 1½ |
|  | Purchase of property, plant and equipment | 2 |
|  | Sale of property, plant and equipment | 1 |
|  | Interest received | 1 |
|  | Issue of share capital | 2½ |
|  | Dividend paid | 1 |
|  |  | 17 |
|  | Property, plant and equipment note | 1 |
|  | Cash and cash equivalents note | 2 |
|  | Available/Maximum | 20 |

| (b) | Memo format | 1 |  |
|---|---|---|---|
|  | Identify users | 1 |  |
|  | Ability to generate cash | 1 |  |
|  | Ability to repay debts | 1 |  |
|  | Helps decision making | 1 |  |
|  | Easier to understand |  |  |
|  | than the statement of profit or loss | 1 |  |
|  | Aids comparison | 1 |  |
|  | Available | 7 |  |
|  | Maximum |  | 5 |
|  |  |  | 25 |

## Suggested solution

(a)  ELMGROVE – STATEMENT OF CASH FLOWS FOR THE YEAR ENDED 31 MARCH 20X9

|  | $m | $m |
|---|---|---|
| *Cash flows from operating activities* |  |  |
| Profit before taxation | 109 |  |
| Adjustments for |  |  |
| Loss on disposal | 6 |  |
| Depreciation | 43 |  |
| Interest income | (6) |  |
| Interest expense | 17 |  |
|  | 169 |  |
| Decrease in inventories (123 – 176) | 53 |  |
| Increase in trade receivables (95 – 87) | (8) |  |
| Increase in trade payables (126 – 70) | 56 |  |
| Cash generated from operations | 270 |  |
| Interest paid (W2) | (13) |  |
| Income taxes paid (W3) | (62) |  |
| *Net cash from operating activities* |  | 195 |
|  |  |  |
| *Cash flows from investing activities* |  |  |
| Purchase of property, plant and equipment (W1) | (165) |  |
| Proceeds from sale of property, plant and equipment (28 – 6) | 22 |  |
| Interest received | 6 |  |
| *Net cash used in investing activities* |  | (137) |
|  |  |  |
| *Cash flows from financing activities* |  |  |
| Proceeds from issuance of share capital (W4) | 60 |  |
| Dividend paid | (32) |  |
| Net cash from financing activities |  | 28 |
| *Net increase in cash and cash equivalents* |  | 86 |
| *Cash and cash equivalents at beginning of the period* |  | 8 |
| *Cash and cash equivalents at end of the period* |  | 94 |

**Workings**

1 *Property, plant and equipment additions*

### PROPERTY, PLANT AND EQUIPMENT

| | $m | | $m |
|---|---|---|---|
| Balance b/d (NBV) | 264 | Revaluation surplus | 31 |
| | | Depreciation | 43 |
| | | Disposal | 28 |
| ∴ Additions | 165 | Balance c/d (NBV) | 327 |
| | 429 | | 429 |

2 *Interest paid*

### INTEREST PAYABLE

| | $m | | $m |
|---|---|---|---|
| | | Balance b/d | 3 |
| ∴ Paid | 13 | Profit or loss | 17 |
| Balance c/d | 7 | | |
| | 20 | | 20 |

3 *Income taxes paid*

### INCOME TAXES PAYABLE

| | $m | | $m |
|---|---|---|---|
| | | Balance b/d | 54 |
| ∴ Paid | 62 | Profit or loss | 47 |
| Balance c/d | 39 | | |
| | 101 | | 101 |

4 *Issue of shares*

| | $m |
|---|---|
| Issue of shares | |
| Share capital (plus premium) 31/3/X9 | 230 |
| Share capital 31/3/X8 | 120 |
| Increase | 110 |
| Debentures converted into shares | (50) |
| Shares issued for cash | 60 |

IAS 7 requires that investing and financing activities that do not require the use of cash, such as converting debt to equity, should be excluded from the statement of cash flows.

(b) MEMO

To:     Memorandum to the directors of Elmgrove
From:   AN Accountant
Date:   1.4.20X9

Subject: Major benefits to the users of financial statements from the publication of statements of cash flows.

The users of financial statements can basically be divided into the following groups.

(i)   Shareholders
(ii)  Management
(iii) Creditors and lenders
(iv)  Employers

The needs of these groups are not identical and hence not all benefits listed below will be applicable to all users.

**Benefits**

(i) Statements of cash flows direct attention to the survival of the entity which depends on its ability to generate cash.

(ii) Statements of cash flows indicate the ability of an entity to repay its debts.

(iii) They give information which can be used in the decision making and stewardship process.

(iv) They are more easily understood than statements of profit or loss that depend on accounting conventions and concepts.

(v) Statements of cash flows give a better means of comparison between different companies.

# 29 CPP and CCA

> **Tutorial note.** It is unlikely that a detailed computation will be asked for, but you must have an understanding of the principles of CPP and CCA, the differences between them and the ways in which they try to improve on HCA.

(a) In accounting, the value of income and capital is measured in terms of money. In simple terms, profit is the difference between the closing and opening statement of financial position values (after adjustment for new sources of funds and applications such as dividend distribution). If, because of inflation, the value of net assets in the closing statement of financial position is shown at a higher monetary amount than net assets in the opening statement of financial position, a profit has been made. In traditional accounting, it is assumed that a monetary unit of $1 is a stable measurement; inflation removes this stability.

CPP accounting attempts to provide a more satisfactory method of valuing profit and capital by establishing a stable unit of monetary measurement, $1 of current purchasing power, as at the end of the accounting period under review.

A distinction is made between monetary items, and non-monetary items. In a period of inflation, keeping a monetary asset (eg trade receivables) results in a loss of purchasing power as the value of money erodes over time. Non-monetary assets, however, are assumed to maintain 'real' value over time, and these are converted into monetary units of current purchasing power as at the year end, by means of a suitable price index. The equity interest in the statement of financial position can be determined as a balancing item.

The profit or deficit for the year in CPP terms is found by converting sales, opening and closing inventory, purchases and other expenses into year-end units of $CPP. In addition, a profit on holding net monetary liabilities (or a loss on holding net monetary assets) is computed in arriving at the profit or deficit figure.

CPP arguably provides a more satisfactory system of accounting since transactions are expressed in terms of 'today's money' and similarly, the statement of financial position values are adjusted for inflation, so as to give users of financial information a set of figures with which they can:

(i) Decide whether operating profits are satisfactory (profits due to inflation are eliminated)

(ii) Obtain a better appreciation of the size and 'value' of the entity's assets

(b) CPP and CCA accounting are different concepts, in that CPP accounting makes adjustments for general inflationary price changes, whereas CCA makes adjustments to allow for specific price movements (changes in the deprival value of assets). Specific price changes (in CCA) enable a company to determine whether the operating capability of a company has been maintained; it is not a restatement of price levels in terms of a common unit of money measurement. The two conventions use different concepts of capital maintenance (namely operating capability with CCA, and general purchasing power with CPP).

In addition CPP is based on the use of a general price index. In contrast, CCA only makes use of a specific price index where it is not possible to obtain the current value of an asset by other means (eg direct valuation).

(c)     In CCA, holding gains represent the difference between the historical cost of an asset and its current cost. If the asset is unsold, and appears in the statement of financial position of a company at current cost, there will be an 'unrealised' holding gain, which must be included in a current cost reserve. When the asset is eventually sold, the profit (equal to the sale price minus the historical cost) may be divided into:

(i)     An operating profit which would have been made if the cost of the asset were its current value

(ii)    A *realised* holding gain which has arisen because of the appreciation in value of the asset between the date of its acquisition and the date of its sale

# Index